DEFENDING NORMANDY
VOL.1A
GERMAN CHAIN OF COMMAND, LXXXIV. AK. & INFANTRY DIVISIONS ON THE COTENTIN

Published in 2024 by Panzerwrecks Limited

Design by Toni Canfora
Maps by Niels Henkemans
Printed by Finidr. s.r.o.
Website www.panzerwrecks.com

Panzerwrecks Limited
Great Priors
Church Street
Old Heathfield
Sussex TN21 9AH
United Kingdom
lee@panzerwrecks.com

©2024 Henkemans. All rights reserved. No part of this publication may be reproduced or transmitted in any form or by any means, electronic or mechanical, including photocopy, recording or any information storage and retrieval system, without permission in writing from the publisher. Mention of company names or individual people are only included for historical documentation purposes. We recognise that some of the company names or designations mentioned in this publication may be registered trademarks or protected under copyright law. Their use in this publication is strictly for historical/technical documentation and does not constitute or imply endorsement of the holders of these titles. The purpose of this book is to document the history of World War 2. The author and publisher distance themselves from fascism, anti-Semitism or racism in any way.

Table of Contents

Introduction — 5

Part 1: German Chain of Command — 14

  German Command Structure in Normandy — 15
    Oberbefehlshaber West — Heeresgruppe D — 70
    Heeresgruppe B — 17
    7. Armee (AOK 7) — 17
    LXXXIV. A.K. — 23

  LXXXIV. Armee-Korps: **Normandy from 1941 to D-Day** — 33
    Höhere Kommando LX and *Generalkommando LXXXIV. A.K.* — 33
    1941: Arrival in Normandy — 34
    1942: Arrivals and Departures — 39
    1943: Reinforcements and Reorganisations — 46
    1944: Setting the Stage — 64

  Generalkommando LXXXIV. A.K.* and *Korpstruppen — 78
    Generalkommando LXXXIV. A.K. — 79
    Korpstruppen — 81

Part 2: *Heer* Infantry Divisions — 88

  The *Heer* Infantry Division — 89

  77. Infanterie-Division — 108
    Organisation and Equipment — 108
    History — 121
    Combat — 127

  91. Luftlande-Infanterie-Division — 158
    Organisation and Equipment — 158
    History — 170
    Combat — 178

Appendix — 218
  The organisation of 7. Armee from D-Day to 24 July — 219
  Glossary — 220
    German Military Symbols — 221
    Comparative Table of Ranks — 222
    Terminology and Abbreviations — 223

Index — 227

Endnotes — 240

Introduction

This book is about the German Army in the Normandy campaign. While entire libraries could be filled with books about the battle for Normandy, surprisingly few of them examine the individual formations that fought there in detail. This is indeed the case for the armed forces of the Third Reich, and it signifies a serious shortcoming in the historiography of this decisive campaign of the Second World War. While it is certainly possible to research and write about any topic from a limited perspective, such an approach will fail to provide a full understanding of the subject at hand. Applying this observation to the topic of this book, how can one fully appreciate the stories told and the sacrifices made, if so little is known about the defending German forces?

There are, of course, many reasons for this failure in the historiography, but the fundamental problem still remains. Questions concerning German units[1] in Normandy — where they were located, their respective strengths, how they operated — are seldom asked. Myths and rumours are repeated and quickly turn into accepted "facts." Much is assumed, little is discussed and even less is researched or proven. The time has come to start afresh by examining the official wartime records — many of which have been overlooked — rather than simply following what has been published and cannot necessarily be trusted as accurate.

This volume (and series) is therefore not a traditional campaign narrative, but a detailed study of the many German units that fought on the Cotentin Peninsula. By examining their organisation and individual histories, this book aims to provide much needed context to better understand what took place on the peninsula, why, and how.

The Cotentin Peninsula

This area of northwest France is part of the *département* (county) of La Manche, itself part of the Normandie region (previously Basse-Normandie). The peninsula extends 45 km northwest into the English Channel (also called La Manche in French) and has a width of about 40 km. The name Cotentin is derived from the former capital, Coutances, and is sometimes also referred to as the Cherbourg Peninsula or the Normandy Peninsula. The latter is also used to refer to a much larger area of Normandy.

Strategically, the most important town is the deepwater port of Cherbourg, which was a key objective in June 1944. The town's prewar population was about 39,000. Today, its infrastructure still includes a military and commercial port, the latter having been a point of departure for immigrants to the United States. Apart from the naval base (*Arsenal*), the wider area was home to three military airfields of which Maupertus (aka Théville in German records) to the east was the most important. Other smaller harbours on the peninsula include Barfleur and St. Vaast-la-Hougue on the east coast and Barneville-Carteret and Portbail on the west. These were mainly fishing ports.

The peninsula has an extensive road network of which the N13 Highway, connecting Cherbourg to Paris, is the most important. The highway runs 6-7 km inland from the east coast, before turning further inland towards Cherbourg. Along this highway are the smaller towns of Valognes, Montebourg, Ste. Mère-Église and — in the southeast — Carentan. All of these were dwarfed by Cherbourg with prewar populations of 5,000, 1,500, 1,000, and 3,500, respectively. In 1944, the highway went straight through these localities but today goes around them. Other important towns, further to the west, are Bricquebec (pop. 2,500) and St. Sauveur-le-Vicomte (pop. 2,000), which cover the western approaches to Cherbourg. The south of the peninsula includes La Haye-du-Puits (pop. 1,500), Lessay (pop. 1,000), and Périers (pop. 2,500).

Lessay and Périers lie along, but outside, the peninsula's southern boundary as defined in this book. This also applies to the low-lying terrain of the Lande de Lessay, south of the town of Lessay. Despite their varying sizes, all these towns were critical crossroads in 1944 and often connected to each other by railway. The single-track routes included: Carentan - La Haye-du-Puits; Coutances - Périers - Lessay - La Haye-du-Puits - St. Sauveur-le-Vicomte - Bricquebec - Sottevast; La Haye-du-Puits - Carteret; and a line running from Montebourg along the east coast to Cherbourg. Today this network has all but disappeared with only the twin-tracked Paris - Cherbourg line, running roughly parallel to the N13 highway, remaining. The traces of the old network remain though, as many routes were turned into cycle paths.

Much of the peninsula is hedgerow country, with its pastures and orchards, known locally as *bocage*. Today many hedgerows and orchards have been removed, opening up the terrain, yet visibility remains limited. Wooded areas are relatively few in number and small in size. The woods around

Cherbourg, along with the Bois de Limors and Forêt de Mont-Castre in the south featured in the fighting. The fighting for the Forêt de Mont-Castre was particularly intense.

The Cotentin's coast varies from cliffs and rocks to long stretches of sandy beaches. The northern coast is mostly rocky, while on the west coast long beaches are interrupted by rocky outcrops and backed by hills. Much of the east, including Utah Beach, consists of a long sandy beach with low dunes protecting the land, followed by a stretch of low-lying ground some 2 km wide. Behind this the terrain slopes gently, becoming increasingly hilly to the north and northwest of the peninsula. North of Utah Beach, the Montebourg - Quinéville Ridge dominates the approach to Cherbourg.

The northeastern corner of the peninsula also consists of low-lying terrain from which a range of hills rise that surround Cherbourg. The town, in the centre of the north coast, is surrounded by a semi circle of hills. To its west is the Jobourg Peninsula, which forms the northwest corner of the Cotentin; this region, which includes the Cap de la Hague, is barren and open.

The centre and south of the Cotentin is generally hedgerow country with gentle slopes, but there are also areas of low ground with meadows. Around La Haye-du-Puits is a cluster of dominating hills and ridges, including Hill 121, Hill 131, Mont-Castre, La Poterie Ridge, and Montgardon Ridge.

The Cotentin has several important waterways, with the Douve and Merderet Rivers dividing much of the centre, flowing from the northwest to the southeast, meeting near Carentan and reaching the sea in the Vire Estuary. Here they are joined by the Taute River, which emerges past the town from the southwest. All three rivers are bordered by wide stretches of low ground. Such areas cover the wider area around Carentan, the Prairies Marécageuses de Gorges to the west and the Prairies Marécageuses stretching towards the west coast from the Douve near Pont-l'Abbé. These areas are prone to flooding, especially in winter, and are jointly referred to as Le Marais (the marsh).

Further south, the base of the peninsula is formed by the rivers Ay and Sèves and low-lying ground that together form an almost continuous line between the west coast and the Prairies Marécageuses de Gorges and Taute. In addition to these more prominent features, numerous streams and brooks intersect the higher ground. Although small, they proved to be obstacles for mechanised forces and formed natural defence lines. Before the invasion, German forces took advantage of the low-lying terrain — basically by preventing drainage — which further restricted movement. These inundations were significant behind Utah Beach and along the Merderet, Douve and Taute Rivers. Even if not directly underwater, these measures made much of the ground soft and waterlogged and impassable for most vehicles.

All of these natural and man-made features had an influence on where and how the battle for the peninsula was fought. In the gently rolling terrain, it was the combination of rivers, streams, marshland and inundations that determined where many battles were fought during the first few weeks of the Normandy campaign. Hills and ridges were of secondary importance, but this changed once the fighting moved closer to Cherbourg, and especially at La Haye-du-Puits, where they became tactically significant.

Literature

For a campaign as extensively studied as Normandy, remarkably little has been written about the German forces involved. There are exceptions, which primarily involve either the *Heer* (Army) and *Waffen-SS Panzer* and *Panzer-Grenadier* divisions, or particular battles. The two dozen or so of the less "glamorous" infantry divisions and wide variety of smaller formations usually get very little, if any, attention. Many campaign books provide some basic information on the German formations, but it is questionable how much is the result of original research rather than a repetition of what has already been written and casually assumed to be correct.

Three books in particular have been important in the development of our detailed knowledge of German troops in the Normandy campaign. All three were the result of ground-breaking research and help to illustrate how the study of German formations has evolved.

The first English language attempt to address the German forces on the Cotentin in any detail was probably Gordon A. Harrison's *Cross-Channel Attack* (1951), an official publication from the history department of the United States Army. Harrison did an excellent job determining the general strength of German formations and the development within their armed forces in the years preceding the invasion. Yet German forces were not his primary concern, and detail was generally lacking. Moreover, his focus was on infantry formations in general, meaning independent[2] *Panzer* and artillery units were not covered in any depth. At the same time, it suffered from several notable inaccuracies.

Perhaps the first major attempt to fill the "*Panzer* void" was Eric Lefèvre's *Panzers in Normandy Then and Now* (1983). The book was an illuminating work on armour that showed not just the vehicle types but the formations that fielded them, but it did not cover armour in the infantry divisions or all of the small independent armoured formations.[3] In the decades after its publication, historians have uncovered numerous errors in the book. Still, Lefèvre's work was a significant step in the evolution of Normandy *Panzer* research.

The lack of attention to individual German infantry formations and particularly smaller units was largely corrected by Niklas Zetterling's *Normandy 1944 — German Military Organisation, Combat Power and Organisational Effectiveness* (2000). The research was of a high standard with a voluminous number of footnotes and sources; yet it was not a conventional narrative history. Its analysis relied heavily on statistics, which formed the basis of the book rather than the fighting. The book began with an introduction looking at German formations in general, their records and armoured vehicles; it continued by discussing most of the individual *Heer* (Army), *SS*, and *Fallschirmjäger* (lit. 'paratrooper', but referred to as 'airborne in the book per Allied traditions/practice) formations in varying detail. For those with a more academic disposition, the appendices embraced discussions on topics such as German combat effectiveness, anti-tank weapons, and the importance of Allied air forces.

While an excellent reference work, it was far from complete. Among the book's few weaknesses was its lack of attention to construction troops, *Heer* and *Kriegsmarine* (German Navy) coastal artillery, and the many *Flak* formations in Normandy. Zetterling attributes these shortcomings to a lack of source material and the relatively minor importance of these units, especially in relation to the focus of his book. The book offered few details on the fighting itself, which was not his purpose for writing it, as is indicated by the book's subtitle. However, this was also where his work proved vulnerable. A more in-depth study of the fighting would have revealed errors in some of his sources and offered more accurate information about when units arrived and where they fought. Moreover, as his book focussed on strength and combat performance, it generally only examined the period shortly before, during and after the fighting. Some answers can only be found by going back further, with the second half of 1943 being particularly significant.

Nevertheless, errors in Zetterling's book were few and minor. Most appear to be the result of either a lack of information or problems within the source materials. In fact, the overall quality of the research was of such a level that I am confident to use the information presented by Zetterling when no other sources are available. Still, the reader will notice that his work is only noted occasionally in this book. The reason for this is simple: In the course of my research many of his sources have been examined directly.

The Approach to This Series

Work on this book began in 2007. My research was facilitated by the fact that, starting about 2000, major photographic and film archives began to digitise their images and were accessible via the internet. Private photos also began to surface on a variety of websites, adding to a rapidly expanding wealth of material that offered unique opportunities for studying World War II outside of the archives.

History and scale modelling forums were quick to recognise this exciting new research environment and became meeting grounds for professional historians, experts and enthusiasts from all over the world. One field that gained particular attention was German armour in Normandy, already a popular subject. Together, online archives were mined, the results shared and discussed in public, with experienced researchers contributing material from traditional work in the archives. This was a period of rapid development of our understanding of German armour in Normandy and also a school of learning for many enthusiasts — including this author — on the possibilities of doing their own research. Perhaps more importantly, communities were formed that have since mentored and encouraged enthusiasts to become leading experts and published authors.

The initial wave of digitalization and focus on photographic evidence slowed around 2004-2005, requiring a different approach to continue the work. At the same time, I became increasingly focussed on the Cotentin Peninsula, a generally unpopular and understudied area of Normandy. This turned my research into a largely individual project, relying on available literature to continue the work. In 2006-2007, this resulted in a number of online articles about German armour on the peninsula and a role as expert in a documentary for the National D-Day Museum (USA). Research gradually widened to embrace all German and American units on the peninsula, an activity aided by the digitalization of period documents including orders, after-action-reports and studies.

By 2010 it was clear that the available records and literature were still insufficient to fully document the German side of the events. Therefore, the only way to make further progress was to turn to the archives. Since then, materials in German, English, French, and Dutch were sourced from archives often with the help of local researchers, scholars, and friends in the historical community. With the addition of digitised German and Russian archives, this has produced a wealth of German records any individual alone would have trouble collecting. Together with Allied intelligence, these records made it possible to write this book to reconstruct the German forces and fighting on the Cotentin.

While Allied operations to capture Cherbourg — conducted by the US VII Corps under the First US Army — were a vital part of the Normandy campaign, the opposing German forces have traditionally been poorly researched. Even though most of the fighting on the Cotentin took place under *LXXXIV. Armee-Korps* (84th Army Corps[4] / *LXXXIV. A.K.*) and they will feature prominently, this book is not a study of the corps; it is about a specific part of the Normandy Campaign. Elements with the corps on D-Day but outside of the peninsula, will generally not be examined.[5] Yet, developments anywhere along the front regularly affected other areas. This makes it both difficult and necessary to determine what will and will not be covered.

Geographically, the peninsula is clearly defined, except for its southern boundary. Here, I could have limited my research to the boundaries of the American advance when Cherbourg and the north of the Cotentin were liberated in late June. Yet, this would put the battle for Cherbourg in a vacuum, giving as it did valuable time to the German defenders for reorganizing their forces and building up their defences along the south of the peninsula. As a consequence, the fighting in that sector was particularly heavy in July. It was also important because it contributed directly to the American breakthrough in Operation Cobra at the end of the month. Ultimately the fighting on the Cotentin was about more than just the liberation of Cherbourg. Understanding the battle requires corresponding boundaries.

The history of the fighting has provided suitable geographic limits, which largely correspond with the geographic boundaries of the region. For most of the fighting in June and July, the *LXXXIV. Armee-Korps* (Army Corps / *A.K.*) was in command of the area west of the Vire River. The corps clearly distinguished two main areas. On the right (south and east) was the reinforced *17. SS-Panzer-Grenadier-Division "Götz von Berlichingen" (17. SS-Pz.Gren.Div. / GvB),* which occupied the area between Baupte and the Vire. On the left (west and north) was an assortment of divisions and other units that covered the approaches to the west coast and Cherbourg. After the Cotentin was split in mid-June, the left sector was withdrawn to the south to cover the line to the west coast; it was then referred to as the *Nordfront* (Northern Front) of the *LXXXIV. A.K.* The line here faced north, attempting to block the advance of the US VIII Corps out of the peninsula towards Périers. This town, with its important crossroads, was also threatened by the advance of the US VII Corps from Carentan, against the *17. SS-Pz.Gren.Div.* The corps' east wing, roughly the area between the Taute and Vire Rivers, saw little activity in June. Further east, beyond the Vire, the US V Corps moved inland from Omaha Beach, resuming its advance towards St. Lô in early July, with the US XIX Corps to the west attacking in the direction of St. Lô. In their areas east of the Vire, both corps faced stubborn resistance from the *II. Fallschirm-Korps* (2nd Airborne Corps / *II. Fs.K.*). To support the US First Army's advance on the town, XIX Corps attacked between the Taute and Vire Rivers on 7 July leading to heavy fighting. This area, specifically the St. Lô – Périers road, ultimately became the jumping off point for Operation Cobra.

Simply put, by early July, *LXXXIV. A.K.* was under attack by three American corps: two towards Périers and one towards St. Lô. The VII and VIII Corps both halted in mid-July once the VIII Corps had reached the next German defence line, the *Wasserlinie* (Waterline). This line, also referred to as the "Lessay-Sèves sector," ran from Lessay to St. Germain-sur-Sèves and was dominated by the Ay and Sèves rivers. To the east, the VII Corps had advanced along the Carentan-Périers isthmus, formed by the Sèves and Prairies Marécageuses de Gorges on the right (west) and Taute River on the left and had established contact with the VIII Corps. The *LXXXIV. A.K.* faced these two corps, following a line between the Ay and Vire Estuary, mostly consisting of waterways. In this book, the *Wasserlinie* and Taute River will be regarded as the southern boundary of the fighting on the Cotentin and mid-July as the moment when it came to its end. This also means that the area between the Vire and Taute will not be covered, with a few exceptions.[6] If units operated in both sectors of the corps, their involvement on the Cotentin will be examined in detail, and their role in the other areas will be included as well. This will be more relevant for subsequent volumes.

Together, the volumes will look at dozens of different formations, most ranging from battalion to division-size. To help explain how these units developed into the formations they were at the time of the invasion, introductions will be provided for the general organisational category or branch of service to which they belonged. In this first volume, this is done for the infantry divisions.

However, a top-down examination, covering all levels of the German chain-of-command, will first be made for the forces involved. This will provide an understanding of the structure of the formations and commands, down to corps level. This volume will then continue with a study of German infantry divisions. Future volumes will look at more divisions (*SS* and *Fallschirmjäger*) and smaller independent units. All of these formations will be discussed individually, and attention will be given to the many non-German formations in the area as well as construction troops and engineers, (coastal) artillery, (anti)tank elements, and *Flak* units. This also means that the *SS*, *Luftwaffe*, and *Kriegsmarine* (often referred to in this work as *Marine*) will feature more prominently in future volumes.

Although the pre-invasion history of the *LXXXIV. A.K.* will be covered in detail, the corps is not the focus of this study. A basic overview of the corps' history after the invasion will still be included, while much of its history will naturally be covered via study of the various major formations that fought under it. In particular, this is the *77., 91., 243., 353.,* and *709. Infanterie-Division* (Infantry Division / *I.D.*). By following the *353. I.D.*, it is possible to track the corps in its retreat from *Operation Cobra* in late July almost to its final destruction in the Falaise Pocket in the second half of August.

Not all of the corps' important sectors and periods will be covered in detail. Since the fighting around Carentan and on the road to Périers was dominated by *Luftwaffe* and *Waffen-SS* troops, these events will be covered in another volume. This will include formations such as the *2. SS-Panzer-Division "Das Reich"* (*2. SS-Pz.Div.* / *Das Reich*), the *17. SS-Pz.Gren.Div.*, *Fallschirmjäger-Regiment 6* (Airborne Regiment 6 / *FJR 6*) and the *5. Fallschirmjäger-Division* (5th Airborne Division / *5. Fj.Div.*). Due to the geographic constraints of this study, the fighting in the Calvados by the *LXXXIV. A.K.* will not be covered. This includes the role of the *352.* and *716. I.D.* on D-Day and the fighting by the temporarily subordinated *II. Fallschirm-Korps* east of the Vire.

Re-examination of the German Army in Normandy

This book was inspired by Zetterling's work and is built from the ground up. It is not a re-examination of the existing literature, but a re-examination of the original records. This approach offers a fresh perspective and makes it possible to incorporate records that have not been used and shed a different light on the fighting in Normandy. Since German sources form the foundation, the results are biased towards a German point of view, which is not necessarily accurate or complete. Considering how much has been written from an Allied perspective, this book serves to improve the balance and allows a valuable comparison to the dominant Allied-centric approach.

Although substantial, the research for this book cannot cover all existing records. This is largely due to the sheer enormity of such a project, not simply to time or financial constraints. Information is scattered over many hundreds of thousands — if not millions — of pages and held in numerous repositories in different countries. Because of these practical issues, the research effort has focussed on records that could reasonably be expected to deliver a useful amount of relevant information. Still, there is undoubtedly much more information in the archives. As Zetterling wrote: "It is a vast topic and much research remains to be done. Perhaps this work will provide some encouragement to spur such efforts." It certainly did for me.

The majority of the research presented here is based on official records from German commands and formations. Four archives were significant in my search for records: The US National Archives and Records Administration (NARA), the German *Bundesarchiv, Abteilung Militärarchiv* (BAMA), The Central Archives of the Ministry of Defence of the Russian Federation (CAMO) and, to a lesser extent, the UK National Archives (UKNA).[7] The microfilm collection at NARA has provided a large percentage of these documents, which are identified by a series of letters and numbers. The T-number indicates the exact microfilm collection, the R-number identifies the roll and the F-number is the frame number. In some cases, the rolls do not include frame numbers; in such cases, the folder number of the document — if available — has been given.

Ideally, the research for this book would have included the records of all formations and their sub-units. Many of their documents did not survive the war and those that still exist, mostly at the *Bundesarchiv*, tend to be incomplete. For practical reasons the research began by focusing on the records of higher level commands; moreover, it eventually became clear that sufficient detail could be obtained from them. Low-level unit records have been examined when available and for units not sufficiently covered by other units or commands. In many cases, the records for these smaller units are missing or incomplete, leaving gaps that may be reduced in the future.

The book presents a new understanding of the German Army in the West. To achieve this objective, it was not enough to just study the situation on and around D-Day. Indeed, it was necessary to take both a broader view and to look back further. The German records examined cover the period from 1940 to the end of the Normandy campaign, with the period from mid-1943 onwards of particular importance. Geographically, it is no surprise that the records of the *7. Armee* (7th Army, with the headquarters referred to as *Armee-Oberkommando 7* or *AOK 7*) and the *LXXXIV. A.K.* (headquarters: *Generalkommando LXXXIV. A.K.*) are the most relevant. These pertain to the fighting in Normandy and earlier preparations, and often include orders from higher headquarters like the *Oberbefehlshaber West* (Commander-in-Chief West / *Ob.West*), the *Oberkommando des Heeres* (High Command of the Army / *OKH*) and the *Oberkommando der Wehrmacht* (High Command of the Armed Forces / *OKW*). The records of *AOK 7* provide an invaluable overview of the context in which the corps operated and its war diary (*Kriegstagebuch* / *KTB*) has been examined from January 1943 onwards. For the second half of 1943, the *KTB* includes an immense collection of supporting documents. During this period, many formations arrived, were established or were reorganised; developments that shaped the army into the fighting force that faced the Allied armies on D-Day. While of less significance and, therefore not examined to the same level of detail, the first half of 1943 still yields some valuable information, especially for a number of smaller units. Records from *LXXXIV. A.K.* are available from its arrival in Normandy in 1941 to the end of 1943. These files offer a good overview of the problems faced by the corps, the arrival and departure of units and the development of the defences in its sector. Unfortunately, corps records for 1944 are scarce, meaning that vital information on the final preparations for the invasion and on the fighting either no longer exists or has to be gleaned from other sources.

Even the combined records of the *7. Armee* and the *LXXXIV. A.K.* do not answer every question. Fortunately, the records of *Ob.West* and *Heeresgruppe B* (Army Group B / *H.Gr. B*) provide complementary data, as do those of the two other corps under the *7. Armee*: The *XXV. A.K.* (25th) and the *LXXIV. A.K.* (74th) in Bretagne. Additionally, records of corps and other commands outside of *7. Armee* have been studied, including several major formations beyond Western Europe but with a link to the units fighting in Normandy. Of course, *OKH* and *OKW* records also provide key information. At the highest level, these two organisations were responsible for the creation, disbandment, authorisation and development of most of Germany's armed forces. All of these sources still only cover the Army and, to a lesser extent, *SS* and *Fallschirmjäger* units. Detailed information on the *Luftwaffe* and *Kriegsmarine* has to be found elsewhere. This is a challenge for the *Luftwaffe*, whose ground forces played an important role in the fighting, but have few surviving records and are insufficiently covered by other headquarters.

The overall organisation of a unit can often be found in the form of a graphic representation of its order of battle, known as a *Gliederung*. These came in different forms, of which the *Grundgliederung*, *Sollgliederung* and *Kriegsgliederung* are the most important. A *Grundgliederung* provides a standard organisation for a specific type of formation, such as a standard infantry division. A *Sollgliederung* (*Soll* = authorised) shows the intended or authorised organisation of a unit, and could vary significantly from the *Grundgliederung*. The *Kriegsgliederung* is arguably the most important since it shows the *Ist* (actual strength) of a unit. Still, all these orders of battle only show the heavy weapons (mortars, artillery, etc.) and machine guns of the subunits, not the small arms. Totals for the these are sometimes listed separately, particularly on *Kriegsgliederungen*. A *Kriegsgliederung* often comes as part of a *Zustandsbericht*, a status report of a unit, which typically includes statistics on weaponry, mobility and personnel (as well as an overall assessment by the commander). When available, these are a good starting point in understanding a unit's strengths and weaknesses.

Another source is the so-called *Feldpostübersicht*. This collection of records provides a near complete overview of the German field post numbers. Changes in these are useful in understanding how units developed, especially if the information cannot be found elsewhere. Rather than referring to individual microfilm rolls, the general term *Feldpostübersicht* will be used. Several websites offer the same information in a more convenient form.

Other than from these records, information has been gathered from personal accounts or Allied records. Most of these were obtained from various national archives and specialised websites. These sources include after-action reports, G2 or S2 (intelligence) reports, prisoner interrogations and the famous "secret recordings" of prisoners of war held in the United Kingdom.[8] ULTRA records — intercepted and decrypted German communications — have also been used as replacements for lost German records. Most of these were obtained from the UKNA.

Of these, the prisoners' statements are arguably the most problematic. Most of their information was from memory, albeit given soon after capture. By its nature, their testimony is vulnerable to mistakes, misinterpretation and omissions, accidental or intentional. Their accounts cannot be ignored, as German units often did not meet their authorised Tables of Organisation & Equipment (*Kriegsstärkenachweisung* / *KStN*), so prisoner information is one of the few sources of actual strength and equipment. This is especially true at platoon level and below. Using these accounts requires a constant evaluation of their reliability, which can vary greatly. At their best, they provide valuable information that cannot be found elsewhere. These prisoner interrogations were obtained from NARA and UKNA.[9]

Publications are another complicated source of information. Although countless articles, books and studies have been written, most lack proper source references, making it difficult to judge their accuracy. This renders them mostly unusable, except where their facts are particularly well-established or important.[10] In some cases, they are used to illustrate misunderstandings or myths.[11] Among the most useful published research is the multi-volume *Verbände und Truppen der Deutschen Wehrmacht und Waffen-SS im Zweiten Weltkrieg 1939-1945* (Organisations and Forces of the German Armed Forces and *Waffen-SS* in the Second World War 1939-1945) by *Georg Tessin*. The research is exceptional and Tessin's volumes remain the standard — albeit basic — overview of nearly every German formation, making them a useful framework. The information provided by Tessin is generally accepted at face-value, although sources are not included and mistakes have been found. Other publications used in this book are mainly related to accounts from key personnel (such as the Foreign Military Studies),[12] for copies of original documents, or for details that were either too complex or of insufficient relevance to justify additional research.

Even with all available sources, it is impossible to cover all units with the same level of detail. For some units there is an abundance of information, while hardly anything can be found for others. This explains differences in the coverage of different periods and sectors.

Notes on Style

German military terminology is used throughout the text and readers unfamiliar with the German language may find it slightly intimidating. These words primarily concern frequently used terms or those with no good English equivalent, including weapons, specific types and names of formations, etc. A glossary is included and explanations are also provided in the text or endnotes. There still remain several peculiarities and choices that would benefit from an explanation.

The correct period German numbering system for formations is used throughout. This means that Roman numerals are used for corps, battalions and platoons and Arabic numerals for the rest, including companies. Roman numerals for corps should not be an obstacle for the reader as only numbers below 10 and *XXV.* (25th), *LXXIV.* (74th) and *LXXXIV.* (84th) are used on a regular basis. When first listed, Roman numbers are accompanied by Arabic numerals to aid the reader. In some cases the German military opted not to follow the standard use of Roman numerals. For example, *XXXXVII.* (47th) was used rather than *XLVII*. When such exceptions are encountered, the book will also follow the German practice. Since infantry regiments (regardless of their subbranch) are often mentioned in the text, their sub-units are typically designated in abbreviated fashion, e.g., *II./921* for the *II./Grenadier-Regiment 921* (2nd Battalion of *Grenadier-Regiment 921*); *2./6* for the *2./Fj.Rgt. 6* (2nd Company of *Fallschirmjäger-Regiment 6*) or *III./38* for *III./SS-Pz.Gren.Rgt. 38.* (3rd Battalion of *SS-Panzer-Grenadier-Regiment 38*). For other units, the numbers will always be accompanied by at least an abbreviation. An exception is made for named regiments, e.g., *III./D* for the *III./SS-Pz.Gren.Rgt. 3 "Deutschland"* or *I./DF* for *I./SS-Pz.Gren.Rgt. 4 "Der Führer"*. These examples

Introduction

also illustrate the German use of the period ("."), which turns a number into an ordinal number. As such, *II.* means 2nd and *6.* means 6th.

A note needs to be made about the many battlegroups, as these can create confusion. These forces typically had no official organisation or designation. Some were numbered after their division but most were named after the commander, combined with a prefix such as *Kampfgruppe* (battlegroup / *KG*), *Unterkampfgruppe* (subordinate battlegroup / *U.KG*) *Gruppe* (group / *Gr.*) or *Untergruppe* (subordinate group / *U.Gr.*). The use of these terms was inconsistent and adds to their complexity. This is especially true where descriptions changed over time but the commander remained the same. To lessen this problem I have employed a standardised system of four terms, even if they deviate somewhat from the terms actually used at the time:

1. The term *Gruppe* will be used to describe formations above divisional size (e.g., *Gruppe Hellmich*, *Gruppe König*, *Gruppe von Schlieben*). These all included at least the main body of a division reinforced by elements from other formations, resulting in a force larger than a division in size.
2. A battlegroup at or below divisional size or command will be described as a *Kampfgruppe*. These can be either: a) a battered division (e.g., *KG 243. I.D.*); b) a deliberately formed force to operate away from its division (e.g., *KG 265*); or, c) a force still operating within the context of its division or serving under another (e.g., *KG Keil, KG Rohrbach, KG Eitner, KG Müller*). This leaves the option open for a *Kampfgruppe* existing within a Kampfgruppe.
3. In cases where *Kampfgruppen,* rather than divisions, formed the basis of a *Gruppe*, the term *Untergruppe* will be used (e.g., *U.Gr. Eitner* and *U.Gr. Lewandowski* in *Gruppe König*). It should be noted that the designations of battlegroups under *Gruppe König* changed several times. To reduce confusion, they will be referred to as *Untergruppen* from 19 June 1944 onwards (e.g., *KG Eitner* becomes *U.Gr. Eitner*). This ends with the disbandment of *Gruppe König* in early July. The battlegroups then revert to being called *Kampfgruppen*.
4. *Unterkampfgruppe* will only be used for comparatively small battlegroups that were part of a *Kampfgruppe* (e.g.: *U.KG Hoffmann* in *KG Keil*).

Many battlegroups were referred to by both their number and commander's name (e.g., *KG 275* or *KG Heintz*, and *KG 243. I.D.* or *KG Klosterkemper*). This will be highlighted when necessary.

Most units are presented with a graphic representation (*Gliederung*) of their organisation (order of battle), heavy weapons and machine guns. These can be difficult to understand, which is why the symbols are explained in the glossary. Please note that the units are numbered right to left, not left to right. A *Gliederung* represents the view a unit's commander has when inspecting his troops on a parade ground. From that perspective, the units would in fact appear to be numbered left to right. Gun calibres, which are common on the *Gliederungen* and in the text, follow the German practice of using centimetres, even if they are foreign. Indeed, many elements were equipped with captured (heavy) weapons. This is indicated by a letter abbreviation of the country of origin. These too can be found in the glossary. In the case of the Soviet Union this was (r), for Russia. For ease of reading, "Russia" is also typically used in the book when referring to the Soviet Union.

Dates are displayed using the European standard, while using German-style annotations since these are most common in the sources used. Thus, 8.6.44 means 8 June 1944, not 6 August. Times are provided in a 24-hour format, with 15:20 meaning 3:20 PM. Well-known geographical names are typically provided in the English version as most readers will find these easier to understand. This particularly applies to locations outside of western Europe, e.g., Warsaw instead of Warszawa. French names are used for French locations. Since the names of quite a few French locations have changed since the war, the modern version is typically also provided. To understand German records, Allied period maps are far less useful, as they contain fewer geographical names than their German and French counterparts. Most French WWII-era names are available through the 1950's maps on remonterletemps.ign.fr, while contemporary names can be found through www.geoportail.gouv.fr.

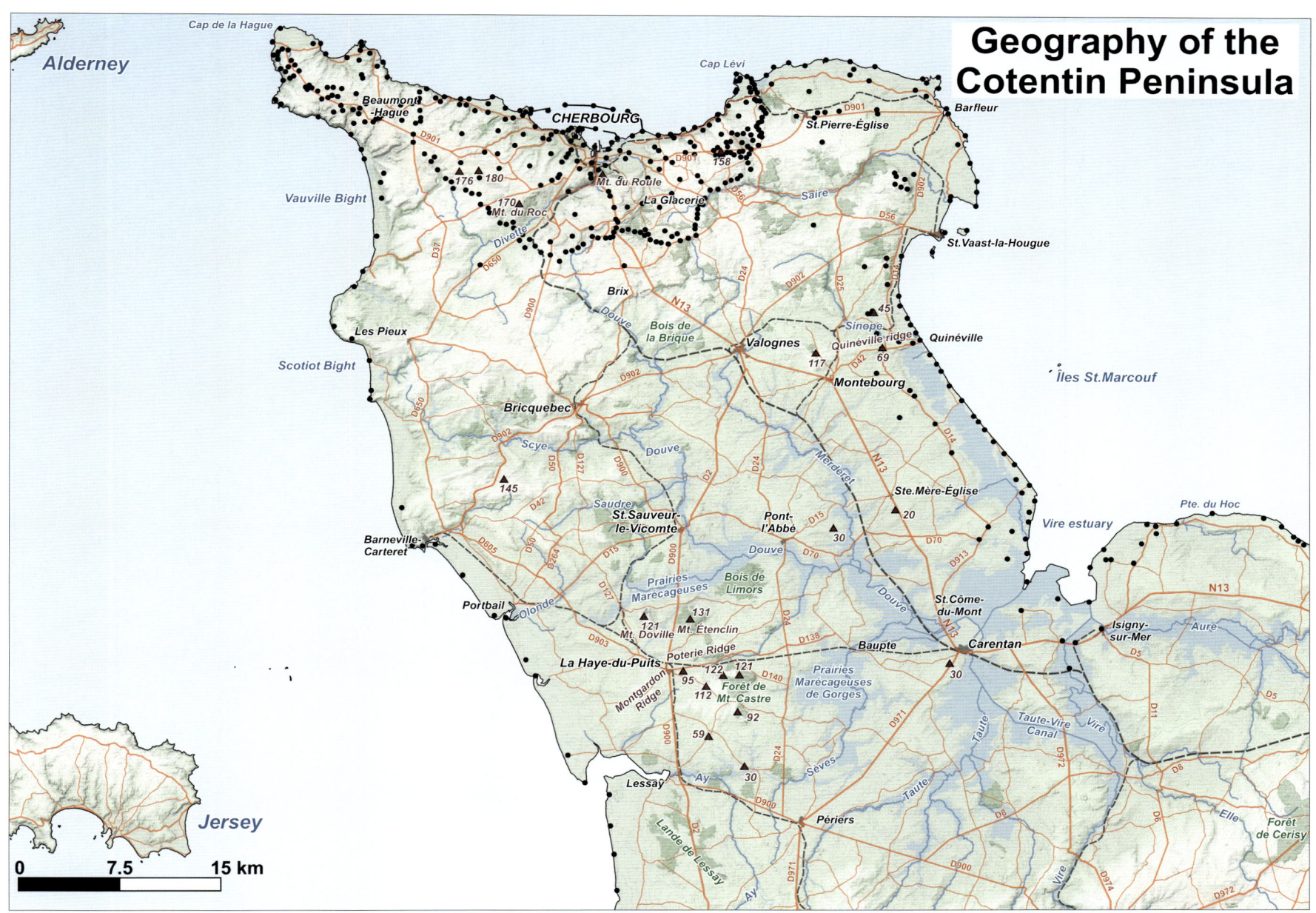

The terrain of the Cotentin Peninsula had a profound effect on the fighting. At the base of the peninsula and behind Utah Beach waterways restricted the avenues of advance. Further west and north, the terrain became increasingly hilly. Resistance nests augmented the natural obstacles and were primarily established along the coast and the Cherbourg Landfront.

Part 1:
GERMAN CHAIN OF COMMAND

German Command Structure in Normandy

Oberbefehlshaber West — Heeresgruppe D

German ground forces in the West were commanded by the *Oberbefehlshaber West* (*Ob.West*). Instead of a separate headquarters, *Heeresgruppe D* (Army Group D / *H.Gr. D*) concurrently served as *Ob.West*.[1] To avoid confusion with *H.Gr. B*, *H.Gr. D* will generally be referred to as *Ob. West*. This corresponds with period documents and, in **September 1944**, the designation *H.Gr. D* was removed altogether.[2]

At the time of the invasion, two major forces were under *Ob.West*: In southern France, *Armeegruppe G* ((ad-Hoc) Field Army Group G, consisting of the *1. Armee* and the *19. Armee*) commanded by *Generaloberst* (*Gen. Obst.*) Johannes Blaskowitz[3]; in the north, *H.Gr. B* under the command of *Generalfeldmarschall* (*Gen.Feldm.*) Erwin Rommel. There were also two smaller forces under *OKW* reserve: *Panzergruppe West* (Armour Group West / *Pz.Gr.West*, which was later designated as the *5. Pz.Armee*)[4] and the *1. Fallschirm-Armee* (1st Airborne Army), which was put under the command of the *OKW* after the invasion.[5]

The commander-in-chief of *Ob.West* on D-Day was *Gen.Feldm.* Gerd von Rundstedt, who held the post from **March 1942** until replaced by *Gen. Feldm.* Günther von Kluge on **2 July 1944**. In turn, von Kluge was relieved of his command on **17 August**.[6] The next day, on his way back to Germany, he committed suicide near Metz.[7] His successor, *Gen.Feldm.* Walter Model, remained in command until **4 September**, when von Rundstedt once again became *Ob.West*.[8]

In late **September 1942**, *General der Infanterie* (*Gen.d.Inf.*) Günther Blumentritt (*Generalmajor* (*Gen.Maj.*) at the time) was appointed as the Chief of Staff of *H.Gr. D* and *Ob.West*. He held this important position until **9 September 1944**.[9] Useful to our understanding of the fighting in Normandy, Blumentritt survived the war, composed several monographs, commented on other officers' writings and, in general, featured prominently in the US Army's Foreign Military Studies (FMS) program.

Left: Gen.Feldm. Gerd von Rundstedt, Oberbefehlshaber West. (BArch, PERS 6/300568)

Centre: Gen.Feldm. Günther von Kluge replaced Feldm. von Rundstedt as Ob.West and later also Feldm. Rommel as commander of H.Gr.B. (NAC)

Right: Gen.Feldm. Erwin Rommel, Commander of Heeresgruppe B. (NAC)

Left: Gen.Obst. Friedrich Dollmann, Commander of 7th Army. (BArch, PERS 6/299566)

Centre: SS-Obergruppenführer Paul Hausser, Commander of 7th Armee after Gen. Dollmann's death. (Collection Michael Miller)

Right: Gen.Maj. Max Pemsel, Chief of Staff AOK 7. (BArch, PERS 6/300333)

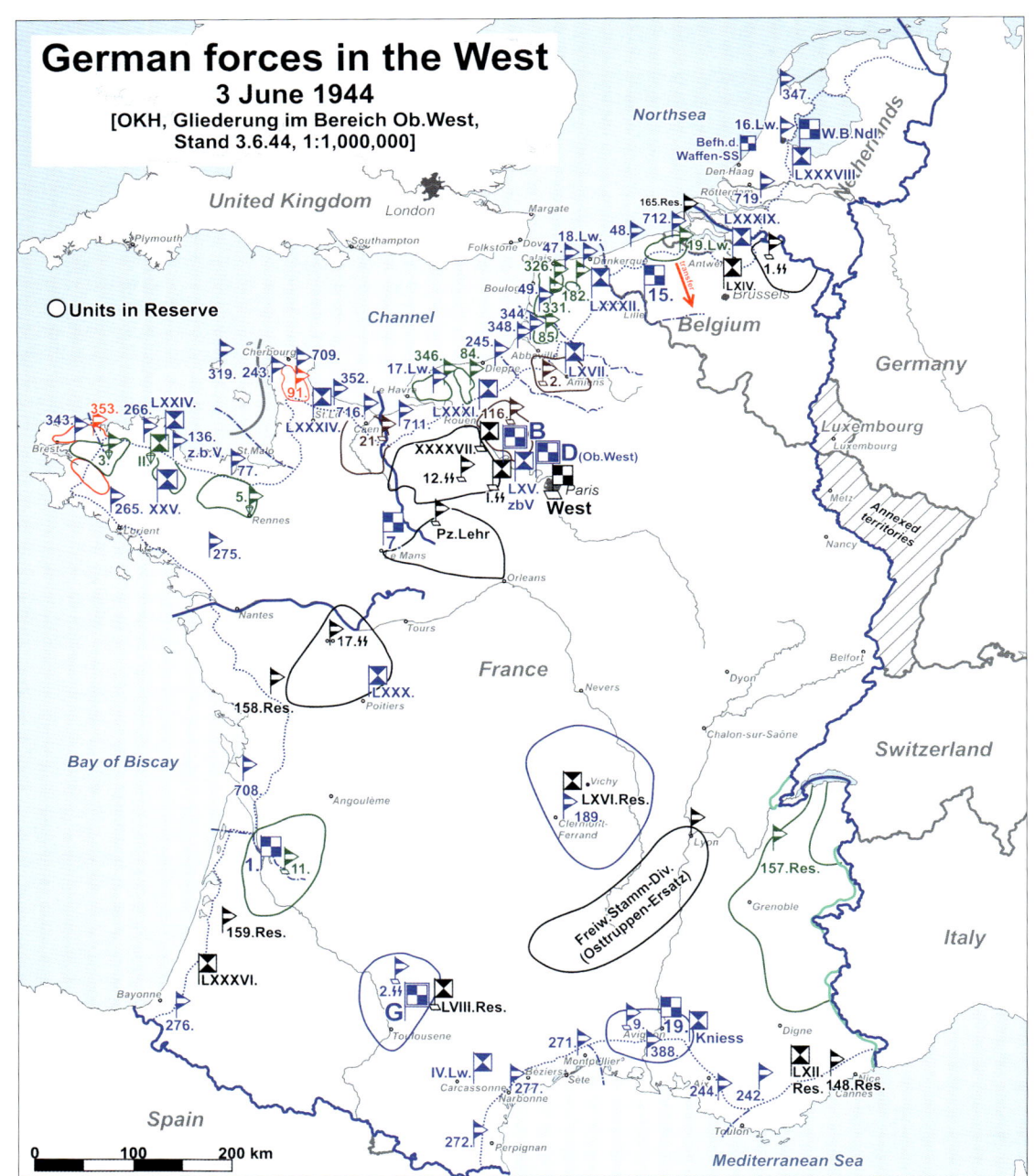

On D-Day most German forces in the West were gathered along the Channel coast. Reserves were generally further inland and were available at different command levels. This included army-corps reserves (green), field-army reserves (red), Army Group B reserves (brown) and OKW reserves (black).

Heeresgruppe B

On D-Day, *H.Gr. B* under Rommel had operational control of the north of the *Westfront* (Western Front).¹⁰ This included the *Wehrmachtbefehlshaber Niederlande* (Commander of the Armed Forces in the Netherlands), the *15. Armee* in Belgium and northern France, and the *7. Armee* in Normandy and Bretagne.¹¹ Rommel commanded *H.Gr. B* until wounded by an Allied air attack on **17 July**. *Ob.West*, *Gen.Feldm.* von Kluge, then also assumed command of *H.Gr. B*.¹² On **18 August** both positions were taken over by *Gen. Feldm.* Model.¹³

H.Gr. B was established on **6 November 1943** as *Heeresgruppe zur besonderen Verwendung* (for special employment / *zbV*). Hitler tasked this special-purpose headquarters with inspecting the defences in the west and preparing plans for counterattacks against enemy landings. Also known as *Sonderstab Rommel*, the headquarters answered directly to Hitler.¹⁴ After inspecting the defences in Denmark, Rommel turned his attention to the *Ob.West* sector in **December**. This created a complicated situation as Rommel's command was operating outside the structure of *Ob.West*. As a partial solution, Rommel's headquarters was placed under *Ob.West* (instead of the *OKW*) without losing its original assignment.¹⁵ On **12 January 1944**, *H.Gr. zbV* was redesignated *H.Gr. B* and given operational command over the forces in the Netherlands, the *15. Armee* and the *7. Armee*.¹⁶

On D-Day, *Pz.Gr. West* (*General der Panzertruppen* Leo Freiherr Geyr von Schweppenburg (*Gen.d.Pz.Tr.*)) was transferred from *OKW* to *H.Gr. B*,¹⁷ but its staff was largely destroyed on **10 June**.¹⁸ It was not until **2 July** that a rebuilt headquarters was able to take over the east of the front from *AOK 7*.¹⁹

7. Armee (AOK 7)

On D-Day, the *7. Armee* was responsible for the defence of Basse-Normandie and Bretagne. It was commanded by *Gen.Obst.* Friedrich Dollmann until his death on **28 June**, whereupon *General der Waffen-SS* (aka *SS-Obergruppenführer / Ogruf.*) Paul Hausser took over.²⁰ *Gen.Maj.* Max Pemsel remained the field army's chief of staff until late **July**, when he was replaced by *Oberst (Obst.)* Rudolf-Christoph Freiherr von Gersdorff.²¹

Much of the field army's *KTB* still exists, providing details about preparations before the landings as well as the fighting. It is also well represented in the FMS. Monographs were written by both Hausser and Pemsel, with Pemsel a frequent commentator on the writings of officers of units subordinated to *AOK 7*.

In early **1944**, three army corps were part of the *7. Armee*, each defending its own coastal sector. The area from Caen to Granville was held by the *LXXXIV. A.K.* under *General der Artillerie (Gen.d.Art.)* Erich Marcks. It was this corps that faced the invasion on D-Day. The Channel Islands were also part of the corps' area.²² In early **April**, the corps' left boundary was extended south to the Sélune River at Pontaubault.²³

The next area, extending to Plouescat in Bretagne, was defended by the *LXXIV. A.K.* (74th Army Corps) under the command of *Gen.d.Inf.* Erich Straube. On D-Day, the *77. I.D.* was in the area around St. Malo up to St. Brieuc; with the *266. I.D.* further west.²⁴ The final coastal sector was held by the *XXV. A.K.* (25th Army Corps) under *Gen.d.Art.* Wilhelm Fahrmbacher. This stretched as far as St. Nazaire on the Loire River. The area around Brest

On 18 May Rommel inspected the coastal defence sectors of the 77. I.D., before attending a meeting at II. Fs.K. headquarters. Here he can be seen flanked by corps commander Gen.d.Flieger Meindl and 7th Army commander Gen.Obst. Dollmann (seated). (NAC)

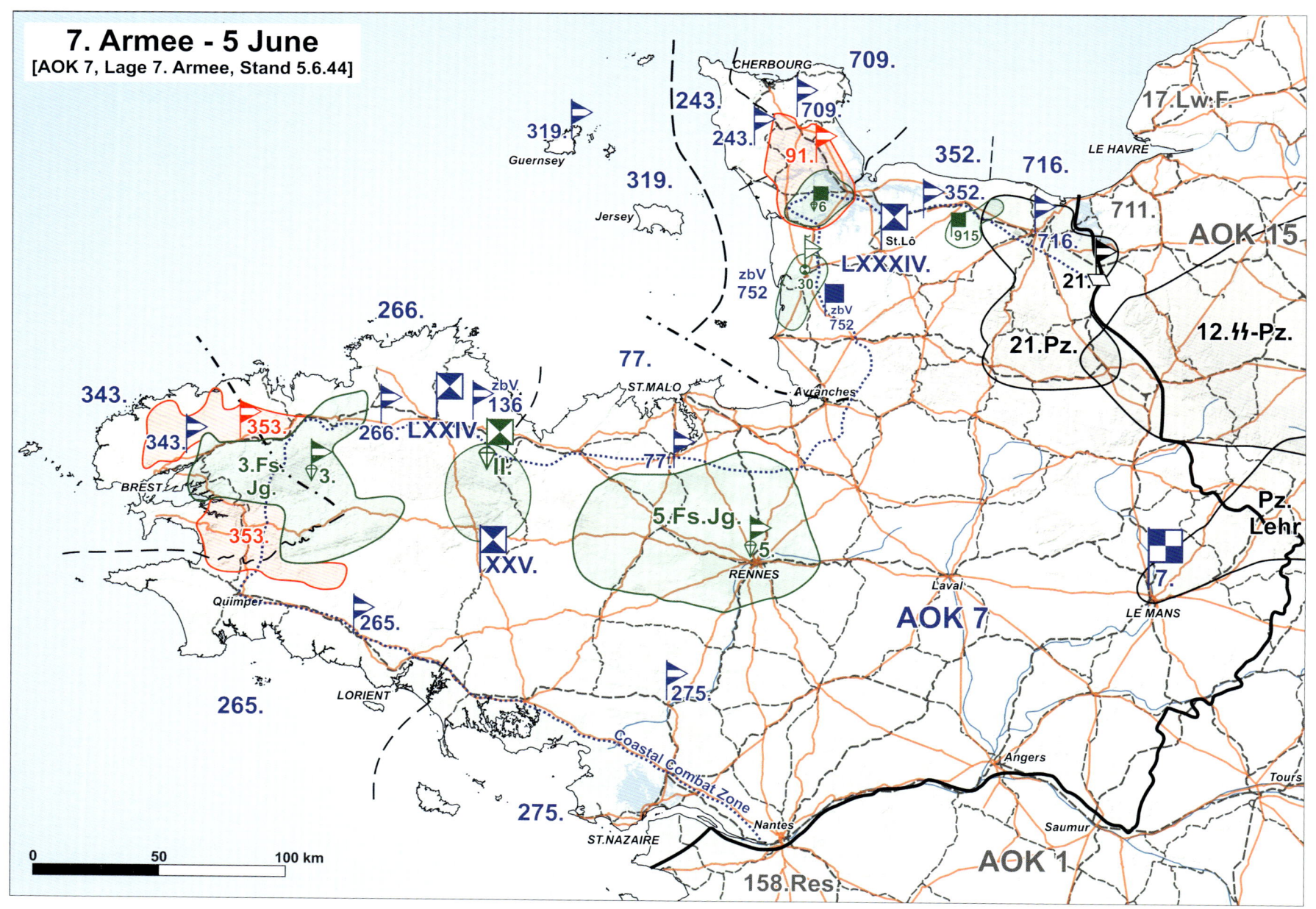

On D-Day four army corps were stationed in 7th Army's sector. They would provide the majority of the troops that saw action in the western part of Normandy in June and July 1944.

On 10 June the headquarters of Panzergruppe West were knocked out by Allied air attacks, forcing 7th Army to remain in charge of most of Normandy. Only the area east of the Orne was handled by 15th Army. On the Cotentin heavy fighting took place west of the Merderet, on the Montebourg front and around Carentan. In the Calvados the German lines were still not continuous (Caumont gap) and at risk of Allied exploitation.

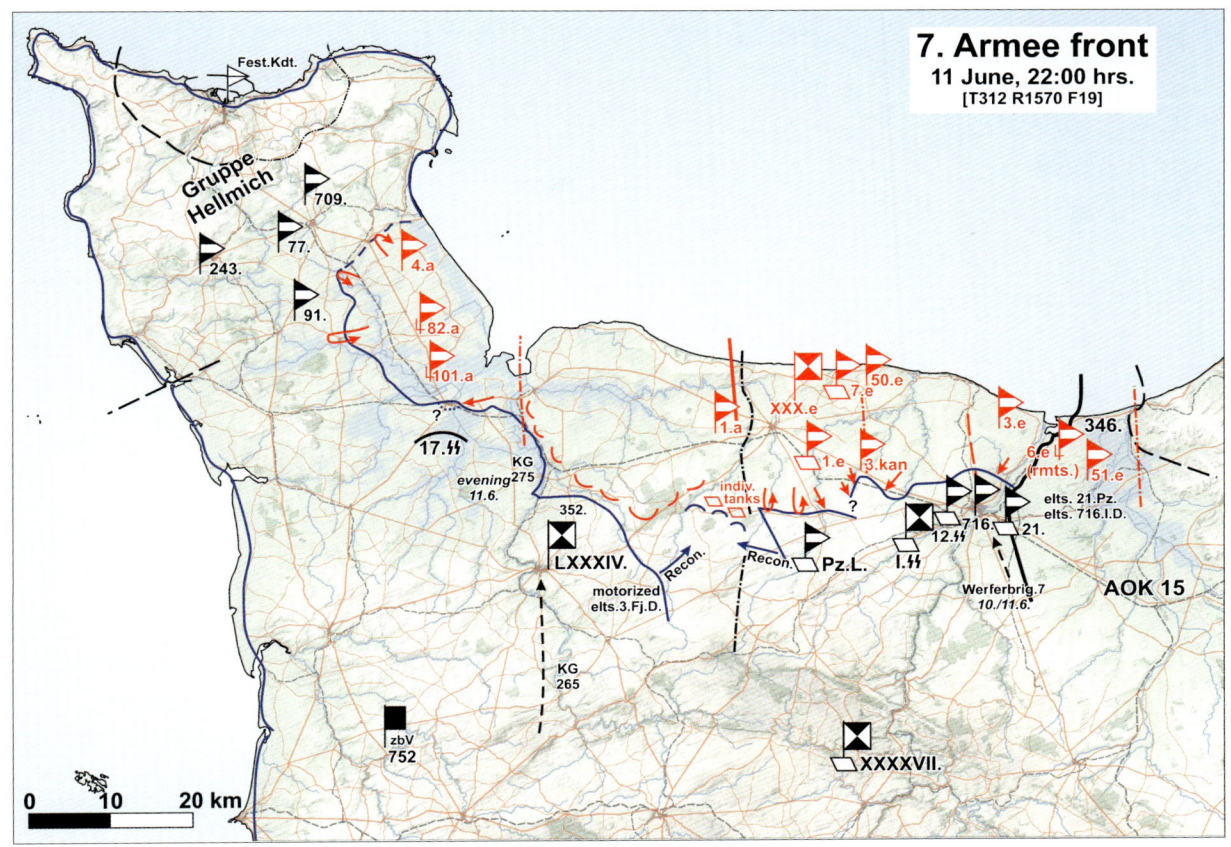

was defended by the *343.* and *353. I.D.* The Quimper-Lorient sector was held by the *265. I.D.* and the remaining sector by the *275. I.D.*[25]

In **May 1944**, the *II. Fs.K.* arrived in Bretagne.[26] This corps, under *General der Flieger (Gen.d.Fl.)* Eugen Meindl, was stationed inland and dispersed over a wide area.[27] The quality of its troops varied, with the *3. Fj.Div.* combat-ready by the time of the invasion and immediately sent to the front, while the *5. Fj.Div.* was still largely untrained. The corps was unusual in having substantial organic corps troops, including a reconnaissance battalion and an assault-gun brigade.[28] Most of the *2. Fj.Div.* arrived only after the corps had moved to the front, so the division was attached to the *XXV. A.K.*, just as the *3. Fj.Div.* had been, when it initially arrived in Bretagne before the *II. Fs.K.* headquarters.[29]

After D-Day, the troops in Bretagne remained under the command of *AOK 7*, becoming the primary source of reinforcements for the west of the front through **June** and **July**. The *II. Fs.K* — or rather its headquarters, assigned corps troops and the *3. Fj.Div.* — was sent to Normandy on **7 June**, reaching the front a few days later.[30] The corps took over the St. Lô area as the right flank of the *LXXXIV. A.K.* before assuming its own command. It remained there and under *AOK 7* throughout **June** and **July**. In the second half of **July**, the *LXXIV. A.K.* headquarters was ordered to the front to serve under *Pz.Gr.West*. The headquarters of the *XXV. A.K.* took over its sector in Bretagne on **26 July**.[31] The *XXV. A.K.* remained under the command of *AOK 7* until **5 August** when it was put directly under *H.Gr. B*.[32]

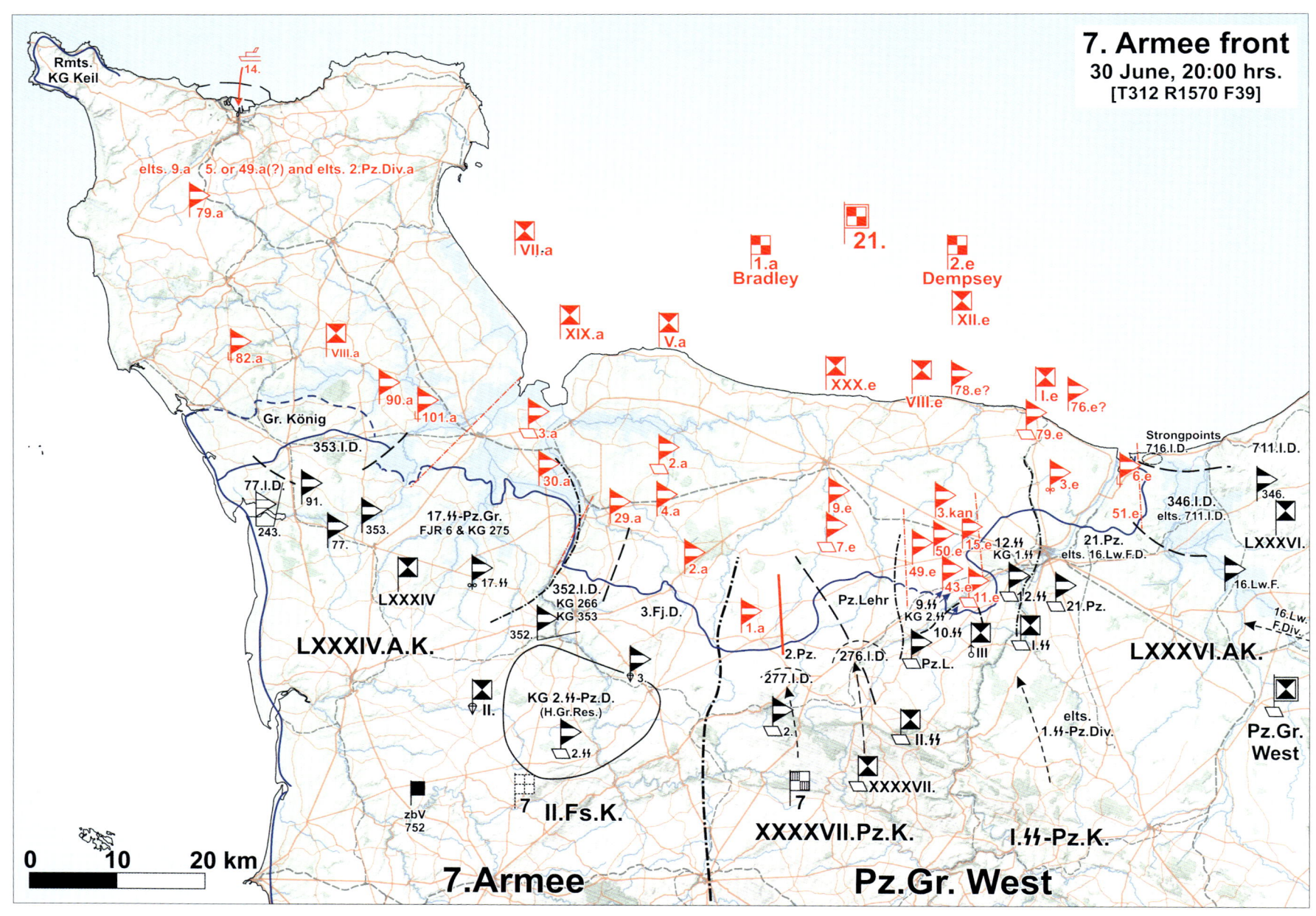

In late June Panzergruppe West became operational again and took over the eastern part of the front in early July. 7th Army continued to focus on the area west of the Vire River with the LXXXIV. A.K. and the II. Fs.K.

Immediately after the invasion, new corps headquarters and troops were quickly sent to the front to reinforce the *7. Armee*. On the afternoon of D-Day, the *I. SS-Panzer-Korps* (*I. SS-Pz.K.*) was the first to be attached.[33] Upon arrival, the corps assumed control of the area east of the Arromanches - Brécey line. The *716. I.D.*, the *21. Pz.Div.*, the *12. SS-Pz.Div. "Hitlerjugend"* and the *Panzer-Lehr Division* (Armoured Instructional Division / *Pz.Lehr-Div.*) would be attached to the corps.[34]

On **7 June**, *AOK 7* was notified that *Pz.Gr.West* — redesignated the *5. Panzerarmee* (*5. Pz.Armee*) in August — was attached to it.[35] The *Panzergruppe*, more or less a field-army command itself, was ordered to assume command of the entire Calvados front as far as Carentan and St. Lô. Its mission was to destroy the enemy southeast of Bayeux, while sealing off advances around Caen and in the area held by the *352. I.D.*[36] The presence of *Pz.Gr.West* would enable *AOK 7* to focus on the left-hand sector of the invasion front and its responsibilities in Bretagne.

Pz.Gr.West took command of the *I. SS-Pz.K.* on the evening of **9 June**.[37] Its headquarters was attacked by Allied aircraft the following evening and put out of commission. The staff sustained heavy personnel losses and was withdrawn from the front to be reconstituted.[38] In turn, the *I. SS-Pz.K.* took command of the sector and returned to *AOK 7* command.[39]

The second corps to reinforce *AOK 7* after the invasion was the *XXXXVII. Pz.K.* (47th Armour Corps), which was ordered to the front on **9 June**.[40] Occupying the area between the *II. Fs.K.* and the *I. SS-Pz.K.*, the corps' forces finally closed the "Caumont Gap" in mid-**June**, establishing a continuous frontline for the first time since the invasion.[41]

In mid-**June**, another corps headquarters was sent to the front. The headquarters of the *LXXXVI. A.K.* (86th Army Corps) was brought up from Dax on the Bay of Biscay and took over the sector east of the Orne River on **20 June**.[42] This area had been assigned to the *LXXXI. A.K.* (81st Army Corps) since **11 June**, which put the sector under *AOK 15*, a situation which changed with the arrival of the new corps headquarters.[43] The *LXXXI. A.K.* was relieved and the boundary of the *7. Armee* extended to the mouth of the Seine.[44]

On **12 June**, the *II. SS-Pz.K.*, which had been attached to *Heeresgruppe Nordukraine* (Army Group North Ukraine), was ordered to transfer to *H.Gr. D* immediately.[45] Needing time to regroup, the corps went into position in Normandy on **28 June**.[46] At that moment, the *I. SS-Pz.K.* was facing the

The I. SS-Panzerkorps played a key part in the fighting in the eastern half of the beachhead. Here we see its commander, Obstgruf. Dietrich, informing Feldm. von Rundstedt during a visit before the invasion. Behind his hand is Brigf. Witt, the commander of the 12. SS-Panzer-Division. (NAC)

British Epsom Offensive, which had started on **26 June** and which the corps could not contain without support.[47] The *II. SS-Pz.K.* received orders to launch a counterattack the following day. (For the counterattack, it was attached to the *I. SS-Pz.K.* and *Pz.Gr.West*.)[48] Further complicating matters, the corps commanding general, *SS-Obergruppenführer* Hausser, was ordered to succeed Dollmann as commander-in-chief of *AOK 7* earlier that day. The field army, however, considered it necessary for Hausser to remain at the front to ensure the corps was deployed correctly.[49] Meanwhile, the corps itself was taken over by *SS-Ogruf.* Wihelm Bittrich.[50]

The rebuilt staff of *Pz.Gr.West* was again operational on **28 June**, assuming command of the *I.* and *II. SS-Pz.K.*, the *XXXXVII. Pz.K.* and the *LXXXVI. A.K.*[51] *Pz.Gr.West* remained under *AOK 7* until 00:00 on **2 July**, when it was put directly under *H.Gr. B.*[52]

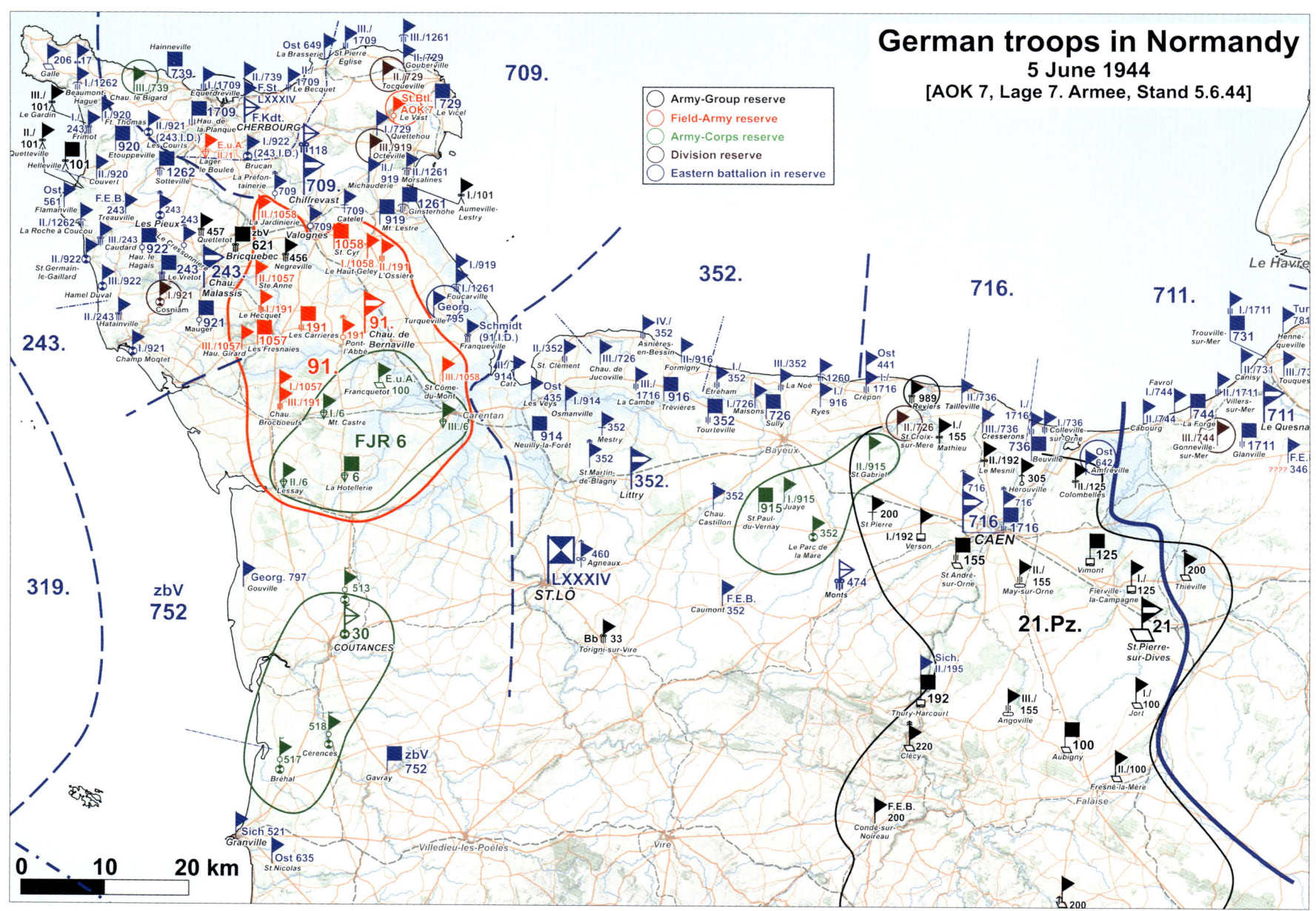

On D-Day there were five divisions stationed in Normandy under the LXXXIV. A.K. The 91.LL.D. was army reserve and the 21.Pz.D. was Army Group B reserve. The heaviest presence of troops was on the Cotentin to protect the important harbour of Cherbourg.

LXXXIV. A.K.

On D-Day, the *LXXXIV. A.K.* defended the Cotentin as well as the Calvados, giving it the dubious honour of facing all of the landings. The corps faced the British 21st Army Group (General Montgomery), which attacked with the US First Army (General Bradley) and the British Second Army (General Dempsey). To counter the invasion, new commands and forces were rushed in, allowing the corps' sector to be quickly reduced in size. By **18 June**, it was limited to the area west of the Vire River. Apart from the final days, the corps would remain under *AOK 7* throughout the battle for Normandy. For most of **June** and **July**, its main opponent was the US First Army, which first brought in the VII Corps and grew to include the VIII and the XIX Corps. The V Corps operated east of the Vire and only encountered the *LXXXIV. A.K.* briefly.

While the *LXXXIV. A.K.* and its development prior to the invasion will be examined in more detail later, for now the discussion will be limited to its role at the time of the invasion and during the fighting. As the most important command at the front on D-Day, this analysis will illustrate how its command developed during the summer of **1944**, which divisions fought under the corps and in which battles and engagements it participated.

On D-Day, the corps was commanded by *Gen.d.Art.* Marcks, who had held the position since **1 August 1943**.[53] Well acquainted with the area and the forces under his command, he was widely regarded as a highly capable and inspirational leader.[54] Late on the morning of **12 June**, while on his way to *Gruppe Hellmich*, he was fatally wounded in a fighter-bomber attack.[55]

Following his death, the corps went through a series of commanding generals. Initially, *Gen.d.Fl.* Meindl took command. This was a logical step, since his *II. Fs.K.* was attached to the corps and Meindl was now the senior commander in the sector. Later that day, *Gen.d.Art.* Fahrmbacher, the commanding general of the *XXV. A.K.*, was ordered to succeed Marcks, which he did at 06:00 on **13 June**.[56] The *XXV. A.K.* was, in turn, taken over by *Generalleutnant (Gen.Lt.)* Dietrich von Choltitz.[57]

These arrangements were short-lived. Fahrmbacher led the corps up to and during the American breakthrough to the west coast of the Cotentin, with Hitler hindering his efforts to withdraw as many troops as possible.[58] Von Choltitz took command on **18 June,** when Fahrmbacher fell ill.[59] Von Choltitz remained in command until relieved by *Gen.Lt.* Otto Elfeldt on **30 July**.[60] This change had been ordered by higher headquarters and was not approved of by Hausser or von Kluge.[61] In **August**, the corps was trapped in the Falaise Pocket. The headquarters was unable to break out and Elfeldt was taken prisoner.[62] The corps headquarters was officially disbanded in **November**.[63]

The corps is well represented in the FMS. Fahrmbacher, von Choltitz, Elfeldt and *Oberstleutnant (Obstlt.)* Friedrich von Criegern (Chief of Staff), all prepared studies.[64] In 1954, the corps chief-of-staff for intelligence, *Major der Reserve (Maj.d.R.)* Friedrich Hayn, published *Die Invasion: Von Cotentin bis Falaise* (The Invasion: From Cotentin to Falaise), which included many of his experiences. Very few corps records for **1944** have survived, but the summer of **1944** is fairly well covered in the records of *AOK 7* and *H.Gr. B*. ULTRA records provide details that cannot be found elsewhere.

At the time of the invasion, the corps consisted of six infantry divisions and numerous smaller formations. The east of the Calvados coast was held by the *716. I.D.*, with the *352. I.D.* on the western part of the coast. The north and east coast of the Cotentin were defended by the *709. I.D.*, while the *243. I.D.* was located along the west coast and on the north coast west of Cherbourg. In the centre of the peninsula was the *91. Luftlande-Infanterie-Division* (91st Airmobile Infantry Division / *91. LL.D.*) as a field-army reserve, reinforced by *Fallschirmjäger-Regiment 6* (Parachute Regiment 6 / *FJR 6*). The final division in the corps sector was the *319. I.D.* on the Channel Islands. The coast south of Barneville was defended by a group of foreign forces recruited from the Eastern Front and security elements commanded by *Grenadier-Regimentsstab zbV 752* (Grenadier Regimental Headquarters for Special Purposes 752). Located inland in the Coutances-Granville area was *Schnelle Brigade 30* (Mobile Brigade 30), an additional infantry reserve of *H.Gr. B*. The *21. Pz.Div.* was also in the sector, around and south of Caen, as a field-army group reserve.[65]

Prior to the invasion, *AOK 7* had realised that the corps headquarters would need support, if the Cotentin and Calvados were attacked simultaneously. In the event, *AOK 7* intended to bring up the *LXXIV. A.K.* headquarters from Bretagne to take over the Calvados, allowing *LXXXIV. A.K.* to concentrate on the Cotentin.[66] This plan was approved by Rommel on **10 May**. In fact, the field army already wanted the *LXXXIV. A.K.* to concentrate just on the Cotentin, and intended to relocate the corps headquarters to the centre of the peninsula.[67] On **12 May**, *Gen.d.Art.* Marcks presented a map of the intended repositioning following the arrival of the *91. LL.D.* In line with the ideas of

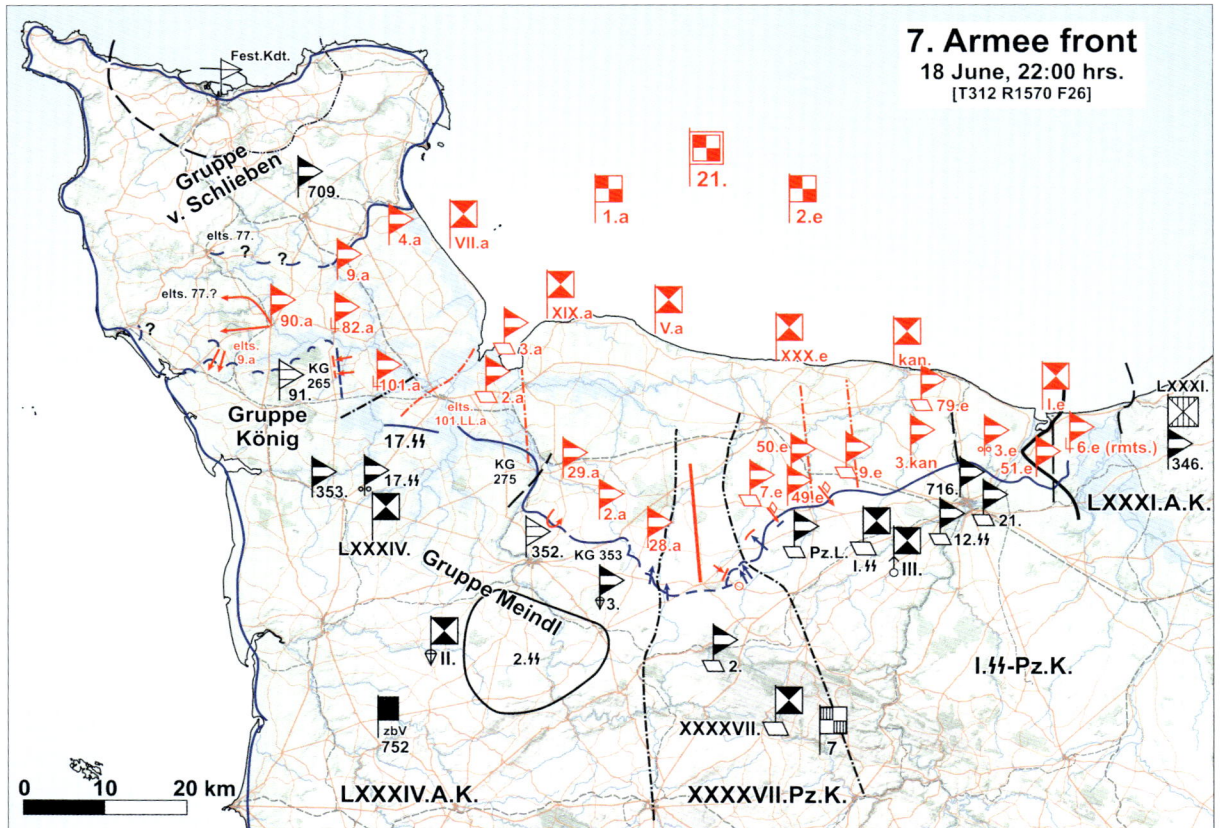

The Westfront on the Cotentin collapsed on 16 June, separating Gruppe von Schlieben and Gruppe Hellmich. Following Hellmich's death, Gruppe König was tasked with sealing off the base of the peninsula while Gruppe von Schlieben defended Cherbourg.

AOK 7. It included an (ad-hoc) corps headquarters at Orglandes.[68] In reality, nothing changed before the invasion, and no second corps headquarters was available to ease the corps' burdens. Instead, *Gen.d.Art.* Marcks issued instructions should the peninsula be cut by Allied forces: The senior commander in the area, *Gen.Lt.* Hellmich of the *243. I.D.*, would assume command of all forces in the sector.[69]

In his post-war monograph, *Gen.Lt.* von Schlieben *(709. I.D.)* viewed this as an unfortunate decision, since the necessary communications equipment was not available. In addition, *Gen.Lt.* Hellmich would still be responsible for his own division. Von Schlieben felt that there should have been a separate corps headquarters to command the three divisions.[70] He was clearly not alone, but the decision was beyond Marcks' control and his solution was arguably a reasonable alternative. *Gen.Lt.* von Schlieben also felt that Hellmich remained preoccupied with his own division, making him reluctant to withdraw forces from the west coast, since he was concerned about additional landings.[71] Despite this, it appears that the troops holding the west coast were reduced quicker than von Schlieben realised, and he may not have appreciated how much of the *243. I.D.* was reinforcing the *91. LL.D.* west of the Merderet.[72] At 22:00 on **8 June**, only two infantry and two artillery battalions from the *243. I.D.* remained on the west coast.[73] Moreover, *Gen.Lt.* Hellmich was not given control over the forces on the Cotentin until that evening.

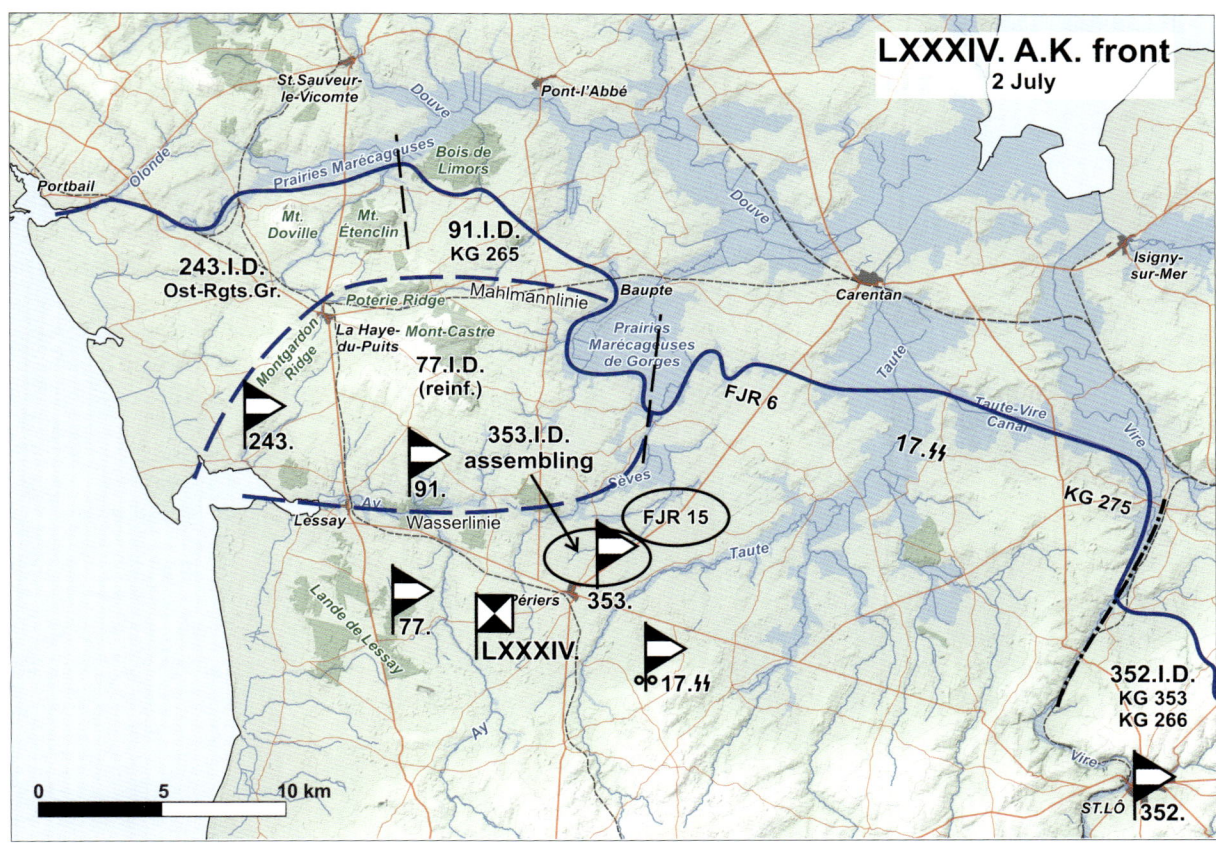

As American forces focussed their attention on the capture of Cherbourg, the LXXXIV. A.K. used the opportunity to establish its defences along the base of the peninsula. In early July Gruppe König was dissolved and the 91.LL.D. and 243.I.D. assumed responsibility of their sectors. The 353.I.D. left the Mahlmann-Linie and the 77.I.D. took control of the line.

June — Invasion

Following the invasion, the *II. Fs.K.* was quickly placed in direct support of the *LXXXIV. A.K.*[74] It was common practice in the German military to make use of the existing command structure, even if a new force occupied a similar level of command.[75] The new corps, which took over command of the *352. I.D.*, also fielded the *3. Fj.Div.* and the *17. SS-Pz.Gren.Div.*, although it did not actually take command at the front until **12 June**.[76]

In the Caen sector, *Pz.Gr.West* and a number of corps headquarters assumed command soon after D-Day.[77] This limited the *LXXXIV. A.K.* to the area west of Bayeux and, when the *XXXXVII. Pz.K.* arrived a few days later, its front was further reduced to the area west of the Balleroy - Vire line.[78] The *II.*

Fs.K. remained subordinated to the corps until **18 June**.[79] Except for a short period after the arrival of the *II. Fs.K.*, the boundary between the two corps was formed by the Vire River, a situation that continued until late **July**.[80]

Faced by the difficulties of this long frontline, the corps decided to simplify the command structure. *Gen.Lt.* Hellmich was given command of the troops on the Cotentin on the evening of **8 June**, with his force being known as *Gruppe Hellmich*.[81]

The next morning, Marcks proposed to *AOK 7* that the *II. Fs.K.* be placed under the command of *Pz.Gr. West*, allowing his corps to focus on the Cotentin. The recommendation was not approved.[82] On the evening of **11 June**, *H.Gr. B* informed *AOK 7* of plans to reduce the burden on the corps headquarters. The intention was to bring another corps headquarters to Normandy. Together with the *II. Fs.K.*, it would form *Armee-Gruppe Marcks* (as a kind of an ad-hoc field-army), with the headquarters of the *LXXXIV. A.K.* taking over-all command of this force.[83] The plan had been inspired by Marcks' extensive knowledge of the area, but his death on **12 June** appears to have put a sudden end to it.[84] No ad-hoc field-army was created, nor were any changes made to the over-all organisation in the west of Normandy.[85]

In the period from D-Day to **14 June**, the US VII Corps was able to expand its Cotentin (Utah Beach) beachhead. In the north, the Americans reached Montebourg and seized the high ground east of the town. To the south, they advanced beyond Carentan and made contact with troops coming from Omaha Beach (V Corps). Troops also crossed the Merderet River and began their push to the west coast of the peninsula.[86] German reinforcements, in particular the *77. I.D.*, were unable to contain the beachhead. With the ever-increasing threat of an American breakthrough to the west coast, elements of *Gruppe Hellmich* were split off on **15 June** to form a second force: *Gruppe von Schlieben*.[87] Officially, this was to allow *Gruppe Hellmich* (aka *Südgruppe* or Southern Group) to focus on the *Westfront* of the beachhead, while *Gruppe von Schlieben* (aka *Nordgruppe* or Northern Group) assumed responsibility for operations on the *Nordfront*.[88] In reality, an American breakthrough to the west coast was already expected. The plan meant that *Gruppe von Schlieben* would remain in the north around Montebourg and ultimately withdraw into *Festung Cherbourg*, while *Gruppe Hellmich* would move south to establish a new defensive line for the *LXXXIV. A.K.*[89]

In response to the critical situation east of St. Sauveur-le-Vicomte, where US forces were pushing west, forces were gathered under *Obst.* König, commander of the *91. LL.D.*[90] This included the elements south of the Douve River and the Prairies Marécageuses. This force later became known as *Gruppe König*.

On **18 June**, when the peninsula had been cut, *Gruppe von Schlieben* (*709. I.D.* and elements from other divisions) was put directly under *AOK 7* command.[91] The *II. Fs.K.* was relieved from its attachment to the *LXXXIV. A.K.*[92] Changes to the corps boundaries also released the *17. SS-Pz.Gren.Div.* — reinforced by *FJR 6* and *Kampfgruppe 275* (aka *KG Heintz*), which had been west of the Vire — from the *II. Fs.K.* and put it under the *LXXXIV. A.K.*

The corps now had two main sectors. *Gruppe König*, better known as the *Nordfront*, extended north from the Prairies Marécageuses de Gorges to the Douve River and then west to the coast. Meanwhile, the reinforced *17. SS-Pz.Gren.Div.* defended the area east of the Prairies Marécageuses de Gorges up to the Vire River. Both *Gen.Lt.* Hellmich and *Gen.Maj.* Stegmann (*77. I.D.*) were killed around this time, leaving *Obst.* König in charge of the *Nordfront*.[93]

What followed was a period of relative calm, allowing the troops to regroup and to organise their defence. The fresh *353. I.D.* (minus elements deployed elsewhere) arrived to reinforce the corps and became the backbone of the *Nordfront*. *Gruppe König* was again disbanded on **1 July**, and command of the frontline divided between the *91. LL.D.* on the right and the *243. I.D.* on the left.[94] To their rear, a new defensive line was formed by the *77. I.D.* and the *353. I.D.*; it became known as the *Mahlmann-Linie* after the commander of the *353. I.D.*

July — Holding On

In early **July**, three American corps from the First US Army launched their offensives against the *LXXXIV. A.K.*[95] This began on **3 July** with the VIII Corps attacking the *Nordfront*, followed the next day by assaults from the VII Corps along the Carentan-Périers isthmus; the objective of both was Périers. Further east, the XIX Corps crossed the Vire and Taute-Vire Canal on **7 July**.[96] As reinforcements, the *2. SS-Pz.Div.* was attached to the corps, largely on the *Nordfront* and in the corps' centre, along the Carentan-Périers highway.

To the east, the Americans started to advance between the Taute and Vire Rivers, threatening to outflank the important town of St. Lô from the west. In response to this, the *Pz.Lehr-Div.*, and gradually much of *5. Fj.Div.* (*FJR 15* was already on the *Nordfront*), were transferred to the area, but the situation continued to deteriorate.[97] Since the entire corps was under attack, *AOK 7* again considered deploying another corps headquarters to take over part of its sector, but this was not done.[98]

Despite the reinforcements, the American advance pushed the German front back. By mid-**July**, the *Nordfront* had pulled back to the *Wasserlinie* — also known as the Lessay - Sèves sector — and the front there again went quiet, allowing the *77. I.D.* headquarters to be sent back to Bretagne. The fighting continued on the corps' right flank. East of the Vire, the *II. Fs.K.* lost St. Lô, while the *LXXXIV. A.K.* elements between the Vire and the Taute were forced back to the Périers - St. Lô highway, suffering heavy casualties. In this sector, the Americans temporarily halted their attacks.[99]

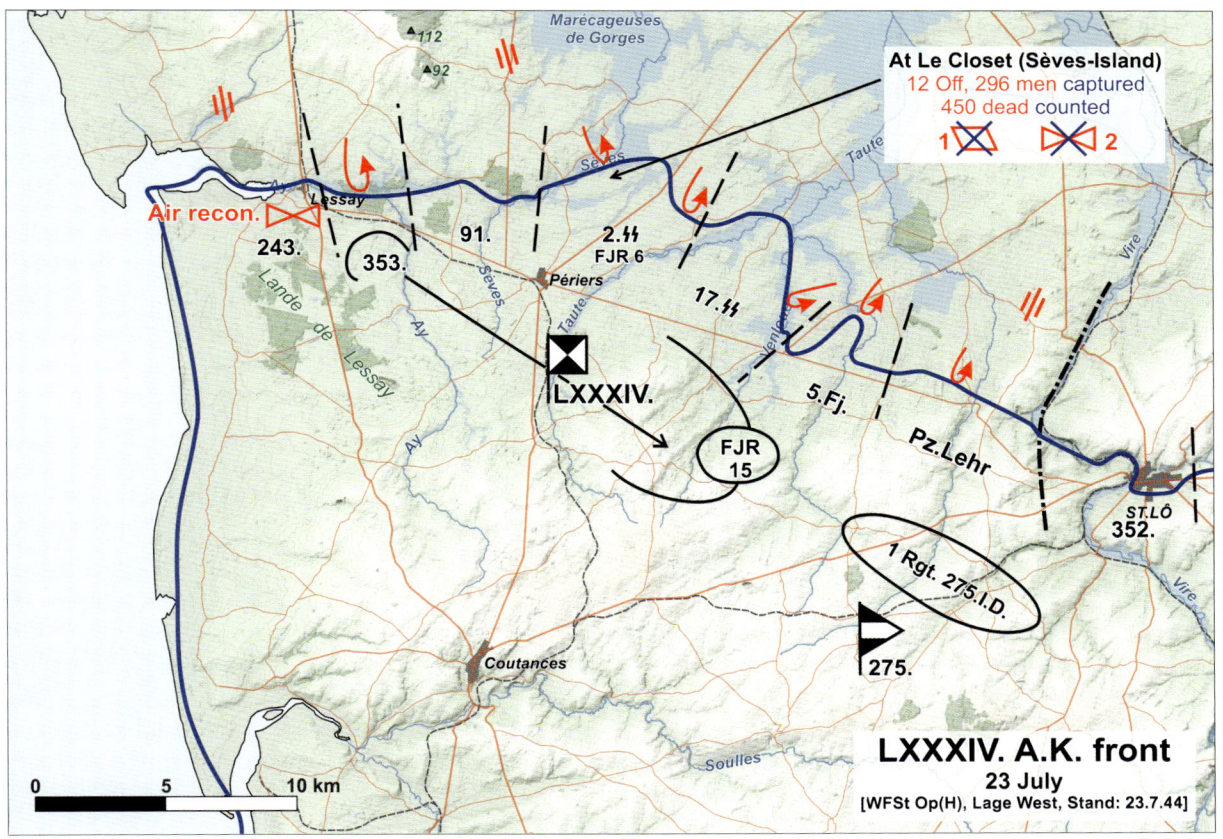

West of the Vire River, the US First Army's offensives of early July gradually forced back the LXXXIV. A.K. By mid-July the corps' Nordfront had to be withdrawn to the Wasserlinie. East of the Taute River, US troops reached the Périers - St.Lô highway. From there they would break through with Operation Cobra.

The corps took advantage of the relative quiet to reorganise. By **24 July**, the *243. I.D.* (to the west) and the *91. LL.D.* held the *Nordfront*, while the Carentan - Périers highway was defended by the *2. SS-Pz.Div.* The corps' right flank, largely following the St. Lô - Périers highway, was covered by the *17. SS-Pz.Gren.Div.*, the *5. Fj.Div.* and the *Pz.Lehr-Div.* (to the east). The *353. I.D.* was moved from the *Nordfront* to the corps' right flank, where it was held in corps reserve south of the highway, behind the *SS* and *Fallschirmjäger* divisions. Elements of the newly arrived *275. I.D.*, being held as a field-army reserve, were on the boundary with the *II. Fs.K.*, behind the *Pz.Lehr-Div.* and the *352. I.D.*[100]

On **25 July**, the Americans unleashed Operation Cobra, which shattered the corps' lines west of St. Lô. Faced with impending encirclement, the corps was ordered to withdraw most of its forces to the southeast. However, the Americans managed to encircle several German divisions in a pocket — known as either the "La Baleine" or "Roncey" Pockets — west of their primary advance on Avranches. While most of the divisions were able to escape, they sustained significant losses in equipment and personnel. Some units headed south, where they unsuccessfully tried to stop the American advance and their breakout from Normandy at Avranches.[101] After Operation Cobra, the *91. LL.D.* ceased to exist as a fighting force.[102] The battered remains of the *Pz.Lehr-Div.*, the *2. SS-Pz.Div.* and the *17. SS-Pz.Gren.Div.* linked up with the *XXXXVII. Pz.K.*, which was pushed into the gap between the *LXXXIV. A.K.* and the *II. Fs.K.*[103]

August — Retreat and Decimation

After several days of bitter combat, the corps was able to impart some order around **1 August** while in the vicinity of Villedieu-les-Poêles.[104] The corps essentially consisted of the remnants of the *243.* and the *353. I.D.*, a regiment from the *363. I.D.*, and a reinforced battlegroup from the *116. Pz.Div.* (*Kampfgruppe Lüder*) on the left (south). The *XXXXVII. Pz.K.* was now in position on the right, but there was no neighbour to the left. Instead, the corps sector continued far to the south and lacked a continuous frontline or contact with friendly forces. Units from the *275. I.D.* and the *5. Fj.Div.* were in the area, but contact with them was soon lost due to continued withdrawals, the American advance and the arrival of new German commands. On **30 July**, the respective headquarters of the two divisions were placed directly under *AOK 7*.[105] Even so, significant elements of the *275. I.D.* remained with the corps, mostly attached to the *353. I.D.*[106]

In an effort to re-establish some control at the front, the corps was reinforced by the *363. I.D.* and the *116. Pz.Div.* on **2 August**.[107] Additional reinforcements were on their way in the form of the *84. I.D.*, and it began arriving in the area of Sourdeval, on the corps' left flank, on **3 August**.[108]

Generally speaking, the first week of **August** was characterised by a fighting withdrawal. This allowed time to prepare for the German armoured counterattack to recapture Avranches — *Unternehmen Lüttich* — which would be staged to the corps' south.[109] A strengthening of the corps and a shortening of the lines of the *7. Armee* allowed the *LXXXIV. A.K.* to relieve the *XXXXVII. Pz.K.* on **4-5 August** and re-establish contact with the *II. Fs.K.* to the right.[110] In turn, the armoured corps took over the left wing of the *LXXXIV. A.K.* from Chérencé-le-Roussel to the southeast. This shift in forces allowed the *XXXXVII. Pz.K.* to relieve the *84. I.D.*, which became available to the *LXXXIV. A.K.*[111] The *84. I.D.* then sought to relieve the *116. Pz.Div.*, but this proved difficult and was not completed until **6 August**.

Once all transfers had been completed, the corps sector consisted of the *363. I.D.* on the right (north), the *353. I.D.* (with parts of the *275.* and the *243. I.D.*) in the centre, and the newly arrived *84. I.D.* on the left. The sector now stretched southwest from Vire to St. Pois, then southeast to the Sée River.[112]

The German armoured offensive opened on **7 August** but ground to an abrupt halt the next day. During this period the *LXXXIV. A.K.* faced intense enemy pressure that lasted for several more days. Its front was pushed back to the south and east, away from Vire and across the Vire-Sourdeval highway. Around Vire (*363. I.D.*), the corps witnessed heavy fighting and suffered setbacks that threatened the resumption of the Avranches offensive. To counter the threat, battlegroups from the *1. SS-Pz.Div.* "LSSAH" and the *Pz. Lehr-Div.* — *Kampfgruppe Schiller* and *Kampfgruppe Hauser*, respectively[113] — were moved up to support the counterattack on **10 August** and rebuild a frontline. Another reinforcement, *Kampfgruppe Dobeneck* from the *331. I.D.*, also participated, and it remained with the *353. I.D.* instead of returning to its division.[114]

Any German hopes of resuming the attack towards Avranches were rapidly overtaken by events. To its south, the *7. Armee* was being outflanked by US forces, which were pushing east and reached Argentan on **12 August**. At the same time, British, Canadian and Polish forces drove southeast towards Falaise from the Caen area. Together, these advances threatened the main body of German troops in Normandy with encirclement and annihilation. The *7. Armee* began a retreat eastward that would take the corps all the way to the Dives River.[115] During the retreat, heavy fighting took place to the rear of the *LXXXIV. A.K.* and the *7. Armee*, as Allied troops attempted to close the pocket by advancing from the north and south along the Caen-Argentan road, and further east, along the Dives River. In these areas, elements from the *5. Pz.Armee* and *Pz.Gr. Eberbach* fought to keep escape routes open.

Starting on the night of **10 August**, corps' operations were characterised by confused withdrawals at night and efforts by day to hold on to the collapsing front. The corps' route took it through Tinchebray-Bocage, south past Flers, then between Landigou and Briouze, and on to the Orne River. On the night of **17-18 August**, it crossed the river between St. Croix-sur-Orne and Putanges. The following night (**18-19 August**), the forces in the pocket pulled back across the Falaise - Argentan highway and adjacent railway, while to their rear (east), the pocket had already been sealed shut along the Dives River.[116] Only a breakout could save the corps now.

Conditions became increasingly desperate, forcing a number of reorganisations and emergency measures that affected the corps.[117] On **16 August**, the *363. I.D.* was reassigned to the *II. Fs.K.*, leaving the corps with only the *84. I.D.*, the *353. I.D.* and parts of the *275.* and the *331. I.D.*[118] On **17 August**, the *10. SS-Pz.Div.* "Frundsberg" was temporarily attached, and it deployed to keep the Orne River crossings open for the retreating *7. Armee*.

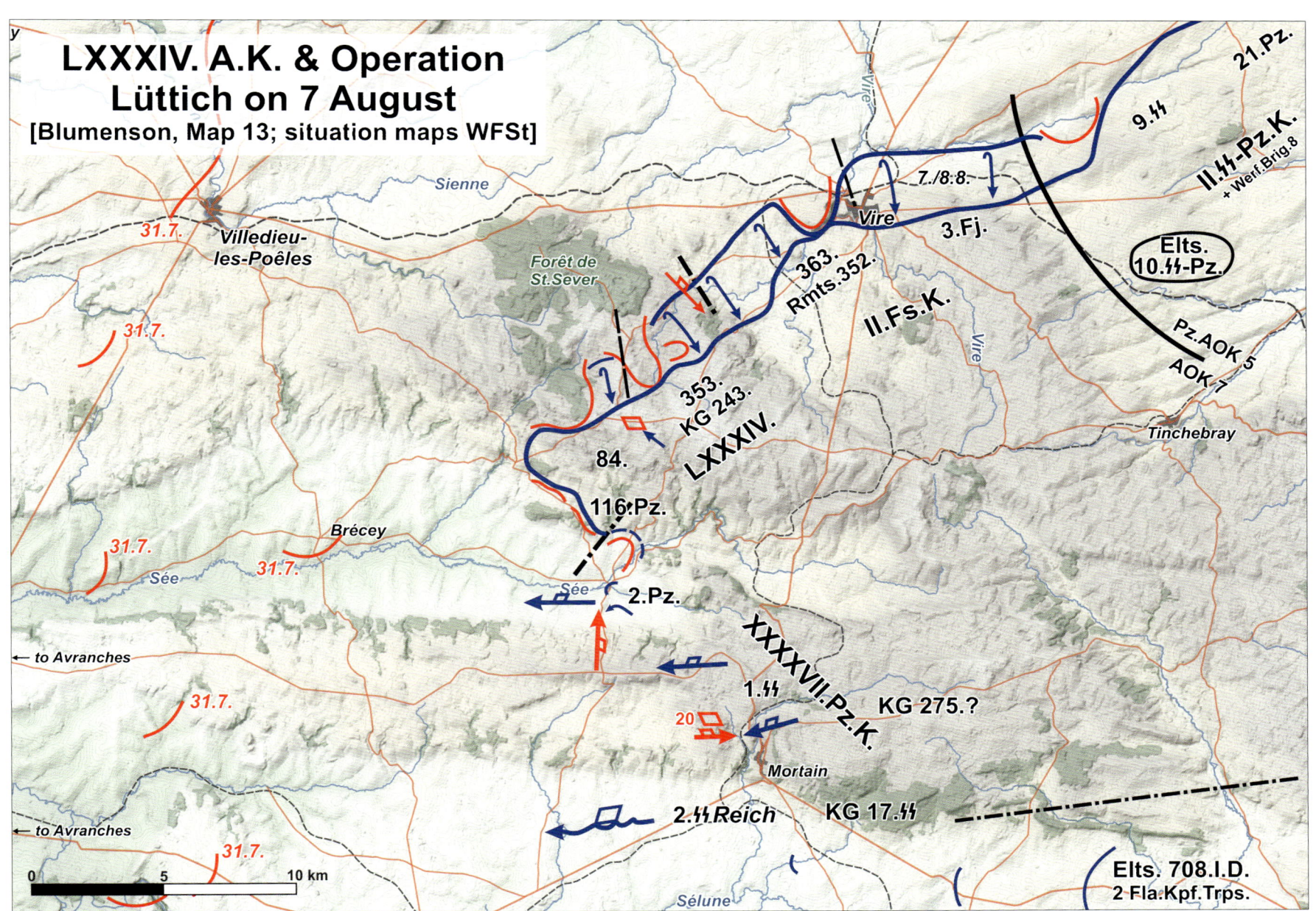

In early August Operation Lüttich attempted to restore the German front in Normandy by reaching Avranches and cutting off the US forces which had broken out into open country. The LXXXIV. A.K. was not directly involved in the operation but protected the right rear of the attack, facing heavy enemy attacks.

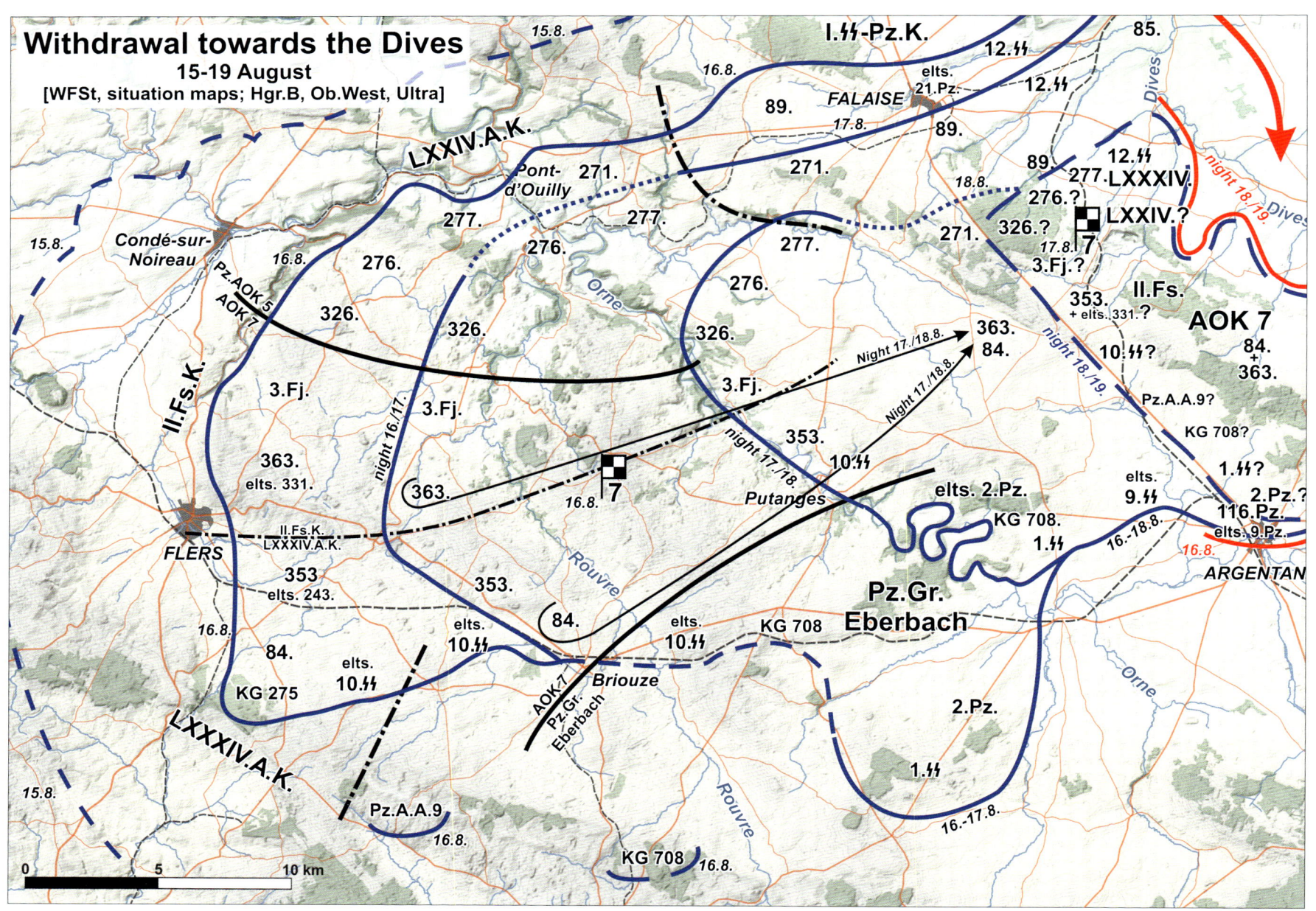

After the failure of Operation Lüttich, the German troops in Normandy were forced to withdraw east. During the retreat, LXXXIV. A.K. held the south-westernmost front of what became known as the Falaise pocket. After giving up its troops, the corps headquarters briefly took command over forces holding the northernmost part of the pocket, south of Falaise.

The same night, the *84. I.D.* was transferred to the *5. Pz.Armee*, where it (together with the *363. I.D.*) reinforced the *LXXIV. A.K.*, which was in serious trouble defending the northwest of the pocket.[119] The *LXXXIV. A.K.* had been ordered to defend the Orne region with the reinforced *353. I.D.*, but early on **18 August** this division was put under the command of the *II. Fs.K.*, thus leaving the corps devoid of forces.[120] The headquarters was now ordered to assume command of the pocket's northern front.[121] Here, the *89. I.D.* (in the west) and the *12. SS-Pz.Div.* (in the east) had become separated from their own corps (*I. SS-Pz.K.*), which was mostly outside of the pocket. Both divisions were placed under the *LXXXIV. A.K.*[122] The status of the *271. I.D.*, even further west, is unclear, but it was presumably attached to the corps as well. The *10. SS-Pz.Div.* was supposed to follow the corps headquarters to the northern sector of the pocket and conduct a counterattack, but its movements were delayed and the attack never took place.[123] Ignoring orders to wait for reinforcements, the commander of the *89. I.D.* opted to pull his division out of the pocket on the night of **18 August**.[124]

The following afternoon (**19 August**), the *277. I.D.* — which was now on the left-hand boundary of the *12. SS-Pz.Div.* following the withdrawal of the *89. I.D.* and the *271. I.D.* — was also put under the corps, but quickly returned to *LXXIV. A.K.* control.[125] *AOK 7* ordered a coordinated breakout for the following night. The corps would cover the northern flank of this breakout attempt, which would be spearheaded by the *II. Fs.K.* The *LXXXIV. A.K.* headquarters would then move through the hole punched through the enemy encirclement by the airborne corps and cross the Dives River.[126] After its breakout, the corps headquarters was to move to Château de Broglie and await new orders.[127]

At this time, the *10. SS-Pz.Div.* was expecting orders for its withdrawal from the corps, but it could not establish contact. Left without orders, the division staged its own breakout.[128] Meanwhile, for the coordinated breakout, the *277. I.D.* relieved the *12. SS-Pz.Div.* at the front, while the latter was placed under the operational control of the *II. Fs.K.* The relief was completed by 02:30 hours on **20 August**,[129] and the corps and the *12. SS-Pz.Div.* began their breakout soon after.[130] Congested roads caused delays, and the corps headquarters failed to cross the Dives before dawn. As a result, it was unable to escape and much of the headquarters — among it, *Gen.Lt.* Elfeldt, *Obstlt.* von Criegern, *Maj.* Viebig (Chief of Staff for Operations) and *Maj.* Hayn (Chief of Staff for Intelligence) — were taken prisoner on **20-21 August**. The corps headquarters would be formally disbanded on **2 November 1944**, never to be rebuilt.[131]

The end of the corps came with the destruction of its headquarters. Many of the staff officers were captured along the Dives River, including its final commander, Gen.Lt. Elfeldt. (NARA)

LXXXIV. Armee-Korps: Normandy from 1941 to D-Day

The previous chapter provided an overview of the organisation and order of battle of the *LXXXIV. A.K.* at the time of the invasion and its role in the fighting. The status of the corps on D-Day was the result of developments in the years preceding the invasion. Since the corps headquarters had already arrived in Normandy in the spring of **1941**, its history helps to build understanding of how the German defence of Normandy evolved.

The corps was initially designated as *Höheres Kommando zbV LX* (60).[1] This meant that it was essentially a corps headquarters, but it was only suitable for secondary fronts and static warfare. These types of headquarters generally lacked corps troops, in particular a signals battalion.[2]

This chapter explores the history of the corps in Normandy up to D-Day. It encompasses several general developments but will mostly address changes in the corps, such as troop transfers, arrivals and relocations within its corps boundaries. In most cases, the focus will be on divisions, regiments and battalions, but a number of headquarters and smaller units will be examined too. Although the corps records offer a wealth of detail about the Channel Islands, these will be ignored unless relevant to the situation on the mainland.

Höheres Kommando LX and Generalkommando LXXXIV. A.K.

The corps headquarters was established on **15 October 1940** as part of a larger effort to create new commands. *H.Kdo. LX* was formed on **15 October 1940** and was part of a larger effort to create new commands that could be used at fortified or secondary fronts. It was formed in *Wehrkreis Prag* (Military District of Prague), using cadre personnel from *Wehrkreis I*. Soon after its formation, the corps moved to northeast France. It stayed there from **November 1940** to **March 1941** before moving to the Channel Coast, where it still was on D-Day. On **15 May 1942**, its status was changed from a *Höheres*

Left: Gen.d.Kav. Rudolf Koch-Erpach was in command of the corps when it was transferred to Normandy in the spring of 1941, but was transferred to XXXV. A.K. within days. (BArch, PERS 6/300020)

Centre: Gen.d.Inf. Max von Viebahn actively commanded the corps from 31 March 1941 until 14 December. (Author's collection)

Right: Gen.d.Art. Hans Behlendorff replaced Gen. von Viebahn in December 1941 and was formally appointed as its commander on 1 January 1943. (BArch, PERS 6/299384)

Left: Gen.d.Art. Gustav von Zangen assumed command of the corps on 1 April 1943 until he swapped positions with Gen.d.Art. Erich Marcks on 1 August. (BArch, PERS 6/301429)

Right: Gen.d.Inf. Wilhelm Wetzel commanded the corps for some two weeks in August and September 1943 while Gen. Marcks was on leave. (BArch, MSG 109/2947)

Kommando to become a full corps headquarters (*Generalkommando*). At that time, it was redesignated as *Gen.Kdo. LXXXIV. A.K.*[3]

The corps had a series of commanding generals. When it arrived in Normandy in late **March 1941**, it was commanded by *General der Kavallerie* (*Gen.d.Kav.*) Rudolf Koch-Erpach.[4] On **31 March**, he was reassigned to a different corps and succeeded by *Gen.d.Inf.* Max von Viebahn.[5] Later that

German forces in the occupied West
5 April 1941
[Gen.St.d.H, Op. Abt., Lage 5.4.41 abends, 1:1,000,000]

After the Armistice of July 1940, German forces occupied much of France. Later in the war the combat troops would increasingly be focussed along the coast, but in 1941 the whole of occupied France was divided over individual divisions.

At this time the West was divided over Army Group A and D. Each comprised a number of field armies which in turn had a number of army corps subordinated to them. Normandy fell under 9th Army, which in turn was subordinated to H.Gr. A. To the south, 7th Army was responsible for the southwest coast of France under Army Group D. This field army soon also became responsbile for Bretagne, replacing 6th Army. By D-Day, 7th Army was responsible for Normandy and Bretagne.

year, von Viebahn was given sick leave and was replaced by *Gen.Lt* Hans Behlendorff on **14 December** who was promoted to *Gen.d.Art.* three days later.[6] On **1 January 1942**, he was formally appointed commanding general and remained in command until **1 April 1943**, when *Gen.d.Art.* Gustav von Zangen took over.[7] Von Zangen was in command for four months until, on **1 August 1943**, he swapped positions with *Gen.d.Art.* Erich Marcks of the neighbouring *LXXXVII. A.K.* (87th Army Corps).[8] Between **18 August** and **2 September**, *Gen.d.Art.* Marcks was on leave, with *Gen.d.Inf.* Wilhelm Wetzel replacing him. Marcks returned on **3 September** and was in command of the corps on **6 June 1944**.[9]

1941: Arrival in Normandy

In the spring of **1941**, preparations were made to transfer the corps headquarters to Normandy to relieve the *XXXXIII. A.K.* (43rd Army Corps) along the Channel Coast, with the corps formally assuming command at 00:00 hours on **6 April**. The headquarters adopted a cover name: *Gen.Kdo. XXXXIII. A.K. Abt. T.*[10] The cover name was indicated by *Abt. T*, in which the *T* most likely stood for "*Tarn*", meaning camouflage. The intention was to conceal any changes in the German organisation while the actual *XXXXIII. A.K.* was transferred to participate in the invasion of the Soviet Union, Operation Barbarossa.

In its new role, the corps was subordinated to *AOK 9 (Abt. T)* — another cover name. In reality, *AOK 9* had already left to join the Barbarossa invasion force and was replaced by *AOK 15* in **April**. The same applied to *H.Gr. A (Abt. T)*, which was in fact *H.Gr. D*.[11] With the start of Operation Barbarossa on **22 June**, the cover-names of the commands in the west lost much of their purpose.[12] On **5 July**, the corps reverted back to its actual designation.[13]

Immense in geographical size, the corps' sector stretched from the mouth of the Seine to Mont-St. Michel — a total of 365 km of coast, not including the depth of the Seine Estuary or the Channel Islands with their 105 km of coastline.[14] On the mainland, the corps essentially covered the departments of Manche and Calvados on the coast and Orne further inland. The corps' southern boundary was also that of the *15. Armee*. As such, the left neighbour was the *XXV. A.K.* (*AOK 7*), with *H.Kdo. XXXII* on the right.[15]

The corps headquarters established itself at Thury-Harcourt. As it arrived, the corps took control of a number of divisions and smaller formations already in the area. In addition to its forces, a significant number of *Luftwaffe* and *Kriegsmarine* units were present, including coastal batteries — such as *Marine-Batterie Brommy*, *York* and *Hamburg* (Naval Battery…), which were stationed around Cherbourg under *Marine-Artillerie-Abt. 260* (Naval Artillery Battalion 260) — and *Flak* elements.[16]

Of the Army formations, the three infantry divisions were the most important. On the right (east) the *225. I.D.* (with *Infanterie-Regiment 333, 376* and *377* (Infantry Regiment… / *IR*) and *Artillerie-Regiment 225* (Artillery Regiment 225 / *AR*) covered the coast from the mouth of the Seine to Dives-sur-Mer.[17] The *57. I.D.* (*IR 79, 199* and *217* and *AR 157*) was responsible for the coastal areas of the Orne river and Arromanches - Port en Bessin. The mouth of the Vire had been defended by the *6. I.D.* until the area was taken over by the *57. I.D.*,[18] when the former was redeployed. The *216. I.D.* (*IR 348, 396* and *398* and *AR 216*) was stationed on the Cotentin and responsible for much of the peninsula. This included most of the east, north and west coasts. The southern part of the west coast of Manche had previously been

With its important headquarters, St. Lô received a number of command bunkers, including this signals installation. (NARA)

In April 1941, H.Kdo. LX took control of much of Lower Normandy: Départments Calvados, Manche and Orne. Up to D-Day the corps would have many different divisions under its command.

Shown here is the army corps' after the transfer of the 225. I.D. sector to a neighbouring corps late in the month. The 319. I.D. was the first division to arrive that would still be with the army corps on D-Day.

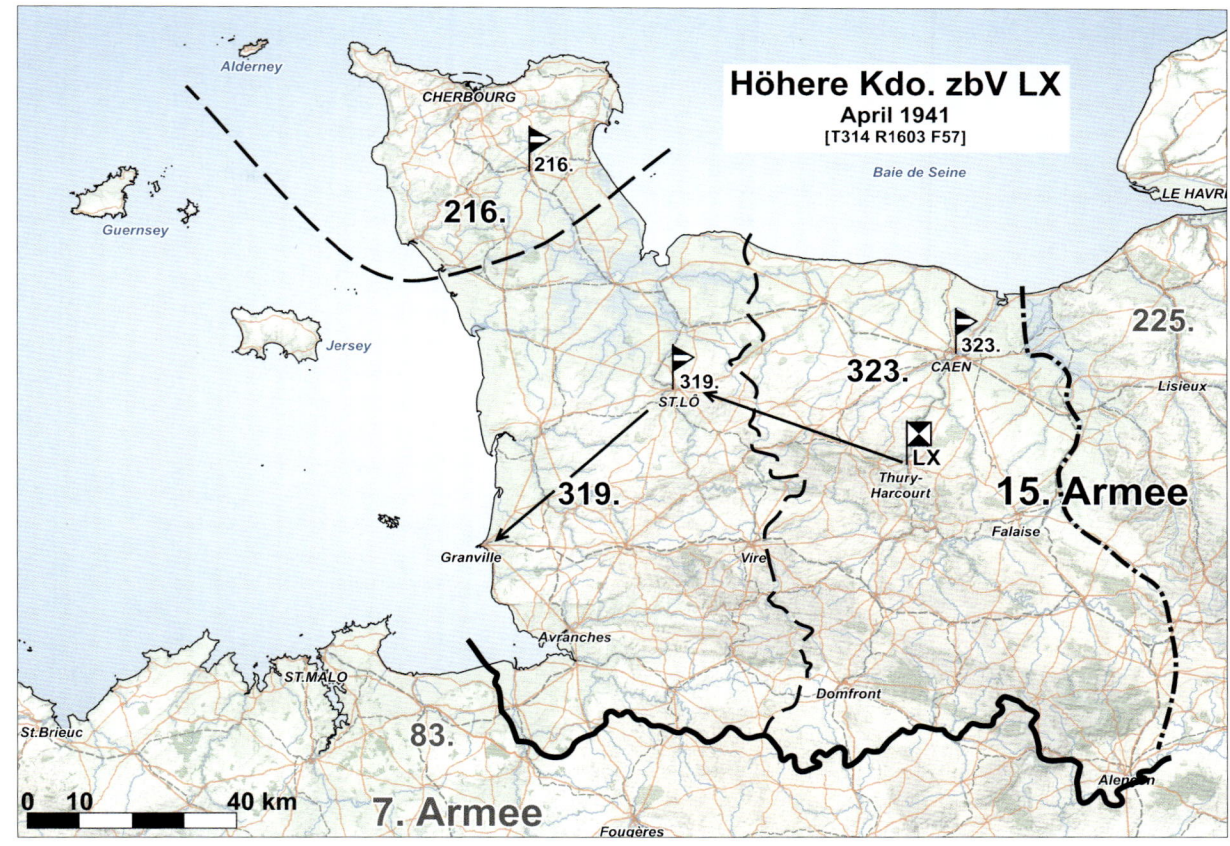

under 6. I.D. control, but it had been taken over by the 216. I.D.; moreover, the Channel Islands were also part of the division's sector.[19]

The 57. I.D. was already destined to leave, with the 323. I.D. (IR 591, 593 and 594 and AR 323) on its way from Germany to relieve the division.[20] It was not alone. The 319. I.D. (IR 582, 583 and 584 and AR 319) was also despatched from the *Reich* to relieve elements that had temporarily taken over from the 6. I.D. This covered an area between the Channel Coast on both sides of the Vire Estuary and the west coast of Manche from Portbail to Mont-St. Michel.[21] The 323. I.D. soon completed the relief of the 57. I.D. and formally took over on **9 April**, while the 319. I.D. assumed control of its sector the following day.[22]

Orders from *AOK 9 (T)* on **18** and **21 April** resulted in a new organisation of the field army. On **30 April**, the 225. I.D. and its sector were taken over by the neighbouring corps, *H.Kdo. XXXII*. This reduced the area held by the corps and its new eastern boundary would stay almost the same until D-Day. Orders were also given to change boundaries within the corps area. The 323. I.D. boundary was to be extended west, to Pointe et Raz de la Percée, reducing the sector of the 319. I.D. The field army designated St. Lô as the new location for the corps headquarters, closer to the centre of its redrawn boundaries. This required the headquarters of the 319. I.D., which was in the town, to move to Granville. This was carried out on **25 April**, with the corps headquarters moving to the St. Lô area on **28-29 April**.[23]

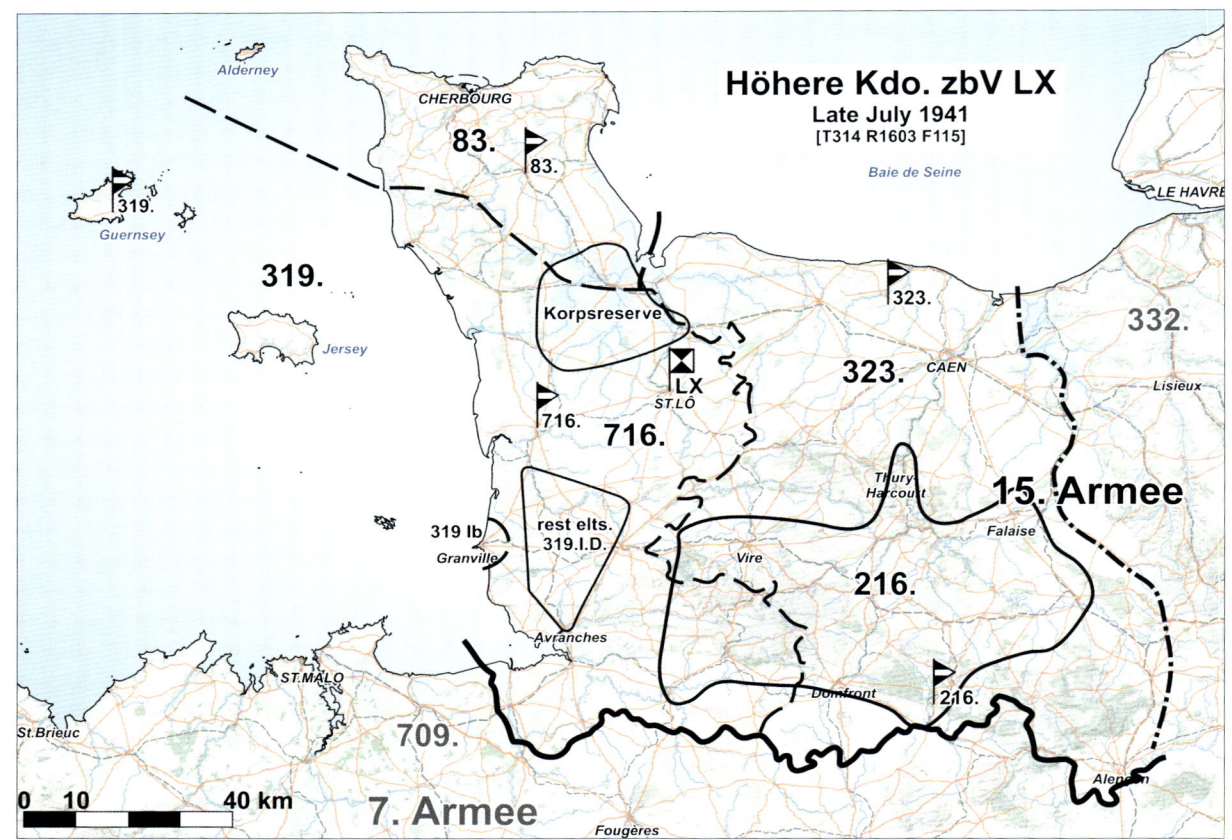

The arrival of the 716.I.D. allowed the 319.I.D. to move to the Channel Islands in force. There it remained until the end of the war. On the Cotentin the 83.I.D. relieved the 216.I.D. around Cherbourg, which then assembled in the southern part of the corps sector before moving to the east.

To the southwest of the corps, the 709. I.D. held the northeast coast of Bretagne. This division would transfer to Normandy towards the end of the 1942.

On **26 May**, *AOK 9 (T)* issued orders to withdraw the *216. I.D.* from coastal defence duties, where it had languished since the summer of 1940. The division was to be relieved by the *83. I.D.* (*IR 251, 257* and *277* and *AR 183*), which was being brought up from the neighbouring *AOK 7*. Once relieved, the *216. I.D.* would be sent to the rear of the corps for training.[24]

On **2 June**, the first elements from the *83. I.D.* arrived at the corps. On **9 June**, the division took over the *216. I.D.* area, with its relief completed on **12 June**. Two days later, the *216. I.D.* had assembled in its new area, which encompassed Cuilberville - Condé-sur-Noireau - Falaise - Argentan - Bagnoles-de-l'Orne - Domfront - Mortain - St. Sever-Calvados.[25]

Gen.d.Inf. Viebahn inspected the Channel Islands defences in the last week of **May**.[26] On the afternoon of **2 June**, *AOK 9 (T)* informed the corps that a report about the islands was to be sent to *H.Gr. D* that evening, to be presented to the *Führer*. Hitler then ordered the islands reinforced, with the corps receiving orders to that effect on **19 June**.[27] Since the *OKH* expected an attack as soon as the summer of **1941**, the measures were to be carried out immediately.[28] The decision was to increase troop numbers on Jersey and Guernsey to one infantry regiment and one light artillery battalion each.[29] This required much of the *319. I.D.*, with the result that the regiment that had been a corps reserve — apparently *IR 582* — was again placed at the disposal of the division. To replace the redeployed forces, the corps would receive the *716. I.D.* (*IR 726* and *736* and *Art.Abt. 656*) as its new reserve.[30]

The 83. I.D. was relieved by the 320. I.D. around Cherbourg in December 1941. Further south, the 711.I.D. had relieved the 716.I.D. in November, but the division would not remain the army corps for long.

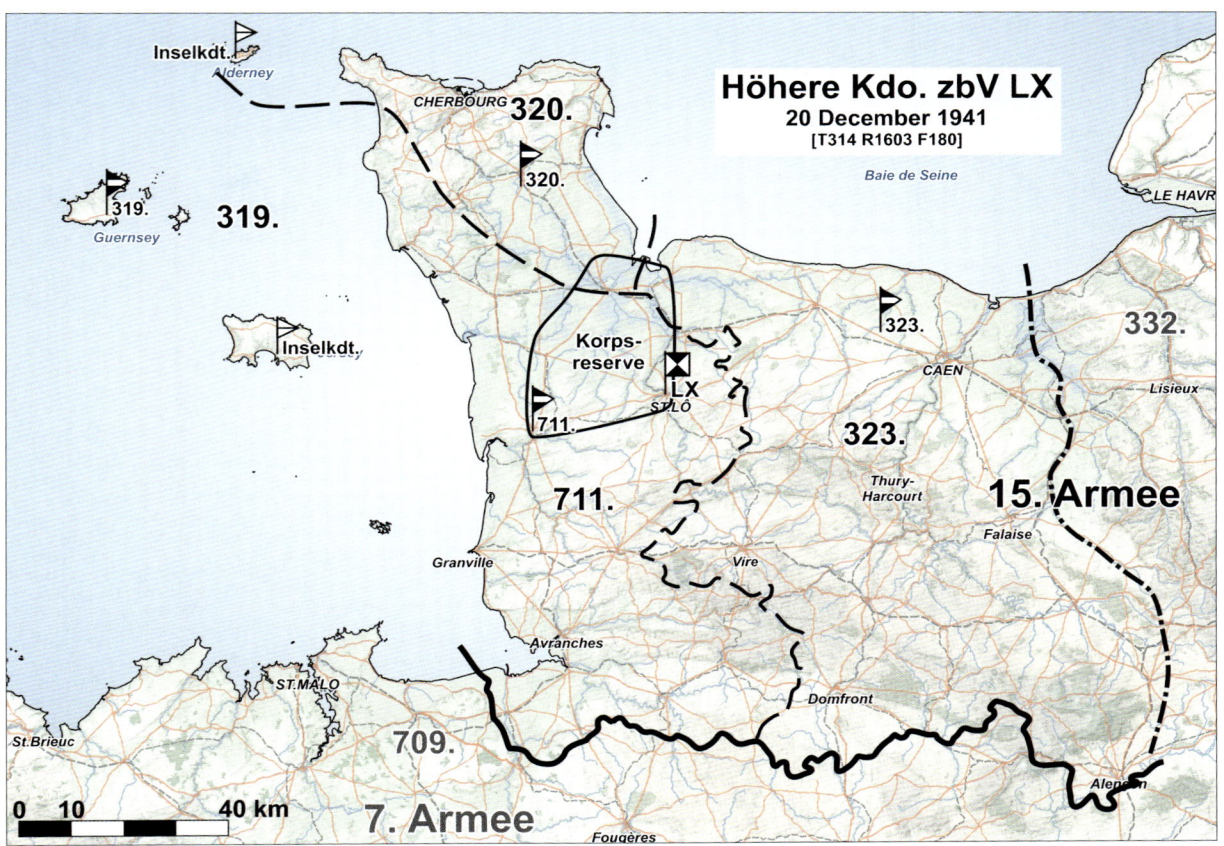

Reinforcement of the Channel Islands was completed on **24 June**, largely by the aforementioned *319. I.D.* Guernsey was occupied by *IR 584* and *Maschinengewehr-Btl. 16* (Machine-Gun Battalion 16 / MG-Btl. 16).[31] Jersey was held by *IR 582*. Alderney was defended by a reinforced company of *IR 277* from the *83. I.D.*[32]

By **23 June**, the *716. I.D.* had arrived in the area of Carentan, La Haye-du-Puits, and Coutances - Marigny - St. Lô, with its headquarters in Coutances. The division needed time to train before it could be used as a corps reserve. On **26 June**, the *319. I.D.* transferred command over its sector on the mainland to the *83. I.D.*, which took over both sides of the Vire Estuary. The *I.* and *II./ IR 583* from the *319. I.D.* remained and were attached to the *83. I.D.* The *II./ AR 319* was transferred to Jersey and replaced by the *I./AR 319*, which was no longer part of the corps reserve. The *319. I.D.* sector along the west coast of Manche was taken over by the *716. I.D.* Again, elements from the *319. I.D.* — namely the *III./IR 583* and *Pionier-Bataillon 319* (Combat Engineer Battalion 319 / Pi.Btl. 319) stayed and were attached to the new division.[33] The divisional quartermaster stayed on the mainland at Granville.[34] *Panzerjäger-Abteilung 319* (Anti-tank Battalion 319 / Pz.Jg.Abt. 319) was transferred to the Carentan area as a corps reserve. The divisional headquarters was finally relocated to Guernsey on **27 June**, with the division staying on the Channel Islands until the end of the war.[35]

July brought changes resulting from the reorganisation the previous month. On **12 July**, the corps ordered the withdrawal of the *I.* and *II./IR 583* from the Vire sector. The 1st Battalion was relieved by the *323. I.D.* and the 2nd Battalion by the *83. I.D.* As a result, the boundary between the two divisions became the Vire River. To the southwest, the *III./IR 583* and *Pi.Btl. 319* were relieved by the *716. I.D.*, which was now deployed along the west coast. *Pi.Btl. 319* returned to divisional control and was transferred to the Channel Islands. The three battalions from *IR 583* became available again. The regiment was assembled in the Airel - St. Côme-du-Mont - Périers - Fougères area. Reinforced by the *I./AR 319* and *Pz.Jg.Abt. 319*, it became a corps reserve.[36]

There were no significant troop movements in the corps sector during **August**. An exception was the arrival of five batteries with captured artillery pieces to reinforce the coastal defences. One 15 cm and three 10.5 cm batteries arrived on the Cotentin and another 10.5 cm battery moved to the Calvados.[37] The Cotentin received *Heeres-Küstenbatterie 316, 317, 318* and *275*. All were armed with French artillery and the 15 cm guns belonged to the latter battery. The battery in the Calvados was *Heeres-Küstenbatterie 315*.[38] The four light batteries were later redesignated as *Stellungs-Batterien (Küste)* (Static Batteries - Coastal)

September, while quiet, marked another noteworthy change: For the first time, the corps was directly affected by the needs of the Army in the East (Ostheer). Hitherto, preparations for the East had mainly resulted in the transfer of entire divisions, but they now had a direct impact on the individual divisions within the corps. Orders arrived to hold the 5th company from the second regiment of three divisions (*83.*, *319.* and *323. I.D.*) ready for the Replacement Army (*OKH/Chef H Rüst u BdE*) (*OKH*/Head of Army Armaments and Commander-in-Chief of the Replacement Army).[39] On **8 September**, these companies left to form infantry regiments for the *2.* or *5. Pz.Div.* The companies were not immediately reconstituted.[40]

The officer corps was also affected. As a one-time measure, the corps was to identify all officers above the bare minimum.[41] This did not include divisions of the 3rd Wave (such as the *216. I.D.*), supply personnel or staffs down to battalion level. In addition, the divisions were to keep cadre personnel to rebuild the 5th Company the regiments had handed over and also keep a number of officers serving as the officers-in-charge of local areas. Officer training was increased to compensate for the expected loss of officers.[42]

Hitler was still preoccupied with the Channel Islands and ordered their reinforcement. In **October**, the *IR 583*, *Pz.Jg.Abt. 319* and the *I./AR 319* were transferred to the Channel Islands.[43] The *319. I.D.* was also reorganised and strengthened, which included absorbing elements from other divisions.[44] Stripped of troops from the *319. I.D.* on the mainland, the corps now had to form a new reserve. *IR 348* (*216. I.D.*) was selected, reinforced by *Pz.Jg.Abt. 216* and the *II./AR 216*. Throughout the month, these formations arrived in the intended sector.[45] The infantry regiment was designated a field-army reserve, rather than a corps reserve,[46] but was incomplete: Its 2nd Battalion, 11th Company and other units were away from the division, serving under *Übungsverband Le Havre* (Training Formation Le Havre), which was experimenting with amphibious landings.[47]

On **4 November**, AOK 15 ordered the *711. I.D.* (*IR 731* and *744* and *Art. Abt. 651*) to relieve the *716. I.D.* on the coast. This was conducted gradually to maintain a continuous defence, with the new division taking command on **28 November**. The *716. I.D.* then left the corps.[48] The corps also ordered a minor change in the boundary between the *83.* and the *323. I.D.* Instead of following the Vire River, the new line ran about halfway between the Vire and Douve Rivers.[49]

The order was finally given on **10 December** to transfer the *216. I.D.*, which had been a field-army group reserve, to the Eastern Front. The first elements were loaded on **15 December**, and the transfer was completed on Christmas day. The transfer once again affected the reserves. *IR 348* was gradually relieved by *IR 744* of the *711. I.D.* It was intended to move *Pz.Jg.Abt. 323* to Carentan - Isigny-sur-Mer as part of the corps reserve.[50]

The *216. I.D.* was not the only division to leave. On **16 December**, the *83. I.D.* was ordered to be relieved by the *320. I.D.* (*IR 585, 586,* and *587* and *AR 320*). The first units arrived on **18 December**. Five days later, the new division reported that it had taken over Alderney; by Christmas, it had assumed command of the remaining sector of the of *83. I.D.* By **7 January 1942**, the *83. I.D.* had left the corps sector.[51]

Although it arrived in **November**, the *711. I.D.* did not stay with the corps for long. In a meeting at *AOK 15* on **29 December**, the planned transfer was announced, and the division would not be replaced. To compensate for the loss of the division, the corps was ordered to prepare a number of options for reorganisation.[52] This resulted in two interim and two final plans, which differed depending on the availability of *MG-Btl. 17*.[53]

1942: Arrivals and Departures

On **8 January 1942**, *AOK 15* ordered the transfer of the *711. I.D.* By then, the corps' plans had been finalised and, on **11 January**, it issued warning orders concerning the reorganisation. The *320. I.D.* was to take over the sector of the *711. I.D.* in addition to its own. This happened on **22 January**, and the transfer of the *711. I.D.* was complete by **24 January**, the division becoming the corps' right-hand neighbour.[54]

To reduce the strain on the *320. I.D.* — now responsible for two divisional sectors — the responsibility for Alderney was transferred to the *319. I.D.*

On **12 January**, the commander of the *III./584* assumed acting command of the island, until a formal commander could be appointed. To secure the island, the *III./584* and a platoon from the *2./Pi.Btl. 319* were transferred on **27 January**. The following day, these elements relieved the *III./587*, which returned to the mainland on **29 January** and assembled at St. Croix-Hague. The designated commander for Alderney arrived on **27 January**.[55]

Since the status of corps reserve had been given to the *711. I.D.*, a new reserve had to be formed. This fell to the *323. I.D.* in the form of *IR 593*, the *III./AR 323* and *Pz.Jg.Abt. 323*. The establishment of the reserve was reported to *AOK 15* on **22 January**.[56]

February was a quiet month for troop movements, with only the *II./585* moving from Brix to La Haye-du-Puits on **2 February**.[57] The month marked the start of the fortification of the mainland. Efforts in the corps area had largely been restricted to the Channel Islands, but in **December 1941** Hitler ordered the west coast of German-held Europe to be turned into a New *Westwall*.[58] The hope was that, when finished, a minimum number of forces would be able to stop a major Allied landing.[59]

But there was a serious problem: Manpower and equipment was limited by more urgent demands. As a result, fortification of the coast had to be limited for the short term. To address this, the project followed several principles:[60]

1. The construction of field-fortifications and fortified strongpoints in the most vulnerable areas was to continue.
2. Long-range artillery was to be sited to protect areas where the enemy could establish bridgeheads. Artillery would also be used to secure facilities and areas that were considered essential for German operations.
3. Army and *Kriegsmarine* efforts to protect the coast would be supported by the *Luftwaffe*, including the deployment of *Flak* elements.
4. Efforts to reinforce the coast should not significantly interfere with other operations, either planned or in progress, or with existing armament programmes.
5. The forces on the coast should only be sufficient for its defence; hence, as the fortification of the coast increased, the number of troops could be reduced.

In his capactiy of Supreme Commander West, Feldm. von Rundstedt paid regular visits to inspect the coastal defences. (NAC)

Of course, not all areas had the same importance. The highest priority was given to Norway, followed by the Belgian and French coasts. Individual areas of each of these coastlines had differing levels of priority. The highest priority was much of the Channel coast, the area south of Brest and from Quiberon to the Gironde. Second priority was given to the peninsulas of Normandy and Bretagne. Although landing conditions in these areas were considered unfavourable, this changed for post-landing operations, and each area's major ports favoured the establishment of bridgeheads. For the *LXXXIV. A.K.*, these new orders were added to the existing plans for the Channel Islands, which continued unaffected.[61]

To assist fortification efforts, the corps was assigned *Festungs-Pionier-Stab 11* (Fortress Engineer Headquarters 11 / *Fest.Pi.Stab 11*) on **27 January**. It was stationed at Caen and its commander, *Obstlt* Bernhardt, reported for duty on **2 February**. Two groups were attached to the headquarters: *Fest. Pi.Abschn.Gr. I/11* (Fortress Engineer Sector Group I/11 / *Fest.Pi.Abschnitts-Gruppe I/11*) and *II/11*; both were deployed on the Cotentin, in the area of the *320. I.D.* The *II/11* was stationed on the peninsula's east coast, with its headquarters in St. Vaast, roughly in the area of *IR 586*. The *I/11* was deployed on the north coast in the area of *IR 587*, with its headquarters in St. Sauveur-le-Vicomte. These groups led the work and liaised with the divisional commander. They were also responsible for construction supplies, albeit in accordance with instructions given by *Obstlt.* Bernhardt. Construction was undertaken by the *Organisation Todt* (*OT*).[62]

Fest.Pi.Stab 11 also took on an advisory role for the corps as well as directly for the *323. I.D.* (in the Calvados). *Festungs-Bau-Bataillon 89* (Fortress Construction Battalion 89) was attached to the fortress engineer headquarters and was also deployed in the *323. I.D.* area. Little time was wasted, and on **15 February**, the corps headquarters presented its first proposal to *AOK 15* for expansion of the coastal defences. This proposal had been discussed with *Obstlt.* Bernhardt in the preceding days.[63]

In mid-**February**, *Ob.West* received orders to form four divisions of the 19th Wave, while other divisions were to be equipped and expanded for deployment to the Eastern Front. Depending on the elements involved, they were to be ready by **15 May** or **1 June**.[64] The *323. I.D.* was selected to be upgraded for service in the east, while the *320. I.D.* received orders to provide cadre for one of the new divisions, the *370. I.D.* Specifically, it would supply personnel for an infantry regiment and an artillery battalion. Other units included a company each for an engineer and anti-tank battalion, and several support elements.[65]

On **11 March**, *AOK 15* ordered the relief of the *323. I.D.* by the returning *716. I.D.* This necessitated the execution of one of the scenarios that had been drawn-up in **December**, with *MG-Btl. 17* being assigned to reinforce the corps. The first units from the *716. I.D.* arrived on **20 March** and started relieving the *323. I.D.* three days later.[66] The division also took over the *Vire* sector.[67] Following its relief, the *323. I.D.* was moved to the area of *H.Kdo. XXXVII*, where it would remain until its preparations for the east had been completed; in the meantime, it was categorised as a field-army reserve. The division's final units left the *H.Kdo. LX* area on **28 March**.[68]

The departure of the *323. I.D.* once again eliminated the designated corps reserve. The *716. I.D.*, as a division of the 15th Wave, had only two infantry regiments and was therefore unable to supply a reserve. Instead, the *320. I.D.* supplied *IR 586* which, in turn, necessitated further changes. On **20 March**, the *IR 587* sector was extended to the right, to south of Barfleur. This relieved the *III./586*, which, in turn, relieved the 1st Battalion of the regiment, which was in reserve at Montebourg. The 1st Battalion was then moved to La-Haye-du-Puits and designated as a corps reserve. The *III./585* (divisional reserve) moved from La Haye-du-Puits to Brix. On **21 March**, the *III./586* was transferred as corps reserve to St. Jean-de-Daye. A week later, *MG-Btl. 17* — elements of which had arrived on **17 March** — relieved the *II./586*, allowing it to join its regiment as corps reserve in Coutances. The regimental headquarters also moved to Coutances.[69]

AOK 15 informed corps headquarters of a new directive from Hitler, *Führerweisung Nr. 40*, on **24 March**.[70] The order stated that if enemy landings occurred, they were likely to take place on the Cotentin or Brest Peninsula; as a result, all available reserves were to be transferred west of the Caen-St. Nazaire line. These reserves were the *24. Panzer-Division* and parts of the *7. Flieger-Division* (7th Air Division / *7. Fl.Div.*). Of these, the airborne division was sent to the corps. On **27 March,** an advance party from the division arrived, and it was decided to position it in the area of Falaise - Torigni-sur-Vire - Villedieu-les-Poêles - St. Hilaire-du-Harcouët - La Ferté-Macé - Argentan. The first elements arrived on **29 March**. The division was designated the field army's reserve and was directed to report to the corps for deployment in case

On the Channel Islands, the 319.I.D. also assumed command over Alderney in January 1942. On the mainland, the 711. I.D. was extracted, its sector taken over by the 320. I.D. in December 1941. The 716. I.D. returned to the corps in March and would remain with the army corps up to D-Day. Upon arriving the division took over Départements Calvados and Orne from the 323. I.D. It also became responsbile for the entire Vire estuary and thus part of the Cotentin. In the corps' rear area the 7. Flieger-Division arrived as a major temporary reserve force in the same period.

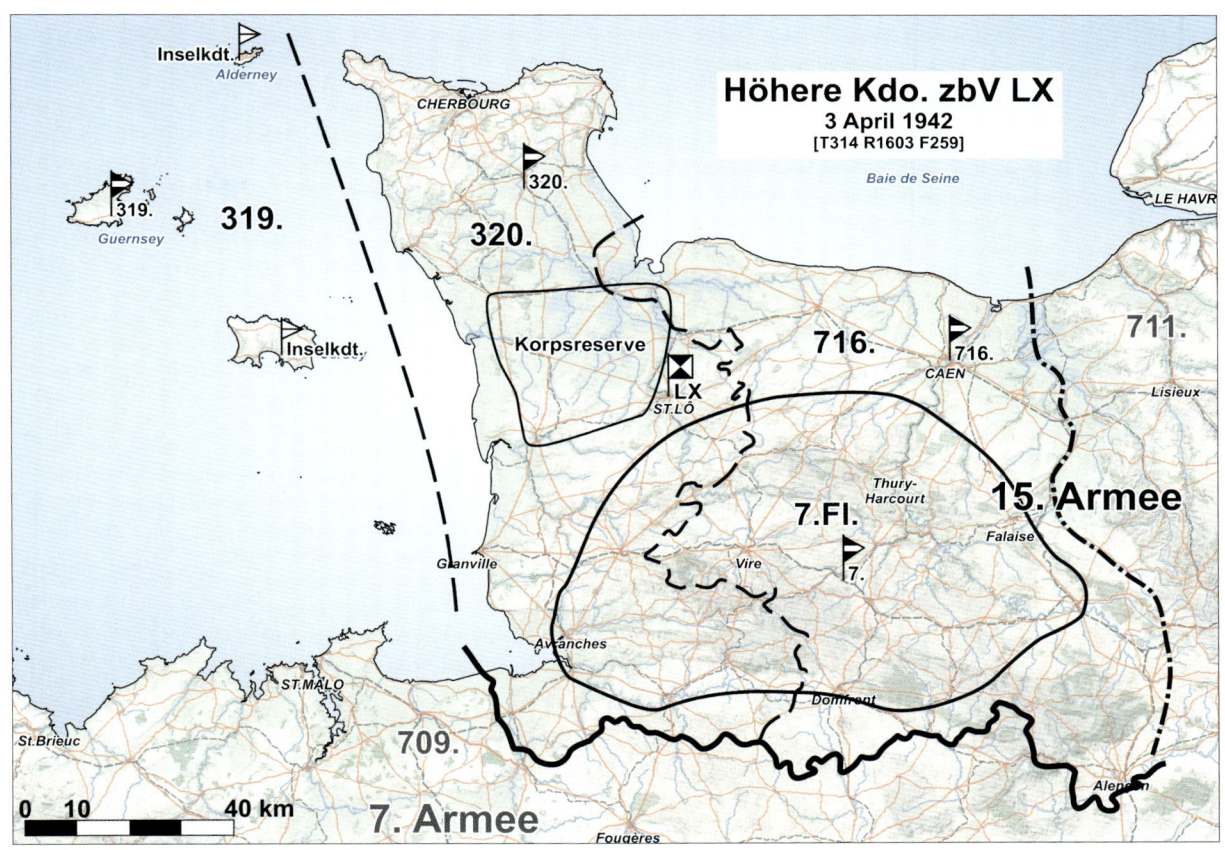

of an enemy landing.[71] The division's organisation was fluid, but in the spring and summer of **1942**, *Fallschirmjäger-Regiment 1, 3, 4* and *5* were (sometimes temporarily) attached to the division.[72]

In **April**, the corps reserve (*IR 586* and *II./AR 320*) was put at the disposal of *H.Kdo. XXXVII* in the Pas-de-Calais. On **20 April**, it was ordered to be transferred to that headquarters. This left *H.Kdo. LX* without a reserve once again. In case of an invasion, the corps headquarters could request the *7. Fl.Div.* to supply a reinforced regiment as a corps reserve. On **29 April**, the following elements were selected for this: *FJR 4* (with its 1st and 3rd battalions), two batteries from *Fallschirm-Artillerie-Regiment 1* (Airborne Artillery Regiment 1 / *Fs.Art.Rgt. 1*), a company from the *Fallschirm-Panzerjäger-Abteilung* (Airborne Anti-tank Battalion / *Fs.Pz.Jg.Abt.*), a company from the *Fallschirm-Pionier-Bataillon* (Airborne Combat Engineer Battalion / *Fs.Pi.Btl.*) and half of *Luft-Nachrichten-Abteilung 7* (Air Force Signals Battalion 7 / *Luft-Nachr.Abt. 7*). On **28 April**, the commander of *FJR 4* took command of this corps reserve, and his headquarters moved to Coutances the following day. After the transfer of the *II./586*, the *III./FJR 4* was moved to Coutances and the artillery to the Villedieu-les-Poêles area, while the *I./FJR 4* remained in Torigni.[73]

Components of the airborne division were frequently dispatched for training to other regions. On **24 April**, *FJR 1* was ordered to the training area at Châteaudun, just outside the corps sector, for jump training.

Transport started on **27 April** and was completed on **3 May**.[74] After training, *FJR 1* reoccupied its previous locations by **28 May**. Now it was the turn of *FJR 3* to move to Châteaudun. On **14 May**, *FJR 4* was ordered to Wittstock (Germany) for jump training. To relieve it, *FJR 5* was attached to the division. It assumed the *FJR 4* sector and became corps reserve. This was completed on **23 May**.[75]

Between **1-3 May**, the units raised for the 19th Wave divisions (*370.* and *371. I.D.*) were transferred. The *320. I.D.* provided cadre troops for the *370. I.D.* and the *716. I.D.* did the same for the *371. I.D.*[76]

On **28 May**, the corps was informed that it had been redesignated as *Gen. Kdo. LXXXIV. A.K.* as of **15 May**.[77] The corps retained that designation until its destruction in **1944**.

During **May**, *Ob.West* introduced a new system subdividing the coastline into Coastal Defence Sectors (*Küstenverteidigungsabschnitte / KVA's*). Each *KVA* was organised in a number of *Küstenverteidigungsgruppen* (*KVG's*), which were further subdivided in *Küstenverteidigungsuntergruppen* (*KVU's*). The coast occupied by *AOK 15* was divided into nine main sectors: *KVA "A"-"J"*.[78] Two of these involved the corps. *KVA "H"* covered the Calvados, while Manche, including the Cotentin, was designated as *KVA "J"*. The lettering system started over in *AOK 7*, with Bretagne being divided into *KVA "A"-"C"*.[79] This system became awkward when *H.Kdo. LX* left the command of *AOK 15* on **21 May** and was subordinated to *AOK 7*.[80] *KVA "H"* and *"J"* were not redesignated.

On **20 May**, *Ob.West* ordered the establishment of a headquarters for *Artillerie-Kommandeur 118* (Corps Artillery Command 118 / *Arko 118*) to coordinate artillery planning. Its commander, *Gen.Maj*. Kruse, arrived on **18 June** and the formation of the headquarters was complete by **20 June**. It was located in St. Lô, collocating with the corps headquarters. Among Kruse's forces was *Heeres-Küsten-Artillerie-Abteilung 832* (Army Coastal Artillery Battalion 832 / *H.K.A.A. 832*), which joined the corps in mid-**May**. The battalion's 3rd Battery was the first to be ready for action near St. Marcouf on **15 May**.[81] The other two batteries moved to the Calvados.[82]

On **9 June** *Fest.Pi.Stab 11* moved from Caen to Hémevez on the Cotentin. Three days later, *Fluganwärter-Bataillon II* (Flight Candidate Battalion II) arrived east of Cherbourg.[83] It was used to provide security for *Luftwaffe* installations, including a number of airfields on the Cotentin: Cherbourg-See, Querqueville, Théville and Lessay.[84] Between **22-26 June**, *FJR 5*, a corps reserve, went to the training area at Châteaudun. It was exchanged for *FJR 3*, which became a corps reserve in the Coutances - Avranches - Tessy-sur-Vire – Torigni-sur-Vire area.[85] At the end of **June**, the reinforced *IR 586* returned from its deployment in *KVA Calais* and relieved the *I.* and *III./585* on the west coast. The regiment did this under the code name "*Division 586*". On **29 June**, the *I.* and *II./586* arrived in the coastal area of *IR 585*. Other forces that had been in *KVA Calais* — the *III./586* and the *4./AR 320* — were ordered by *AOK 7* to the company commander school at Camp d'Avours as instructional personnel.[86]

Following the example of the army in creating static battalions and the formalisation of improvised formations, the corps established a number of new units throughout the month. Between **10-20 June,** men were reassigned from the *319.*, *320.* and *716. I.D.*, as well as from the headquarters company of the corps headquarters itself, to form a reconnaissance troop: *Aufklärungs-Schwadron 84*. The troop reported directly to the corps, allowing it to carry out its own reconnaissance. *Kraftfahr-Kompanie 84* (Motor-Transportation Company 84) was also created. This company was established to ensure the mobility of the corps reserve in the event of an invasion.[87] The company was attached to the corps headquarters, but its platoons were placed under the operational control of reserve battalions and batteries.[88]

July 1942 was even busier. First, the relief of the *I.* and *III./585* by the *I.* and *II./586* was completed. The fictitious "*Division 586*" was established along much of the west coast of Manche. The battalion staffs used the symbols of a regiment, while the regimental staff pretended to be a division. The regimental headquarters moved to Périers, and the headquarters of the 1st and 2nd Battalions moved to Granville and Carteret, respectively. After being relieved, *IR 585* took over the role of corps reserve, reinforced by the *II./AR 320*. This did not include the regiment's 2nd Battalion, which remained divisional reserve. The 1st Battalion moved to the area around La Haye-du-Puits, while the 3rd Battalion moved to the Sainteny - St. Fromond area. The regimental headquarters remained in Coutances, while the *II./AR 320* was quartered in Périers and St. Sauveur-Lendelin. When the commander of *IR 585* took command of the corps reserve, *FJR 3* was released and reverted to being the field-army group reserve.[89]

In preparation for possible Allied landings, *Ob.West* decided to return corps units that were stationed elsewhere. The reinforced *III./586* returned to the area of St. Hilaire-du-Harcouët - Fougères on **10-11 July** and became the field-army reserve. *FJR 5* returned from the training area at Châteaudun and took up positions in the Avranches - Brécey - Ducey area between **12-14 July**. *FJR 4* arrived from Germany to be deployed in the area of Villers-Bocage - Aunay-sur-Odon – Caumont no later than **15 July**.[90]

Additional corps reinforcements included *Fluganwärter-Bataillon V and VII*[91], which moved to Caen - Bretteville and Lessay, presumably to the airfields of Carpiquet and Lessay. Other *Luftwaffe* units included two companies from the *I./Luft-Nachr.Rgt. 53*. *Infanterie-Ersatz-Bataillon 226* (Infantry Replacement Battalion 226 / *Inf.Ers.Btl. 226*) also arrived and was split between Caen – Alençon for security duties under *Feldkommandantur 723* (Field Administrative Command 723) (Caen) and *916* (Alençon).[92] The battalion headquarters and several companies left in early **September**.[93]

As always, there were minor movements within the corps area that are insignificant.[94] An exception is *Korps-Nachr.Abt. 460* (Corps Signals Battalion 460), which was ordered by *Ob.West* on **28 July** to disperse to reduce losses from enemy air attacks. Hitherto, the entire formation had been stationed at a former French military installation. While the battalion remained in and around St. Lô, its companies dispersed in line with orders.[95]

July witnessed the beginning of changes that would affect the corps by the end of **1942**: Another levy for the Eastern Front. To this end, on **7 July**, *OKH* ordered the reorganisation of the divisions from the 13th and 14th Wave, including the *320. I.D.*[96] The division's reorganisation involved creating a number of elements: A proper signals battalion, a third battery for each artillery battalion, reinforcement of the infantry regiments with heavy-weapons companies and stronger divisional support units.[97]

Personnel requirements for the Eastern Front were different from those in the west, and this had consequences for other divisions from the *LXXXIV. A.K.* An extensive exchange of personnel among the divisions occurred in the autumn, with officers, non-commissioned officers (NCO's) and men deemed unfit for the Eastern Front being removed from the *320. I.D.*, along with only surviving sons and fathers of five or more children. Men were also transferred into or from divisions outside of the corps. For example, the corps was to transfer 1,000 men to the Eastern Front in exchange for soldiers with frostbite.[98]

On **3 August**, the *III./586* and the *4./AR 320* (previously a field-army reserve) returned to corps control. On orders from *AOK 7*, the two elements moved to Tourlaville and Brix respectively to work on construction of the Cherbourg defences. These forces became a corps reserve and reported to its commander (*IR 585*), whose headquarters moved to Blanchelande later that month. In another move, the headquarters of the *III./585* moved to Le Dézert. A number of batteries from *AR 320* took up new positions and the *II./AR 320* headquarters moved to La Haye-du-Puits. A significant change in **August** was the departure of the *II./Fs.AR 1* on the **7th**.[99]

The immediate displacement of the *7. Fl.Div.* to the St. Lô - Balleroy - Torigni area was ordered and carried out on **5 September**. On **28 September**, new orders called for the division's withdrawal, the transfer beginning on **1 October** and completing on the **7th**.[100]

Although there were no significant developments regarding the defences in Normandy, change was coming. Throughout **August** there had been meetings in Germany at the highest level to discuss the coastal defences. The limited plans of the previous year were replaced by a much more ambitious scheme. Hitler ordered a "*Westwall*-like" fortification of the coast, which became known as the *Atlantikwall*.[101] Plans envisaged the construction of 15,000 defensive structures. Much of the project would be carried out in the winter of **1942-1943** and everything was to be ready by **1 May 1943**.[102] These ambitious plans turned out to be far too optimistic.[103]

During this period (up to August 1942), the *Kriegsmarine* decided which ports to fortify, with eight on the west coast of Europe given top priority. In Normandy, these included Cherbourg (as a large port), with Caen and Granville (as smaller ports). Nearby, but outside the corps sector, St. Malo and Le Havre were included.[104]

In **September**, the *LXXXIV. A.K.* learned that it had been assigned a construction programme amounting to 1,200 structures. Of these, 270 would be built in *KVA "H"*, including 20 for the Navy and 50 for the *Luftwaffe*. More were planned for *KVA "J"*, with Cherbourg having a total of 930 structures, including 60 for the Navy and 270 for the *Luftwaffe*. Of these 930 constructions, 445 would be built in the Cherbourg area, with 300 intended for the Army, 55 for the Navy and the remaining 90 for the *Luftwaffe*.[105]

On **12 September**, *Ob.West* specified a number of projects as high priority. In the Calvados, this included 40 positions around Caen and the mouth of the

Orne; on the Cotentin and around Cherbourg this applied to 220 structures. To give an idea of the scale, the Army required 86,100 m³ of concrete for 123 projects; the Navy 29,400 m³ for 42 projects; and the *Luftwaffe* 38,500 m³ for 55 projects.[106]

Festungs-Pionier-Kommandeur XIV (Fortifications Engineer Commander XIV) had contributed to the fortification of the Channel Islands since late 1941 and, as part of the preparations for the *Atlantikwall*, the corps appointed its commander, *Obst.* von Marnitz, as its engineer advisor. He stayed with the corps staff for 17 days in **September**. During this period, the final boundaries of the Cherbourg defences were determined.[107]

The corps received new forces in early **October** to compensate for the transfer of the *7. Fl.Div.* Starting on **1 October**, *SS-Rgt. "Der Führer"* (*"DF"*) of SS Division *"Das Reich,"*[108] reinforced by an artillery battalion, an anti-tank company and a *Flak* battery, was sent to the area of Caumont - Torigni - St. Lô - Canisy.[109] This force arrived by **7 October**.[110] A second reinforcement also arrived. It was the *II./Pz.Rgt. 202*, which moved to the area of Coutances - St. Sauveur-Lendelin - Périers. All of these elements were designated field-army reserves.[111]

On **9 October**, the corps was notified that the entire SS Division *"Das Reich"* would be transferred to Normandy as a field-army-group reserve; in addition, the *165. Division* (*165. Div.*) would be deployed as part of the Cherbourg defences. The *SS* division would be deployed to the area St. Lô - Coutances - Villedieu-les-Poêles - Vire - Balleroy with the move to be completed by **11 October**.[112] The *165. Div.* was deployed in the Cherbourg defensive sector and placed under the operational control of the *320. I.D.*[113] It was essentially an understrength division formed from training and replacement units and had little more than an infantry regiment and an artillery battalion. Its major subordinate elements were better known as *IR Reithinger* and *Art.Abt. Römer*.[114]

Additionally, an *Ob.West* reserve was brought up in the form of *gepanzertes Artillerie-Regiment 1* (*gep. AR 1*) a self-propelled artillery formation. It was transported by rail to Mayenne and completed its move on **11 October**.[115] It was to be positioned so that it could be rapidly sent to either Bretagne or Normandy.[116]

On **12 October**, the corps headquarters decided that the commander of the *165. Div.* would be given control of the entire Cherbourg Defence Zone, including both the land and see defences. This meant that *IR 587* and the *II./585* (divisional reserve of the *320. I.D.*) were subordinated to this commander as well.[117] The division's transfer was completed on **17 October**; the next day, the division commander, *Gen.Lt.* von Schacky auf Schönfeld, was formally installed as commander of the Defensive Zone of Cherbourg. The division relieved the *III./586*[118] on **18 October**, which then moved to near Montebourg. By **19 October**, the division assumed full command of its sector.[119]

On **23 October,** the corps received orders to reorganise the *319.* and *716. I.D.* as static divisions by **1 December**.[120] The corps was less than enthusiastic with this, as it meant the infantry regiments would lose their heavy machine guns, light mortars and anti-tank rifles, leaving them with only medium mortars and light machine guns (MG's) for counterattacks.[121]

The pace of activity increased in **November**. On **30 October**, the corps learnt it would receive the *348. I.D. (bodenständig)* (static / *bod.*) and spent much of **November** preparing for its arrival. However, on the **22ⁿᵈ**, it was informed that the transfer would not take place.[122]

Other developments actually did affect the corps strength. On **7 November**, the *II./Pz.Rgt. 202* received orders to move to Rennes (Bretagne), where it would take over from the *6. Pz.Div.*, which was being redeployed. On the **13ᵗʰ**, final orders arrived to transport the battalion by rail, and it left over the next three days. The corps was notified on **17 November** that *"Das Reich"* (now reclassified as a SS-Pz.Gren.Div.) and *gep. AR 1* would transfer to the *XXV. A.K.* in Bretagne.[123] The artillery regiment arrived in the Rennes area on the **21ˢᵗ**.[124] Corps records do not mention when the *SS* division started its move, but it appears that it was probably on **26 November**.[125] On **14 December,** the movement was reported complete.[126]

More positively for the corps, it was informed on **17 November** that it would be reinforced by *Pz.Abt. 223*, stationed near Carentan. Its first components arrived on **20 November.**[127] By the **23ʳᵈ**, the headquarters was located in St. Côme-du-Mont.[128] Elsewhere on the Cotentin, the *III./586* relieved *MG-Btl. 17* on **16 November**. The MG battalion took over the former positions of the *III./586* around Montebourg and became a corps reserve.[129] Two days later, the *II./585* took over the sector of the *II./587*.[130]

This was insignificant compared to changes throughout the next few weeks. For months, efforts had been underway to increase the combat strength of the *320. I.D.* and prepare it for the east. On **22 November**, the corps was informed

As of June 1942, LXXXIV. A.K. was no longer subordinated to the 15th Army, but to the 7th Army instead. This arrangement continued up to D-Day. With only two divisions permanently stationed on the mainland, the 165. Div. was brought up to reinforce the Cotentin in October. The new division took over Defence Sector Cherbourg. South of St. Lô, SS Division "Das Reich" arrived as a temporary reserve force in the same period.

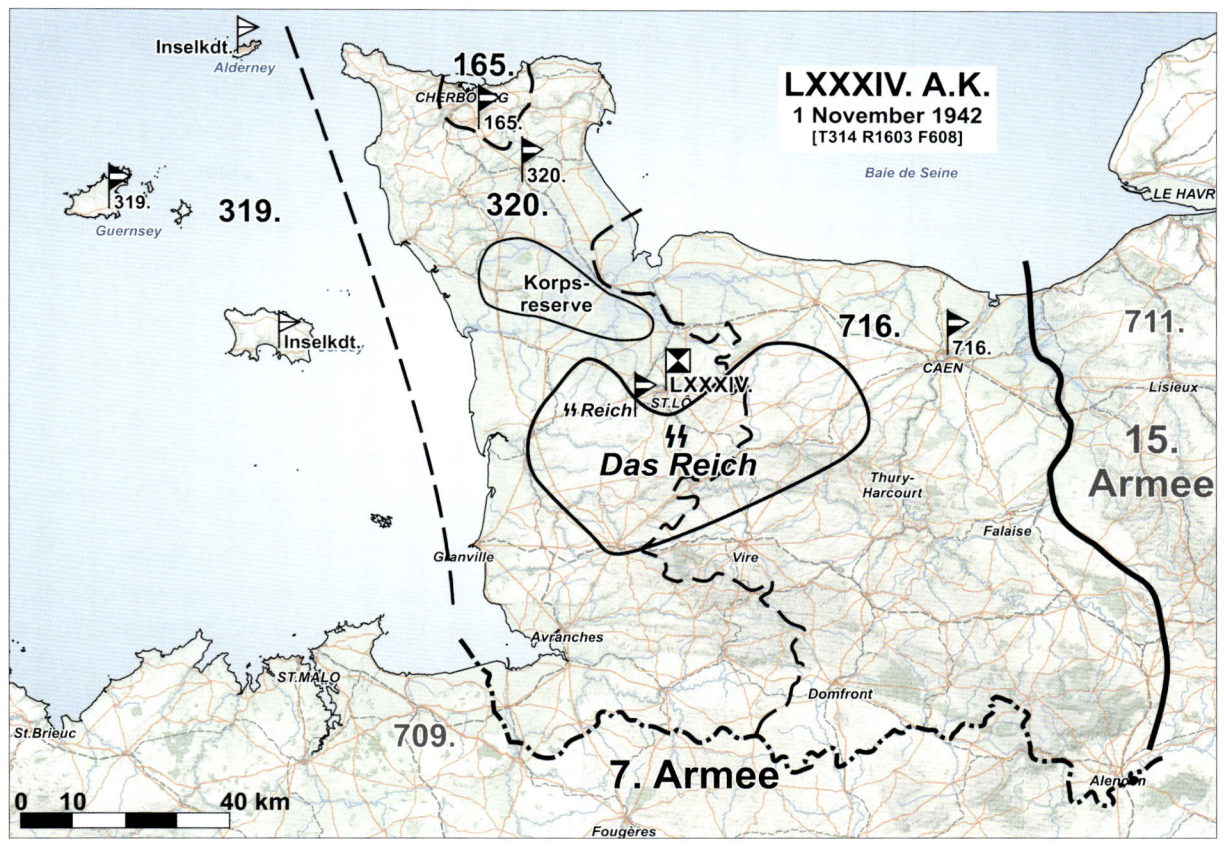

that the division would be withdrawn after **5 December**, while the *709. I.D.* (*Grenadier Regiment 729* and *739* (*GR*) and *Art.Abt. 669*) would be brought up from the neighbouring *LXXXVII. A.K.* as a replacement.[131] Unlike the *320. I.D.*, the new division had just two infantry regiments, meaning the corps sector had to be reduced in size. The left boundary was moved north from Mont-St. Michel to the line Les Salines - Bricqueville-sur-Mer - Cérences. South of this line, the *346. I.D.* of the *LXXXVII. A.K.* relieved the *I./586*.[132]

The *709. I.D.* was expected to arrive between **27-30 November**. Although the exact departure date of the *320. I.D.* was unclear, it was decided that the *709. I.D.* would relieve it anyway. The *320. I.D.* assembled in the rear area, awaiting transfer to the Eastern Front.[133] *MG-Btl. 17* was to relieve the *II./585* on the Jobourg Peninsula before **29 November**. The *II./585* would then be temporarily moved to Montebourg.[134] *GR 729* was to relieve elements of the *320. I.D.* along the northern and east coast of the Cotentin, including the *III./587*, the *III./586* and the *II./585*.[135]

The *165. Div.* was also affected by new the arrival, as *GR 739* was ordered to Cherbourg to command the defensive sector there. The regiment was to do this gradually, while the *165. Div.* would move to the west coast of the Cotentin, the former sector of *GR 586*.[136] *Art.Abt. 669* (*709. I.D.*) was to take over the positions of the *I./AR 320* (*320. I.D.*) on the east coast. The artillery from the *165. Div.* was placed under the operational control of the *709. I.D.* As such, *Art.Abt. Römer* would relieve most of the *II./AR 320*.[137] Part of the order was later changed. On **29 November**, it was announced that *Heeres-Küsten-Artillerie-Abteilung 755* (Army Coastal Artillery Battalion 755 / *H.K.A.A. 755*) — a battalion headquarters with three batteries — would be transferred to the *LXXXIV. A.K.*[138] This allowed for a change of plan. Instead of *Art.Abt. 669*, the coastal artillery battalion would relieve the *I./AR 320*, while *Art.Abt. 669* would relieve the *II./AR 320* on the Jobourg Peninsula. This meant that *Art.Abt. Römer* could be used as a reserve.[139]

The first *320. I.D.* and *165. Div.* units were relieved by the *709. I.D.* on **28 November**.[140] On **6 December**, the *709. I.D.* completed its move, and command of the entire coastal sector of the *320. I.D.* was taken over by the *709. I.D.* and the *165. Div.*[141] The transfer of the *320. I.D.* to *H.Gr. Süd* (Army Group South) in Russia finally started on **28 December** and was completed on **8 January 1943**.[142] The *709. I.D.* was the third division attached to the *LXXXIV. A.K.* until D-Day.

In the *716. I.D.* sector, few changes took place in **December 1942**. The most significant was the relief of the *II./736* by the *III./736* on **6 December**.[143] In contrast, the first two weeks of the month were characterised by movements on the Cotentin related to the arrival of the *709. I.D.* On **1 December**, its commander, *Gen.Maj.* Nake, temporarily assumed command of the *320. I.D.* elements still in his area.[144] The following day, the *II./GR Reithinger* relieved the *I./586* on the west coast.[145] On **4 December**, *MG-Btl. 17* was attached to the *709. I.D.* and the *I./729* took over from the *III./586*, which moved to Lison two days later.[146]

Command of the Cherbourg defences was taken over by the commander of *GR 739*, *Obst.* Manussi, on **5 December**. The *165. Div.* established itself to the south, and its headquarters moved to Périers, while the *III./GR Reithinger* relieved the *II./586* near Carteret.[147] Over the next few days, more formations from the *165. Div.* and the *320. I.D.* were moved. On the **7th**, the *III./587* arrived in the area of St. Pierre-Église and the *I./GR Reithinger* near St. Sauveur-Lendelin.[148] The *I./GR Reithinger* became a corps reserve.[149]

A number of artillery reinforcements arrived on the Cotentin. On **8 December**, the transport of *H.K.A.A. 755* was reported to be on schedule, ultimately arriving at Valognes and relieving the *I./AR 320* on **10 December**.[150] The headquarters was located in Château de Tourville, with its batteries in Grasville, Azeville and Lestre.[151] The same day, the commander of *H.K.A.R. 644* — a regimental command & control headquarters rather than an actual regiment — took over duties as the divisional artillery officer of the *709. I.D.*[152]

On **28 December,** the corps reserve — the *I./GR Reithinger* with the 13th and 14th companies of the regiment — moved to the La Haye-du-Puits - Neufmesnil - Lithaire area. The next day, the headquarters and parts of *Art.Abt. Römer* moved to Airel and St. Fromond to establish two new self-propelled batteries (4th and 5th).[153]

1943: Reinforcements and Reorganisations

In the first weeks of **1943**, the most noteworthy activities concerned the departure of the *320. I.D.* On **11 January**, with *165. Div.* remaining at the base of the Cotentin Peninsula and west coast, it was announced that it, along with the *182. Div.*, would stay in their current areas and form the basis for the *282. I.D.* by **1 March**. Although a *Luftwaffen-Felddivision* was initially expected to replace the *165. Div.*, it became clear there would be no replacement, with the result that the division's departure would require the corps to reorganise.[154]

Although several headquarters and battalions were moved in **January**, this was not related to the plans for the *165. Div.* Most of the changes involved infantry formations in the two coastal divisions. On **3 January**, the *GR 729* headquarters moved from Montebourg to Château de Pépinvast, near Le Vast, then moved several days later to Le Vast itself.[155] On **4 January**, the *I./729* headquarters moved to Octeville-l'Avenel and that of the *III./729* to Montebourg.[156] The next day, the headquarters of the *III./739* moved to St. Croix-Hague, while in the Calvados, the headquarters of *Pi.Btl. 716* moved to Caen.[157] On **17 January**, the *II./GR Reithinger* was relieved by the regiment's 1st Battalion and the *I./729* by the *III./729*.[158] On **27 January**, the *I.* and *II./739* swapped positions, with the 1st Battalion going to Cherbourg and the 2nd Battalion to Digosville. In the Calvados, the same happened with the *I.* and *II./726*, the former moving to Isigny and the latter to Bayeux. The *III./739* and the *II./726* became the divisional reserve.[159]

On **29 January**, the corps ordered a change to the boundary between the *716.* and the *709. I.D.* While minor, it did move *Stellungs-Batterie (K) 316* (Static Battery (Coastal) 316) to the *716. I.D.*[160] There had already been a number of artillery changes earlier in the month. On **8 January**, the *Art.Abt. Römer* staff moved to St. Fromond, and on the **17th**, *H.K.A.R. 644* moved to Valognes.[161]

The 709.I.D. arrived in December 1942, relieving the 320.I.D. in Manche. The new division would still be with the army corps on D-Day. After the arrival of the 709. I.D., the 165. Div. temporarily took over parts of Manche, but the left corps boundary had to be moved north to compensate for the reduction in troops. This turned the Avranches - Granville sector over the neighbouring corps.

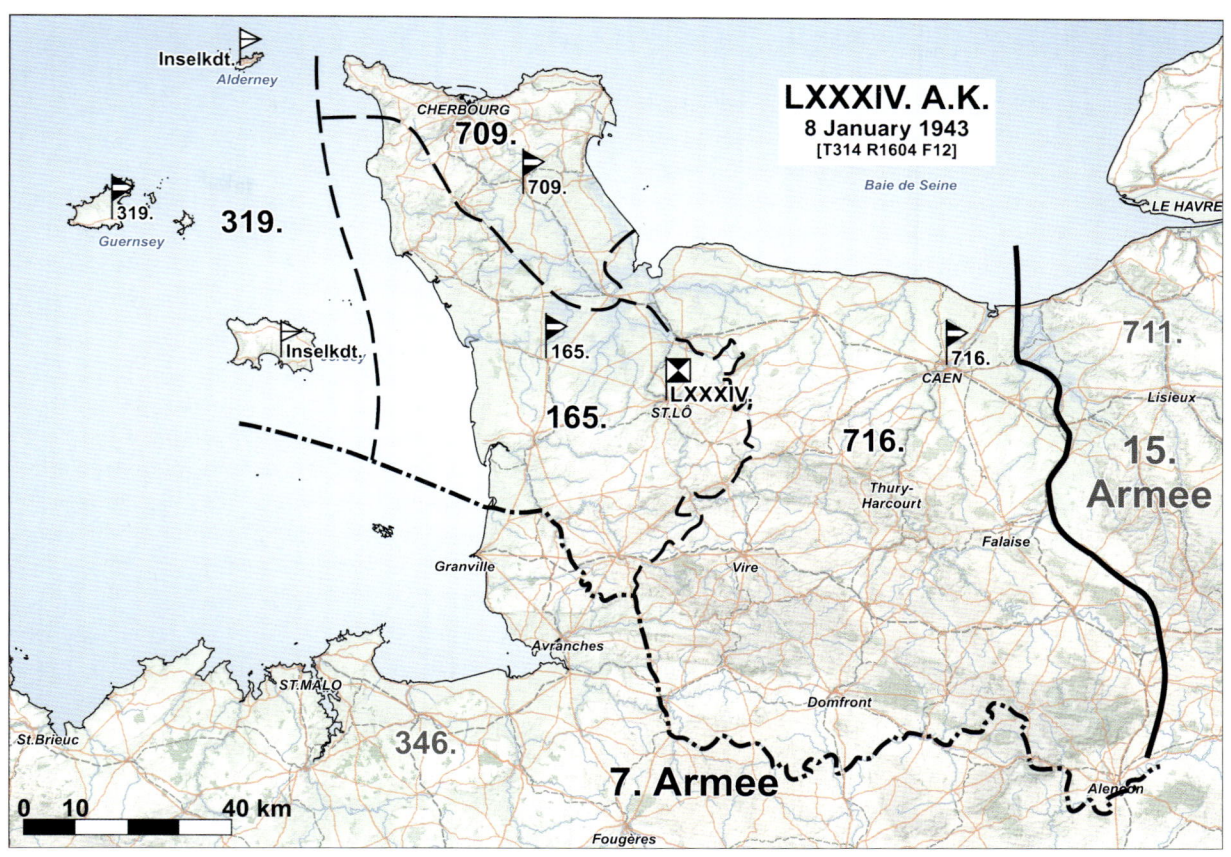

The armoured elements of the corps also underwent some changes. On **16 January**, the headquarters of *Pz.Abt. 223* moved from Houesville to Coigny.[162] The battalion was redesignated as the *I./Pz.Rgt. 100* on the **19th**.[163]

On the last day of the month, *AOK 7* announced the expected arrival of a *Turk-Bataillon* (Turkic Battalion), which would be deployed on the west coast of Manche.[164] Two more Turkic battalions were earmarked to join the *XXV. A.K.* in Bretagne. After being trained and acclimatised, they would gradually relieve German formations. If this initial test case was successful, it was expected that more would follow.[165]

The corps also set to work building mobile forces. The *709.* and *716. I.D.* were each instructed to prepare a reinforced regiment for deployment in vulnerable areas. Each was to include an infantry regiment (using battalions from different regiments), two anti-tank platoons, an anti-tank company and the divisional artillery battalion with three batteries. The *716. I.D.* would provide "*Rgt. Krug*" (the commander of *GR 736*), which meant one battalion had to be withdrawn from the coast. This was not an issue for the *709. I.D.* "*Rgt. Rohrbach*" (the commander of *GR 729*) only required two infantry battalions, since *MG-Btl. 17* could be used as the third battalion in the reinforced regiment. This force was further strengthened by *Aufkl.Schw. 84*. Both reinforced regiments were to be fully motorised, albeit in an ad hoc manner, using *OT* assets, organic vehicles, motor transport columns and vehicles from naval transport troops.[166]

German Chain of Command

Significant changes took place in **February**. On the Cotentin, the headquarters of *Pi.Btl. 709* moved to Château de l'Ermitage, northwest of Ruffosses, on **19 February**. Four days later, the *I./729* was relieved as a corps reserve in Montebourg by the *II./729*. The 1st battalion moved to the northeast of the peninsula.[167] In the Calvados, the *II./726* relieved the *I./736* on the **24th**.[168] On **28 February**, orders arrived for the disbanding of *Fluganwärter-Btl. V* by **1 March**.[169]

More notable changes arose from the anticipated departure of the *165. Div.*, with the *709. I.D.* preparing to take over its coastal area.[170] Preparations included the movement of a number of units. On **2 February,** *MG-Btl. 17* moved to near St. Croix-Hague and became the divisional reserve, while the *III./739* was sent to the Jobourg Peninsula.[171]

On **11 February**, *Ob.West* ordered the *165. Div.* to be consolidated with the newly forming *282. I.D.* in the area of *AOK 15*. This was to begin on **19 February** and completed by the **25th**, with more detailed orders to follow from the corps.[172] To make this possible, the headquarters and 2nd Battalion of *GR 739* was to move into the sector of the *165. Div.* so it could be relieved before noon on the **17th**.[173] The movement of *GR 739* to the *165. Div.* area affected the Cherbourg defensive sector, since the commander of *GR 739* had also been its commander. To replace him, *AOK 7* assigned a new officer (who reported to the *709. I.D.*) to take over the defences: *Obst.* Blumentritt.[174] The corps also ordered the division to establish a headquarters for him. The army intended to designate the organisation as a static (*bodenständig*) entity, including the associated rights and responsibilities.[175] *Obst.* Blumentritt took command on **17 February**.[176]

On **15 February**, the *I./739* was ordered to La Haye-du-Puits. When the *Turk-Btl.* arrived, it would move to the town and the *I./739* would relocate to Blanchelande.[177] On the **16th**, the *II./739* moved to Cherbourg, while the 1st Battalion was transferred to the sector of the *165. Div.*[178] The following day, the headquarters of *GR 739* and the battalion relieved *GR Reithinger*.[179] The regimental headquarters moved to Périers and the battalion headquarters to La Haye-du-Puits.[180] *GR 739* was to disguise itself as *"Division 739"*, with the battalion posing as a regiment in La Haye-du-Puits.[181] The *Turk-Btl.* announced in **January** turned out to be *Georgisches-Infanterie-Bataillon 797* (Georgian Infantry Battalion 797 / *Georg.Inf.Btl. 797*).[182] Arriving on **17 February**, it was initially split between Bricquebec and Périers, before moving to its deployment area around La Haye-du-Puits and the west coast on the **23rd**.[183] On **20 February**, the *165. Div.* handed over command of its coastal sectors to *GR 739* and left the corps two days later.[184] *Art.Abt. Römer* remained with the corps to be reconstituted and redesignated as *schwere Artillerie-Abteilung 450* (Heavy Artillery Battalion 450 / *s.Art.Abt. 450*).[185]

On **17 February**, corps headquarters was notified that it had been assigned three bicycle reserve battalions.[186] Intended for reconnaissance and security duties, they were *Reserve-Radfahr-Abteilung 2, 11* and *17* (*Res. Radf.Abt....*).[187] The three battalions were to be put under a regimental headquarters — *Reserve-Radfahr-Regiment 30*. Following its formation, the headquarters was to be stationed in Argentan. *Res.Radf.Abt. 2* would be located in Cérences, while *Res.Radf.Abt. 11* would be in Bricquebec and *Res. Radf.Abt. 17* in Lessay.[188] The three battalions arrived on the **24th-25th**.[189] *Res. Radf.Abt. 11* ultimately moved to Les Pieux instead of Bricquebec.[190]

More significant news arrived on **4 February**, when *AOK 7* announced that the corps would receive a number of fairly large elements. The first group would consist of two partial formations, intended to be ready for employment by **1 April**, while preparing for eventual expansion to full divisions.[191] Another large reinforcement was an artillery-brigade. *Ob. West* had ordered that *gepanzertes Artillerie-Regiment 1* (*gep.AR 1*) would again leave its sector around Rennes and return to Normandy, along with the other elements of *gepanzerte Artillerie-Brigade 1,* to which it belonged. This brigade consisted of a headquarters, two regiments (with six batteries each) and a battalion with another six batteries. The brigade was directed to assemble in the area of Flers - Mortain - St. Hilaire-du-Harcouët - Fougères - Domfront (exclusive).[192]

The corps responded by selecting areas for the two formations that eventually were to become divisions. *Gep.AR 1* was redesignated *Art.Rgt. zbV 621* and was to be sent to the western sector of the brigade. It comprised a headquarters and two semi-separate battalions: *s.Art.Abt. 456* and *457*. The brigade headquarters and a second regiment would be grouped together in the north, and the remaining battalion in the southeast.[193] *Art.Rgt. zbV 621* arrived on **17 February**.[194] The arrival of the artillery regiment resulted in a major reinforcement for the corps: six self-propelled *15 cm s.F.H. 13* (*schwere Feld-Haubitze 13* / Model 13 Field Howitzer). These guns would be used to build two batteries, one in Montebourg and the other in La Haye-du-Puits.[195] An earlier plan to form these batteries

Self-propelled artillery was uncommon in infantry divisions. 7th Army, however, received a number of 15 cm s.F.H. 13 on Lorraine tractors, which it used to strengthen several of its divisions. On D-Day six guns were still in service with the 716. I.D. and additional pieces could be found in Bretagne. (USAHEC via Panzerwrecks)

with *s.Art.Abt. 450* may explain why they were initially designated the 4. and 5./*s.A.A. 450*.[196] The new batteries had no place in the battalion's reorganisation and were soon referred to as separate equipment batteries and later designated as *gepanzerte Geräte-Batterie 709* and *716*.[197-198]

On **10 February**, *AOK 7* informed the corps it would receive only one of the formations intended for reconstitution as a division.[198] It would still require much more attention than the artillery brigade. It had been decided to rebuild the divisions from the *6. Armee*, which had been destroyed at Stalingrad. Within *AOK 7*, six divisions were to be reconstituted: The 76., 113., 305., 371. and 389. I.D., as well as the *16. Pz.Div*.[199] The partial formation sent to the *LXXXIV. A.K.* turned out to be the *389. I.D.* It would be reconstituted initially as a *Kampfgruppe*, then mature into a full division. The battlegroup was to be ready by **1 April** and the full division by **1 September**.[200] It would generally assemble in the area of Balleroy - St. Martin-des-Besaces - Villers-Bocage. A much larger area was selected for the division: Balleroy - Percy - Évrecy - Noyers-Bocage.[201] Elements from the *389. I.D.* started to arrive on **7 March**.[202] Over the ensuing weeks, the "division" grew in size as more men arrived.[203]

The bicycle formations that arrived in **February** were soon redesignated, initially becoming *Schnelle Abteilungen* instead of reserve bicycle battalions.[204] Later that month, they were also renumbered: *Schnelle Abt. 2, 11* and *17* became *Schnelle Abt. 518, 517* and *513*, respectively.[205] On **9 March**, the corps learned that the regimental headquarters had been redesignated as *Schnelle Brigade 30*.[206] The brigade moved several times that month. On **3 March**, *Schnelle Abt. 517* moved to the area of Les Pieux - Rauville-le-Bigot, while the brigade headquarters went from Argentan to Coutances on **12 March**.[207]

Other movements within the corps sector were limited. One involved the *s.Art.Abt. 450* headquarters moving from St. Fromond to Le Ham on **9 March**.[208]

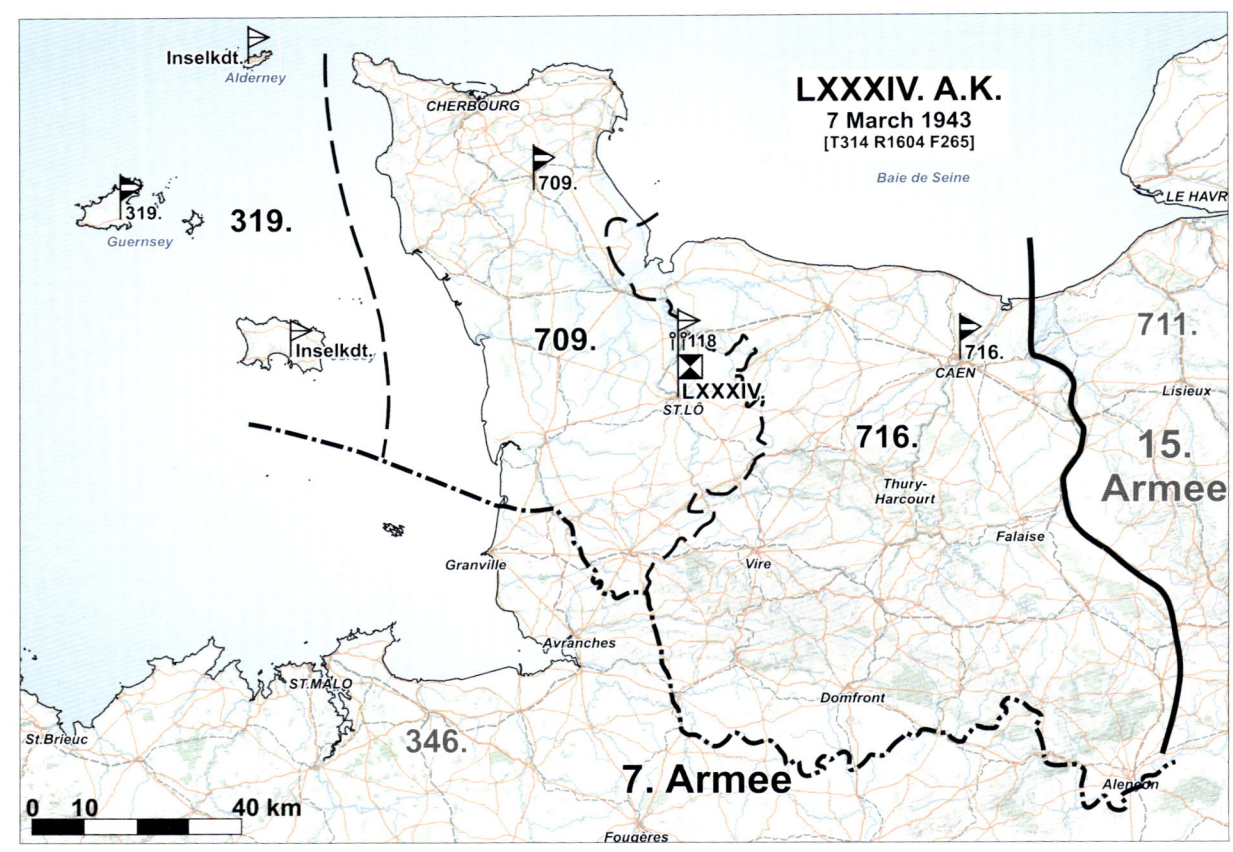

With the extraction of the 165.Div. in February 1943, the 709.I.D. took control over the rest of Manche, within the corps sector. Once more the LXXXIV. A.K. was reduced to just two divisions on the mainland and the 319.I.D. on the Channel-Islands.

There were some new arrivals. On **13 March**, *Sicherungs-Regiment 5* (Security Regiment 5 / *Sich.Rgt. 5*) arrived in the area of Le Dézert with two battalions reinforced by a tank company from *Pz.Rgt. 100*.[209] The regiment did not stay with the corps for long: On **26 March**, *AOK 7* transferred the regiment and the tank company to the *XXV. A.K.*[210] This move was completed three days later.[211] Another temporary reinforcement was *Sturmgeschütz-Abteilung 905* (Assault Gun Battalion 905 / *Stu.Gesch.Abt. 905*, which arrived on the **22ⁿᵈ** and was transferred to *AOK 15* on **10 April**.[212]

April brought minor changes among the divisions and their subordinate forces. On **9 April**, the *II.* and *III./729* swapped positions — the 3ʳᵈ Battalion moving to Montebourg and the 2ⁿᵈ Battalion covering the coast between St. Vaast-la-Hougue and Ravenoville.[213] On **10 April**, the *II./736* headquarters relocated from Bénouville to St. Aubin-d'Arquenay.[214] Three companies from the *I./Pz.Rgt. 100* moved southwest of Carentan on **12 April**, and *Schnelle Abt. 517* to Bricquebec the same day.[215]

A major change took place on the Cotentin at the end of the month. On **20 April**, *Obst.* von Rohr took charge of the Cherbourg Defence Zone (he was officially installed as commander on the **27ᵗʰ**).[216] *Obst.* Blumentritt resumed his role as the Commissioner for the Construction of the *Atlantikwall* for the sector and, in **May**, the corps headquarters requested that he report to *Obst.* von Rohr.[217]

On **23 April**, *Georg.Inf.Btl. 797* relieved the *I./739* on the west coast, the

The 7. Flieger-Division returned as a reserve in April 1943 and elements of Schnelle Brigade West were stationed in the southern corps sector. Both soon left, but this did not apply to the 389.I.D. After its destruction at Stalingrad, its remnants were used to rebuild the division over the summer of 1943.

Reserve Bicycle Regiment 30 had been redesignated as Schnelle Brigade 30 in March and its HQ moved from Argentan to Countances later in the month.

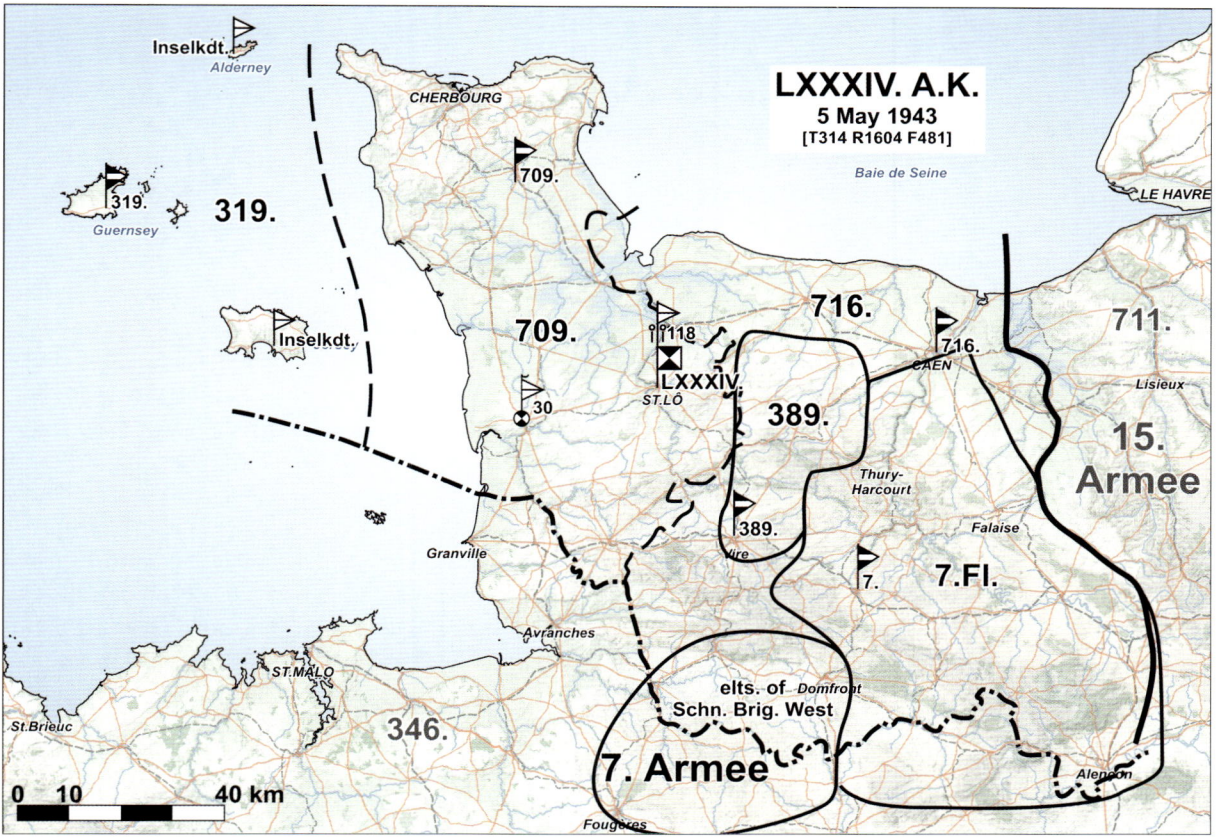

latter being designated a corps reserve near La Haye-du-Puits.[218] On **29 April**, *MG-Btl. 17* moved north of Valognes and *Pi.Btl. 709* to Sideville - St. Croix-Hague. Both battalions were a divisional reserve. In the Calvados, the *I./736* relieved the *II./736* on the coast, the latter becoming a divisional reserve.[219]

Gep.Art.Brig. 1, which had arrived in the preceding months, was designated part of *Schnelle Brigade West* (Mobile Brigade West / *Schnel.Brig. West*) which later became the *21. Pz.Div.* In **April**, as additional units arrived, some of the brigade's elements left the corps. Orders were issued to temporarily move the two battalions from *AR. 621* to Bretagne, replacing artillery formations that had been transferred to *AOK 15*.[220] The orders called for their departure on **3 April**, and they left around that time.[221] On **8 April**, a division formerly in the sector returned: the *7. Flieger-Div.* It completed its move on the **22nd** and became a reserve of the field-army group.[222]

The *389. I.D.* continued to grow in size and, as a result, new sectors were selected for its constituent elements, moving to their new sectors by **20 May**.[223] The divisional headquarters moved to Canisy; the headquarters of *GR 544* and *546* were in Carentan and St. Jean-de-Daye, respectively, while the headquarters of *AR 389* was in Torigni-sur-Vire.[224]

The *7. Fl.Div.* did not stay with the corps for long: on **26 May**, it began its transfer to *Heeresgruppe Südwest* and was redesignated as the *1. Fallschirmjäger-Division* (*1. Fj.Div.*). *Schnelle Brigade West's* departure for the *XXV. A.K.* was also reported on **29 May**, with *Art.Rgt.Stab 621* moving to Rennes.[225]

Other than the departure of the airborne division and the mobile brigade, **May** was relatively quiet, seeing only a few units from the *709.* and the *716. I.D.* moved. On **8 May**, the *II./726* relieved the *I./736* on the coast.[226] On **13 May**, the *OKH* ordered the *LXXXIV. A.K.* to establish a headquarters for the *II./AR 716*, which would be part of the *716. I.D.* A similar task was given to the *LXXXVII. A.K.* in Bretagne, which was for the headquarters of the *II./AR 709* — intended for the *709. I.D.*, although then attached to the *343. I.D.*[227] On **23 May**, the *III./729* and *s.Art.Abt. 450* were selected as a labour force to assist with construction of the Cherbourg defences.[228] The *III./729* was moved to Teurthéville-Hague - Tollevast on **29 May**, while most of *s.Art.Abt. 450* moved to the Cherbourg area on **2 June**.[229]

May also marked the start of permanent reinforcements, although many did not arrive for some time. On **17 April**, the corps headquarters contacted *AOK 7* about the situation on the Cotentin, which it considered unsatisfactory. It noted that the transfer of the *320. I.D.* and the *165. Div.* had not been compensated despite the arrival of the *709. I.D.* In fact, compared to the earlier situation, six fewer infantry battalions were deployed on the peninsula. The arrival of *Georg.Inf.Btl. 797* did little to change this, and the corps requested two static fortress battalions to occupy the Cherbourg defences.[230] Although not directly the result of its concerns, the corps eventually received reinforcements. On **8 May**, orders arrived concerning the establishment of *Festungs-Stamm-Abteilung LXXXIV* (Fortress Cadre Battalion LXXXIV / *Fest.Stamm-Abt. LXXXIV*), a static formation for the Cherbourg defences. Its first significant personnel transport arrived three days later. Formation of the battalion — a headquarters and four companies — was completed on **1 June**.[231]

Concerns about the Cotentin persisted. On **5 June**, the *709. I.D.* received news that *Ob.West* had requested that the Replacement Army assign an additional infantry regiment and a light artillery battalion to the division. These were to come from one of the new static divisions being formed before **1 August**. No decision had yet been made about a regimental artillery headquarters or the strengthening of the divisional supply troops.[232] Nonetheless, there were a number of promising developments for the artillery. Both the *709.* and the *716. I.D.* came one step closer to having proper artillery regiments when *Art.Abt. 669* and *656* were redesignated as the *I./AR 669* and the *I./AR 656*. The *II./AR 709* and the *II./AR 716* were also redesignated as the *II./AR 669* and the *II./AR 656*.[233]

On **5 June**, two coastal artillery headquarters moved. The headquarters of *H.K.A.A. 832* moved to Isigny-sur-Mer and *H.K.A.A. 404* to Tocqueville.[234] Otherwise, most of the corps' infantry battalions stayed in place, although the *I./736* relieved the *III./736* on the coast on **17 June**, the latter becoming the divisional reserve.[235]

The formation of the *389. I.D.* continued and, on the **8th**, *Pi.Btl. 389* moved to the engineering school at Angers.[236] Despite not being fully formed, the division had to hand over certain units. On **28 June**, the *II./544* left to help build the *334. I.D.* and other elements were transferred on the **29th**.[237]

Unusual new arrivals came in the form of elements from the *24. Pz.Div.*, being reconstituted in *AOK 15*.[238] On **1 June**, *Panzer-Grenadier-Regiment 21* (Armoured Infantry Regiment 21 / *Pz.Gr.Rgt. 21* / *PGR 21*) and *Panzer-Artillerie-Regiment 89* (Armoured Artillery Regiment 89 / *Pz.Art.Rgt. 89* / *PAR 89*) arrived in the eastern portion of the corps, staying in the general Falaise area until **13 August**.[239]

It was obvious that fighting would not necessarily occur in the *LXXXIV. A.K.* area, meaning that the corps might have to provide reinforcements for others. On **28 June**, the corps headquarters introduced plans for locations outside the corps boundaries that might be attacked. Preparations were made to rapidly transfer forces to other commands. A similar system was employed by other corps in *AOK 7*, the measures went into effect on **1 July**.[240] The contingency plans featured three courses of action, identified as measures.

Contingency Measure I called for the withdrawal of entire divisions; for the *LXXXIV. A.K.*, this meant the *716. I.D.* (minus the *II./AR 656*). Command of its sector (*KVA Calvados*) would be taken over by *Arko 118* as *Division Kruse*. *KVG Caen* would be taken over by the headquarters of *H.K.A.R. 645*; *KVG Bayeux* by *Fest.Pi.Stab 11*. Control of sub-sectors would be allocated to reserve battalions from the *709. I.D.* and *Fest.Bau-Btl. 11* (the redesignated *Fest.Bau-Btl. 89*). In case the *346. I.D.* was moved from the neighbouring *LXXXVII. A.K.*, but the *716. I.D.* remained in place, *KVU Granville* would be taken over by the *709. I.D.* by deploying the battalion held as a corps reserve at La Haye-du-Puits.[241]

Measure II was less extensive, with the corps only transferring a reinforced regiment and reinforced battalion. The regiment was envisaged as an ad hoc formation, combining elements from the *709.* and *716. I.D.* The headquarters would be provided by *GR 739*; the three battalions drawn from

The 389.I.D. continued to expand, providing an increasingly powerful reserve in the corps sector. To the east elements of the 24.Pz.Div., another 'Stalingrad division', were temporarily stationed in the rear area of the corps.

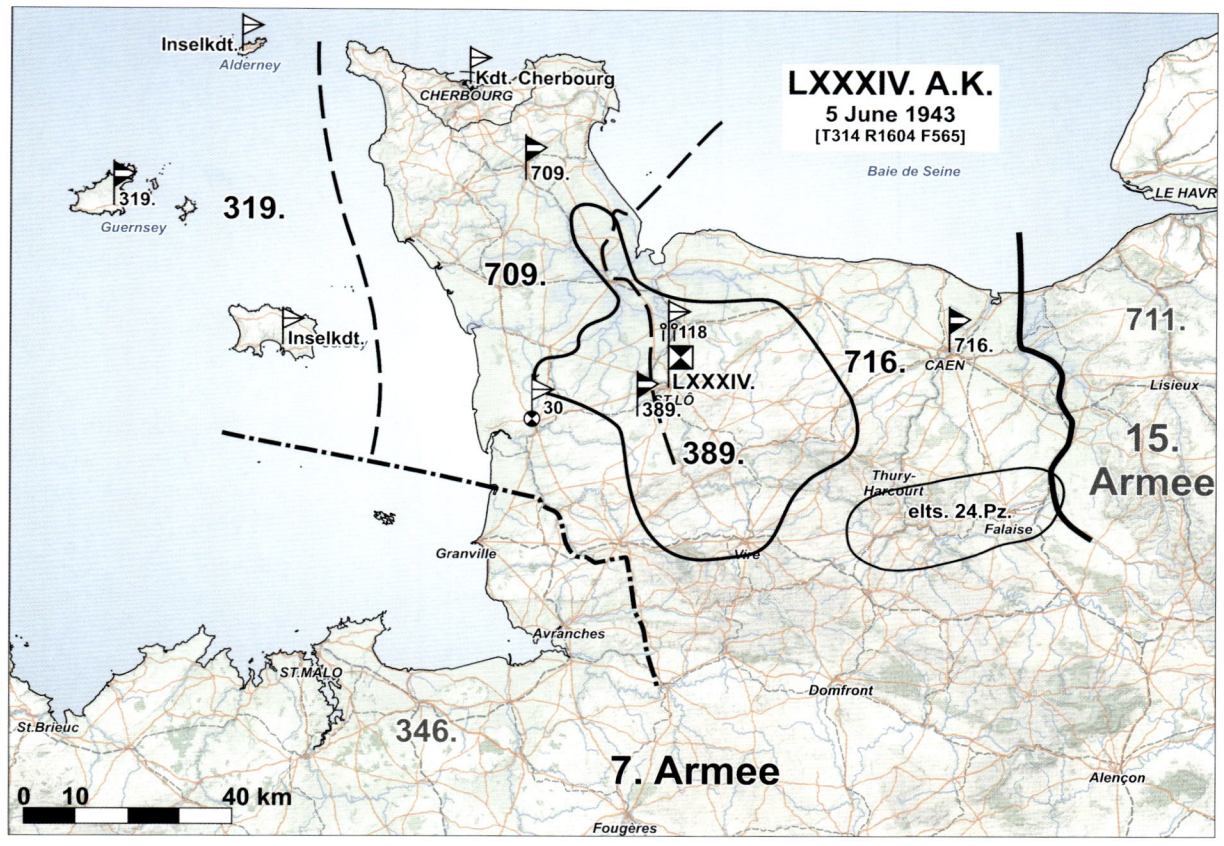

both divisions. The latter were two corps reserve battalions from the *709. I.D.*, along with the battalion held in division reserve in Bayeux (*716. I.D.*). The regiment would also include an ad hoc artillery battalion formed from the two divisions; the *I./AR 656* would provide the headquarters. An engineer and an anti-tank company from the *716. I.D.* would complete the reinforced regiment. The (separate) reinforced battalion would also come from that division. The battalion in divisional reserve in Caen was chosen for this along with an anti-tank platoon from *GR 736*.[242]

Measure III was the least disruptive of the three scenarios. It concerned the transfer of divisional and corps reserves to a neighbour. If this were the *LXXXI. A.K.* (on the right), it would receive the two divisional reserve battalions from the *716. I.D.* and anti-tank platoons from its two regiments. If the *LXXXVII. A.K.* (on the left) were to be reinforced, the divisional reserve battalion at Bayeux (*716. I.D.*) and the corps reserve battalion in La Haye-du-Puits (*709. I.D.*) would be used. Both battalions would have an anti-tank platoon attached.[243]

July passed quietly. In the Calvados, the *I./726* relieved the *III./726* on the coast on **6 July**.[244] The *I./729* moved to Montebourg as a corps reserve on the **17th**, and the *III./729* moved to Tocqueville.[245] On **27 July**, *Pi.Btl. 389* returned from Angers and was billeted in Le Molay.[246]

On **11 July**, the *709.* and *716. I.D.* learned that *OKH* had ordered *Ob. West* to form regimental artillery headquarters for the two divisions, enabling them to finally establish proper artillery regiments.[247] On **17 July**, orders were issued for deployment of *s.Art.Abt. 450* as a field-army group reserve, with the battalion to be spread throughout the interior of the Cotentin with batteries in La Haye-du-Puits and Flottemanville. The headquarters was to be in Le Ham and one battery in *KVU Barfleur*.[248] By **24 July**, the battalion headquarters had transferred to Urville, with the three batteries going to Bolleville, Flottemanville and Canteloup.[249] On the last day of the month, the battalion received orders to be ready to move at 20:00. To compensate for the impending departure, the self-propelled batteries from the *709.* and the *716. I.D.* were ordered to Bolleville and Flottemanville, respectively.[250]

The first components of *s.Art.Abt. 450* departed on **5 August**, the remainder the day after.[251] The same day, *gepanzerte Geräte-Batterie 716* was sent to Bolleville, while the battery from the *709. I.D.* moved to Flottemanville on the **7th**.[252] *Gepanzerte Geräte-Batterie 716* returned to its division on **21 August**, moving to Sommervieu in the Calvados and becoming a divisional reserve.[253] Later that month, both batteries were redesignated with *716* becoming *Batterie Graf Waldersee* and *709 Batterie Reichenau*.[254]

Bttr. Graf Waldersee's return to the Calvados was made possible by the arrival of reinforcements announced in mid-**August**. All of these ended up on the Cotentin and comprised both field-army-group and field-army reserves. The former included *Art.Rgt. zbV 621* with *s.Art.Abt. 457*, with both elements arriving on **21 August**. The regimental headquarters moved to La Haye-du-Puits, while two of the battalion's batteries took up positions around Urville; the third battery was in Bolleville.[255] A light artillery observation battalion also joined the corps, *leichte Beobachtungs-Abteilung 33 (le.Beob.Abt. 33)*, arriving in Bricquebec on **20 August**.[256]

The field-army reserves were provided a reinforced regiment and a smaller but no less interesting formation called *Einsatzverband 390* (Operational Formation 390).[257] It was re-established by *AOK 7* in mid-**August** and consisted of the headquarters of a militia battalion, *Landesschützen-Bataillon 390 (Ldsch.Btl. 390)* and its 1st Company. The 2nd Company had been formed from the field army's alert unit and *Armee-Nachr. Abt. 531*. Orders called for the organisation to be ready for transport on **20 August**, and it arrived in the Cherbourg defensive sector on the **22nd**.[258] It was first staged near Mesnil-au-Val, moving southwest of La Glacerie on **31 August**.[259] The formation was used as a security force around Cherbourg and assisted in the construction of the sector's defences. It also guarded V-weapons sites.[260-261]

The reinforced regiment that arrived on **23-26 August** originated from the *384. I.D.*, another division destroyed in Stalingrad.[261] The regiment was formed from the headquarters of *GR 535* and comprised one battalion from each of the division's three regiments (*GR 534, 535* and *536*) plus an ad hoc anti-tank company. Other elements included the *II./AR 384*, plus an engineer and an anti-tank company.[262] Its headquarters moved to Ste. Mère-Église with the *II./535* staged to the south and east of the town. The *III./534* was positioned around La Haye-du-Puits and the *II./536* northeast of St. Sauveur-le-Vicomte. The *II./AR 384* ended up in the northern portion of the peninsula, between Cherbourg and Canteloup.[263] The 384. I.D. itself was being rebuilt in Bretagne under XXV. A.K.

Within the corps sector, several battalions were repositioned. On **23 August**, *Pi.Btl. 709* moved to Les Pieux, with the *I./739* moving to the area of St. Croix-Hague as a divisional reserve.[264] Two days later, the *I./544* of the *389. I.D.* moved to Sainteny – Carentan. For the time being, the division would remain with the corps, although orders were received to prepare for its departure.[265] On **31 August**, *Ob.West* requested the division be ready to entrain with 48 hours' notice.[266]

Developments in **September** related primarily to the departure of the *389. I.D.* Additionally, there were some minor movements, departures and new arrivals. On the **27th**, the bulk of *Schnelle Abteilung 517* moved to Périers.[267]

On **13 September**, the corps was informed of the intention to send a regiment from the *243. I.D.* to the area of Caen - St. Lô as a field-army reserve. It would be supported by *s.Art.Abt. 456*, which itself was a field-army-group reserve.[268] The battalion arrived on **16 September** and dispersed over a wide area north of La Haye-du-Puits.[269] It reported to *AR 621*, as did *s.Art.Abt. 457*.[270]

Some moves were part of a grander scheme. On **4 September**, the corps notified *AOK 7* of the planned reorganisation of its reserves in preparation for the arrival of a reinforced regiment from the *242. I.D.*, the reinforcement requested for the *709. I.D.* by *Ob.West* in June. Initially, the plan envisaged moving the *II./536* within the corps area, although the battalion left the corps on **12 September**.[271] Other reserves did move as planned. On **18 September**, *leichte Beobachtungs-Abteilung 33* moved to St. Sauveur-le-

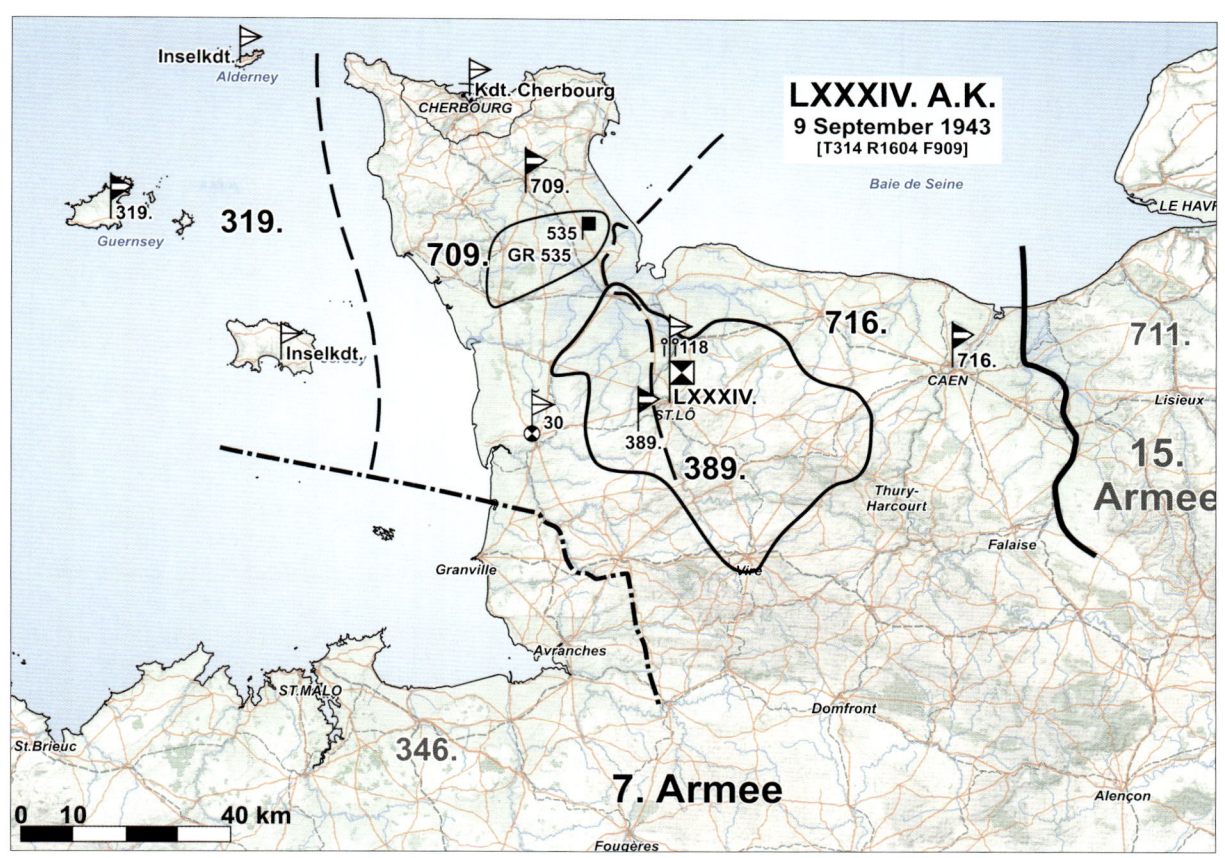

The arrival of the reinforced GR 535 (384.I.D.) in August provided the corps with a reserve force at the base of the peninsula. Again this was only temporary. The rest of the division was rebuilt elsewhere after its destruction at Stalingrad.

Vicomte and the headquarters of *GR 739* moved to Bricquebec on the **25th**.²⁷² *AOK 7* decided that the *I./729* would stay in Montebourg until the regiment from the *242. I.D.* arrived.²⁷³

While few movements concerned the *389. I.D.*, an exception was *AR 389*, which moved on **11 September**. The headquarters and the 4th Battalion went to Torigni-sur-Vire, with the 1st Battalion going to the Périers area, the 2nd around Tilly-sur-Seulles and the 3rd around Colombières.²⁷⁴

Although the *389. I.D.* was about to depart, it was still required to relinquish some units. In accordance with a direct order from Hitler (*Führerbefehl*), it had to provide an infantry battalion, an engineer platoon, an anti-tank platoon and an artillery battery for a division in the East.²⁷⁵ The battalion and battery selected were the *III./546* and the *8./AR 389*, both of which were ordered to be replaced at once. The infantry battalion and battery did not leave the division immediately.²⁷⁶ Indeed, the artillery battery's transfer was cancelled altogether in **October**, with the *III./546* transferred to the *19. Pz.Div.* on **8 November**.²⁷⁷

Of the remaining subordinate elements, some would still not follow the division to the east. In mid-**September**, the *OKH* decided that the divisional reconnaissance battalion, the re-established *III./546*, the *III./AR 389* and a transport column would stay in France.²⁷⁸ This was soon expanded to include the self-propelled company of *Pz.Jg.Abt. 389* (its 1st Company).²⁷⁹ The elements that remained would form a *Kampfgruppe*. To command this force, the *OKH* would provide a regimental headquarters with its attendant company.²⁸⁰ On **19**

September, *AOK 7* informed the corps that the *389. I.D.*'s transfer would start the next day.[281] The movement was concluded on the **26th**.[282]

Several of the division's elements still in Normandy were moved on **25 September**. *Aufkl.Abt. 389* moved to the area of Marigny - Marchésieux and the new *III./546* to St. Jean-de-Daye.[283] Disposition of the remaining elements from the *389. I.D.* was also directed by *Ob.West* on **25 September**: They would form a *Kampfgruppe* as the basis of a new division. Initially, the force would be designated *Kampfgruppe Normandie* (later becoming the *352. I.D.*). Additional units would come from the *356. I.D.* (*AOK 19*), which was ordered to release the *II./869* and the *III./871* and a company from *Pz.Jg.Abt. 356*. Although the *Kampfgruppe* would establish the nucleus of the new division, the divisional and other headquarters elements, a signals battalion and supply troops were to be transferred from the Army in the East.[284] Until the arrival of the division staff, *Oberstleutnant* Heine, the adjutant of the corps headquarters, was put in acting command. The headquarters was located in Le Dézert and the *Kampfgruppe* as a whole designated as a field-army reserve.[285]

A busy **October** for the corps began with the arrival of *GR 922* from the *243. I.D.* While the division was transferred to Bretagne, the regiment and its two ad hoc battalions was sent to the Cotentin, arriving near Carentan on **1 October**. The battalions were formed by combining the three bicycle companies in each of two divisional regiments and designating them as the *IV./920* and the *IV./922*.[286] The next day, the regimental headquarters and the headquarters of the 4th Battalion were in Carentan, while the headquarters of the *IV./920* was in Sainteny.[287]

On **3 October**, the corps informed the *709. I.D.* about the impending arrival of the reinforced regiment from the *242. I.D.*, now identified as *GR 919* and the *II./AR 242*. Upon arrival, these elements would be incorporated into the division and the artillery battalion redesignated as the *III./AR 669*.[288] The regiment would serve as a corps reserve, with the headquarters and one battalion around Ste. Mère-Église and the other two battalions near Montebourg and La Haye-du-Puits.[289]

The arrival of the artillery battalion was just one of the changes made to the artillery on the Cotentin in **October**. The first orders were issued on the **3rd**. The *III./AR 669* was deployed near Les Pieux to defend the coast north and south of Cap de Flamanville. *Geräte-Batterie Osteck* was to be positioned near the coast to provide flanking cover southwest of Osteck. *Stellungs-Batterie (Küste) 317* (Positional Battery (Coastal) 317 / *St.B.(K) 317*) would move to the Cherbourg defences, taking over from the *II./AR 384*. The battery itself would be replaced in *KVU Barfleur* by *Geräte-Batterie Fort du Roule*.[290]

On **5 October**, a minor change was made. Only two batteries from the *III./AR 669* moved to Les Pieux, while the 3rd Battery took over the role of *Stellungs-Batterie (Küste) 317* until *Gerate-Batterie Fort du Roule* arrived.[291] As planned, the remainder of the artillery battalion deployed in the area of Les Pieux on the **6th** to defend the coast north and south of Cap de Flamanville, with the *III./AR 669* headquarters reported in Les Pieux the following day.[292]

Plans were also made for a new naval battery. Two guns arrived from the Channel Islands and moved to the positions of *Geräte-Batterie Fort du Roule*, which was about to move. These guns would be taken over by the Navy and later expanded to a full battery. The battery would then move to the caverns at Fort du Roule under *Marine-Artillerie-Abteilung 260* (Naval Artillery Battalion 260 / *M.A.A. 260*).[293] This battery ultimately became *Marine-Küsten-Batterie Fort du Roule*.

Changes to the artillery on the Cotentin did not end there. On the **12th**, the headquarters of *s.Art.Abt. 456* moved to Vindefontaine.[294] Further north, the headquarters of the *I./AR 669* and *Eisenbahn-Artillerie-Abteilung 681* (Railway Artillery Battalion 681 / *E.Art.Abt. 681*) (performing duties in a coast artillery role) swapped positions on **22 October**. The former was now in Équeurdreville, the latter in Beaumont-Hague.[295] Around this time, the corps was also informed that the equipment batteries with the *709.* and the *716. I.D.* had been formally approved.[296] Although no numbers were mentioned, this may have involved as many as 10 batteries.[297]

Infantry formations also went through a number of changes. On **6 October**, the *I./729* moved to St. Martin-d'Audouville, with the reinforced *GR 919* arriving the same day. On the **9th**, the regiment's three battalions were reported south of Fauville, Montebourg and La Haye-du-Puits, respectively. The regimental headquarters was in Ste. Mère-Église.[298]

The regiment's arrival enabled a series of changes announced in Corps Order No. 6 (**11 October**). The boundary between the *709.* and the *716. I.D.* was redrawn, with control of Carentan and the south of the peninsula's east coast assigned to the *709. I.D.* To enable this, another battalion from the division was deployed in *KVG Cotentin-Ost*. An additional reinforcement for the Cotentin was *Georg.Inf.Btl. 795*, which was due to arrive shortly for use as a divisional reserve in the Cherbourg land defences, with the exception of one company going the coast.[299]

These orders were soon followed by Corps Order No. 7 (**17 October**). The *319.*, the *709.* and the *716. I.D.* were each instructed to prepare one battalion (*II./582*, *I./739* and *II./726*, respectively) for transfer to the Eastern Front. At the same time, the planned arrival of two eastern battalions was reported.[300] *Ost-Btl. 439* was to be deployed in *KVU Bessin* and *Ost-Btl. 627* on Jersey. Before the latter battalion arrived, its task was given to *Ost-Bataillon 643* (East Battalion 643 / *Ost-Btl. 643*).[301] On the Cotentin, the *I./739* was to be relieved by *MG-Btl. 17* as divisional reserve. *GR 919* would remain as a corps reserve and its 2nd Battalion was to be moved to the area of Montebourg - St. Germain-de-Tournebut – St. Martin-d'Audouville.[302]

On **17 October**, the *I./729* moved to the Beuzeville-au-Plain - Ste. Marie-du-Mont area to take over the division's new sector, while the *II./919* moved to Flottemanville (south of Valognes).[303] The boundary between the *709.* and the *716. I.D.* was finally redrawn on **19 October**. Everything north of the Canal du Port de Carentan was transferred to the *709. I.D.*; as a result, the entire east coast of the Cotentin was now under that division. This sector — known as *KVG Cotentin-Ost* — was held by *GR 729*. While the 1st Battalion assumed command of *KVU Marcouf*, the 2nd Battalion took charge of *KVU St. Vaast* and the 3rd Battalion did the same in *KVU Barfleur*. The regimental headquarters was in Montebourg and the 1st Battalion in Beuzeville-au-Plain.[304] On the **25th**, the headquarters of the *II./729* was in Octeville-l'Avenel and the *III./729* in Tocqueville.[305] Other divisional elements also changed locations. On the **23rd**, the *I./739* moved to Bricquebec and, the next day, the *II./919* to St. Germain-de-Tournebut.[306] *MG-Btl. 17* also displaced. On the **26th**, the battalion was staged around St. Croix-Hague, with the headquarters in Le Bigard, west of Tonneville.[307]

Further east, *KVA Calvados* was reorganised. The *I./736* was relieved by the *III./736*. On **21 October**, the *I./736* was in Le Mesnil and the *III./736* in St. Aubin-d'Arquenay. In *GR 726*, the 3rd Battalion relieved the 2nd Battalion. On the **21st**, the three battalion headquarters were in Maisons, Bayeux and Isigny. The *I./736* was a divisional reserve and the *II./726* a corps reserve.[308]

The first of the new eastern battalions arrived on **13 October**: *Georg.Inf.Btl. 795* and *823*.[309] *Georg.Inf.Btl. 795* was reported on the Cotentin, the other on Guernsey.[310] On **14 October**, the former battalion was in the area of St. Croix-Hague - Beaumont-Hague, with headquarters in Nacqueville. As planned, it became a divisional reserve of the *709. I.D.*[311] On the **22nd**, parts of *Ost-Btl. 439* arrived in Bayeux, completing the move on the **28th**.[312] On **30 October**, the battalion was east and northeast of Bayeux, with the headquarters in St. Vigor-le-Grand. On the **27th**, *Ost-Btl. 643* arrived in Grouville-la-Fontaine on Jersey. Four days later, the corps received another eastern battalion, when *Ost-Btl. 642* arrived in Caen.[313] The next day (**1 November**), it was quartered in the Beauregard Barracks, northeast of the town.[314]

The formation of the *352. I.D.* continued apace. On **3 October**, the *II./869* and the *III./871* started arriving, completing their movement on the **5th**.[315] On the **4th**, the headquarters of the fusilier battalion relocated to Feugères, while the *II./869* was in Amigny and the *III./871* in Gorin-l'Epinay-Tesson. The *1./Pz.Jg.Abt. 356* was billeted in St. Fromond.[316] Orders were given to transfer elements of *Pi.Btl. 371* (in Bretagne) to *KG Normandie* to form the cadre for *Pi.Btl. 352*.[317] These arrived on **13 October**.[318]

Alongside the new arrivals, the corps continued to hand over formations. On **18 October**, transfer of the reinforced *GR 535* was completed, having apparently begun on the **6th**.[319] The arrival of *Georg.Inf.Btl. 823* on Jersey allowed the *II./583* to transfer to the east, an exchange ordered on **26 September**.[320] The battalion was initially sent to St. Malo on **23 October** before leaving for the Russian Front on the **27th**.[321]

Another noteworthy change was a reorganisation of engineers and construction troops, ordered by *AOK 7* on **3 October**. *Fest.Pi.Stab 19* and *Fest.Pi.Abschn.Gr. I/14* and *II/14* were transferred from the Channel Islands, while on the mainland *Fest.Pi.Abschn.Gr. II/11* left the *709. I.D.* area; all of these elements then left the field army.[322] The forces from the Channel Islands left on the **8th**, including *Fest.Pi.Btl. 19*.[323] Although the *II/11*'s departure is not mentioned in the corps records, it was no longer listed within the organisational documents of fortress engineer and construction forces of **15 October**.[324]

The reorganisation left *Fest.Pi.Abschn.Gr. I/11* with the *709. I.D.*, the *III/11* with the *716. I.D.* and the *II/19* on the Channel Islands with the *319. I.D.* All three were commanded by *Fest.Pi.Stab 11*, which moved to St. Lô and was earmarked to receive more troops. *Bau-Pi.Btl. 59* and a company from *Bau-Pi.Btl. 158* were anticipated in early **October**, along with a company each from *Fest.Pi.Stab 9* and *19* later in the month. These elements were

Known as Battery Crisbecq by the Allies, Marine-Küsten-Batterie Marcouf provided the heaviest firepower along the east coast of the Cotentin Peninsula. Its 21 cm guns, however, failed to have a significant impact on the fighting. The battery's heavy fortifications nonetheless allowed it to be used as an infantry strongpoint to oppose the American advance north. (NARA)

to reinforce the east coast of the Cotentin, from the mouth of the Vire to south of St. Vaast, by constructing fortified positions. Most were located in Bretagne, but the *2./Bau-Pi.Btl. 158* came from the Channel Islands, arriving in La Madeleine on **15 October**.[325] *Bau-Pi.Btl. 59* arrived in Montebourg on the **12th** and moved to Château de Courcy in Fontenay-sur-Mer on the **24th**.[326]

The status of the additional reserves was also clarified. *AR 621* (*s.Art. Abt. 456*, *s.Art.Abt. 457*, and *le.Beob.Abt. 33*) remained as a field-army-group reserve to be in general support of counterattacks by corps and divisional reserves and reinforce artillery support in general. Priority was given to *KVG Cotentin-Ost*, then *KVG Cherbourg* and *KVU Jobourg*.[327]

The field-army reserve consisted of the *I./Pz.Rgt. 100* and *Einsatzverband 390*. The tank battalion was to prepare for operations against enemy troops on the east coast and airborne landings in the area of Carentan - Lessay - St. Sauveur-le-Vicomte - Ste. Mère-Église. *Einsatzverband 390* would continue as a security force in the interior.[328]

The corps reserves included *KG Normandie* and *GR 922*. *KG Normandie* was directed to plan for operations in several directions: through Le Molay to Bayeux; along the Vire River to the area east of Isigny; through Carentan or Baupte to Ste. Marie-du-Mont; and against the west coast in the direction of Lessay - La Haye-du-Puits. *GR 922* had two missions: To support the fighting on the east coast and in *KVU Vire* and to secure the bridges at Carentan, thereby keeping the Douve crossing between Étienville and Carentan open for reserves moving north. *GR 919* could be employed in support of the fighting on the coast but also to secure the area of Blosville - Étienville - La Haye-du-Puits - St. Sauveur-le-Vicomte - Ste. Mère-Église from airborne landings. Priority was given to the northern Prairies Marécageuses in conjunction with *AR 621* and the *I./Pz.Rgt. 100*. The regiment was also to be prepared to be transferred to the *716. I.D. Aufkl.Schw. 84* reported directly to *GR 919*. The corps reserve of *GR 726*, reinforced with *Bttr. Resi* and *Graf Waldersee*, received its orders from the *716. I.D.* and was to be prepared to move to the west coast via Airel. *Schnel.Brig. 30* had the status of corps reserve, but was still attached to the *LXVII. Res.Korps* (established in **1942** to command reserve divisions and formations under *Ob.West.*). It was to prepare for deployment on the west coast, to protect the boundary with the *346. I.D.* and to defend against airborne landings in the Lande de Lessay.[329]

Since a number of changes had occurred, it was necessary to update the orders for Contingency Measures I-III introduced in **June**. New orders were issued on **9 October** and primarily involved changes in officers, forces and designations. Overall, little changed but the arrival of *GR 919* provided the corps with a standing reserve regiment, which had consequences for the relief force for the transfer of the *716. I.D.* in Contingency Meausure I. While Contingency Measure II no longer required an ad hoc regiment, nothing changed for the artillery battalion.[330] On the same day, orders came in to prepare to form a reserve engineer battalion for the corps. It was to consist of *Fest.Pi.Btl. 11*, *Gesteinsbohr-Kompanie 28* (Rock Drilling Company 28) and *Baustoff-Kolonne 429* (Building Material Column 429). This battalion would be used for special assignments. If necessary, it could be employed tactically. It would also play a part in Contingency Measure I.[331]

The relocation and arrival of artillery elements was undoubtedly important, but even more basic changes took place towards the end of the month. The boundary change between the *709.* and the *716. I.D.* focussed attention on an issue in the *LXXXIV. A.K.*'s organisation of its coastal artillery. The change was necessitated by the transfer of *St.B.(K) 316* to *709. I.D.*, increasing the number of batteries under *H.K.A.A. 755* on the east coast to six, but its headquarters had already struggled to command five batteries. As no other solution was available, the corps requested another *H.K.A.A.* headquarters.[332] The *709. I.D.* was informed of this request on **30 November**. A new headquarters would allow (*Artillerie-*)*Gruppe Zerweck* (artillery under the commander of *H.K.A.A. 755*, *Major* Zerweck) to be disbanded, and the division was instructed to start preparations.[333] That day, orders were also given to the *716. I.D.*, noting that *H.K.A.R. 645* would leave the division and be attached to the *709. I.D.* Instead, the commander of *AR 656* would become the division artillery officer.[334] The coastal artillery in the Calvados would be commanded by *H.K.A.A. 832*.[335]

October 1943 marked the end of reinforcing the *Atlantikwall* rather than bringing in more forces. Compared to **1942**, the forces had been weakened by the demands of the Eastern Front. Since **October 1942**, 34 infantry divisions, 2 airborne divisions, 12 armoured divisions and 5 armoured infantry divisions had been transferred from the west. This did not account for the individual weapons, separate batteries and battalions and personnel that had also been sent east. Although many elements had been replaced, the quality was far below that of **1942**.[336]

On **28 October**, *Feldm.* von Rundstedt sent a 49-page report to the *OKW*, explaining in detail the poor condition of the defences in *Ob.West* and identifying shortcomings. Significant defences were not possible across large parts of the front when only "security" forces were often available. For *AOK 1* and *AOK 19*, the situation was worse and only reinforced "observation" was possible. He noted:[337]

One should not be surprised if our defences are unsuccessful in defeating an Allied invasion, regardless of the Atlantikwall and efforts of the troops and their commanders.

Things needed to change, and fast. Hitler responded by issuing *Führer* Directive No. 51 on **3 November**. This finally prioritised defences in the west and would form the basis of changes that took place in the months before the invasion.

The reorganisation of the artillery under *LXXXIV. A.K.* proceeded. On **6 November**, the corps addressed the latest plans for the artillery received from *AOK 7*. In the *716. I.D.* sector, *H.K.A.A. 832* was to be redesignated *H.K.A.A. 761*. As the sector had no need for a regimental headquarters, *H.K.A.R. 645* would be transferred to the Cotentin and be redesignated *H.K.A.R. 760*. *Eisb. Art.Abt. 681* was the first headquarters staff assigned to the regiment in its new sector. The other regimental headquarters on the peninsula, *H.K.A.R. 644*, was to be redesignated *H.K.A.R. 762* — its 2nd Battalion was formed from *H.K.A.A. 755* and the 3rd Battalion from *H.K.A.A. 404*.[338]

On the same day, the corps was informed of plans from *Marine-Gruppe West* to position a modern 21 cm battery near Quinéville and a 15 cm battery around Port en Bessin.[339] Ultimately, these were established as *Marine-Batterie Marcouf* and *Marine-Batterie Longues*, part of *M.A.A. 260*.[340]

In late **October**, the corps headquarters informed the *709. I.D.* that the preparations of *AR 621* for supporting the division were inadequate for the east coast of the Cotentin. It was not enough to plot positions on paper, instead it was deemed necessary to construct actual positions that could be

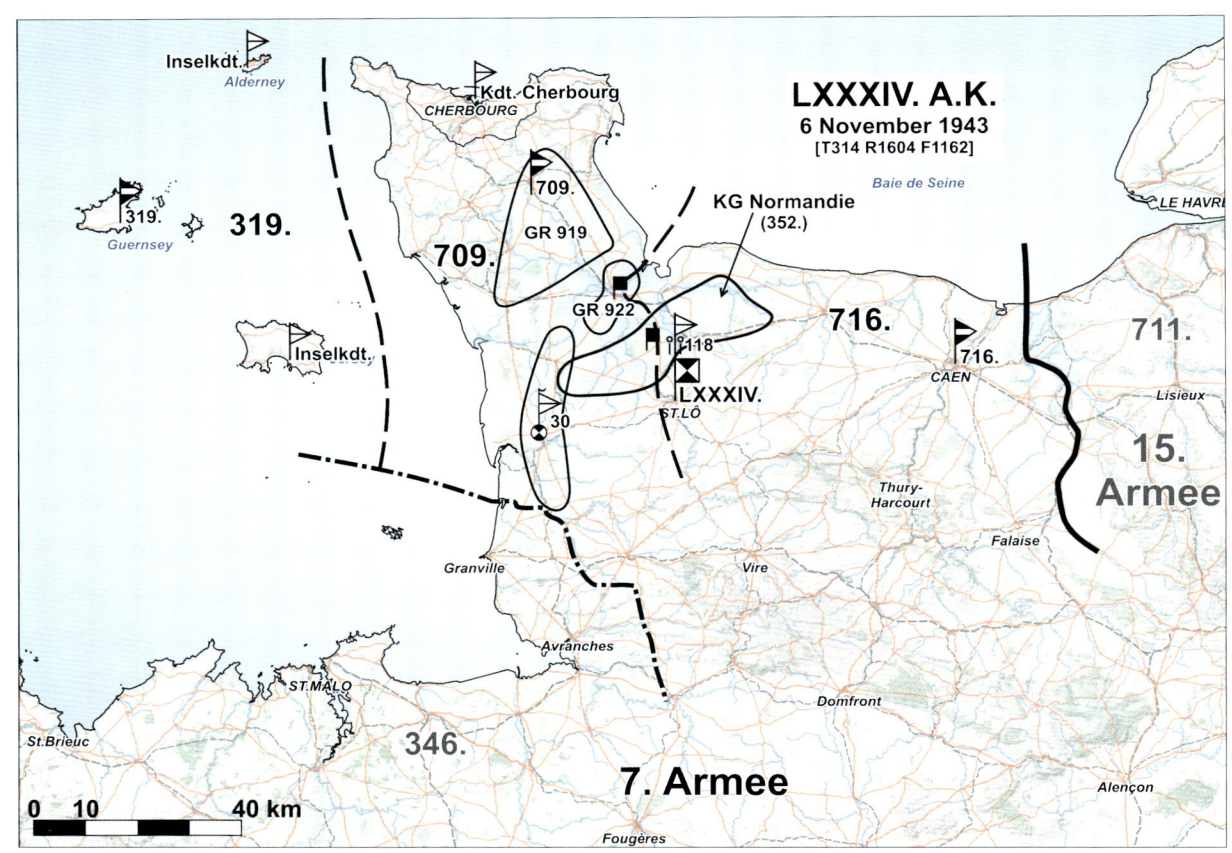

The departure of the 389. I.D. in October 1943 weakened the corps sector. Using elements of the division, KG Normandie was formed, which would over time expand to become the 352. I.D. To provide more immediate and permanent reinforcements, GR 919 joined the 709. I.D.

It was originally used as a reserve force, but still allowed the 709. I.D. to take control of the southeast corner of the Cotentin from the 716. I.D. The situation around Carentan further improved with the arrival of GR 922 (an ad-hoc regiment from the 243. I.D.).

used as required.[341] As a result, on **8 November**, *AR 621*, with *s.Art.Abt. 456* (minus its 3rd Battery) and *s.Art.Abt. 457*, were temporarily moved to the peninsula's east coast. This move was to be coordinated by the *709. I.D.* and, although the troops would report to the division, the regiment remained a field-army-group reserve.[342] On **12 November**, *AR 621* and its two battalions conducted the move. The regimental headquarters moved to Le Vast and the headquarters of *s.Art.Abt. 456* to Michauderie, west of Quinéville. Its two batteries were in position northeast of Montebourg. The *s.Art.Abt. 457* headquarters moved to La Pernelle, and its three batteries were northwest of Quettehou.[343] The previous day, an artillery change had also been made in the Calvados, with *H.K.A.A. 832* moving to La Cambe.[344]

As in the preceding months, the *352. I.D.* continued to evolve. In addition to its role in the formation of new and larger units, its combat-ready forces stayed as a reserve force. In the event of an attack, the old *Kampfgruppe* would be reassembled quickly.[345] Among the new formations created in **November** was *Pi.Btl. 352*. Initially formed on the **2nd**, it moved to Trévières six days later.[346] More important were plans for command of the division. The headquarters of the *223. I.D.* was sent from the east to St. Lô to form the divisional staff. The provisioning of signals and supply troops and artillery was yet to be determined. The orders included designations for the three infantry regiments: *GR 914, 915* and *916*.[347]

An advance party from the *223. I.D.* headquarters arrived on the **8th**.[348]

The main body of the headquarters arrived on **16 November** and was located in Canisy.[349] Four days later, as the headquarters of the *352. I.D.*, it took command of *KG Normandie*.[350] The same day, several divisional formations were redesignated: The *II./869* to *II./914*; the *III./871* to *I./915*; the *III./546 (neu)* to *I./916*; *Divisions-Füsilier-Bataillon (Aufklärungs-Abteilung) (Div.Füs. Btl. (A.A.))* added the number *352*; and the *III./AR 389* became the *III./AR 352*. Finally, the company with towed anti-tank guns became *Pz.Jg.Kp. 352*.[351]

The *223. I.D.* personnel did not command the *352. I.D.* for long. On the **27th**, it was learned that it would be relieved by the headquarters from the *321. I.D.* and that this division would supply many of the missing personnel for the new division.[352] Among the first formations to arrive (**29 November**) were the headquarters and elements of *Nachr.Abt. 352*.[353]

As well as changes in location for the artillery, there were other movements in the corps area, some the result of departing formations. These movements could have been more significant, but on **3 November** the previous order to transfer three infantry battalions to the east was reduced to just the *I./739*, which departed on the **12th**.[354] On **2 November**, the *I./Pz.Rgt. 100* was transferred from the *AOK 7* sector.[355] Its departure meant changes among the reserves at the base of the Cotentin and, on **6 November**, new plans were announced. Since *GR. 922* would stay in Normandy, the *IV./920* would move to the area previously held by the *I./Pz.Rgt. 100*. In turn, *Div.Füs.Btl. (A.A.) 352* was to move to the area of Tribehou - St. Georges-de-Bohon - Méautis - Sainteny.[356] Both moves were carried out on the **12th**. The headquarters of the fuselier battalion was located in Château d'Auxais and the *IV./920* moved to Coigny, west of Carentan.[357] It was decided to return *GR. 922* to its division in Bretagne to train for about four weeks, the transfer to be carried out in early **December**. Upon its departure, *Div.Füs.Btl. (A.A.) 352* would move to the Carentan area.[358] Other changes for the corps included moving the *III./736* to Château Jucoville, north of La Cambe, on **11 November**.[359] A number of headquarters elements constructing the defences moved to St. Lô in **November**. On **6 November**, *Fest.Pi.Stab 11* was the first to move, followed by *Fest.Nachr.Stab 10 zbV* on the **19th**.

Three battalions joined the corps in **November**. On **12 November**, *Pi. Btl. 346. I.D* arrived in Cherbourg and was in Mesnil-au-Val the next day.[360] On **27 November**, the battalion began its temporary move to the Calvados. The next day, the headquarters was reported in Le Molay. On **18 November**, *Ost-Btl. 649* arrived in Cherbourg; the following day, its headquarters was in Château Digosville. Another eastern battalion reached Bayeux on the **27th** (*Ost-Btl. 630*).[361]

The final reinforcement for **November** was *schwere Stellungs-Werfer-Abteilung 103* (Heavy Positional Rocket Launcher Battalion 103) / *s.St. Wfr.Abt.103*). On the **30th**, the corps learned that the battalion would move to Carentan as a field-army reserve by **15 December** and deploy in the Orglandes - Étienville - St. Jores area.[362]

During **November**, the quality and improvement of the defences was assessed and plans made for the coming months. Many of these involved troops that had recently arrived or were expected. For example, labour for the Cherbourg defences was to be provided by three companies from *Georg. Inf.Btl. 795* and *Ost-Btl. 649* and two companies from *MG-Btl. 17*. All would be used four days a week for that mission. *GR 919* was to work three days a week to increase the depth of the main line of defence and the so-called "2nd Position". Headquarters elements, reserves and supply troops would do the same.[363] For the *716. I.D.*, the battalions in corps and divisional reserves in Caen and Bayeux were to be used three days a week as well. *Ost-Btl. 439* and *642* would be used four days a week.[364]

The plans prioritised certain sectors for improving the depth of the defences. On the east coast of the Cotentin, these were the areas between the lines Audouville-la-Hubert - Ste. Mère-Église - Reigneville in the south, and St. Vaast-la-Hougue - Quettehou - Teurthéville-Bocage in the north. On the west coast, a similar area stretched from the Jobourg Peninsula to the line Carteret - St. Sauveur-le-Vicomte. Two similar areas were chosen in the Calvados: The area between the Orne and the defensive positions around Carpiquet airfield and the area between Bayeux and Isigny, including both towns.[365]

The use of dedicated engineer and construction troops was complicated by the start of work on the *V-weapons* sites. A new headquarters was tasked with the preparations for them, commonly referred to as *Sonderbauten* (special structures). It was commanded by *Gen.Maj.* Hellwig, the supervisor of "camouflage" in the broadest sense and military security at *Ob.West*.[366] He was assisted by officers from *AOK 7* — *Major* Mayer-Krapoll in particular — and *Fest.Pi.Kdr. XIX*. The new headquarters reported to the *LXXXIV. A.K.* and was directed to work with *Fest.Pi.Stab 11*.[367] As the *V-weapons* programme was both secret and controlled by the *Luftwaffe*, there were issues in coordinating

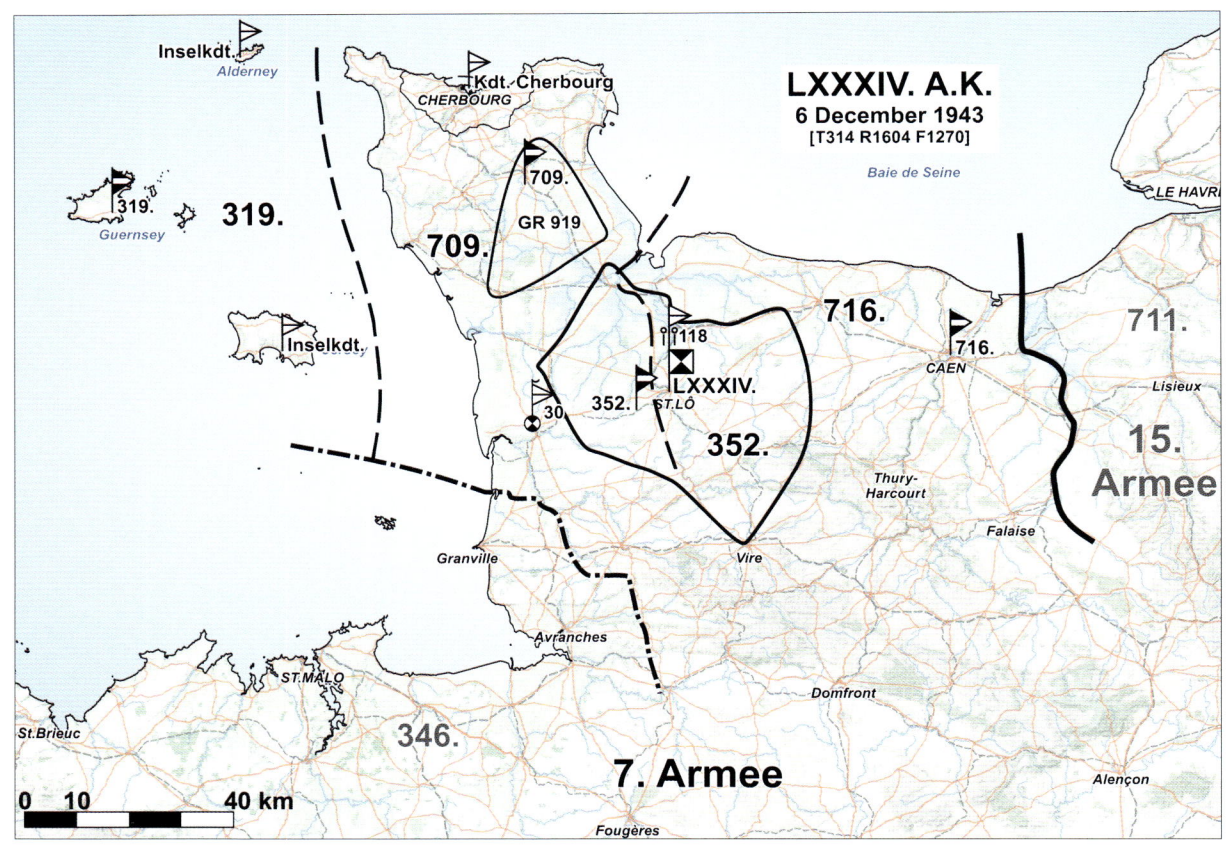

By December 1943 KG Normandie had become the 352 .I.D., although its development into a fully operational division would still take more time. The division took over the Carentan area from GR 922 which left to rejoin its division in Bretagne. By D-Day the 352. I.D. was still with the LXXXIV. A.K., holding part of the Calvados coast.

the programme. Due to a lack of information, it was difficult to incorporate the *V*-weapons sites in a "2nd Position" and to guarantee their protection by Army elements. Conversely, the *Flak* belt to protect the sites on the Cotentin roughly matched the rear boundary of the Cherbourg defensive sector. This allowed them to be incorporated into the over-all defensive planning.[368]

It was announced on **26 November** that the corps would receive the reinforced *II./Sicherungs-Regiment 195* (Security Regiment 195 / *Sich.Rgt. 195*), which would be dispersed throughout the area Villers-*Bocage* - Le Molay - Airel - Brix - La Haye-du-Puits - Pont-Hébert, with its headquarters in Airel.[369] Its arrival may have been related to the *V*-weapons programme. On the same day, the corps was informed that *Einsatzverband 390* would be relieved by the *II./Flieger-Rgt. 90* (Aviation Regiment 90 / *Fl.Rgt. 90*), the redesignated *Fluganwärter-Btl. II* that would guard and protect *Luftwaffe* installations. Considering the activities of its predecessor, these installations probably included the *V*-weapons sites. The headquarters would be located in St. Pierre-Église near Théville airfield. The corps was instructed to transfer *Einsatzverband 390* to Le Mans no later than **1 December**.[370]

Plans for transferring reserves to other corps were updated in **October** and rescinded on **12 November**. The new orders from *AOK 7* no longer included plans for possible extraction of a division or reinforced regiment (Contingency Measures I and II). Contingency Measure III was altered and apparently no longer included the transfer of forces to *KVG Granville*.

Conversely, the number of forces available for the *LXXXI. A.K.*, was increased to include a regimental headquarters with attendant support elements and two reinforced battalions. *GR 726*, would provide the headquarters and headquarters company and motorisation would be by its division. The reserve battalions from *GR 726* and *736* would also be included, as was *Bttr. Resi* and the anti-tank platoon from *GR 726*. Mobility for these units would be provided by *Kraftfahr-Kompanie 84*. On the coast, the headquarters of *GR 726* was to be replaced by an ad hoc headquarters formed from *Fest.Pi.Stab 11* and *Korps-Nachr.Abt. 460*.[371]

The transfer of *GR 922* to Bretagne began with the *IV./922* on **30 November** and was complete in early **December**.[372] The *IV./920* left on **2 December,** with the headquarters following two days later.[373] As planned, *Div.Füs.Btl. (A.A.) 352* moved to Carentan on the **2nd**.[374]

Most new arrivals in **December** were for the establishment of the *352. I.D.* On **1 December**, a large number of headquarters elements from the *321. I.D.* arrived, including division staff and the fusilier and engineer battalion staff. A mixture of support and supply elements also arrived.[375] More forces joined the division on the **3rd** and **4th**, including the headquarters of *GR 589*, which was used to form *GR 915*.[376] The *321. I.D.* continued to arrive throughout the month. On **5 December**, this included the headquarters of the *I./AR 321* and personnel for a number of batteries.[377] Between **4-9 December,** the *223. I.D.* headquarters left the corps.[378] At 12:00 on **6 December**, the headquarters of the *321. I.D.* officially took command of the *352. I.D.*[379] Three days later, *Pi. Btl. 352* was sent to Angers for training.[380] *GR 914* and *915* were in Remilly and Le Dézert, respectively, while the *II./AR 352* moved to Cerisy-la-Forêt on **19 December**.[381]

On the Cotentin, *MG-Btl. 17* relieved the *III./739* on **5 December**, the latter becoming a divisional reserve with its headquarters in Le Bigard and three companies in St. Croix-Hague, with the fourth supporting *MG-Btl. 17*. The headquarters of *MG-Btl. 17* was in Beaumont-Hague and its companies in the surrounding area.[382] Changes were also made to the artillery on the Cotentin. On **13 December**, *H.K.A.R. 645* was moved to Sotteville.[383] Five days later, *s.Art.Abt. 456* moved to Émondeville, its three batteries positioned east of the village.[384] On the **22nd**, *Eisenbahn-Batterie 722* (Railway Battery 722 / *E-Bttr. 722*) was transferred from Cherbourg to Torigni-sur-Vire, 10 km southeast of St. Lô.[385] This was in line with concerns about its suitability against sea targets.[386]

New arrivals in **December** included the reinforced *II./Sich.Rgt. 195*; its move was announced in **November**, and it started arriving on **1 December**, completing on the **4th**. On **3 December**, the battalion headquarters was in Airel.[387] On **19 December**, it was reported that the battalion had deployed on security duty, with the headquarters still in Airel.[388] For unknown reasons, the planned transfer of *Einsatzverband 390* on **1 December** was not carried out as ordered; it finally left on **17 December**.[389]

An interesting *Luftwaffe* arrival in **December** was the 23rd Battery of the *IV./Flak-Rgt. 155*, which arrived in Bricquebec on the **22nd**. With the rest of its battalion, it would operate the V1 installations on the Cotentin. The battery command post was established at the Trappist Monastery 2 km west of Bricquebec.[390]

Reorganisation of the artillery was started in November, but on **19 December** the *OKH* finally issued detailed orders to reorganise much of it under *Ob.West*. These orders involved the establishment and redesignation of battalions and batteries, as well as the issuance of new equipment and weaponry. For the *LXXXIV. A.K.*, this included the *709. I.D.* Its *AR 669* (aka *AR 709*) was redesignated *AR 1709* while the *716. I.D.*'s *AR 716* was redesignated *AR 1716*.[391] The coastal artillery was also redesignated. The numbers mentioned in **November** (*760*, *761* and *762*) were not used at all. In the Calvados, *H.K.A.A. 832* became *H.K.A.A. 1260* and, on the Cotentin, *H.K.A.R. 644* and *645* were redesignated *H.K.A.R. 1261* and *H.K.A.R. 1262*, respectively. Within *H.K.A.R. 1261*, the headquarters of the 1st Battalion had to be established, whereas the 2nd and 3rd Battalions were formed from the redesignated *H.K.A.A. 755* and *404*. The regiment was composed of existing batteries, with the exception of the 10th Battery, which was a new formation with 17 cm guns. In *H.K.A.R. 1262*, the 1st battalion was also built around a newly formed headquarters, while the 2nd Battalion was formed from *E.Art.Abt. 681*. The 4th and 5th Batteries were new units, with the former equipped with 17 cm guns and the latter issued Russian 12.2 cm guns.[392]

While activity in Normandy continued, critical decisions were made in Berlin about the *Atlantikwall*. Aware that time was running out, Hitler changed his focus to the provisional completion of the coastal defences, with tactically significant projects given precedence. Completed fortifications were to be properly finished and camouflaged, but new allocations of concrete were destined for the construction of artillery and anti-tank gun casemates.[393] The reason for this was the expectation that Allied forces would have air superiority. This meant all batteries without sufficient *Flak* had to be protected with concrete. Because adequate defences required large numbers of anti-aircraft guns — far more than were available — nearly every battery was affected by these orders. The construction of concrete positions was not ideal since armoured turrets were not available, which meant that guns would be installed in casemates that allowed for only limited traverse. Nonetheless, protection was prioritised over all-round fire.[394]

The *LXXXIV. A.K.* was informed of the general plans in late **December**, and *Ob.West* ordered the *Atlantikwall* to be ready by **1 March**. The construction of casemates was the priority. As a result, the construction capacity would be increased at the expense of those further to the rear and by limiting the use of concrete for other types of structures. Work on any construction that would not be completed before **1 March** was to be halted at once. The actual decisions on this were reserved for the corps commanding generals after consultation with armed forces representatives.[395]

The corps ordered a conference for **31 December**, including the chiefs-of-staff for operations of the *709.* and *716. I.D.*, as well as a representative from the headquarters of the *LXV. A.K. zbV*, which was responsible for operational use of the *V-weapons*.[396] Two topics were discussed: a) which constructions would continue and which would be stopped; and, b) the use of manpower and material given the interests of the *LXV. A.K. zbV*, the discontinuation of work on *Marine-Batterie Gréville*, and plans for new naval batteries.[397] The personnel working on the Gréville battery were redirected to the east coast of the Cotentin to build what would become *Marine-Batterie Marcouf*.[398]

The plans for the construction of casemates were developed and, in mid-**January**, the *OKW* ordered construction of 3,000 casemates, to be ready by **30 April**.[399] The *LXXXIV. A.K.* was to construct 300 fortified gun emplacements. Since time was of the essence, the corps and divisions would ensure that fortress engineer elements were informed of the exact positions of the pillboxes and their guns before **5 February**. While work continued to finish certain fortifications, this work was not to interfere with the casemate programme. Ammunition storage and command posts for the casemated guns would only be considered after the emplacements and the other fortifications were complete.[400]

1944: Setting the Stage

In early **January**, the corps made plans for deployment of its reserves, including formations that were expected that month. Among these were the *243. I.D.*, a reinforced regiment from Germany (*GR 1021*), and *schwere Stellungs-Werfer-Abteilung 103*.[401] While the planning did not go entirely as intended, the reinforcements did arrive.

The most significant reinforcement was the *243. I.D.* (*GR 920, 921* and *922* and *AR 243*), with its transfer to Normandy starting on **7 January**.[402] It was preceded by *Pi.Btl. 243*, while two other battalions, the *II./921* and the *I./922*, stayed in Bretagne for the time being.[403] On **10 January**, new locations for many of the division's headquarters were reported. The divisional headquarters and signals battalion were both in Périers. *GR 920* moved to Carentan and its two battalions to La Coquerie and St. Côme-du-Mont (2nd Battalion). *GR 921* went to Château Rupalet, with the 1st Battalion in Gorges and the 3rd Battalion in Montsurvent. The headquarters of *GR 922* was in Le Dézert, while the 2nd Battalion moved to St. Jean-de-Daye and the 3rd Battalion to Colombières. *AR 243* moved to Chau. Perron with its three battalions around Les Oubeaux, St. Sauveur-Lendelin and Sainteny.[404] Eight days later, *GR 921* moved north. Its headquarters moved into a château 4 km west of St. Sauveur-le-Vicomte; its 1st Battalion in a château 2 km north of the same town and the 3rd Battalion to La Haye-du-Puits. The *III./AR 243* followed the regiment and occupied positions around Pont-l'Abbé, where its headquarters was situated.[405] The *II./AR 243* moved to the Lessay area on the **22nd** with the command post in the town.[406] The next day, new positions for most of *GR 921* were reported. Its 3rd Battalion was in Château Les Désert (east of La Haye-du-Puits). The headquarters of the *I./921* did not move, with its companies in an arc north of St. Sauveur-le-Vicomte.[407] The final notable headquarters movement was *Feldersatz-Bataillon 243* (Field Replacement Battalion 243 / *Feld-Ers.Btl. 243*) to Château Rupalet, south of St. Sauveur-Lendelin, on the **24th**, with its four companies in the surrounding area.[408]

The corps received several battalion-sized formations, most of which were announced late in **1943**. Among these was *s.St.Wfr.Abt. 103*; although delayed (original intended arrival date was **15 December**), its transfer to the corps finally began on **3 January**. It arrived in Vindefontaine the following day.[409] On **11 January**, it was redesignated as the *III./s.St.Wfr.Rgt. 101*.[410] Another battalion to join the corps was *Panzer-Abt. 206*, arriving in Falaise on **17 January**.[411]

Several V1 launch sites were built on the northern part of the Cotentin Peninsula. Where possible they were incorporated in the Cerbourg Landfront. This one was positioned east of the N13 highway, near Château du Pannelier. The position was captured by the US 79th ID in June 1944. (NARA)

A significant number of new arrivals were (construction) engineer elements. On **6 January**, *Pi.Btl. 243* arrived in Le Molay, replacing *Pi.Btl. 346* and reinforced by the *1./Pi.Btl. 265 (265. I.D.)*.[412] Officially, the new battalion would be deployed in the "2nd Position" line, reporting to *Fest.Pi.Abschn.Gr. Beger*, but this appears to have been cover for work on the *V*-weapons sites.[413]

The construction troops and workers announced in **November** arrived in **January**.[414] *Bau-Pi.Btl. 803* arrived in Le Molay on the **19th** to replace *Ost-Btl. 630*, which left the *LXXXIV. A.K.* on **9 January**.[415] It was transferred to *AOK 15* to reinforce the *346. I.D.*, which had to leave an infantry battalion in Bretagne.[416] Until then, the eastern battalion had been supporting *Fest. Pi.Abschn.Gr. Beger* on *V*-weapons sites in the Calvados.[417] As its replacement, *Bau-Pi.Btl. 803* would also be under Beger's fortress construction formation and therefore unavailable to improve the corps' defences. A similar formation, *Bau-Btl. 802*, arrived on **19 January**, with its headquarters in St. Pierre-Église.[418] It was intended for large-scale mine-laying on the Cotentin.[419]

Further support for work on the "2nd Position" was to be from 2,850 men of the former French labour service; also promised in **November**, it is not clear whether they ever arrived. Plans to relieve workers on the *V*-weapons sites with 1,000 German military convicts[420] so the former could be used on the coast did not materialise.[421] In view of the increasing threat of invasion, it is clear that *AOK 7* had priorities that competed with the *V*-weapons sites, which relied on engineers and construction troops already in short supply. Indeed, in **March**, the army voiced its concerns to *H.Gr. B*, questioning the use of limited Army resources on these *Luftwaffe* projects.[422]

Development of *V*-weapons plans may also explain why new positions were reported for the II./*Sich.Rgt. 195* on **13 January**. The battalion headquarters was in Thury-Harcourt and some of the companies near the Caen - Falaise highway, with others around the Forêt de Cerisy.[423] Both areas were associated with the *V*-weapons programme.[424]

Most of the other movements concerned the *709. I.D.* This was largely due to *GR 919* taking over the area south of *GR 729*, which essentially led to dividing the east coast into a sector held by *GR 729* (*KVU St. Vaast*) and another by *GR 919*. (*KVU Marcouf*). On **6 January**, elements of the *I./919* started to relieve the *I./729*. The next day, the *GR 729* headquarters was in Beuzeville-au-Plain and *GR 919* in Le Ham.[425] As a result, the *I./919* became responsible for what would soon become Utah Beach. More moves followed and, on **19 January**, the headquarters of *GR 919* moved to Montebourg, its 2nd Battalion to Octeville-l'Avenel and its 3rd Battalion to Le Ham. At the same time, the headquarters of *GR 729* moved to Le Vast, closer to the centre of its reduced sector. The *I./729*'s return to its regimental sector was not reported, but on **15 February** it was in Quettehou. It may have arrived in January.[426]

Little changed regarding the *352. I.D.*, except the *I.* and the *IV./AR 352* moving on **8 January**. The headquarters of the 1st Battalion moved to Tessy-sur-Vire and St. Martin-des-Besaces.[427] Near the end of the month, *AOK 7* announced new plans. At least two battalions from the artillery regiment were to be used in *KVU Bessin* starting on **1 February**. The artillery in this sector was considered weak and these two battalions were intended to strengthen it.[428]

On **8 January**, several artillery formations moved: *Arko 118* to Valognes and the headquarters of *AR 621* to La Haye-du-Puits. The entire *le.Beob.Abt. 33* took up new positions and moved its headquarters to Percy.[429] Another battalion that moved in its entirety was *Schn.Abt. 517*, its headquarters moving to Bréhal on **9 January**.[430]

January marked the beginning of a new division: the *77. I.D.*, which was to be established in the *LXXXIV. A.K.* sector. The division was formed around the reinforced *GR 1021* and transferred to Caen between **17-19 January**. Its 1st Battalion moved to Lantheuil, the 2nd Battalion to Martragny and the 3rd to Mouen, while *Art.Abt. 1021* took up positions in Bretteville.[431] On **21 January**, the regimental headquarters was reported in Fontenay-le-Pesnel and *Art.Abt. 1021* in Putot-en-Bessin.[432]

There was another development that would affect the *352. I.D.* (and the *243. I.D.*) over the coming months. On **13 January**, *Ob.West* ordered the creation of anti-tank battalions for the two divisions, in addition to the *353. I.D.* in Bretagne. The corps were informed two days later. The battalions would consist of a headquarters, a self-propelled company, an assault-gun company and a *Flak* company.[433]

On **4 February**, the three corps of *AOK 7* were instructed that Hitler had declared a number of defensive sectors (*Verteidigunsbereiche*) to be fortresses (*Festungen*),[434] effective immediately. For the *LXXXIV. A.K.*, this meant the port of Cherbourg.[435] Although Hitler's decision was made on **19 January**, with *AOK 7* receiving the news two days later, the information was apparently not passed on to the corps for quite some time.[436] The delay may have been caused by *Ob.West* needing to prepare new orders. Rules and regulations had to be provided for the fortresses, including orders regarding the role of the fortress commanders.[437] The change in designation from Cherbourg being a defensive sector to being a fortress did little to improve the port's defensive capabilities. Indeed, this was illustrated by the words of *Gen.Maj.* Sattler, the fortress commander, who arrived in **April**:[438]

As little as a three year old boy will grow a beard when he is declared to be a man, just as little will a town become a fortress by being declared a fortress.

Other orders had a more direct effect. Having visited on **29 January**, *Feldm.* Rommel concluded that there was an imbalance between reserves and frontline troops in the *716. I.D.* sector and the right flank of the *709. I.D.* In his opinion, the front needed more troops and the *243. I.D.* moved further north.[439] *AOK 7* responded with new orders on **6 February**, deploying *Ost-Btl. 439* and *642*, as well as *Georg.Inf.Btl. 795* and the *III./739*, on the coast. The *77., 243.*, and *352. I.D.* would prepare to attack towards the coast within hours of an enemy landing. To accomplish this, movement of the divisions closer to the coastline (with the exception of the *77. I.D.*) was necessary.[440] The *243. I.D.* was positioned in the area of Carentan - Montebourg - Bricquebec – Lessay. The sector selected for the *352. I.D.* covered Bayeux - Trévières - Isigny - St. Lô. The corps had already suggested moving two of the division's artillery battalions towards the coast and *General* Dollmann, *7. Armee* commander-in-chief, agreed.

The formation of the *77. I.D.* continued unabated, with most of its headquarters elements and subordinate formations arriving between **5** and **12 February** (most of them drawn from the 355. I.D.). The divisional headquarters arrived on the **8th**, as did *Nachr.Abt. 223*; *Gen.Lt..* Poppe took command of the division on the **11th**.[441] The division established its headquarters in the area of St. Martin-de-Fontenay, south of Caen.[442] On the **10th**, the headquarters and the 2nd Battalion of *AR 355* arrived, as did the headquarters of *Pz.Jg.Abt. 355*, and *Pi.Btl. 355*. The four headquarters elements were located in Bretteville-l'Orgueilleuse, Rots, St. Sylvain and Cormelles-le-Royal, while the signals battalion was in May-sur-Orne.[443] Over the next few days, a number of supply elements and medical services arrived. The headquarters of *GR 336*, for the division's second infantry regiment, arrived on the **12th** and moved to Troarn.[444]

To the west of the *77. I.D.*, the entire *352. I.D.* relocated to an area that stretched from Airel in the west to east of Bayeux. The divisional headquarters was established in Littry.[445] On **15 February**, the new locations were reported. *GR 914* moved to l'Epinay-Tesson, with its 1st Battalion in Mestry and its 2nd Battalion in Le Mesnil-Véneron; *GR 915* moved to Trévières, its 1st Battalion to Cussy and its 2nd Battalion to Bernesq. The new headquarters of *GR 916* was St. Paul-du-Vernay with the 1st Battalion headquarters in Château de Juaye, south of Bayeux, and the 2nd Battalion in Parfouru. The artillery moved nearer the coast. *AR 352*'s headquarters was further inland at Tournières, as was the 4th Battalion at Montfiquet. Its remaining three battalions were in Étréham (1st), Neuilly-la-Forêt (2nd) and La Noé (3rd). *Feld-Ers-Btl. 352* moved to Caumont and *Div.Füs.Btl. (A.A.) 352* to Tilly-sur-Seulles. The remaining two battalions, *Pz.Jg.Abt. 352* and *Nachr.Abt. 352*, took up positions in Airel and Château Castillon, respectively.

On the **3rd**, the *I./736* relieved the *III./736* on the coast and moved its headquarters to Colleville-sur-Mer. The *III./736* became a divisional reserve, with its headquarters in Le Mesnil.[446] A number of eastern battalions were now transferred to the coast as well. On **8 February**, *Ost-Btl. 642* took command of *KVU Meuvaines* and was followed by *Ost-Btl. 439* on **11 February**. The latter took over the Vire Estuary, with its headquarters at Resistance Nest 94 (*Widerstandsnest 94 / Wn. 94*).[447] On the **13th**, the *II./726* moved to Ryes as divisional reserve.[448] *KVG Bayeux* was then formally reorganised on **17 February**. The *I./726* became responsible for *KVU Bessin*. To its west was *KVU Percée*, held by the *III./726*. The final sector, *KVU Vire*, was the responsibility of *Ost-Btl. 439*. Alongside these developments, the Calvados was reinforced by *s.Art.Abt. 989* on **6 February**. The headquarters moved to Amblie and its three batteries were nearby in Reviers and Colombiers-sur-Seulles.[449]

On the Cotentin, *MG-Btl. 17* moved from the Jobourg Peninsula to the area around Le Bigard on **7 February**.[450] Its place on the peninsula was taken by *Georg.Inf.Btl. 795*, which had been held in reserve. Another reserve battalion, the *III./739*, was moved to *KVU Vauville*, south of the peninsula.[451] The headquarters of the *II./729* moved to Tocqueville on **9 February**, with its companies positioned around the village.[452] On **27 February**, the *III./AR 1709* was transferred from the west coast to the St. Pierre-Église area.[453] Individual companies also were transferred, among them both the 1. and 2. *Pz.Jg.Kp. 709*. The first moved to Teurthéville-Bocage on **1 February**; the second to Bricquebec on the **18th**.[454]

At the base of the Cotentin, there were changes for the *243. I.D.* Two companies of the newly arrived *Pz.Jg.Abt. 243* moved to the Sainteny area on **2 February**[455] and were joined by the battalion's 3rd Company on the **27th**.[456] On **15 February**, the headquarters of *GR 922* moved to St. Sauveur-le-Vicomte and its 2nd Battalion to La Haye-du-Puits. The *I.* and *II./AR 243* also took up new positions: The *I./AR 243* at Ste. Marie-du-Mont and the *II./AR 243* at Hatainville (northwest of Barfleur).[457]

There were two noteworthy departures from the corps. On the **12th**, *le. Beob.Abt. 33* left, followed by the *III./s.St.Wfr.Rgt. 101* the following day.[458] Meanwhile, the *2./Nachr.Abt. 460* moved to Le Dézert on **24 February**.[459]

Work to improve the defences was still a high priority, and plans were made for large-scale mine laying. On **3 February**, the corps intended to use *Pi.Btl. 243* for this, along with *Bau-Pi.Btl. 802* and two eastern battalions. If *Fest.Pi.Gr. 107 (Beger)* needed a replacement for *Pi.Btl. 243*, the corps would allocate one of the eastern battalions.[460] Three days later, *AOK 7* ordered the reinforced *Pi.Btl. 243*, *Pi.Btl. 352* and the engineer company of *GR 1021* to be used for laying minefields.[461] *Pi.Btl. 243* appears to have continued to support *Fest.Pi.Gr. 107*, although for two days a week it would work on minefields. It planned to return to its division for mine laying when *Bau-Pi.Btl. 94* joined *Fest.Pi.Gr. 107* after **15 March**.[462] *Bau-Pi.Btl. 803* stayed with *Gruppe Beger* throughout this time. The battalion headquarters moved to Haut Mesnil, near one of the *V*-weapons sites, on **2 February**. Some of its companies were already in the area, and the remaining companies joined the battalion there as well.[463]

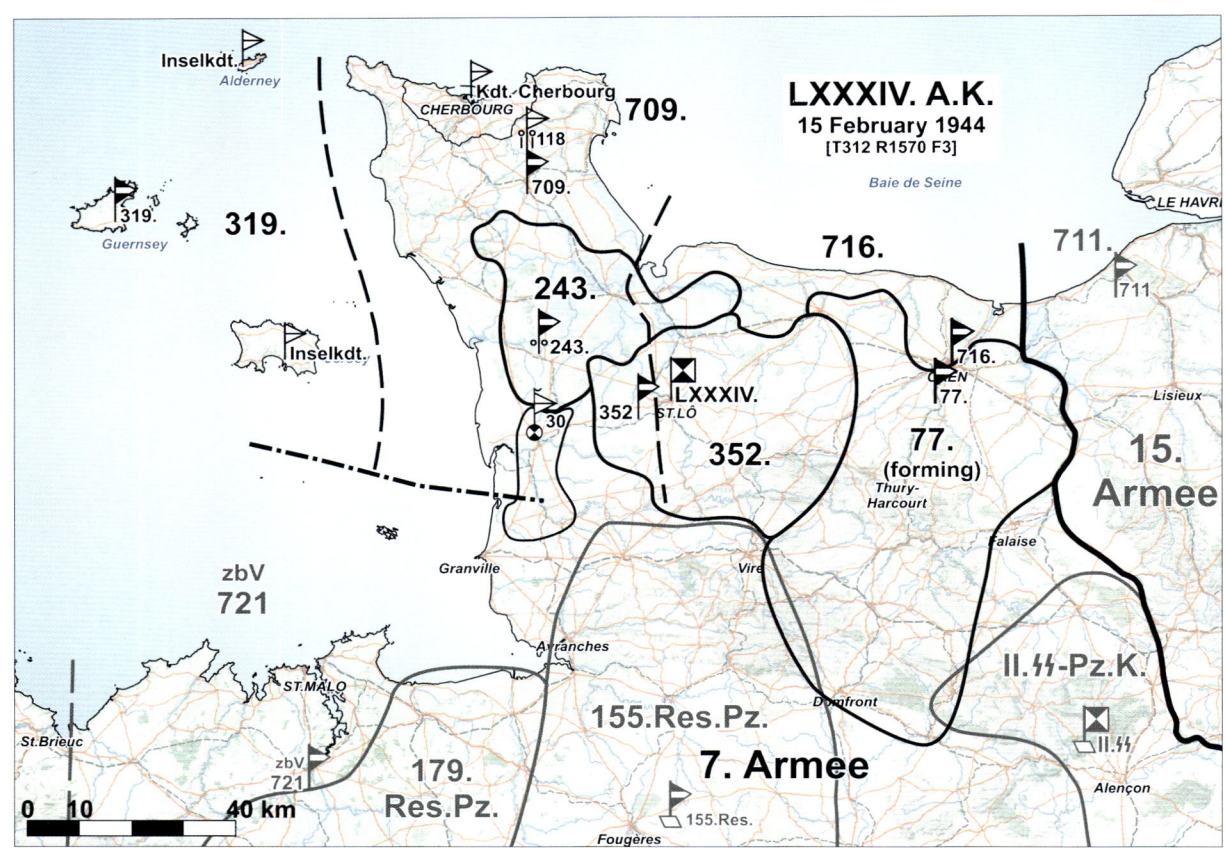

In January 1944 the LXXXIV. A.K. was reinforced by the arrival of the 243. I.D. which went into position along the base of the Cotentin. Further north the 709. I.D. was joined by Arko 118 to coordinate the artillery on the peninsula. Around and south of Caen the formation of 77. I.D. began.

During this period a number of formations were stationed just south of the corps' own elements. To the southeast were elements of the 2nd SS Panzer-Korps, while further west were parts of the 155. and 179. Res. Pz.Div. These divisions would soon leave the area to be used to (re)build the 9th and 116th Panzer-Division.

February was relatively quiet for the corps. There were no significant arrivals for the *77. I.D*, which continued its establishment. The main changes in the division involved the anti-tank elements. The headquarters of *Pz.Jg.Abt. 177* (*Pz.Jäg.Abt. 355*) was transferred, with the division receiving an anti-tank company from the *352. I.D.* instead.[464] Another change involved *Pi.Btl. 177*, which was sent to Angers for training on **2 March**.[465]

A major change to the corps' organisation occurred on **19 March**, when the *352. I.D.* took command of *KVG Bayeux*, relieving the *716. I.D.*, although some of the latter's forces remained.[466] The associated movements of the division towards the coast are poorly recorded, but *GR 914* and *915*, respectively, became responsible for the Vire Estuary and the coast up to the *716. I.D*. On **8 April** the headquarters of *GR 914* were at Neuilly-la-Forêt and its two battalions at St. Germain-du-Pert (1st) and Catz (2nd). Of *GR 915*, 1st battalion had moved to Ryes and 2nd battalion to Formigny. *Pz.Jg.Abt. 352* had taken over Mestry from *I./914*, while *II.* and *IV./352* had established themselves at Isigny-sur-Mer and Asnelles, respectively.[467] During March, the *352. I.D.* was strengthened by the arrival of the *3./Pz.Jg.Abt. 352* on the **2nd** and the return of *Pi.Btl. 352*. The battalion arrived from Angers on **5 March** and moved to Isigny.[468]

On **24 March**, the Cotentin was reinforced with the two battalions from the *243. I.D.* that had previously been in Bretagne. The battalions were sent to *Festung Cherbourg* and reported to the *709. I.D. The II./921* moved to Hainneville and the *I./922* to Tourlaville.⁴⁶⁹ Due to their deployment in the interior defences, they became known as the *Landfront* battalions.⁴⁷⁰ Little changed for the rest of the *243. I.D.*, except for some company and supply troop moves.⁴⁷¹

The corps received three separate battalions to improve defensive positions. *Ost-Btl. 441* and *Ost-Btl. 561* arrived on **8 March**, with *Landes-Bau-Pionier-Btl. 17* following on the **16ᵗʰ**.⁴⁷² *Ost-Btl. 561* moved to the Cotentin and was located in the area of Nacqueville - Querqueville on **9 March**.⁴⁷³ On the **22ⁿᵈ**, its headquarters moved to Flamanville, and the companies deployed along the west coast of the Cotentin.⁴⁷⁴ *Ost-Btl. 441* went to the Calvados coast and, on **9 March,** the headquarters was in Bayeux.⁴⁷⁵ On the **18ᵗʰ**, *Landes-Bau-Pionier-Btl. 17* headquarters was in St. Laurent-sur-Mer and its companies on the coast.

One of the most significant developments for the *LXXXIV. A.K.* in **April** was a sector change. Its left border with the *LXXIV. A.K.* was moved south to a line running from Pontorson to the bight 3 km west of the Canal du Couesnon. The area north of this line left *KVA "A1"* and became part of the new *KVA "J2"*, which stretched north to the line St. Sauveur-le-Vicomte - Barneville - Cap de Carteret. The rest of the Cotentin (*709. I.D.*) became *KVA "J1"*. In command of "J2" was *Gren.Rgts.Stab zbV 752*, an ad hoc regimental headquarters with no organic battalions. The transfer had been ordered for **1 April**, but it did not go into effect until 18:00 on **2 April**.⁴⁷⁶ The headquarters was reported in Cérences on **16 April,** and it was reported in Gavray the next day.⁴⁷⁷

The new boundaries put much of *Georg.Inf.Btl. 797* in *KVA "J2"* under *Gren.Rgts.Stab zbV 752*. The new southern boundary also meant that the corps took over a number of formations already in the area. This included *Ost-Reiter-Abt. 281* (Eastern Mounted Battalion 281 / *Ost-Rtr.Abt. 281*), which arrived in Granville on **17 February**, and *Sicherungs-Bataillon 521* (Security Battalion 521 / *Sich.Btl. 521*), which arrived on **22 March**.⁴⁷⁸ Bretagne was experiencing an increase in *Résistance* activity, and *Ost-Rtr.Abt. 281* was considered essential for anti-*Résistance* operations, so its return to Bretagne was requested.⁴⁷⁹ Corresponding orders were issued on **25 April**, stating that the battalion would be relieved in Normandy by another eastern battalion.⁴⁸⁰ On the **28ᵗʰ**, the headquarters of *Ost-Rtr.Abt. 281* moved to Queron, south of Granville, possibly in preparation for its transfer, which would take place in **May**.⁴⁸¹

On the Cotentin, the *709. I.D.* was joined by *Fla-Kp. 709* on the **4ᵗʰ**. It was initially located in Pépinvast and then on the La Pernelle heights a week later.⁴⁸² On **11 April**, the entire *Art.Rgt. zbV 621* was moved: The headquarters to Bricquebec and the battalions nearby. *S.Art.Abt. 456* took up positions around Négreville. The headquarters of *Art.Abt. 457* moved to Quettetot, and its batteries further north.⁴⁸³ *Art.Rgt. zbV 621* was joined by *le.Beob.Abt. 33*, which returned to the corps on **22 April**. The headquarters and two batteries moved to Bricquebec and a third to Sortosville.⁴⁸⁴ Other changes affected the *243. I.D.* The *GR 920* headquarters moved to Franquetot (Château Franquetot, northwest of Blosville) on **5 April**,.⁴⁸⁵ In *Festung Cherbourg*, the *II./921* moved to Les Courts on the **8ᵗʰ** and most of its companies to resistance nests established in the Cherbourg defences.⁴⁸⁶ Further south, *Pi.Btl. 243* relocated to Montmartin-sur-Mer on **20 April**.⁴⁸⁷ It stayed there briefly, then moved to Blainville-sur-Mer on the **25ᵗʰ**.⁴⁸⁸

In the Calvados, *Fla-Kp. 716* also joined its division on the **4ᵗʰ**, when it arrived at Anisy. Other changes in the Calvados included arrival of *Bau-Pi.Btl. 94*. On **11 April**, the battalion joined *Fest.Pi.Gr. 107*, with its headquarters in Balleroy before moving two days later to Littry.⁴⁸⁹ On **16 April**, *Pz.Abt. 206* moved southeast of Bayeux, with the headquarters in Carcagny. Three more battalions were moved on the **20ᵗʰ**: The *II./726* moved to Colombières as a divisional reserve, the *III./736* to Cresserons and *Ost-Btl. 441* to Le Mesnil.⁴⁹⁰ On **21 April**, *KVG Caen* was redesignated as *KVA "H1"* while *KVG Bayeux* became *KVA "H2"*.⁴⁹¹

In the Caen area, the *III./AR 177* joined the *77. I.D.* on **10 April**, and it was located in Vieux, with the *II./AR 177* reported in Bellengreville, a few kilometres to the east. This situation changed later in the month, when the entire division was transferred to the *LXXIV. A.K.* in Bretagne, taking over the St. Malo sector (*KVA "A1"*) on **6 May**. This altered the corps' left boundary, which now ran along the Douer and Sélune Rivers to Pontaubault (*LXXIV. A.K.*) and Tombelaine Island (*LXXXIV. A.K.*).⁴⁹² To replace the *77. I.D.*, the *21. Pz.Div.* was transferred from Bretagne and the south of Manche to south of Caen.⁴⁹³ This began on **26 April** and was completed on the **30ᵗʰ**.⁴⁹⁴ Since its positions at this time are poorly documented, the locations of this division will only be provided around D-Day.

Although the corps had steadily received eastern battalions, and several had been deployed on the coast in accordance with Rommel's orders, concerns grew about their usefulness and reliability. In late **April**, AOK 7 informed its three corps of the issue. The *Osttruppen* were deemed unsuitable for important coastal sectors and could only be used in the rear or to build

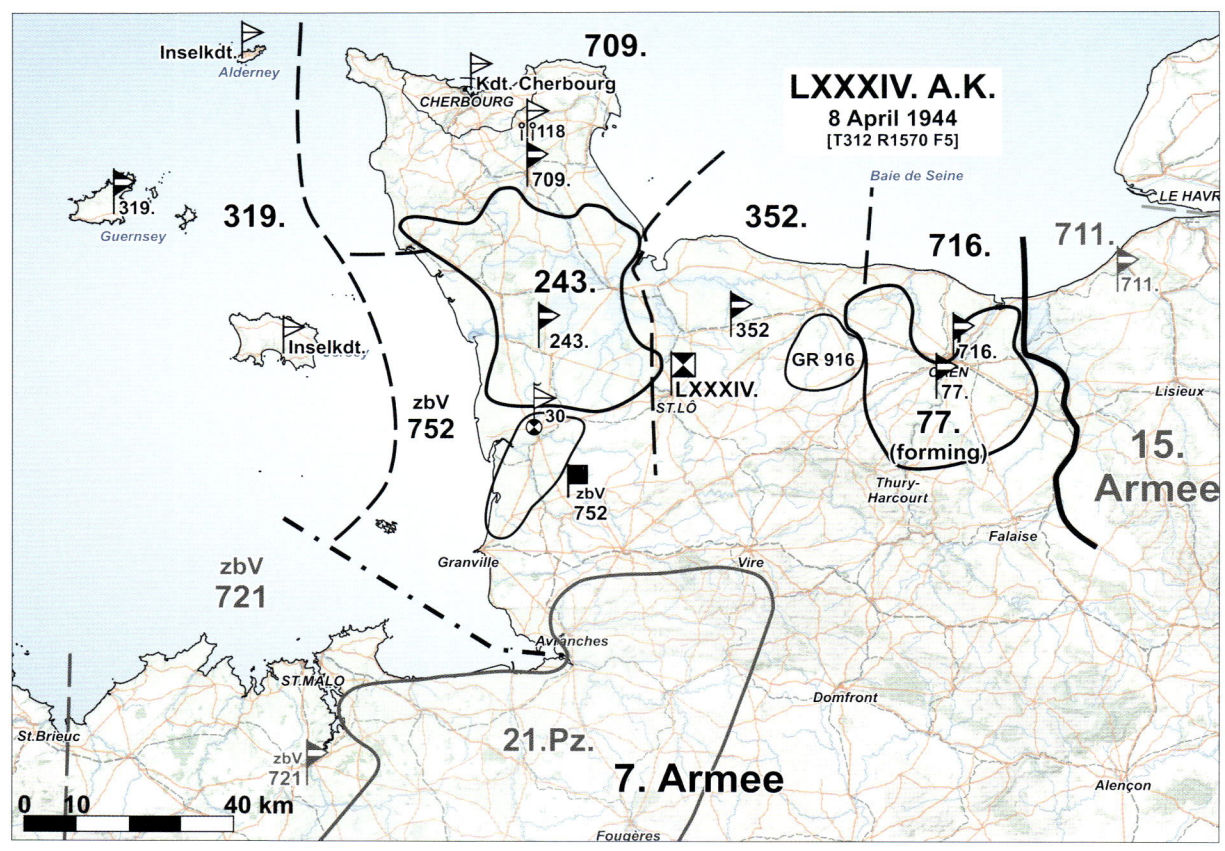

In March the 352 .I.D. took over part of the Calvados coast from the 716 .I.D. It kept GR 916 inland as a reserve force. In April GR zbV 752 assumed command over the southern coast of Manche and the Avranches - Granville sector fully returned to LXXXIV. A.K. control.

fortifications. Therefore, a number of battalions had to be relieved as soon as possible. In Normandy, this applied to *Georg.Inf.Btl. 795* on the Jobourg Peninsula. The corps was also ordered to determine if other battalions might need to be relieved, specifically *Ost-Btl. 439* and *Georg.Inf.Btl. 797*.[495]

On **1 May**, *AOK 7* sent its latest report to Rommel's *H.Gr. B*. The coast between the army's eastern boundary and Cap de Carteret was deemed sufficiently secure. Especially so if the time until early **June** was used to complete defensive works northwest and northeast of Bayeux and to install additional beach obstacles and minefields. As part of the invasion preparations, flooding around the Dives, either side of the Vire and along the east coast of the Cotentin, was in full effect. The arrival of the *21. Pz.Div.* in the east of the corps sector meant there was now a substantial reserve for areas under threat of airborne landings around Caen.[496]

Yet, serious problems remained. The area between Cap de Carteret and Mont-St. Michel was only lightly occupied — even if the threat of sea landings in this region was considered limited — while troops to oppose airborne forces to the rear were hardly available. *AOK 7* suggested that both weaknesses could be remedied by transferring a combat-ready, division-sized formation[497] to the St. Lô - Coutances - Avranches – Vire area.[498]

AOK 7 also assessed the problem faced by the *LXXXIV. A.K.* in case of a simultaneous attack against the coastal sectors of Caen and Bayeux in the Calvados and against the Cotentin. In this scenario, the corps headquarters would struggle to coordinate the fighting. In that eventuality, the field army proposed to transfer another corps headquarters and corps artillery command to the Calvados to command the *716. I.D., 352. I.D., 21. Pz.Div.*, and possibly the *711. I.D.* (*AOK 15*). The field army intended to use the nearby headquarters of the *LXXIV. A.K.* for this, provided that Bretagne was not under attack. In fact, *AOK 7* had already requested the immediate transfer of *Arko 474* to coordinate artillery in the Calvados.[499]

On **3 May**, the staff of *GR 922* moved to Pierreville. The next day, in accordance with plans to strengthen the beach obstacles, much of the *243. I.D.*'s infantry was sent to the coast. Infantry companies from *GR 920* were put to work on the east coast of the Cotentin, while three companies from *GR 921* and eight from *GR 922* were deployed on the west coast between Flamanville and Portbail; the two *Landfront* battalions remained with the *709. I.D.*[500] Further south, *Ost-Btl. 635* arrived in the Granville area on **5 May**, replacing *Ost-Reiter-Abt. 281*, which left the corps on **6 May**.[501] The headquarters of *Ost-Btl. 635* moved east of St. Nicolas. On the Cotentin, the headquarters of the *II./H.K.A.R. 1262* moved to La Roche à Coucou (southwest of Les Pieux).[502] *Pi.Btl. 243*, which had arrived on the west coast of Manche in **April**, continued its activities in the area; on **8 May**, it moved from Coutances to Granville.[503] Later in the month, it returned to its division, and its place in *KVA "J2"* taken by the *1./Pi.Btl. 319*.[504]

Plans for new arrivals were reexamined in the first week of **May**. *AOK 7* and the *LXXXIV. A.K.* had apparently been notified of the imminent arrival of *s.St.Wfr.Rgt. 101*, and both commands prepared for its deployment.[505] On **6 May**, *H.Gr. B* confirmed that the regiment would join the corps soon. It was decided, presumably in line with existing plans, that the regiment's headquarters and two of its battalions would be deployed within the right-hand sector of the *709. I.D.* and another battalion in the Vauville Bight.[506] *AOK 7* was also notified that its request to transfer *Arko 474* to the Calvados had been approved.[507] It would be used to coordinate the artillery in *KVA "H1"* and *"H2"* and prepare for a possible future arrival of another corps headquarters (*LXXIV. A.K.*)[508]

On **6 May**, the corps was informed that Hitler was still worried about the defences on the Cotentin and had ordered its immediate reinforcement with an airborne regiment, *Pz.Abt. 206* and *Sturmbataillon AOK 7* (*St.Btl. AOK 7*).[509]

On **7 May**, the corps received further information and orders. Major changes were planned for the *243. I.D. GR 920* was to deploy in the right-hand sector of *KVG Bricquebec*, along with parts of the *709. I.D.* already in the area. The regiment was attached to the *709. I.D.* for the duration of this mission.[510] While the rest of the *243. I.D.* was under divisional control, orders were issued to move the bulk of the division north, through the Prairies Marécageuses. There, it would defend its new sector against possible airborne landings. The assembly area would be regarded as a combat sector, meaning the personnel would dig in with their weapons at the ready day and night. The high ground was to be occupied and villages avoided. An additional task concerned preparations for a counterattack against enemy landings on the coast. In its new mission, the division would lose its previous role as field army reserve and report directly to the corps.[511]

Orders for *Pz.Abt. 206* called for its deployment between Cap de la Hague and Cap de Carteret, where it would dig in to reinforce the coast. Further south, *St.Btl. AOK 7* would move south of La Haye-du-Puits, an area also at risk of airborne landings. Its mission and manner of deployment were identical to the *243. I.D.*[512]

The orders concerning the airborne regiment were expanded to include the entire *2. Fj.Div.* Upon arrival, it would immediately deploy south of the *243. I.D.*, establishing contact with the assault battalion and receiving the same mission. Until the arrival of sufficient airborne elements, the measures already taken in its sector by the *243. I.D.* remained in place. Although *FJR 6* was immediately transferred from Germany, the rest of the division would not follow until after a short reorganisation.[513]

The new orders revealed another reinforcement for the Cotentin: *Panzer-Ersatz-und-Ausbildungs-Abteilung 100* (Tank Replacement and Training Battalion 100 / *Pz.E.u.A.Abt. 100*). This battalion was to be prepared to quickly intervene in the event of an airborne landing.[514]

On the **8th**, the corps headquarters was informed that it would not receive the *2. Fj.Div.* after all. Instead, it had been assigned the *91. Luftlande-Infanterie-Division* (91st Airlanding Infantry Division / *91. LL.Div.*) (*GR 1057* and *1058* and *AR 191*), which would become a field-army reserve.[515] This division had been earmarked for Bretagne, and its first elements had arrived on **5 May**, before being redirected to Normandy.[516] Instead, the *XXV. A.K.* would receive the *2. Fj.Div.*, which was not yet available. In fact, it still had to be relieved on other fronts before it could begin to reorganise its forces.[517]

The field army offered more details on how to reinforce the Cotentin. As planned, *GR 920* would be in the Vauville Bight, deployed to enable its heavy infantry weapons to cover the beach. *Pz.Abt. 206* would dig in behind the Surtainville Bight under the *709. I.D.*[518]

The *243. I.D.* (minus *GR 920*, the *II./921*, the *I./922* and the *I./AR 243*) would be sent to the area of Colomby - Les Pieux - Barneville - Pont-l'Abbé. One regiment each would be positioned behind the Sciotot Bight and the Surtainville Bight, both located between Flamanville and Barneville. Again, their heavy infantry weapons were to be positioned so that they could cover the beach. The divisional artillery stayed in its positions on the east (*I./AR 243*) and west coast (*II./AR 243*) of the Cotentin; the 3rd Battalion was to be used against airborne landings and be prepared for mobile employment in the divisional sector. The division's move was to begin immediately.[519]

The *91. LL.Div.* was to be positioned south of the *243. I.D.*, in the area of Carentan - Ste. Mère-Église - Barneville - St. Sauveur-Lendelin. One regiment would be deployed near the coast on either side of Portbail and another in the area then held by *GR 920* and south of Ste. Mère-Église. According to the new plans, *St.Btl. AOK 7* was to deploy on the hills north of La Haye-du-Puits and report directly to the *91. LL.D. Pz.Ers.u.Ausb.Abt. 100* would move to the area around Baupte, attached directly to the *LXXXIV. A.K.*[520]

By **9 May**, the plans had been refined. On Rommel's orders, the *243. I.D.* was to take command of *KVG Bricquebec* — the area of *KVA "J1"* west of *Festung Cherbourg* — which put *GR 920* back under its control. Despite its new mission, the division was still the corps reserve. Further south, the *91. LL.D.* would take over the area previously held by the *243. I.D.* There, two regiments would be deployed: One on either side of Portbail and one on the east of the Cotentin. The *243. I.D.* artillery was to be relieved by the *91. LL.D.* The orders for *schweres Stellungs-Werfer-Regiment 101* were also revised: Two battalions (instead of one) were to be sent to the west coast and just one to the east coast. Finally, it was announced that the corps would still receive *FJR 6*, even though the rest of the *2. Fj.Div.* was to be transferred to Bretagne.[521] The next day, the regimental sector was announced: Lessay - Périers – Gorges.[522]

Between **9-11 May**, Rommel paid another visit to the *LXXXIV. A.K.* Dollmann, the commander-in-chief of the *7. Armee*, used the occasion for a three-day tour of Normandy of his own to inspect the defences and confer with Rommel and the *LXXXIV. A.K.*[523] In case of an attack on the Cotentin, *H.Gr. B* intended to use the *12. SS-Pz.Div.* and a rocket-launcher brigade. Rommel also stated that *Art.Rgt. 621* would remain on the Cotentin and move to the east coast within several days. Moreover, the *243. I.D.* would remain on the coast, even in the event of an attack — a decision that effectively ended its role as a reserve. Instead of digging in behind the coast, *Pz.Abt. 206* was to move onto the Jobourg Peninsula for mobile deployment against airborne landings. Further south, *FJR 6* and *Pz.E.u.A.Abt. 100* were attached to the *91. LL.D.*[524]

Feldm. Rommel's plans to reinforce Normandy went further than simply fulfilling Berlin's orders to strengthen the Cotentin. The forces south of the peninsula were weak and armour would have difficulty arriving in time. To rectify this, he intended to position the *12. SS-Pz.Div.* around St. Lô. At the same time, Rommel also reconsidered his plan to deploy the *21. Pz.Div.* on the coast. To be able to intervene on the Cotentin, he considered moving an advance guard from the division to the area south of Montebourg.[525] His plans for the two divisions failed to materialise, and it left much of Normandy without armoured support.

Following the new orders, the headquarters of the *243. I.D.* moved to Château Malassis on **13 May** and took command of *KVG Bricquebec*.[526] The same day, new locations were reported for nearly every headquarters within the division. *GR 920* was moved to the Vauville Bight; its headquarters was located in Étoupeville, with the regiment's two battalions southeast of Vauville (1st) and Hau. Couvert (2nd). *GR 921* took over the coast around Barneville; its headquarters moving to (Hôtel) Mauger, 3 km east of Barneville, and its two available battalions to Cosniam (1st, today La Maison Quoniam) and Champ Moqtet (3rd, today La Chalerie). For *GR 922*, the regimental headquarters was in Hau. le Haquais, with its two battalions 1 km southeast of Le Rozel (2nd) and 3 km southeast of Surtainville (3rd). The headquarters of *Feld-Ers. Btl. 243* moved to Tréauville.[527] The *AR 243* headquarters was in Chambert, with battalions in Hatainville (2nd) and Caudard (3rd).[528] Two days later, the regimental headquarters moved again, this time to an area southwest of Le Vrétot.[529] The 1st Battalion remained in Ste. Marie-du-Mont until it moved to Frimot on the **19th**.[530] The majority of *Pz.Jg.Abt. 243* left the area southwest of Carentan on **11 May** and moved between Barneville and St. Sauveur. The battalion headquarters was 2 km north of Barneville, with the 1st Company near Hameau aux Petits (north of Besneville) and the 2nd Company nearby in Le Pont aux Moines.[531] On the **13th**, the headquarters moved north to

La Commanderie, east of Grosville.[532] The last battalion to move onto the Cotentin was *Pi.Btl. 243*, arriving in Les Pieux on the **22nd**.[533]

The constant changes for the employment of *Pz.Abt. 206* are reflected in its movements on the Cotentin. On **10 May**, it arrived east of Bricquebec, near the Surtainville Bight.[534] Three days later, following the decision to use the battalion on the Jobourg Peninsula, the headquarters was reported in "Galle" (presumably Hameau ès Galle), north of Beaumont-Hague.[535] As the *243. I.D.* took command of its new sector, a number of elements in the area were attached, among them *Ost-Btl. 561* and *MG-Btl. 17*. Since **February**, *MG-Btl. 17* had been stationed around St. Croix-Hague, within the in-land defences.[536] On **2 May**, its machine-gun companies were distributed throughout the wider Cherbourg area, but still within the "fortress" perimeter.[537] Later that month, the machine-gun battalion moved to the Jobourg Peninsula to relieve *Georg. Inf.Btl. 795*, and its headquarters was in Beaumont-Hague on **13 May**.[538] The transfer of *s.St.Wfr.Rgt. 101* began on **10 May**[539] and was completed by the **12th**. It headquarters was in Helleville the next day. It was joined by its 2nd and 3rd Battalions, which moved to Quetteville and Le Gardin, respectively, located on the southern and northern end of the Vauville Bight.[540] On the east coast of the Cotentin, the 1st Battalion moved to Aumeville-Lestre and then to the Tilly area on the **20th**.[541]

The first trains carrying the *91. LL.D.*'s troops, vehicles and equipment arrived on **10 May** and the division's transfer to Normandy was completed on the **15th**.[542] The positions of most of its headquarters elements were reported between **14-16 May**. The divisional headquarters was established in Château de Bernaville, southwest of Ste. Mère-Église. The positions of *GR 1058* and most of *AR 191* were reported on the **14th**. The headquarters of *GR 1058* was at St. Cyr, southeast of Valognes; its 1st Battalion was nearby in Le Haut Gaillon. The other battalions were some distance away. The 2nd Battalion was in La Jardinerie on the Cherbourg - Bricquebec road, while the 3rd Battalion was at the base of the Cotentin on St.Côme-du-Mont. *AR 191* was also dispersed: The headquarters in La Ligue, northeast of St. Sauveur-le-Vicomte; The 1st Battalion in Blandamour; the 2nd Battalion in L'Ossière, west of Montebourg. Finally, the 3rd Battalion. was in the Bois d'Étenclin, north of La Haye-du-Puits.[543] *GR 1057*'s headquarters first moved to La Barrière-du-Lude, and it continued to a position 2 km west of St. Sauveur-le-Vicomte on the **16th**. The same day, the headquarters of the *I./1057* and the *III./AR 191* moved to a Château 2.5 km northeast of La Haye-du-Puits (presumably Château Brocboeufs). The *II./1057* moved to Ste. Anne, southeast of Bricquebec, and the headquarters of the *III./1057* was reported to be at a crossroads between St. Sauveur and Portbail.[544]

Other attached units arrived around the same time. On the **14th**, the headquarters of *FJR 6* was north of Gerville-la-Forêt.[545] Two days later, it was in the woods west of the Périers - St. Jores road, around l'Hôtellerie.[546] Its three battalions formed a triangle between Carentan, La Haye-du-Puits, and Lessay. The 1st Battalion was at the northern edge of the Forêt de Mont-Castre; the 2nd Battalion east of Lessay; and the 3rd Battalion 3 km southwest of Carentan, south of the Périers road.[547] *Pz.E.u.A.Abt. 100* reached the area of Baupte on **10 May**.[548] The next day, its headquarters was in Appeville before moving to Francquetot on the **14th**.[549] Further west, *St.Btl. AOK 7* arrived north of La Haye-du-Puits on **10 May**;[550] its headquarters reported its location at Château Brocboeufs on the **11th**. Its companies and single battery formed an arc around the town, occupying the hills to the north and east.[551]

Despite the frantic activity on the Cotentin, **May** was mostly quiet for the *709. I.D.* Initially, only a few companies were relocated and the *III./919* moved to Tocqueville.[552] *Ost-Btl. 561* and *MG-Btl. 17* were attached to the *243. I.D.* when that division took over *KVG Bricquebec*. As ordered, *Georg.Inf. Btl. 795* had been relieved on the Jobourg Peninsula, making it available to the *709. I.D.* On the **13th**, it assembled in Le Bigard before being transferred to the southeast of the peninsula for deployment around Turqueville - Beuzeville-au-Plain under *GR 919*.[553] The change in sectors also put elements from *GR 739* under the *243. I.D.*, albeit only briefly. On the **6th**, the headquarters of *GR 739* moved to Sotteville, northeast of Les Pieux, putting it in the middle of the new division when the sectors changed.[554] On the **22nd**, the headquarters moved to Hainneville within *Festung Cherbourg*.[555] On **26 May**, the final battalion from *GR 739*, the 3rd, was relieved on the coast. It moved to the area of St. Croix-Hague - La Pasquerie - Château du Bigard (headquarters), where it was a corps reserve, along with the *14./739*.[556] Although *St.Btl. AOK 7* was initially deployed around La Haye-du-Puits, it moved to Le Vast on **16 May**.[557] This presumably allowed the *III./919* to be transferred back to its regimental sector on the **17th**, when it moved to Octeville-l'Avenel.[558] The next day, *Pz. Jg.Abt. 709* moved to Câtelet (east of Valognes) — likely because its previous position now fell under a different division.[559]

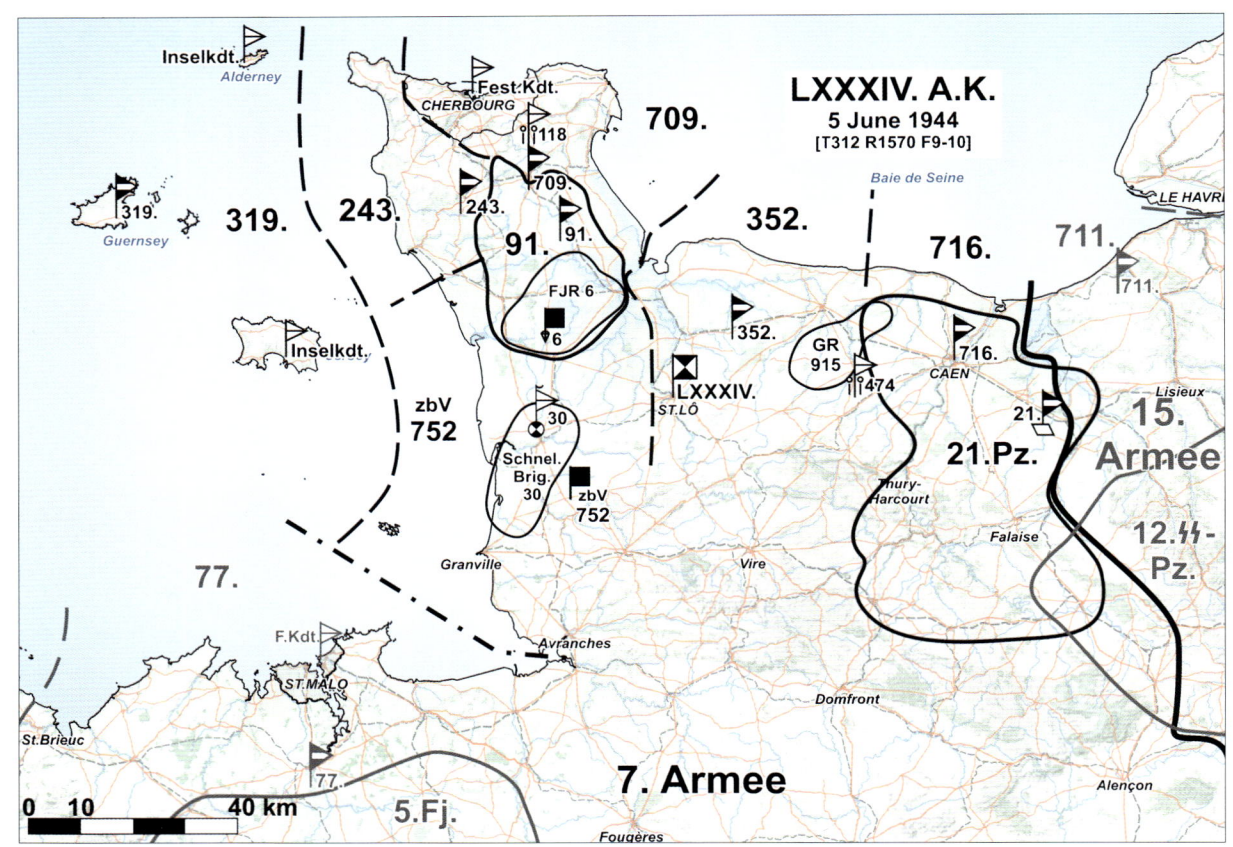

The troop strength in Normandy continued to increase. In May the 91. LL.D. and FJR 6 arrived on the Cotentin, while the 243. I.D. took over the west coast of the peninsula. The 21.Pz.Div. moved to the area around and south of Caen where it relieved the 77.I.D. which moved to Bretagne.

In the Calvados GR 915 and 916 rotated their positions, leaving the reinforced 915 inland as army-corps reserve and 916 on the coast.

The net result was that the Cotentin had been significantly reinforced. Indeed, by **21 May**, all reinforcements had arrived, all unit movements had been carried out and all elements had been deployed.[560]

The changes on the Cotentin were of little significance for the Calvados and the south of Manche. In the *352. I.D.* sector, *GR 916* and *915* swapped positions, a move completed on **1 May**. This put *GR 916* on the coast, with *GR 915* becoming a corps reserve.[561]

On the **3rd**, the *3./Pz.Jg.Abt. 352* moved to Pont-l'Abbé on the Cotentin, probably to defend the bridges across the Douve.[562] On the **19th**, the *II./915* moved to St. Gabriel. On **27 May**, the headquarters of *GR 915* was south of St. Sauveur-Lendelin and that of the *I./915* in La Motinerie, west of St. Sauveur.[563]

On the **29th**, the *I./915* moved again, this time to St. Malo-de-la-Lande, west of Coutances.[564] *Div.Füs.Btl. (A.A.) 352* was also transferred to Manche; on the **27th**, it reported its location in Bréhal, near Granville and, on the **29th**, in Les Verges, northeast of its previous position.[565] Other changes on the west coast involved *Georg.Inf.Btl. 797*, with some of its companies moving on **8** and **17 May** and the battalion headquarters moving to Gouville-sur-Mer on the **20th**.[566] These changes appear to have put the entire battalion under *Gren.Rgt. zbV 752*.

It was an uneventful month for the *716. I.D.* On the **4th**, the *II./726*'s headquarters moved to Ste. Croix-sur-Mer.[567] On the **8th**, *Ost-Btl. 441* was transferred to the area around Amfreville, north of Ranville.[568] There were concerns about the quality of *Ost-Btl. 642*, which was deployed on the coast northeast of Bayeux. As a result, it was to be sent to the Coëtquidan Training Area for additional training. The only option to relieve it was *Ost-Btl. 441*, already on a major deployment. As a result, *AOK 7* requested the return of *Ost-Btl. 630* from *AOK 15*, since the battalion from the *346. I.D.* that it had left behind in Bretagne in January had already rejoined its division. Lacking a suitable replacement, the corps was ultimately forced to relieve *Ost-Btl. 642* with *Ost-Btl. 441*.[569] This was carried out on **May 29**, with the battalions essentially swapping positions.[570] The headquarters of *Ost-Btl. 441* was in Crépon and that of *Ost-Btl. 642* in Amfreville.[571] *Ost-Btl. 642* was never sent to Coëtquidan.

A number of batteries changed position. On **6 May**, the *3./AR 1716* moved to Merville.[572] On **29 May,** two of *H.K.A.A. 1260*'s three batteries were repositioned: The 1st Battery to St. Aubin-d'Arquenay and the 2nd northeast of Cricqueville-en-Bessin (the famous Pointe du Hoc battery).[573] Other artillery changes took place further south. On **30 May**, the 1st Battery of *Eisenbahn-Artillery-Abteilung 725* (Railway Artillery Battalion 725 / *Eisb. Art.Abt. 725*) joined the corps and was located in St. Germain-de-Tallevende, south of Vire.[574] Earlier in the month, *le.Beob.Abt. 33* had moved. Although its transfer from the Cotentin has not been not found in the *AOK 7* daily reports, it was in Torigni-sur-Vire from at least **22 May**.[575] Based on ULTRA records, this move appears to have taken place on or shortly before **15 May**.

A number of changes affected the corps headquarters itself, of which the most significant was the arrival of *Arko 474* to command the artillery in *KVA* "H1" and "H2". On **13 May**, it was located in Tilly-sur-Seulles.[576] Four days later, the headquarters of *Nachr.Abt. 460* moved to Agneaux, west of St. Lô, while its 3rd Company moved to Le Mesnil-Rouxelin, north of St. Lô.

The changes in May had a significant effect on reserves. The *91. LL.D.* and the *21. Pz.Div.* were available for use throughout the *Ob.West* area. The *243. I.D.* was no longer a reserve outside of the *7. Armee*. This also applied to *Schnel.Brig. 30*. The *352. I.D.* could be transferred to *AOK 1*, if its sector were attacked. Among the artillery, *Art.Rgts.Stab 621*, with *s.Art.Abt. 456 and 457* and *le.Beob.Abt. 33*, were general reserves for use throughout *Ob.West*. This also applied to *s.St.Wfr.Rgt. 101*, although at some point the whole entry for the regiment was removed from the list of reserve units, suggesting its reserve role may have been cancelled, possibly before the invasion.[577]

In the last few days before the invasion, there was still time for reinforcements. The *II./Fallschirmjäger-Ersatz-und-Ausbildungs-Regiment 1* (Airborne Replacement and Training Regiment 1 / *Fj.Ers.u.Ausb.Rgt.1*) arrived in Cherbourg on **2 June** and was spread out over the Cotentin. The headquarters and two companies were located 6 km southwest of Cherbourg; the remaining three companies were in the areas of Valognes, St. Sauveur-le-Vicomte and La Glacerie.[578] The final changes on the Cotentin occurred on **5 June**, when *GR 739*'s headquarters relocated south of Hainneville and two batteries from *Art. Rgt. 1709* also changed positions.[579]

Meanwhile, there was a major reinforcement in the Calvados. Elements of the *352. I.D.*, which had moved to Manche in **May**, returned to the Calvados on **2 June**, when the *I./915* and *Div.Füs.Btl. (A.A.) 352* took up their old positions.[580] On **4 June**, *Flak-Rgt.32 (LW)* arrived with two battalions to address the anti-aircraft shortage, particularly between Bayeux and Isigny. *Gemischte Flak-Abt. 497* was sent northeast of Isigny, while *le.Art.Abt. 90* moved to the Bayeux area.[581]

Because the records do not record all troop movements, they therefore do not provide an accurate picture of the situation on D-Day. For the forces on the Cotentin, this will be corrected in the chapters about specific formations, but this will not be done for the Calvados. Instead, the sectors held by the *352. I.D.*, the *716. I.D.* and the *21. Pz.Div.* will be examined here. To provide a complete overview, this will also include positions that have already been mentioned.[582]

The headquarters of the *352. I.D.* was still in Littry and *Nachr.Abt. 352* was southeast, in Château Castillon. Northwest of the headquarters were *Pz.Jg.Abt. 352* (in Mestry) and *Pi.Btl. 352* (St. Martin-de-Blagny). The headquarters of *AR 352* was in Tourteville (northeast of Trévières, today Teurteville), with its four battalions deployed near the coast. *Feld-Ers.Btl. 352* was still in Caumont. The western sector of the division (*KVU Vire*) was held by *GR 914*; its headquarters in Neuilly-la-Forêt and battalions mostly around the Vire Estuary. The 1st Battalion was in Osmanville, with the 2nd Battalion in Catz. The sector was reinforced by *Ost-Btl. 439* in Les Veys and the *II./AR 352* in St. Clément. The sector from Grandcamp to Asnelles-sur-Mer was also held by the division, yet this was complicated by the fact that there were also elements of the *716. I.D.* there. As such, the area from Grandcamp to Cabourg (*KVU Percée*) was the responsibility of *GR 916*. From there, the sector to Asnelles (*KVU Bessin*) was covered by *GR 726* (*716. I.D.*), which was attached to the *352. I.D.* In the *GR 916* sector, the regimental headquarters was in Trévières. The *III./726* was in Château de Jucoville, northwest of La

Cambe, and the *II./916* in Formigny. Artillery was provided by the *IV./AR 352* in Asnières-en-Bessin and the *III./1716* in La Cambe. In the division's final area of responsibility, the headquarters of *GR 726* was in Sully, northwest of Bayeux, with the *I./726* nearby in Maisons and the *I./916* in Ryes. The *352. I.D.* had two artillery battalions in the area. The headquarters of the *I./AR 352* was still in Étréham, while the 3rd Battalion was still in La Noé. Another artillery headquarters in this area was *H.K.A.A. 1260* at Ryes.[583] Further inland, *GR 915* and *Div.Füs.Btl. (A.A.) 352* were grouped together as a corps reserve south and east of Bayeux. The regimental headquarters was in St. Paul-du-Vernay; its 1st battalion in Juaye and its 2nd Battalion in St. Gabriel. *Div.Füs.Btl. (A.A.) 352* was in Le Parc de la Mare.[584]

The remainder of the Calvados coast was in the hands of the *716. I.D.*, with most of the divisional headquarters in Caen. This also included *Nachr.Abt. 716*, *AR 1716* and *Pi.Btl. 716*. Elements from the *716. I.D.* in the neighbouring sector of the *352. I.D.* left little more than *GR 736* and divisional artillery to defend its stretch of coast. However, there were a number of reinforcements from the *21. Pz.Div.*, which will be mentioned separately.[585] The headquarters of *GR 736* was in Beuville (north of Caen) along with the *I./AR 1716*.[586] The left flank of *GR 736* stretched from Asnelles-sur-Mer roughly to Graye-sur-Mer (*KVU Meuvaines*). It was held by *Ost-Btl. 441*, located near Crépon, as was the *II./AR 1716*. The *II./726* was further inland as a divisional reserve in Ste. Croix-sur-Mer. The next sector ran to roughly St. Aubin-sur-Mer (*KVU Seulles*) and was commanded by the *II./736*, with its headquarters in Tailleville. The headquarters of *s.Art.Abt. 989* was located further to the rear, in Reviers. The next coastal sector (*KVU Luc*) was held by the *III./736*, with its headquarters in Cresserons. The final sector, running from Ouistreham, including the mouth of the Orne on the right flank (*KVU Orne*), was held by the *I./736* with its headquarters in Colleville-sur-Orne, southwest of Ouistreham. *Ost-Btl. 642* was located in Amfreville, east of the Orne. This battalion was not deployed on the coast.[587]

The *21. Pz.Div.* continued to move elements in **May**, but no major changes were reported at the beginning of **June**. At the time of the invasion, the divisional headquarters was in St. Pierre-sur-Dives and the signals battalion in Thiéville. *PGR 125*'s headquarters was located to the northwest, around Vimont; its two battalions near Fierville-la-Campagne (1st) and Colombelles (2nd). The other mechanised infantry regiment, *PGR 192*, had its headquarters in Thury-Harcourt. Its 1st Battalion was southwest of Caen at Verson, arriving on **13 May**;[588] its 2nd Battalion was north of Caen at Le Mesnil. *Pz.Rgt. 100* was in Aubigny (north of Falaise), with its 1st Battalion in Jort and its 2nd Battalion in Fresné-la-Mère (east of Falaise). The bulk of the artillery was in *Pz.Art.Rgt. 155*, with its regimental headquarters in St. André-sur-Orne. The regiment's 1st Battalion was near the coast, north of Mathieu. The headquarters of both the 2nd and 3rd Battalions were south of Caen, in May-sur-Orne and Angoville. *Pz.Jg.Abt.200*'s headquarters was also close to the coast, in St. Pierre, east of Tilly-sur-Seulles. The division's *Flak* battalion, *Heeres-Flak-Abt. 305*, was in Hérouville-St. Clair (north of Caen). *Pz.Pi.Btl. 220* was well south of Caen, with its headquarters in Clécy. To the southwest was *Feld-Ers.Btl. 200*, with its headquarters in Condé-sur-Noireau. The southernmost sector was held by *Pz.Aufkl.Abt. 21* near Briouze, some 50 km south of Caen. The situation map for **5 June** puts *Stu.Gesch.Abt. 200* further north, in the area of Putanges, although much of it may actually have been in the Cagny area.[589]

Soon the preparations of the *LXXXIV. A.K.* and its forces would be put to the ultimate test: D-Day.

Opposite: From the arrival of the first German forces in June and July 1940, Lower Normandy and the Channel Islands were controlled and occupied by a large series of commands and formations. This was especially true for the first year when the area was divided between two different army groups. The situation became more stable with the arrival of Höh.Kdo. LX, but up to the invasion many divisions would still make their way to and from Normandy.

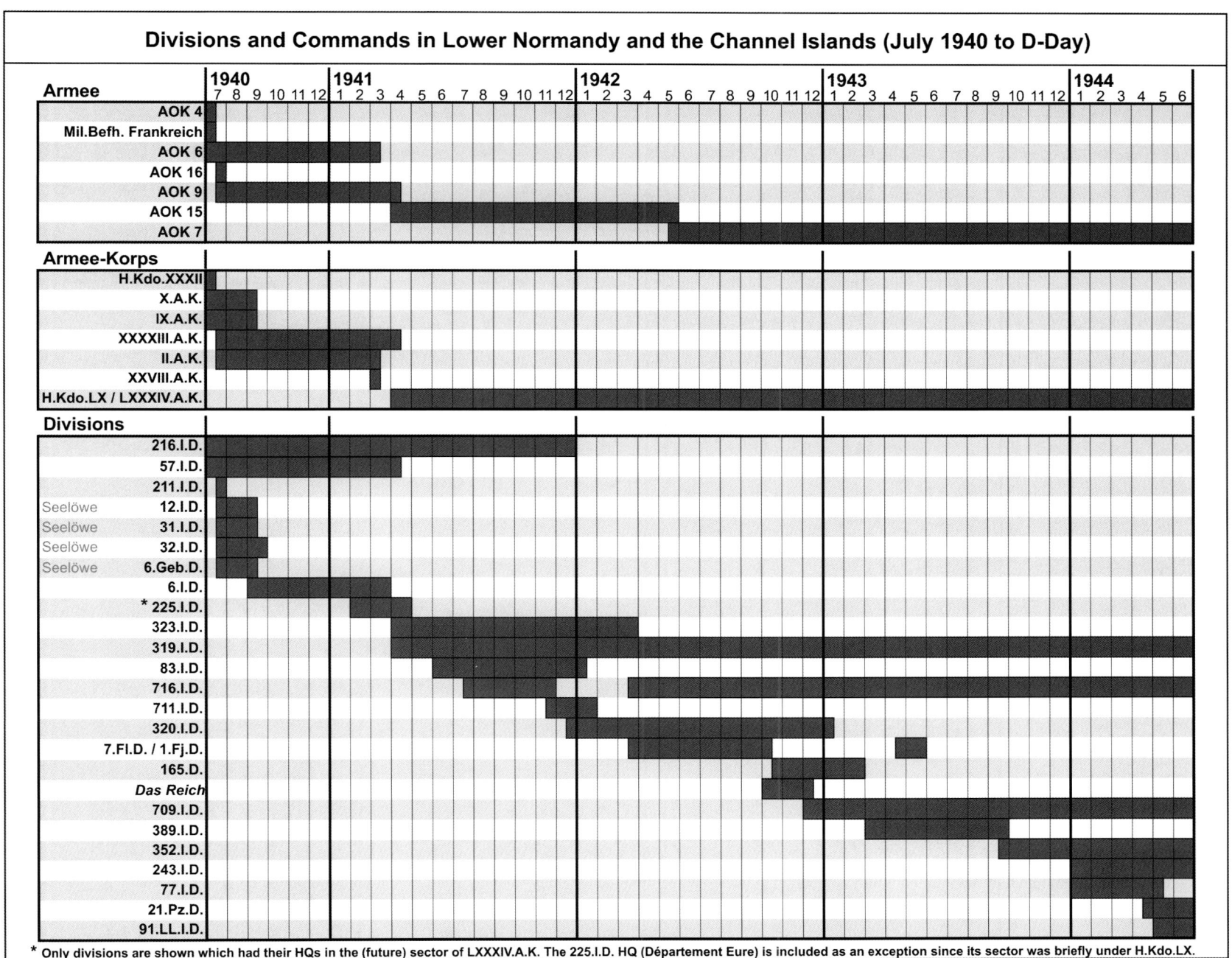

Generalkommando LXXXIV. A.K. and Corps Troops

Left: Gen.d.Art. Erich Marcks commanded the corps until his death on 12 June. (BArch, PERS 6/300187)

Centre: Following Marck's death, Gen.d.Fl. Eugen Meindl took acting command of LXXXIV. A.K. in addition to his own II. Fs.K. (NAC)

Right: Gen.d.Art. Wilhelm Fahrmbacher commanded LXXXIV. A.K. from 13-18 June when he returned to his XXV. A.K. in Bretagne. (BArch, PERS 6/299620)

The *LXXXIV. A.K.* played a major role in the Normandy fighting during the summer of **1944**. Although attention is usually focussed on its combat formations, it is also important to understand the corps headquarters (*Generalkommando*) in command of the German defence. This not only includes the headquarters itself, but also includes formations known as corps troops that were permanently assigned to it. Finally, there were the units and commands that were placed under its operational control during the invasion.

Corps troops typically included a mapping detachment (*Korps-Kartenstelle*), a signals battalion (*Korps-Nachrichten-Abteilung*), military police section (*Feldgendarmerie-Trupp*) and army post office (*Feldpostamt*). To coordinate the subordinated artillery, many also had an artillery commander with a staff (*Artillerie-Kommandeur* or *Arko*).[1] This was the case with the *LXXXIV. A.K.*, with the exception that it lacked an organic post office. It did have an organic motor transport element, *Kraftfahr-Kompanie 84 (Kf-Kp. 84.)*

On **1 April 1944**, the corps headquarters plus its mapping detachment,

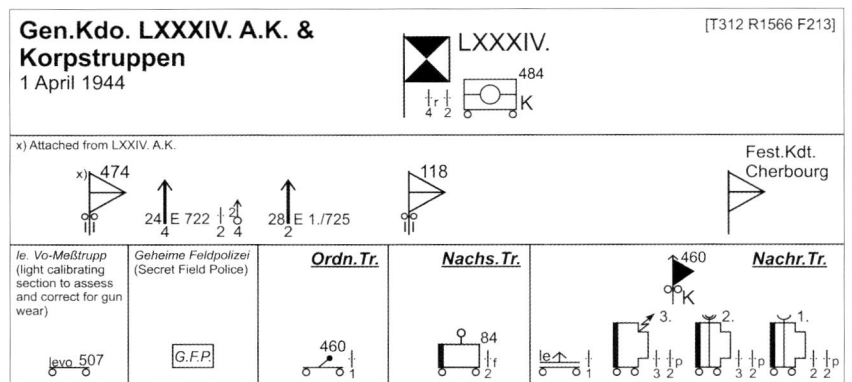

A wide variety of units was directly subordinated to corps headquarters. This included a number of specialised headquarters, a signals battalion, railway-artillery batteries, as well as smaller support elements.

military police section and the transport company had a personnel strength[2] of 583 officers and men.[3] Unfortunately, little is known about the mapping detachment (*Hauptmann* Jühne) and the military police, as the order of battle does not include their manpower. It does show that *Feldgendarmerie-Trupp 460* was armed with a light machine gun (MG). The headquarters itself had two German and four Czech light MG's.

The headcount of 583 does not include *Korps-Nachr.Abt. 460 (mot)*, or *Arko 118*. In addition to these formations and staffs, the headquarters commanded some less common formations, including a Fortress Commander for Cherbourg (*Festungs-Kommandant Cherbourg*) with his own staff. In **May 1944**, a second *Arko* (*Arko 474*) was attached to the corps.

Over the years, other organic units had supported the corps and, although they no longer existed at the time of the invasion, are worth discussing. These are *Aufklärungs-Schwadron 84* (Reconnaisance Troop 84 / *Aufkl.Schwd. 84*) and the commander of the corps' supply elements (*Kommandeur der Korps-Nachschubtruppen 460*).

The corps had two railway batteries reporting to it on D-Day. Although they do not appear to have supported the corps during the fighting on the Contentin, they should be included for completeness.

Left: Gen.d.Inf. Dietrich von Choltitz commanded the corps for the remainder of June and most of July. (BArch, PERS 6/299513)

Right: Gen.Lt. Otto Elfeldt took over the corps on 30 July and remained in charge until the corps' destruction in the Falaise pocket. (BArch, PERS 6/299605)

Generalkommando LXXXIV. A.K.

Although the organisation of the *LXXXIV. A.K.* staff is not included in corps records, there existed only one *Kriegsstärkenachweisung* (Table of Organisation and Equipment / *KStN*) for such formations: *KStN 12 (1 March 1942)*. Because officer records from the staff match this organisation, there is no doubt that it was used.

KStN 12 in itself is straightforward, but the situation was complicated by a number of updates. These did not significantly affect the core organisation of the headquarters, which was organised into six distinct groups:[4]

a) At the top was the commanding general (*Kommandierender General*) and his chief-of-staff (*Chef des Generalstabes*). Both had personal orderlies.
b) Tactical operations were directed by the command section (*Führungsabteilung*), which was divided into operations (*Ia*) and intelligence (*Ic*). The operations section was led by the operations officer, also referred to as the *Ia*, who had an assistant, the *erster Ordonnanzoffizier (O1)*[5] and a Cartography and Surveying officer (*Ia-Meß*). Additionally, there were two NCO's and three clerks and draftsmen. In February 1943, this section also included a specialist officer, an additional clerk (NCO) and an additional draftsman. The operations officer was the senior general-staff officer under the chief of staff. The intelligence section was led by the *Ic* (third general staff officer), aided by the *O3* and *O4* and one or more interpreters (officers). Lower ranking personnel included two NCO's and two enlisted. These were clerks or draftsmen.
c) The weapons officer section actually only had a gas officer (*Stabsoffizier für Gasabwehr*), assisted by an NCO and enlisted soldier serving as clerks.
d) The quartermaster section (*Quartiermeisterabteilung*) was reduced in strength in November 1943, although it did not affect its overall organisation.[6] It was organised into several groups of which the quartermaster was the largest. It comprised the quartermaster himself (*Qu*), his assistant (*O2*) and specialist officers for ammunition, equipment and fuel supply. The rest of the personnel consisted of five NCO's and two men. Three NCO's were specialists, and the remainder were clerks. In December 1943, the section was expanded by adding two branches. The first was fuel, consisting of a specialist officer, two officials, two NCO's and six clerks (including three women). The second, for signals equipment, was handled by a specialist officer, supported by an assistant, an NCO, and two clerks (including one female). Added to this core were a number of specialist areas, such as the corps administrative officer (*IVa*), the corps surgeon (*IVb*), the corps veterinarian (*IVc*) and corps engineer (*V*). Combined, they had a strength of three officers, three officials, five NCO's, and six men. On special order, additional officers (including assistants for the *IVb* and *IVc*) and an armed forces official (Wehrmachtsbeamte) could be added to compensate for reductions in personnel.
e) The adjutant's section consisted of the adjutant (*IIa*), the main office (*Hauptbüro*) and the military court (*III*). The adjutant and *IIb* were supported by four clerks (two NCO's and two men).[7] The main office had two officials and two men. The military court consisted of two officials (including a judge) and two clerks (one NCO and one man).
f) All these groups, of course, could only operate with support of the *Hauptquartier*, the HQ — sometimes referred to as the *Stabskompanie*. This was divided into five groups. In overall command was the *Kommandant*, supported by three NCOs, including a *Hauptfeldwebel*, and a medical NCO. Other personnel consisted of 15 men. Financial matters were handled by the *IV Z*, which consisted of a *Beamte* (*Zahlmeister*, paymaster), an NCO, and a clerk. Supplies were managed by the rations section (*Verpflegungsstaffel*), led by the rations officer (*Verpflegungsoffizier*). His personnel included two NCO's (including

a cook) and five men (including three cooks). Transportation was the responsibility of the motor transport section (*Kraftfahrstaffel*). The officer in charge was aided by three NCO's, who had specific tasks: One organised the use of vehicles, another distributed fuel and the third handled the maintenance. The section was subdivided into three more areas. Staff cars and lorries were in a group with 3 NCO's and 25 men — all 28 being drivers or assistant drivers. The motorcycles were part of another sub-group with a strength of 6 NCO's and 25 men; all 31 were motorcycle riders. A small motor-vehicle workshop formed the third group, and it consisted of one NCO and three men. Security for the headquarters was provided by the guard section (*Infanteriestabswache*). It was led by an NCO with two section leaders (also NCO's). There were 12 enlisted men, including 10 men as riflemen (or manning two machine guns).

Apart from this core, the *KStN* allowed room for additional specialised staff officers (including their staffs). When required, these could be assigned by special order. Examples were the artillery staff officer (*Stabsoffizier der Artillerie / Stoart*), staff officer for anti-tank operations (*Stabsoffizier für Panzerbekämpfung / Stopak*) and engineer staff officer (*Stabsoffizier der Pioniere / Stopi*). According to the *KStN*, these officers were typically supported by two NCO's and two men, although the *Stopi* was also assisted by an official. Of these, the *LXXXIV. A.K.* only appears to have had a *Stopi* on D-Day.

Another change to the *KStN* was introduced in **April 1944**, with the introduction of a national socialist guidance section. This consisted of the national socialist leadership officer (*Nationalsozialistischer-Führungsoffizier / NSFO*) and a clerk.

Whereas the addition of a *NSFO* was universal, certain changes were corps specific. For example, on **7 June 1944**, the *OKH* issued orders to augment the staffs of the corps engineer sections in several corps, including the *XXV.*, the LXXIV. and the *LXXXIV. A.K.*, with an additional officer, official, NCO and two men.[8]

All the changes and exceptions make it difficult to determine the theoretical strength of a specific corps headquarters. The last known detailed report from the *LXXXIV. A.K.*, dated **21 December 1943**, listed a strength of 16 officers, 6 officials, 35 NCO's, and 94 men.[9] Its precise strength and composition at the time of the D-Day invasion are not known.

While they were not part of the corps headquarters itself, *KStN 12* specifically stated that the mapping section, military police and post office should be attached for provisions and supplies, which illustrates the close ties between these entities.[10] In **December 1943**, the first two were included in the rations headcount for the corps headquarters. Other corps troops included were the reconnaissance squadron, the motor-transport company and the commander of the corps supply troops.

The headquarters in St. Lô was defended by a *Luftwaffe Flak* platoon, which was under the operational control of the corps headquarters.[11] It had a personnel strength of 1 officer, 3 NCO's, and 18 men. It was also included in the ration count for the corps. Around the time of the invasion, this platoon was presumably the 4th Platoon of the *4./le.Flak-Abt. 996*.[12]

Left: The grave of Gen. Marcks before he was reburied at the German war cemetery at Marigny. (NARA)

Gen. Marcks' grave at the German war cemetery at Marigny. (Sean Claxton)

Left: Gen.Maj. Kruse, the first commander of Arko 118. Having been relieved by Obst. Hamann, the general briefly commanded the 343.I.D. in Bretagne. (BArch, PERS 6/300076)

Right: Obst. von Rohr was put in command of Defence Area Cherbourg on 20 April 1943. He remained in charge until the arrival of Gen.Maj. Sattler in April 1944. (BArch, PERS 6/300501)

Corps Troops

Artillerie-Kommandeur 118 (Arko 118)

Arko 118 was in charge of the artillery in the corps sector and had the status of a brigade headquarters. *Ob.West* ordered its establishment in **May 1942**, and its formation was completed on **20 June**.[13] For much of its existence, the headquarters was listed as a motorised formation, assisted by a signals platoon from the *2./Div.Nachr.Abt. 301*.[14] Despite its designation, the battalion was not a divisional formation. Instead, it was to provide communications between coastal artillery positions and the local *Arko*. In the last known order of battle, dated **1 April 1944**, *Arko 118* had a strength of 18 officers and men, but it did not list the signals platoon.[15]

Gen.Maj. Kruse, appointed on **10 June 1942**, was the first commander.[16] On **17 July 1943**, he was succeeded by *Oberst* Hamann.[17] Kruse was transferred to *Arko 474* in Bretagne and made commander of the *343. I.D.* shortly thereafter.[18]

Formation of the *Arko* removed the need for a staff artillery officer within the corps headquarters. In the *LXXXIV. A.K.*, this position appears to have been less than stable. In **February 1942**, it had been held by an *Oberleutnant* commandeered from the headquarters of *AR 323* (*323. I.D.*).[19] The corps received a more senior officer in *Maj.* Heine, when he was assigned on **5 March**.[20] It appears that he was soon replaced by *Arko 118* and Heine became the *IIa* of the corps headquarters.[21]

For most of its time in Normandy, *Arko 118* was based in St. Lô. In **January 1944**, it moved to the Valognes area, joining the headquarters of the *709. I.D.*[22] This apparently shifted the focus of the *Arko* more to *KVA "J"* (Manche). Simultaneously, *Obst.* Hamann doubled as the artillery officer (*Artillerie-Führer / Arfü*) of the *709. I.D.*, responsible for this coastal sector.[23]

On **13 June**, the headquarters of *H.K.A.R. 1261* took over as the artillery command and control element of the *709. I.D.*[24] *Arko 118* could have returned to the *LXXXV. A.K.* but the corps commanding general, *Gen.* von Choltitz, believed *Arko 474* to be more efficient and wished to keep it.[25] Thus, *Arko 118* was listed under the *II. Fs.K.* on **22-23 June**. After that, it reported directly to *AOK 7*.[26] *Obst.* Hamann left his position on **10 July**, apparently due to health issues, and was succeeded four days later by *Obst.* Seifert.[27] In **October**, the *Arko* was redesignated *Arko 484* and then renamed *Arko 486* in **November**.[28]

Arko 118's transfer to the Cotentin in **January 1944** left the Calvados coast without an *Arko*. To resolve this, *Arko 474* was brought up in mid-**May**. As the name suggests, it belonged to the *LXXIV. A.K.* in Bretagne. In Normandy, the *Arko* commanded the artillery in the Calvados, *KVA "H1"* and *"H2"*.[29] The headquarters was commanded by *Obst.* Mertz and had a combined strength of 19 officers and men.[30] After the invasion, it served as the *Arko* for the *LXXXIV. A.K.* and, unlike the corps headquarters, survived the fighting.[31]

Festungs-Kommandant Cherbourg

The *Festungs-Kommandant Cherbourg* (Fortress Commander) was in command of *Festung Cherbourg* and had the status of a brigade headquarters.[32] At the time of the invasion, the position was held by *Gen.Maj.* Sattler, who was appointed in **April 1944**.[33] According to the last known order of battle, his staff had a strength of 25 men.[34]

Sattler stayed in command until **23 June**, when Hitler appointed *Gen. Lt.* von Schlieben (the commander of the *709. I.D.*) as commander of the town and fortress, with Sattler kept to assist him.[35] Von Schlieben was taken prisoner on **26 June** and Sattler followed when he surrendered the Arsenal the following day.[36]

The position of fortress commander was a recent creation, given that Cherbourg was only declared a *Festung* by Hitler in **January 1944**.[37] Prior to this, it had been designated as *Verteidigungsbereich Cherbourg* (Defence Area

Cherbourg / *V.B. Cherbourg*). Initially, the role of the designated commander was more a consequence of being the senior officer rather than a planned position.[38]

This changed in **February 1943**, when *AOK 7* assigned *Obst.* Blumentritt, as the Commissioner for the Construction of the *Atlantikwall* for *V.B. Cherbourg*. The *LXXXIV. A.K.* decided to designate him commander of the Defensive Zone as well, while *AOK 7* asked higher headquarters to declare the position of commander to be "static" (meaning both sector bound and permanent). The *709. I.D.* was to establish a headquarters and report on its composition.[39] On **22 March**, *AOK 7* asked *Ob.West* for a static commander and battalion for each of the *U-Boot* bases (*V.B. Brest*, *Lorient* and *St. Nazaire*) and *V.B. Cherbourg*.[40] These were promised on the **25th**.[41] A new commander, *Obst* v. Rohr, arrived in **April** and assumed command of *V.B. Cherbourg* on the **20th**.[42] In his original capacity as construction commissar, *Obst.* Blumentritt was subordinated to the new commander.[43]

On **26 March**, *AOK 7* specifically requested *Ob.West* for headquarters elements for these commanders.[44] In Normandy, the *LXXXIV. A.K.* had created such a headquarters in **February** and, in **March**, it sent a provisional *KStN* to *AOK 7* for approval.[45] On **1 April**, an official *KStN* was introduced instead: *KStN 94(W)*. In **June,** the *OKW* modified it for *Ob.West*.[46] Although neither version of this *KStN* has been found, similar versions have survived and are close to the corps' proposal, matching the modifications perfectly.[47] By combining the proposal with surviving records, the following organisation emerges.

The command was divided into three sections: the *Gruppe Kommandant* (headquarters), *Festungs-Nachrichten-Kommandant* (fortress signals commander) and *Festungsnachrichtenstaffel* (fortress signals section)[48] The over-all headquarters had four officers: The commander, his adjutant, a facility officer (*Standortoffizier*) and an assistant. They would be assisted by an official, two NCO's and two men. The messenger section (*Meldestaffel*) was led by an NCO and four messengers with bicycles. The motor vehicle section (*Kraftwagengruppe*) consisted of two drivers and presumably two vehicles for transportation.[49]

The *OKW* change in **June** added a signals commander to the over-all organisation, consisting of a commander and a second officer. They were assisted by an NCO, a telephone operator, a clerk and a draftsman. A vehicle was available for this element.[50] The signals section had the most manpower. It was led by an NCO in command of two telephone sections (*Fernsprechtrupps*), presumably a small section (*kl. Fernsprech-Trupp*) with an NCO and three men and a medium one (*mittl. Fernsprech-Trupp*) with an NCO and four men.[51]

The corps' *KStN* proposal from March would have given the latter section a strength of 24 men, with another 7 for the fortress signals commander. The lower ranks would be provided by the *709.* and the *319. I.D.*[52] The available *KStN's* give a strength of 34 men, including the fortress signals commander.[53]

On **19 January 1944**, *V.B. Cherbourg* was reclassified as *Festung Cherbourg*,

Gen.Maj. Robert Sattler commanded Festung Cherbourg from April 1944 until 23 June when Gen.Lt. von Schlieben (709.I.D.) was given responsibility for the defence of the fortress by Hitler. Sattler surrendered the Arsenal on 27 June. (NARA)

although this does not appear to have changed the organisation. On **27 March**, *Ob.West* asked *OKW/OKH* to approve its suggestion for a new *KStN* for the fortresses under its command. The proposal essentially called for the same organisation as outlined above. The intended signals section organisation was very specific, however. *Ob.West* wanted a medium wireless section, 80 medium wave (motorised) (*mittl. Funktrupp 80Mw (mot)*), six backpack wireless sections, type A (motorised) (*Tornisterfunktrupp A (mot)*), a light telephone operator section, type 20 (motorised) (*le. Fernsprech-Betriebstrupp 20 (mot)*), a medium wire section, type 12 (motorised) (*mittl. Feldkabeltrupp 12 (mot)*) and a medium telephone maintenance section (motorised) (*mittl. Fernsprech-Instandhaltungstrupp (mot)*). This would give a combined strength in the section of 10 NCO's and 30 men. [54, 55]

In response, the *OKH* issued a preliminary *KStN* on **22 April** and instructed the Replacement Army to quickly form the elements needed for the fortresses in *Ob.West*. The existing structure was to be dissolved upon the arrival of the *Festungs-Kommandant* staff. The existing personnel and equipment were to be transferred to the incoming headquarters, with the *OKH* only supplying personnel to fill the remaining positions. The exact signals equipment for the signals section depended on what was already available, as the *OKH* would not issue any.[56]

The new *KStN Kommandant einer Festung* from the *OKH* also included elements that had not been in *Ob.West's* proposal. In addition to the modified headquarters, fortress signals commander and signals section, there was a command and supply detachment (*Führungs-u.Versorg.Abt.*), a messenger and vehicle section (*Melder- u.Kfz.Staffel*) and a partially motorised military police section (*Feldgendarmerie-Trupp (tmot)*).[57]

The headquarters would be formed by the fortress commander and a number of officers from the command and supply detachment. This included an officer for operations (*Sachbearbeiter Ia*), an officer for logistics (*Sachbearbeiter Ib*), an artillery officer (*Stoart*), an assistant (*Ord.*), a fortress engineer officer (*Pi.Offz. Fest.Pi.*) and a medical officer (*Sachbearbeiter IVb*). There were two officials: a paymaster and a fortress engineer for defences (*Zahlmeister* and *Wallmeister*). Finally, there were seven NCO's and seven soldiers. No vehicles were provided except for eight bicycles. All motor vehicles were pooled in the messenger and vehicle section.[58]

The signals commander section would consist of the commander and an officer assistant.[59] The signals commander was also in charge of the signals section. The officers were aided by an NCO and three men. *Ob.West* had requested a specific organisation for the section, but the *OKH* did not agree. Instead, it decided that no new signals equipment would be assigned and that the existing equipment in the fortresses should be used. Rather than dictate the rank structure of the section, the *KStN* only gave the number of personnel: 5 NCO's, and 15 men to operate telephone equipment, with the same number of NCO's and men for the radios.[60] The totals matched that of *Ob.West*, although it had asked for more radio personnel.[61]

The messenger and vehicle section was led by an NCO with a light motorcycle and eight light motorcycles for the seven messengers. Another group of messengers (also one NCO and seven men) was allocated bicycles. Other motor vehicles in the section included three staff cars and a lorry for ammunition and equipment. There were four drivers for these.[62]

The military police section was a relatively large unit commanded by an officer, who led 25 NCO's and 7 men. The section was allocated three light MG's and six bicycles, nine light motorcycles, and six motorcycle-sidecars.[63]

As little information is available about the composition of the Cherbourg "fortress", it is unclear to what extent the *KStN* was followed. In fact, the newly approved headquarters staff never arrived in Cherbourg. On **26 July**, the headquarters was redesignated as the Commander in the Defensive Area of La Rochelle and the Replacement Army was instructed to send it there.[64]

This confusion regarding the organisation makes it difficult to assess the actual elements in Cherbourg. Some documents were found on *Gen. Maj.* Sattler when he was captured, and these offer some information. In addition to the general, the headquarters staff consisted of four officers, three of whom had been attached for duty and had multiple roles. As planned, there was an engineer officer / liaison officer from *Fest.Pi.Stab 11*.[65] The fifth officer in direct support of the general was *Obst.* Reiter, who served as both the commander of *Art.Rgt. 1709* and as artillery officer of the fortress. His headquarters and two of his battalions were located in the fortress and the third was to the east.[66]

Communications were controlled by the fortress signals commander. This position was held by *Obstlt. d.R.* Kohtz, aided by two officers.[67] Actual operations were conducted by a dedicated fortress signals section, which was commanded by Kohtz and had a strength of about 50 men. This meant is was close to the *KStN*. Reportedly, the men who operated the telephones or radios were organised into groups of four or five, suggesting they were organised into squads. Some of the squads were attached to *709. I.D.* companies and others to companies from *Festungs-Stamm-Abteilung LXXXIV* (Fortress Cadre Battalion LXXXIV / *Fest.Stamm-Abt. LXXXIV*).[68]

Information on the messenger and vehicle section and the military police section, which were both part of the *KStN*, has not been found. It is likely that the former did exist in one form or another. The existence of a military police unit, in addition to the one already stationed in Cherbourg (*Feldg.Tr. 583*), is unlikely.

Korps-Nachrichten-Abteilung 460

Communications at corps level was by *Korps-Nachrichten-Abteilung 460*, which had been raised in **November 1940** within the jurisdiction of the Armed Forces Commander for Bohemia-Moravia, with personnel supplied from Military District I. Since the battalion was originally established for *H.Kdo. zbV LX*, the predecessor to the *LXXXIV. A.K.*, it received the number "460", combining "60" with the typical "400" used by corps troops. It stayed with the corps until destroyed in the summer of **1944**.[69] Its field post office numbers were cancelled on **16 January 1945**.[70]

The battalion comprised three companies.[71] Although not mentioned by Tessin, it also had a signals supply column. All units received their field post office numbers numbers in the same period, suggesting the signals column was raised early on as well. In **1943,** a 4th Company was temporarily listed under the field post number of the headquarters.[72]

On **1 April 1944**, the battalion was commanded by *Maj.* Benzmann and had a personnel strength of 602 men. It consisted of the headquarters, three companies and a supply column, all of which were motorised. On paper, the 1st Company was a telephone company, the 2nd a field cable company and the 3rd a radio company.[73]

Later that month, the battalion was reorganised on orders from the *OKH*. The headquarters was to follow *KStN 805 n* (**1 October 1943***)* and four *KStN's* from **1 January 1944** were selected for the other units. The field cable company (*Feldfernkabel-Kp.(mot)*) used *KStN 843*, including the full complement of 12 field-cable squads. *KStN 833* (corps telephone operator company / *Kps.Fe.Betr.Kp.(mot)*) and *KStN 860* (corps radio company / *Kps. Fu.Kp.(mot)*) were used by the other two companies. The column used *KStN 872* (*Kps.-Nachr.Kol.(mot)*).[74] The companies and trains were all motorised.

Despite the situation on paper, personnel from the 1st Company stated that they were the wire-laying and maintenance company, consisting of three wire platoons, each divided into three sections. Each section had 1 NCO and 10 other ranks armed with rifles but no machine guns.[75] This apparently differed at higher levels within the company, which reportedly possessed two German and two Polish machine guns.[76] Each section had two lorries and each platoon had two cable lorries, each carrying 6 km of cable.[77]

There is little information on the other units in the battalion. On **1 April 1944,** the 2nd Company was armed with three German and two Polish machine guns, while the 3rd Company had one less German machine gun. The signals supply column was armed with one machine gun.[78]

The battalion headquarters and the 3rd Company were primarily located in or around St. Lô and were still there on D-Day.[79] The 1st Company. left St. Lô in the autumn of **1943,** moving to Torigni-sur-Vire; one section was sent to Valognes in early **June 1944** and put under the signals troops from the *709. I.D.*[80] The 2nd Company relocated to Le Dézert in **February 1944** and was presumably still there when the invasion started.[81]

Kraftfahr-Kompanie 84

The *LXXXIV. A.K.* possessed a number of small organic support units. Little is known about them, but *Kraftfahr-Kompanie 84* (Motor Transport Company 84 / *Kf.Kp. 84*) is an exception. It was raised as part of the efforts to bring about mobility for static elements (*Beweglichmachung*) in **June 1942** to guarantee deployment of the corps reserves in case of an invasion.[82] It reported directly to the corps and used the same field post number as the headquarters, with a letter added to distinguish it from the staff elements.[83]

Although it was initially formed using rented motor vehicles driven by French civilians, it appears that it had military personnel by the time of the invasion, as civilians were no longer mentioned.[84] The company was poorly armed and, on **1 April 1944**, its heaviest weapons were two French machine guns.[85]

A POW from the company gave details on its strength and organisation. It consisted of four platoons, each with two transport sections. These had a

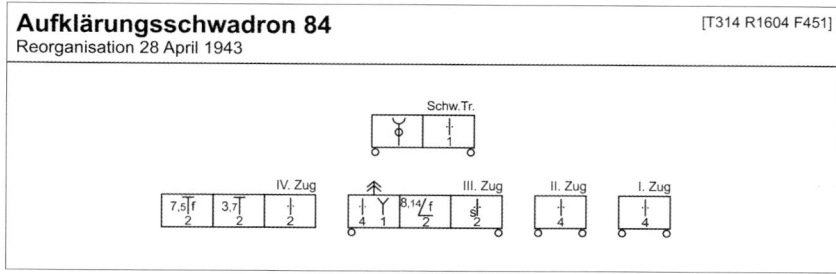

Aufklärungsschwadron 84 was reorganised in the spring of 1943. It consisted of an HQ section and four platoons. The first two were infantry platoons while the third was a mixed heavy platoon with a mortar, a heavy MG and an engineer section. The fourth Zug was an anti-tank platoon.

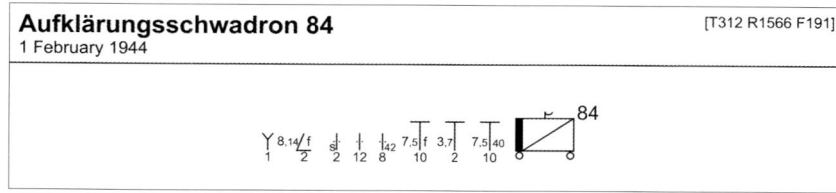

By February 1944 the Schwadron had taken in 10 Pak 40 anti-tank guns. This was a step towards the formation of additional anti-tank companies for the 709. and 716.I.D., which ultimately led to the disbandment of the Schwadron.

strength of about 10 drivers under an NCO. There were approximately 10 vehicles, plus a staff car for the NCO.[86] This is reasonably close to a strength report from **November 1942**, when the company consisted of 1 officer, 4 NCO's, and 62 men.[87]

Apparently, the company had no German lorries, the vehicles being a mix of different makes and models. One section alone had Dodge, Citroën, Saurer, Renault, Morris and Ford lorries, ranging from 1.5-tonne (Morris) to five-tonne (Saurer). Although the vehicles were not new, they were reportedly reliable.[88]

Aufklärungs-Schwadron 84

Some units supporting the corps in earlier years no longer existed by D-Day. One such unit was *Aufklärungs-Schwadron 84* (Reconnaissance Troop 84 / *Aufkl.Schwd. 84*), a curious formation. It was formed in **June 1942** for reconnaissance in the greater corps sector. To form the troop, personnel were gleaned from the *319.*, the *320.*, the *716. I.D.* and the headquarters company of the corps headquarters.[89]

The troop was last listed on an order of battle dated **1 February 1944** and was a motorised formation with substantial heavy equipment. Weaponry included a flamethrower, 2 French medium mortars, 2 heavy machine guns[90] and 20 light machine guns, including 8 *MG 42's*. There were also 2 "French" 7,5 cm Pak 97/38's, 2 3,7 cm Pak's and 10 7,5 cm Pak 40's.[91]

According to the last known orders from **April 1943**, the fully motorised troop should have consisted of an headquarters with a light telephone section, two infantry platoons, one mortar/engineer platoon and an anti-tank platoon.[92] A soldier of the troop confirmed much of this organisation. According to him, the first two platoons were infantry, the third a mortar platoon and the fourth an anti-tank platoon.[93]

The troop was commanded by *Hptm.* Hümmerich. He joined the corps on **6 June 1942** and was designated an acting commander (*mit der Führung beauftragt / m.d.F.b.*)[94] of the troop soon thereafter.[95] No orders or dates have been found regarding its disbandment, but late in **1943** the troop was selected to form an organic anti-tank company for the *709. I.D.* *Hptm.* Hümmerich ultimately became commander of *Pz.Jg.Abt. 709*, while other elements were transferred to *Pz.Jg.Abt. 716*.[96] These developments presumably led to the end of the troop and may explain why, on its last organisational document, it was listed as having 10 heavy AT guns.[97] On **1 December 1943**, it had only two light anti-tank guns and two medium ones, which had been the case for most of **1943**.[98]

Kommandeur der Korps-Nachschubtruppen 460

Another element no longer listed on the last order of battle before the invasion was the *Kommandeur der Korps-Nachschubtruppen 460* (commander of the corps supply troops). It was created through command channels in **April 1943**, located in La Meauffe in **May**, and formally established in **August**. Formed from the staff elements of *Nachschub-Kolonnen-Abt. Bauer zbV*, it was an ad hoc formation under *AOK 7* and organised into four horse-drawn transportation sections (30-tons each).[99] These sections appear to have been combined into two 60-ton sections: *Große Fahrkolonne 697* and *698*. Although belonging to the *7. Armee*, both reported to the *LXXXIV. A.K.*, which explains why they are listed under the supply troops of both headquarters.[100]

The arrival of the supply transport sections at the *LXXXIV. A.K.*, combined with the presence of *Kf.Kp. 84*, may have created a need for a command element. Since the staff of *Abt. Bauer* was available, using it for the establishment of the new headquarters would have been a logical solution. According to Tessin, the headquarters was destroyed in the fighting of **1944**, but this is unlikely.[101] The order of battle of the corps last listed it on **1 February**, and it had vanished by **1 April**.[102] Its field post number was cancelled on **4 April**, suggesting that it had been disbanded in **February-March**.[103] This is no surprise, since both of the subordinate supply sections had left in late **November 1943**.[104] As such, *Kf.Kp. 84* was the only organic supply/transport unit at the time of the invasion, leaving little need for a headquarters.[105]

Miscellaneous Elements

On D-Day, the corps had two railway batteries attached to it. One had been located in the corps area for many years: *Eisenbahn-Batterie 722* (Railway Battery 722 / *E.Bttr. 722*). On **1 April 1944**, the battery had a strength of 220 men and was outfitted with four *24 cm "Theodor Bruno" Kanone (E)*, with additional weaponry including two machine guns and four 2 cm *Flak*.[106] It was in Cherbourg for several years, but this changed in **September 1943**, when the guns were deemed unfit for coastal defence. This was primarily due to their excessive range, making it difficult to engage landing troops or land targets.[107] On **23 December** the battery moved to Torigni-sur-Vire.[108]

The *1./Eisenbahn-Artillerie-Abteilung 725* (Railway Artillery Battalion 725 / *E.Art.Abt. 725*), joined the corps before D-Day, arriving in St. Germain-de-Tallevende (4 km south of Vire) on **30 May**. It had two *28 cm "Neue Bruno" K. (E)*.[109]

It proved difficult to direct the guns against the Cotentin. On **6 June**, attempts were made to move the two guns to St. Lô. From there, they could interdict Allied shipping crossing the Banc de Madeleine on the approach to Utah Beach. Railway damage delayed the movement.[110]

Some of the railway guns were near Bayeux when the invasion began and were then withdrawn towards Villers-Bocage. Ultimately, it appears that neither battery was used to support operations on the peninsula and both were soon reassigned to *Höheres Artillerie-Kommando 309* (Higher Artillery Command 309 / *Harko 309*),[111] which was fighting in the Calvados. Since the guns' mobility depended on the damaged railway network, it proved difficult to withdraw the guns and most were lost in the area of Villers-Bocage, Guilberville and Vire. The three remaining guns from *E-Bttr. 722* were blown up in Vire on **5 August**. Days before, the surviving gun from the *1./E.Art.Abt. 725* was recovered in St. Germain-de-Tallevende and taken to Domfront via Mortain.[112]

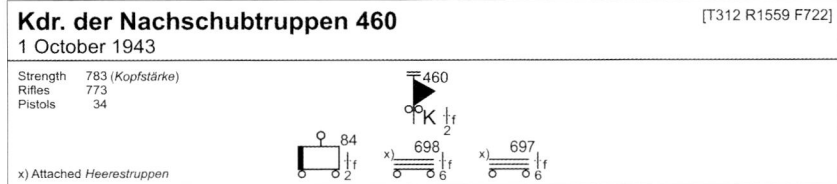

The HQ of the commander of the corps supply troops existed only for a brief period. At its peak it consisted of Kraftfahr-Kp. 84 and two heavy (60 tonnes) transport columns. Although the latter were shown as motorised, they appear to have been horse drawn.

One of the guns from Bttr. 722(E), captured between Villers-Bocage and Guilberville. (NARA)

Part 2:
HEER INFANTRY DIVISIONS

(Archives du Calvados 10Fi/2, photo 126 Fama, France et Atlantic, Berlin)

The Heer Infantry Division

Supported by numerous artillery formations and a miscellany of other units, the infantry divisions made up the backbone of the German coastal defences in the west. The situation on the Cotentin was no exception, but was not restricted to the coastal frontline of **June 1944**. Particularly in the *bocage*, the fighting would be dominated by the infantry, whether from an infantry, airborne or mechanised division.

Before discussing the individual *Heer* infantry divisions on the Cotentin, it is important to examine some of their key characteristics and developments in the months prior to the invasion. Despite many differences, a lot of the problems faced by these divisions were similar. From late **1943** until D-Day, many underwent reorganisation and attempts to increase their strength and mobility as far as circumstances would allow.

The Organisation of the Infantry Divisions

Unlike their American opponents, German infantry divisions on the Cotentin were far from uniform. Some had been raised as early as **1941**, others as late as **January 1944**. More significantly, they had been raised in different mobilisation iterations or "waves" (*Wellen*), meaning the divisions were based on a variety of base organisational documents. The resulting differences could relate to their intended use. For example, divisions such as the *243.*, the *265.* and the *709. I.D.*, were classified as static (*bodenständig*) and not intended for standard deployment; therefore, there were differences in their structure, armament, manpower and mobility compared to regular infantry divisions. In addition, many divisions were changed over time, further increasing their diversity and complexity.

Some changes resulted from modifications made to the structure of the infantry divisions, the most important occurring in **1943-1944**. At lower levels, units were affected by changes made to the *KStN's*. This was an on-going process, accounting for the units' latest requirements, as well as the availability of equipment and personnel. This can make it a challenge to ascertain the authorised strength of a formation at a specific time.

In **1941**, prior to the excessive losses on the Eastern Front, a "typical" German infantry division consisted of three infantry regiments, an artillery regiment and divisional troops consisting of anti-tank, reconnaissance and engineer elements. Added to these were a variety of support troops. The infantry regiments (redesignated as grenadier regiments in the autumn of 1943) had three battalions each, with each battalion organised into three rifle companies and one heavy company. An infantry-gun company and an anti-tank company were assigned as the 13th and 14th Company. Reconnaissance (sometimes equipped with bicycles) and engineer platoons were with the regimental staff. There was more variety among the divisional anti-tank and reconnaissance formations, with many divisions having both types of battalions. The anti-tank battalions (*Panzerjäger-Abteilungen / Pz.Jg.Abt.*) had up to three companies, while reconnaissance battalions (*Aufklärungs-Abteilungen / A.A.*, with some later called *Radfahr-Abteilungen / Radf. Abt.*, literally, bicycle battalions) typically consisted of two mobile infantry companies with a heavy company in support. Such a battalion could therefore be regarded as a 10th infantry battalion in the division. Not all divisions had both anti-tank and reconnaissance battalions; some just had a single battalion combining these elements. These were initially known as the *Panzerjäger- und Aufklärungs-Abteilung* and later as a *schnelle Abteilung*.[1] The artillery regiment was typically organised with three light battalions and one heavy battalion, each with three batteries armed with four howitzers or cannons. The organisation of the engineer battalion (*Pionier-Bataillon / Pi.Btl.*) was also standard, and it typically consisted of three companies and support column. Some battalions also had a bridging column but these were removed later in the war.[2]

Even before the outbreak of war there had been differences among the infantry divisions. Once the fighting started losses, transfers, reorganisations, new iterations, manpower and equipment shortages and changing conditions resulted in ever increasing diversity among German infantry divisions. This included differences in the number of infantry battalions. By **1943**, it was considered necessary to standardise divisions and their sub-units. On **5 August 1943**, a new base organisation for nearly all infantry divisions was introduced: The *"Infanterie-Division neuer Art" / Inf.Div.n.A.* (new type).[3] Initially, it only applied to the organisations in the East, but was extended to most divisions in the West on **2 October**.[4] The new type of infantry division signified an effort to establish more uniform formations and to compensate for increasing personnel problems. The new type of division marked a clear

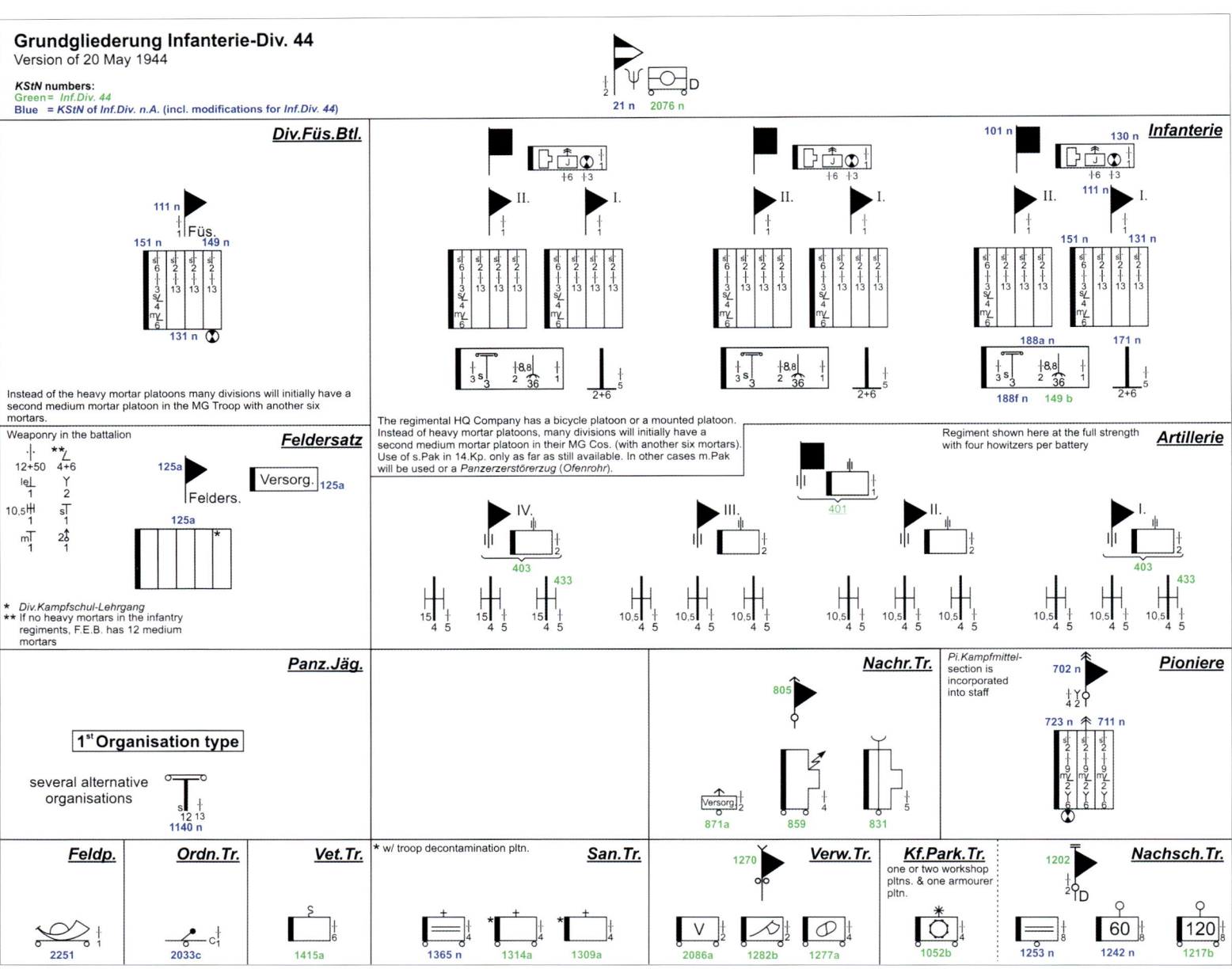

By the time of the invasion, the Infanterie-Division 44 (Type 44) had become the standard organisation of regular German infantry divisions. It was a further development of the Infanterie-Division neuer Art which had been introduced in 1943.

shift between the early war divisions and those of the final years. The base documents introduced many changes, of which no longer having 9 or 10 infantry battalions per division was arguably the most significant. All standard infantry divisions would now have seven infantry battalions, including a fusilier battalion (*Füsilier-Bataillon / Füs.Btl.*) in place of a reconnaissance or bicycle battalion. The new organisation also added a field replacement battalion (*Feldersatz-Bataillon / Feld-Ers.Btl.*) as standard.[5] The *353. I.D.* is a good example of a division raised as an *Inf.Div.n.A.*

With the introduction of the *Inf.Div.n.A.*, many of the associated *KStN*'s were replaced or updated.[6] Still, they were not final and, as before, changes continued to be made. Minor changes were usually manually added to a *KStN*, which explains why many have corrections and writing on them. This typically included the official order number and date of the change. Changes to organisational documents and *KStN*'s were usually minor, but on **4 March 1944** further reductions were made to the *Inf.Div.n.A.*, leading to a new base document: The *Infanterie-Division 44 (Inf.Div.44)*. The OKH stressed that, except for the supply troops, this new structure did not affect the over-all organisation of the division nor the combat strength of the infantry. The over-all number of heavy weapons in the division also remained unaffected. Although this may have been technically correct, it did not conceal the fact that the change further reduced the overall manpower and number of machine guns. Compared to the original *Inf.Div.n.A.*, the number of light machine guns in each infantry regiment was reduced by 24. This was done by reducing the number of reserve machine guns in the rifle companies (minus 18) and by having fewer light machine guns in the 14th Company (minus eight), while adding one to both battalion headquarters (plus two). The changes made to the infantry battalions also applied to the *Füs.Btl.* (minus eight).[7]

To effect these changes, alterations were made to many *KStN*'s. In most cases minor modifications sufficed, but for some units, an entire *KStN* had to be reworked or replaced. This was the case for the artillery and the *Feld-Ers.Btl.* (also abbreviated *F.E.B.*), while the reorganisation of the supply troops would be ordered later.[8] This appears to have delayed the actual reorganisation to *Inf.Div.44*. In the meantime, the divisions were simply ordered to carry out the reductions immediately.

The implementation date for *Inf.Div.44* was ordered for **20 May 1944**, apparently because all *KStN*'s and reorganisation plans had been drawn up. Now, almost all infantry divisions were ordered to reorganise according to this new organisational concept and associated *KStN*'s.[9] On **27 May**, *AOK 7* ordered its corps to carry out the required reorganisations, which had to be complete by **1 July**.[10] With the Allied invasion less than two weeks away, it is questionable to what extent these orders were actually implemented.

As was the case with the *Inf.Div.n.A.*, exceptions were made, most notably for the static divisions, which were to keep their existing base documents and old *KStN*'s, unless specifically ordered otherwise. A second group of divisions, those with a special base document, were to implement the new *KStN*'s while keeping their old over-all organisation.[11] There were also exceptions for specific divisions, and all divisions of the 25th wave – including the *77. I.D.* and the *91. LL.D.* – were part of this group. Although they had been raised after introduction of the *Inf.Div.n.A.*, they did not follow that structure nor that of the *Inf.Div.44*. Instead, they were considerably weaker. The elements that were present followed the same *KStN*'s as standard divisions, unless there were reasons to deviate from this such as in the *91. LL.D.*[12]

The Infanterie-Division 44

By combining the *KStN*'s with the order of battle of a division it should be possible to determine its authorised strength (*Soll-Stärke*) in detail, although such a level of detail is not relevant to this introduction. Instead, only the combat elements will be discussed, and only so far as it concerns overall organisation of the units, their manpower and heavy weapons.[13] The signals battalion (*Nachrichten-Abteilung / Nachr.Abt.*) was also considered a combat branch, but it will not be dealt with here because it had a largely supportive role; the divisional anti-tank elements will be discussed as a separate topic. Individual divisions will be covered later, with detail on their combat and non-combat formations, as well as actual, rather than theoretical, strength.

The examination of *Inf.Div.44* can best begin with the divisional headquarters, which was considered part of the combat troops. This helps to understand how the division was led. The command group was organised into eight specific sections, some of which were subdivided further. The first two groups were formed by the divisional commander and the command staff, which comprised the *Ia* (operations group) and *Ic* (intelligence group). The former included the *Ia* (first general staff officer for operations) with his assistants, the *O1* (*1. Ordonnanzoffizier*) and a gas-protection officer (*Gasschutzoffizier*). The *Ic* included the *Ic* himself (divisional intelligence officer), an *NSFO*, an assistant intelligence officer, the *O3* (*3. Ordonnanzoffizier*), and two further officers as assistants/interpreters.[14]

The third group was formed by the quartermaster section and consisted of four officers, among them the *Ib* (second general staff officer for logistics) and his assistant, the *O2* (*2. Ord.Offz.*). The next four groups were the *IVa* (*Intendant* or administrative officer), the *IVb* (division surgeon), the *IVc* (division veterinarian) and the *V* (motor vehicle officer).[15]

The largest section of the staff was the office of the adjutant, divided into five groups: *Adjutant* (*IIa*); divisional court (*III*); divisional clergy (*IVd*) (one Catholic priest, one Protestant minister); the headquarters commandant; and the divisional band. The headquarters commandant section was the largest of these and included the *IVz* (paymaster), the supply trains, the motor vehicle section, the staff car section, the motorcycle section, the vehicle maintenance section and the headquarters guard (armed with two light MG's).[16]

The divisional headquarters had a total strength of 23 officers, 10 officials, 61 NCO's and 92 men. Divisions without an anti-tank battalion had an extra officer for anti-tank defence.[17] The structure also provided provisions for a divisional mapping detachment, field police and field post office.

The fighting core of an infantry division was its infantry regiments (*Grenadier-Regiment / Gren.Rgt. / GR*). In an *Inf.Div.44*, there were three, each consisting of a headquarters and headquarters company, two infantry battalions, an infantry-gun company (13th Company) and an anti-tank company (14th Company).[18] The regimental headquarters was fairly spartan: 7 officers, 1 NCO and 16 men. The officers included the commander, his adjutant, two assistants, a special-duties officer, the regimental veterinarian and a second veterinarian assistant. There were no heavy weapons.[19]

The regimental headquarters company (*Stabskompanie / St.Kp.*) was more complex. It included a company headquarters (*Gruppe Führer*), a signals platoon (*Nachrichten-Zug*), an engineer platoon (*Pionier-Zug*), a mounted (*Reiter-*) or bicycle platoon (*Radfahr-Zug*) and, finally, the trains (*Troß*). The company had an authorised strength of 3 officers (commander, signals officer and engineer officer), two officials (paymaster and master armourer), 29 NCO's and 163 men. The engineer platoon was the largest element in the company and consisted of a platoon headquarters section and six subsections with one light machine gun. The mounted/bicycle platoon was composed of a headquarters and three sections, each with one light MG. The remaining light MG was issued to the trains.[20]

All infantry battalions shared the same organisation: A headquarters, three rifle companies (*Schützenkompanie / Sch.Kp.*) and a heavy company, identified as either a *MG-Kp.* or a *schwere Kp.*[21] To avoid confusion with regimental heavy weapons companies, this book opts to use the former term. Unlike the regiments, battalions did not have a headquarters company, just a headquarters section; it included the command group, a signals section and trains. The total strength was 4 officers (commander, his adjutant, an assistant/signals officer and a battalion surgeon), 2 officials (paymaster and master armourer), 13 NCO's, and 58 men. The only light MG assigned was part of the trains.[22]

In the *Inf.Div.n.A.*, it had been intended to equip the rifle companies with 16 light MG's and two medium mortars.[23] This was changed with the *Inf.Div.44*

A MG42 used as a heavy machine gun in its tripod configuration. (NARA)

to 13 light MG's, 2 heavy MG's and no mortars.[24] Each rifle company included the command group, three platoons, a heavy MG section and the trains. Combined company strength was 2 officers (the commander and one platoon leader), 21 NCO's (including two platoon leaders), and 119 men. The platoons had three sections, each with one NCO, eight men and a light MG. A fourth MG was kept as a reserve at platoon level, one fewer than the *Inf.Div.n.A.* The two heavy MG's were part of the heavy MG section and the remaining light MG was in the trains. An infantry section's small arms included two machine-pistols, a pistol and six rifles.[25] One of the machine pistols was used by the platoon leader and, in practice, the second was a self-loading/semi-automatic rifle: The *Selbstladegewehr 41*, also known as the "G41" or, later on, the "G43". The standard rifle was the *Karabiner 98k* (*K98k*), but one was issued with a telescope and another with a grenade-launcher (*Schießbecher*).[26]

The *Inf.Div.n.A.* had introduced a MG company that differed in weaponry from previous iterations, although it was realised it would take time to accomplish this. In their final configuration these companies were to be armed with eight heavy MG's, three light MG's and four 2 cm *Flak* in mounts for ground combat. For the time being, the companies would be armed with 12 heavy MG's, three light MG's and four heavy mortars.[27] The *Inf.Div.44* eventually changed this to six heavy MG's, three light MG's four heavy mortars and six medium mortars. This removed the mortars from the rifle companies, while two heavy machine guns were transferred to each of those. It was clear that it would be impossible to immediately provide the divisions with sufficient heavy mortars, so the MG company typically had a second platoon with another six medium mortars.[28] The companies consisted of the command group, a heavy MG platoon with six heavy MG's, two platoons with medium mortars (six mortars each) and the trains with one light MG. This gave the company an authorised strength of 2 officers (commander and the heavy MG platoon leader), 40 NCO's and 182 men.[29]

The 13th Company (*Infanterie-Geschütz-Kompanie / I.G.Kp.*) was outfitted with infantry guns; it was composed of the command section, three platoons with light infantry guns, one platoon (4th) with heavy infantry guns and the trains. Authorised strength of the company was 3 officers (commander, and the platoon leaders of the 1st and 4th platoons), 32 NCO's and 157 men. Although most of the heavy weapons and machine guns were in the gun platoons, the trains had a single light MG. Each of the gun platoons possessed two infantry

The 15 cm s.I.G.33 was the standard heavy gun in the 13th Co. The light guns could either be 7.5 cm or 7.62 cm pieces. (NAC)

guns (either light or heavy) and one light MG. In the light platoons, the guns were horse-drawn, while the heavy platoon relied on the *Raupenschlepper Ost* (*RSO*), a light fully tracked prime mover.[30]

The anti-tank company (the 14th Company or *Infanterie-Panzerjäger-Kompanie*) was composed of several *KStN's*. It consisted of the command section and trains, a platoon of anti-tank guns and two platoons with anti-tank rocket launchers. The company boasted an authorised strength of 4 officers (commander and three platoon leaders), 22 NCO's and 142 men. There were no heavy weapons within the command section, but the trains had a single light MG. Both followed *KStN 188a n.*[31] The anti-tank gun platoon had three 7.5 cm heavy anti-tank guns and three light MG's. The platoon was motorised, using *RSO's* to tow the anti-tank guns. The employment of heavy anti-tank guns was limited to units that still had them, otherwise these platoons were equipped with medium anti-tank guns or organised as anti-tank rocket platoons.[32] Two of the latter platoons (*Panzerzerstörerzug*) were already standard in such companies. These were equipped with the *Raketenpanzerbüchse 54*, more commonly known as the *Ofenrohr* (stove pipe) or the *Panzerschreck*. The platoons were organised into three sections, each with six launchers, for a total of 18 launchers per platoon. The only light MG was kept at platoon level.[33]

The fusilier battalion introduced with the *Inf.Div.n.A.*, remained part of the

Inf.Div.44. Essentially a seventh infantry battalion, it was similar in organisation to a regular infantry battalion, consisting of a headquarters, three rifle companies and a MG company. These used the same *KStN's* as the infantry battalions, except for one of the rifle companies, which was equipped with bicycles.[34]

This type of company had the same manpower as a regular infantry company, with 2 officers (commander and platoon leader), 21 NCO's, and 119 men. The organisation was also identical, with a command section, three rifle platoons, a heavy MG squad and trains. The light MG's were distributed among the three platoons (each with three squads with one light MG each); three light MG's were held by the command section as a reserve, and the final one was with the trains. The two heavy MG's were in the heavy MG squad.[35]

The organisation of the artillery regiment was straightforward. It consisted of a regimental headquarters and headquarters battery, three light battalions and one heavy battalion. Each battalion had a headquarters and headquarters battery and three batteries with four howitzers each. Due to shortages, some batteries only had three guns.

The regimental headquarters was relatively small, with a total strength of six officers, two NCO's, and nine men. The headquarters battery included the command section, a signals platoon, a workshop for weapons and equipment and the trains. The heaviest weapon was a single light MG in the trains. The battery had an authorised strength of 1 officer, 2 officials, 22 NCO's, and 68 men.[36]

The headquarters of the light and heavy battalions used the same *KStN* and were identical. Both had a strength of six officers (commander, adjutant, liaison officer/assistant, battalion surgeon and veterinarian), three NCO's, and eight men.[37]

Two Americans examine an Ofenrohr, aka Panzerschreck. (NARA)

A number of captured 7.5 cm Pak 40 A/T guns at the Isigny-sur-Mer collection point. (NARA)

The headquarters battery of both types of battalion were similar but manifested a few differences. Each included a command section, a signals platoon, a survey section (*Artillerie-Vermessungstrupp*), a supply section (one light MG), battery trains (for the headquarters and the headquarters battery, armed with one light MG) and battalion trains. With the exception of the signals platoon and supply section, these elements were identical for the light and heavy battalions. The light battalions had an additional element: A vehicle workshop with a strength of one NCO and five men.[38] Compared to the signals platoon of a light battalion, the heavy battalion had an additional radio section to communicate with aircraft, adding an NCO and four men to its total. The heavy battalion also had six more men in its supply section. Due to these differences, the headquarters and headquarters battery of a light battalion had an authorised strength of 8 officers (including the headquarters battery commander and a signals officer), 2 officials (master armourer and paymaster), 25 NCO's and 111 men, while a heavy battalion had 116 men.

Just like the battalion headquarters and headquarters batteries, the light and heavy howitzer batteries shared a similar organisation. They were organised in a command section (with a battery headquarters section including forward observation elements), a signals platoon, a line battery (*Gefechtsbatterie*) with the actual howitzers, and trains. With much heavier guns in the heavy batteries, the line battery required more personnel (an extra NCO and 32 men) than the light batteries. The trains of the heavy batteries also had two more men. This provided for an authorised strength of 3 officers (commander, forward observer and gun battery officer), 26 NCO's, and 84 men in the light batteries, and 3 officers, 27 NCO's, and 118 men in the heavy batteries. Both light and heavy batteries were equipped with five light MG's; these were divided among the command section (one), the line battery (three) and the trains (one).[39]

The *Pionier-Bataillon* in the *Inf.Div.44* had a standard organisation of a headquarters (partially motorised), two "regular" engineer companies and a bicycle company.[40] Because of the special nature of these battalions, the headquarters was rather complicated. It included the command section, a signals platoon, an ordnance section, a motor vehicle workshop and two trains (combat and supply). The four light MG's were divided equally among the command section and the combat trains. These elements resulted in an authorised strength of 6 officers (commander, staff officer, adjutant, special-duties officer, battalion surgeon and veterinarian), 3 officials (paymaster, engineer and master armourer), 14 NCO's and 60 men.[41]

The engineer companies consisted of the command section, three platoons, a heavy MG section, a mortar section and the trains. Each platoon was issued three light MG's. The heavy MG section was armed with two heavy MG's, while the mortar section fielded two medium mortars. There were no heavy weapons with the trains.[42] Although not listed in the *KStN*, the companies also had six flamethrowers.[43] All told, the companies had an authorised strength of 3 officers (commander and two platoon leaders), 26 NCO's, and 150 men. These numbers in men and weapons were identical for the bicycle engineer companies. The presence of 146 bicycles was in marked contrast to the 11 bicycles in the standard companies.[44]

The organisational document for the *Feldersatz-Bataillon* (Field-Replacement Battalion) simply shows a headquarters, a supply company and five companies, the first of which served as the divisional combat school.[45] Although this is a good reflection of its organisation, its internal structure was rather more complex. The battalion was formed around cadre personnel (*Stammpersonal*), who were organised into a headquarters and supply company. Incoming replacements formed the replacement section (*Ersatzstaffel*).[46]

The headquarters consisted of a command section and a training section. The command section consisted of the commander and his adjutant, along with two enlisted personnel. Most of the battalion's key personnel were in the training section. The battalion's 13 officers were 5 company commanders and 8 platoon leaders. The 78 NCO's included eight platoon leaders, 5 company first sergeants and 60 section leaders. In addition, there were five messengers and clerks.[47]

The supply company included a command section, an administrative section that supported the battalion as a whole and a weapons section. The latter was authorised the battalion's heavy weapons: 50 light MG's, 12 heavy MG's, 6 8 cm mortars, 4 12 cm mortars (or another 6 medium mortars instead), a *le.I.G.18*, a 5 cm anti-tank gun, a 7.5 cm heavy anti-tank gun, a 2 cm *Flak*, 6 flamethrowers and a *le.F.H.18*. The company had an authorised strength of 2 officers (commander and medical officer), 1 official (paymaster), 19 NCO's and 53 men.[48]

The replacements were in the *Ersatzstaffel* (replacement section), which existed outside the battalion staff and supply company. The section had an authorised strength of 750 NCO's and men.⁴⁹ In practice they would be combined with the cadre personnel and battalion's weaponry to create the battalion's companies.

Divisional Anti-tank Troops

As the war progressed, the anti-tank capabilities of infantry divisions became a concern. Measures were taken that resulted in a complete reorganisation of the anti-tank elements, bringing changes to many divisions in Normandy.

In **July 1943**, the *OKH* introduced plans to reorganise the anti-tank forces in the east. The divisional anti-tank battalions would consist of a headquarters and signals platoon, a company with 12 towed heavy AT guns, a company with either 14 self-propelled AT guns or assault guns (*Sturmgeschütze*) and a company with 12 2 cm or 9 3.7 cm *Flak*. Because it was understood that this type of battalion could only be built up gradually, the infantry divisions would initially form a divisional anti-tank company with 12 heavy AT guns, while another six heavy anti-tank guns would be distributed among the regimental anti-tank companies.⁵⁰ This general reorganisation was later summarised by the Inspector General of the Armoured Forces, *General der Panzertruppen* Guderian.⁵¹

> *The decisive importance of anti-tank defence made a fundamental change in the armament of the anti-tank battalions necessary. Therefore, on my initiative, the reorganisation of the anti-tank battalions began, and the first objective was to equip one company of each battalion with either assault guns or self-propelled anti-tank guns.*

Although the plans were initially for the Army Forces in the East (*Ostheer*), this type of anti-tank battalion was incorporated into the *Inf. Div.n.A.* and later into the *Inf.Div.44*, ultimately affecting all regular infantry divisions. In the *Inf.Div.n.A.*, the core of the divisional anti-tank units was the company of towed anti-tank guns. Depending on availability, this element could be expanded to battalion size to include a headquarters, a *Flak* company and a company with either SP anti-tank or assault guns. Many divisions initially started with just a single company and then went on to establish complete anti-tank battalions.⁵²

In **January 1944**, the formation of an anti-tank battalion was ordered for several infantry divisions within *Ob.West*, including a number of *Inf.Div.n.A.* The organisation of these battalions would differ from earlier plans: Its 1ˢᵗ Company would be equipped with self-propelled anti-tank guns instead of motorised ones; the 2ⁿᵈ Company would receive assault guns; and the 3ʳᵈ Company remained a *Flak* company.⁵³

Following the introduction of the *Inf.Div.44*, fresh orders were issued on **25** and **30 March 1944** addressing the anti-tank capabilities of the infantry divisions in general.⁵⁴ This was especially urgent, for it was realised that the gap between production numbers and losses of heavy AT guns would mean that the *Inf.Div.44* could not be equipped as intended. It was estimated that the divisions would, on average, be equipped with 22 motorised heavy AT guns during **1944**; as an alternative, they could have 12 heavy anti-tank guns and 10 assault guns.⁵⁵

As the situation varied between divisions and fronts, guidelines rather than strict rules were offered. Priority was given to establishing at least one fully equipped company of 12 motorised AT guns within the battalion. If more than 12 heavy AT guns were available within a division, the additional guns could be assigned to the AT company of each infantry regiment to establish an additional platoon with three guns. As an alternative, a division was allowed to form a second company within the battalion, as long as the battalion was not planned to be issued assault guns in the foreseeable future. The field replacement battalion could, if required, receive a heavy AT gun as well. This gun could be used for training and as a reserve. Light and medium anti-tank guns ⁵⁶ were only allowed in the regimental anti-tank companies; *3.7 cm Pak* and captured AT guns were considered excess and not taken into consideration when it came to a unit's strength.⁵⁷

Production numbers of the *Ofenrohr* (*Raketen-Panzerbüchse 54 / RPzB.54*, aka *Panzerschreck*) would enable two platoons in the regimental anti-tank companies to be equipped with 18 each. The regimental anti-tank platoons that could not (yet) be equipped with anti-tank guns were also to be outfitted with these weapons.⁵⁸

The changes to the organisation of the anti-tank battalion, which began in mid-**1943**, largely ended with the activation of the *Inf.Div.44*, which included four possible organisational variations for the divisional anti-tank troops. For each division, the *OKH* would decide which type of organisation it was to follow. These consisted of one or more types of units, selected from a total of eight *KStN*'s. The options varied from divisions having no more than a

The anti-tank elements of a Type 44 infantry division could have a number of organisations and several types of weaponry. In strength and mobility they varied from a single towed anti-tank gun company to a full battalion with three self-propelled companies, armed with a mixture of assault guns, anti-aircraft, and anti-tank guns.

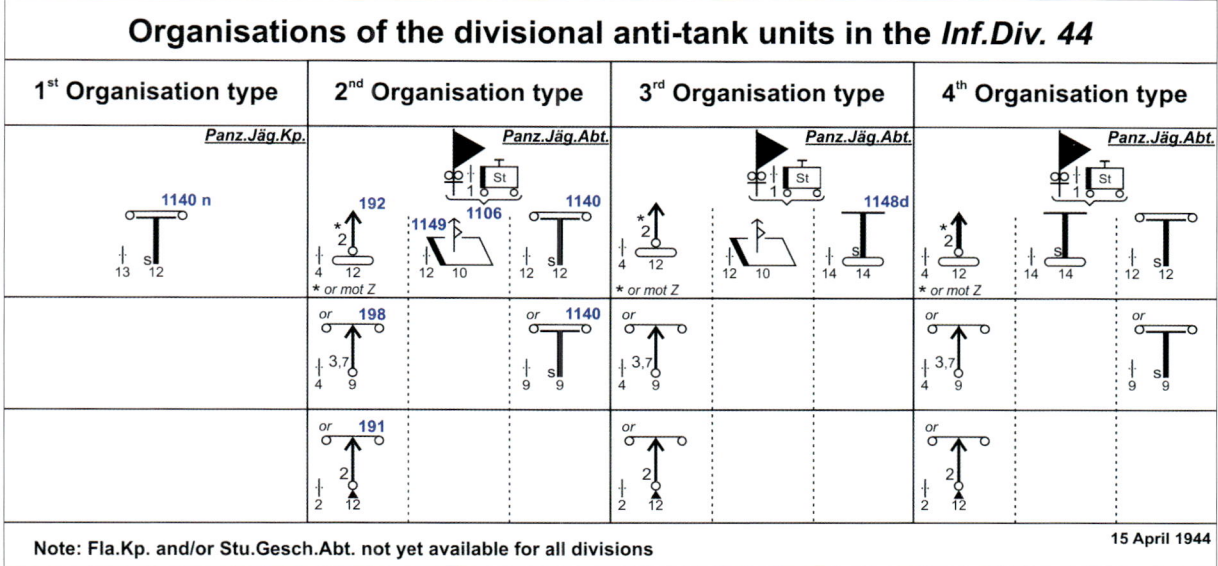

single anti-tank company to those fielding a full battalion (with three possible configurations and additional options).[59]

For obvious reasons, only the battalion-sized elements (variations 2 - 4) required a headquarters and headquarters company, which followed *KStN 1106*.[60] The headquarters itself had a strength of five officers (commander, adjutant, officer assistant, battalion surgeon and motor-transport officer), three NCO's and eight men. The headquarters company consisted of a signals platoon, a maintenance section (one light MG), and three trains elements; it had an authorised strength of 1 officer (signals officer), 3 officials (maintenance, master armourer and paymaster), 18 NCO's, and 47 men.[61]

The type 1 organisation consisted of a single separate anti-tank company with 12 heavy AT guns. In accordance with *KStN 1140n*, the company was motorised and included a command section, four platoons (each with three 7.5 cm AT guns and three light MG's) and trains (one light MG). The company had a total authorised strength of 3 officers (commander and the platoon leaders of the 1st and 2nd platoons), 1 official, 28 NCO's and 152 men.[62] When such a company was part of a battalion (2nd or 4th type of organisation), *KStN 1140* applied.[63] This called for a command section, three platoons (each with four 7.5 or 7.62 cm AT guns and four light MG's), a maintenance section and three trains elements. This gave a total strength of 3 officers (commander and two platoon leaders), 27 NCO's and 131 men.[64]

All iterations of the anti-tank battalion also included a 3rd Company (*Flak*).[65] Three different *KStN's* were possible for this. *KStN 191* called for 12 motorised 2 cm mountain *Flak*, while *KStN 192* included the same number of self-propelled 2 cm *Flak*; and *KStN 198* included nine motorised 3.7 cm *Flak*. In practice, there were exceptions where both towed and self-propelled 2 cm *Flak* were part of the same company, or where the 3.7 cm anti-aircraft guns were self-propelled. The *243.* and the *353. I.D.* are examples of such deviations. All of these companies were organised with a command section, a signals section, three gun platoons (with either four 2 cm *Flak* or three 3.7 cm *Flak*), and three trains elements (including two light MG's). Only the 3.7 cm company had an ammunition section. While all the companies had two officers (commander and 1st platoon leader), the remaining personnel varied between 29-34 NCO's and 111-116 men.[66]

The organisation of the self-propelled anti-tank companies (3rd and 4th types of organisation) followed *KStN 1148d*.[67] The command section was equipped with two self-propelled 7.5 or 7.62 cm AT guns (each with a light MG). These vehicles were more commonly known as the *Marder*, of which several types existed.[68] The three platoons each had four *Marders* for a total of 14 self-propelled guns in the company. Other elements were a maintenance section and three trains elements. This resulted in an authorised strength of 3 officers (commander and the platoon leaders of the 1st and 2nd platoons), 54 NCO's and 79 men, although personnel could be increased by two NCO's and 17 men in motorised (towed guns) rather than self-propelled battalions.[69]

The assault gun companies (2nd and 3rd organisational types) followed *KStN 1149*, which replaced both *KStN 446a* (an artillery *KStN*), and *1159* (for 14 assault guns rather than 10).[70] The companies were organised into a command section (one assault gun with a 7.5 cm main gun and one light MG), three platoons (three assault guns each), a vehicle maintenance section (one light MG) and two trains (one light MG). These elements gave the company an authorised strength of 3 officers (commander and the platoon leaders of the 1st and 2nd platoons), 44 NCO's and 72 men.[71]

The introduction of assault guns in infantry divisions was relatively new. As assault artillery, these weapons had originally been assigned to the artillery branch. In the spring of **1943**, assault guns also began to appear under the armour branch.[72] In both *Panzer* divisions and *Panzer-Grenadier* divisions — the latter still designated as *Inf.Div. (mot)* at the time — they were issued in lieu of tanks.[73] During the summer of **1943**, anti-tank assault gun companies (*Panzerjäger-Sturmgeschütz-Kompanien*) became part of infantry divisions as well. As anti-tank elements these assault guns were also part of the *Panzertruppen*.[74] The different branches were reflected in the uniforms worn, although official uniform regulations were not always practiced in the field. In the *Panzer* and *Panzer-Grenadier* divisions and separate anti-tank units, the crews wore black uniforms; in the infantry divisions these were field grey, like the *Sturmartillerie*. The crews of the *Sturmartillerie* continued to wear *Litzen* (a decorative flourish) on their collars, while the *Panzerjäger* crews wore the death's head of the *Panzertruppen*.[75] The *Waffenfarbe* (branch colour) also differed, the *Panzertruppen* using pink, the artillery red.[76]

In **February 1944**, many assault gun formations were redesignated. The companies in the infantry divisions were redesignated as an *Abteilung* (detachment in this context) and renumbered by adding 1000 to the number of the parent anti-tank battalion.[77] For example, the *2./Pz.Jg.Abt. 353* became *Stu.Gesch.Abt.1353*. This was little more than a name change, as they continued to be part of the battalion and employed as its 2nd Company.

Of course, the development of the divisional anti-tank troops also affected the infantry divisions of *AOK 7* in the year before the invasion. The shortage of heavy AT guns explains the condition of the infantry divisions up to **February 1944**. At that time, no division possessed an operational anti-tank battalion. Instead, many had a divisional anti-tank company with towed AT guns, consistent with the *Inf.Div.n.A*. Many of the static divisions did not even have such a company, nor did the newly raised *77. I.D.* (25th wave).[78]

As noted, the static divisions were exceptions in the efforts to standardise infantry divisions and this affected their anti-tank troops as well. In Normandy, the *709.* and the *716. I.D.* had been earmarked since late **1942** to receive self-propelled heavy anti-tank companies. When these weapons failed to arrive promptly, temporary measures were taken, including the use of lighter guns and static weapons. In **November 1943**, the SP guns finally arrived, actually adding to an already confusing organisation of the divisions' anti-tank troops. By D-Day, however, both divisions had a company of towed anti-tank guns, a company with self-propelled anti-tank guns, and a *Flak* company. This organisation was closest to the 4th type of anti-tank organisation, yet with fewer self-propelled anti-tank guns. Only one of the battalion equivalents had a headquarters.[79] Other static divisions, such as the *265. I.D.*, were much weaker, lacking divisional or regimental anti-tank companies, or both. In these divisions, platoons of regimental anti-tank companies were frequently used to man static guns, another clear difference compared to regular infantry divisions.[80]

Some of the non-static infantry divisions in the *7. Armee* also possessed an anti-tank battalion on **6 June 1944**. The formation and organisation of three of these battalions had been ordered in **January 1944** as part of a group of nine divisions under *H.Gr. D*, albeit without the headquarters company, which was not introduced until later. For *AOK 7*, this affected the divisions of the 21st wave (*352.* and *353. I.D.*) and the *243. I.D.*. These went from having a single anti-tank company to an entire battalion, signifying that they would have a headquarters and three companies. The 1st Company was to receive 14 *Marder* self-propelled *7,5 cm Pak 40's*, while the 2nd Company would field 10 assault guns. The weaponry for the 3rd Company, the *Flak* company, was not yet determined for these divisions;[81] in practice there just were two options — 12 2 cm *Flak* or 9 3.7 cm *Flak*. The organisation of these battalions is surprising, since it matches the 3rd type of organisation of the *Inf. Div.44,* which was not formally introduced until the spring of 1944.[82]

Unlike the *352.* and the *353. I.D.*, the divisions of the 25th wave were raised in early **1944** and, at that time, were merely authorised to have an anti-tank company.[83] Since these divisions were (mostly) to use the same *KStN*'s as the *Inf.Div.n.A.* and *44*, their anti-tank units followed the same principles, resulting in companies with 12 motorised heavy AT guns. This applied to divisions such as the *77. I.D.* and the *91. LL.D.* The appearance of a *Flak* company and headquarters in some of these divisions suggests that the single company was only a start, not dissimilar to how the 21st wave divisions had begun.[84]

Manpower

The theoretical organisation of the infantry divisions does not tell the whole story about their actual strength, and depended ultimately on their equipment and the quality of their personnel. The Eastern Front — beginning as early as **September 1941** and continuing to late **1943** — had been a constant drain on manpower from the west.[85] These transfers of personnel to the forces in the east had a significant impact on both the quantity and quality of the forces in the west. Many formations were stationed, formed, or reconstituted in the west and then sent (or sent back) to the east.[86] The issue also affected formations that remained in Western Europe.

The harsh conditions in the East (and North Africa) of course were much more demanding than those in occupied western Europe, meaning that a lower standard of men could be accepted for divisions in the west, particularly in the static divisions. This included men who were not considered to be fit for regular service (*kriegsverwendungsfähig*). As a result, the most able men were often removed from divisions in the west and sent to the east, leaving lower quality personnel — among them men classified as "fit for garrison duty in the field" (*garnisonverwendungsfähig Feld,* or *g.v.F.*) or merely "fit for garrison duty in the zone of interior" (*garnisonverwendungsfähig Heimat,* or *g.v.H.*) — in the divisions of *Ob.West.* In return for its able-bodied troops, the west typically received replacements that were not (or no longer deemed) fit for service on the Eastern Front. These exchanges occurred on a regular basis and, over the years, involved tens of thousands of men from the *7. Armee* alone.[87] Among the replacements for divisions in the west were also many young soldiers and recruits. In **December 1943**, 13,240 soldiers in the *7. Armee* sector were born in 1925 and another 7,106 in 1926 — a total of 15.3% of the on-hand strength of the field army.[88] Many of these young men arrived as part of an exchange that began in late **August** and was intended to furnish 18,000 men (born **1906-1924**) for the east while replacing them with the same number of recruits born in **1925**.[89]

The veterans, who were no longer fit for service in the east, had among them older men and men suffering from severe frostbite.[90] German personnel who had spent time in Soviet captivity formed an additional group, since they risked severe punishment by the Soviets, if they were recaptured.[91] Some men enjoyed a special status that exempted them from serving on the Eastern Front: These included last surviving sons and fathers of five or more children.[92] In practice, the level of protection varied from being exempt from service all together to not serving on the frontline. Yet as the war progressed, the protected status of most groups was withdrawn. For example last surviving sons lost their special status in **September 1943**.

Despite the influx of young soldiers, the average age of personnel within the divisions in the west remained relatively high. In **July 1943**, the average age of the NCO's and men in the *709.* and the *716. I.D.* was 33. Only about 15% and 11% respectively of the personnel in these two divisions had experience on the Eastern Front.[93]

In **October**, the *Ob.West* assessed the personnel of its static divisions. The planned arrival of men born in 1925, intended to make up an average of 20% of personnel, lowered the average age. The remaining men were often born in 1907 or even earlier, but were also men with frostbite, men unsuitable for the Eastern Front, and Polish personnel of German heritage (*deutsche Volksliste III / dVL III*). The average age of personnel by rank was as follows: battalion commanders, 45¼; company commanders, 35; platoon leaders, 31; NCO's, 30; enlisted personnel, 30-31.[94] This can be compared to the authorised maximum age of NCO's and men in the combat formations of such divisions, which was officially set at 36 years.[95] There is little reason to assume that the average age had reached this limit by D-Day.

A particular group of men deserves additional attention: Members of the so-called *Deutsche Volksliste III*. This was one of four categories used to classify inhabitants of annexed regions of Poland who were of German descent. These were "former" Poles who had "volunteered" to become "Germans". Although men of this group could be conscripted into the German armed forces, the number of such men who made it into the Army in occupied Europe was relatively few at the time of the invasion. In **March 1944**, the number of *dVL III* men serving on the various fronts amounted to about 78,000. Over half of these were with *Ob.West* (*H.Gr. D*), which had close to 40,000 men from that list and constituted about 5.5% of its total strength.[96] In **March 1944**, 8,778 men from *dVL III* served within the *7. Armee*.[97] In contrast, the numbers varied between 0.4-0.6% in the four field-army groups in the east.[98] Other theatres such as Norway (3.9%), Italy (2.6%), and the Balkans (2.8%) had a modest percentage of such troops.[99]

Both the men themselves and their German "brothers-in-arms" generally regarded these troops as Poles rather than Germans.[100] Their reliability was often questioned, as underscored by the regulation for their use in the east. This state of affairs was not restricted to men from *dVL III*. Similar issues affected men from other annexed territories, such as the Alsace and Lorraine, Luxembourg and Lower Styria (part of modern-day Slovenia).[101] Combined, the men from these regions amounted to just over 38,000, or about half the number of the *dVL III* men.[102] In **March 1944**, the *7. Armee* reported just 1,415 men from these territories.[103]

More complex is the issue of men from regions *not* annexed by Germany but still conscripted into the German Armed Forces. Rüdiger Overmans' research has produced the following figures for men conscripted into the German armed forces from outside the greater *Reich* (including annexed regions): East and Southeast Europe (Poland, Hungary, Romania, Yugoslavia), 846,000; France (Alsace-Lorraine), 136,000; others from Western Europe, 86,000. These figures can be compared to a total of 17,300,000 conscripted by the services from 1939-45 (which included 1,306,000 Austrians and 588,000 men from annexed territories in East and Southeast Europe).[104]

Apart from many Germans, Austrians and Poles, prisoners taken in Normandy also spoke to the presence of Czechs, Romanians, Slovenes, Yugoslavs, etc. or prisoners who identified themselves as such.[105] This illustrates the presence of ethnic Germans living outside the *Reich* (*Volksdeutsche*), next to German nationals (*Reichsdeutsche*) in various units. Prisoner accounts generally indicate that the morale of the *Volksdeutsche* was lower than that of *Reichsdeutsche*, but it is difficult to assess the difference or consequences. This is complicated by the fact that numbers were only reported for a few specific groups, like *dVL III*, making it difficult to determine just how many *Volksdeutsche* served in Normandy, their percentages within certain units or how well they performed.

Following *Führer* Directive No. 51, the defences in the west became a priority in late **1943**; as a result, the personnel situation began to improve. Although personnel exchanges of men with frostbite continued, this was compensated for by the arrival of more combat-capable replacements of NCO's and men. By the end of the first quarter of **1944**, *AOK 7* concluded that, for the first time in a long time, it had not been weakened by transfers in any significant way.[106]

Developments among the officers contributed to a palpable improvement. In late **1943**, many officers had been old and lacking combat experience. This changed as older officers and those whose health was seen as "not crisis proof", started to be replaced by younger, combat-experienced officers; moreover, the east-west exchange of officers was halted completely in **February 1944**. By the end of **March**, the average ages of commanders in the static divisions of the *7. Armee* were: 42.7 (infantry battalions), 44.7 (artillery battalions), 34.5 (infantry companies) and 32.5 (artillery batteries). This can be compared to regular infantry divisions, where the average ages of these groups were: 37.5, 36.5, 30.0, and 30.2 years, respectively. *AOK 7* deemed the officer situation *"fully satisfactory"*, with about 60% bringing experience from the Eastern Front.[107]

Over the years the east-west exchanges had not only reduced the quality of the troops, but it also undermined the cohesion and continuity of the formations affected. This was not simply a matter of an exchange of individual men, as transfers might affect entire formations. In some cases, infantry divisions in the west had to relinquish one or more battalions to help build other formations or for service in the east.[108] This not only affected the battalions, but also other components of the division, which had to exchange men who were "eastern capable" for men who were not. This meant that divisions could lose a battalion-sized number of their best soldiers at one fell swoop.[109] In certain cases, these transfers caused a permanent reduction in the number of battalions in a division. In the autumn of **1943**, several divisions of *AOK 7* surrendered battalions without seeing them reconstituted. Instead, some received battalions of "eastern volunteers", better known as *Osttruppen*, which hardly counted as adequate replacements.[110]

In general, on D-Day, divisions in the west still consisted of a disproportionately large number of both younger and older soldiers, men from *dVL III* and other soldiers deemed unfit for service in the east. But this is only a sweeping observation. Putting it into actual numbers for each individual division is difficult due to a lack of records. Of the six divisions discussed in this book, only basic age statistics have been found for the three (then) static divisions and only for **1943**.[111] This means that understanding German manpower requires considerable reconstruction effort, for which only limited information is available. In the summer of **1944**, Allied intelligence faced the same problem, which it addressed by analysing the tens of thousands captured during that period.[112] Although this gave an overall impression as to age, origin and year of mobilisation, the statistics did not address individual units. It also generally has a bias towards those serving on the frontline and, in consequence, were more likely to be captured. To better understand individual units, the Military Intelligence Research Section (MIRS) also analysed captured pay books for a number of divisions.[113] While useful, this approach is not without its own limitations; the sample sizes vary between divisions and, again, has a bias towards men at the front. For this book, it is also problematic that the *91. LL.D.*, the *265. I.D.* and the *709. I.D.* were not among the divisions covered by the study.

To still be able to address all six divisions, the author has obtained additional information by examining records about men killed in action (KIA)[114] and missing in action (MIA) in the summer of **1944**. Two collections made this possible: The German Red Cross lists from the 1950's of those still missing (*Vermisstenbildliste*) and official war-time "death cards".[115] As is the case with the captured pay books, these two collections are still clearly biased towards men more likely to be at the front, but arguably less so than the MIRS study: Death cards tend to be more complete for those operating behind the front, while the lists of the missing cover all elements of a division, including rear area support units, which were less likely to come into direct contact with Allied ground forces. As such, both data sets provide information the captured pay books are unlikely to deliver. It must still be noted that, as in the MIRS study, the KIA/MIA sample sizes differ between divisions. Bias towards frontline troops also varies as this depends on how the fighting developed, who was committed, the location and the time. When looking at the average age (approached here as "average year of birth") the numbers of the KIA/MIA samples are clearly several years lower than those of **December 1943**.

Since it is unlikely that this difference accurately and fully reflects changes in personnel composition, it should be taken as an indication of the samples' bias. As the MIRS study likely includes a large percentage of pay books obtained from POW's — whereas the KIA/MIA numbers focus on fatalities — the two studies could be complementary to one another as individual years were under/over-represented at different rates among those killed and captured.[116] This nonetheless still means a bias towards frontline troops.

At first glance, the MIRS study may seem to have an advantage over the KIA/MIA numbers, as it was based on larger samples. Yet, a larger sample does not automatically equal a better sample. In fact, the MIRS numbers generally appear to have a stronger bias towards younger personnel than the KIA/MIA approach. The data underlaying the latter allows for a more thorough analysis as birthdays and units can be linked to individuals, while such details are not available for the MIRS study, which merely presents age groups. Age groups, however, can be misleading. This is most apparent for MIRS' important 1910-24 age group. In the six divisions, it accounts for some 40-60% of personnel and covers the 15 year period when men can be considered to be in their military prime. However, upon closer examination using the KIA/MIA numbers, the build-up within this group is remarkably different between the divisions. For example, 19% of the entire *353. I.D.* was born in 1924, while the numbers for that year in the five other divisions vary from less than 1% to 5%. This shows why age groups need to be appropriately sized to be useful. 5-year age groups will be used here as they are deemed more suitable. Since those born in 1924 still included many 19-year-olds on D-Day, that year will be considered part of the youngest age group, which covers 1924-26 (and in rare cases also 1927). This also allows for a more detailed look at these individual years, which are the only ones that stand out in size when looking at the six divisions. Also, at these young ages, two years do make a considerable difference, both physically and in length of military service, making it useful to be able to distinguish between them.

Although the personnel ages of the individual divisions will be covered in more detail in their own chapters, some general observations can already be made. Among the mobile infantry divisions, a difference emerges between the two 25th wave divisions (*77.* and *91.*) on the one hand and the *353. I.D.* on the other. Raised in early **1944**, the former two had about 35% born in or after 1924, while this was up to 52% for the *353. I.D.* Nearly 70% in the *77. I.D.* and the *91. LL.D.* were aged 30 or younger. For the *353. I.D.*, this was almost 80%. Since no earlier personnel statistics have been found, it is difficult to value the samples, but a bias towards frontline troops is to be expected. This is probably less of an issue for the *77. I.D.* where some rear-area elements and staffs were cut off and then killed or captured in mid-June.

The importance of the various age groups in the two static divisions (*265.* and *709. I.D.*) was rather different from the mobile infantry divisions. They stand out with about 55% being more than 30 years old, and only some 45% being 30 or younger. Those born in 1924 or later, nonetheless, still amount to some 23% of all manpower. With nearly all born in 1925 (and 2% in 1924), this percentage was close to the intended 20%. The most difference between the two divisions can be found for the age range of 25-35. Combined, these averaged around 35%, but the number of men in the 25-30 range and 30-35 range differed considerably between the divisions. Here the accuracy of the sample should be questioned, especially for the *265. I.D.*, which only committed a battlegroup to Normandy. This is, however, better discussed in the divisions' own chapters. The two oldest age groups (35-40 and 40+) were again similar in importance between the two divisions and accounted for some 26% and 6% of the men, respectively.

The formerly static *243. I.D.* still retained many characteristics of a static division with only 45% being 30 years old or younger. Yet it had a different spread compared to the two static division: More men of the preferred years of 1919-24 and fewer from 1925 and 1926. In fact, the latter two years do not appear to have reached 20% in this division, despite an expected over-representation in the sample. At 31%, the age group 1909-13 was the largest of the division, followed by 1904-08 (23%). Both of these were close to the *709. I.D.* Compared to the two static divisions, the oldest age group was less significant in the *243. I.D.* and more akin to regular infantry divisions.

	1924	1925	1926
77. ID.	4.9%	19.4%	9.3%*
91. LL.D.	2.2%	31.3%	2.5%
243. I.D.	0.8%	11.4%	1.3%
265. I.D.	1.5%	22.3%	0.8%
353. I.D.	19.0%	6.7%	26.5%
709. I.D.	1.8%	20.7%	0.0%

Table 1: Troops born 1924 or later per division. (Based on 1,525 KIA/MIA. * Incl. 1927)

	Sample Size	Average YOB	≤1903	1904-1908	1909-1913	1914-1918	1919-1923	≥1924
77. I.D.	247	1918	0.8%	9.3%	23.5%	15.8%	17.0%	33.6%
91. LL.D.	278	1918	2.9%	11.5%	15.8%	15.1%	18.%	36.0%
243. I.D.	237	1914	1.3%	22.8%	31.2%	14.3%	16.9%	13.5%
265. I.D.	130	1914	6.2%	26.2%	19.2%	14.6%	9.2%	24.6%
353. I.D.	464	1920	1.9%	7.1%	12.3%	11.9%	14.7%	52.2%
709. I.D.	169	1914	5.3%	25.4%	27.2%	10.1%	9.5%	22.5%

Table 2: Age distribution (Based on 1,525 KIA/MIA)

Mobility

Lack of mobility, particularly motorisation, was a widespread problem in the German armed forces and generally poor among the infantry divisions. Only certain formations within the divisions were motorised, as called for by their *KStN*. Examples include the anti-tank battalions, portions of the infantry anti-tank companies and the signals battalions.[117]

Mobility also varied between different types of infantry divisions, and it was virtually non-existent among the static divisions, which by definition were considered immobile.[118] For example, a static rifle company had just three horses (one for the commander and two for the field kitchen) and six bicycles.[119] This can be compared to a rifle company (new type), which had 27 horses and 3 bicycles (no motor vehicles).[120]

Determining the number of horses in static divisions is difficult, as their organisations tended to be non-standard. For the *265. I.D.*, the authorisation was reported as 1,603 horses.[121] Numbers are not available for the *709. I.D.*, but it probably had 1,600-1,700 horses.[122]

The example of the rifle companies not only illustrates the lack of mobility in a static division, but shows that even a new type rifle company relied almost entirely on horse transport and movement on foot.[123] This also applied to the *Inf.Div.44*. In these divisions, despite being considered fully capable of displacement on their own, motorisation was limited to certain elements. Most men still marched on foot and much of the artillery and heavy equipment was horse-drawn, limiting the divisions' mobility. This dependency on horses is obvious from the example given by the *OKH* for

Throughout the war, German infantry divisions relied heavily on horses for transportation. This applied to almost all elements, including artillery, infantry and supply. The vehicles used included a wide variety of wagons, carts and limbers. Here we see an Ersatzfeldwagen 40 or 43 that was captured in the area of St. Côme-du-Mont after D-Day. (NARA)

a "standard", albeit somewhat understrength, *Infanterie-Division 44*.[124] These divisions required 802 riding horses, as well as 2,535 regular, 523 heavy, and 119 very heavy draught horses, for a total of 3,797 horses. The divisions also had 1,365 horse-drawn wagons and carts. Another 498 carts were not directly horse-drawn, but could be coupled to those that were. For various purposes there were also 728 bicycles. This does not mean there was no motorisation, but it was limited: 154 motorcycles, 14 *Kettenkräder*, 167 (staff) cars, 370 lorries, 10 assault guns, 9 buses, 58 *RSO's*, 10 halftrack lorries (*Maultiere*), and 3 halftracked prime movers.[125] The numbers for a 25th wave division were considerably lower: 2,495 horses, 125 motorcycles, 12 *Kettenkräder*, 161 (staff) cars, 283 lorries, 26 *RSO's*, 2 *Maultiere*, 4 buses, and 16 halftracked prime movers. Much of this was due to having a smaller complement of artillery.[126]

Mobility problems were not just a matter of quantity, but they were also affected by quality and variety. In **July 1943**, the *709. I.D.* had 320 motor vehicles of an astounding 180 different types.[127] Even if these vehicles were new, the maintenance of so many types must have been a logistical nightmare.

The limited mobility of German infantry divisions — static divisions in particular — made it more difficult to move elements or send in reinforcements. To remedy this, the *LXXXIV. A.K.* established a motor vehicle company (*Kf. Kp. 84*) in mid-**1942** to provide the division and corps reserves with better transportation. In this manner, certain elements received (non-organic) semi-permanent motorisation support.[128] Still, when reserves had to be transferred outside the corps area, additional vehicles would have to be commandeered from the divisions without regard to their needs.[129] If still insufficient, vehicles would also be provided by other armed forces or *OT* elements.[130]

This situation lasted until late **1943**, when a programme to improve mobility of some infantry elements was introduced as a result of *Führer Directive No. 51* (**3 November**). The directive called for a counterattack to hit an invasion with massive force. It was therefore critical to build the available division-sized forces into high grade, offensive and fully mobile formations. This was to be achieved by the rapid allocation of sufficient troops and equipment and via vigorous training. Counterattacks would enable these forces to parry any expansion of the enemy beachhead(s) prior to hurling them back into the sea. Such an approach might call for bringing up troops from coastal sectors that had not been attacked.[131] It would, however, take considerable effort to turn such elements into ad hoc assault formations.

On **8 November** *Ob.West* informed its senior commanders of the *Führer Directive* and its implications. Like other major commands under *Ob.West*, *AOK 7* was instructed to propose which coastal divisions would immediately begin preparations to be made mobile. It was always understood that this would only allow a limited number of divisions to attain that status. Even so, *AOK 7* was ordered to select a minimum of two divisions.[132] Three days later, *AOK 7* proposed the *243.* and the *346. I.D.* for increased mobility. In addition, the field army pointed out that preparations had also been made, circumstances permitting, to withdraw further divisions from the coast.[133]

Although motorisation was preferred, it simply could not be achieved with the available vehicles. On **11 November**, *AOK 7* informed *Ob.West* that there were insufficient resources to provisionally make both divisions mobile, at the same time. An additional two-thirds of the tonnage required for a single division was still needed.[134] Of course, many vehicles also had to be assigned to divisions that were being formed in the field army's area of responsibility, meaning that the demand for vehicles was considerably higher than just the requirement for increased mobility.

The overall process to enhance the mobility of formations is covered by the general term *Beweglichmachung*.[135] It refers to measures taken to increase mobility above that of the *KStN*. This additional mobility could involve horses, bicycles and motorisation, the latter often in a field-expedient fashion (*behelfsmäßig*). Charts that show these efforts for certain elements typically list them as bicycle or (partially) motorised formations. When no symbols are shown it means that additional horse transportation was received or planned.

The equipment needed was, by definition, non-organic and did not affect the organisation. This means that units could look the same on paper but have a different organisation. This mobility enhancement was sometimes identified on organisational documents by adding (*Bew.*) to an element's designation. The differences between units is also reflected in the definitions used by *AOK 7* in **April 1944**.[136]

For example, there were differences between fully motorised units, which had organic mobility, and similar units outfitted with additional vehicles. This also applied to (organic and non-organic) partially motorised units. In addition to motor vehicles, mobility efforts could include horses and horse-drawn vehicles. Bicycle units could have organic mobility but also improved mobility with motorised trains. There were also formations that received bicycles but were only considered "bicycle mobile", and not actual bicycle units. These did not have motorised trains.[137]

The fighting elements of some units could also be loaded onto lorries or other motor vehicles (*verlastet*) and transferred by transport columns. This particular method of transport could even include their horses and horse-drawn vehicles. It still resulted in limited mobility on arrival and required support from local commands until support elements arrived. In case horses of combat units were not brought along, these could be replaced by a provisionally motorised trains element, which would then remain with the unit after its arrival.[138]

Since these efforts concerned mobility beyond the existing *KStN*'s, practical problems arose. Drivers were needed, but the *KStN*'s did not allow for such personnel. This may seem like a minor issue, but it was a serious problem. The enhanced mobility of an entire static division required 1,000 men as drivers and related jobs, and all of them had to be drawn from the divisional troops, seriously reducing their combat strength.[139] When units with (*KStN*) horses were upgraded to motor vehicles, the former horse elements could, in theory, provide drivers. Yet, the (non-organic) motor vehicles were by no means guaranteed to stay, and many units had to keep their horse transport in reserve. This meant that personnel for the motor vehicles still had to be taken from the combat troops.[140] Detailed orders to address this problem were not issued until **7 May 1944**.[141]

Although some static divisions in *H.Gr. B* were made mobile in a provisional fashion, they did not attain the mobility of a regular infantry division. These formerly static divisions were capable of movement but ill-suited for mobile warfare given their *ad hoc* mobility, problematic interaction between units and significantly lower number of vehicles (only about 70%) compared a regular infantry division.[142] One exception was the *243. I.D.* It acquired special status and underwent modifications to transform it from a static status to being fit for mobile deployment (*beweglicher Einsatz*), which included a motorised artillery regiment. As a result of the improvements, the division's artillery was superior in mobility to a regular infantry division.[143]

In **February 1944**, the mobility efforts were extended to include divisions of the 21st through 25th waves, which were already considered fully mobile by nature, even if that largely meant moving by foot and horse transport. In the *AOK 7* sector, this was the *77.*, *275.*, the *352.*, and the *353. I.D.* In each division an infantry regiment, the fusilier battalion (if available), the engineer battalion and a supply platoon would receive bicycles.[144]

A document dated **12 May 1944** illustrates the organisational disparity between the divisions of the *7. Armee* by listing the *Beweglichmachungs-Tonnage* — the mobility tonnage above that of the *KStN*. The *243. I.D.* had 1,180-tonnes; the *709. I.D.* 144-tonnes; the *353. I.D.* 76-tonnes; the *77. I.D.*, however, was still short 60% of its *KStN* tonnage.[145] Yet it should be pointed out that these numbers are misleading, because all these divisions had a different base organisational document. Still, the figures for the two static divisions reveal a great disparity between the 243. and the 709. I.D. The numbers also illustrate the fact that, except for the *243. I.D.*, additional mobility was quite minimal. The equipment available was simply not enough to outfit all subordinate elements, let alone divisions. Ultimately, mobility was only augmented for a small proportion of most divisions. In certain cases, these were used to form a mobile *Kampfgruppe*. In this way, the *Beweglichmachung* and formation of *Kampfgruppen* often went hand in hand.

Kampfgruppen

The defence of the *Atlantikwall* presented German commanders with a serious dilemma: The wall had to be manned along its entire length, but any landing would only attack a small section. With but a limited number of troops, forces were thinly spread. As a result, rapid reinforcement would be needed to stop an invasion, if it were not stopped on the beaches[146]. An order from **March 1944** again emphasised the urgency of this problem:[147]

Experiences from the fighting in Italy show it is crucial to quickly deploy mobile and strong formations against enemy landings.

Following *Führer* Directive No. 51, some static divisions started their conversion to fully mobile formations, but this could not be achieved for all of them. Even if it had been possible, their own sectors still needed to be defended against additional landings. A partial answer to this was the formation of *Kampfgruppen* within divisions, usually a reinforced infantry regiment. The war diary of *AOK 7* records this process with the battlegroups and the efforts to make them mobile being among the most discussed topics in the months preceding the invasion. Initiatives to increase the mobility and strength of the divisions were made with the divisional battlegroup taking precedence over the rest of the division.

The emphasis placed on the *Kampfgruppen* (and mobile divisions) was further reinforced by the thorough preparations made to rapidly despatch them to the front. Rail transportation was preferred and detailed plans were drawn up, with the transfer of each force receiving a code name.[148] Loading of trains was also practised to minimise the loss of time when things turned serious.[149]

Since railway problems were likely to arise in an invasion, plans also had to be established for motor transportation. This was not an easy task due to the lack of vehicles. Unless a solution was found, the only alternative would be movement by foot, horse or bicycle. As one measure, special motor transport companies were organised to provide transportation as needed. This allowed some flexibility as a limited reserve for transportation. Such a company already existed in the *LXXXIV. A.K.*, while the formation of one in the *XXV. A.K.* got underway in **November 1943**. In some cases, the (re)organisation of these transport units meant that some units within divisions again lost their motorisation.[150]

The formation of battlegroups was vital for static divisions and divisions that were still forming. For static divisions, a mobile *Kampfgruppe* enabled elements to support other sectors. Since these divisions were largely deployed on the coast, pulling out an infantry regiment meant that a large sector would have to be taken over by the remaining troops. A practical solution was found by building an ad hoc infantry regiment using forces from several other regiments.[151] This would leave smaller areas to be taken over by the remaining regiments, making the preparations simpler. It also meant that more anti-tank and infantry gun companies could be included in the *Kampfgruppe* — even at the cost of weakening the rest of the division. An example of this is the *Kampfgruppe* of the *265. I.D.*, which took all of the division's mobile regimental anti-tank guns.

This organisation of *Kampfgruppen* from bits and pieces of an entire division may give a false impression of a lack of coherence. For example, the organisation of *Kampfgruppe 265* was completed by early **February 1944** and changed little over time. A regimental headquarters was in charge of the force, while its artillery was under the command of one of the division's battalions. All in all, the division's battlegroup was a well-organised formation and even received training to operate as an integrated force.[152]

The divisions of the 21st to 25th waves, which were formed between the autumn of **1943** and the invasion, already had battlegroups well before the mobility measures began to affect them. It was standard practice that divisions, in the early phases of being established or reconstituted, were ordered to organise their combat-ready elements into *Kampfgruppen* that could be used in an emergency. The latest examples of this in the *7. Armee* area were the *77.* and *275. I.D.*, but this applied earlier to the *352.* and the *353. I.D.*, and to other divisions earlier in the war.[153] As these divisions approached their authorised strength and mobility, their need for the battlegroups largely disappeared as the invasion drew nearer.

In a *Kampfgruppe* (or division), one of the infantry battalions was typically selected as the advance guard (*Voraus-Bataillon*), the spearhead with the best mobility. If available, this would be the fusilier battalion. Barring that, it was one of the regular infantry battalions.[154] Unfortunately, much of the planned mobility of the advance guard was eliminated before the invasion. In **February 1944**, these battalions were still intended to be motorised;[155] but by early **May**, this had been reduced to bicycles with only a motorised trains element.[156] After **19 May**, it was even considered that the trains would forego their motorisation in favour of horse transportation.[157] To what extent these changes were implemented in the short period before the invasion is not clear.

In **May 1944**, dedicated *Kampfgruppen* remained only in the *77.*, the *265.*, the *266.* and the *275. I.D.* For the *77.*, the *266.*, the *243.*, the *352.* the *353. I.D.* and the *91. LL.D.*, it was also possible to move the entire division, while the *343.*, the *709.*, and the *716. I.D.* were no longer earmarked to furnish mobile reinforcements at all.

Infantry on the Cotentin

The existence of *Kampfgruppen* helps to explain which reinforcements were sent to the front shortly after the invasion and, to a point, how they were used. The *265.*, the *266.* and the *275. I.D.* quickly deployed their *Kampfgruppen*. The latter two (initially) supported the *352. I.D.*, while *KG 265* was at the base of the Cotentin. Although the entire *353. I.D.* was sent to Normandy, its unbalanced levels of mobility meant that some units reached the front before others, resulting in formation of a battlegroup as a consequence rather than as a planned intention. Moreover, this battlegroup reinforced the *352. I.D.*, while the remainder of the division was at the base of the Cotentin peninsula. Another reinforcement for the Cotentin was the entire *77. I.D.*

The author hopes this introduction to German infantry divisions has provided a better understanding of their characteristics and the problems they faced before and during the fighting. Along with the *91. LL.D.* and the *243.* and the *709. I.D.*, which had all been deployed on the Cotentin on D-Day, the *77.* and the *353. I.D.* and *KG 265* provided the bulk of the German infantry that fought on the peninsula. Additional infantry came from three separate battalions: *Sturmbataillon AOK 7, Maschinengewehr-Bataillon 17* and *Festungs-Stamm-Abteilung LXXXIV*. While all of these divisions will all be examined in this book, the three battalions will be covered in a future volume, as will the eastern troops. Eight eastern (infantry) battalions participated in the fighting on the Cotentin, many of which were attached to, or even incorporated into, infantry divisions. *Gren.Rgt. zbV 752*, a heterogeneous collection of security forces and *Osttruppen*, will also be covered alongside these formations, since it had a similar background.

The variety of motor vehicles used by the Wehrmacht is well illustrated by this collection point on the Cotentin. Note the Renault UE tractor and woodgas truck on either side of the ambulance and the (tracked) RSO on the left front. (NARA)

77. Infanterie-Division

The *77. Infanterie-Division* was formed on **15 January 1944** as part of the 25th wave. It was built around elements stationed at Münsingen in Military District V (Württemberg and Baden), which would also provide replacements for the division.[158] Later that month it moved to France and *AOK 7* was given responsibility for forming the division.[159] After its formation near Caen, the division moved to St. Malo in late **April**-early **May**, staying in the area until shortly after D-Day.[160] As one of the divisions closest to the invasion front, it was among the first reinforcements sent to Normandy.[161]

The division's first commander was *Gen.Lt.* Walter Poppe, who took command on **11 February**.[162] On **25 April**, he was succeeded by *Gen.Lt.* Bruno Ortner, who was only technically in charge for about a week and appears never to have actually taken up the assignment.[163] On **1 May**, *Gen. Maj.* Rudolf Stegmann was appointed the new commander.[164] The general would lead the division until his death on **18 June**.[165] He was succeeded by *Obst.* Rudolf Bacherer, one of the regimental commanders.[166] In **August**, the remnants of the division were destroyed in the fighting in and around St. Malo and Bacherer was taken prisoner.[167]

As the division's formation largely took place in the sector of *AOK 7*, the field army's war diary offers detailed information on its organisation and problems encountered during the formation process. Its transfer to Bretagne and return to Normandy after the invasion is covered by both field army and *LXXIV. A.K.* records.

After the war *Gen.Lt.* Poppe wrote an overview of the division's history as part of the Foreign Military Studies. For the period after his transfer, his study appears mostly based on information provided by the divisional intelligence officer, *Oblt.d.R.* Schreihage, with additional information from the operations officer, *Obstlt.i.G.* Seiffert. Although largely written from memory and lacking detail, it provides a useful overview of the division's operations. Some additional information can be found in a brief account by Schreihage, which was used in a book written by the corps intelligence officer of the *LXXXIV. A.K.* Among the handful of other records is a combat report from one of the regiments, written by its adjutant. While this was probably a reconstruction, it offers details that cannot be found elsewhere, even though it appears to be written largely from memory (with the help of some official documents and perhaps personal notes). Taken together, these records allow for a reasonably thorough assessment of the division, although details of the actual fighting remain scarce. This applies to both its operations in Normandy and the final engagements in Bretagne.

Left: Gen.Lt. Poppe was the first commander of the division. (BArch, PERS 6/300364)

Centre: Gen.Maj. Stegmann commanded the division during its first battles in June.

Right: Obst. Bacherer assumed command of the divisions after Stegmann's death. He had been awarded his Knight's Cross in October 1943 and would receive Oakleaves for his actions in Normandy. (BArch, MSG 2/7759)

Organisation and Equipment

The six divisions of the 25th wave shared a similar background. All were formed around an existing reinforced regiment.[168] Although some were officially raised in Germany, five of the divisions were formed elsewhere. One was established in Norway (*89. I.D.*), two under *AOK 15* (*84.* and *85. I.D.*), one largely under Supreme Command Southwest in Italy (*92. I.D.*) and one in Germany (*91. I.D.*).[169] The *77. I.D.* was the only one to be formed in the area of *AOK 7*. The core personnel for the new division were provided by the reinforced *GR 1021*; this formation's combat elements consisted of an infantry regiment with three battalions, an artillery battalion with two batteries and an engineer company.[170]

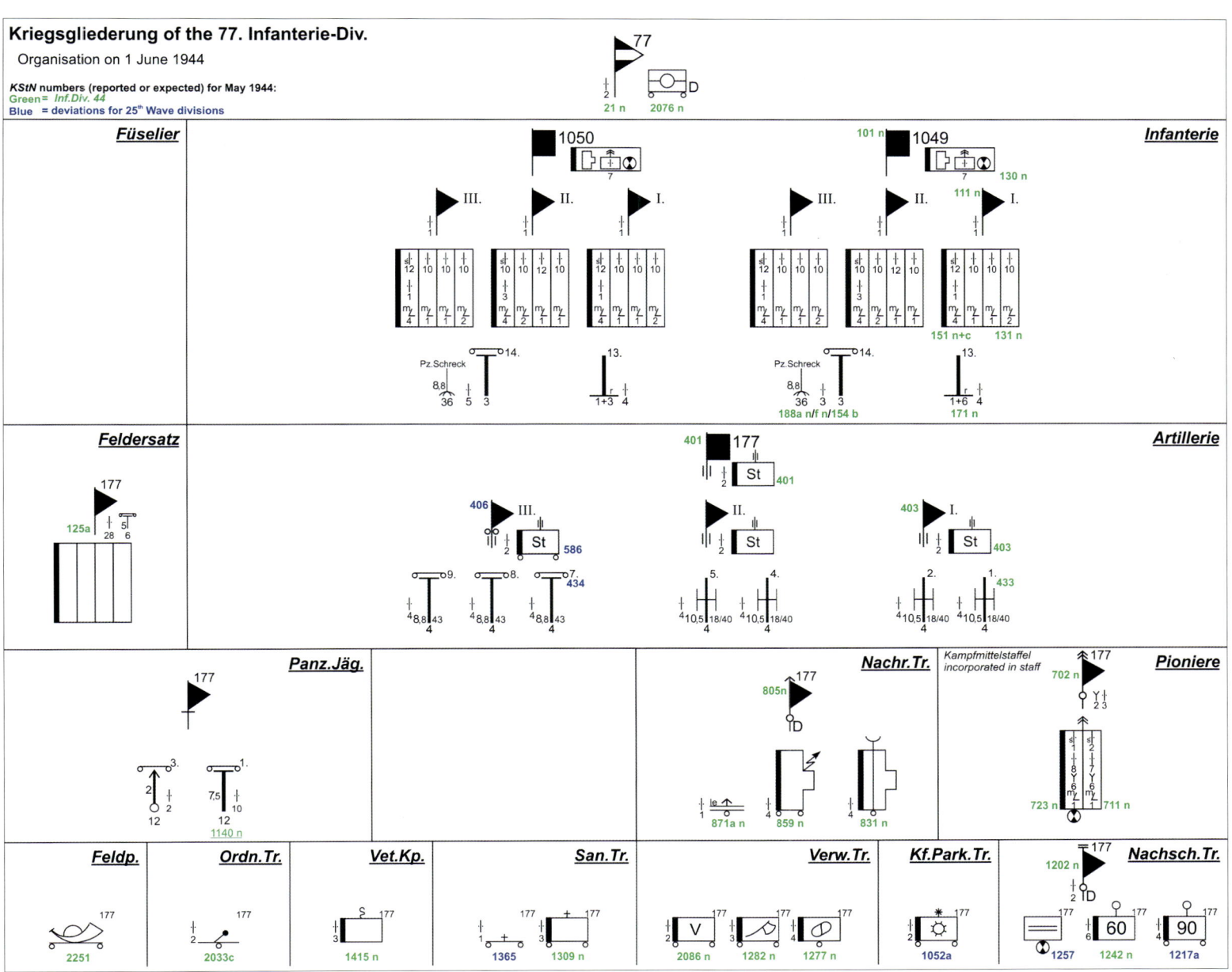

On D-Day the 77.I.D. was a prime example of a 25th Wave division but it was not yet fully formed. Especially the latest changes ordered to increase its strength had not yet been carried out.

The regiment's arrival at the *LXXXIV. A.K.* had been anticipated since early **January**. The corps had been informed that it would be attached to it upon arrival. At this time, it was still a separate formation, but it would be subordinated to the *709. I.D.*[171] As such, the corps headquarters intended to deploy the regiment behind the northern sector of the west coast of the Cotentin.[172] On **15 January**, however, the regiment was given a new destination: The area west and south of Caen.[173] Three days later, *AOK 7* informed the corps that it would establish the *77. I.D.* in that area.[174] The regiment, which had yet to arrive, was already absorbed by the new division. In addition to *GR 1021*, the divisional and artillery headquarters of the disbanded *355. I.D.*, along with various support elements, were to be used to form the division.[175] These had been intended to form the *364. I.D.* (21st wave), but its formation was never completed and elements reassigned to the *77. I.D.*[176] The remainder of the troops came from a variety of sources.[177] All of the formations, with the exception of the infantry regiments, were redesignated and received the number "177".[178]

The *AOK 7* war diary of **9 February 1944** records an order to *AOK 7* for establishing the division: *Befehl für Aufstellung der 77. Inf.Div. (25. Welle)*. This document provides detailed information concerning the division's organisation, the elements involved, and the *KStN* numbers. The field army was given the task of getting the division ready for deployment by **15 April**, with the organisational buildup to be completed by **1 March**.[179] The base organisation documents used for divisions of the 25th wave resulted in some of the weakest infantry divisions of the war, considerably weaker than the *Inf. Div. n.A.*[180] (Allied intelligence referred to them as "pocket divisions".) In light of these differences, it is important to examine the theoretical organisation of the division before analysing its actual situation on D-Day.

The division had an authorised strength of just two infantry regiments (*GR 1049* and *GR 1050*), while an *Inf.Div.n.A.* would have three. The former was the redesignated *GR 1021*, while the latter used the headquarters and headquarters company of *GR 336*.[181] *GR 336* originally belonged to the *161. I.D.*, but it had been subordinated to the *355. I.D.* for some time.[182] The battalions in *GR 1050* were drawn from the *364. I.D.*; the *I.* and *II./973* became the *I.* and *II./1050*, respectively, while its third battalion was formed from *Füs.Btl. 364*.[183] The division also received two companies from *GR 1032*, which was used to build divisions of the 25th wave.[184]

The two regiments of a 25th wave division each had three battalions instead of two (two being standard with the *Inf.Div.n.A.*). The battalions boasted the

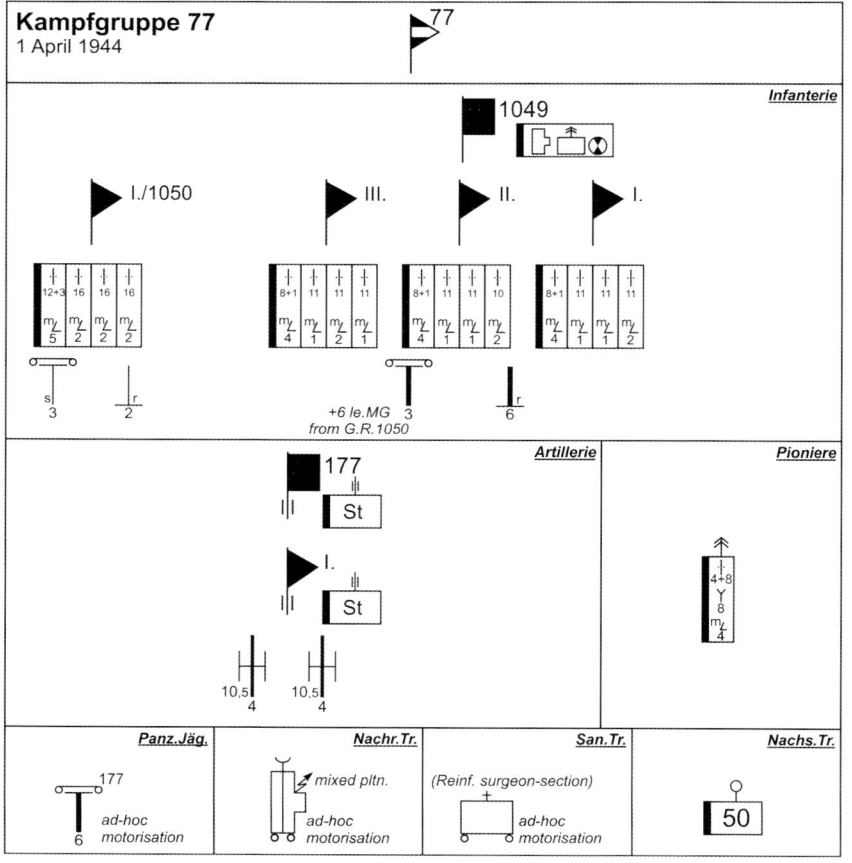

As was standard practice, the combat-ready elements of the division were formed into a Kampfgruppe as soon as possible. As the division grew in size and strength the battlegroup decreased in importance.

same standard organisation of three rifle companies and one heavy company and were based on the same *KStN*'s as regular infantry divisions. The rifle companies were to be equipped with 16 light MG's and two medium mortars; the heavy (MG) companies would receive six medium mortars, three light MG's and 12 heavy MG's.[185] In the spring of **1944**, the *KStN*'s for these types of companies were changed: The rifle companies would now have two heavy MG's (taken from the MG company) and 13 light MG's, while mortars were removed from the rifle companies and assigned to the heavy company. The plan was to have six medium and four heavy mortars per heavy company, as well as six heavy MG's and three light MG's. If heavy mortars were not available, there would be an additional six medium mortars instead.[186]

Infantry regiments in divisions of the 25th wave also possessed heavy weapons companies. In a similar fashion to the *Inf.Div.n.A.*, the plans called for the 13th Company to be equipped with two heavy and six light infantry guns and five light MG's. The 14th Company was an infantry anti-tank company, outfitted with one motorised AT platoon of three *7,5 cm Pak 40*'s and two tank destruction platoons (*Panzerzerstörer-Züge*) with 18 *Ofenrohre* (*Panzerschrecks*) each. These companies also had six light MG's.[187]

Similar to a division of the 25th wave, an *Inf.Div.n.A.* also had six infantry battalions, yet these were distributed over three regiments.[188] This meant that divisions of the 25th wave saved a regimental headquarters and headquarters company and two heavy weapons companies, resulting in a lower ratio of heavy weapons to infantry since they used the same *KStN*'s.[189] Despite having six infantry battalions, the infantry strength of the *77. I.D.* was below that of a standard *Inf.Div.n.A.* or *44*; and although 25th wave divisions were supposed to eventually have a fusilier battalion and a field-replacement battalion, the original organisational documents for these divisions accounted for neither.[190] On **25 May**, however, *Ob.West* was ordered to form these battalions for the four 25th wave divisions, which included the *77. I.D.*[191] On **30 July**, the plans were cancelled once again due to the situation in Normandy and personnel shortages.[192] No information on a fusilier battalion has been found, but a field-replacement battalion had been formed within the division.

As with many recently formed divisions, initial plans did not call for an anti-tank battalion, but only for a single anti-tank company: *Pz.Jg.Kp. 177*. This company would be armed with 12 motorised heavy AT guns and 13 light MG's. As usual it would follow *KStN 1140n*, resulting in four platoons, each with three guns. Personnel were to be gleaned from divisions of the 21st wave, which were transitioning from a single divisional towed AT company to a full AT battalion without towed anti-tank guns.[193] Personnel from *Pz.Jg.Kp. 352* (*352. I.D.*) were indeed transferred to the *77. I.D.* on **11 March**.[194]

The divisional artillery was *Art.Rgt. 177*. Its regimental headquarters was formed from *AR 355*, while the *II./AR 355* and *Art.Abt. 1021* would become the *II.* and *I./AR 177*, respectively. The 3rd Battalion would be a new formation.[195]

Because *AR 177* belonged to a division of the 25th wave, it was relatively weak. It would only have two light battalions instead of the typical three. This in itself was not a problem, as there only were two infantry regiments (albeit with three battalions) to support, but the battalions would only field two batteries each, rather than three. Although the motorised "heavy" battalion (3rd Battalion) would have three batteries, it would not be allocated the usual heavy howitzers. Each battalion would have a headquarters battery, in addition to the one at the regiment. In the battalions, each headquarters battery was issued with two MG's, while the regimental headquarters battery had just one. All the gun batteries were equipped with four howitzers or cannons and five MG's. As in most infantry divisions, the light battalions were horse-drawn, which restricted their mobility.[196] As there were only two batteries per battalion, the regiment had only 16 *10,5 cm le.F.H.18/40*'s, instead of the 36 in an *Inf.Div.n.A.* or *Inf.Div.44*.[197]

This problem was partially addressed by an updated organisational document for 25th wave divisions. No extra battalion or batteries were authorised, but the divisions' artillery battalions were authorised six guns per battery instead of the usual four.[198] This development is noted in the records of the staff of the artillery inspectorate at *OKH*, which state that batteries with six guns were considered impractical. Still, the novel idea would be tested by four divisions of the 25th wave (*77., 84., 85.* and *92. I.D.*). The reorganisation was to be carried out before **15 July**. The orders were issued on **5 June**, but cancelled on **22 June**.[199] As a result, the *77. I.D.* fought in Normandy with the typical four guns per battery.

There were no changes to the *III./AR 177* before the invasion. The initial organisation document had already called for a motorised battalion with three batteries, each equipped with four 8.8 cm AT guns, although the guns could also be *Flak*, depending on availability.[200] Again, this was typical among divisions of the 25th wave. Although the number of guns was identical to the heavy battalion in the *Inf.Div.n.A.*, the choice of 8.8 cm guns was in contrast to the standard *15 cm s.F.H.18*.

The orders from **5 June** and the revised base document reveal the intention to reequip these battalions (*77., 84., 85.* and *92. I.D.*) with *s.F.H.18's*, although the orders specified that only the 7th and 8th Batteries were to be reequipped.[201] On **22 June**, this reorganisation was rescinded for the *77. I.D.*[202] Like the expansion of the light batteries, planning was overtaken by events.

The final combat formation in the base document was *Pi.Btl. 177*. It consisted of just two companies, one with bicycles. The battalion headquarters and ordnance section were partly motorised and armed with four light MG's. Each company was to have six flamethrowers, two heavy MG's, nine light MG's and two medium mortars.[203]

A regular *Inf.Div.n.A.* or *44* was authorised three engineer companies, and the organisation of the 25th wave divisions was later updated to three.[204] On **25 May**, *Ob.West* ordered the formation of these third companies for its four 25th wave divisions.[205] Although the orders were cancelled on **30 July**, there are indications that the formation of a *3./Pi.Btl. 177* had started.[206]

Having established the theoretical organisation of the *77. I.D.*, it is easier to understand its condition on D-Day. The actual combat organisation (*Kriegsgliederung*) of **1 June** offers the last known overview of the division and will form the basis of the strength of the division's units. It is part of the monthly status report (*Zustandsbericht*), which provides additional details on manpower, armament and other equipment.[207] Figures also exist for the situation on **1 May** and help us to understand some of the developments that took place in the month or so prior to the invasion.[208]

Additionally, information obtained from prisoners offers details that cannot be found in official records. Although these often cannot be confirmed or conflict, some are included for interest, particularly when they indicate deviations from the situation on paper.

On **1 June**, the division reported a strength of 10,257 men. There were 246 officers, a shortage of 25; 1,573 NCO's, a shortfall of 232; and 7,395 men, a surplus of 610. The number of foreign volunteers (*Hilfswillige / Hiwi's*) was 1,400, four above the authorised strength.[209] The authorised numbers may be too low, as they do not reflect the formation of a new battalion: *Feld-Ers. Btl. 177*. Not counting the headquarters and supply company, it would have

required 750 NCO's and men in replacements alone. Yet it is still interesting to compare these figures to those of **1 April**, when the division had 588 German personnel above the authorised levels and a shortfall of 1,222 *Hiwi*'s, indicating that a significant number of the latter had arrived over a two-month period.[210]

As can be expected, most of the men came from Military District V, mainly Ulm and Konstanz.[211] Because of its origins there, the division was more formally known as the *Württembergisch-Badische 77. I.D.* (Württemberg - Baden).[212]

The available records do not allow for a full understanding of the age build-up of the division. An analysis of 247 KIA/MIA[213] shows that 34% were 20 years old or younger (born in or after 1924), 33% were 20-30, and another 33% were 30-40. The group more than 40 years old (born 1903 and earlier) came in at less than 1%. Those of the preferred age of 20-35 made up 56% of the division and were leaning somewhat towards the older age group (about 42% of the combined age group).

	≤1903	1904-1908	1909-1913	1914-1918	1919-1923	1924	1925	≥1926
KIA/MIA	0.8%	9.3%	23.5%	15.8%	17.0%	4.9%	19.4%	9.3%

Table 1: Age distribution in the *77. I.D.* (Based on 247 KIA/MIA)

The MIRS numbers, based on a study of no less than 1,454 pay books, varied somewhat from the KIA/MIA figures.[214] The exact bias of the two samples is difficult to establish. Being cut off in mid-June, certain headquarters and rear-area elements came into contact with American ground forces. As a result, both the MIRS and KIA/MIA numbers may better represent the division as a whole than for most divisions, where such elements remained well behind the front. Even so, about 70% of the KIA/MIA sample concerns personnel from the infantry regiments, which contained only roughly half the division's manpower. To what extent the MIRS study is more balanced is impossible to say without the underlaying data, but its higher percentages of young personnel could suggest an even stronger bias towards frontline troops. Still, except for the 1910-24 group, the differences between the samples are relatively small and both can be used as an indication of the division's general age build-up.

	Sample size	≤1909	1910-1924	1925	≥1926
MIRS	1,454	16.5%	49.2%	22.1%	12.2%
KIA/MIA	247	14.2%	57.1%	19.4%	9.3%
Difference	1207	-2.3%	7.9%	-2.7%	-2.9%

Table 2: Comparison of age groups in the *77. I.D.* between MIRS and KIA/MIA numbers.

On **1 June**, the division had 439 MG's, a shortfall of 35 (71 heavy MG's and 368 light ones). The authorised levels of AT guns and artillery was 31 and 17, respectively; of these, 30 and 16 were available. Some of these deficiencies were apparently due to the new field-replacement battalion, which increased the authorised levels of both AT guns and artillery by one.[215] The authorised levels for these two categories may seem odd, but the artillery regiment was equipped with 12 AT guns in its 3rd Battalion. This raised the expected number of AT guns in the division and reduced the number of artillery pieces. The report does not specify a shortage of mortars and infantry guns, although these figures were reported on **1 May**. At that time, the division only had 48 mortars although it was authorised 76. There were only 8 light infantry guns, instead of 12, and none of the 4 heavy infantry guns.[216] Two heavy infantry guns arrived before 1 June, but the number of mortars had still not increased by then. Due to formation of the field-replacement battalion, the mortar deficiency must have increased by another 12.[217]

The division's on-hand small-arms weaponry included: 5,039 rifles, 565 *G41* self-loading rifles, 65 sniper rifles, 90 rifle-grenade-launchers, 490 machine pistols and 1,825 pistols. This still left a shortage of weapons. A considerable number of these had already been allocated, but had yet to arrive: 1,360 *K98k* rifles, 100 *G41* and 211 *G43* self-loading rifles, 75 sniper rifles, 4 *7,62 cm I.KH.290(r)'s* (German designation for the Soviet 7.62 cm field piece) and 2 *s.I.G.33's*.[218]

The order of battle shows that, as per the *KStN*, there were two MG's with the divisional headquarters.[219] This is confirmed by members of the division, who stated that there was a bicycle platoon, which could use lorries for long distances.[220] This is unexpected, since such a unit was neither part of the orders from **February** nor the *KStN,* and it is not listed on the base document of **1 June**. If this platoon did exist, it may have been the start of the fusilier battalion. Without more information, it cannot be ruled out that it was in fact the bicycle platoon from a regimental headquarters company.

Some detailed information is available regarding the vehicles of the division's operations staff. Reportedly, *General* Stegmann used a *Kfz. 21* and the *Ia* had both a *Volkswagen* and a Jaguar at his disposal. In addition, there were eight other staff vehicles, three lorries, a command vehicle (a modified bus) and a map-printing vehicle for the division's map section.[221]

On **1 June**, both *GR 1049* (*Obst.* Bacherer) and *GR 1050* (*Obst.* Brandt) were not yet fully equipped. In each battalion, most of the three rifle companies had just 10 MG's and one medium mortar. Exceptions to this were the *6./1049* with 12 MG's, while the *1.* and *9./1049* and the *9./1050* had two mortars. All six MG companies were equipped with four medium mortars and 13 MG's. In the 2nd Battalion of each regiment, these companies had 10 heavy MG's and three light MG's, while the other companies had 12 heavy MG's and 1 light MG. On **1 May**, the *6./1049* was listed with bicycles but a month later none of the companies were shown as bicycle units.[222]

In both regiments, the headquarters company included engineer, signals and bicycle platoons.[223] According to an officer in *GR 1049*, the headquarters company in his regiment was commanded by an officer, assisted by a number of lower ranks. The company headquarters section leader was a *Feldwebel*. There was also a first sergeant, a medical NCO, a despatch rider with a bicycle, 2 messengers without bicycles, 2 clerks, a paymaster, an assistant armourer, 2 field cooks, a rations man and 15 drivers. Company transportation consisted of 23 horses and 7-10 wagons.[224] There were reportedly three lorries in the headquarters company of *GR 1050*.[225]

Each headquarters company had eight light MG's.[226] According to the order of battle of **1 May**, the engineer platoon in each regiment had seven light MG's, although the base document of **1 June** simply shows eight MG's for the entire company.[227] The large number of MG's in the engineer platoon is largely supported by prisoners. Reportedly, these platoons had three sections, each subdivided into two half sections. Each half section had a MG, for a total of six. Other weapons in the sections consisted mainly of *K98k* rifles and some machine pistols. There was very little engineer equipment available, most of which had to be borrowed. One account notes that the sections consisted of one officer and 12 men. The number of men may be correct but the section leaders were undoubtedly NCO's.[228] The bicycle platoon was listed without heavy weapons.[229] Prisoners stated it had a strength of 30 men and comprised three sections. All the men had bicycles. It is also claimed that the platoon had three light MG's, while the rest of the weaponry was *K98k* rifles.[230] Little is known about the signals platoon. It reportedly used backpack wireless (*Tornister-Funkgerät k* aka a *Karl Gerät*). For telephone communication there were two 10-line switchboards.[231]

The battalion headquarters were listed with just one MG each, which corresponds to the *KStN*.[232] Men from the division stated that these staffs included a messenger section, a signals section and transport. Combined, the battalion headquarters reportedly had a strength of 34 men.[233] Compared to the *KStN*, this was low. Although the battalions were horse-drawn, there were other forms of transport available. For example, the battalion headquarters of the *I./1050* had a motorcycle, a staff car and 10 bicycles, which corresponds closely to the *KStN*.[234]

As previously stated, each battalion had three rifle companies and one MG company.[235] The rifle companies were organised into three platoons with three sections each.[236] Mortars are rarely mentioned by the men. Reportedly, they were organised into a mortar section in addition to the regular platoons, in line with the old *KStN's*.[237] The sections in the rifle platoons had a strength of one NCO and seven or eight men and were armed with a light *MG 42*, a machine pistol, a grenade launcher and rifles. Some magnetic hollow-charge anti-tank charges (*Hafthohlladungen*) were available, although the reported numbers varied from one per platoon to one per section.[238] An officer from the *1./1050* said that all companies in his battalion had anti-tank mines, although he did not know how many. His own company had 20.[239] In action, *Faustpatronen* (a type of single-shot hollow-charge anti-tank weapons, often referred to as the *Panzerfaust*) were issued to several companies, but it is not possible to say to which and in what quantity.[240]

There were three MG platoons and one mortar platoon in the MG companies. Each MG platoon had two sections. These were led by an NCO in charge of 10 men. Each section had two heavy *MG 42's* and personal weapons, including one machine pistol, six rifles and six pistols.[241] Little information is available for the mortar platoons, but they apparently had four to six medium mortars.[242]

Information about the personnel composition of the infantry battalions is vague, and figures vary in detail and numbers, which raises serious doubts as to their reliability. The companies in the *III./1050* supposedly varied in strength from 123 to 185 men;[243] conversely, the *2./1049* had a strength of just 100 men. The men in this company ranged in age from 18 to 37; of these, one third were Poles, and there were 15 Russians, presumably *Hiwi's*.[244] The men in the *III./1049* were quite young with 80% born in 1926. Some were Poles and a number were convalesced wounded.[245]

In accordance with the *KStN's*, the companies of the infantry battalions were heavily dependant upon horse transport. For example, the rifle companies in the *III./1050* each had around 22 infantry carts and seven four-wheel wagons (commonly referred to as a *Panjewagen Pleskau*); the *12./1050* had about 18 carts (*Infanteriekarren 8 / If.8*), 3 MG carts (identified as *If.1*), 6 *Panjewagen Pleskau* and 6 mortar carts (*If.9*).[246]

1./1050 is said to have had 24 If.8 carts (they were moved in groups of four behind a single horse) and 5 supply 2-horse wagons. In total the company had about 20 horses.[247]

As a whole, III./1050 had 36 light and 118 heavy draught horses and 10 riding horses. For individual transport, the men used bicycles.[248]

In late **May**, both infantry regiments formed a regimental combat school (*Kampfschule*, also known as an instructional company or *Lehr-Kompanie*.).[249] These companies were formed by taking a (reserve) section from each company. This included a mortar- and machine-gun-section as well as a tank destroyer platoon (*Panzerzerstörer* (*Ofenrohr*)) from the 14th Company The new companies were reportedly fully equipped with bicycles.[250] This development may also explain why most accounts do not mention mortars in the rifle companies. Some of the MG companies are said to have had the authorised six mortars, which also suggests that mortars were taken from the rifle companies. It is also possible that the new *KStN's* were already being followed, although this is not evident from the **1 June** order of battle.

This document does show that the infantry gun company of *GR 1049* had six Russian infantry guns issued as light infantry guns, while the *13./1050* only had two.[251] These guns were the *7,62 cm I.KH.290(r)* and were standard in a 25th wave division; orders show four were to have been sent to the division before **1 March**.[252] Records show that all the heavy infantry guns were still lacking as late as **13 May**, but one heavy gun was listed in each company on **1 June**. Another two heavy guns and four *7,62 cm I.KH.290(r)'s* were to be issued to the division but had not yet arrived.[253]

Further details on these companies are provided by a *Leutnant* from *GR 1049*, although admittedly he was uncertain of the facts. According to him, the *13./1049* had four Russian 7.62 cm guns instead of six. The guns were divided between two platoons. In addition, the company obtained a single Russian 12.2 cm gun, which was part of a third platoon.[254] This information is confirmed in part by an *Oberleutnant* from the same regiment, who agreed that the company had two light platoons and one heavy, but stated that all were equipped with two guns.[255] Due to these two accounts, the existence of just four light guns seems plausible. It may indicate the *13./1050* had received two guns from *GR 1049* to even out the number of guns in both regiments, while they both awaited the arrival of their remaining guns.

Information on the *13./1050* is limited, making it difficult to verify any claims. An officer from the regiment claimed that the company had three platoons with 7.5 cm infantry guns. Reportedly, each platoon had two sections with one infantry gun each.[256] Another claim concerning the *13./1050* was that it had three Russian 7.62 cm infantry guns, two or three *7,5 cm le.I.G.18's*, and possibly a heavy gun.[257] Ignoring the calibre of the guns, the claims support the presence of more than two light guns in this company.

On **1 June**, the 14th company of both regiments was listed with three platoons each. Both companies were armed with three motorised AT guns and both had two tank destruction platoons with a total of 35 (*14./1050*) or 36 (*14./1049*) *Ofenrohre*.[258] Although the type of anti-tank guns is not noted, these were *7,5 cm Pak 40's*. There had been six with the infantry in **February**.[259] According to an officer from *GR 1050*, these guns were towed by *RSO's*, which matches the *KStN*.[260] In addition to *RSO's*, *Kettenkrad* motorcycle halftracks were apparently used to move the guns at the front.[261]

The use of the *Ofenrohr* platoons is rather more obscure and, in practice, they may have been divided among other units. The single tank destroyer platoon from the regimental instructional company would already account for half the *Ofenrohre* of its parent company (one of the two platoons in the 14th Company).[262] It has also been said that each battalion had *Ofenrohre*.[263] This could be possible, if the remaining platoon were divided among the three battalions. This would be fairly simple, since each platoon consisted of three sections with six launchers.

In addition to the three platoons, the *Pak 40's* and *Ofenrohre*, the companies probably had additional anti-tank weapons. There are indications that there were *5 cm Pak 38* medium anti-tank guns. These first appeared on a **February** order of battle and, at that time, there were six with the *14./1049*.[264] These disappeared in **March**, only to reappear on **1 May** with the anti-tank company.[265] It is possible they had been retained until the opportunity arose to give them a new role. The order of battle of **1 May** suggests that *5 cm Pak's* may have been transferred to the 14th Companies from *Pz.Jg.Kp. 177*.[266] This is supported by an officer from *GR 1050*, who stated that there were two *5 cm Pak* in the *14./1050* in addition to the *7,5 cm Pak 40's*. These two guns were towed by two ammunition lorries for long-distance moves.[267] An officer from *GR 1049* believed that the *14./1049* also had *5 cm Pak's*.[268] On the order of battle of **1 June**, six motorised *5 cm Pak's* were listed with the field-replacement battalion and not with the 14th Company[269] Identifying the use of the *5 cm Pak* is complicated by contradictory information about the number and types of platoons in the regimental anti-tank companies. One claim is that the *14./1049* had three platoons, two with four *5 cm Pak's* each, and one with two *7,5 cm Pak 40's*.[270] Another source says that the *14./1050* had one light platoon and two heavy platoons. All the AT guns were supposed to be 7.5 cm, but apparently not all platoons possessed the same weapons.[271] Another source supports the theoretical organisation of the *14./1049*, but claims that the *14./1050* had four platoons.[272]

Without further evidence, it is assumed that each 14th Company matched the *KStN*, but that both tank-destroyer platoons may have been detached to other units within the regiment. It is also probable that both companies had some *5 cm Pak's*, which may have formed an additional platoon. This would be in line with official orders that allowed the use of medium AT guns in the regimental anti-tank companies, but no longer at divisional level.[273]

It is not just the regimental anti-tank troops that is confusing, the same is true for *Pz.Jg.Abt. 177*. The divisional anti-tank troops around D-Day differed from the organisation envisaged in the order of **9 February**, which called for just a single AT company.[274] In effect, an anti-tank battalion with multiple companies was in the process of being formed about the time of the invasion. On paper this would have resulted in a battalion with a headquarters, an AT company and a *Flak* company. The invasion appears to have prevented the battalion from being fully formed, although most of the individual elements existed nonetheless.

While it is not clear when the decision was made to form the battalion, it was probably in late **March** or early **April**. Ironically, a battalion headquarters had already been listed on the order of battle of **18 February**, but it left on **7 March**. Around the same time, an AT company was listed as a cadre unit.[275]

The presence of this headquarters in **February** shows that an AT battalion headquarters had arrived, despite the fact that it was not needed, since the division was only authorised an AT company. The headquarters originated from *Pz.Jg.Abt. 355* and arrived with the remnants of the *355. I.D.* to form the *77. I.D.*[276] Because the headquarters was not required for the new division, the *OKH* issued orders on **21 February** to move it (7 officers, 24 NCO's, and 72 men) to Mielau (Mława, Poland), where it would report to the Replacement Army.[277] This sequence of events is illustrated by the headquarters' field post number. The designation listed under the original number of the staff of *Pz.Jg.Abt. 355* was changed to *Pz.Jg.Kp. 177* on **17 March**, but was changed back to "*Pz.Jg.Abt. 355* two weeks later. As it is common for these numbers to be changed with a delay, this would tie in with the staff leaving around **7 March**. When, later on, it was decided to form a battalion after all, the transfer of the headquarters turned out to have been premature. It was not until **20 May** that the post office number was changed to "*Stab Panzerjäger-Abteilung 177*". Since the post office number of the former *Pz.Jg.Kp. 177* had already been changed to the *1./Pz.Jg.Abt. 177* on **17 April**, the decision to form the battalion must have been taken some time earlier.

It is not clear when the headquarters returned to the division, but it was reportedly on its way from East Prussia to Dinan when the invasion commenced.[278] It appears it arrived in Bretagne soon after the division left for the front. On **17 June**, *AOK 7* was able to commit the maintenance and weapons sections of the headquarters.[279] This seems to confirm the headquarters' arrival, or at least parts of a headquarters company. The context of the document indicates that these elements operated far away from the front and the division, which was fighting on the Cotentin. This is confirmed by the fact that, on **28 June**, the maintenance section was 2 km north of Le Mans.[280] On **1 July**, the *7. Armee* requested 30 motor vehicles from the senior quartermaster in the west for *Pz.Jg.Abt. 177*.[281] Although the request may have been the result of losses suffered on the Cotentin, it seems more likely it was related to the incomplete formation of the battalion or to an ill-equipped battalion headquarters and headquarters company.[282]

Although the evidence shows that the division lacked a fully formed anti-tank battalion when the invasion began, individual companies were available. The absence of a headquarters also seems to have caused the division to use these companies differently than intended. This is especially true for the *Flak* company, officially the 3rd Company. The very existence of the company was a deviation from the orders of **9 February**. In fact, the base document for 25th wave divisions does not list that type of company in any form. The presence of *Fla-Kp. 177* makes clear that at least some 25th wave divisions were assigned such companies. (The same occurred with the *91. LL.D.*, although the company in that division remained a separate unit.)[283] It is not clear when the decision was made to add *Fla-Kp. 177* to the division, but it was probably in **February** or **March**. It was assigned a post office number on **17 April**.

While little is known about the company, it had 12 2 cm guns and probably followed a standard *KStN*.[284] After all, divisions of the 25th wave were to use the same *KStN's* as the *Inf.Div.n.A.* or 44, which included these companies. Thus, it was likely based on *KStN 191*, which should mean three platoons each with four 2 cm guns. On **18 April**, the division received 12 *2 cm Flak 38's*, and the next day the *3.(Fla)/Pz.Jg.Abt. 177* was sent to the division.[285] The company was not listed on the **1 May** order of battle, but it is present on **1 June**. At that time it had two light MG's and 12 motorised 2 cm *Flak*.[286]

It appears that the company was not used as a single formation. It has been reported that three guns were available to the division, six were sent to *GR 1050* and the remaining three may have been attached to *GR 1049*.[287] The only reference to the company in the Normandy fighting is from the order of battle of *Kampfgruppe 91. I.D.* on **17 July**. At that time, the company was attached to the *III./AR 177*.[288] From **20 July** onwards, it appears to be listed as the *9./AR 177*.[289]

As noted, *Pz.Jg.Kp. 177* (*Hauptmann* Hiller) was formed as planned in the **9 February** orders.[290] It was formed with personnel from *Pz.Jg.Kp. (motZ) 352*, which was transferred to the division as a cadre unit on **11 March**.[291] The company became available when the *352. I.D.* was ordered to form an AT battalion that did not include towed guns. *Pz.Jg.Kp. 177* received its post office number on **4 April**; on **17 April** it was redesignated as the *1./Pz.Jg.Abt. 177*.[292]

The arrival of six *Pak 40's* was reported on **17 March**, and it appears that the company received its last six guns on **6 April**.[293] These guns must have been earmarked for the company, as the infantry regiments had already received their heavy AT guns. On **1 June**, the company was listed with 12 motorised heavy AT guns and 10 light MG's.[294] The company reportedly had a strength of 184 men; 27 were Russian, five or six were Poles, and the rest were German.[295]

Prisoner information confirms that the AT guns were divided among four platoons. Each gun had a crew of eight. Additional weapons included a number of light *MG 42's*, *Panzerfäuste* and a single hollow charge (*Hafthohlladung*).[296] As planned, the company was motorised. All guns were towed by *RSO* prime movers, of which the company had 12. In addition, the company had a 4.5-tonne diesel lorry, six 3-tonne Ford V-8 lorries, nine *Volkswagens*, and a *Kettenkrad*.[297]

While this explains the organisation of the company, the **1 May** base document requires attention. Oddly, it showed two AT companies among the divisional anti-tank troops, rather than one. One company was armed with the typical 12 *7,5 cm Pak 40's*; the other with 12 *5 cm Pak 38's* and 6 MG's. Both companies were motorised except for six of the 5 cm guns, which were "immobile". The document has an interesting handwritten note: "with the 14th Company?"[298] This suggests a possible reinforcement of the anti-tank companies in the infantry regiments. Since the heavy AT company was at the core of *Pz.Jg.Abt. 177*, the note suggests that the 5 cm guns were attached or reassigned to the infantry AT companies of the two regiments. On paper, six 5 cm AT guns were with the field-replacement battalion on **1 June**, but in practice these may have been used by the infantry regiments.[299]

Although Zetterling states that six of the 5 cm guns were "static", this does not correspond with the records.[300] The guns are characterised as "immobile" (*unbeweglich*), not "static" (*bodenständig*).[301] This may appear to be a minor difference, but in this context it could mean they belonged to the division, rather than the sector as would be the case with static weapons. This raises the possibility that all 12 *5 cm Pak 38's* accompanied the division to Normandy, provided that some sort of mobility was arranged. Still, only six *5 cm Pak 38's* were listed on **1 June**. After examining the records, it seems most likely that the division had six 5 cm guns available; these were officially part of the field-replacement battalion, but in practice were likely used by the anti-tank companies of the infantry regiments.

In contrast to the anti-tank battalion, the organisation of *AR 177* (*Obst.* Stoltenburg) is quite clear. Its organisation matched the **February** orders, although the *KStN* numbers were changed before the invasion. The numbers of the regimental units and light battalions matched those of a *Inf.Div.44*, but this did not apply to the motorised 3rd Battalion, which used *KStN 406, 586,* and *434* for the headquarters, the headquarters battery and the gun batteries.[302] The regimental headquarters reportedly included six officers: The regimental commander, the adjutant, an officer assistant, a battalion surgeon, a veterinary officer and the commander of the headquarters battery.[303]

The order of battle of **1 June** does not specify the organisation of the regimental headquarters battery, but does show that it had a single MG.[304] According to prisoner statements, the battery included a signals platoon and trains. The signals platoon consisted of six sections: Three telephone sections and three radio sections. The telephone sections each comprised an NCO and six men. Each of the three radio sections was formed by an NCO and three men. The headquarters battery relied on horse-drawn transport. There were six four-horse wagons used by the signals platoon. The rest of the wagons were drawn by two horses. This included a field kitchen, the officers baggage wagon, a wagon for equipment and spares, an orderly room wagon, a rations wagon, two food wagons and a medical wagon.[305]

As planned, each of the three battalions had a headquarters battery armed with two MG's.[306] Little information has been found on these units, except for the 3rd Battalion, whose headquarters battery is said to have included a signals section, an armourer/artificer element (a *Feldwebel*, an *Unteroffizier* and two assistants). The strength of the battery was about 100 men, with an average age of 25. Most of the men were drawn from existing artillery formations that had been in combat. About 95% of the personnel were German, the remainder were Poles.[307]

Although there are few witness accounts as to the composition of the light battalions, official records do provide some information. On the order of battle of **3 February**, the two batteries of *Art.Abt. 1021* were listed as each possessing four *10,5 cm le.F.H.18/40's*.[308] As intended, this battalion was later redesignated as the 1st Battalion of the artillery regiment.[309] Along with the regimental headquarters, the 2nd Battalion was first listed on the order of battle of **18 February**, although it was without weapons.[310] On **17 March**, the division reported the arrival of the remaining eight *le.F.H.18/40's*.[311] For some reason the guns in the 2nd Battalion were only first listed on the **1 May** order of battle. By this time, the light batteries had the authorised number of artillery pieces, but there was still a shortage of machine guns.[312] By **1 June**, all the batteries had four light MG's.[313] The two battalions were horse-drawn and each battery reportedly had 128 horses.[314]

AOK 7 records also provide details on the 3rd Battalion, which was first listed in the order of battle of the field army for **10 April**.[315] It had not been listed before then because it was being formed in Germany (not France like the rest of the division). The battalion was formed at Wiblingen near Ulm in **January-February 1944** and was first identified as *Einheit Baumann*, after its commander *Hauptmann* Baumann.[316] On **29 March**, Military District V was instructed to send the battalion to the division on, or shortly after, **1 April**. Any missing equipment or motor transport would be sent later via rear detachments, with the formation of the battalion to be completed by *Ob.West*.[317]

The **1 May** order of battle shows that the three batteries were equipped with four *8,8 cm Pak 43's* each.[318] No machine guns were available at that time, but on **1 June** each battery had four MG's and two more with the headquarters battery.[319] The artillery pieces were received in **April**, and although they were listed as *Pak 43/41's* in *AOK 7* records, they were actually *Pak 43's*.[320] The artillery capabilities of these anti-tank guns were limited compared to regular artillery pieces, a situation made worse by the fact that no sights for indirect fire were provided. Instead, the guns had been delivered with telescopic anti-tank sights, suitable for direct fire only. The men had not been instructed on how to operate these guns and, prior to D-Day, only one battery had fired.[321]

The 3rd Battalion was the only motorised formation in the artillery regiment and had about 130 vehicles.[322] The battalion collected its transport at Erquy (Bretagne) in **April**. The headquarters company reportedly had 4 *Volkswagens* in the headquarters section and 2 in the signals section and 13 lorries for ammunition and baggage.[323] While impossible to confirm, another source says that the headquarters company had 8-10 V-8 lorries, 2 staff cars and 2 motorcycles. The batteries were each equipped with four halftrack prime movers, either *Sd.Kfz. 7's* or *8's*.[324] Each battery reportedly also had a fuel lorry with a maximum capacity of 1,000 litres carried in five 200 litre barrels. To keep the vehicles operational, each battery had a repair section, consisting of an NCO and three men. Any vehicles they could not repair were sent to a maintenance facility outside of the division.[325]

The regiment's inadequate strength did not go unnoticed. On **24 February** an *OKH* inspector, *General* Buhle, visited the division and was urged to increase the number of batteries in the light battalions to three, but no promises were made.[326] On **25 April**, it was the *LXXIV. A.K.* that contacted the *7. Armee* about the regiment; it wanted to know if the 1st and 2nd Battalions would receive more than their two batteries and if the 3rd Battalion, with its *8.8 cm Pak*, was actually suitable for use as regular artillery. In response, *AOK 7* made clear that the division would not receive additional batteries. The question about the AT guns would be answered at a later date.[327]

In mid-**May**, it was suggested exchanging the *Pak 43's* of the heavy battalion with *Pak 43/41's* from *Pz.Jg.Abt. 200* (*21. Pz.Div.*). Ironically, these guns did have sights for indirect fire.[328] Such an exchange made sense because the *Pak 43* was better suited to anti-tank combat than the bulky *Pak 43/41* on its howitzer carriage. The *7. Armee* order of battle of **18 May** already lists the *Pak 43/41* with the 3rd Battalion, but this was premature since the actual order to carry out the exchange was not given until **25 May**.[329] In **June**, prisoners from the battalion still identified their guns as *Pak 43's*, meaning that the exchange had not taken place.[330] It is possible it had been cancelled because of plans to rearm the battalion with *15 cm s.F.H.18's*.[331] Either way, it does not appear that the battalion's batteries were ever re-equipped.

The order of battle entry of **1 May** for *Pi.Btl. 177* (*Major* Seifert) matches the planned organisation of two companies, including one with bicycles. As intended, the headquarters was partially motorised.[332] On **1 June**, the battalion headquarters had three light MG's and two flamethrowers. Both companies had six flamethrowers and a single German medium mortar. Although both had nine machine guns, the 1st Company had seven light MG's and the 2nd Company eight; the remainder were heavy MG's. For some reason, no bicycles were listed.[333] The engineer equipment included mines and bridging equipment and was carried by motor transport.[334] Each company also had four rubber rafts capable of carrying 12 men.[335]

The companies had a strength of about 160 men each. There were few foreign personnel in the 1st Company, just a single Pole and Slovene; the 2nd Company had 25 Russians and four Slovenes.[336] Men from the 2nd Company stated that the companies consisted of three regular and one heavy platoon. The regular platoons each had a strength of 1 *Leutnant* and 40 men in three sections. Each section was armed with a light *MG 42*, a machine pistol, a self-loading rifle and *K98k* rifles; in addition, there were two *Hafthohlladungen*.

All of this was close to the *KStN*. The heavy platoon is said to have had three sections, although the *KStN* did not call for a heavy platoon. Instead, it authorised a single heavy MG section and a mortar section. The heavy platoon had a combined strength of just one *Feldwebel* and 10-15 men. The first section was a MG section. It was not at full strength with only one light and one heavy *MG 42*, but it also had a self-loading rifle, a machine pistol, rifles, and two *Hafthohlladungen*. The two remaining sections were mortar sections. The types of light weapons in them were identical to those in the MG section, even the number of *Hafthohlladungen*. It has been claimed each of these mortar sections were to have a Russian 12 cm mortar, but only one section actually had one. In addition, it has been said that the 1st Company did not actually possess any mortars.[337] The order of battle of **1 June** raises doubts about the accuracy of those claims.[338]

Prisoners stated that both companies were equipped with bicycles for all the men, but as there are no statements from soldiers of the 1st Company, this cannot be confirmed. The officers and platoon leaders had motor vehicles; several sources also note *Schwimmwagens* and motorcycle combinations. Each company had three lorries: mess, ammunition and weapons.[339] When the battalion moved to the front, the men's personal luggage was carried on their bicycles. The pioneer equipment (of the companies) was left behind except for some mines transported with the field kitchen.[340]

According to two members of the divisional headquarters, the battalion received 36 rocket launchers while in Bretagne. Although the type is not noted, these most likely were 28/32 cm launchers. These weapons were not restricted to the *Nebeltruppen* and commonly used by engineers. Reportedly, the battalion was successful in mounting six of the launchers on a lorry. Special frames were built for this, which allowed them to be mounted on 2-ton lorries within 30 minutes. Although these lorries and their rocket launchers are said to have been used in the Normandy fighting, it is difficult to verify due to a lack of confirmation from battalion personnel.[341]

Yet, there is no question that the division had access to rocket launchers. In mid-**May**, 244 heavy rocket launchers (*28/32 cm schweres Wurfgerät / s.W.G.*) were being allocated to the division's sector.[342] After D-Day, the *5. Fj.Div.* took over this area and, on **18 June**, was ordered to hand over 180 *s.W.G.'s* and report where the remaining 100 launchers would be deployed.[343] This figure is noteworthy, as it signifies that the total launchers in the sector was 36 higher than the 244 noted in **May** — a fact that could support the delivery of this number of launchers to *Pi.Btl. 177*.

The battalion was not unique in building mobile launchers, as there were several other attempts to fit rocket launchers to vehicles in the *7.* and the *15. Armee*. In fact, in **April 1944**, *AOK 7* discussed these experiments with *Feldm.* Rommel and it was suggested to keep 15% of the launchers mobile. The type involved was the *schweres Wurfgerät* (*40* and *41*), the most basic platform for launching 28/32 cm rockets. These could be fired from their transport crates.[344]

As is clear from the preceding examples, the original orders to raise the division were not carried out to the letter. In addition to changes in artillery, the infantry regiments and anti-tank troops, the division formed a completely new battalion: *Feld-Ers.Btl. 177*.[345] On **25 May**, *Ob.West* was ordered to establish these battalions for the four 25th wave divisions in its theatre.[346] A week later, on **1 June**, the battalion was already listed on the division order of battle, although its establishment did not begin until **5 June**.[347] Despite this, the battalion was already listed with 28 light MG's and six motorised *5 cm Pak's*. It was shown with four companies, which were still without personnel. Although all of the division's other formations were listed at full strength in personnel, the field-replacement battalion had 95% of its cadre personnel and apparently no troops for its companies.[348] Initially, the battalion used the field post number of the combat school until an official number was assigned on **16 June**.[349]

The first battalion commander, *Hauptmann Burkhard*, and his adjutant were both captured and provided some information about the battalion. Since mid-February, the *Hauptmann* had been in charge of the divisional combat school and remained there until it was disbanded on **1 June**, when he became the first commander of *Feldersatz-Btl.177*. Despite never having seen the organisational documents of his battalion, the captain was certain it consisted of four companies, including a bicycle company, for a total of about 600 men. The field post number indeed mentioned a headquarters and four companies. The formation of the battalion should have been completed on **15 June**, but for obvious reasons, this was not achieved.[350]

At the time of the invasion, the "battalion" had about 170 men, all cadre personal. This included mostly officers, NCOs and future section second-in-commands, but also clerks, cooks, etc., and all had been drawn from *GR 1049* and *1050*. In addition, there were 14 *Hiwi's* to handle the horse transportation. Weapons were limited to sidearms and five light *MG 42's* retained from the divisional combat school. Because he believed that the regiments would be unable to supply sufficient numbers of men to fill his battalion, *Hauptmann* Burkhard expected the remaining men to arrive from Germany with their weapons, equipment and bicycles.[351] Still, the previously noted formation of regimental combat schools may actually have been a step in the battalion's establishment, as the divisional combat school was usually attached to such a battalion. On **30 July**, the plans to form the field-replacement battalions were cancelled again, but how this affected *Feld-Ers.Btl. 177* is not clear.[352] According to the adjutant, the battalion had already seized to exist by mid-June, having been thrown into battle and absorbed by G.R.1050 after suffering heavy losses.[353]

Some information is also available on the divisional military police, *Feldgendarmerie-Trupp 177* (*Feldg.Tr. 177*). The section had a strength of one officer (*Oberleutnant* Konrad) and 30-32 men; all except four were NCO's. The men were armed with *K98k* rifles and *P08's* (Luger pistols). When on patrol, only the pistol was usually arried.[354] The order of battle lists it as partially motorised and armed with two light MG's.[355] The section reportedly also had four *Schwimmwagens*, a lorry, a staff car and bicycles; however, a former member contradicts this, stating there were 3 staff cars and 30 bicycles.[356]

The division had a motor transport column, *Kraftfahr-Kompanie 177* (*Kf.Kp. 177*) with a capacity of 90 tonnes. It reportedly had a strength of two officers and 45 other ranks with a repair section of four or five men. The company had 32 3.5-tonne V-8 lorries, 2 staff cars and 4 motorcycles. When moving, the lorries did not carry spare fuel for themselves; instead, one or more lorries were always reserved to carry fuel for the other vehicles, transported in 200 litre drums.[357]

Mobility and Beweglichmachung

The company only covered a small amount of the division's motor transport capacity which, at the time of the invasion, was just over 80% of the authorised tonnage.[358] This was an improvement compared to **12 May**, when the division had been at 40%.[359] This suggests many of the 360 motor vehicles allocated by OKH in late **April** had arrived.[360]

The division had an authorised lift tonnage of 695 tonnes, of which, on **1 June**, only 525 tonnes were available (75.5%) and another 50 tonnes (7.2%) in short-term repair. Divisional authorisations included 2 *Maultiere* and 83 cross-country lorries, but only seven of the lorries were available and no *Maultiere*. The situation with regular lorries was better: 203 ready and 20 in short-term repair (authorised 248). The division received all of its 13 prime movers (at least 8-tonne) and 30 of its authorised 58 *RSO's*, with one in repair. Figures are also available for the division's motorcycles and cars. Simply put, there were 4 *Kettenkräder*, 9 motorcycle-sidecar combinations and 88 other motorcycles operational (authorisations of 11, 36 and 106, respectively); another 7 motorcycle-sidecar combinations and 11 motorcycles were in short-term repair. The authorisation documents called for 146 cross-country and 37 non-cross-country cars; of these, there were 118 and 6 in service, with 11 and 8 in repair.[361]

The only transport element above authorised strength was the horses. These were authorised at 2,694, while the actual amount was 2,745, including 11 so-called *Panjepferde*, a type of small, sturdy, horse commonly found in eastern Europe and Russia and appreciated for its resilience and tolerance to extreme weather. Despite the number of horses, the mobility of the horse-drawn elements was only 70%. This was mainly due to a lack of harnesses, wagons and carts.[362]

Kampfgruppe

Like many other divisions in the west, the *77. I.D.* had initially been ordered to immediately prepare a *Kampfgruppe*. When these orders were received, the division was busy forming and training. However, since the division was built around the existing reinforced *GR 1021*, the orders were not unreasonable.

Mobility, of course, was critical for the divisional battlegroups and, in **April**, it was intended to have one infantry regiment as well as the engineer battalion fully equipped with bicycles and motorised headquarters.[363] The order of battle of **1 May** only listed the *6./1049* and the *2./Pi.Btl. 177* as bicycle formations, but it is clear that bicycles were used by the *III./1050* as well.[364] This battalion apparently served as the division's advance guard. It is not clear when it received its bicycles.

The divisional battlegroup slowly evolved until it, on **1 April**, consisted of the following: *GR 1049*, including its 13th Company (with six Russian infantry guns) and motorised 14th Company (with three *7,5 cm Pak 40's*); and the

I./1050 and the regiment's 13th Company (with two guns) and 14th Company (as with the *14./1049*). The artillery component included the headquarters of *AR 177* and its 1st Battalion. Completing the *Kampfgruppe* were a combat engineer company and six *7,5 cm Pak 40's* from *Pz.Jg.Abt. 177*, which at that time were motorised had been motorised in a field-expedient manner.[365]

History

The division was established on **15 January 1944**. The reinforced *Gren.Rgt. 1021*, formed in Münsingen in Military District V on **22 November 1943**, provided the initial core.[366] Working staffs were then set up to transform the regiment and develop any missing elements.[367]

The root of the formation can also be traced to the General Government in German-occupied Poland, where many elements that later joined the division were stationed in the winter of **1943**.[368] For example, the supply troops were stationed near Sandomierz, with other elements at the Deba Training Area.[369] The latter were primarily remnants of the former *355.* and *161. I.D.*, which were intended to provide the core for the *364. I.D.* until its formation was cancelled on **21 January 1944**, whereupon they were reassigned to the *77. I.D.*[370]

Gen.Lt. Poppe was appointed commander of the *364. I.D.* on **15 December 1943**. Following the division's cancellation, he was assigned to the officer manpower pool of Military District IV. It appears, however, that he remained with the *355. I.D.* divisional staff, with the result that when the headquarters was earmarked for the *77. I.D.* in **February**, he became the commander. Having officially assumed command of the division on **11 February** he was relieved in late **April**.[371] One staff officer expressed his approval of the change:[372]

Our previous division commander, Gen.Lt. Poppe, […] had to hold a short conference about the division's exercise and that was terrible. He was a clumsy fellow and talked a lot of nonsense. Any more or less intelligent lieutenant would have been ashamed.

Gen.Lt. Ortner was designated the divisional commander on **25 April** but, on **1 May**, he made way for *Gen.Maj.* Stegmann.[373]

The reinforced *GR 1021* was transported from Münsingen to Caen from **17-19 January** and continued its formation.[374] Most of the forces from the General Government arrived in **February**.[375] On **19 January**, the regimental headquarters was in Brouay;[376] two days later, it was in Fontenay-le-Pesnel, with the 1st through 3rd Battalions in Lantheuil, Martragny and Mouen, respectively. *Art.Abt. 1021* (later the *I./AR 177*) was in Putot-en-Bessin and *Pi.Kp. 1021* in Lasson.[377] The advance party of the *355. I.D.* headquarters arrived on **5 February**.[378] Three days later, the divisional headquarters was in St. Martin-de-Fontenay.[379]

Elements continued to arrive and, on **10 February**, the headquarters of AR 355 was in Bretteville-l'Orgueilleuse; its 2nd Battalion was in Rots. *Pz.Jg.Abt. 355* and *Pi.Btl. 355* were located in St. Sylvain and Cormelles-le-Royal, respectively. The divisional headquarters (now redesignated) was transferred to St. André-sur-Orne and *Nachr.Abt. 177* to May-sur-Orne.[380] The headquarters of the second infantry regiment (*GR 336*, redesignated as *GR 1050*) arrived on **12 February** and was in Troarn.[381] On **27 February**, the *III./1050* (redesignated from the *III./336*) moved to Cagny.[382]

On **2 March**, *Pi.Btl. 177* moved to Angers for training.[383] Five days later, the headquarters of *Pz.Jg.Abt. 177* left the division and the *7. Armee*.[384] Among the arrivals in **April** was the *III./AR 177*, which moved to Vieux on the **10th**. The same day, the *II./AR 177* moved to Bellengreville.[385]

The locations of the other battalions are not found in the daily reports, but a situation map from **8 April** displays them. Since it was not committed on the coast, the division was only responsible for defending its sector against airborne landings. Caen itself remained under control of the *716. I.D.*, but the area around the city was secured by the *77. I.D.*; its divisional headquarters was located in St. André-sur-Orne, with the signals battalion in nearby May-sur-Orne.[386]

GR 1049 was responsible for the sector west of Caen, which stretched southwest of the city roughly to Noyers-Bocage, to Bayeux in the west and Fontaine-Henry in the north. The regiment's sector was divided into a northwest and southwest subsector by the Caen – Bayeux highway. Close to Caen, Carpiquet airfield separated the two areas and from there to Bayeux *AR 177* formed a wedge straddling the highway. The headquarters of *GR 1049* was located southwest of Caen in Baron-sur-Odon; the headquarters of its three battalions were in Lantheuil (1st), Cairon (2nd) and Mouen (3rd). The *AR 177* headquarters was in Bretteville-l'Orgueilleuse; its 1st Battalion in Audrieu and its 2nd Battalion in Rots.[387]

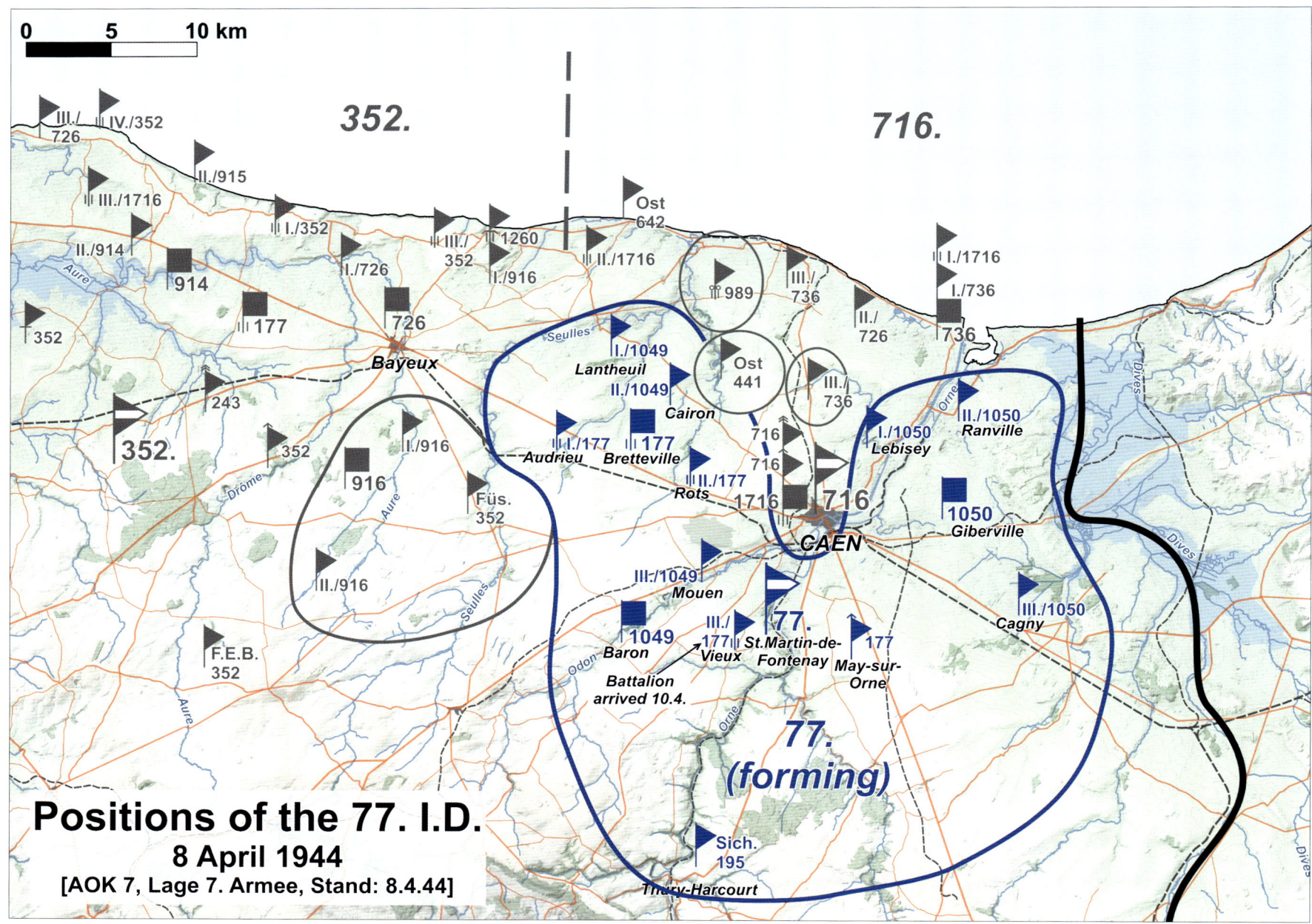

In its early days, the division was stationed around Caen where it served as a reserve to the rear of the 716.I.D.

GR 1050 commanded the area east of Caen. This included either side of the Orne and Caen Canal northeast of the city. From there, the sector continued east to include the villages of Bréville and Troarn. To the southeast, the regiment covered the crucial N13 highway and railway to Paris up to Moult. Its area of responsibility continued further to the south, ending east of the highway to Falaise. The headquarters was in Cuverville, east of Caen. The 1st Battalion was in Lébisey, the 2nd in Ranville and the 3rd in Cagny.[388]

The divisional supply troops covered the southwestern sector, including Épinay-sur-Odon, Hamars and Thury-Harcourt. Wedged between *GR 1049*, *GR 1050* and the supply troops was *Nachr.Abt. 177*, which included Urville and the highway to Falaise in the east and St. André-sur-Orne in the north, while continuing westwards across the Orne River to southwest of Hill 112. The division support command was in Thury-Harcourt.[389]

Positions on D-Day

After initial work up near Caen, the division moved to the *LXXIV. A.K.* in Bretagne, while the *21. Pz.Div.* took over the sector around Caen.[390] In a transportation movement codenamed "Cornflower Movement" (*Bewegung Kornblume*), 29 trains transported the division between **29 April-4 May** to St. Malo and St. Brieuc.[391] The division was to strengthen the coastal defences and continue training to become fully operational.[392] At 12:00 on **6 May**, the division assumed responsibility for *KVA "A1"*, where it would remain until D-Day.[393]

The daily logs of *AOK 7* offer few details on the division's deployment in Bretagne or its precise positions. While much of this information has been provided by situation maps and members of the divisional staff, exact locations for many companies are not known.[394]

KVA "A1" stretched from Pointe de Pordic in the west to the mouth of the Sélune River in the east. The exact boundaries went into effect when the division assumed command of *KVA "A1"* and slightly reduced the sector of the *266. I.D.* while increasing the sector of the *LXXXIV. A.K.* The *77. I.D.* was subdivided into *KVG Lamballe* (*KVU Matignon*, *KVU Pléneuf*, *KVU Yffiniac*), *Festung St. Malo* (*KVU Seefront*, *KVU Landfront Ost*, *KVU Landfront West*) and *KVG Miniac* (*KVU Dol* and *KVU Cancale*).[395]

On **16 May**, the divisional headquarters was established in a hamlet west of St. Hélen;[396] on the **27th**, it moved to Tressaint, where the divisional support command had been since early **May**.[397] The headquarters of *AR 177* was in Château Frêsne west of St. Hélen. *Nachr.Abt. 177* had its headquarters in Lanvallay, east of Dinan. The commander of the supply troops was in Dinan and the division Ib was in Évran, 6 km to the southeast.[398] *Pi.Btl. 177* had its headquarters on the eastern edge of Dinan, with its 1st Company in Pléneuf and its 2nd Company in Dinard. Both companies were employed in the construction of defensive obstacles around the coast. Once the highest level of alert (*Alarmstufe II*) was issued, the companies were to assemble as the divisional reserve, with the 1st Company gathering in the Hénansal area and the 2nd Company in Dinan.[399] The headquarters of *Pz.Jg.Kp. 177* was near Plancoët, along with one platoon of three *7,5 cm Pak 40's* as divisional reserve (4th Platoon).[400] *Gren.Rgt. 1049* defended the western half of the *KVA* and *Gren.Rgt. 1050* covered the east. *Festung St. Malo* was defended by elements of both regiments. The headquarters of *GR 1049* was near the Lamballe railway station, while the headquarters of *GR 1050* was in Miniac-Morvan, between Dinan and Dol-de-Bretagne.[401]

The westernmost sector of *KVA "A1"* was *KVU Yffiniac*. It ran from the western divisional boundary — Pointe du Pornic and the Gouet River — to Yffiniac, at the southernmost point of the Baie de St. Brieuc. The main town in the area was St. Brieuc, just inland. The sector was defended by the *I./1049*, with its headquarters in Yffiniac. The battalion was reinforced by a platoon from the *14./1049* with three *7,5 cm Pak 40's*. This platoon was in place between La Croix and Bout de Ville, northwest of Yffiniac.[402] Barely any information was found as to the locations of the companies. The 1st Company was reportedly in Plérin, with its platoons in resistance nests on the coast. On the left was *Wn.Po. 9* (Les Rosaires),[403] followed by *Wn.Po. 8* (Pte. des Tablettes) and *Wn.Po. 7* (at the mouth of the Ruisseau de Bachelet).[404] (In these resistance nests "Po." refers to KVG Pornic.)

The *II./1049* was responsible for *KVU Pléneuf*, which continued to Pointe de l'Assiette. The battalion headquarters was in a shelter about 1-1.5 km south of Pléneuf-Val-André, possibly *Wn.La. 382* (La. for *KVG Lamballe*).[405] The locations of the companies are not known, but the headquarters of the 6th Company was in Dahoët and elements of the company were at least as far north as the Pointe de Pléneuf.[406] The sector was reinforced by a number of formations, including both batteries of the *I./AR 177*; these were reportedly in concrete emplacements about 1.5 km south-southwest of Pléneuf. The

9th Battery was also located there with its four guns, as was a platoon from *Pz.Jg.Kp. 177* and a static (sector bound) SP battery.[407] The static SP battery was equipped with self-propelled *15 cm Lg s.F.H.13's* mounted on French armoured Lorraine prime movers;[408] it had arrived in the St. Alban area on **31 May**.[409] Attached to the division, it was referred to by different names such as *s.F.H.-Geräte-Bttr. Weber* (Heavy Field Howitzer Equipment Battery Weber) or *schwere Batterie 177 (Sf.)*.[410] The reported locations of the artillery are questionable, as there were no reinforced strongpoints southwest of Pléneuf. There were, however, battery locations to the east-southeast of the town. Another claim says that the battalion headquarters and the 2nd Battery were at La Bouillie (east of Pléneuf), while the headquarters battery and 1st Battery were in surrounding villages.[411] This also better matches R. Rolf's research, who places the 1st Battery at *Wn.La.373* (north of Pléneuf) and the 2nd Battery at *Wn.La.374*. The latter position was casemated and located northeast of l'Hioval, east of Pléneuf, and west of La Bouillie.[412] Additional troops in the area included the SS Military Geology Battalion (*SS-Wehrgeologen-Bataillon*),[413] located around St. Alban with its headquarters, headquarters company and two other companies. This battalion was a corps reserve, but it fell under the division in case of enemy landings at Pléneuf or Erquy.[414]

The next coastal defence sector was *KVU Matignon*, stretching to the bridge in St. Briac; it was held by Volga-Tatar Infantry Battalion 627 (*Wolga-Tatarisches-Infanterie-Bataillon 627*). Its headquarters was in Matignon and protected by the battalion's three *4.5 cm Pak 184/1(r)'s*.[415] The battalion was reinforced by a platoon from *Pz.Jg.Kp. 177* on the St. Jacut-de-la-Mer peninsula. Two guns covered the beach southwest of the village; the third was on the east of the peninsula, covering the northeast. Artillery was provided by the *III./AR 177*; its entire 8th Battery and half of the 7th Battery were in position northeast of Pléhérel defending the Baie de la Fresnaye to the southeast. The final artillery element was *Ost-Bttr. 582*, in position near l'Hôpital (east of Matignon);[416] it was armed with four *10 cm le.F.H.316 (j)'s*, two *Flak 30's*, and one *Flak 38*.[417]

Festung St. Malo had coastal defences and land-based frontage. The boundaries of the fortress ran from the bridge at St. Briac to the south (via the eastern edge of Pleslin); then east over the bridge at Le Port St. Hubert; north to St. Jouan-des-Guérets, La Massuère and back to the coast at Pointe de la Varde. The headquarters was in the citadel and the front divided into three sectors, each defended by a battalion. The I./1050 defended the coast (*KVU Seefront*) between St. Briac and Pointe de la Varde; its headquarters was in Dinard and it had relieved the I./857 (346. I.D.) on **19 May**.[418] The 1./1050 was in Paramé, and took part in mining the seafront east of St. Malo. The company itself was not committed at the front but had a counterattack reserve role.[419] The III./1049 held *KVU Landfront West*, west of the Rance; its sector running from St. Briac to Le Port St. Hubert. The battalion headquarters was southwest of Pleurtuit. The II./1050 was responsible for defence of the eastern portion of the interior lines (better known as *KVU Landfront Ost*). It covered the area from Pointe de la Varde to St. Jouan-des-Guérets and had taken over this sector on **30 May**. Its headquarters was at *St.P. Ra.234* ("Ra." for *KVG Rance*: 1.3 km southwest of Paramé church)[420] as was the 8th Company, while the 5th Company was held in reserve 0.5 km north of the church. The church at St. Servan provides a reference point for the remaining two companies: The 6th Company was 0.8 km to the northeast and the 7th was 2 km to the southeast.[421] Of course, the defence of the fortress was supported by a variety of other formations, among them the garrison (*Festungs-Stamm-Kompanie LXXIV*) and a mix of artillery and *Flak*. The latter consisted of *H.K.A.R. 1266*, *H.K.B. 1271*, various units of *Marine-Artillerie-Abteilung 608* (*M.A.A. 608*) and *le.Flak-Abt. 912*, while the harbour commander of *St. Malo* also contributed troops.[422]

KVU Cancale stretched east from Pointe de la Varde through Cancale to Vildé la Marine and was held by *Ost-Btl. 602*.[423] Although the battalion had been in the St. Malo area for some time, it was not listed under the division on the order of battle of **18 May**.[424] At that time, it was further inland, taking part in an operation under *Div.Kdo. zbV 136* against "terrorists", having moved by train from St. Malo to Guingamp on **11-12 May**.[425] The battalion was sent back to St. Malo on **24-25 May** and, the next day, it took over from the II./1050, which was transferred to the land defences of *Festung St. Malo*.[426] On **27 May**, the battalion's new positions were reported, with its headquarters in *St.P. Ra.110*, west of St. Coulomb; the 1st Company was 1.5 km northwest of Cancale church, the 3rd Company 0.6 km south of La Guimorais, the 4th Company in St. Coulomb and the 2nd Company in reserve in La Ville Garnier.[427] The battalion was reinforced by a platoon from *Pz.Jg.Kp. 177* and although its exact positions are not known, the guns were trained on the shore of Cancale. Extra artillery was courtesy of the *II./AR 177*, whose headquarters was in a shelter on the southern edge of St. Coulomb, with two batteries in concrete emplacements 2-3 km south of

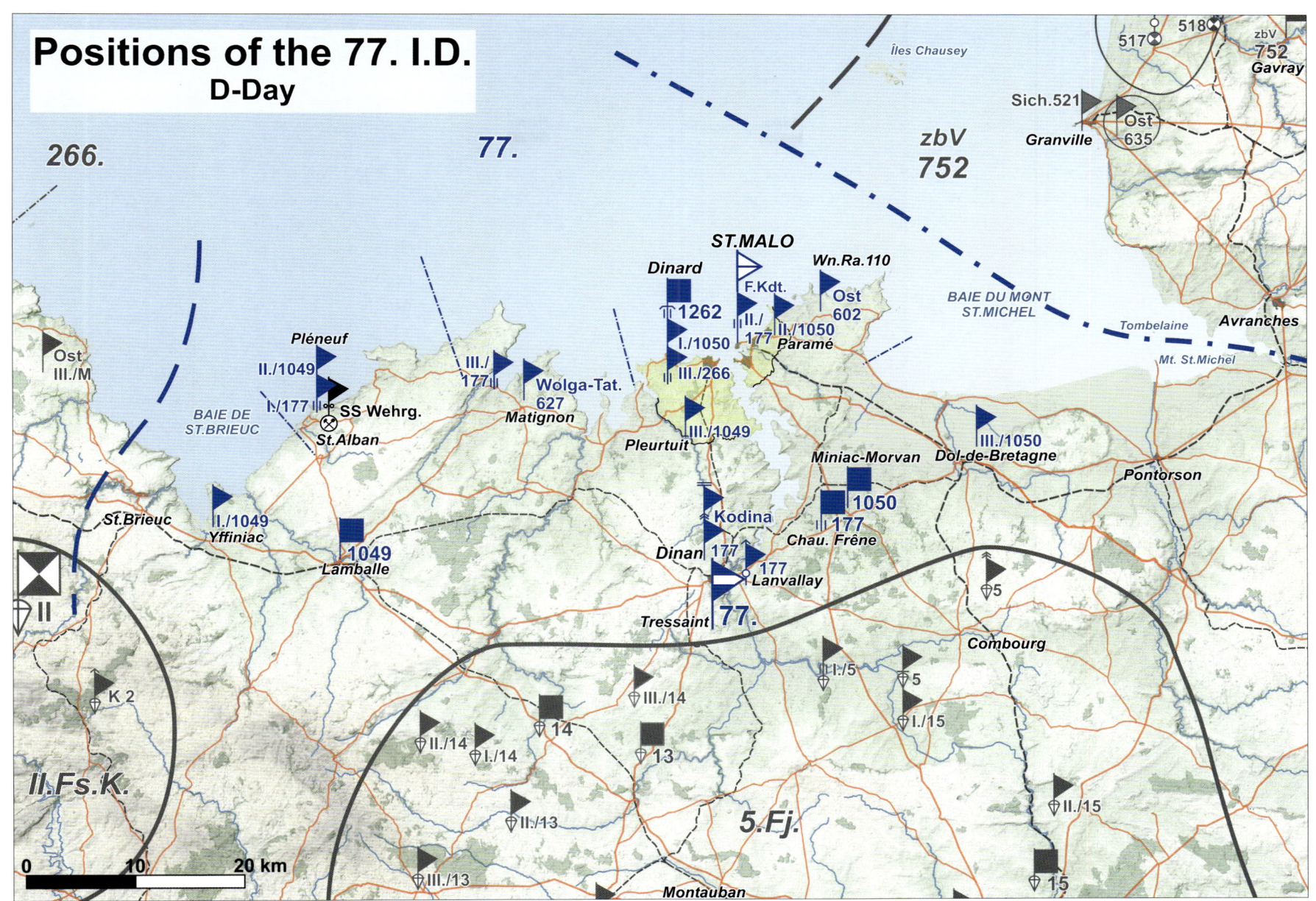

In Bretagne the division was responsible for KVA 'A1'. Its main strength was assembled around Festung Saint-Malo. To further strengthen the coastal defences, two eastern battalions were attached to the division. To the rear the 5.Fj.D. was still in the early phases of its formation.

the town.[428] More specifically, the 5th Battery has been linked to *Wn.Ra.110* (1 km west-southwest of St. Coulomb).[429] This information is in conflict to the 5 June situation map which puts the battalion HQ at St. Malo instead. An unusual artillery reinforcement was provided by battery "Ara" of the 1st Italian Naval Infantry Division. Arriving on **30-31 May**, it took up positions just south of Cancale in *Wn.Ra.100* armed with four British 7.5 cm anti-aircraft guns, the Vickers-Armstrong Model 31, known to the Germans as the *7,5 cm Flak M 35(h)* or *(d)*. Critically short of ammunition, the battery had just 30 rounds.[430]

The final divisional coastal sector was *KVU Dol*, running from Vildé la Marine to the mouth of the Sélune River. The boundary with the *LXXXIV. A.K.* was formed by the Douer and Sélune rivers, Pontaubault (*LXXIV. A.K.*), and the island of Tombelaine (*LXXXIV. A.K.*). The sector was named after Dol-de-Bretagne, one of the larger towns in the area and the location of the headquarters of the *III./1050*.[431] Artillery support was limited and consisted of only half of the *7./AR 177*. One of its 8.8 cm AT guns was in Le Vivier-sur-Mer, the other in Vildé la Marine. A platoon from the *14./1050* was near Mont-St. Michel with three *7,5 cm Pak 40's*. Mont-St. Michel itself was defended by three sections from the *III./1050*, each armed with a single light MG. Despite having been assigned to *LXXXIV. A.K.* in April, Rocher de Tombelaine, a small island in the middle of the Baie du Mont-St. Michel, was defended by a *Flakvierling 38* and two sections from the *III./1050* with one light MG each. Reserves in the *KVU* were the regimental training company in Pontorson and an infantry section from another company at the battalion headquarters in Dol.[432]

Several issues regarding artillery positions have already been noted, and there is room for more doubt. The battery locations of the *III./AR 177* conflict with the last known official report, dated **16 May**. The staff officers who reported their locations may have been wrong or they were right and there was a later move that was not recorded. Either way, based on the original report, the 8th Battery was in *KVU Matignon*, but positioned further east, near St. Cast-le-Guildo, with its four guns. The 7th Battery may not have had any guns in the sector, since all four were reported in *KVU Dol*; two were in the area of Vildé la Marine and the other two near Cherrueix. The 9th Battery was not positioned in *KVU Pléneuf*. Instead, half of the battery was near Erquy (in the north of the sector) and the other half near the southern boundary in the area of Hillion (north of Yffiniac).[433]

As previously mentioned, the division's sector was assigned a large number of heavy rocket launchers and, in mid-**May**, 244 launchers were being positioned. While not all locations are known, 80 were placed in support of *Festung St. Malo*, in groups of 20 in an arc south and east of the town. The locations of 20 of these launchers (with the *II./1049*) was not reported. An additional 20 launchers were sited in groups of five around Canvale in *KVG Miniac*. Launchers were also in *KVG Lamballe* but, unfortunately, numbers or locations have not been discovered.[434]

Operation Landgraf

In early **May**, *Feldm.* Rommel's *H.Gr. B* ordered a diversionary operation: *Aktion Landgraf*. In Bretagne, this meant the creation of fictitious divisions by the *XXV.* and the *LXXIV. A.K.* in an effort to convince the Allies that German forces in Bretagne were more robust than they actually were. The *XXV. A.K.* "created" the *101. I.D.*, while the *LXXIV. A.K.* did the same with the *285. I.D.*[435] (The *285. I.D.* was later changed to the *264. I.D.*)[436] The operation was coordinated by *Div.Kdo. zbV 136*. To simulate the divisions, troops were selected from the *77.* and the *266. I.D.* The *77. I.D.* sent only weak elements: the combat school of both infantry regiments, as well as parts of the bakery and veterinary companies. A battery from the *III./AR 177* was also meant to participate, but it lacked sufficient fuel. The operation lasted from **13-29 May**, the troops then returned to their parent formations.[437]

Reserve Role

On **31 May**, the division received orders to prepare for two possible deployments. The first called for the withdrawal of the entire division, minus the battalion in *Festung St. Malo* (*I./1050*); the second only affected the divisional battlegroup.[438] During this period, the division was considered for operations throughout *Ob.West*; for example, in the sectors of *AOK 1, 15, 19* or in the Netherlands as *Ob.West* reserves. In these scenarios, the entire division would be used. In case of operations in *AOK 7*, the *Kampfgruppe* would be available rather than the entire division.[439]

Combat

On **6 June 1944**, the division was still in the St. Malo area. As one of the divisions closest to the invasion front, its use was an obvious possibility, and that evening *Feldm.* Rommel ordered the *Kampfgruppe* to prepare for combat.[440] The situation became urgent when large airborne landings were reported between Lessay and Coutances on the night of **6-7 June**.[441] These reports turned out to be inaccurate, but by then the *77. I.D.* (and much of the *II. Fs.K.*) was on the move.

At 08:50 on **7 June**, Rommel ordered the *17. SS-Pz.Gren.Div.* and the *77. I.D.* to address the threat. The *SS* division was ordered to Villedieu-les-Poêles, while the entire *77. I.D.* was to be sent north along the coast as quickly as possible. Although the transfer potentially increased the risk of landings in Bretagne, Rommel viewed this as unlikely since the enemy already seemed fully committed in Normandy. The division was to be relieved by elements of the *II. Fs.K.* At 09:15, *AOK 7* informed the *LXXIV. A.K.* of these decisions. The *77. I.D.* forces in St. Malo and the eastern battalions were to remain in place. The rest were to be relieved by the *5. Fj.Div.* However, the corps reported that there was a shortage of two or three battalions to relieve the division, so the *I./1050* (*Hptm.* Ries) would stay in St. Malo until it too could be relieved.[442]

An hour later, the field army notified the *II. Fs.K.* of the developments. The *5. Fj.Div.* was to displace two or three battalions to relieve the *77. I.D.* More significantly, the corps, including its corps troops, had been selected to lead the operations on the west coast of Manche. The *3. Fj.Div.*, the *77. I.D.*, and the *17. SS-Pz.Gren.Div.* were placed under the operational control of the the airborne corps for this. *Gren.Rgt. zbV 752*, which was already in the area, would also come under the corps headquarters. Upon arrival, the corps was to report to the *LXXXIV. A.K.*[443] Meanwhile, the *5. Fj.Div.* was directed to take over *KVG Lamballe* with a three-battalion regimental force. One battalion each would relieve the *77. I.D.* in *KVU Pléneuf* and *KVU Yffiniac*; the other would be moved up to the area of Miniac as a reserve for use in the fortress or in *KVU Dol*.[444]

The first battalion to leave was the *III./1050*, under *Hptm.* Kuhle. It was to move at once to Granville without first being relieved; once there, it was to report to *Gren.Rgts.Stab zbV 752*. As it waited in its assembly area near Pontorson, it was attacked by Allied aircraft, but losses were limited to one man wounded and one horse.[445] At 14:00 on **7 June**, the battalion left for Granville.[446] The men rode in single file with one company setting off every hour. The distance between platoons was 500 m and 10 m between bicycles. When planes appeared the men would take cover in the ditch to the right of the road. By advancing spread out in this manner, the task of the attacking enemy aircraft was made more difficult. Indeed, the tactic was successful and the battalion did not lose a single soldier during the march. This method, of course, meant that the men arrived piecemeal, taking a few hours for all troops to assemble.[447]

By the evening of **7 June**, the airborne landings near Coutances had still failed to be confirmed. Therefore, *AOK 7* requested *H.Gr. B* to redirect the *17. SS-Pz.Gren.Div.* to St. Lô, so it would have flexibility to deploy the division as required. The request was not approved.[448] About midnight, the *77. I.D.* was informed that *Kf.Abt. LXXIV*, with two companies having a transport capacity of 120 tons each, would be assigned to the division for transport.[449]

It was not until 08:30 on **8 June** that the field army could inform Rommel that the west coast of the Cotentin was free of the enemy. This allowed for a new deployment of the *II. Fs.K.*, with Rommel ordering it to move towards St. Lô with two divisions, and the *77. I.D.* was informed at 11:35. To speed up its advance, *AOK 7* ordered it to march both day and night.[450]

At 08:00 on **9 June**, the *5. Fj.Div.* took command of *KVA "A1"*.[451] That morning, the *77. I.D.*'s mission was changed again. *Gen.* Marcks informed *AOK 7* that he considered the division's transfer to the Cotentin to be of decisive importance. He had gained the impression that the *709. I.D.* would be unable to hold back the American drive on Cherbourg. Marcks' request was approved — the division attached directly to his *LXXXIV. A.K.* and sent north to Valognes.[452] There it would strengthen the front southwest of Montebourg on both sides of the Merderet River.[453]

Naturally, it took several hours for everyone to be informed of this change. The *III./1050* had arrived in Granville and was briefly attached to *Gren.Rgt. zbV 752*, before being redirected to St. Lô, the new direction for the *II. Fs.K.* At 13:00 on **9 June**, the initial company departed in the direction of Villedieu-les-Poêles. The decision redirecting the division to Valognes only reached the battalion after after one of its company's departure. The new orders sent the battalion to St. Sauveur-le-Vicomte. *Maj.* Kuhle sent a motorcycle to intercept the company, while the others left in the new direction: Through Coutances, Lessay and La Haye-du-Puits to St. Sauveur-le-Vicomte. The intial company joined the rest of the battalion just south of Coutances.[454]

Many of the towns on the route from Bretagne to St. Sauveur had been bombed, hindering the German advance. All roads leading to Coutances had been hit and a long detour was necessary to find a bridge to cross the Soulles River and bypass the town. The situation in La Haye-du-Puits was problematic as well. Bicycles were able to get through the town, but it was impassable for motor vehicles such as the major's *Schwimmwagen*. Despite the obstructions, the first company arrived at St. Sauveur at about 22:00 and the last at 03:00-04:00 on **10 June**.[455]

Although the *III./1050* had suffered little from aerial attack on its way to the front, this was not the case for the entire regiment. As *Obst.* Brandt recalled:[456]

We were simply thrown into the beachhead, coming up from Bretagne. [We were] quickly issued bicycles and put in motion. In two days, we travelled about 170 km on bicycles. Our trains came later. Some of the heavy weapons were loaded onto lorries and buses. They were all shot to pieces by aircraft, because we had to travel by day. My entire 14th Company was completely wiped out. Weapons, Ofenrohre, Pak — everything destroyed. In the 13th Company, they knocked out my s.I.G.'s.

At the end of the day, the *LXXIV. A.K.* reported that the division's transfer was on schedule. The *II./1049* (*Hptm.* Lausberg) would leave during the night, using motor transport.[457]

All of this illustrates how the division did not move or arrive as a single force, so it is no surprise that its units were committed to battle in a piecemeal fashion. This complicates the task of following the division's operations and troop movements. It is easier to examine the activities of the individual battalions.

As the first of the divisional units arrived on the peninsula on **10 June**, the bulk of the division was still north of Coutances.[458] The lead battalion, the *III./1050*, was attached to the *91. LL.D.*, where it was first listed as an separate battalion.[459] However, it took until 19:00 on **11 June** before the lead battalion was reported as deployed on the Merderet River and covering the arrival of the rest of the division.[460] In reality, it was simply inserted into the line as a reinforcement for the *91. LL.D.* This helped to protect the arrival of the rest of the division, but did little for its intended sector. Instead, other units from *GR 1050* were used to relieve the Montebourg front.

The *III./1050* operated with elements of the *243. I.D.*, which were supporting the *91. LL.D.*[461] It had been committed soon after its arrival, but was it not identified by the Allies until **13 June**, when the US 90th ID captured several of its men near La Lande - Les Landes. By that time, the 9th Company was said to be down to 30-40 men, and the 10th and 11th Companies had also sustained serious losses.[462]

Four days later, the US 82nd AB, which fought north of the Douve River, reported that it had captured 73 men from the battalion, a good indication that it had been deployed against the southern end of the Merderet bridgehead.[463]

The main body of the division was further north. When it arrived in the late morning of **10 June**, the lead elements of *GR 1050* (excluding the *III./1050*) made contact with scattered airborne forces along the line St. Cyr - Montebourg.[464] After clearing the area, the troops began to feel increasing enemy pressure along the Montebourg front and sustained their first losses to artillery fire.[465] On the morning of **11 June**, it was reported that the divisional command post was in St. Jacques-de-Néhou and that the division had reached St. Sauveur-le-Vicomte. It was to be deployed on both sides of the Merderet.[466] By the end of the day, the command post had moved to Le Poiré (5 km southwest of Valognes).[467]

Upon arrival, the main body of the division took up positions on both sides of the Merderet, although this may have been a gradual development.[468] To the left of the division was the reinforced *709. I.D.*, with the reinforced *91. LL.D.* on the right. The exact boundary with the *91. LL.D.* is unclear, but it may have moved south as more troops arrived.

Obst. Bacherer (the commander of *GR 1049*) had operational control of the divisional front. *Kampfgruppe Brandt* (the commander of *GR 1050*) was a sub-group that held the left flank and relieved *KG Hoffmann* southwest of Montebourg.[469] Here the lines ran from Montebourg south to Éroudeville, then south-west along the railway to Le Ham. The principal line of defence was the edge of Montebourg (now held by *U.KG Hoffmann*) and the railway line (*KG Brandt*), with the area to the Montebourg - Le Ham road at best only lightly held.[470] The rest of the divisional sector presumably continued south, along the west bank of the Merderet, although this may have evolved as more of the division's troops arrived, and the *91. LL.D.* was forced to commit more troops to the south.

On the division's front, *GR 1050* had no control over either the *III./1050* or the *I./1050*, which remained in St. Malo. To strengthen the stripped down regiment, the *III./1049* (*Maj.* Gärtner) had been attached just after the start of the invasion.[471] This meant that *KG Brandt* consisted of the *II./1050* (*Hptm.* Indlekofer) and the *III./1049* when it moved into the line southwest of Montebourg; its arrival allowed the troops of *KG Hoffmann* to return to their parent formations.

Preparations to take over from *KG Hoffmann* began on the evening of the **11th**, the relief beginning that night with a single battalion (*II./1050*). This battalion was also the first element of *KG Bacherer* to see action, although the Allies failed to identify its presence.[472] Not all elements from *KG Hoffmann* were relieved, with *St.Btl. AOK 7*, a separate formation, staying at the front and reporting to *KG Brandt*. It remained in place and held the left wing of *KG Brandt*, having contact with Montebourg (now defended by *U.KG Hoffmann*) on its left flank and the *II./1050* on its right.[473]

This means that the right flank of *Gruppe Brandt* should have been formed by the *III./1049*, but it was likely never used east of the Merderet. Instead, it seems more likely that it was used to relieve *Kampfgruppe Simon*, which had been pushed back to the west bank of the river from the Le Ham area.[474]

On the division's right, *GR 1049* apparently only had the *I./1049* available, given that the *III./1049* was with *KG Brandt* and the *II./1049* was far behind in its march to the front. Allied forces west of the Merderet first identified the *I./1049*, and soon thereafter the *III./1049*, supporting the idea that this battalion held the right flank of *KG Brandt*.[475]

Exactly when these battalions reached the front is not clear, but it was probably a gradual process and some units may have initially been held in reserve. At some point, the *III./1049* returned to its regiment, but again, when this occurred is not clear.[476] It would make sense if the battalions were back under their regimental command when both were forced into action and fighting side by side on the northern flank of the Merderet bridgehead.

While *KG Bacherer* was fighting north of the Douve, the *II./1049* was still unavailable, even though it was moving to the front. Higher commands were concerned about the defence of Cherbourg, so orders were given to move a battalion there to replace one of the Landfront battalions, which had been pulled out on **9 June**. The replacement battalion was to arrive on the night of **12 June**, but it was unable to do so.[477]

In fact, only one battalion was available for Cherbourg: The *II./1049*, indicating that the others were already committed. The battalion was still too far south to quickly reach the strategic port city and, in any case, was not given sufficient time to do so. Early on **13 June**, the 508th Parachute Infantry Regiment (508th PIR of the 82nd AB) crossed the Douve River and pushed south towards Baupte, opening a gap in the German lines and establishing a front south of the Douve. This was an immediate threat, and the battalion was brought up by motor transport to close the gap.[478] Additional support arrived later in the form of *Kampfgruppe 265*.[479] That afternoon, *AOK 7* instructed the *LXXXIV. A.K.* that: a) the gap had to be closed and, b) the battalion had to be pulled out again and — in accordance with a direct order from the *Führer* — dispatched to Cherbourg.[480]

Considering conditions at the front, the orders were contradictory. The daily logs of *AOK 7* are unclear as to whether the battalion was pulled out in the night and sent to Cherbourg. Evidence reveals this did not happen.[481] At 18:40 on **14 June**, the battalion held Prétot and became part of *KG Eitner*, while the *II./AR 177* provided support to the battlegroup.[482] The infantry battalion was still attached to *KG Eitner* on **18 June**, indicating that it remained south of the Douve.[483] In fact, *AOK 7* records still link the battalion to *U.Gr. Eitner* towards the end of the month.[484]

The last battalion to reach the front was the *I./1050*. It was relieved in St. Malo by the *III./FJR 13* on **12 June** and left for the front that evening. The troops that had stayed with the self-propelled battery were also attached. The battalion reached Périers on **17 June**.[485] By then, the rest of the division had seen heavy fighting, and the battalion arrived too late to come to its aid north of the Douve.

Little has been recorded about the fighting in the division's own sector. East of the Merderet river, the *II./1050* reportedly held out against continual American attacks on **13-14 June** that failed to achieve palpable results from the German perspective.[486] In fact, US forces between the Merderet and the Carentan - Montebourg highway had already reached their objectives and were simply holding their positions.[487]

West of the Merderet, it seems that the *I./1049* was drawn into battle first, followed by the *III./1049*. To what extent this was due to the expansion of the bridgehead or to relieve elements of the *91. LL.D.* is not clear; however, the division appears to have successfully held the north of the bridgehead against the US 90th ID. This division first identified the *I./1049* around Gourbesville on **15 June**. The next day, it identified the *III./1049* north and northwest of the village.[488]

77. Infanterie-Division

The *77. I.D.* held its ground, but further south the front was collapsing and the Americans were advancing to the west coast. With only half of its battalions available, the division could do little to intervene and the scattered positions of its forces frustrated its staff. A staff officer later explained the untenable situation for the German troops to *Maj.* Kuhle:[489]

We did everything possible. We told the corps, told Hellmich: We will gladly take over a larger sector with our strong battalions, only to be able to join up with [you] Herr Major [Kuhle, III./1050] again. We wanted to take over the entire sector, so that [you] Herr Major would form our right flank. But they did not agree to that. We told them: Please, we just relieved Bataillon Mügge [II./1057]. Please give us back Maj. Kuhle. We have already taken over the sector — that of the entire force of Klosterkemper [GR 920] — we have taken it over with a battalion. The complete sector of Simon [GR 921] and Mügge we took over with a battalion. Just a part of Mügge's force was in between [the division and the III./1050]"

On Kuhle's left flank, there were still 30 men with *Hauptmann* Siepmann (*II./922*, part of *KG Simon*), and *Bataillon Mügge* was to the left of this small force.[490]

Yes, we took over a part of Mügge['s force]. Siepmann was already under us. When the big gap of 3-4 km was torn, then we simply subordinated Siepmann to us, with the entire battalion.

It was exactly the same with Lausberg [II./1049] as he was taken from us: We asked the corps [about the battalion] three or four times a day. It was just the same with Hptm. Ries [I./1050] who was in the fortress [St. Malo]. We asked the corps every day: "The division requests information as to the present location of the I./1050: When can it be expected to arrive at the division?" Never got an answer.

The division's fate was not only determined by the crisis developing in the *91. LL.D.* sector, but also by a difference of opinions between headquarters on how to conduct the fighting on the Cotentin. As a result, its chances of escaping the Cotentin were severely diminished.

On the morning of **14 June**, *Gen.* Dollmann discussed the situation with *Feldm.* Rommel, who noted that the centre of gravity had shifted from the northern portion of the beachhead to the west. The field marshal ordered that all forces available in the north be used to prevent the Cotentin from being cut off; he also observed that three divisions need not remain on the peninsula. Two divisions would suffice for Cherbourg, an apparent reference to the *709.* and the *243. I.D.* The neck of the peninsula had to be kept open at all costs; to accomplish this, the *77. I.D.* was to reinforce the western sector and Rommel decided that the battalion earmarked for Cherbourg had to be returned to the division.[491]

AOK 7 responded by issuing orders to the *LXXXIV. A.K.* An enemy breakthrough at La Haye-du-Puits and Périers was to be prevented at all costs; the *77. I.D.* was to be withdrawn from either side of the Merderet and used to strengthen the *Westfront*. In the event of an impending breakthrough around Valognes or the cutting of the Cotentin, the troops in the north (*709. I.D.*, *243. I.D.* and *91. LL.D.*) were to move to *Festung Cherbourg*, either by order of the corps or — in an emergency — on *Gen.Lt. Hellmich's* authority.[492] The *77. I.D.* was not to be cut off on the peninsula.[493]

The corps dispatched liaison officers to inform the divisions involved. The orders included plans to divide forces on the Cotentin into a *Gruppe von Schlieben* and a *Gruppe Hellmich*.[494] *Gruppe von Schlieben* would defend Cherbourg; *Gruppe Hellmich* would try to hold the western sector or, if unable to do so, build a defensive line across the base of the peninsula. Preparations were to begin at once. This included sending the trains to the rear and selecting positions in the new sector for the artillery and command posts.[495]

For the time being, the division remained on the Merderet front. To the southwest, the situation took a turn for the worse on **15 June**. A gap opened up east of St. Sauveur-le-Vicomte, which required the attention of *AOK 7*. *Gen.Maj.* Pemsel (the chief of staff for *AOK 7*) considered the *77. I.D.* to be the best option for dealing with the crisis. This would also enable it to be reassembled as a whole, since two battalions were already deployed to the south and another was coming up from St. Malo. At 10:30, *AOK 7* informed *H.Gr. B* that it was unlikely the entire division could be withdrawn, as all of its elements were already deployed and pulling them out would result in the collapse of the front. As a result, the decision was made to reinforce the *Westfront* with elements of the *91. LL.D.*[496]

Just after midnight on **16 June**, *AOK 7* informed Rommel's army group about the dire situation on the Cotentin. It concluded that the enemy's operations south of Orglandes pointed to their intention to cut

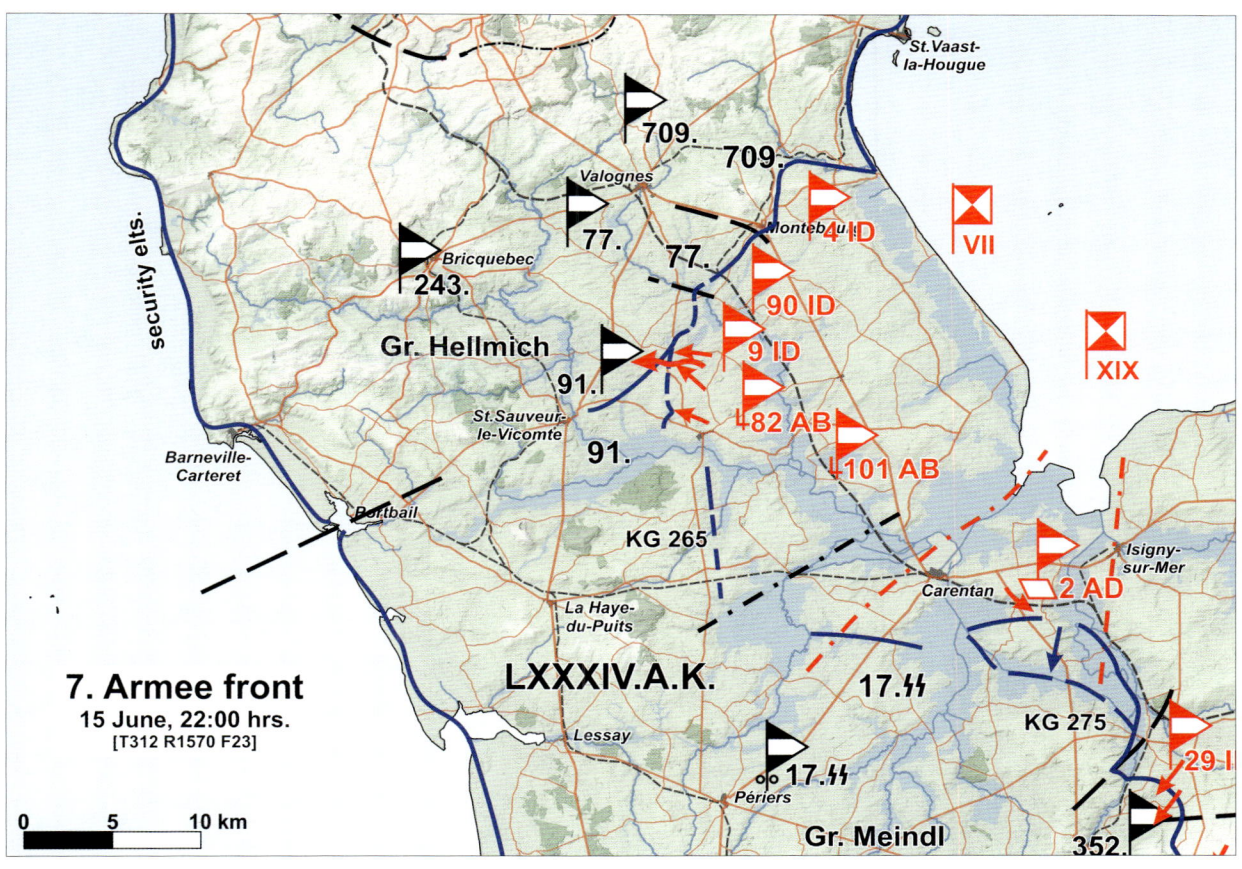

The 7th Army situation map of 15 June is one of their few showing a sector for the 77.I.D., but not very accurately. In reality the division's right boundary was west of the Merderet River where it opposed the 90th ID around Gourbesville. To the southwest, the front of the 91.LL.D. was about to collapse.

off the peninsula. To prevent forces from becoming trapped, the field army requested a rapid decision to pull back the northern sector to Cherbourg and the western sector to the south.[497] To enable this, the corps carried out a reorganisation of its troops on the Cotentin. As previously arranged, parts of *Gruppe Hellmich* were split off to form *Gruppe von Schlieben*. The two groups became responsible for the western and norther sectors, respectively; they were also known as the *Nordgruppe* (Schlieben) and *Südgruppe* (Hellmich). The boundary between the two was the line Ste. Mère-Église - Orglandes - Ste. Colombe (*Gruppe von Schlieben*) – St. Jacques-de-Néhou.[498] This put the 77. *I.D.* with *Gruppe von Schlieben*, but in light of previous considerations it was clearly intended to join *Gruppe Hellmich* when possible.

The situation on the *Westfront* became increasingly perilous on **15-16 June**. The front was pushed back and a new screening line established along Gourbesville - Orglandes - south to La Bonneville - Crosville - then to the Douve River.[499] American forces were now within reach of St. Sauveur-le-Vicomte.

As urged earlier by the corps, the 77. *I.D.* had prepared to withdraw its battlegroups either to Cherbourg or to the south. It was now time to act.[500] At 10:00 on **16 June**, there was a meeting at the divisional command post. The officers were instructed that the division would move south, bypassing the enemy. Although preparations were made for this plan, orders arrived from higher headquarters that afternoon resulting in its cancellation. The division was now compelled to remain where it was against the wishes of almost everyone.[501]

131

At 10:35, *Gen.* Fahrmbacher called *AOK 7* and informed it that *Gruppe von Schlieben* and *Hellmich* had been formed. The main threat was to the area defended by *Gruppe Hellmich*, where a collapse of the line and a breakthrough to the west were expected within hours. The commanding general urged that the *77. I.D.* be allowed to move south. This would leave only the *709. I.D.* to defend Cherbourg, but the fortress did not have enough supplies to support a larger number of troops. The withdrawal of the *77. I.D.* would also necessitate a withdrawal to Cherbourg, a contingency plan referred to as *Bewegung Cherbourg* (Movement Cherbourg). *AOK 7* understood the request and, although such a move required its authorisation, the field army compromised by stating that everything on the Cotentin intended for mobile warfare, including all mobile artillery, was to be moved south in time to evade an enemy breakthrough.[502]

Although the situation was growing increasingly desperate, the corps' request was not approved. At 10:50, *Gen.Lt.* Hans Speidel, the chief-of-staff of *H.Gr. B*, informed *AOK 7* that a *Führer* order forbade *Bewegung Cherbourg*. The forces were to stay where they were. The *LXXXIV. A.K.* was at once informed of Hitler's decision.[503] *Gen.* Fahrmbacher could do little more than point out to *AOK 7* that a collapse of the front was now imminent. Indeed, at 13:00 he informed his superiors at *AOK 7* that the enemy had opened a 5 km wide gap between Étienville (Pont-l'Abbé) and Orglandes.[504]

A short while later, Pemsel informed Speidel that the only way to salvage the situation would be to pull the *77. I.D.* out and strengthen the front around St. Sauveur. As a result, the withdrawal to Cherbourg would also be necessary. These actions would have to be decided by *Feldm.* Rommel, who was then at the *LXXXIV. A.K.* to personally assess the situation. In any case, no decision was made and, at 15:35, *Gen.* Fahrmbacher reported that St. Sauveur-le-Vicomte had been lost.[505]

At 16:50, *Feldm.* Rommel, at the corps headquarters, was informed of Hitler's orders by *Gen.* Dollmann. Dollmann inquired if the corps could transfer at least some troops from the north into the gap; in response, Rommel decided that minor elements of the *77. I.D.* could be moved south.[506]

At 17:30, Pemsel spoke again with Speidel about the deteriorating situation on the peninsula. In addition to the gap at St. Sauveur, vigorous enemy aerial reconnaissance was reported along the west coast — an ominous sign. Despite the situation, Speidel could only repeat that Hitler's order remained in effect. For his part, Pemsel insisted that the withdrawal to Cherbourg needed to be carried out at once; he also observed that the more troops committed to the fortress, the sooner its ammunition and supplies would run out.[507] This was another argument supporting a decision to move more troops to the south.

Acutely aware that time was being wasted, *Gen.* Fahrmbacher tried to force a decision. At 17:45, after Rommel had left, he told Pemsel of the situation on the Cotentin and the outcome of the meeting with Rommel. Based on the meeting, the *77. I.D.* was to be attached to *Gruppe Hellmich* and deployed west of St. Sauveur to prevent a breakthrough to the west and south. Simultaneously, this would force *Gruppe von Schlieben* to withdraw to Cherbourg. *Gen.Lt.* Pemsel again referred to the *Führer* order and demanded an unequivocal answer as to whether Rommel had issued these orders. *Gen.* Fahrmbacher had to admit that Rommel had not actually done so. He asked *AOK 7* to respond with a decision that evening.[508] His attempt to use the vacuum in decision making following Rommel's departure had failed.

In captivity, *Maj.* Viebig (the corps *Ia*) later explained the situation. Although Rommel had agreed that all troops able to leave should evacuate the Cotentin, he was still bound by his orders to keep everything in place. *Gen.* Fahrmbacher asked if the dire situation meant that they should disobey their orders. Rommel apologised, but said he simply could not do so.[509] As *Maj.* Hayn the (corps *Ic*) quoted him: "Against a *Führerbefehl* even I am powerless!"[510]

At 19:15, *H.Gr. B*. again repeated to *AOK 7* the explicit orders from the *Führer* not to retreat to Cherbourg. This was forwarded to the corps, which was also informed that detailed orders would be given after a meeting with Rommel, who was due to arrive at the *7. Armee* headquarters.[511]

The meeting with Rommel started at 21:20, with Dollmann, Pemsel and Rommel discussing the developing crisis. The field marshall called Speidel and *Gen.Lt.* Blumentritt (chief-of-staff of *H.Gr. D*) and informed *Feldm.* von Rundstedt of the measures to be taken regarding the situation on the Cotentin. Rommel decided that the *77. I.D.* had to send troops to St. Sauveur-le-Vicomte immediately and prevent an enemy advance along the road to Cherbourg. Reserves could be deployed as required, but there was to be no retreat. Moreover, the troops had to continue holding the positions of the *77. I.D.*[512] Based on these decisions, *AOK 7* issued fresh orders to the *LXXXIV. A.K.*:[513]

> *Everything has to stay where it is, however, those parts of Gruppe [von] Schlieben and the 77. I.D. that can be pulled out have to be deployed at St. Sauveur to block the road to Cherbourg. A withdrawal cannot take place."*

As the day progressed, the *77. I.D.* came under mounting pressure. It encountered its first armoured opposition around Orglandes and, during the evening, *GR 1049* again reported attacks on its right flank.[514] Time was growing short, but nothing changed until the next morning.

At 10:35 on **17 June**, as *Feldm.* Rommel and von Rundstedt were conferring with Hitler at his headquarters in Soissons, a new *Führer* order arrived at *AOK 7*: *Bewegung Cherbourg* had finally been authorised but with strict conditions.[515] Rommel issued new orders:[516]

> *The Nordgruppe of the LXXXIV. A.K. (Gruppe [von] Schlieben) may execute a fighting withdrawal from its current positions, but this can only begin under strong enemy pressure. The enemy advance has to be delayed by all possible diversions.*

The *LXXXIV. A.K.* was informed of the decision at 11:00. The corps reported to *AOK 7* that there was fighting in St. Sauveur and that a move south would begin only under pressure, in accordance with Hitler's orders for Cherbourg.[517] Since Hitler's order authorised a withdrawal to Cherbourg, it offered the possibility of moving the *77. I.D.*, which Rommel had wanted since **14 June**. At corps level — and presumably at *AOK 7* and *H.Gr. B* — the withdrawal of *Gruppe von Schlieben* to Cherbourg and *Gruppe Hellmich* to the south were seen as two sides of the same coin. Now that the *Führer* order authorised the first movement, the latter was also considered approved.[518] But, moving the *77. I.D.* would accelerate the collapse of the front between Montebourg and the west coast; hence, it would clash with Hitler's intention of holding Cherbourg as long as possible. For commanders at the front, however, the priority was different than Hitler's — to prevent an American breakout from the Cotentin Peninsula. The *77. I.D.* was urgently needed for that task.

According to *AOK 7*, Rommel ordered two battalions from the division to St. Sauveur to build a new front.[519] This was more significant than it sounds, as it affected most of the division's infantry north of the American advance. Although the communications log of *AOK 7* does not mention orders regarding the transfer of the *77. I.D.*, around 14:30 the field army again pointed out to the *LXXXIV. A.K.* that all units used for mobile operations should be pulled out.[520] The corps interpreted this as approval for the division's transfer to *Gruppe Hellmich*.[521]

In effect, little actually changed, as *Gen.* Stegmann had already issued his withdrawal orders early on **17 June**. The objective was clear:[522]

> *The 77. I.D. breaks contact with the enemy at 10:00 on 17 June (if clear weather, only during the evening of the 17th) and will reach without pause [the] area [of] La Haye-du-Puits.*

To enable this, *Obst.* Stoltenburg, the commander *AR 177*, was to form a screen line to cover the division's withdrawal. For this he was assigned *Pi. Btl. 177*, the combat school of *GR 1049* (both units equipped with bicycles), and the *III./AR 177*. The force would establish a line from Magneville, via Hau. Gaillot and Hau. Quettier, to the railway crossing 2 km southwest of St. Sauveur-le-Vicomte. This line had to be in place by 10:00. The division would withdraw behind this security line. Two routes were selected for the combat troops. *KG Bacherer*, consisting of *GR 1049* (minus the 2nd Battalion), *Btl. Siepmann (II./922)* and *Pz.Jg.Kp. 177*, would take route A: La Croix des Aulnays - Magneville - Le Carrefour - St. Jacques-de-Néhou - Le Pont aux Moines - Besneville - St. Sauveur-de-Pierrepont. *KG Brandt*, with his *GR 1050* (minus the 1st and 3rd Battalions) and the *I./AR 177*, would take route B: La Croix des Aulnays - l'Étang-Bertrand - Bricquebec - Fierville-les-Mines - Gouttière - crossroads of D264 and D903 - crossroads of D903 and D137 (east of Les Fosses) - St. Nicolas-de-Pierrepont. Route C ran across the main roads from Bricquebec via Barneville and Portbail to St. Lô-d'Ourville.[523] This longer route was reserved for the more mobile units.[524]

The division acted quickly. The trains and vehicles not belonging to the combat troops were ordered to march south, through Bricquebec, Barneville and La Haye-du-Puits. The new sector for the trains was to be in the area of Lessay - Périers - Laulne.[525] In line with these orders, *Pz.Jg.Abt. 177* established a blocking position south of Colomby - Magneville to protect the rear, while the *III./AR 177* did the same east of St. Jacques-de-Néhou.[526] However, American armour had already broken through parts of these lines by 15:00.[527]

GR 1049 was to leave a sizeable rearguard on the line and move via Bricquebec and St. Jacques-de-Néhou to St. Sauveur. *GR 1050* would move through l'Étang-Bertrand to Bricquebec, then follow *GR 1049*.[528] The divisional support units had started to move south during the day and many managed to reach La Haye-du-Puits.[529] The combat units waited until about 23:00 and used the darkness to their advantage. They caught a break when they reached the bridge across the Scye southeast of Le Valhue (D900). Here, the 9th ID had failed to establish a roadblock to protect the rear of its 60th IR; this oversight enabled *GR 1049* to cross the stream and surprise the 1/39th IR, which had been attached to the 60th IR and the 60th Field Artillery Battalion (60th FA).[530] In St. Jacques-de-Néhou, the regimental spearhead encountered American troops and the engineer platoon attacked to push the enemy out of the town.[531] The fighting was intense, forcing the Germans to bring up infantry and artillery support. Bitter fighting took place between 04:00-06:00 on **18 June** and although the Americans were forced back, the road stayed closed and the regiment had to find a different route.[532]

Further west, *GR 1050* had its own problems. Unlike *GR 1049*'s route, the 60th IR had set up roadblocks on the Scye bridges south of Bricquebec to protect its lines of communication. At 03:00, two vehicles from *GR 1050* (presumably from the regimental "bicycle" platoon under *Leutnant* Weustermann) struck mines on the D50 south of Les Perques. The regimental engineer platoon was ordered to clear the road, with *Obst.* Brandt personally leading the effort. The Americans opened fire when the men were just 40 metres away, hitting the platoon. Despite German claims, no US armour took part in this action. The roadblock was held by a platoon from the 60th IR's anti-tank gun company and half of the anti-tank-mine platoon. Just as with *GR 1049*, the road remained blocked.[533] The regiment turned around, moved west, and reached the Bricquebec - Barneville road. *Obst.* Brandt went ahead to locate new routes but failed to return;[534] he had been taken prisoner.[535] In the darkness, parts of the regiment and division lost contact with the lead battalion (*II./1050*). Southwest of Bricquebec, the battalion was forced to take cover at dawn because of Allied air cover. The battalion slipped into the woods southwest of Bricquebec. The regiment was forced to wait until dark before it could resume its attempt to break out through Barneville.[536]

Further east, components of *AR 177* attempted to cross the bridge over the Scye on the D127 at 05:00. This was the site of another roadblock — similar in strength and organisation to the one on the D50 — and the Germans were stopped by American fire. The lead vehicles were destroyed, forcing the rest to fall back. This action also resulted in a number of officers from the divisional staff being captured by the Americans.[537]

At about 06:00, *Gen.Maj.* Stegmann was fatally wounded by an Allied strafing attack several hundred metres southeast of Bricquebec, while directing the retreating vehicles.[538] The wounded general was carried southwest with the artillery units.[539] The *Ia*, *Major* Seiffert, temporarily assumed command of the division.[540]

The column sought to escape to the south on the Bricquebec - Barneville road (D90). Elements of the 60th IR, however, had already reached the high ground (Hill 145) northeast of the crossroads at Maison Bosquet and spotted the German column below. As the head of the column reached the crossroads, the infantry, tank destroyers and all of the divisional artillery opened fire.[541] The Germans were stopped as the American fire skilfully crept along the road. When the firing stopped, destroyed German artillery, prime movers, vehicles, dead horses and all manner of other material stretched a distance of 9.5 km. The destruction continued north, but the road there could not be examined because the wreckage had made it impassable. German personnel losses had been light, but in the chaos Stegmann went missing, his ultimate fate unknown to his men and German headquarters.[542]

The division's efforts to escape were thwarted everywhere by US forces, and the situation was becoming increasingly desperate. Around 08:00, officers of the *II./1050*, at the head of the division, scouted ahead to check the situation in Barneville. They soon discovered that motorised American troops were already in the town and that the northwest entrance was blocked by infantry. Even the coast was in enemy hands, eliminating that possibility as well.[543] Few options remained.

At 13:00, *Obst.* Bacherer arrived in the rest area. Elements of *GR 1049* were pulled from St. Jacques-de-Néhou and a *Kampfgruppe 77. I.D.* was formed with Bacherer in command. Artillery support and anti-tank weapons were no longer available. At 22:00, the colonel briefed his officers. The situation was bleak butt not without hope. They would not surrender, but try to break out. At 22:30, the *Kampfgruppe* made its move. Villages, crossroads and American artillery positions were carefully bypassed.[544] Several *Volkswagens* and two radio lorries were pushed silently through the first American line.[545]

At about 10:00-11:00 on **19 June**, the force reached the railway east of Barneville and came upon American forces. The men were given a few hours rest in a sunken road; rain and cloud cover offered welcome protection from Allied aircraft. An American bivouac was just 500 metres away.⁵⁴⁶ As the men were resting, a surviving radio lorry managed to contact the *LXXXIV. A.K.* and reported the situation and the unit's plans: At 13:00, the *Kampfgruppe* would attack at St. Lô-d'Ourville. The German troops believed they had been discovered by reconnaissance planes, as nearby American troops prepared for an attack. The *Kampfgruppe* fell back a few kilometres to evade the American movements. With the support of some approaching assault guns, an American position near Villot was overrun from the rear. At the Ollande River, there was still a risk that all efforts to escape had been in vain. The *II./1050* valiantly stormed the bridge, seizing it intact along with 12 Jeeps and 120 prisoners. The battalion commander, *Hauptmann* Indlekofer, was later awarded the Knight's Cross (*Ritterkreuz*).⁵⁴⁷

Although it had taken a few days, *Obst.* Bacherer had finally succeeded in leading a group of 1,200-1,400 men — albeit without their heavy weapons — south through American lines. About 400 of these were frontline troops.⁵⁴⁸ Although most of the men belonged to the *77. I.D.*, personnel of the *91. LL.D.*

Not all troops from the 77.I.D. were able to break out. These officers were captured and photographed on the Place Ste.Anne in Bricquebec. (Alamy)

and the *243. I.D.* were also in the group.⁵⁴⁹ On **11 August**, *Obst.* Bacherer was awarded the Oakleaves (*Eichenlaub*) to his Knight's Cross.⁵⁵⁰

Even though the escape could be viewed as a success, the division's move south was controversial. Berlin had intended to use it to defend Cherbourg, but senior commanders on the ground felt that the division was clearly needed to help prevent an American advance to the south and out of the peninsula. Rommel's order from **14 June** was an excellent example of this thinking.

Officially, the final move to St. Sauveur was an attempt to prevent the Cotentin from being cut off and isolated. Even if this had been a realistic goal, it also meant that contact with *Gruppe von Schlieben* would be lost, ultimately forcing its withdrawal to Cherbourg, a move that was authorised by Hitler early on **17 June**. That evening, contact between the *Nordgruppe* (von Schlieben) and *Südgruppe* was only being maintained by weak covering forces.⁵⁵¹ Taking additional troops from the right of the *Nordgruppe* (i.e., *77. I.D.*) would have predictable results.

It appears everyone directly involved was well aware of the consequences of Rommel's orders, but kept quiet and played along.⁵⁵² As late as 10:30 on **18 June**, *AOK 7* had informed *H.Gr. B.* that it had put *Gruppe von Schlieben* directly under its command and that it was to continue fighting along with the *709. I.D.*, the *77. I.D.* and weak forces from the *243. I.D.*⁵⁵³ In reality, the *77. I.D.* had already begun to withdraw southwest on **17 June** and had been fighting its way through overnight.⁵⁵⁴ As a result, the reference to "elements of the *77. I.D.*" was misleading.

In his post-war monograph, *Gen.Lt.* von Schlieben was very clear about the situation and refuted the accuracy of the *AOK 7* records:⁵⁵⁵

> *[On 17 June] the remaining units of the 77. I.D., which had briefly been attached to me, were withdrawn and moved off to the south. [...] There remained only the 709. I.D. with the badly battered GR 922.*

The general specifically addressed the report of 10:30 on **18 June**:⁵⁵⁶

> *It must be said that in reality no closed formations of the 77. I.D. had belonged to Gruppe [von] Schlieben since the evening of 17 June. The report goes too far and creates a false impression by considering some wounded who had been left behind or stragglers as "forces".*

77.Infanterie-Division

The withdrawal of the *77. I.D.* to the south had never been formally ordered by the highest command levels. To the contrary, the *OKW* had ordered the division to move north to defend Cherbourg.[557] An infuriated Hitler demanded answers. He wanted to know what orders had been issued by *Ob.West*, *H.Gr. B*, *AOK 7*, and the *LXXXIV. A.K.* about the forces that were to defend Cherbourg. Above all, he wanted to know who had ordered the regiment and/or the *77. I.D.* to break out to the south.[558]

His questions were passed down the chain of command and, on **22 June**, *AOK 7* and the *LXXXIV. A.K.* discussed the division's breakout:[559]

Gruppe Hellmich with the subordinated 77. I.D. had orders, in case of an enemy breakthrough at Valognes or the threat of the Cotentin being cut, to turn south. Before this measure could be taken, the front of the 243. I.D. [here presumably meaning Gruppe Hellmich] had collapsed by the enemy advance through St. Sauveur. Thereupon, after carrying out the ordered transfer of battalions to Gruppe [von] Schlieben, the [remaining] elements of the 77. I.D. broke out to the south at their own initiative and led by Obst. Bacherer. Obst. Bacherer had to decide to either try to reach Gruppe v. Schlieben — which would have been possible — or to break through to the south. He decided on the latter, even though this was considerably more difficult.

Previously, Gen. Stegmann had intended to move [his division] to strengthen the front west of St. Sauveur. He was however killed before this could be accomplished. The decision to break out was taken by Obst. Bacherer.

Gen. Fahrmbacher, who had returned to the *XXV. A.K.* after having been replaced as commander of the *LXXXIV. A.K.* on the **18th**, specified that, as ordered, one battalion had been transferred to *Gruppe von Schlieben*.[560] Presumably, he was referring to the "Cherbourg battalion", which was most likely never sent to Cherbourg. It is also possible his reference is to the *II./1050* on the Montebourg front, but that battalion had also moved south.

Based on the information received from the corps, *AOK 7* informed *H.Gr. B* later on the **22nd**:[561]

The 77. I.D. arrived on the peninsula piece by piece. The first elements arrived on the Nordfront on 12 June. It remained there until 16 June. Two battalions were committed, a third was ordered to Festung Cherbourg. These battalions were severely affected [in the fighting]. Because the enemy shifted his centre of gravity to the west, the field army was forced, on orders from the commander-in-chief of H.Gr. B [Rommel], to transfer two battalions to strengthen the front at St. Sauveur. These battalions, however, arrived too late and were surrounded. In view of the situation, the commander of GR 1049, after the divisional commander had been seriously wounded and gone missing, decided to break out to the south.

That evening, Rommel informed *Ob.West*. The field marshall presented the events as the inevitable result of an unfortunate combination of factors:[562]

At 22:00 [on 17 June] an order was sent by telegraph that the Nordgruppe of the LXXXIV. A.K. was only to commence a fighting withdrawal to Festung Cherbourg when under heavy enemy pressure.
At this time, elements of the 91. LL.D., the 77. I.D., the 243. I.D. and the 709. I.D. belonged to the Nordgruppe.
On 18 June, the commander of the 77. I.D., as directed by H.Gr. [B], had orders to turn south/southwest from the direction of l'Étang-Bertrand (8 km south of Valognes (sic)) with the two available battalions from the 77. I.D. and establish a defensive front at St. Sauveur-le-Vicomte that faced east in order to eliminate the threat of a breakthrough to the west. Already in the area of St. Jacques [-de-Néhou], it came into contact with the enemy, who had advanced there. The divisional commander was seriously wounded and missing. Because of the situation, the commander of the 709. I.D. placed these elements of the 77. I.D. under his command to protect the flanks. A strong enemy advance, roughly along the road that led to Bricquebec from the southeast, separated these elements of the 77. I.D. from the 709. I.D. It was through this development that the enemy cut off the battalions — which had been intended and ordered by the commander of the 709. I.D. to stay with the 709. I.D. — from the Nordgruppe, rather than through a "deliberate breakout to the south." [The force was] surrounded by the enemy and pushed towards the Südgruppe. Subsequently, [it] broke through weaker enemy forces to the south/southwest.

The version of events as reported by Rommel was well phrased. It conveniently omitted the fact that the *77. I.D.* had been made part of the *Südgruppe* and that no real forces from the division were supporting the *Nordgruppe*. Moving troops to St. Sauveur had also opened a gap with the *Nordgruppe*.

Questioning Rommel's account would have been difficult. Contact with the troops had largely been lost, forcing them to act on their own initiative or to follow previous orders. Key individuals were also not available: *Gen.* von Schlieben was cut off in Cherbourg; *Gen.* Hellmich and Stegmann had both been killed; and *Gen.* Fahrmbacher had been replaced by *Gen.* von Choltitz and was back in Bretagne.

Berlin did not readily accept the explanation provided by von Rundstedt and, on **26 June**, *Feldm.* Keitel (chief of staff of the *OKW*) ordered a formal investigation into the responsibility of *H.Gr. B*, *AOK 7*, the *LXXXIV. A.K.* and Stegmann for the breakout. Von Rundstedt responded by formally appointing *Gen.d.Art.* Theissen and *Generalrichter*[563] Freiherr von Beust to investigate the matter. A staff-officer from the *LXXXIV. A.K.* confirmed that a formal inquiry was carried out. According to him, a provost marshall from the *OKH* arrived at the corps with a complete staff. Their investigation was underway when an unexpected message arrived from Keitel:[564]

On personal request of Feldm. Rommel, I have ordered the cancellation of the enquiry regarding the 77. I.D.

And that was the end of it. Rommel had taken the opportunity to discuss the matter with Keitel when visiting Hitler on **29 June**, convincing him to close the case. Theissen concluded that the matter had been insignificant to the outcome of the battle for Cherbourg.[565] The corps and division could move on.

Holding the *Nordfront*

The time and energy spent assessing the escape of the *77. I.D.* was an unwelcome distraction for the corps, which faced more pressing matters. While the fighting for Cherbourg raged to the north, the situation in the south of the peninsula was relatively quiet. Now was the time to reorganise the troops and strengthen the defences at the base of the Cotentin. This also applied to the *77. I.D.*, with the period after the breakout being used to reorganise the division. On **20 June**, the remnants of the division assembled in the area of Angoville-sur-Ay - St. Germain-sur-Ay, northwest of Lessay.[566] Two battalions stayed at the front: The *II./1049* and the *I./1050*, the latter taking over the extreme left flank of the corps on **19 June**.[567] The relief of this battalion by *Wolga-Tat.Inf.Btl. 627* began on **28 June** and, the following day, orders were given for the *II./894 (265. I.D.)* to relieve the *II./1049*.[568]

On **24 June**, the divisional headquarters was established at Haut Gue, southeast of Lessay;[569] it remained there until it moved to La Valaisserie on **4 July**.[570] *Obst.* Bacherer remained the acting division commander.[571]

To understand the extent of the reorganisation, it is necessary to examine the condition of the surviving units — which ones were stranded on the peninsula and which managed to break out. Two battalions had been south of the Douve: The *I./1050* and the *II./1049*. The latter had been in action there since **13 June**, and the former was still moving up from St. Malo. On **18 June**, both were listed among the forces south of the American breakthrough.[572]

As noted, the *III./1050* had quickly been transferred to the *91. LL.D.* when it arrived on the Cotentin. On **18 June**, the battalion was with the forces south of the American breakthrough to the west coast, suggesting it escaped with the remnants of the *91. LL.D.* and the *243. I.D.* Its losses, however, had been severe. The escape of the battalion comports with *Gen.* Fahrmbacher's assertion that only three infantry battalions and the divisional staff had been north of the breakthrough.[573] Based on evidence, the three battalions noted by Fahrmbacher were the *I.* and *III./1049* and the *II./1050*. *Obst.* Brandt (captured on **18 June**) was bitter about the use of his regiment on the Cotentin Peninsula.[574]

That's how we were thrown in and the [entire] 77. I.D. exactly the same. They sent one of my battalions [III./1050] 12 days ahead. I had no idea where it was. When I found out where it was by chance, they said: "Well, there's nothing left of that battalion!" The same happened with my second. They smashed it up just the same. The first [I./1050] which, thank God, came too late to be encircled, and is now on the southern front, that will be destroyed too, sooner or later.

On **21 June**, it was reported that only 60 men of the division were in the Cherbourg fortress — too few for a battalion in reserve.[575] This again reinforces doubts as to whether the battalion was ever sent to the fortress. Von Schlieben also stated that none of the division's organised units were with him there.[576]

77.Infanterie-Division

The artillery and anti-tank losses for the division can also be ascertained. Harrison's *Cross-Channel Attack* clearly overestimates its losses:[577]

This column [west of Hill 145], and others near Barneville and Le Valdecie, presumably included much of the 77th Division artillery, which was wholly lost in the attempt to evacuate it to the south.

This claim was likely based on German records, which seem to have been an overly pessimistic estimate in the chaos following the retreat from the Cotentin.[578] Although the division did lose guns in the breakout, the artillery regiment was not "wholly lost". An inspection of the destroyed column by the US 9th ID only found a few artillery pieces.[579] This is supported by a German report from **27 June**, suggesting the loss of half the regiment's artillery.[580]

These more accurate figures can be explained by the deployment of the artillery and anti-tank troops. On **17 June**, *Pz.Jg.Abt. 177* and the *III./AR 177* had established a screening front to protect the division's left flank as it

One of the artillery pieces lost to the US barrage on the Bricquebec - Barneville road. As the markings on the inside of the gun shield show, this le.F.H.18/40 was gun 'B' of 1./AR 177. (NARA)

moved south;[581] these elements are therefore likely to have sustained losses. Conversely, both formations were motorised, meaning they were also better able to disengage and escape the peninsula than horse-drawn units.

Evidence also indicates that the *I./AR 177* was deployed in the north, supporting the division. As it was largely horse-drawn, the chances that it escaped with minimal losses is low. By contrast, the *II./AR.177* was supporting *KG Eitner* in mid-**June** and in all likelihood was never north of the Douve.

On **27 June**, during a period of relative calm south of the Douve, the *LXXXIV. A.K.* was able to better assess the strength of its attached elements, including the *77. I.D.* Personnel losses in the division amounted to 34% of the infantry, 20% of the artillery, 22% of the engineers and 23% of the anti-tank troops.[582] These figures signify that the division still possessed one medium strength infantry battalion (300-400 men) and three weak battalions (100-200 men).[583] Divisional records offer more detailed numbers for *GR 1050*, which sustained the following losses: Headquarters Company: 17%; 1st Battalion: 34%; 2nd Battalion: ca. 40%; 3rd Battalion: 72%; 13th and 14th Companies: ca. 50%.[584] Such figures are not available for *GR 1049*, but its 3rd Battalion had reportedly suffered heavy losses, as did *Pi.Btl. 177* and *Feld-Ers.Btl. 177*. The *II./1049*, however, was still in fairly good condition.[585] Information on *Feldgendarmerie-Trupp 177* was intercepted by ULTRA in the form of an urgent request for 15 NCO's and men for the section, suggesting personnel losses of around 50%.[586]

As only four infantry battalions were mentioned on **27 June**, it raises the question as to why the division's other two battalions were not included. It appears that the *III./1049* and the *III./1050* suffered losses of such a scale that they were disbanded. This would match the fate of *Feld-Ers.Btl. 177*. Yet, upon closer examination, this does not explain the two battalions missing in the report. Instead it is more likely that the four battalions listed were only those available to the division at that time; several of the division's battalions only returned around **28 June**.[587] On **27 June**, the charts of *AOK 7* still listed the *I./1050* holding the left flank of *U.Gr. Klosterkemper (243. I.D.)*.[588] The *I./1050* was finally relieved by *Wolga-Tat.Inf.Btl. 627*, which was listed under the *Kampfgruppe* the next day.[589] Further east, the *II./1049* was relieved by the *II./894* of *U.Gr. Eitner*, as ordered on **29 June**.[590] Considering the battles they were involved in, both the *II./1049* and the *I./1050* can be expected to have been at least "medium strength" at this time. This means they cannot be part of the three weak and one medium strength battalions on **27 June**. This supports the possibility that it was these two battalions that were not included in those numbers, simply because they were not with the division.

The **27 June** report also covers losses of weapons and equipment, which were much worse than that of manpower. 70% of the division's machine guns and 85% of its AT guns had been lost.[591] Of 18 *7,5 cm Pak 40's* before the invasion, only three remained, although they were still motorised. *AR 177* is not mentioned directly, but the available artillery pieces show it still existed, if only at half-strength. The division was still equipped with eight *10,5 cm le.F.H.18/40's*, basically one complete light battalion. Six 8.8 cm AT guns were available in the *III./AR 177*, although still without sights for indirect fire (*Rundblick Fernrohr*). Four *7,5 cm Feldkanone 16 neuer Art (F.K.16 nA's)* were also available;[592] these were probably former anti-landing guns stripped from coastal defence positions, as there had been 16 of them in the *709. I.D.* sector on **1 April 1944**.[593] The four guns were likely used as replacements for heavy weapons companies in the infantry regiments. It appears that the *I./AR 177* lost all its guns on the Cotentin. Photographic evidence reveals that elements of 1st Battery were in a column attacked by artillery fire called for by 9th ID. The 2nd Battery may have abandoned its guns at Ste. Colombe, where the 9th ID captured a four-gun battery; it was complete, including horses, but without crews.[594] German records do not give information on this battalion until the second half of **July**. At that time, it was considered an emergency infantry reserve and had no guns.[595]

A sense of the division's personnel losses can be gathered from the fact that, by **5 July**, 1,166 of its men had been counted in POW cages in the UK — too early a date to include prisoners captured after **3 July**. Of the losses in **June**, only a minority could have been from units south of the Douve. A closer examination reveals the division's catastrophic withdrawal. The number of men captured was greater than the 1,027 POW's from the *91. LL.D.*, a division that had been in heavy fighting for longer than the *77. I.D.* To illustrate the relative number of prisoners, they can be calculated as a percentage of the authorised strengths (if available). As expected, the greatest losses were among the infantry, and *GR 1049* and *1050* had 514 (19%) and 355 (13.1%) captured, respectively. More telling is the capture of 211 men (16%) from *AR 177*. These POW figures were more than any other division sent to Normandy as reinforcements and were much higher than those of the

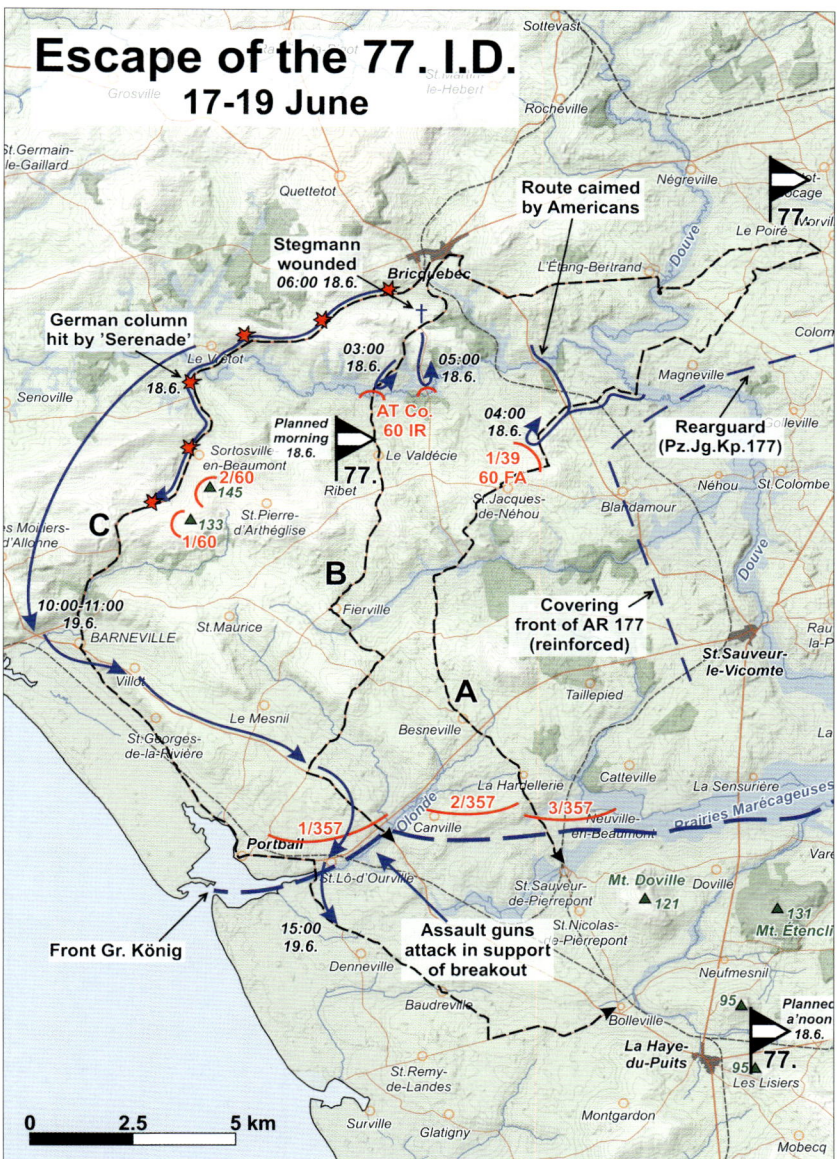

The escape of the 77.I.D. was complicated by the advance of the US 9th and 90th ID. The division suffered heavy losses in its breakout attempt before its survivors managed to join Gruppe König.

91. LL.D. Also taken prisoner were 6 men from the divisional headquarters, 41 from *Pi.Btl. 177* (9.3%), 15 from *Pz.Jg.Abt. 177*, 8 from *Feld-Ers.Btl. 177*, and 16 support troops.[596]

With *Gruppe König* holding the frontline, the *77. I.D.* and the fresh *353. I.D.* were to defend the *Mahlmann-Linie*, being built some distance to the rear. *AOK 7* intended the *77. I.D.* to anchor the left wing of this line; moreover, the *LXXXIV. A.K.* had begun work on additional defensive lines further to the rear. The northernmost of these was the so-called *Wasserlinie* (Water Line) or "Lessay - Sèves sector", which took advantage of the Sèves and Ay Rivers sealing off much of the base of the peninsula.[597] For the time being, this third line did not concern the division.

The situation map of **29 June** showed the division had moved into the *Mahlmann-Linie*, establishing a line stretching from the coast to the La Haye-du-Puits - Lessay highway. The *I./1050* was committed on the right, the *II./1050* in the centre, and the *I./1049* on the left.[598]

The battered division was prioritised for replacements, followed by the *91. LL.D.* and the *243. I.D.* This decision related to the plan to pull the *353. I.D.* from the *Mahlmann-Linie*. The *77. I.D.* would then take over the entire line.[599] The other two divisions were already in action on the forward line, which made it difficult to send them replacements.

The first replacements were in *Marschbataillon zbV 362*; then, on **5 July**, the *1./Festungs-Stamm-Reserve Ob.West* was reported as on its way.[600] Both groups consisted of men born in 1906 at the earliest, and many were in their late thirties.[601] The former had been formed in Kempten (Bavaria) and reportedly totalled 1,100-1,200 men, although officially the figure was 722. The battalion also included young soldiers from the class (*Jahrgang*) of 1926. When it reached Versailles, it was split up — possibly into march units for the journey to the front.[602] It arrived at the release point at Argentan on **29-30 June**.[603] This may have included one group of about 600 men, which was sent towards Coutances on 28 June; on **8 July**, it became the *III./1049*. Apparently, the "new" battalion included few men originally with the division. In the 9th Company, a medic was reportedly the only man who had previously served in the regiment.[604]

The grave of Gen. Stegmann at the Orglandes military cemetery. The general was posthumously promoted to Generalleutnant. (Sean Claxton)

Bricquebec after the liberation. The main square is the Place St.Anne where the officers were photographed. (NARA)

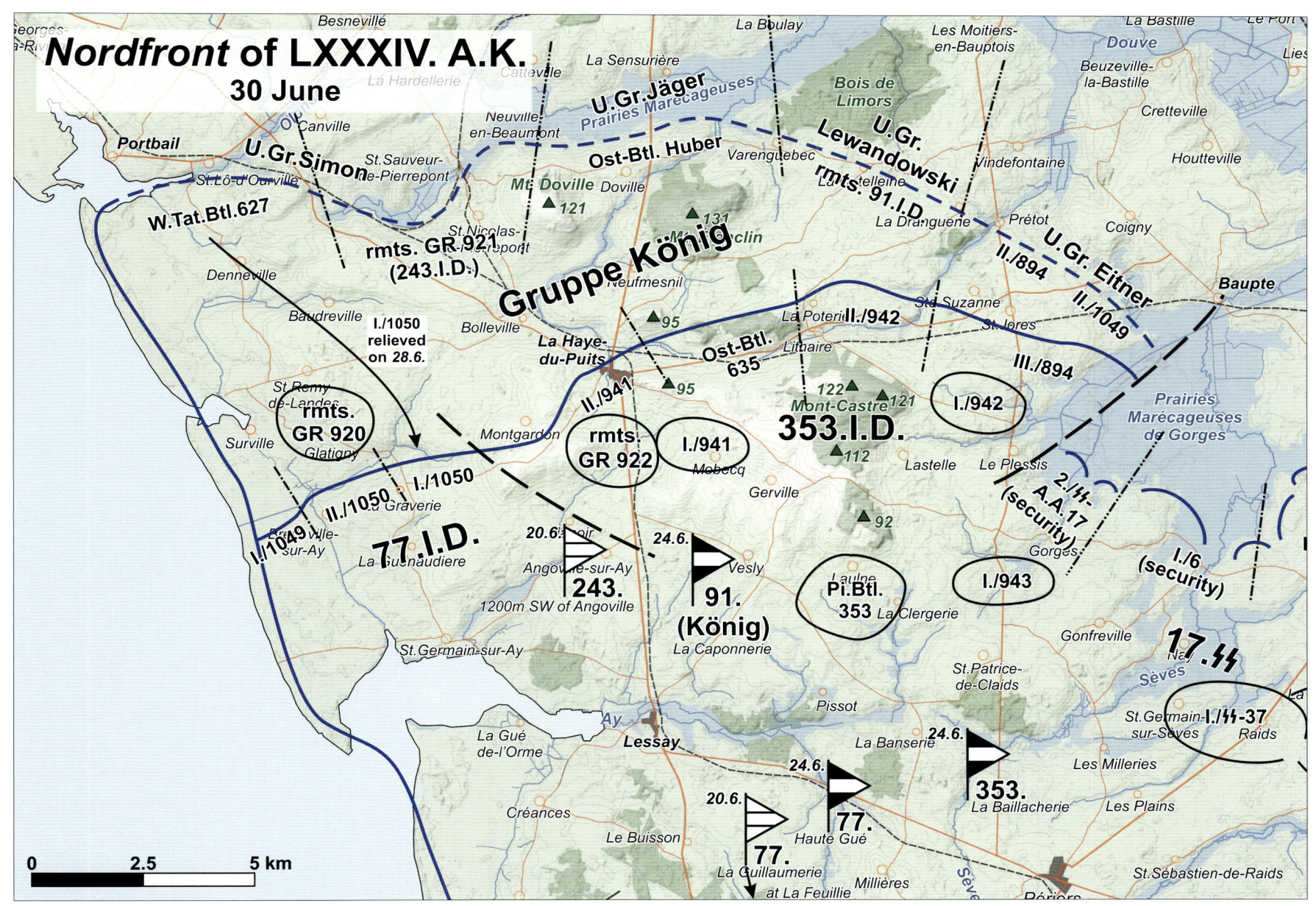

To prepare for the next American offensive, LXXXIV. A.K. established a number of defence lines. The weak forward line was held by Gruppe König. To the rear, the 77. and 353.I.D. built the Mahlmannlinie, where the 77.I.D. initially held the left wing with three battalions.

Information on the reorganisation of *GR 1050* is also available in detail. After *Obst.* Brandt was captured, *Hptm.* Indlekofer (commander of the *II./1050*) took acting command of the regiment until a higher ranking officer could be despatched. Due to its prohibitive losses, the 3rd Battalion was disbanded, leaving only its cadre (the battalion disappeared from the order-of-battle). In what was now a common practice in the German Armed Forces, regimental support units were scoured to obtain men for the combat units. *Feld-Ers.Btl. 177* was disbanded as well. The troops made available were used to reinforce the 1st and 2nd Battalions. Little, however, could be done for the regimental heavy weapons companies; both had lost all their weapons and equipment, and it would take time for replacement guns to arrive.[605]

On **29 June**, the *LXXXIV. A.K.* issued new orders for the defence of its front. *Gruppe König* would be disbanded and, instead, the *91. LL.D.* and the *243. I.D.* would assume command. The boundary between the *77. I.D.* (on the *Mahlmann-Linie*), the *91. LL.D.* (on the actual front) and the *17. SS-Pz.Gren. Div.* to their right was a line running from east of St. Aubin-du-Perron - St. Sébastien-de-Raids - Le Hommet (*77. I.D.*) - Baupte (*91. LL.D.*). This would go into effect with the departure of *SS-Pz.Aufkl.Abt. 17* from the southwest of the Prairies Marécageuses de Gorges. On the front, the *II./1049* would be relieved by the *II./894* and return to its division.[606]

These changes were related to the planned withdrawal of the *353. I.D.* from the *Mahlmann-Linie* around **30 June**; The *77. I.D.* was given responsibility for the entire line, with its centre of gravity around the Forêt de Mont-Castre. This would block most of the direct routes to Périers. Despite its relief, the *353. I.D.* still left elements on the defensive line: The *I./942*,[607] the *II./942*, *Pi. Btl. 353* and some artillery. Some of those elements were committed behind the *91. LL.D.*; others behind the *243. I.D.*[608]

The organisation and deployment of the *77. I.D.* at this time is unclear, as information is limited and often conflicting. Simply put, *GR 1049* was used on the left flank and "*GR 1050*" on the right. The latter was now an ad hoc formation, led by the former commander of the *II./1049*, Hauptmann Lausberg. As such, it was known as *KG Lausberg*. His troops included the headquarters and signals platoon from *GR 1050* and the *II./1050*. Additional infantry was provided by the *I./1049* and the *I./942* (*353. I.D.*); two-thirds of *Pz.Jg.Abt. 353* was also available with eight assault guns, six *Marders* and four *3,7cm Flak*. The *I./AR 353* provided artillery support.[609]

The composition of *GR 1049* is not clear, but it included the *I./1050*, which was apparently deployed on the regiment's right flank.[610] It is also likely that the regiment included the *II./1049*, which had been relieved from *U.Gr. Eitner*. The status of the *I.* and *III./1049* at this time is unknown. Since the *III./1049* was apparently reconstituted, this may indicate that its remnants had been divided among the *I.* and *II./1049*, much like what happened to the *III./1050*.[611]

The right boundary of *KG Lausberg* was the line Baupte - centre of the Prairies Marécageuses de Gorges - Le Hommet; its left boundary was the road that ran from Ste. Suzanne along the eastern edge of the Forêt de Mont-Castre to Lastelle. The front in this sector ran along the Carentan - La Haye-du-Puits railway. The *I./1049* was deployed on the right and in contact with *SS-Pz. Aufkl.Abt. 17* on the left flank of the *17. SS-Pz.Gren.Div.* The *I./942* held the left of the battlegroup and the *II./1050* was in reserve 800 metres southwest of Beau Coudray.[612]

On **3 July**, the US VIII Corps launched its offensive against the *Nordfront*, with the initial objective of taking the Lessay - Gorges line, before pushing on to the high ground at Coutances. The corps attacked with three divisions abreast. On its right (west) was the 79th ID, while the 82nd AB advanced in the centre and the 90th ID on the left.[613] This meant that the *77. I.D.* would primarily face the 90th ID, which initially committed its 358th IR on the left (east) with the intention of advancing south along the St. Jores - Périers road (D24). To the right, the 359th IR would take Mont-Castre and link up with the 79th ID south of La Haye-du-Puits. Once these tasks were accomplished, the reserve regiment (357th IR) would conduct a passage through the lines of the 358th IR.[614]

To oppose the American offensive, the *353. I.D.* hurried back to the *Mahlmann-Linie* and was positioned between the *77. I.D.* on the right and the *243. I.D.* on the left.[615] During the day, American forces penetrated to a depth of 500-800 metres. In response, the *II./1050* counterattacked, preventing a breakthrough but failing to clean up the penetration. A new enemy advance cut the battalion off at Carrefour St. Jores and most of its men were taken prisoner with only small groups escaping to German lines. The Americans pressed their attacks, threatening to cut off *KG Lausberg*. Swift German counterattacks again managed to seal off the penetrations but, even with support of the neighbouring *I./1050*, they could not push the Americans

On the eastern wing of the Nordfront the forward line and Mahlmann-Linie joined. Having relieved the 353.I.D., the 77.I.D. held the latter line behind the 91.LL.D. and absorbed the remnants of that division and KG 265 by then end of 4 July.

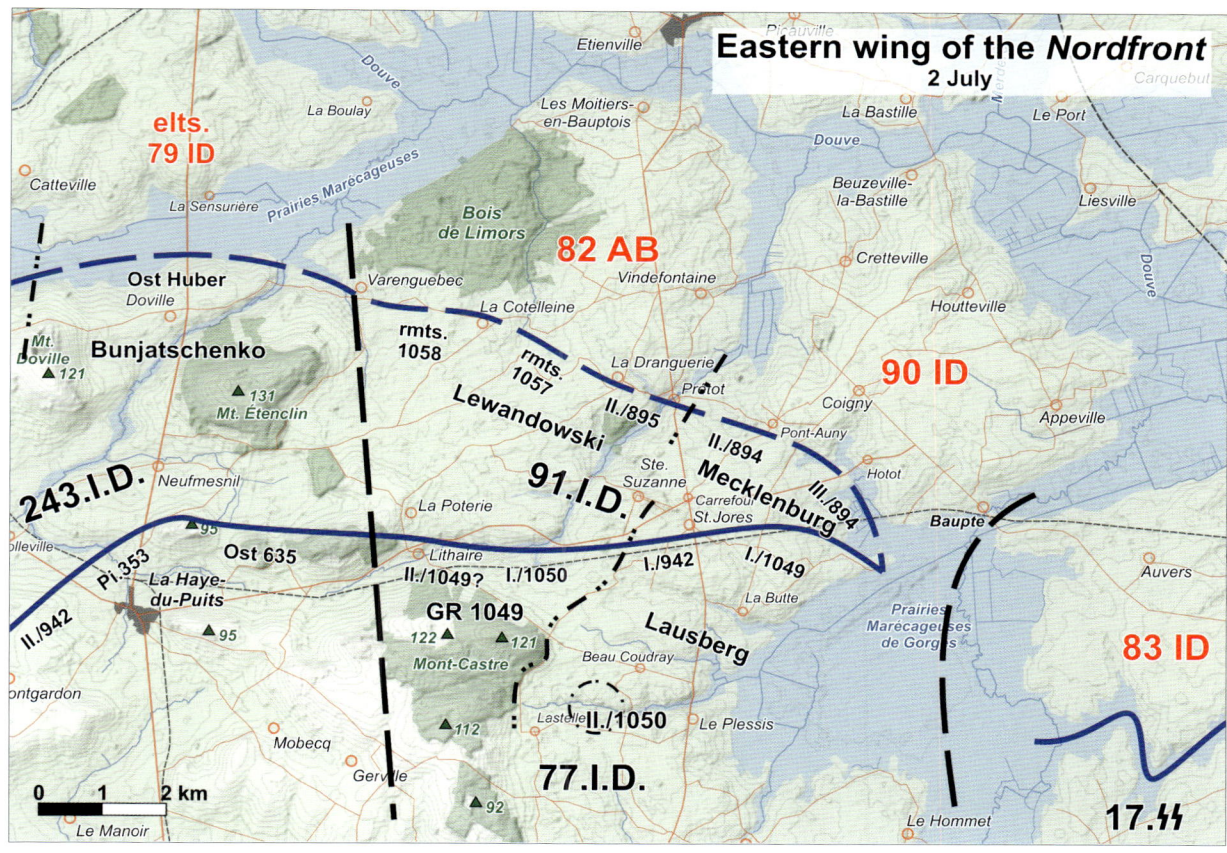

back. In *KG Lausberg*'s sector the situation stabilised after dark, when US forces pulled back to defensive positions.[616]

In response to these events, a series of measures were taken, among them the withdrawal of the *I./942* for return to its division.[617] The *77. I.D.* was ordered to take over the troops and sector of the *91. LL.D.*, which was being pushed back to the *Mahlmann-Linie*. No longer in command of troops, the *91. LL.D.*'s headquarters was put at the disposal of LXXXIV. A.K.[618] The boundary between the *77.* and the *353. I.D.* ran roughly north-south from Varenguebec to Mobecq; this put the Forêt de Mont-Castre and the hamlet of La Poterie in the sector of the *77. I.D.* and Lithaire and the Bois de la Poterie in that of the *353. I.D.*[619]

The fighting, which continued during the night, led to minor incursions that were sealed off before dawn on **4 July**.[620] On the division's right flank, *Obstlt*. Dropmann arrived as the new commander of *GR 1050*. This brought an end to *KG Lausberg*, but its troops stayed under *GR 1050*.[621] The fighting continued throughout **4 July**, focussed on St. Jores. With effective artillery support, the division conducted a successful defence and eliminated three enemy incursions, but only by committing its final reserves. By evening, however, the division was unable to prevent or eliminate new advances around Les Rivières, St. Jores (where the Americans reached La Butte) and La Poterie.[622]

The newly arrived *Obstlt*. Dropmann was heavily involved in the action and already credited with destroying two Shermans with a *Panzerfaust*. Facing intense pressure, a new defensive line was cobbled together from La Butte to the northeast corner of the Forêt de Mont-Castre, via the D140. The assault guns of *Pz.Jg.Abt.* 353 had suffered such heavy losses from artillery fire that they could no longer offer support.[623] *AOK* 7 ordered that the lines be held at all costs to prevent the enemy from advancing from St. Jores to La Butte.[624]

The fighting went on through the night, particularly in the area of La Butte and La Poterie. A lack of forces meant enemy spearheads could no longer be cleaned up. On **5 July**, the Americans resumed their attacks. The 358th IR was considered too depleted to continue and was relieved by the reserve regiment, the 357th IR, which attacked towards Périers. Despite modest defensive successes, the only corps reserve, the *I./941* (*Hptm.* Rogge), had to be used against an attack at Le Fry (west of St. Jores) on the *77. I.D.*'s left flank. The battalion's immediate counterattack was halted when the Americans struck its flank from St. Jores. Further west, the *II./941* was committed in the Bois de la Poterie.[625]

Throughout the day, the corps was ordered to hold the *Nordfront* and oppose enemy advances south and southeast of La Poterie and the Bois de la Poterie. Reinforcements were on their way, including *FJR 15* (*5. Fj.Div.*) which was moving to the area north of the Forêt de Mont-Castre, where the American penetration was considered the main threat.[626] The regiment would be under the operational control of the *77. I.D* and deployed on its left flank.[627] This way, it could relieve the *I./941*, which would return to its division.[628] Another reinforcement was a powerful battlegroup from the *2. SS-Pz.Div.*, which was not specifically earmarked to support the division, but rather the *Nordfront* in general. The *III./SS-Pz.Gren.Rgt. 4 "Der Führer"* was ultimately deployed southwest of La Haye-du-Puits, *SS-Pz.Aufkl.Abt. 2* southeast of the town and the *III./SS-Pz.Gren.Rgt. 3 "Deutschland"* at Mont-Castre.[629]

On **6 July**, the *77. I.D.* faced an American attack from the area of La Butte, through Beau Coudray and towards Le Plessis, but it was repulsed along the line Le Plessis - La Vilette - Hill 41. Another US attack was launched from St. Jores via La Rivagerie towards the crossroads east of Mont-Castre. This attack thwarted the division's own attempt to launch an attack from the south against Mont-Castre and Hill 121. To the left (west), *FJR 15* was able to recapture Hill 122 on the northern edge of the forest, although the situation on the divisional front remained critical. Allied artillery and air attacks, coupled with continuous ground assaults and counterthrusts, cost the division its final reserves. On the boundary with the *353. I.D.*, US forces had attacked southwest from the Forêt to Hill 112 (Mt. de Mobecq). During the day, the planned counterattack of *Das Reich* was delayed by Allied air activity, with the result that, by dusk, the battlegroup had reached the area northeast of Mobecq but had yet to begin its attack.[630]

In the early hours of **7 July**, the *77. I.D.* was able to recapture the main line of resistance in the area of Le Plessis after heavy fighting, in the process cutting off two companies of the 357th IR (90th ID) south of Beau Coudray.[631] Further west, *FJR 15* managed to push American troops out of the Forêt and seized Hill 121 and 122. Around 05:20, the *III./Deutschland* finally counterattacked to the west of the forest and reached the railway south of Halte la Guillaumerie in front of Hill 122. The battalion was attached to the *77. I.D.* for the attack and established contact with *FJR 15* at Hospice on the western edge of the forest. American troops, however, were still to the south of Mont-Castre.[632]

The fighting dragged on into the evening with serious encounters in the Forêt, where Hill 122 was recaptured by US troops. Even so, the American positions on Mont-Castre were precarious. Further east, US attempts to free their encircled forces failed. The *77. I.D.* continued to hold the line north of Beau Coudray and cleared the pocket, capturing 265 men and five officers. Some distance to the west, the division fought off an attack from the area of La Rivagerie.[633] In the eyes of *AOK* 7, the division had distinguished itself enough in the last few days to be mentioned in the Armed Forces Daily Announcement, a view shared by *H.Gr. B*.[634]

Temporary defensive successes could not conceal the fact that losses were steadily mounting. American records offer an insight into the division's losses in early **July**. On **3-6 July**, the VIII Corps captured 118 of the division's men. Four were from *GR 1049*, 74 from *GR 1050* (66 from the *I./1050*), and 40 from *Pi.Btl. 177*.[635] The *LXXXIV. A.K.* reported that its front had become a patchwork of units composed of whatever troops and reserves that could be scraped together and committed. Several units were consolidated and underwent battlefield reconstitution.[636] An example is the *III./1049*, reconstructed virtually from scratch around **8 July**, then redeployed almost at once. Initially, the *9./1049* was in reserve, but soon its three platoons had to be sent to reinforce the 11th Company[637]

The rate of losses meant that, sooner or later, there would not be enough men to hold the front, forcing a withdrawal to shorten the lines. For the

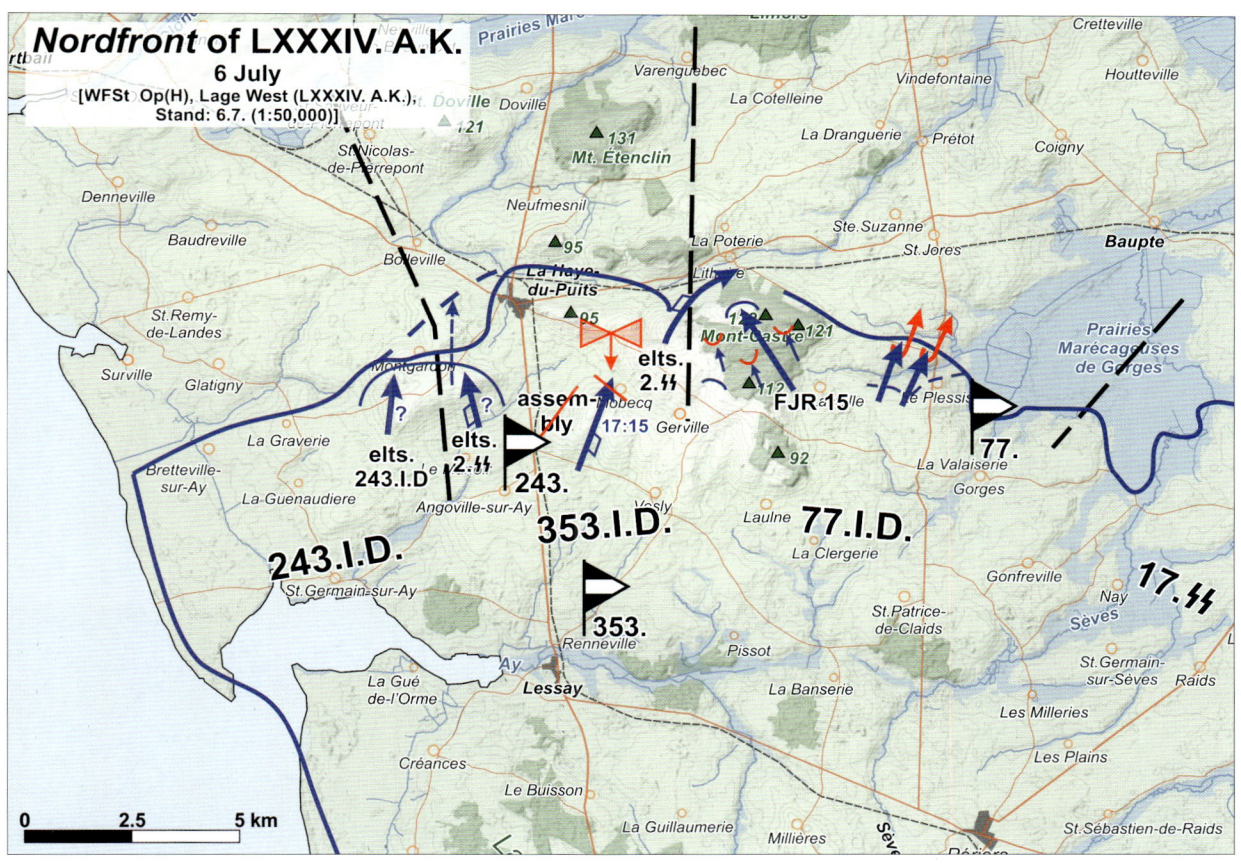

6 July saw some of the heaviest fighting along the Nordfront as FJR 15 and the Das Reich battlegroup threw in their weight. On the east flank, the 77.I.D. remained heavily engaged against the 90th ID along the road to Périers.

time being, the counterattacks of *FRJ 15* and the battlegroup of *Das Reich* had bought precious time and, unlike *Gen.* von Choltitz, the divisional commanders still thought it possible to hold the lines. In view of the situation, especially the expected withdrawal of *Das Reich* battlegroup, *AOK 7* notified *H.Gr. B* that reserves were needed for the *Nordfront*. Without them, an urgent withdrawal would have to be considered.[638] This view was supported by Rommel, but could only be carried out if absolutely necessary, while the right flank, the front of the *77. I.D.*, would need to be held regardless. To strengthen the *LXXXIV. A.K.*, it was decided that the rest of the *5. Fj.Div.* would be brought up from Normandy to relieve the *77. I.D.*[639]

H.Gr. B spoke of an "exchange", suggesting a possible return of the *77. I.D.* to Bretagne. Although the original orders have not been found, this was part of a larger plan to relieve and rebuild battered divisions. In the first two weeks of **July**, this primarily concerned the *77. I.D.*, the *91. LL.D.* and the *352. I.D.*[640] As early as **27 June**, Hitler had ordered the *275. I.D.* to be brought up to *AOK 7*'s front and to have the division's coastal sector taken over by the *77. I.D.* and the *91. LL.D.* On **5 July**, these initiatives were considered impossible due to reality of the fighting.[641]

There were no significant attacks on the *Nordfront* on **8 July**. Minor assaults were repulsed, while German efforts to clear the Forêt and close the gap to the west of the forest continued, the latter being stopped by an American counterattack. It proved impossible to pull out the *Das Reich* battlegroup;

similarly, the *5. Fj.Div.* was still earmarked for the *Nordfront*, but the situation there did not allow the *77.I.D.* to be pulled out either way. Tension mounted as the division commanders were losing confidence that they could continue to hold on to their positions.[642]

Fighting in the division's area on **9 July** was at first erratic. In the evening, it was struck on its left flank but that was successfully defended by *FJR 15*.[643] Despite the arrival of replacements, the division's strength had decreased further. This forced the consolidation of *GR 1050* with *GR 1049*, leaving just one operational regiment. The division suffered another blow with the unfortunate loss of *Obstlt*. Dropmann, who was severely wounded. In the few days he had fought with the regiment, he had distinguished himself and was later awarded the Knight's Cross.[644] The commander of this mixed force became *Maj.d.R.* Karsten.[645]

Although the fighting in the division's sector had been limited, the corps became increasingly worried about the gap between La Haye-du-Puits and Mont-Castre, where the *Das Reich* battlegroup was being withdrawn. On the night of **9-10 July**, the lines of the *353. I.D.* were pulled back to La Tourelle - the crossroads at Mobecq - Florimond - Mont du Tot (high ground southwest of the D528 and D136 crossroads). This freed up the *SS Kampfgruppe* and contact between the *353. I.D.* and the *77. I.D.* was re-established.[646] The boundary between the divisions now ran from Le Val to the northwest via Laulne and La Tourelle to the Abbaye de Blanchelande (south of Hill 131).[647] Again, little changed in the sector of the *77. I.D.*, except for the destruction of American forces that had entered the southern part of the forest.[648]

On **10 July**, the combat strength of the *77. I.D.*, including *FJR 15*, was reported as 1,840 men, covering a 10 km front.[649] That evening, the *LXXXIV. A.K.* and *AOK 7* discussed a number of measures. Among them was a possible leadership change for the division (*Obst*. Steinmüller). Another matter

An atmospheric picture showing the brutal hedgerow fighting of the 90th ID around Mont-Castre. (NARA)

concerned the potential disbanding of the *91. LL.D.*, with its artillery and transport being reassigned to the *5. Fj.Div.* and the remainder of the division to the *77. I.D.*.[650] Neither of these plans were carried out.

Early on the morning of **11 July**, after a night of heavy fighting on Mont-Castre, the division's front stretched roughly from Beau Coudray to La Tourelle (southwest of Mont Castre).[651] The *77. I.D.* witnessed heavy fighting on the eastern edge of the forest. In the centre of the *Nordfront*, the *353. I.D.* was facing increasing difficulties; therefore, *AOK 7* requested permission to pull the front back that night to the line Gonfréville - Gorges - the high ground at Hill 92 - Vesly - Angoville-sur-Ay - St. Germain-sur-Ay. Without a timely withdrawal, the forces, especially the artillery, risked being lost. Hitler approved this later that afternoon but stressed that it should not be regarded as a step towards the *Wasserlinie*. Control of the line Gonfréville - Gorges, in the sector of the *77. I.D.*, was considered of vital importance, because a breakthrough there would strike the rear of *FJR 6* and elements of *Das Reich* and *Götz von Berlichingen* defending the Carentan - Périers isthmus. Gonfréville was already under threat from enemy advances on the isthmus and a withdrawal of the *Nordfront* to the *Wasserlinie* was under consideration.[652]

The withdrawal took place on the night of the **11th**.[653] On **12 July**, the division repelled several attacks on both sides of Gorges. On the front of the *353. I.D.*, the Americans established a 1 km-wide penetration east of Vesly and moved south, where they were confronted by German reserves. In view of the overall situation, *AOK 7* requested permission from *H.Gr. B.* to pull its front back to the *Wasserlinie* and strengthen the right flank. This move was to be executed no sooner than the night of **13-14 July** and protected by a strong rearguard.[654]

As noted, in an effort to rebuild several battered infantry divisions behind the front, Hitler had decreed the immediate withdrawal of the *77. I.D.*, the *91. LL.D.* and the *352. I.D. AOK 7* responded by informing *H.Gr. B* that relieving the *77. I.D.* was no longer possible. Its planned relief by the *5. Fj.Div.* on **14-16 July** had become impossible, as this newly introduced division was in action on the right flank of the *LXXXIV. A.K.*.[655]

On **13 July**, the *77. I.D.* beat back a series of American attacks around St. Germain-sur-Sèves and northeast of Laulne. US forces, however, achieved several penetrations on the boundary with the *353. I.D.* and to the west, requiring all available reserves to seal them off.[656] Early that afternoon, the *LXXXIV. A.K.* requested permission to withdraw to the *Wasserlinie* and, at 17:00, this was approved by *H.Gr. B*. An enemy advance to the new lines was to be delayed as long as possible by rearguard action. *AOK 7* relayed orders that the *Wasserlinie* was to be resolutely defended and that any further withdrawal was unthinkable. For the moment, the withdrawal would decrease enemy pressure, while allowing time to reorganise.[657]

To occupy the new line in an orderly fashion, it was decided to pull back by disengaging rather than doing so under pressure. The plans altered the northern part of the division's boundaries. On the left (*353. I.D.*), they would now run along the line Coutances - Muneville-le-Bingard-Millières, and then continue as before. The right boundary (with *Das Reich*) was redrawn to run from Courcy - St. Sauveur-Lendelin - Périers – Gruchy - the crossroads 1.3 km southwest of Gonfréville - Le Hommet and then continue as before to Baupte. The divisional headquarters was established at Cuve (0.5 km south of Millières).[658] The withdrawal to the *Wasserlinie* was also seen as an opportunity to finally relieve and rebuild the *77. I.D.*. That evening, *H.Gr. B* ordered the divisional headquarters, signals and support troops to be pulled back to the area around St. Malo, while the combat troops were to be withdrawn step by step. *AOK 7* challenged these orders, as it considered the withdrawal of any part of the division to be out of the question given the crisis, but the orders were not revoked.[659] In Bretagne, the division was to be reconstituted under *Obst.* Bacherer.[660]

The withdrawal to the *Wasserlinie* was completed by the morning of **14 July**, despite the headquarters of the *III./1049* being cut off during the move; as a result, some of the troops around Laulne only managed to reach German lines on **17 July**. To the east, in order to comply with the new lines, the left flank of *Das Reich* was pulled back behind the Sèves. The *Nordfront* was quiet throughout the day, the enemy advancing deliberately and only making weak contact with the German outposts.[661] The lull allowed for an assessment of the condition of the *LXXXIV. A.K.*. On the *Nordfront*, the infantry strength of the *77.* and the *353. I.D.* had dropped dangerously since the beginning of the American **July** offensive. This also applied to *FJR 15*, which now had a combat strength of just 447 (all ranks); but the shattered regiment was recommended for the Armed Forces Daily Announcement.[662] Despite the order to transfer elements of the *77. I.D.* to St. Malo, this required time, and preparations only started after the withdrawal.[663]

Along the *Nordfront*, the German outposts continued to hold out on **15 July**. An exception was the left flank, where Hill 30 (east of Pissot) was lost,

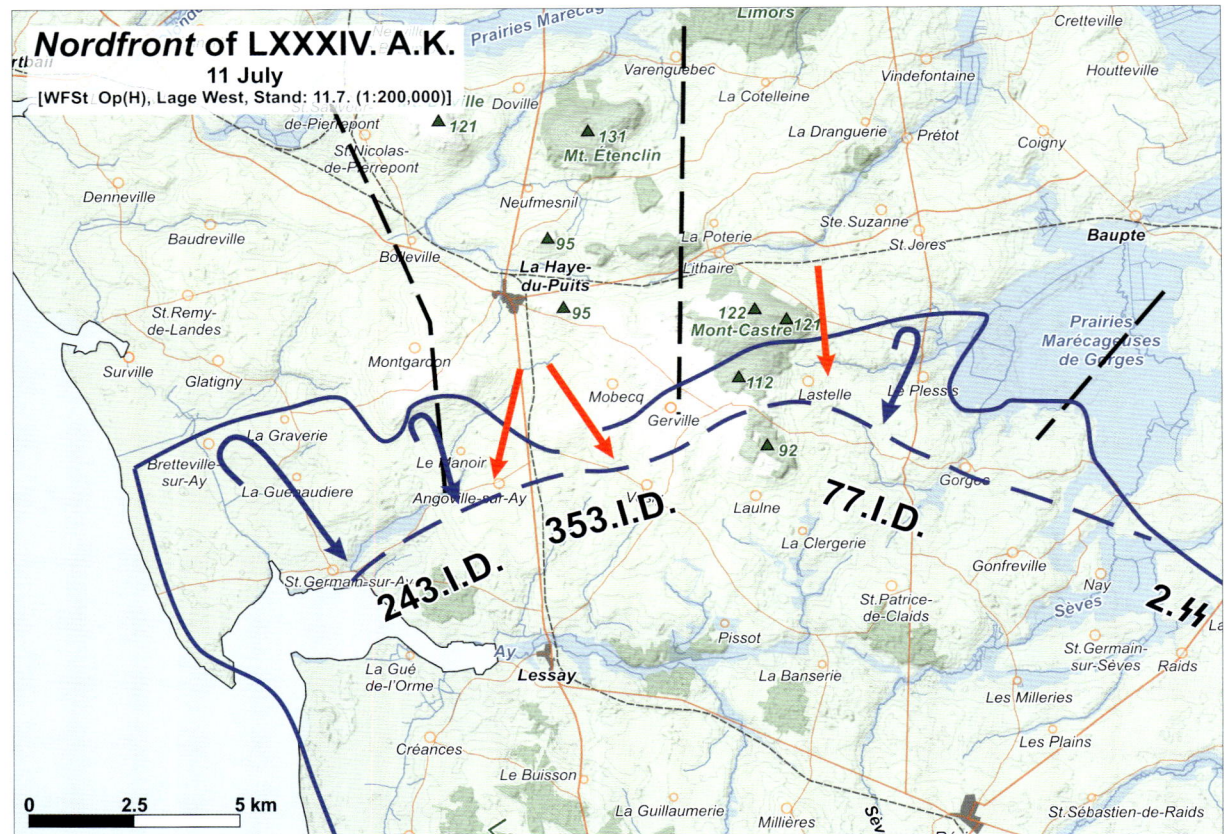

By 11 July the Nordfront was no longer able to hold on to the main positions of the Mahlmann-Linie. To gain some control of the situation the lines had to be pulled back, although it was not yet needed to withdraw to the Wasserlinie.

meaning the Americans had reached the *Wasserlinie*.[664] The command post of the *77. I.D.* was moved to Le Temple (3 km west-southwest of St. Sauveur-Lendelin).[665]

The next few days were mostly quiet.[666] Late on **16 July**, the division held its front with two (organic) battalions (probably the *I.* and *III./1049* under the command of *GR 1050*) and *FJR 15*, while *KG 265* was in reserve behind the right flank.[667]

The withdrawal of combat troops and transfer to St. Malo had yet to be carried out. On **17 July**, the entire divisional sector, including all (attached) troops, was put under the command of the *91. LL.D.*, which thus became operational again.[668] This initiative relieved the headquarters and support elements of the *77. I.D.*, which began their move to St. Malo the next day.[669] Most of the withdrawn elements assembled in the area of Villedieu-les-Poêles, where they remained until **23 July**.[670] The divisional command post was in Le Fresne, southwest of Noirpalu.[671]

The complexity in interpreting POW numbers means it is difficult to determine the division's losses since the start of **July**. By **14 July**, 1,286 of its men were prisoners in the UK, just 120 more than in **June**. This suggests a significant delay between capture, arrival and identification in the UK. This leaves questions as to the extent of the delay and the actual number of men captured. The number of prisoners from *GR 1049* and *1050* had increased by just 24 and 37, respectively. This could be due to men captured by the 90th ID on **4-5 July**: 22 men from *GR 1049* and 34 from *GR 1050*. More problematic was the increase in POW's from *Pi.Btl. 177* in the UK (just three) despite the capture of 38 men on **5 July**. This illustrates that not all prisoners were promptly shipped to the UK. In another example, the number of soldiers from *AR 177*, who arrived in the UK, increased by 56 to 267; yet there is no reason significant numbers of men from this regiment would have been encountered by the VIII Corps in early **July**.[672] Instead, it seems likely that they were captured in the fighting around Cherbourg or captured earlier during the Allied breakthrough to the west coast. These data show that prisoner numbers in the UK are often difficult to link to actual losses or specific actions in the first half of **July**. It is worth noting that the number of prisoners outside of these combat units did not increase at all. Unfortunately, no figures are available for the division's personnel losses in the first half of **July**.

When the *91. LL.D.* became operational again on **17 July**, its composition was recorded and this also sheds light on the composition of units on the front of the *77. I.D.* Operational infantry included the entire *FJR 15* and *GR 1050* (with headquarters company), with a motley collection of other units. These troops under *GR 1050* mainly consisted of the *I./1049* (with two companies and a company formed from remnants of the *II./1049*) and the *III./1049*, apparently with what remained of the *II.* and the *III./894* also attached (strength of one company). The *I./1049* was supported by the 13th Company of both *GR 1049* and *1050*, while the *III./1049* had support from the *13.* and the *14./896* and the *14./1050*. Since the *14./896* was listed as a company, it may have included the AT platoons of both the *14./894* and the *14./895*. The reserves and emergency units under the *91. LL.D.* were grouped under the headquarters of *GR 1049* (with the headquarters company). The troops included the *II./1050* with a headquarters and four companies, the remnants of the *I./1050* (one company), and the *14./1049* (platoon-sized) with anti-tank guns and *Ofenrohre*. What remained of the *I./AR 177* was also part of these forces and included the headquarters and a "battery/company". *Pz.Jg.Kp. 177* still existed as a company. Other elements included the

---

In order to rebuild to 77.I.D. in Bretagne, its troops at the front were put under the command of 91.LL.D. Having lost most of its assigned troops, the 77.I.D. elements formed the bulk of this division, with FJR 15 and KG 265 providing much of the additional forces.

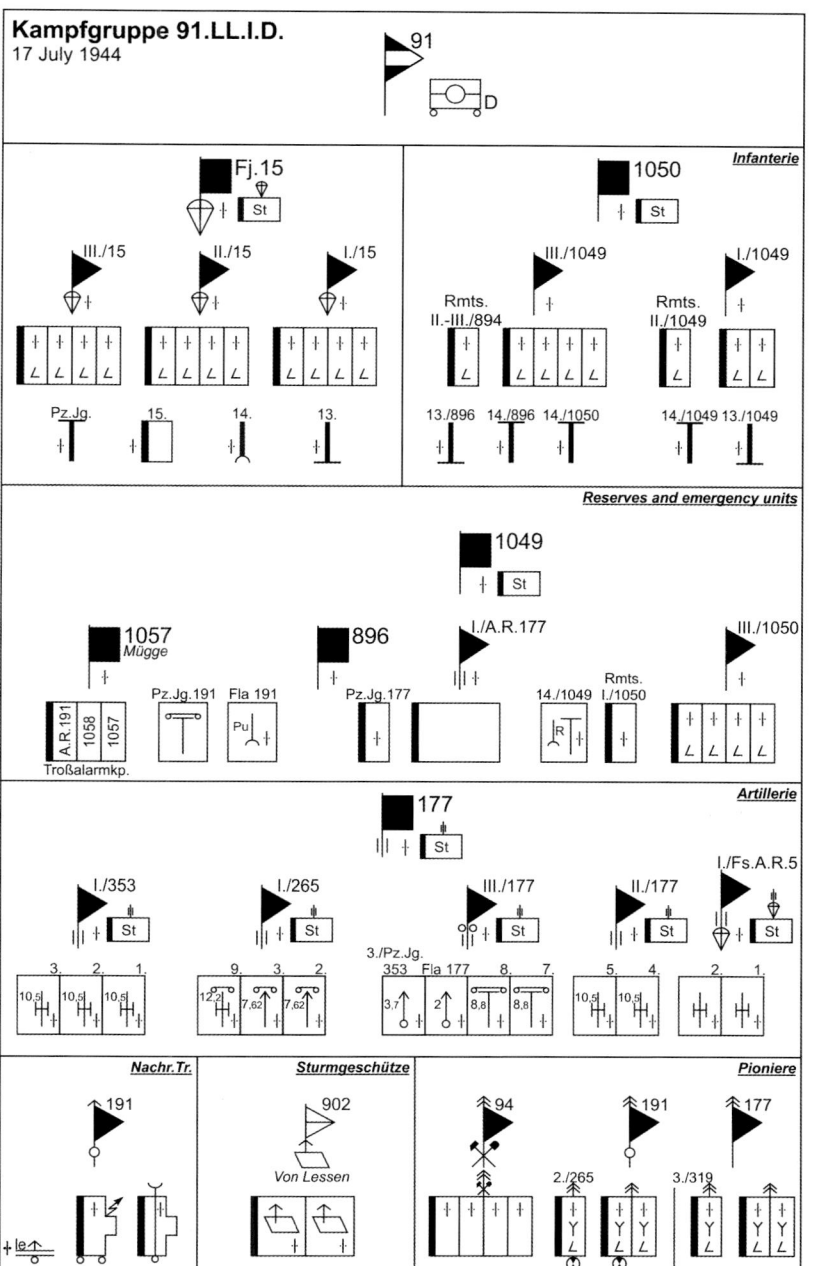

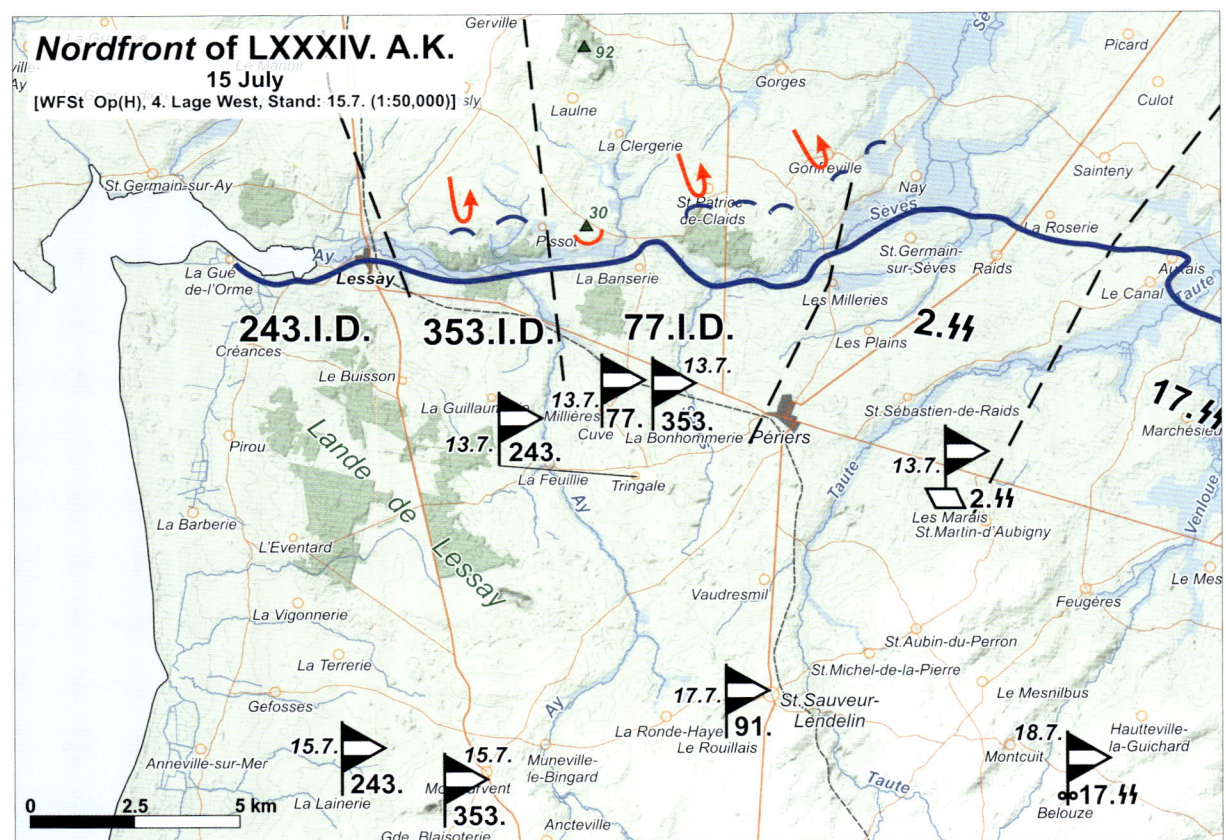

After the withdrawal to the Wasserlinie, the 77.I.D. continued to hold a sector. This ended when its troops were taken over by the 91.LL.D. This allowed the 77.I.D. to be withdrawn to Bretagne to be rebuilt. Most of its combat troops stayed at the front, where they could not be spared.

headquarters of *GR 896* and *1057*. The latter had three emergency companies formed from the trains of *GR 1057, 1058* and *AR 191*. The final units under *GR 1049* were the platoon-sized *Pz.Jg.Kp. 191* and *Fla-Kp. 191* with the *8,8 cm Raketenwerfer 43*, referred to as the *Puppchen*. The artillery was under the headquarters of *AR 177* (with the headquarters battery) and included five battalions, each with a headquarters and headquarters battery. These were the *I./Fs.AR 5* (aka *Fs.AR 5*) with two batteries; the *II./AR 177* with its 4th and 5th Batteries; the *III./AR 177* with its 7th and 8th Batteries; the *I./AR 265* with three batteries; and the *I./AR 353*, also with three batteries. Also reporting to the artillery were *Fla-Kp. 177* and the *3.(Fla)/Pz.Jg.Abt. 352*, which had been in Pont-l'Abbé on D-Day. The final 77. I.D. unit under the *91. LL.D.* was *Pi.Btl. 177*; it had been reinforced by the *3./Pi.Btl. 319* and existed next to the reinforced *Pi.Btl. 191* and *Bau-Pi.Btl. 94*.[673]

On **20 July**, *FJR 15* left the division and the infantry now consisted of *GR 1049* and *1050* (each with a headquarters company). The headquarters of *GR 1049* had taken over its battalions from *GR 1050* again, except for the *II./1049*. Heavy weapons support was from the 13th Companies of *GR 1049* and *1050*, both at company strength. Anti-tank guns came from 14th Companies of *GR 894, 896, 1049* and *1050*. The first three were only at platoon strength and the *14./1049* was armed with just *Ofenrohre*. The infantry from *GR 1050* was composed of just three companies, each formed from the remnants of larger forces: The *I./1050*, the *II./1049* and the *II.*

and the *III./894*. Heavy weapons were limited to the anti-tank gun platoon of the *14./895* and an anti-tank company from the *5. Fj.Div.* The reserve and emergency units were now just the *II./1050* and the *I./AR 177*. The *II./1050* had four companies and the *I./AR 177* now had a 1st and 2nd "Battery/Company". It was reinforced by *Pz.Jg.Kp. 177*. The artillery had not changed much, although the *I./Fs.AR 5* had left. *Fla-Kp. 177* had become the 9th Battery of the *III./AR 177* and was supported by the *3./Pz.Jg.Abt. 352*. The *I./AR 265* had been reinforced by attaching the *13./896*. There was a minor change among the engineers. Unlike on **17 July**, the headquarters of *Pi.Btl. 177* was now listed as partially motorised.[674]

LXXXIV. A.K. records show that on **23 July** five infantry battalions from the *77. I.D.* were still subordinated to the *91. LL.D.* Two were classified as average (*mittelstark*), one as weak (*schwach*) and the last two as worn out (*abgekämpft*).[675] These units can be identified by using the earlier records and data for **26 July**. The two "average" battalions were the *III./1049* and the *II./1050*; both still had four companies. The weak battalion was apparently the *I./1049*, with two companies: 1st Company and the combined 2nd and 4th Companies. The battalions listed as worn out were the *II./1049* and the *I./1050*, both reduced to company size.[676]

The equipment in the *77. I.D.*'s regimental heavy weapons companies for **17-23 July** has not been established, but it appears they had lost all motorisation. The *14./1049* was initially listed as an *Ofenrohr* and AT gun platoon. The other three companies (*13./1049* and *13.* and *14./1050*) were still listed as companies, although with no more details.[677] On the **20th**, the AT guns disappeared from the *14./1049* and, in their place, the *14./1050* was listed with *5 cm Pak's*.[678]

The **23 July** document has information regarding the condition of the *77. I.D.* artillery, which was also supporting the *91. LL.D.* Another document, dated **21 July**, illustrates the organisation of the corps' artillery in much more detail.[679] It shows that *AR 177* was in fairly good condition: 4th and 5th Batteries still had three and four 10.5 cm howitzers, respectively; the 3rd Battalion had three batteries, with the 7th and 8th Batteries both possessing three 8.8 cm guns and the 9th Battery seven 2 cm and two 3.7 cm *Flak*.[680] The *Flak* obviously came from the *3.(Fla)/Pz.Jg.Abt. 177* and *3.(Fla)/Pz.Jg.Abt. 352*.[681]

On **26 July**, the organisation of the *91. LL.D.* was reported one last time. As expected, it still consisted largely of units from the *77. I.D.* along with troops from the original *91. LL.D.*, the *353. I.D.* and *KG 265*. The infantry was divided between *GR 1049* and *1050*. The regiments included what remained of their organic elements in addition to attached units. *GR 1049* had both its 1st and 3rd Battalions, with the same (organic) strength as listed on **23 July**. Both regimental heavy weapons companies were also present. The 2nd Battalion had returned to the regiment, but it was still only one company strong. This also applied to the remnants of *GR 894*. *GR 1050* had two operational battalions: The *II./1050* and the *III./1058*, each with four companies. What remained of the *I./1050* was still just company-sized. In addition to the two regimental heavy weapons companies, an anti-tank company from *FJR 15* and a mountain infantry gun company from the *91. LL.D.* were also available. The latter seems to have supported the 3rd Battalion.[682] The "regiment" was now led by *Oberst* Wittenberg, who had taken command on **11 July** (the unit was also known by his name).[683] As noted, *AR 177* still possessed four of its organic batteries and was under the command of an *Artillerie-Führer*, who also controlled most of *AR 353*. *AR 177* was reinforced by three batteries of the *I./AR 265* (2nd, 3rd and 9th Batteries) and the *13./896*. In the *III./AR 177*, the 9th Battery was designated as a *Flak* battery with 2 cm guns, with the *3./Pz.Jg.Abt. 352* supporting the battalion as an separate platoon. The status of the *I./AR 177* had not changed; as before, it was still part of the emergency forces of the *91. LL.D.*, as was *Pz.Jg.Kp. 177*. The organisation of the engineers was also unchanged since the **20th**.[684]

As a result of *Operation Cobra*, *Ob.West* ordered the *Nordfront* to be moved back during the night of **26 July**.[685] This marked the start of a withdrawal along the west coast of Manche that continued until the *91. LL.D.* and the *77. I.D.* elements crossed the Baie du Mont-St. Michel under cover of darkness.[686] Their arrival in Bretagne was reported by *Maj.* Seiffert (operations officer of the *77. I.D.*) on the morning of **31 July**.[687] After reaching Pontorson, they were handed over to the headquarters of the *77. I.D.* (*Gruppe Bacherer*), which had arrived some days before.[688]

The *91. LL.D.* was no longer fit for combat. The *77. I.D.*, however, was being reconstituted and, with the arrival of the *91. LL.D.*, was reinforced by the returning units. This was not as impressive as it may seem. Of the combat troops that had survived in Normandy, only the headquarters of *GR 1049* and *AR 177* managed to rejoin the division.[689]

77.Infanterie-Division

Back in Bretagne

The period the division spent in Bretagne in **July**-**August** is beyond the scope of this book. However, a brief history is required because it was disbanded soon after. Simply put, the period was characterised by efforts to rebuild the division and by combat operations. Situation maps first show the division in the St. Malo area on **23 July**, although records indicate it actually arrived around **26 July**.[690]

Efforts to rebuild *GR 1050* appear to have begun in late **July**. While still at the front, the *II./1050* absorbed what was left of the regiment. The trains of the 1st and 3rd Battalions withdrew to Dol-de-Bretagne to meet 1,200 men coming up from La Rochelle and intended for the two battalions.[691] This new cadre included men from *Marschbtl. 158*, a battalion pulled together from the *158. Res.Div.* in Luçon, north of La Rochelle. It had at least three (possibly four) companies with an estimated 240-300 men each. The battalion was transported by train to Rennes and then to Dol-de-Bretagne, arriving at the end of **July**.[692] Before reconstitution could begin, the troops were overrun and the majority taken prisoner.[693]

On **5 August**, with American forces advancing into Bretagne, the *OKH* still planned to transfer the division to somewhere else in Southern France for reorganisation as an *Inf.Div.44*.[694] While illustrating that there were still plans for the future of the division, the timing of the order hardly made this realistic. The division (now under the *XXV. A.K.*) had been forced back into action at the end of **July**.

On **25 July**, the headquarters of the *LXXIV. A.K.* had been ordered to Normandy, turning over command of its sector to the *XXV. A.K.* at 12:00 on **26 July**. Returning from Normandy, the *77. I.D.* would be deployed in *KVA "A1"*. Upon arrival, the division took command of the sector, as had been the case before the invasion.[695]

On the afternoon of **26 July**, the divisional headquarters, signals battalion and parts of the supply troops arrived in Tressaint, where the headquarters was located.[696] The next day, the *XXV. A.K.* ordered the division to take command of *KVA "A1"* at 18:00. *Ost-Btl. 602, Sicherungs-Bataillon 1220 (M)* (with men suffering from gastrointestinal ailments: *M = Magenkranken*) and *Festung St. Malo*, were placed under the operational control of the *77. I.D.*, and it was ordered to begin security operations in the area up to the Merdrignac - Rennes - Avranches road.[697]

The situation in Normandy continued to deteriorate and, on **30 July**, *AOK 7* ordered *Obst.* Bacherer to take command in Avranches. Later that day, the colonel was ordered to form a battlegroup with the task of defending Avranches and preventing an enemy breakout into Bretagne.[698] The colonel even received a personal phone call from *Feldm.* von Kluge, who declared the mission to be of vital importance to the war. Bacherer asked which troops would be offered, given that his division had not yet been rebuilt. The answer was sobering: The field marshall could offer nothing — the division would have to scrape together whatever it could.[699] A battery of *Stu.Gesch.Brig. 341* was put at his disposal along with the *III./897* (*266. I.D.*), which was on its way to St. Malo.[700]

The *XXV. A.K.* issued formal orders for the operation at 01:30 on **31 July**. The river crossings north of Avranches were to be kept open at all costs, and the enemy prevented from entering Avranches.[701] Bacherer, however, had already reported enemy armour in the town at 21:30.[702] During the night, his command post relocated to Pontorson, closer to Avranches.[703] With no significant German elements in the area, the task facing the division (or what remained of it) was an impossible one. As Bacherer later recalled:[704]

I had orders to hold Avranches with a thousand men, paratroopers and everything you can imagine that they had raked together, with one battery which only arrived the next day.

His modest collection of forces included elements from the *5. Fj.Div.* and *Stu.Gesch.Brig. 341*, with support from the *266. I.D.* and *Fj.Ers.u.Ausb. Rgt. 2* expected to arrive later that day.[705] Moreover, the *2. Fj.Div.* was ordered to prepare two reinforced battalions, a regimental headquarters, one light battery and anti-tank weapons to support *Gruppe Bacherer*.[706] At 02:35, the order was changed for the airborne division to provide just one battalion instead of two.[707]

Events now moved swiftly. Avranches was reported to have fallen at 01:00 on **31 July**.[708] In response, *Feldm.* von Kluge ordered the town to be retaken at once.[709]

The initial reports were false, as the town had only been reached by light US forces, which set up outposts in the south and east outskirts.[710] To secure the town, *Obst.* Bacherer dispatched a makeshift battalion of paratroopers (*5.*

Fj.Div.) and an assault-gun battery and ordered the bridge across the Sélune at Pontaubault to be secured by at least one assault gun. *Obstlt.* Jäger, who had commanded different battlegroups in Normandy, was put in command of this force and, at 04:35, his troops secured the bridge.[711]

A few kilometres to the north, the situation at Avranches was confusing. According to German reports, the road through town was clear of the enemy at 06:00; the crossings north of the town secured by the *5. Fj.Div.* By 07:00, German assault guns had made contact with US armoured cars (apparently south of Avranches).[712] With the town clearly not firmly in German hands, the attack ordered by von Kuge started around 12:30; but by 15:00 it was clear that the attack had failed. Significant enemy machine-gun fire, supported by armour and aircraft, was too much to overcome. The assault gun battery suffered considerable losses. As for *Obstlt.* Jäger, he had disappeared, forcing Bacherer to take over.

Now the Americans pushed south from Avranches, towards the Sélune river. According to German reports, after the first two enemy tanks crossed the Pontaubault bridge at 17:00, it was destroyed by Allied aircraft. If true, this meant that the German troops north of the river were trapped, with the bridge at Ducey offering the only possible escape route.[713]

However, reports of the destruction of the bridge were also false, and spearheads from the 4th Armored Division rumbled across it to form a defensive perimeter.[714] The Americans finally had their vital bridgehead for the breakout from Normandy. In response, *Gen.* Fahrmbacher ordered Bacherer to defend the approaches to St. Malo and delay the enemy advance, specifically around Dol-de-Bretagne. Meanwhile, *Obst.* König was sent to take over the defence of Rennes.[715]

On the morning of **1 August**, Bacherer's forces stopped an armoured attack along the Pontaubault - Dol-de-Bretagne highway. That afternoon, they were forced to pull back when enemy armour broke through to within 400 metres of the command post, which was moved to Miniac-Morvan.[716] *AOK 7* then ordered elements of the *77. I.D.* to reinforce *Festung St. Malo*.[717]

On **2 August**, *Gruppe Bacherer* was holding the Dinan - Dol line, blocking the southeastern approaches to St. Malo while conducting reconnaissance towards Pontorson. Dol-de-Bretagne was found to be clear of enemy troops.[718] Further south, *Gen.Lt.* Spang (*266. I.D.*) took over the defence of the Rance on both sides of Dinan. He was given a variety of troops to form *Kampfgruppe Spang*; apart from elements of the *265.* and the *266. I.D.*, these included *KG Wittenberg*, named after the colonel, who had been appointed local area commander for of Dinan. This battlegroup included a regimental headquarters of the *2. Fj.Div.*, the *III./Fj.Rgt. 7*, the *3./Fs.AR 2*, and *Sich.Btl. 1220 (M)*.[719] *KG Bacherer* stayed east of the Rance and, on **3 August**, moved its command post north to St. Joan-de-Guérets.[720]

Due to the rapidly changing situation, *Gen.Lt.* Spang was ordered to withdraw to Brest the next day. As a result, *KG Spang* was disbanded, although troops in the Dinan area were ordered to stay put; when forced to do so, they would pull back into *Festung St. Malo*.[721] *Obst.* Bacherer was directed to break through with headquarters staff to Brest (after completing his current mission).[722] That evening, *Gruppe Bacherer* was holding the line Châteauneuf-d'Ille-et-Vilaine – St. Méloir-des-Ondes, with combat outposts in the area of Dol-de-Bretagne, Miniac-Morvan and Dinan.[723]

Obst. Bacherer was unable to leave St. Malo and, on **6 August**, his battlegroup was placed under the fortress commander of St. Malo, a move later formally approved by *H.Gr. B*.[724] *Obst.* Bacherer assumed command of the fortress west of the Rance (*Rance West*), his command post in a bunker complex in the south of Dinard. His remaining troops followed him, crossing the Rance in locally acquired boats.[725] The next day, the force was incorporated into the defences of the fortress.[726] As before the invasion, *Obst.* Stoltenburg became the artillery commander for the entire position.[727] Meanwhile, *Obstlt.* Jäger had reemerged, leading a battlegroup in the fortress east of the Rance (*Rance Ost*). On **6 August**, all infantry in the sector, including the naval and scattered units, were put under his command. To the rear, additional naval units and *Ost-Bataillon 602* were assembled, while Jäger's command post was in Josefsberg, east of St. Malo.[728] Over the following few days, *Festung St. Malo* was cut off completely, and the German lines pushed back.[729] *Obstlt.* Jäger was taken prisoner on **10 August**.[730]

On **14 August**, the Americans launched a new attack west of the Rance and achieved a significant advance at Pleurtuit, reaching Dinard. Although the situation was growing desperate, *Gruppe Bacherer* continued to defend the town and the strongpoint *Feste Paulus* (*Ra.145*, on the Pointe de la Garde Guérin, west of St. Lunaire).[731] The troops around Dinard received orders to withdraw to *Feste Paulus* and hold it to the last round. A mixed force of some 700 men reached the site, exceeding both the supply and combat

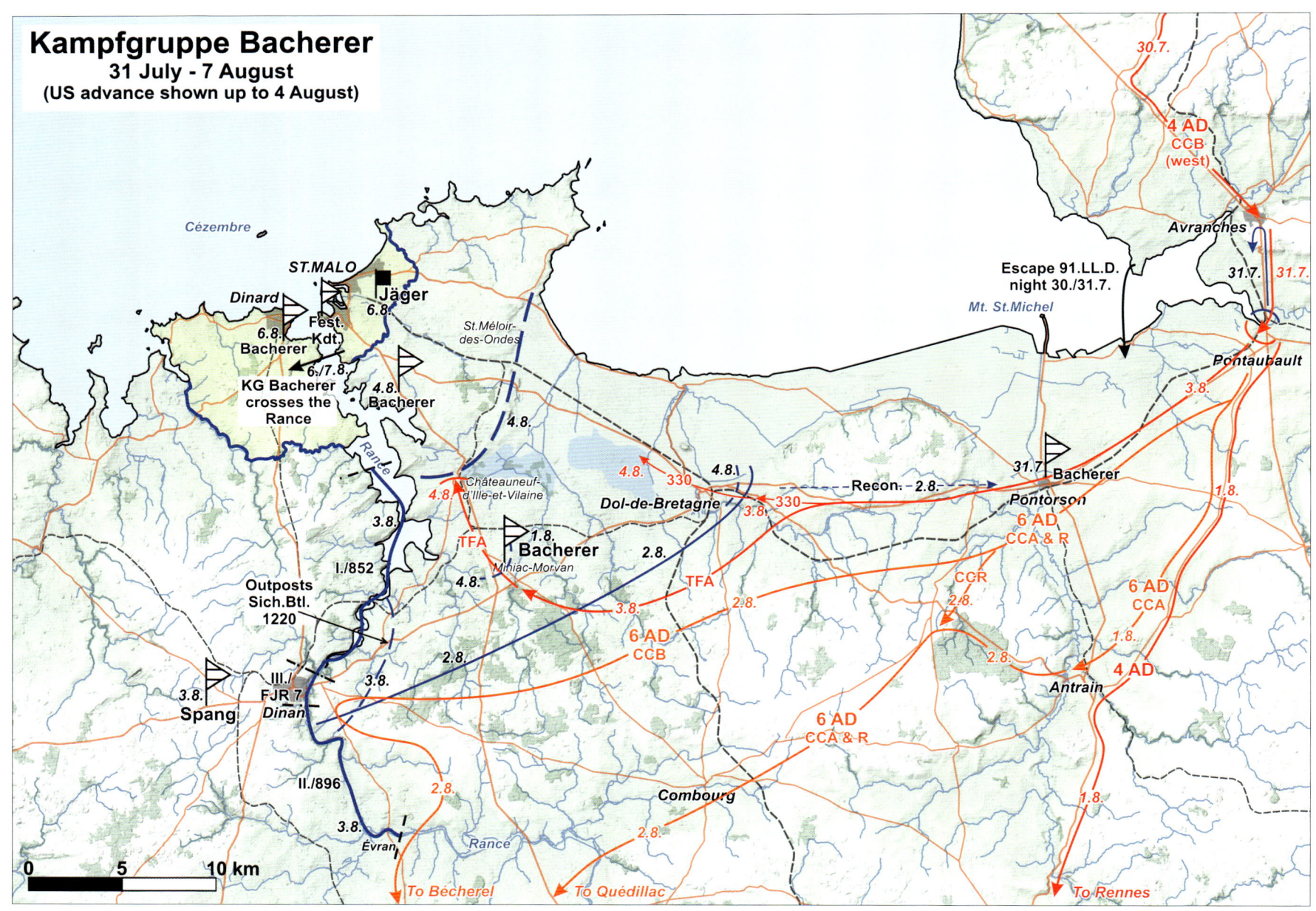

The US advance to Avranches forced the 77.I.D. back into action. As Gruppe Bacherer, the division tried to secure the town but could not prevent a breakout into Bretagne. Instead, the battlegroup defended the approaches to St. Malo before crossing the Rance and taking control of the western part of the Festung.

Festung St. Malo came under attack from Task Force A (TFA, 6th TD Group), before the 83rd ID threw in its full weight, supported by the 121st IR (8th ID). The fortress fell to the Americans on 17 August, after Bacherer had already surrendered on the 15th. The island of Cézembre continued to resist until 2 September.

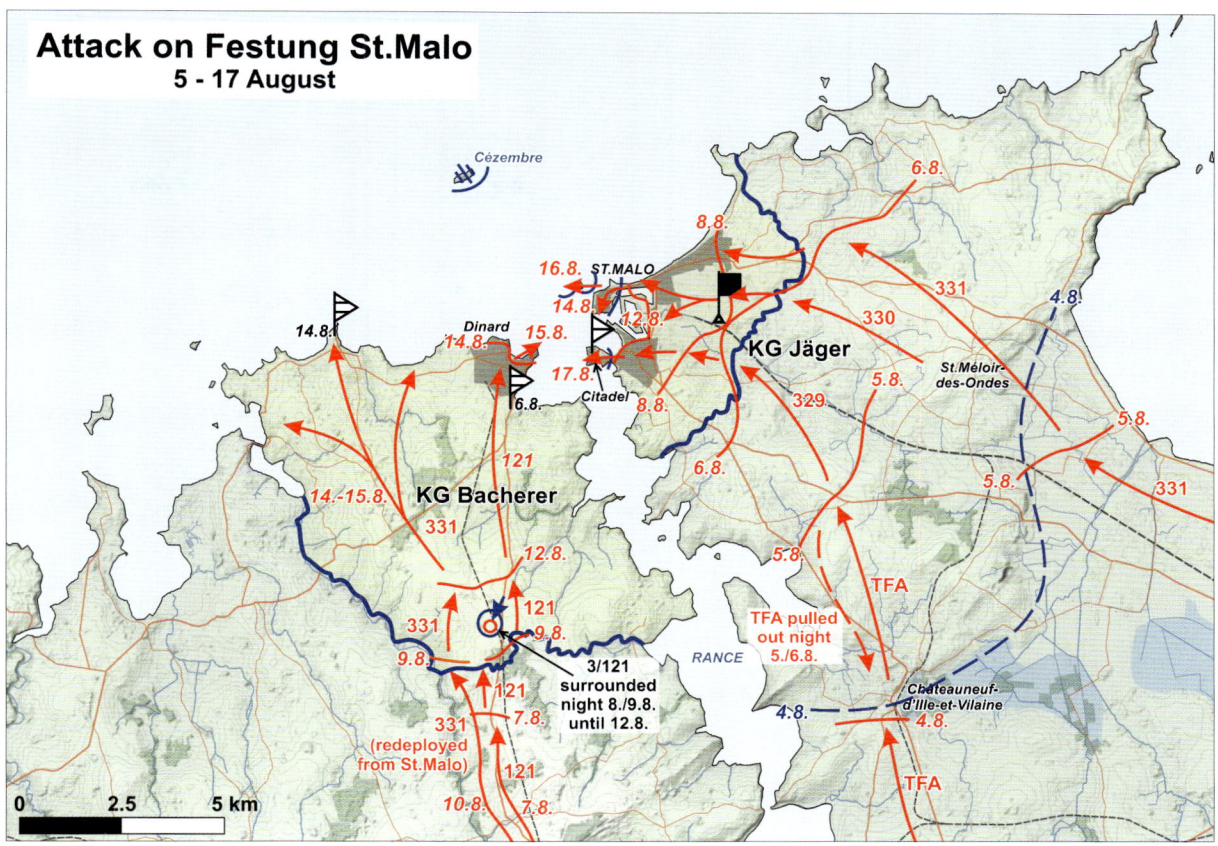

capabilities of the complex. The NCO's and men were therefore given the option of surrendering before the American assault and about 300 took the opportunity to do so.[732]

On **15 August**, the Americans cleared the town of Dinard and the surrounding area.[733] *Feste Paulus* also came under attack and, lacking adequate ventilation, soon became untenable. Just before 16:30, *Obst.* Bacherer ordered the white flag to be raised and the position surrendered. The 350 survivors marched off into captivity.[734]

East of the Rance, the St. Malo citadel (Cité) finally surrendered on **17 August**, ending resistance in the area. Only the island of Cézembre held out until **2 September**.[735]

Despite the destruction of his division, *Obst.* Bacherer was proud of its accomplishments. In captivity he boasted to a fellow prisoner:[736]

It was a well-known fact that the 77th Division was by far the best in the whole of the 7th Field Army. [Good] Old Dollmann had already written to tell my wife that. But it was not because the officers or the other ranks were better, but because the people from Baden are good soldiers and because from its very formation it had been created from only first-class officers and NCO's. Nearly all the NCO's had the eastern campaign medal, and nearly all of them had been awarded the Iron Cross First Class in the east. But the fundamental reason was the absolutely clear orders that Stegmann gave, as to which I advised him, based on the experiences I had gained in the east last year.

77.Infanterie-Division

The battle for *Festung St. Malo* marked the end of the *77. I.D.* (What remained of the division was still estimated at 3,000 men on **1 September**.)[737] The division was formally disbanded on **13 September**.[738] On **20 November**, the reassignment of the remaining elements was reported. Little more than support troops remained and their locations were largely unknown – often an indication that their destruction had not yet been confirmed. Exceptions were the headquarters of *Pz.Jg.Abt. 177* and the *3.(Fla)/Pz.Jg.Abt. 177*. Both had become part of *Pz.Jg.Abt. 189 (89. I.D.)* and redesignated accordingly.[739]

Their survival indicates that they had not been with the division around St. Malo. Indeed, *AOK 7* ordered the company to carry out road patrols in early **August**, which typically refers to a mobile *Flak* role. This likely put it behind the front, which may well have enabled it to escape encirclement and destruction in Normandy.[740]

This was also the case with *Pi.Btl. 177*, which has been linked to the fighting around Paris in late **August**.[741] Despite escaping Normandy, it would also be formally disbanded after being annihilated in the summer of **1944**.[742]

Men from the 331st IR (83rd ID) fight their way throught the streets of Paramé. (NARA)

US Troops at a road sign in Paramé on the the eastern outskirts of St.Malo. (NARA)

91. Luftlande-Infanterie-Division

The *91. Luftlande-Infanterie-Division* (*91. LL.D.*) was a peculiar formation.[1] It had been raised as a regular infantry division of the 25th wave on **15 January 1944** and initially stationed at the training areas at Baumholder and Bitch in France.[2] In **March**, it was ordered to convert to a *Luftlande-Division* (Airlanding).[3] Despite its designation, it was a unit of the Army and not the Air Force.

As an airlanding division, it was to be transported by air, landing by glider or flown into an airfield, rather than jumping from aircraft like an airborne division. It was outfitted with special weaponry and partially organised for airborne landings.[4] According to *Major* von der Heydte (commander of *Fj. Rgt. 6*), it was intended to use the division and his regiment in a combined operation in northern Europe (*Unternehmen Tanne* or *Fichte*).[5] The operation was never carried out and, in **May 1944**, the division was sent to France to defend against airborne landings.

When the division was established, *Gen.Lt.* Bruno Ortner was put in acting command, officially becoming commander on **10 February**.[6] On **25 April**, he was succeeded by *Gen.Maj.* Wilhelm Falley, who was promoted to *Generalleutnant* on **1 May**.[7] Falley was killed on D-Day while returning to his command post;[8] he was replaced a few days later by *Obst.* Eugen König, who stayed in command until the division's destruction in the summer of 1944.[9]

The division is poorly covered in the records. *Obst.* König contributed a monograph to the FMS program, but his study offers little more than a brief overview of events.[10] No other significant personal accounts have been found. Due to the division's late arrival in the 7. *Armee* sector, its pre-invasion history is also poorly covered in the records of *AOK 7* and the *LXXXIV. A.K.* (whose records are mostly missing for **1944**). Among the surviving materials in the archives are a number of orders-of-battle, which illustrate the division's composition in the Normandy campaign.[11] There remains a lack of information about where and how the units operated and their boundaries.

A history of the division published in **2017** uses a lot of information from the German Federal Archives, but it does not offer much detail on the actual fighting.[12] For this volume, a study of records held in other archives has produced detailed information and much of the division's organisation has

Left: Gen.Maj. Bruno Ortner, the division's first commander. (BArch, PERS 6/300319)

Centre: Gen.Maj. Wilhelm Falley, shown here with the Knight's Cross he had been awarded on 26 November 1941. (BArch, PERS 6/299624)

Right: Obst. Eugen König had been decorated with the Knight's Cross in August 1942, followed by Oakleaves in November 1943. (BArch, MSG 2/7763)

been gathered from captured documents. Additional documents and prisoner statements help identify where certain elements operated. Together, they provide a reasonable overview of the division's organisation and operations.

Organisation and Equipment

As a regular division of the 25th wave, the *91. LL.D.* started life in a fashion similar to the *77. I.D.* It was established around an existing reinforced grenadier regiment, *GR 1025*, which was formed at Baumholder in **November 1943**.[13] In addition to infantry, it included an artillery battalion, an engineer company and other units.[14]

Warning orders for the division's establishment were announced by the *OKH* on **15 January 1944**, to be initially completed by **1 March**. Responsibility for raising the division was given to Military District XII (Wiesbaden), where the Baumholder Training Area was located. The military district used the reinforced regiment as the foundation for the division, while elements of reinforced *GR 1032* were also used. The latter regiment was divided up to help form the new 25th wave divisions, with Military District XII receiving the regimental headquarters, the *II./1032* (minus its 5th and 6th

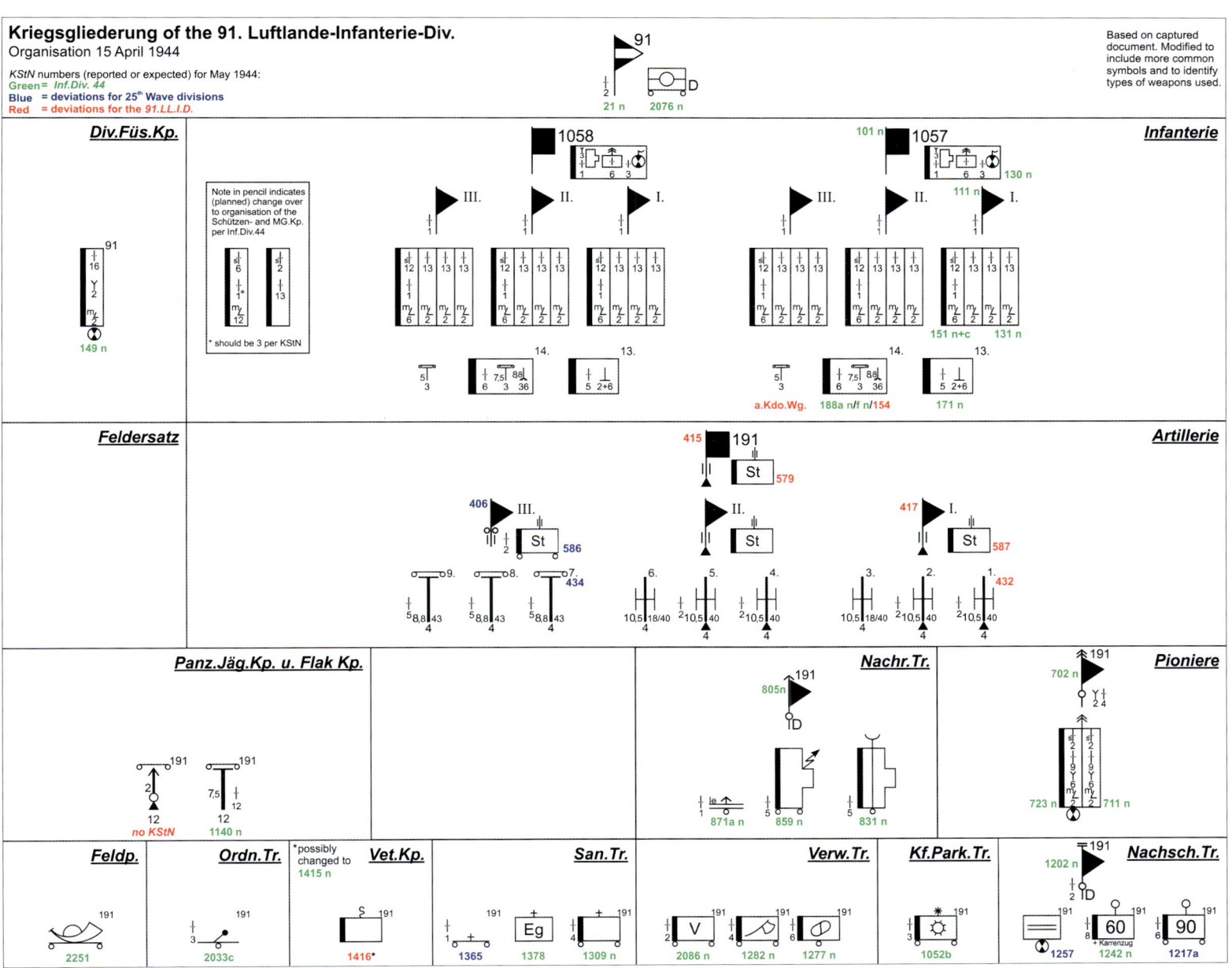

The Order of Battle of the 91. LL.I.D. with KStN numbers. Apart from later changes, this should give a good representation of the division's strength and organisation on D-Day. (UKNA, WO 219/5229)

Companies), a platoon each from the 13th and 14th Companies and a platoon from *Pi.Kp. 1032*.[15] In addition, the military district could call on *Division Nr. 172* and *Nr. 462* from the Replacement Army, both of which were located in the district. These divisions would primarily provide men for the infantry, engineers and artillery.[16]

The district was also ordered to form the divisional headquarters by **1 May**.[17] Most of the support elements were new, the majority being raised in Military Districts XII and VII (Munich). Some individual elements were also raised by Military Districts II (Stettin), XI (Hannover), XIII (Nuremberg) and XXI (Posen, today Poznań in Poland). The medical troops were selected from the *355. I.D.*, and the transportation company and veterinary company were also existing units, provided by Military Districts XXI and VI, respectively. All new units were to be operational by **15 April** and the division as a whole by **10 May**.[18]

As a division of the 25th wave, the authorised organisation was weak but straightforward. There were two infantry regiments, each with a headquarters company, three infantry battalions and two heavy weapons companies. The 13th Company was to consist of six light and two heavy infantry guns, while the 14th Company would have a heavy AT platoon with three motorised heavy Pak and two tank-destroyer platoons with Ofenrohre. The artillery regiment included a headquarters and headquarters battery; the guns were in two light battalions and one "heavy" battalion, each with a headquarters battery. The light battalions had two batteries of four light field howitzers each; the heavy battalion was to be motorised, with each of its three batteries equipped with four 8.8 cm guns, preferably the AT version. The engineer battalion was to consist of two companies, one of which one would use bicycles. The division would also have an AT company with 12 motorised heavy AT guns.[19] When the reinforced *GR 1025* became part of the new division, its units were redesignated with the number "191". The only exception was the regiment itself, which was allotted the number "1057". The second infantry regiment had the number "1058".[20]

Compared to an *Inf.Div.n.A.* or 44, the divisions of the 25th wave were lower in strength. Although there were six infantry battalions, these were distributed among two regiments, which reduced the number of heavy weapons companies. Personnel strength was also decreased by the absence of fusilier and field-replacement battalions, while the engineer battalion had just two companies instead of three. All of these missing components were later added in an update to the base documents. The artillery regiment was particularly weak, given that there were only two light battalions with just two batteries each and a rather feeble "heavy" battalion. While the artillery regiment of a regular division would have 36 *10,5 cm le.F.H. 18* and 12 *15 cm s.F.H.18*, that of a 25th wave division only had 16 light guns and 12 8.8 cm AT or *Flak* guns.[21] It should also be pointed out that 25th wave divisions only had two infantry regiments to support rather than the typical three, although there were still a total of six infantry battalions.

On **4 March**, elements were specified that were to be reequipped and reorganised for airlanding deployment and, thus, would differ from a regular 25th wave division. Among them were both infantry regiments as well as the headquarters of *AR 191* and its 1st and 2nd Battalions. Parts of *Nachr.Abt. 191* and *Pi.Btl. 191* were also earmarked for airlanding use but not reequipped. *Pz. Jg.Kp. 191*, the *III./AR 191* and the rest of the signals battalion, as well as all trains and logistics elements, were envisaged for traditional use.[22]

The purpose of changes was to have weapons that could be delivered by glider. In the infantry regiments, the heavy infantry-gun platoon (13th Company) would be replaced by a mortar platoon with four medium mortars; the heavy anti-tank guns of the 14th Company would be replaced by *Ofenrohre* and handheld AT weapons. In the artillery regiment, the guns would be replaced with the lighter *7,5 cm Gebirgsgeschütz 36*, a mountain gun.[23]

To enhance mobility, air-mobile elements were to receive 400-500 light infantry carts *(If.8)*, around 150 *Kettenkräder* and about 25 staff cars. The fuselages of *GO 242* and *DFS 230* gliders were brought to Baumholder for training purposes.[24]

On **25 May**, *Ob.West* was ordered to form a fusilier battalion, a field-replacement battalion and a third engineer company for the division. It seems, however, that the division had already begun to form the fusilier battalion using "command channels". Such formations were formally budgeted by the same order.[25] On **5 June**, orders were issued to strengthen the artillery of 25th wave divisions, but the *91. LL.D.* was excluded.[26] This had no impact on the division, as its artillery already exceeded that of regular 25th wave divisions.

A proper order of battle for the division around D-Day has not been found; none exist in the *AOK 7* daily logs, probably because of the division's late arrival. Other German records include a base organisational document for **6 June**, but it only shows the overall organisation and does not provide numbers of weapons.[27] A useful alternative is an order of battle from **15 April**, which was captured in Normandy.[28] Although it precedes some *KStN* changes introduced with the *Inf.Div.44* in **May**, it does provide numbers for the heavy weapons already present. Of course, these numbers may have increased before the invasion.

Without a status report, it is difficult to determine the division's manpower, weapons and mobility. Captured documents offer some details on the weapons and mobility, but without authorised numbers their value is limited. For small arms and mobility, a basic comparison can be made between the on-hand strength and the authorised strength of a standard 25th wave division for **4 May**, before the formal introduction of the *Inf.Div.44*.[29] It should also be remembered that the *91. LL.D.* was a non-standard formation. To reconstruct the division's organisation on D-Day, the base documents of **15 April** and **6 June** will be used and combined with prisoner information and other records.

Zetterling estimates the division had no more than 7,000 or 8,000 men when it was sent to France. This figure seems low compared to similar divisions, and the number given by the quartermaster of the *7. Armee* on **2 May** was 10,700.[30] Numbers illustrating the various age groups and level of experience in the division have proven to be elusive. In mid-June an Allied examination of pay books found one third of the division to be under 19 years of age and a similar percentage more than 30[31]. The examination of 278 men KIA/MIA[32] in the summer of 1944 paints a similar picture: 27% were 30-40 years old, 34% were 20-30, and 36% were aged 20 or younger (born 1924 or later). Personnel more than 40 (born 1903 or before) was limited to 3%. It is worth noting that the preferred personnel of 20-35 years old amounted to 50% of the division, with a relatively even spread among the three 5-year age groups it encompassed. Still, it must also be noted that the sample is somewhat biased towards infantry regiments; these would have contained about half of the division's manpower, yet account for some 60% of the sample. The youngest personnel in the division are therefore likely over-represented but not by much. It is also clear that, compared to the *77. I.D.*, the *91. LL.D.* had a considerably higher percentage of men born in 1925, while 1924 and, especially, 1926 were smaller. An explanation for these differences has not been found.

	≤1903	1904-1908	1909-1913	1914-1918	1919-1923	1924	1925	1926
KIA/MIA	2.9%	11.5%	15.8%	15.1%	18.7%	2.2%	31.3%	2.5%

Table 1: Age distribution in the *91. LL.D.* (Based on 278 KIA/MIA)

Captured figures for small arms, presumably from **March**,[33] reveal that the division was armed with 1,901 pistols, 7,616 rifles, and 928 machine pistols. The standard authorisations for these weapons was 1,731, 6,397 and 1,132, respectively. The on-hand strength for machine guns was 351 light and 76 heavy and, on **15 April**, the division had 416 and 76. The figures can be compared to a standard authorised strength of 422 and 76, respectively, but do not take into account the fusilier company, which was shown to have 16 light MG's. On the order of battle, the artillery regiment was listed with 25 light MG's, 17 below standard strength, which could account for the machine guns in the fusilier company.[34] At 76, the number of heavy MG's on the order of battle matched the authorisations of a standard 25th wave division (in its original configuration without a fusilier company). The division's 78 medium mortars (*8,1 cm Gr.W. 34's*) matched the authorisations, when the fusilier company is included.

A major concern for the division at the time of the invasion was the availability of (and experience with) signals equipment. Due to the division's late arrival, *AOK* 7 could only begin issuing this equipment in **May**, a process requiring several months for other divisions of the *7. Armee*.[35] As a result, the division was neither fully equipped with or accustomed to the equipment on D-Day. For example, the artillery only received its radio equipment days before the invasion.[36]

Based on the **15 April** order of battle, the divisional headquarters was armed with the authorised number of two light MG's, which were likely in the infantry headquarters guard. The divisional headquarters was supported by the typical mapping section. Information on an element this close to a divisional headquarters is rare. Fortunately, a soldier in this section was captured and reported that it consisted of a *Wachtmeister* and seven other ranks and that its primary task was map printing and duplication.[37]

As indicated, the division had two infantry regiments, *GR 1057* (*Major* von Saldern) and *GR 1058* (*Obst.* Beigang). *GR 1057* was the redesignated

GR 1025 and had given up its 3rd Battalion, which became the *I./1058*. The headquarters of *GR 1058* was provided by *GR 1032* and the *II./1032* became the *II./1058*. Both the *III./1057* and the *III./1058* were created for the division. *Div.Nr. 172* provided *GR 1057* with personnel for its 3rd Battalion headquarters as well as for the 3rd, 7th and 11th Companies. In turn, *Div.Nr. 462* provided the headquarters for the *III./1058* and personnel for its 3rd, 7th and 11th Companies.[38]

Each regiment had a headquarters company, three battalions, an infantry gun company (13th) and an AT company (14th). The battalions consisted of the usual three rifle companies as well as a MG company.[39] Based on the reported on-hand weapons (around **March/April**) and the order of battle of **15 April**, it would appear all companies in the battalions were fully equipped with mortars and each rifle company had its authorised 13 light MG's, the latter figure matching the *KStN* of **1 May 1944**.

The regimental headquarters company included bicycle, engineer and signals platoons. These were armed with three, six, and one light MG, respectively. For some reason, the signals platoon was also listed with three flamethrowers, but these probably belonged to the engineer platoon.[40] Reportedly, the signals platoon had four *Torn.Fu.d2* ("*Dora 2*") radio sections and perhaps four telephone sections. The engineer platoon consisted of five sections and transport means; each section had a strength of an NCO and nine men, its standard weaponry also augmented by a light *MG 42* and a *G41(W)* self-loading rifle. Mobility consisted of about 20 *Kettenkräder*, which transported *Teller* mines.[41]

Few details have been found concerning the infantry battalion headquarters, although they were listed with a single light MG on **15 April**.[42] The leader of the radio section of the *I./1057* stated that he had seven signalmen. Since the battalion did not have telephones on D-Day, it relied on radio and messengers. Battalion headquarters had one "*Dora 2*" radio set and each company also had one; the sets in the companies being operated by men from the battalion headquarters. Transport for the headquarters was reportedly by light motor vehicles and horses. There was a staff car, a *Kübelwagen*, a *Schwimmwagen* and a motorcycle; there were also 15 horses, but that figure seems low when compared to an authorised strength of 33 horses; that duly noted, the motorisation was better than expected.[43]

The rifle companies in the regiments had three regular platoons and a heavy "platoon". The regular platoons consisted of three sections each; they were armed with a light *MG 42*, a grenade launcher, a self-loading rifle (identified as a *G41(W)*) and a sniper rifle.[44] The platoon leaders and company commanders had machine pistols.[45] As authorised, the rifle sections should have had a strength of an NCO and eight men, yet there are claims as high as nine men and as low as four.[46] The 13 light MG's per company that had been listed in April would match the authorised allocations.[47]

Soldiers from *GR 1058* stated that each heavy platoon had two sections, with a total of two heavy MG's and two medium mortars.[48] Men from *GR 1057* do not mention the heavy MG's and give the number of mortars as between one and three.[49] For both regiments, the figures do not fit a *KStN*, unless the three mortars in *GR 1057* were a typographical error. It is also conceivable that weapons were attached from a MG company, which could also explain the presence of both heavy MG's and mortars in *GR 1058*. The rifle companies in *GR 1057* reportedly had 120-130 men per company, with similar numbers reported for *GR 1058*.[50] This would be below authorised strength, for the different versions of *KStN's* called for 140-147 men per company.

The weapons claimed for *GR 1057* seem to match the earlier *KStN*, with mortars but without heavy MG's. Conversely, the information for *GR 1058* (with heavy MG's) already indicates a shift to the latest version, although that *KStN* lacked mortars. This information might indicate that the transition to the new *KStN's* (ordered by *AOK 7* on **27 May**; to be completed on **1 July**) may have begun before the invasion in some parts of the division but had not been completed.[51]

The MG companies in the battalions were composed of three MG platoons and one mortar platoon. They were about 160 men strong. These MG platoons were each armed with four heavy *MG 42's* (or the occasional *MG 34*), while the mortar platoon had six medium mortars.[52] In the *12./1058*, each machine-gun section had a strength of six men.[53] The presence of 6 medium mortars and 12 heavy MG's in these companies suggests that the regiments had not yet transitioned to the new *KStN's*, which would have reduced the number of heavy MG's to 6 and increased the mortars to 12.

Men from the infantry regiments give different numbers about their age and origin. It appears that about half of the division had combat experience in Russia, and the other half were new recruits between the ages of 18-38.[54]

This most likely applies to the infantry regiments as well. About 40% of the men in the infantry were under 20.[55] Another source states that the personnel were largely 18-22 year-olds with a few in their late 30's;[56] this dovetails with another claim that the personnel of the *6./1058* were between 18-38.[57] The average age for the *III./1057* was given as 27.[58]

These age groups are largely supported by the commander of the *3./1058*, who also had a thing or two to say about the quality of his men:[59]

> *My personnel were pitiful, including a man with a crippled hand. Two of them were short-sighted - terrible! They couldn't shoot at all. They couldn't even recognise a man 30 metres away. None of them belonged to a sports club, none of them were Party members, none of them belonged to a gymnastics club; [Only] two of them had a sports badge, I think. The average age was made up, on the one hand, of quite young people, 18 and 19 year-olds, who were not fully developed and without any strength, completely degenerate people; and, on the other hand, of older men over 35, 38 years old, who had already been overworked, family men. The NCO's had been raked up from the district headquarters, railway station guards and transport commands, and the devil only knows where they all came from. The situation was this: In all sections we had MG's, grenade launchers, self-loading rifles and sniper rifles. Good God, to whom shall I give these highly-specialised weapons? When I give someone a self-loading rifle or grenade launcher, then I need someone who can think and act by himself and knows how to handle the weapon.*
>
> *Our training was extremely bad. I always felt more like a duty NCO, not like a company commander."*

There were limited foreign personnel in the regiments. The commander of the *III./1057* stated that only 5% of his men belonged to *Volksliste III*.[60] This was the same for the *I./1058*.[61] On the other hand, the *9./1057* claimed to have had 32 Poles, which would signify a much higher percentage.[62] Of course, not all "Poles" actually belonged to *Volksliste III*. The foreigners in the *6./1058* included some Poles, Russians and two Slovenes. These men were used with the company's transport section, which suggests at least some were *Hiwi's*.[63] Poles with the transport section are also reported for other regimental units.[64] Reportedly, there were 40 Russian *Hiwi's* in the *III./1057*. These men were used at supply points.[65] The headquarters and trains of the *I./1057* had about 15 *Hiwi's*.[66]

With minor exceptions, transport in the infantry battalions was horse-drawn.[67] There were reportedly a few tracked motorcycles (*Kettenkräder*) per battalion for ammunition supply;[68] this may have amounted to one per company.[69] Although a member of the *I./1057* headquarters reported six to eight motor vehicles in each company, this appears to have been incorrect. The vehicles are identified as "*If.8,*" a reference to the single axle small infantry cart. In addition, there were 10 horses[70] — a number that is quite low in comparison to all versions of *KStN 131n*, which allowed for 22-28 horses. The number also seems low because, by **30 April**, both regiments had already received their authorised horses.[71]

Each regiment had two heavy weapons companies: An infantry gun company (13th) and an AT company (14th). These appear to be non-standard. On **15 April**, the 13th Company in each regiment was shown as a typical infantry gun company, adhering to the standard *KStN 171n*.[72] The base document for **6 June**, however, lists them as mountain companies.[73] Since mountain troops were generally equipped with lighter weapons, mountain guns were a logical choice for an airlanding division. The plans to replace the heavy infantry guns with a mortar platoon were apparently not carried out. It must be noted that the **March** on-hand strength report claimed that there were eight *le.I.G.18's* and two *s.I.G. 33's* in the division.[74] This was not enough to fully equip both companies with six light and two heavy infantry guns, but the companies were shown as fully armed on **15 April**.[75] Statements from prisoners suggest that the situation had become more complex by D-Day, making it difficult to determine the type and number of guns.

According to a soldier from the *13./1058*, his company consisted of three light and one heavy platoon. Each platoon was armed with two infantry guns, although calibres varied between the light (7.5 cm) and heavy (15 cm) platoons.[76] This organisation would match the standard *KStN*.[77] Members of *GR 1057* identified the (light) guns in their regiment as "7.5 cm infantry guns (split trail)", without reporting numbers.[78] (The common *7,5 cm leichtes Infanterie-Geschütz 18* did not have such a carriage.) Since these guns are listed as mountain guns in the later base documents, they were most likely *7,5 cm leichtes Gebirgs-Infanterie-Geschütz 18's*, which did have a split trail.[79] The *7,62 cm I.K.H.290(r)*, which was actually standard in 25th wave divisions (four of which the division was supposed to have received before **15 March**) can also be ruled out, as these also did not have a split trail.⁸⁰ Another option would be the *7,5 cm Gebirgs-Geschütz 36*. Although this gun matches both the calibre and type of carriage, it was not considered an infantry gun.⁸¹

The weaponry of the companies is further confused by statements by an officer of the *13./1057*. According to him, the first three (light) platoons each had three guns, rather than two. In the 3ʳᵈ Platoon, these were Russian 7.62 cm guns and in the other two platoons these were German 7.5 cm mountain guns.⁸² The 4th Platoon was the heavy platoon, with the probable two 15 cm guns.⁸³ These figures seem to confirm the existence of mountain guns, but the existence of Russian guns and the number of guns per (light) platoon is surprising. On **18 June**, Russian infantry guns were also shown in *GR 1058*. Both Russian 7.62 cm guns (three) and German 7.5 cm mountain guns (seven) were also listed around **28 June**.⁸⁴ Although the latter information is for both the *13./1057* and the *13./1058*, the number of mountain guns indicates that these were probably used by both regiments. The question remains as to how many of both types were in each company on D-Day.

On **1 July**, the *13./1057* had two 7.5 cm mountain infantry guns and one Russian 7.62 cm infantry gun, while the *13./1058* had five 7.5 cm mountain guns, three Russian 7.62 cm infantry guns and two 15 cm *s.I.G. 33's*. These numbers, which should only show organic equipment, suggest that the officer was correct in his claim that two of the light platoons in the infantry gun companies were outfitted with three German mountain infantry guns each, while the third platoon had three Russian infantry guns. And yet it is unclear where this organisation came from. Had the division simply been assigned specialised guns to replace any *7,62 cm I.K.H.290(r)'s*, but kept those as well? Or had it received permission to expand the companies to three guns in the light platoons?

In the *13./1057*, the light guns were reportedly towed by *Kettenkräder* and the heavy guns by *RSO's*. Once the fighting began, the light guns were horse-drawn. Each platoon also had four handheld AT weapons.⁸⁵ The *13./1058* had a reported strength of about 130-140 men aged 19-35. Foreign personnel was limited to just five or six Russians.⁸⁶

Like the 13ᵗʰ Company, the 14ᵗʰ Company in both regiments did not adhere to the plan of being partially reequipped for air landings. They held on to their heavy anti-tank guns, rather than relinquishing them for additional *Ofenrohre*. Both companies followed the standard organisation of 25ᵗʰ wave and *Inf.Div.44* divisions — a platoon of three *7,5 cm Pak 40's* and two tank-destroyer platoons with 18 *Ofenrohre* each. There was also a fourth platoon with three *5 cm Pak 38's* available to both companies; these platoons had been formed through "command channels".⁸⁷

A soldier from the *14./1057* provided details about his company. It consisted of a "headquarters platoon" and four platoons. The former included six messengers on bicycles, with a horse for the company commander. The platoons each had a strength of about 40 men, but these numbers may only apply to the 2ⁿᵈ and 3ʳᵈ Platoons.⁸⁸

The 1ˢᵗ Platoon was armed with three *7,5 cm Pak 40's* and was motorised, with several *Kettenkräder* and three *RSO's*.⁸⁹ Considering the *KStN*, the *RSO's* were probably used as the prime movers for the guns.⁹⁰ Being tank-destroyer platoons, the 2ⁿᵈ and 3ʳᵈ Platoons were armed with *Ofenrohre*. The soldier actually stated that there were three *Ofenrohr* platoons in his company (that would mean a 4ᵗʰ Platoon), but personnel of the *14./1058* and an officer from the *13./1058* only report (as expected) two platoons.⁹¹ The 3ʳᵈ Platoon of the *14./1057* had three sections of 12 men each and, at platoon level, four NCO's and the platoon leader, an officer.⁹² Each section had six *Ofenrohre*.⁹³ This matched the theoretical strength of 36 *Ofenrohre* per company, and 72 of these had already been reported earlier in the year.⁹⁴ At platoon level, there was a single light MG transported on a four-wheeled cart (one horse), which also carried between 9 and 12 handheld AT weapons. Each section would be issued three or four of these.⁹⁵ The *14./1058* reportedly also had a supply of magnetic hollow-charge grenades, but it is not clear how many or when they arrived.⁹⁶

The individual *Ofenrohre* were operated by a crew of two. The gunner was armed with an *P 08* pistol and the assistant with a *K98k*. The former carried the launcher and a box with two rockets while the latter carried two boxes. Infantry carts (*IF.8*) with additional rounds were kept close to the firing positions, if possible within 50-100 metres. When in combat, it appears that the *Ofenrohr* platoons were parcelled out among the infantry battalions of their respective regiments.⁹⁷ Unless there actually were three *Ofenrohr* platoons, there were not enough platoons to assign one to each battalion. Instead, it is possible that two sections were assigned to each infantry battalion or that *Ofenrohre* were distributed as the situation required.

In the *14./1057*, the transportation of the *Ofenrohr* platoons was horse-drawn. Each section had three *IF.8* carts. These were coupled up and drawn by a single horse. Each cart could carry 16 boxes of rockets, each box holding two rounds.[98] This would require four horses per platoon. The figure of nine *IF.8* is higher than the *KStN*, which allowed for eight per platoon, including two at platoon level instead of the previously mentioned four-wheel cart.[99] In contrast, the *14./1058* may not have used horses at all, as they were not mentioned. This company had 24 *Kettenkräder* and a number of *RSO's*, enough to replace the horses. The company is said to have had a strength of 200-220 men aged 18-36. Again, there were few foreigners, but reportedly there was a Pole or Russian with each AT Gun.[100]

Personnel data for the regiments as a whole is not available for the time of the invasion, but on **26 April** *GR 1058* had a strength of 54 officers, 8 officials, 427 NCO's, 1,905 men and 318 *Hiwi's*, giving it a combined strength (*Hiwi* excluded) of 2,386.[101] This can be compared to an authorised strength of 56 officers, 8 officials, 428 NCO's, 1,952 men and 369 *Hiwi's*, which reveals that the regiment was close to its authorised strength. This is corroborated by the strength report of the *III./1058* from **13 May**: It had 13 officers, 2 officials, 114 NCO's and 616 men (excluding *Hiwi's*), compared to an authorised strength of 13, 2, 124 and 681 (including 100 *Hiwi's*), respectively.[102] No records have been found showing the age groups in the regiments, but in the second half of **March** the average age in *GR 1057* was 26. This had dropped from an average age of 32 due to an exchange of older for younger personnel.[103]

On **30 April**, each infantry regiment was authorised 631 horses, and they had been supplied to the regiments. This figure is slightly below the expected authorisations for a standard 25th wave division of **4 May**, which was 645. On **25 May**, each regiment also had 126 motor vehicles against authorisations of just 51. The surprising difference can be explained by the presence of additional *Kettenkräder*; moreover, it is also possible that some of the vehicles were lighter than intended, requiring more vehicles.[104]

Although the plan had been to provide the division with an additional 400-500 *IF.8* carts, it is not clear this actually took place. For example, on **13 May**, the *III./1058* had just 111 compared to an authorisation of 123. However, this battalion had no less than 43 motor vehicles (with five more en route), compared to an authorisation of just four. With this noted, it only had 135 horses (with 21 more en route) against an authorisation of 184.[105] Considering that, as of **30 April**, the regiment had all its authorised horses, it is possible that deviations from the *KStN's* were in play.

Apart from its two regimental anti-tank companies, the division also had a separate anti-tank company, *Panzerjäger-Kompanie 191*.[106] It had been dispatched to the division on **25 March**, and was commanded by *Olt.* Reimer. The company was outfitted with the expected number of 12 motorised heavy AT guns, distributed among four platoons, and 12 MG's. The AT guns were the standard *7,5 cm Pak 40's*; each platoon reportedly had three *RSO's* for towing the guns.[107]

As with the infantry regiments, the most reliable figures for vehicles can be taken from the report of **25 May**. At that time, the company had 81 motor vehicles compared to an authorisation of just 43. As was typical in these motorised units, there were no horses. The significant difference between authorised and on-hand strength can largely be explained by the presence of 24 *Kettenkräder* versus an authorisation of only one.[108]

The division also included *Fla-Kompanie 191* (*Lt.* Hayn), a motorised mountain anti-aircraft company.[109] This company is noteworthy because that type of unit was not authorised in the base documents of a 25th wave division.[110]

Compared to the Flak 38, the 2 cm Gebirgsflak 38 was an uncommon weapon. It is most easily recognised by its tripod base and curved gun shields. (D. (Luft) T. 1040-1)

91. Luftlande-Infanterie-Division

It appears that its establishment was ordered on **1 March** and completed on **30 March**.[111] A field-post number was assigned on **14 April**, suggesting the company was to be transferred to the division about that time.[112] The transfer apparently took place on **22 April**, although the company had already appeared on the order of battle of **15 April**.[113] The postal number suggests that the company had first been earmarked to become the *4./Pz.Jg.Abt. 22* of the *22. I.D.*[114] However, before the company was sent to this division, it was reassigned to the *91. LL.D.* Although an anti-aircraft company was also formed for the *77. I.D.* (another 25th wave formation), its position within that division was different as it was incorporated within an AT battalion, while the company in the *91. LL.D.* remained separate.[115]

A soldier in the company provided many details, making it possible to examine it in depth. The company reportedly consisted of a command group, support elements and three gun platoons. *KStN 191* would fit this company very well, though the order of battle of **15 April** does not indicate a particular *KStN*. The company had a strength of about 150 men, of which 70% were German. The remainder were Poles, Austrians, Alsatians and Lorrainers. While most had frontline experience, it is ironic that none had mountaineering experience.[116]

The command group and support elements included a number of sections. The signals section was the largest with a *Feldwebel*, two junior NCO's and six men. The company headquarters had three clerks (a *Hauptfeldwebel* and two men). The repair section consisted of an *Oberfeldwebel*, a *Feldwebel* and three men. The armourer/artificers section was composed of a *Feldwebel*, an *Unteroffizier* and two men. Three men made up the supply section. The three gun platoons were each armed with four 2 cm mountain *Flak* and one light *MG 42*. Each gun crew consisted of an NCO and five men. Only HE rounds were available for the guns, and ammunition was in short supply for all weapons, including the rifles. The company reportedly had a large number of motor vehicles; these included five 3-ton Mercedes lorries, four 1.5-ton Steyr lorries to tow the guns, and a fifth lorry to transport the ammunition. The company also had 13 *Volkswagens* and eight motorcycles.[117] That said, these numbers may actually be too low, as the company had 46 motor vehicles compared to an authorisation of 45 on **25 May**. There were no horses.[118]

According to Tessin, a fusilier battalion was formed in **April 1944**, but this was actually just a company.[119] *Divisions-Füsilier-Kompanie 91* was raised by the division on **6 April**.[120] The company reported directly to the division and was used as its reconnaissance unit and, like most of the division, also in an anti-airborne role in Normandy.[121] The order to establish a fusilier battalion was not given to *Ob.West* until **25 May**. As a result, there was no time to form such a battalion before the invasion.[122]

The commander of the company, *Oblt.* Kattermann, was taken prisoner in **June**, and his interrogation provides some detail about the company's organisation.[123] (Much of his information was verified by a medic from the company.)[124] It consisted of a company headquarters section and three platoons.[125] A *Feldwebel* was in charge of the headquarters section, which included six more men who were armed with rifles. The platoons were also led by a *Feldwebel*, supported by three men. Each platoon had three sections. These consisted of a junior NCO and 10 men armed with one light *MG 42*, two machine pistols and rifles.[126]

On **15 April**, the company was listed as having 16 light MG's, 2 medium mortars, and 2 flamethrowers.[127] This was premature, since the machine guns and mortars did not actually arrive until later that month, and no mention was made of any flamethrowers arriving. On **16 April**, the company had a strength of 1 officer, 20 NCO's and 112 men. 12 *Hiwi's* were assigned a week later. The average age of the company was about 22.5 years. For the NCO's, this was a little over 28 years, and for the junior enlisted just under 22. For mobility, the men relied on bicycles, of which there were 124. The motor vehicles assigned to the company were two *Kfz.1's*, one *Kfz. 2*, two *RSO's* and one *Kettenkrad*. In addition, there were four wagons (*E.F.40*) and a field kitchen. The authorised 18 light and two heavy draught horses arrived on **29 April**.[128] Mobility appears to have increased after the transfer to Normandy; the company trains are said to have had eight lorries, which apparently were also used as troop transports.[129] These vehicle numbers can be compared to the situation on **25 May**, when the authorised number of motor vehicles had been five and the on-hand strength had been eight.[130]

Although *(Gebirgs) Artillerie-Regiment 191* (*Obstlt.* Kiewitt) was formed as a typical regiment of a 25th wave division, its final organisation was more complicated. Initially, the artillery regiments of these divisions were to consist of three battalions (two light and one "heavy" (motorised)). Both the light battalions would have two batteries, each with four light guns, and the "heavy" would have three batteries of four 8.8 cm AT guns or *Flak*.[131] Later base documents raised the possibility of equipping the 3rd Battalion with 15 cm heavy field howitzers, but this was not done for the *91. LL.D.*[132]

When the invasion began, the regiment did not match any base document. On **4 March**, its first two battalions were ordered to reequip with the nonexistent *Gebirgs-Haubitze 36*, an error soon corrected to the *7,5 cm Gebirgs-Geschütz 36*.[133] Due to the partial transition to a mountain artillery regiment, it also became known as *Gebirgs-AR 191*. This is reflected in the military postal number that was amended on **11 April**.[134] The previous designation, however, remains more common in the records.

In any case, these developments resulted in both the 1st and 2nd Battalions having three batteries instead of two. Four batteries were equipped with four *10,5 cm Geb.H. 40* each, a type of mountain howitzer.[135] This is confirmed by a report from **27 April**, which states the regiment had received the authorised number of 16 guns of that type.[136] The remaining batteries (3rd and 6th) were armed with the standard *10,5 cm le.F.H.18/40*. These batteries were listed as having been formed through "command channels".[137]

The difference between the batteries with the *Geb.H. 40* and the *le.F.H.18/40* can be explained by looking at the history of the division. The reinforced *GR 1025* had already included *Art.Abt. 1025*, which consisted of a headquarters and two batteries armed with eight 10.5 cm howitzers. When *AR 191* was formed, the battalion became part of it and was redesignated as the *I./AR 191*.[138] The 2nd Battery was reassigned to the 2nd Battalion and redesignated as its 4th Battery. The 1st Battery became the 2nd Battery, and a new 1st Battery was formed.[139] It is not clear if all batteries in the 1st and 2nd Battalions had ever been equipped with regular guns. It is quite likely that the shift to mountain guns was made before any additional (regular) guns had been delivered. This would limit the *le.F.H.18/40's* to the eight pieces in the two batteries from the former *Art.Abt. 1025*.[140] To get these eight regular howitzers into the 3rd and 6th Batteries, artillery pieces were moved from one battery to another. On **7 April**, orders were issued to transfer the 5th and 6th Batteries to the 3rd Battalion, where they would be redesignated as the 8th and 9th Batteries. In turn, the 3rd Battery would become the new 5th Battery. This meant that the 3rd and 6th Batteries had to be reformed. On the same day, four *Geb.H. 40's* each were assigned to the 1st, 2nd and 4th Batteries. This freed up the eight *le.F.H.18/40's* — now in the 2nd and 4th Batteries — for the new 3rd and 6th Batteries.[141]

One of the 10.5 cm le.F.H.18/40's that were used in the 3rd and 6th Batteries. This one belonged to 3rd Battery and was captured at Holdy on D-Day by the 101st AB.
(Mark A. Bando Collection)

91. Luftlande-Infanterie-Division

An excellent photograph of one of the division's rare 10.5 cm Geb.H.40. An 8.8 cm Flak and 7.5 cm Pak can be seen in the background. (NARA, via Steven J. Zaloga)

The 3rd Battalion was not reequipped for airlanding and kept its original 8.8 cm guns while remaining motorised. Since the 8.8 cm guns in 25th wave divisions were supposed to be AT pieces (although *Flak* could be issued), there have been questions regarding the battalion's weapons.[142] The use of *Flak* guns was only ordered for the *92. I.D.*[143] Indeed, all records identify the guns of the *III./AR 191* as AT weapons, but rarely show if they were *Pak 43's* or *Pak 43/41's*.[144] Fortunately, there is a high-level report from **April 1944** that confirms that the *91. LL.D.*, the *77.* and the *89. I.D.* were armed with *Pak 43's*.[145] Although an officer from the *II./AR 191* claimed the guns were 8.8 cm *Flak*, he appears to have been confused by the cruciform base of the *Pak 43*.[146] This shape of carriage was common on many types of 8.8 cm *Flak*.

On **30 April**, the regiment had all of its authorised 943 horses, including 426 pack horses for the mountain guns. On **25 May**, the regiment also had 256 motor vehicles (24 below the authorisation), but the exact types are not known.[147]

Due to its transition to a "mountain" regiment, many of its elements used different *KStN's* from regular infantry divisions. The headquarters

Another view of the same mountain howitzer. (NARA, via Steven J. Zaloga)

and headquarters battery used *KStN 415* and *579*, respectively. In the light battalions these elements used *KStN 417* and *587* respectively, with the gun batteries using *KStN 432*.[148] All were dedicated *KStN's* for mountain artillery. The 3rd Battalion used *KStN 406* for the headquarters, *586* for the headquarters battery, and *434* for the gun batteries. The 3rd Battalion *KStN's* were standard for 25th wave divisions.

The *KStN's* should provide the theoretical organisation of these units, but little detailed information is available on the actual condition of the regimental and battalion headquarters or their headquarters batteries. The regimental headquarters and headquarters battery reportedly had a combined strength of about 100 men. The battery included the usual signals platoon and a survey section (*Artillerie-Vermessungs-Trupp*).[149]

At battalion level, the strength of the headquarters and headquarters battery was lower. The signals platoon had a strength of about 40 men and the survey section consisted of 4 to 6 men.[150] It was estimated that the average age of the artillerymen was 24. Generally, the men were well trained and many had frontline experience. Little is known about the transport in the first two battalions, but according to an officer from the 2nd Battalion, both battalions used horse-drawn vehicles.[151]

The presence of the unusual mountain guns in the 1st and 2nd Battalions caused serious problems, because the guns used different ammunition than the standard *10,5 cm le.F.H. 18's*.[152] Furthermore, ammunition shortages for the *Geb.H. 40* already existed before D-Day. On **10 May**, *AOK 7* requested ammunition from *Ob.West*, but as late as **17 June** none had been delivered. The severity of the problem is apparent from the situation on **5 June**, when the stocks of this ammunition with *AOK 7* were at 22%.[153]

The ammunition shortages were acutely felt during the fighting in Normandy. In fact, the problem became so urgent that a request was made to airlift ammunition from Germany.[154] The guns were ultimately replaced due to this lack of ammunition.[155] The replacement guns were inferior to the howitzers and consisted of a variety of guns taken from coastal defence positions on the west coast of the Cotentin, so-called landing defence guns (*Landeabwehrgeschütze*).[156] These artillery pieces were light field guns of Belgian, Czech and German origin, with calibres around 7.5 cm. Based on reports, these were the *7,5 cm F.K. 235(b)*, the *7,65 cm F.K 17(t)*, and the *7,65 cm F.K.16 nA*.[157] All three types had been present in large numbers on the Cotentin before the invasion.[158] With regard to the *F.K. 235(b)*, it is possible these had been recovered from Hill 121 (Mt. de Doville) and Hill 131 (Mt. Étenclin), rather than taken from the coast. In the summer of **1943**, five such guns had been positioned on these hills.[159]

Pionier-Bataillon 191 (*Hptm.* Bohnenkamp) was similar to the engineer battalions of other 25th wave divisions. All of these battalions were established with just two companies. As was typical, the 2nd Company was equipped with bicycles, and the battalion headquarters was partially motorised to handle the heavy equipment in the combat equipment section attached to the headquarters. On **15 April**, the headquarters was armed with four light MG's and two flamethrowers, while both companies had two heavy MG's, nine light MG's, two medium mortars and six flamethrowers[160] — numbers that matched what was expected. No reports from the battalion have been found, making it difficult to provide more details. Records show that the battalion received 79 horses compared to an authorisation of just 67 by **30 April**. The battalion also had more motor vehicles than called for: 42 (32 authorised).[161]

On **25 May**, the *OKH* informed *Ob.West* that the divisions of the 25th wave should be expanded to have a third company in their engineer battalions.[162] It proved impossible to carry this out in the short time before D-Day and the orders were cancelled on **30 July**.[163]

The orders of **25 May** also called for creation of a field-replacement battalion. Time was short and on D-Day the division merely had a combat school and *Feldersatz-Zug 191* available. The platoon appears to have been an embryonic replacement battalion.

Mobility

Some figures are available on the mobility of the division as a whole. On **30 April**, the authorised number of horses was 2,652, including 426 pack horses in the artillery regiment. The division actually matched these authorisations in all its elements, except for *Pi.Btl. 191*, which exceeded its authorisation by 12. The division therefore had 2,664 horses.[164]

Similar numbers are available for the division's motorisation. On **25 May**, the division, despite an authorised level of 802, had 1,005 vehicles. All elements were above strength except for *AR 191* (down by 24) and *Nachr.Abt. 191* (down by two).[165]

The supply columns had horse-drawn and motorised transport. A driver from *Verpflegungs-Kompanie 191* stated it had 10 3.5-ton lorries, which were used to collect rations for the men and horses; six of the lorries were of German manufacture, the others French.[166] All told, the support units had 335 horses (on-hand quantities matching authorisations) and 184 motor vehicles (Authorised: 161).[167]

The presence of pack horses, mountain howitzers and mountain infantry guns are examples of modifications made to prepare the division for airlanding use. These changes also affected the division's motorisation. This is best illustrated by its use of a large number of the *Kleines Kettenkraftrad* (*Sd.Kfz. 2*). Photographs suggest these vehicles were omnipresent in the area around Ste. Mère-Église, and there was a good reason for this.[168] Before the invasion, the division had a reported total of 160 *Kettenkräder* (and 66 trailers) against an authorisation of just 12. This shows that the **March** plans to provide an additional 150 had largely been met. These additional vehicles were mostly assigned to the infantry regiments, which had 50 each.[169] As previously noted, a member of the *14.(Pzj)/GR 1058* stated that his company alone had 24 of these vehicles, although the *KStN* did not call for any.[170] The regimental engineer platoons are said to have had about 20, even though none were authorised in the *KStN*.[171]

Documents provide detailed numbers on motorisation. While the date of the documents is not clear, it was probably just before the general numbers provided on **25 May**, since the combined total is just 33 vehicles less. In any case, the documents offer a good look at the authorised vehicles at the time of the invasion; for this reason, they are presented here in detail.[172] The numbers provided below are the on-hand numbers, with "(o)" denoting vehicles not specifically developed for the military.

The division had 37 light motorcycles (up to 250 cc) (authorised 3), 89 heavier types (authorised 117) and 16 motorcycle combinations (authorised 42). This gave it a total of 142 motorcycles against an authorised level of 162. There was a greater variety of cars. The division had 88 *Kfz. 1 VW Kübelwagen's* (authorised 107), no *Kfz. 1's* (authorised 3), 42 *VW Schwimmwagen's* (authorised 3), 19 *Kfz. 2's* (radio version)(authorised 6), 1 *Kfz. 3* artillery surveying vehicle (authorised 1), 4 anti-aircraft *Kfz. 4's* (authorised 1), no maintenance *Kfz. 2/40's* (authorised 1), 31 light staff cars (o) (authorised 28), 6 medium staff cars (o) (authorised 7), 1 heavy staff car (o) (authorised 0), 9 *Kfz. 12* prime movers (authorised 2), no telephony equipment *Kfz. 15's* (authorised 8), 13 signal *Kfz. 15's* (authorised 4), 8 wireless *Kfz. 15's* (authorised 2) and 12 wireless *Kfz. 17's* (authorised 1). Combined, this resulted in an on-hand strength of 234 motorised vehicles against an authorisation of 174.[173]

The lorries can be grouped into three categories: up to 2-tonne, 2-3.5-tonnes and 3.5-5-tonnes. The first group included 39 open-top light lorries (authorised 39) and 19 open-top light cross-country ones (authorised 61), but there was no maintenance lorry (authorised 1). The majority of the lorries were in the second group. There were 247 open-top medium lorries (authorised 191), no *Kfz. 42* battery vehicles (authorised 1), 1 signals maintenance *Kfz. 42* (authorised 1) and 4 maintenance lorries (authorised 2). The number of heavy lorries was limited to 8 open-top vehicles (authorised 5), 1 closed-top lorry (authorised 0), 5 closed-top cross-country vehicles (authorised 2) and 40 maintenance vehicles (authorised 40). This gave an on-hand strength of 365 "regular" trucks (authorised 361).[174]

There were also 12 *Kfz. 31* ambulances (authorised 5) and one *Kfz. 100* rotating crane vehicle (authorised 1). Buses included 1 light (authorised 1), 4 medium (authorised 2), and 1 heavy bus (authorised 1). The tracked vehicles included 160 *Kettenkräder* (authorised 12), no *Maultiere* (authorised 1), 13 *Sd.Kfz. 7's* (authorised 16), and 39 *RSO's* (authorised 46).[175]

The division's trailers reflect the high number of *Kettenkräder*, with 66 specialised *Kettenkrad* trailers present without any being authorised. Other trailers included 1 (generator) *Sd.Anh. 24* (authorised 0), 1 *Sd.Anh. 32* with a 3-tonne transport box (authorised 1) and 1 *RSO* trailer (authorised 1). No trailer-mounted 7.5 kVA generator (authorised 1) was available and no *Sd. Anh. 23's* (authorised 2) or *Sd.Anh. 32's* (authorised 48).[176]

History

The division's early history was uneventful. It was stationed in Germany and reported to the Replacement Army.[177] The reinforced *GR 1025* had already been stationed at Baumholder Training Area, which is where the initial formation of the division took place. On **23 January**, the artillery battalion was transferred to the Bitsch (Bitche) Training Area; gradually, more troops arrived at both locations to build the division. On **27 March**, *GR 1058* also moved to Bitsch.[178] The division stayed at these locations until late **April**, when the decision was made to relocate it to *AOK 7*.[179] The dedicated air transport allocation it had originally been given was reassigned to *Fj.Rgt. 6*, which was stationed in Wahn.[180]

The advance party of the division, led by the commander of *Nachr.Abt. 191* (*Hauptmann* Buckreihs), arrived in the *7. Armee* sector on **1 May**.[181] The division followed by train the next day, its transfer taking place under the code name *Bewegung Leonore* and requiring 32 trains.[182] The assembly area was roughly a triangle between Nantes, Rennes and Redon, and it included the high ground between Nantes and Pontchâteau. The division was to deploy in battlegroups, with one regiment moving to the northern front of *KVB Nantes*.[183] The division was given two missions:

- Defend against sea and airborne landings (especially at Lorient and St. Nazaire).
- Prepare for a rapid movement within or outside the *7. Armee* sector.

For defence against airborne landings, the assembly area was to be considered a combat zone. The division was to dig in and be prepared day and night to destroy a "ten-times superior enemy." To do this, the division was to occupy the high ground and avoid the villages. Apart from its local defence role, the division was a field-army reserve and, as such (and for matters related to its formation), was placed directly under *AOK 7* control. For local deployment, it was assigned to the *XXV. A.K.*[184]

On **8 May**, the division was moved in a different direction: La Haye-du-Puits on the Cotentin Peninsula. The *2. Fj.Div.* was sent to the *XXV. A.K.* in its place.[185] The change in orders arrived late, and by **9 May** 17 trains had already been unloaded at the original destination.[186] The remaining trains changed direction and, on **10 May**, the first five arrived in the new sector. Over the next few days that number rose to 12, 19, 23 and 27 and, on **15 May**, the move was complete.[187]

The division's first locations on the Cotentin were reported on **14 May**. The divisional headquarters was established in Château de Bernaville. The headquarters of *GR 1058* was in St. Cyr (4 km southeast Valognes) and its three battalions located in Le Haut-Geley, La Jardinerie and St. Côme-du-Mont. The locations of *AR 191* were reported at the same time. The regimental headquarters was in La Ligue (2 km northeast of St. Sauveur-le-Vicomte), and the battalions in Blandamour, l'Ossière and the Bois d'Étenclin.[188] The positions of *GR 1057* were reported on the **16th**. Its headquarters was located on the main road 2 km west of St. Sauveur-le-Vicomte. The 1st Battalion, together with the *III./AR 191*, had moved to Château Brocboeufs; the 2nd was further north around St. Anne; and the 3rd was on the St. Sauveur - Barneville road, about 1 km east of Besneville.[189]

A conference with *Gen.* Marcks took place at divisional headquarters on **11 May**. The division was briefed on its deployment which, apart from the

Feldm. Rommel leaving the division's headquarters in Château de Bernaville in May 1944. Gen. Falley is on the left, putting on his gloves. (Normandy Institute)

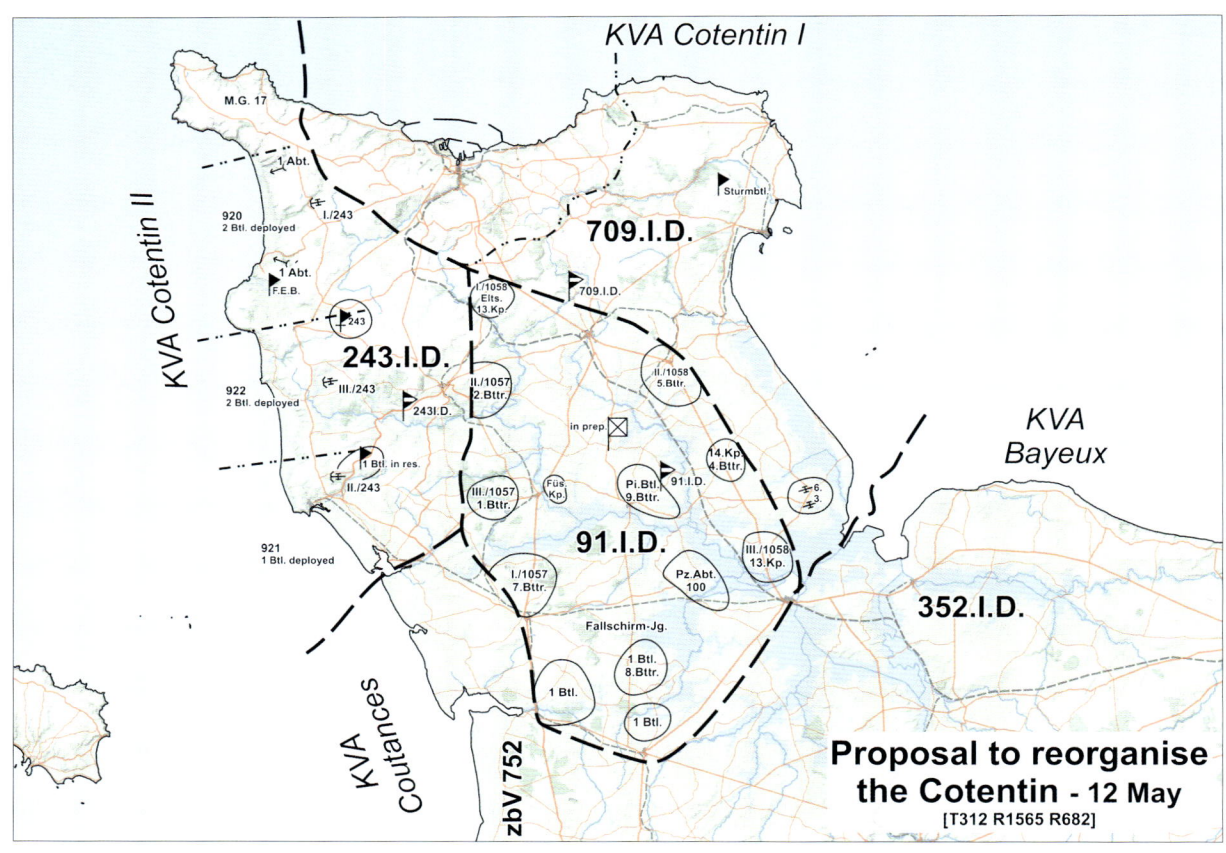

The transfer of the 91. LL.D. to Normandy allowed LXXXIV. A.K. to reorganise its defences on the Cotentin Peninsula. Shown here is the plan to build battalion size battlegroups and position these on the high ground and other important sectors. With the bulk of the division's combat troops deployed along the division's boundary, the support troops (not shown here) were given the task of defending the centre. The two batteries at Ste. Marie-du-Mont are also shown. These supported the coastal defences and where detached from the division. (T312 R1565 F682)

location, was in line with the tactical principles outlined above. Its sector on the Cotentin was considered good for airborne landings, with an expected centre of gravity to the east, the area best suited for amphibious landings. The division was to establish forces in the north and south, while the centre would have less strength. *FJR 6*, which had yet to finish training, would be attached; support would come from *Panzer-Ersatz-und-Ausbldungs-Abt. 100* with one training and four combat companies. Of particular tactical significance were Carentan and the hills along the St. Sauveur-le-Vicomte - La Haye-du-Puits highway. These were the responsibility of *Maj.* Eitner's *I./1057*. His troops could rely on support from three static guns on Hill 131 (Mt. Étenclin) and two on Hill 121 (Mt. de Doville).[190] These were the five *7,5 cm F.K.235(b)'s*

deployed in the summer of **1943**. Whether each hill still had a 3.7 cm Renault FT tank is not clear.[191]

In the north, the division was to coordinate with *Flak-Rgt. 30*, which had formed a protective belt for the *V*-weapons installations close to the land defences of *Festung Cherbourg*. The division would also make contact with units from *AR zbV 621*, which were in reserve around Négreville (*s.Art.Abt. 456*). The high ground at Brix would serve as the observation post. As with most other troops on the Cotentin, the division's troops would be used to construct air-landing obstacles.[192]

On **12 May**, *Gen.* Marcks presented the *LXXXIV. A.K.'s* plans describing how the corps would deploy the division in reinforced battalions (and sometimes companies). The infantry battalions and *Pi.Btl. 191* would each be supported by a battery from *AR 191* or one of the regimental heavy weapons companies.[193] Rather than forming traditional defence lines, these units would operate more or less in isolation. Each force was to split into smaller groups for all-round defence — the method considered most effective for defending against airborne landings. Unfortunately, this type of deployment also made it difficult for the division to quickly assemble strong forces should that needed to be done.[194] The support troops were most likely instructed to deploy in a fashion similar to the combat troops. Although the plan was not followed rigidly, much of it was carried out.

It is not clear to what extend this tactical deployment was based on the division's own input or on guidelines and ideas set by others. This matter deserves some more attention since, in 1952, Chester Wilmot wrote in his influential 'The Struggle for Europe' that the division "had been specially trained for anti-airlanding operations" — a statement since repeated by many other authors. Yet Wilmot did not actually support his claim by evidence and it may even have been solely inspired on the peculiar designation of the division. The claim in itself is problematic as it implies (a) that the division was purposely selected to move to the Cotentin because of its special training and (b) that the division was fully ready to deal with airborne landings. The former overlooks the context in which the transfer took place: a last ditch attempt to reinforce the Cotentin in **May 1944**. By this time very few divisions were available to reinforce the West, and yet, the *91. LL.D.* was first directed to Bretagne and the *2. Fj.D.* to the Cotentin. However, with most of the *2.Fj.D.* not yet available — and the *II.Fs.K.* assembling in Bretagne with what were to become several airborne divisions — it was decided to redirect the *91. LL.D.* to the Cotentin instead. There *FJR 6* was already in place for anti-airborne operations. Being available and having only six infantry battalions, the *91. LL.D.* was arguably the best candidate to supplement the parachute regiment (with which it already had a connection). Any training of the division in anti-airborne warfare would have been a bonus, but suggesting it was well trained for such operations appears to be an exaggeration; The division's training plans do not mention anti-airborne operations, except for those of *GR 1058*. In that regiment such activities were only covered in the eighth of the divisions nine weeks of training (**17-23 April**). That week, the regimental subunits were to receive both specific instruction (theory) and combat training, but in both cases it was only one of several topics on the curriculum. Considering the division's contacts with the *Luftwaffe* (especially formations involved in airborne operations), it is nonetheless possible that the thinking by such organisations about countering such operations influenced the division in ways not reflected in the documents. This may have also have happened after arriving in Normandy, when *FJR 6* was subordinated to the division.

Once under 7th Army, the division was certainly well aware that it could face airborne landings. On **12 May**, *Gen.Lt.* Falley issued instructions to all commanders in his (reinforced) division, laying out 10 basic principles to defeat the expected Allied invasion. They included instructions to keep up morale through propaganda messages and proper care of the men, but also addressed operational issues; four of the principles directly concerned airborne attacks and/or the difficult hedgerow terrain. Through the lowest NCO's, they were to be passed on to the men.

- Since attacks from the air might happen at any time, we need to be at defensive and combat readiness at all times. The troops will dig in to form strongpoints (with reinforced foxholes (*Panzerdeckungslöcher*) for 2-3 men) and forgo the comforts of villages.

- Our weapons […] will only fulfill their purpose when put to their full use, meaning their full repellent potential. For most automatic weapons (incl. sniper rifles!) the character of [the terrain in] Normandy and Bretagne, with its enclosed roads and fields, requires well constructed high placed firing positions: in trees, elevated firing positions (*Hochständen*), in hedgerows transformed into defensive positions, etc. The troops must become excellent and resourceful in this matter.

- The battle against airborne forces (arriving by parachute or glider) will initially be a battle against an enemy superior in number. The German soldier can however rely on the defensive preparations and fighting spirit of his unit, his excellent weaponry, as well as his beliefs and hatred [towards the enemy]. When every German soldier, regardless of where he finds himself at the time of an airborne landing, fully commits himself as a solo warrior (*Einzelkämpfer*), he will prevent the enemy from forming up and contribute to their swift annihilation. This notion must receive particular emphasis in the day-to-day training.

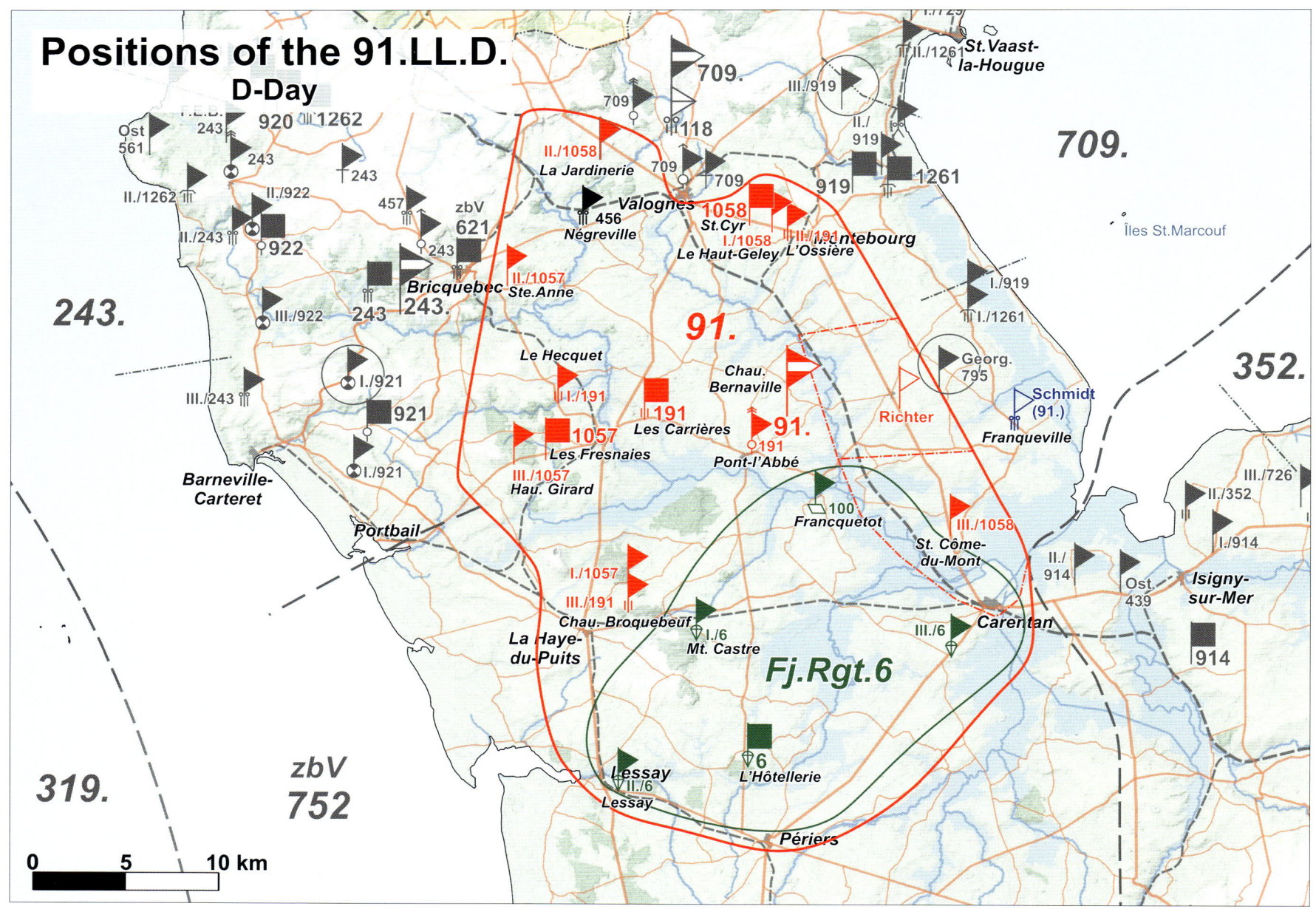

On 5 June the division had taken up its positions. Unfortunately, the boundaries of its battlegroups are only known for KG Richter and KG Diekhoff (III./1058). (T312 R1570 F9)

- In the current terrain, cooperation between all arms and troops within the reinforced companies (this also applies to battalions, etc.) is of utmost importance. This is only possible when the NCO's are properly trained. To improve the low level tactical decision making of NCO's, the reinforced companies are — if possible daily — to provide terrain instruction in the immediate surroundings of the strongpoints; The troops have to be trained in similar fashion (at section and reinforced platoon level).

The German defences continued to take shape and, in early **June**, the *LXXXIV. A.K.* ordered the *I./1057* to the north to form a battlegroup. On **5 June**, the division issued corresponding orders and took the opportunity to make some changes of its own. This involved expanding the sector of *GR zbV 752*, which was responsible for the west coast of Manche from Portbail down to Avranches. On the night of **7-8 June**, *Ost-Btl. 635*, which was under the operational control of *GR zbV 752*, would relieve the *II./Fj.Rgt. 6*, which was positioned around Lessay. In turn, the following night, the airborne battalion was to take over the *I./1057* sector: The hills (Hill 121 and 131) and the highway south of St. Sauveur-le-Vicomte. The headquarters of the *III./AR 191* and the 7th Battery were to stay in the area and report directly to *FJR 6*. The following two nights were to be used by the *I./1057* (*KG Eitner*) to move to its new sector, which is not known; this force consisted of the *I./1057*, some regimental troops and the *I./AR 191* with its headquarters, headquarters battery and 1st Battery. The headquarters of *GR 1057*, with its headquarters company and motorised combat team, would also move, but the location remains unknown. These movements were to be carried out on the night of **8-9 June**.[195]

It is not believed that any of these changes happened before the invasion, but preparations were probably already made. Meanwhile, the same divisional orders included several changes that would go into effect on **6 June**. *KG Kiewitt* (*AR 191*) would be dissolved, although the headquarters was to stay in charge of its sector, at the disposal of the division. Two new *Kampfgruppen* were to be formed. The first was to be made up of supply troops under the command of the supply officer — presumably the *Ib*, *Major* Bartuzat — with the commander of the transportation company (*Oberleutnant* Evers) second-in-command. The second was *KG Bohnenkamp*, named after the commander of *Pi.Btl. 191*.[196]

Positions on D-Day

Despite uncertainty arising from last minute changes, it is still possible to provide a general overview of the division's positions on D-Day. Simply put, it covered the interior of the peninsula, while the *243.* and the *709. I.D.* defended the coast.[197] More specifically, the sector covered by the organic units started around Carentan in the southeast and ran via Montebourg to Brix, south to Besneville, past La Haye-du-Puits, then back east to Carentan.[198] The division headquarters was still north of Picauville.[199]

GR 1058 essentially protected the rear of the *709. I.D.* and was spread out along highway N13. The positions of regimental units had not changed much since the initial report of **14 May**. The *III./1058* (*KG Diekhoff*) was furthest south around St. Côme-du-Mont, where its headquarters was located. The other two battalions were near Montebourg and Valognes.[200] Although these battalions were a long way from the coast, their central positions would enable them strike in all directions, including Cherbourg. The 1st Battalion (*KG Moch*) was in Le Haut-Geley and the 2nd Battalion (*KG Lewandowski*) in La Jardinerie. The former has been linked to the hills north of Montebourg. The regimental headquarters was also to the north, in St. Cyr, between Montebourg and Valognes. Additional units were south of Ste. Mère-Église, including the 14th Company, which covered the Chef-du-Pont - Ste. Marie-du-Mont road (D70) crossroads. The divisional combat school was in the same area.[201]

The *14./1058* had been reinforced with infantry and was known as *KG Richter*, named after the company commander, *Oberleutnant* Richter. On **12 May**, his company had become the nucleus of a fourth battlegroup, despite only having about 200 men. Prisoners state that this consisted of a platoon from the 14th Company, the regimental engineer platoon and various rifle platoons from the 2nd and 3rd Battalions. It also included about 65 of the regiment's *Kettenkrad* operators.[202]

Little information is available regarding the combat school. It appears it was in action in platoon strength with the 14th Company after the invasion.[203] Its purpose was to train platoon leaders, and it was led by *Oberleutnant* Witte from the *7./1058*. In the event of enemy landings, the men were to return to their units or, if that was not possible, to join *Feldersatz-Zug 191* in La Coquerie, south of Ste. Mère-Église.[204] It is likely that these forces supported or were incorporated into *KG Richter*.

Either way, *KG Diekhoff* and *KG Richter* provided depth to the defences of

GR 919, which was responsible for Utah Beach.[205] A map was captured after the invasion showing the sector held by these two forces. In both cases, the flooded fields around the Merderet and Douve Rivers formed the western boundary. The boundary between the two groups ran along the road from Chef-du-Pont to Ste. Marie-du-Mont (D70) as far as the junctions with the D129 and D524 (north of Hiesville). The village, road and crossroads belonged to *KG Richter*; *KG Diekhoff's* sector continued south past Angoville-au-Plain and around Carentan, roughly forming a triangle. *KG Richter's* eastern boundary continued north from the crossroads, running roughly 2 km east of the highway to south of Saussetour, where it then turned west past Fresville to the Merderet.[206] Around Turqueville, this sector may have overlapped with *Georg.Inf.Btl. 795*.

In general, *GR 1057* defended the rear area of the *243. I.D.*, with its regimental headquarters located west of St. Sauveur-le-Vicomte, in Les Fresnaies. The positions had not changed since the report of **16 May**. This still put the 1st Battalion (*KG Eitner*) in the Château northeast of La Haye-du-Puits. The 2nd Battalion (*KG Mügge*) was southeast of Bricquebec in St. Anne, with the 3rd Battalion (*KG Reiter*, previously *Wittner*) east of Besneville in (Hameau) Girard.[207] A former officer of the *2./1057* gave his position as Besneville, but no reliable information has been found regarding other company positions.[208]

These positions match a report by *GR 1057* on **20 May**, which gives an impression of the different sectors. *KG Eitner* was responsible for Hills 121 and 131, and tasked with placing obstacles in the Prairies Marécageuses, west of the highway between St. Sauveur-le-Vicomte and La Haye-du-Puits. *KG Wittner/Eitner* (3rd Battalion) was doing the same south of Besneville, around St. Sauveur and Le Hequet. Further north, *KG Mügge* was assigned the areas around St. Anne and Le Melleret, both east of Bricquebec. The emplacement of obstacles, for which as many as 350 civilian workers were pressed into service, was to be finished by **25 May**.[209]

The deployment of the two regiments largely followed the plans of **12 May**. Unfortunately, the positions of individual companies are not clear, making it difficult to assess how large the battlegroup sectors may have been. Based on the positions of the battalion headquarters, it seems clear that the division's main strength was around the edges of its sector. The situation in the centre remains less clear. Until shortly before the invasion *KG Kiewitt* (*AR 191*) was responsible for the centre of the division.[210] Again, the precise area covered by this force and the units involved is not known. They may have included *Pi.Btl. 191*, although this battalion was to form *KG Bohnenkamp* by **6 June** (based on a pre D-Day plan) when *KG Kiewitt* was dissolved. A second battlegroup, formed from supply troops, was probably located in the centre as well and had apparently been part of *KG Kiewitt*; these troops were probably north or west of *KG Bohnenkamp*.

The positions of *Pionier-Btl.191* are uncertain because they are not mentioned in the daily logs of *AOK 7* or noted on the situation map of **5 June**. The **12 May** map reveals the intention to deploy the battalion in the Pont-l'Abbé area, and this appears to have been the case on D-Day.[211] There were several units in the general area that were not from the division. One was *9./Fj. Ers.u.Ausb.Rgt. 1*. This airborne training and replacement company arrived in St. Sauveur-le-Vicomte on **2 June**, while the rest of its battalion was further north on the peninsula.[212] Another interesting reinforcement was the *3.(Fla)/Pz.Jg.Abt. 352*, armed with self-propelled 3.7 cm *Flak*. It arrived in Pont-l'Abbé on **3 May** and was still there on D-Day.[213] On **10 June**, *Pi.Btl. 191*, *Pz.Jg.Kp. 191*, *3./Pz.Jg.Abt. 352*, and an airborne training and replacement company were part of *KG Bohnenkamp*, but it is not clear when this organisation had gone into effect and may have already happened on the eve of D-Day.[214] The positions of these units could confirm that, on **6 June**, *KG Bohnenkamp* was responsible for defending the area directly north of the Douve, roughly in the area of St. Sauveur-le-Vicomte - Pont-l'Abbé - Beuzeville-la-Bastille. As such, it was probably responsible for the defence of the Douve and Merderet bridges in the area.

The positions of *Pz.Jg.Kp. 191* and other combat companies are also problematic. The plans of **12 May** only showed the position of *Füs.Kp. 91*, which was to be positioned east of St. Sauveur , as confirmed by the company commander.[215] On **21 May**, *Füs.Kp. 91* was attached to *AR 191* (*KG Kiewitt*) for administrative matters. As *KG Kiewitt* was supposedly disbanded before D-Day, the company must have been released from attachment or attached to another battlegroup, perhaps *KG Bohnenkamp*. This could have been confirmed by the company commander, but he only mentioned being part of *KG Kiewitt*.[216]

The map of **12 May** offers no insights into the positions of *Fla-Kp. 191* or *Pz.Jg.Kp. 191*. On **21 May**, *Fla-Kp. 191* was administratively attached to *Pz. Ers.u.Ausb.Abt. 100*, which was between the Douve River and Baupte. The

Flak company was probably in the area.[217] On **10 June**, it was formally part of a force built around a tank battalion (*KG Bardtenschlager*) that still held an area south of the Douve.[218]

On **21 May**, *Pz.Jg.Kp. 191* was administratively attached to *AR 191* (*KG Kiewitt*), which indicates that it was located in the centre of the divisional sector. The company has been linked to St. Sauveur-le-Vicomte and, as mentioned, was part of *KG Bohnenkamp* with at least six guns on **10 June**.[219]

AR 191 was spread out on D-Day. The regimental headquarters was in Les Carrières (1 km northeast St. Sauveur), with the headquarters battery in Rauville-la-Place. The headquarters of the 1st Battalion was to the west in Le Hequet; the 2nd Battalion in l'Ossière, in the *GR 1058* sector. The headquarters of the *III./AR 191* was at the Château northeast of La Haye-du-Puits; this put it in the sector of *GR 1057* and close to *FJR 6*.[220] Considering the plans from **May** and positions of the troops on D-Day, it seems that the 1st Battalion was supporting *GR 1057* and the 2nd supporting *GR 1058*. The plans to leave the 3rd Battalion (and 7th Battery) in place once *FJR 6* took over suggests that it was to operate in a certain sector rather than support a specific formation.

The decision to assign each of the two light battalions to a different regiment reportedly dated back to **April**, when battlegroups had been formed around the two regiments.[221] These plans were permanently changed on **12 May** to focus on battlegroups formed by reinforced battalions, with batteries directly supporting them.[222] The details were not followed to the letter. For example, the 4th Battery operated with the *III./1058* (*KG Diekhoff*), while the earlier plans were for this battery to be in Ste. Mère-Église with the *14./1058* (*KG Richter*).[223] The 5th Battery was near Montebourg as planned, but probably supported the *I./1058* (*KG Moch*) rather than the 2nd battalion.[224] *GR 1057* had the *I./AR 191* in direct support. This makes it possible that, as planned, the 1st Battery supported the *III./1057* (*KG Reiter*) and the 2nd Battery did the same for the *II./1057* (*KG Mügge*).[225] The *I./1057* (*KG Eitner*), which had not yet moved, was supported by the *7./AR 191* and the headquarters of the *III./AR 191*.[226] *Pi.Btl. 191* (*KG Bohnenkamp*) was to receive fire support from the *9./AR 191*, while the guns of the 8th Battery were with *Fj.Rgt. 6* as planned.[227]

Two more batteries from *AR 191* were positioned outside the divisional sector, around Ste. Marie-du-Mont, where they were incorporated into the coastal defences. These were the 3rd Battery at Holdy and the 6th at Brécourt, both with *le.F.H.18/40's*. Combined under a ad hoc headquarters, this battalion was known as (*Art.*) *Gruppe Schmidt* or *Abteilung Schmidt* and included a platoon of infantry from *GR 1058*. On **18 May**, a battery from the assault battalion (*Sturm-Bataillon AOK 7*) was put under Schmidt's command, which was in turn attached to *H.K.A.R. 1261*.[228]

The division's operational strength improved when *Maj.* von der Heydte's *Fj.Rgt. 6* was attached.[229] This regiment covered the southern sector, roughly the area between Carentan, La Haye-du-Puits, Lessay and Périers.[230] It was supported by elements of *AR 191*. The 8th Battery was attached to the paratroopers and the and *13./1057* also appears to have been in the area. Although positioned in Lessay, it seems to have served with its own division during the fighting.[231] The regiment was further supported by the 2 cm anti-aircraft guns of the *3.(Fla)/Pz.Jg.Abt. 243*, which was in Sainteny.[232] The final reinforcement was *Pz.Ers.u.Ausb.Abt. 100*, between Baupte and the Douve River in the *FJR 6* sector. It is not clear how closely the division and regiment operated together. Due to the nature of the landings and the terrain around the flooded Merderet and Douve Rivers, the regiment essentially fought in a separate sector within the first few hours of D-Day. Still, comments from *Obst.* König suggest that the two were in close contact until the regiment was subordinated to the *17. SS-Pz.Gren.Div.* about a week later.[233]

Reserve Role

As the division was intended for airlanding operations, preparations for this began in early **March**. The *I./Luftlandegeschwader 1* and the *I./Luftlandegeschwader 2* were chosen to transport the division by air.[234] These two wings were equipped with *DFS 230* and *GO 242* gliders, respectively. The orders included plans to distribute the division among the gliders and prepare for deployment. Fuselages of gliders and the *Kettenkräder* with their drivers were moved to Baumholder for trials and training.[235]

On **26 March**, *Ob.West* requested the division's transfer to the Reims area, which would facilitate deployment from the area's large airfields.[236] This request was denied, as the division was *OKW-Reserve* and could be used in any theatre. For this role the division was coupled with *Luftlandegeschwader 1*, which had to stay in Strasbourg.[237] However, in late **April** it was decided to send the division to *AOK 7*.[238]

91. Luftlande-Infanterie-Division

Despite its transfer to the west, the division remained *OKW-Reserve* for airlanding deployments. In this capacity, it could be air lifted to Denmark (*"Hanna"*); under *Ob.Südwest* on the Ligurian coast (*"Marder 1"*) or on the Adriatic coast of Italy (*"Marder 2"*); with *Ob.Südost* on the Adriatic coast of the Balkans (*"Forelle 1"*) or in the Aegean (*"Forelle 2"*).[239] With *AOK 7*, the division was a field-army reserve, while the tank battalion and *Fj.Rgt. 6* were corps reserves.[240] The division was a major asset for *Ob.West*. If the need arose, it could be deployed against an invasion in an area stretching from the Netherlands to southeast France.[241]

The bodies of Gen.Lt. Falley and the Ib, Maj.i.G. Bartuzat were initially buried in La Bonneville. Bartuzat was posthumously promoted to Oberstleutnant. (WWII Museum, Medusky Collection)

Today, Gen.Lt. Falley and ObstIt. Bartuzat are two of 10.152 who have been interred at the German war cemetery at Orglandes, less than 5km from where they were killed. (Sean Claxton)

Combat

On the night of **5-6 June**, units from the *91. LL.D.* quickly found themselves confronting the US 82nd and 101st Airborne Divisions. The Allied plan had been for the 82nd AB to land the 505th PIR around Ste. Mère-Église and the 507th and 508th PIR west of the Merderet River. The 101st AB would land its 502nd and 506th PIR behind Utah Beach and the 501st PIR east of St. Côme-du-Mont.[242]

The actual landings were scattered over a wide area, sowing confusion among both American and German forces and having a profound impact on the fighting.[243] Instead of sizeable and well-organised battlegroups, stray paratroopers formed small groups that tried to make their way to their objectives, while the defenders tried desperately to assess the situation. Amongst the ubiquitous hedgerows, danger lurked around every corner, resulting in many minor engagements that continued through **9-10 June**.[244] While most of these encounters were never recorded, a few examples illustrate the situation.

An early victim of the chaos was *Gen.Lt.* Falley, who had not been with his division when the landings began. Like many commanders, he had left the day before to participate in the war games which would be hosted by the *II. Fs.K.* at Rennes on the **6th**. In their meeting, the senior commanders of the 7. Armee would address the topic of airborne landings! Falley took the opportunity to spend the night of **5/6** June at the iconic Mont-St. Michel, about two thirds of the way to Rennes. The adjutant of the *III./1050 (77. I.D.)* made the necessary, last minute arrangements. That night, at 01:15, *AOK 7* declared *Alarmstufe I* (for the field army) and *II* (for the *LXXXIV. A.K.*). The immediate return of the general to his divisions was ordered. After some difficulty, the battalion adjutant managed to get through to the general, who, around 06:00, set off in his Wanderer to return to his division. The message to travel to corps headquarters in St.Lô never reached him. That morning, just short of his headquarters, the car ran into a group of paratroopers. Falley and the division logistics officer, *Major* Bartuzat, were both killed; their wounded driver captured.[245] *Obst.* Klosterkemper, commander of *GR 920 (243. I.D.)*, assumed acting command of the division.[246]

Contrary to normal combat protocols, many of the division's supply troops were in the centre of its sector. Although a deliberated decision, it meant they also came in contact with enemy troops. One such case was *Feldpost-Amt 191*. Its postmen, located at Amfreville, responded in the spirit of anti-airlanding operations and functioned as an independent fighting force on **6-7 June**. During the fighting one man was killed, along with five Americans, who also suffered several wounded and six taken prisoner.[247]

Among the early victims of the airborne landings, albeit outside the division's area, were the two batteries from *AR 191* around Ste. Marie-du-Mont. The landings put them in an isolated position; both were quickly discovered by American troops and put out of action.[248] As a result, they were permanently lost to the division. The loss of the 6th Battery at Brécourt was made famous by the television series *Band of Brothers*. Still, at least 30 men from *Abteilung Schmidt* made it back to German lines. On **24 June**, the battalion was officially reported as disbanded.[249]

Looking at the larger picture, at 01:15 on **6 June** (having been informed of the first airborne landings) *AOK 7* ordered Alert Level II (*Alarmstufe II*) for all of the *LXXXIV. A.K.* By 02:00, the corps had identified the landings from Ste. Marie-du-Mont to Montebourg as one of two centres of gravity (the other being the area of the *716. I.D.*). At 02:15, *AOK 7* updated *H.Gr. B* and requested the subordination of the *91. LL.D.*, which was granted. At 02:35, the division, which was already in action against air landings, was put under control of the corps.[250] During the night, the divisional command post was attacked by an estimated battalion-sized force and evacuated on the order of the *Ia*, *Obstlt.* Bickel. It moved from Chau. de Bernaville to a prepared position in a wooded area; then later to the command post of the divisional supply troops, reportedly near La Bonneville.[251] At 03:30, the corps reported that contact with Ste. Mère-Église had been lost.[252] The small town would become the focal point of the division's operations on **6-7 June**.

At 07:00, the corps notified *AOK 7* that air landings had taken place from Carentan to north of Valognes, and that the *91. LL.D.* would need to clear the area. The corps report was soon followed by the field army's morning report to *H.Gr. B*, informing it of the countermeasures that had been initiated.[253] The *709. I.D.*, with the attached *GR 1058* (minus the southern battalion), was to counterattack from Montebourg in the direction of Ste. Mère-Église to clear the zone east of the flooded area between Carentan and Le Ham (flooded Merderet and Douve). The *91. LL.D.*, supported by *Pz.Ers.u.Ausb.Abt. 100*, would counterattack north and east to clear the area west of the inundated land.[254] In its afternoon report, *AOK 7* informed *H.Gr. B* that *Fj.Rgt. 6* was also taking part in the counterattacks.[255] Simply put, it was to attack the landing area from the south, reinforced by the *III./1058*.[256]

The division's troops and its reinforcements were engaged in three main areas, with the counterattacks mostly in the direction of the airborne forces around Ste. Mère-Église: *GR 1058* attacking from the north, *GR 1057* from the west and *Fj.Rgt. 6* from the south.

German records offer few details about the fighting west of the Merderet on D-Day. American forces in the area, primarily the 507th and the 508th PIR (82nd AB), largely failed to capture or destroy the bridges across the Douve and Merderet, thus failing to secure a bridgehead.[257] By late morning, the Germans had secured the crossing at Pont-l'Abbé, while continuing to press their attacks to the north.[258] In the afternoon, supported by *Pz.Ers.u.Ausb. Abt. 100*, the Germans recaptured Cauquigny on the western end of the Cauquigny - La Fière causeway. Control of this causeway was vital, as it was one of only two roads crossing the flooded Merderet in the area and linked Ste. Mère-Église to Picauville and Amfreville. For the Americans, it was a vital link between the troops east and west of the river. For the Germans, it offered the best route to attack Ste. Mère-Église from the west. A subsequent German tank and infantry assault across the causeway was stopped at La Fière bridge by A/505th PIR (reinforced), preventing *GR 1057* from reaching Ste. Mère-Église.[259]

The German troops fighting west of the flooded area had some success. Not only were the crossings of the Douve still in German hands, but the 82nd AB had been prevented from establishing a reliable link between the troops either side of the Merderet. The Germans had also gained control of most of the area. By the end of D-Day, organised American resistance had been reduced to a few serious pockets, while stray paratroopers roamed the area or established small isolated groups. One pocket was west of Amfreville and south of Gourbesville (*Colonel* Millett, commander of the 507th PIR). Two others were in close proximity: East of Amfreville (Captain Taylor, commander of H/507th PIR) and northwest of Cauquigny (Lieutenant-Colonel Timmes, commander of the 2/507th PIR). The two joined at daybreak on D+2. A fourth was on Hill 30, west of Chef-du-Pont (508th PIR, commanded by Colonel Shanley).[260] These pockets continued to play a part in the fighting over the next few days.

North of the main drop zones, *Obstlt.* Keil (commander of *GR 919*, *709. I.D.*) received reports of thousands of airborne troops landing, and he identified Ste. Mère-Église as the focal point from captured maps. To deal with this, he requested the division release the *I./1058* (*Maj.* Moch) to attack in that direction. His request worked its way up the chain of command and, at 02:30, the *Ia* (*Major* Förster) informed Keil that the battalion had been released.²⁶¹ In fact, the entire regiment had been placed under the *709. I.D.*, and the battalion was to attack the town.²⁶² Since it was not in contact with the division, Keil passed these orders on to the battalion, expecting it to reach the town no later than 07:00. At that time, however, the battalion was still at the southern exit of Montebourg. Keil repeated the attack order immediately.²⁶³

By late morning, *GR 1058* was attacking southeast from positions near Émondeville.²⁶⁴ Around 10:00, it reported to Keil that *Batterie Azeville* (*2./H.K.A.R. 1261*) was surrounded and asked if it should come to the battery's aid. Keil again directed the *I./1058* to attack towards Ste. Mère-Église.²⁶⁵ The attack was launched but failed to reach the town due to stubborn resistance from D/505ᵗʰ PIR at Neuville-au-Plain. Against increasing German pressure, the paratroopers withdrew from the village late in the afternoon.²⁶⁶ By 18:00, it was clear to *Gen.Lt.* von Schlieben (commander of the *709. I.D.*) that the regiment would not reach Ste. Mère-Église on D-Day.²⁶⁷

South of the town, *KG Richter* was isolated by the airborne landings, although it was presumably still in contact with *Georg.Inf.Btl. 795*. It was joined by the *Flak* transport troops, who had left Ste. Mère-Église during the night, withdrawing south.²⁶⁸ During the day, the battlegroup was probably responsible for the pressure against the perimeter of the 82ⁿᵈ AB south of the town. After its attacks had been repulsed, the battlegroup continued to defend the high ground (Hill 20) and, that evening, prevented Task Force Raff from breaking through from the south with its armour. Together with the Georgian battalion, it formed a pocket stretching from Hill 20 to Turqueville.²⁶⁹

Further south, the American landings had isolated the *III./1058* (and the *4./AR 191*) from the other troops east of the Douve and Merderet. During the day, the battalion made contact with *Fj.Rgt. 6*, which was moving up through Carentan, and was attached to the regiment.²⁷⁰ Both elements are covered in the *FJR 6* after-action report, but not in a positive way. To some extend this appears to be a matter of bias from the German paratroopers, for their American counter-parts reported facing considerable opposition upon landing around St. Côme-du-Mont. This applies to both the night and day, at times when and locations where only German army forces were present. Still, the main German weakness, the Americans noted, was not a lack of fire, but a reluctance to leave their firing positions and close-in with the Americans when they were at their most vulnerable.²⁷¹

When the airborne landings began, the commander of *FJR 6*, *Maj.* von der Heydte, tried in vain to contact the division. He did succeed in reaching the *LXXXIV. A.K.* just before 06:00 and received orders directly from *Gen.* Marcks: The regiment was to clear the enemy in the Carentan area and attack north to destroy the enemy that had landed to the rear of the *709. I.D.* (meaning *GR 919*) between Carentan and Ste. Mère-Église.²⁷² At 10:30, Carentan was reported free of the enemy.²⁷³ In early afternoon, its 1ˢᵗ and 2ⁿᵈ Battalions assembled around Raids. (The 3ʳᵈ Battalion was still in heavy fighting south of the Périers - Carentan highway and covering the regiment's eastern and southeastern flanks.) The main body moved north on the highway to St. Côme-du-Mont, where the *III./1058* was dug in. From there, the two battalions were to attack the beachhead, while the *III./FJR 6* stayed in the Carentan area to protect the regiment's rear.²⁷⁴

Additional security was provided by an *Ost-Bataillon* that had moved north of Périers. It was sent towards Carentan to make contact with *GR 914* (*352. I.D.*), which held the division's left flank with the *II./914* and *Ost-Btl. 439*, and to attack south of Brévands.²⁷⁵

Von der Heydte later claimed that the attack by the 2ⁿᵈ Battalion came to within 500 metres of Ste. Mère-Église, but the town was never the objective.²⁷⁶ The regiment's after-action report shows that, around 16:30, he ordered the 2ⁿᵈ Battalion to advance via Château Houesville to the northern edge of Hiesville, while the 1ˢᵗ Battalion's objective was the northern edge of Ste. Marie-du-Mont. This makes more sense, as the battalions could cover each other's flanks, while a move against Ste. Mère-Église would have resulted in a gap of several kilometres. While the German paratroopers were attacking, the *III./1058* was to create a fallback position around St. Côme-du-Mont to cover the rear and flanks of the battalions. To support the attacks, the *4./AR 191* was directed to support the *I./FJR 6* and the 8ᵗʰ Battery the 2ⁿᵈ Battalion. The two battalions were to move out at 19:30 and reached their assembly areas around 17:30. The attacks jumped off on schedule with support from both artillery batteries. Around 23:00, the 4ᵗʰ Battery came under intense naval artillery fire, resulting in 27 casualties and a hasty abandonment of its positions. This left the *I./FJR 6* without artillery support, while the battery, having pulled back beyond Carentan, was not found by *FJR 6* until the afternoon of the **7ᵗʰ**.²⁷⁷

In its evening report, *AOK 7* informed *H.Gr. B* that countermeasures were still underway. The attacks of the reinforced *GR 1057*, *GR 1058* and *FJR 6*, were making slow progress.[278] For the next day, the field army intended to continue its assaults on the bridgehead around Ste. Mère-Église with elements of the *91. LL.D.* and *Fj.Rgt. 6*. In addition, a reinforced regiment from the *243. I.D.* was to be used (*Kampfgruppe Müller*, commander of *GR 922*).[279] By the end of **6 June**, the *91. LL.D.* was regrouping to continue its counterattacks, while the bulk of *GR 1058* was under the *709. I.D.*, allowing the *91. LL.D.* to focus on the west (*GR 1057*) and south (*FJR 6*). Little is known about further reinforcements but, according to *Obstlt.* von Criegern (chief of staff of the *LXXXIV. A.K.*), a second regiment from the *243. I.D.* was moved to the beachhead on the night of **6 June** and attached to the *91. LL.D.* This is not to be confused with *KG Müller* noted above. That battlegroup was attached to the *709. I.D.* for operations on the east coast.[280] It appears that the force that reinforced the *91. LL.D.* was *KG Simon* (commander of *GR 921*). It was moved up to hold the front along the Merderet and the railway, north of where *GR 1057* was already committed[281]

7 June saw the launch of the coordinated counterattack. The main attack against Ste. Mère-Église would come from the north (*GR 1058*). The main attack force consisted of the regiment (minus its 3rd Battalion) reinforced with both assault guns and SP guns from *Pz.Jg.Abt. 243*.[282]

The regiment struck at dawn — the assault guns leading the advance on the highway with the 1st Battalion on the left (east) and the 2nd on the right. The regimental command post was in Neuville-au-Plain. Early in the fighting, several assault guns were knocked out just in front of the town, and the attack stalled. When *Sturm-Btl. AOK 7* arrived, it deployed on both sides of the highway in an effort to reach the two battalions and restart the attack. That afternoon, *Gen.Lt.* von Schlieben arrived at the command post and ordered an immediate attack. *Obst.* Beigang responded by ordering the regiment to attack regardless of losses. The Germans, aggressively counterattacked by the 82nd AB and the 4th ID and supported by tanks, were thrown back. The

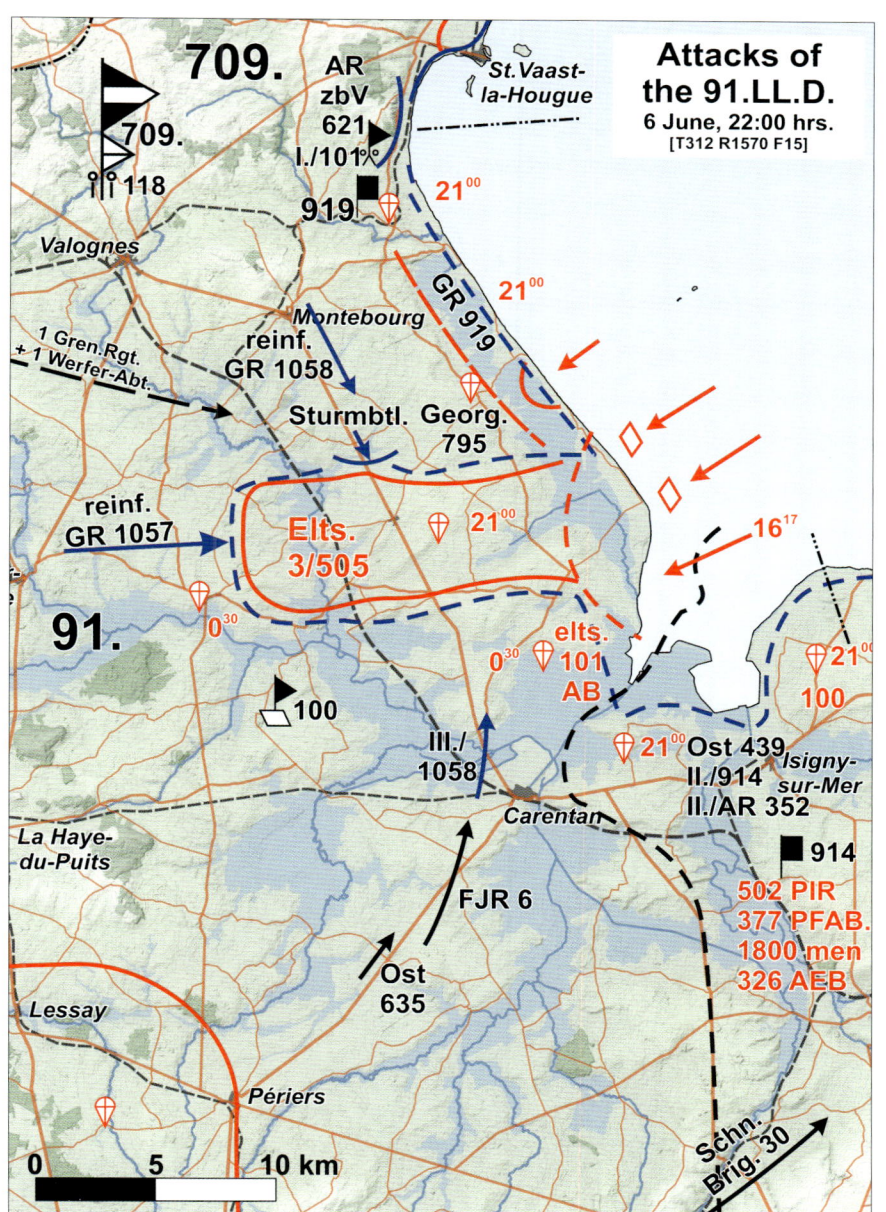

The AOK 7 situation map at 22:00 on D-Day shows the attacks of GR 1057 and 1058, as well as that of other forces. By this time FJR 6 had already joined in the fighting. (T312 R1570 F21)

day left the *I./1058* badly mauled, having lost its headquarters and many of its men.[283] The lack of German records and accounts makes it difficult to assess the American claims, but the battalion disappeared from the charts, supporting the perspective that it lost much of its strength and staff.[284] On orders from von Schlieben, a defensive line was formed 1,200 metres north of Neuville-au-Plain early that evening.[285]

To the west, the *GR 1057* attack (again supported by *Pz.Ers.u.Ausb.Abt. 100*) also started in the morning. Here, the fighting focussed on a small area around the narrow Cauquigny - La Fière causeway, which became a site of bitter combat. Although their situation grew increasingly critical, American forces on the east bank stopped the German attackers, preventing them from encircling Ste. Mère-Église from the west at a critical time.[286]

Away from the causeway, the pocket of Colonel Millett was attacked several times throughout the day, but it defended successfully; conversely, the Timmes' pocket was not attacked, with the exception of erratic mortar fire. Further south, the pocket on Hill 30 came under heavy attack in the morning but, again, the troopers stood their ground.[287]

On the *91. LL.D.*'s southern front, the counterattack by *FJR 6* could not be continued. After midnight, the regiment was surprised by new airborne landings, which were interpreted as a threat to the rear and flanks of its forward battalions. American forces moved between the *I./FJR 6* and the *III./1058*, pushing the company on the right of the latter battalion back towards St. Côme-du-Mont. In the early hours, the airborne battalions were ordered by radio to restore contact with each other and the regiment and to pull back to St. Côme-du-Mont and prepare defences.[288] Contact could not be made with the 1st Battalion, which was cut off around Vierville and virtually annihilated in the ensuing retreat. This left the regiment with its 2nd and 3rd Battalions and the *III./1058* to defend St. Côme-du-Mont.[289] The *II./FJR 6* was ordered to pull back and establish a line from the northern outskirts of Houesville via Beaumont to Les Droueries, where it was to make contact with the *III./1058*.[290] The latter was ordered to move right and hold the line Les Droueries - Basse Addeville - Belle Eneau. Around 08:00, US forces made several advances around Basse Addeville. The *9./Fj.Rgt. 6* was committed to restore the situation on the right flank and, around noon, the *12./FJR 6* was also brought up. To the left, the *10./FJR 6* was inserted into the line of the *III./1058* to clear the area and re-establish a continuous front; this was accomplished by 02:00 on the **8th**.[291] While the exact positions are not clear, von der Heydte suggests a thin defensive line was created 300-500 metres east of the highway, although fighting continued and the lines may have moved further east.[292]

Closer to Ste. Mère-Église, the pocket containing *Georg.Inf.Btl. 795* and elements of *KG Richter* was overrun by the 4th ID. To the southwest, elements from the 82nd AB moved through the isolated Carquebut - Le Port area and found it clear of German troops.[293]

Late on **7 June**, *AOK 7* still officially planned to drive home its attacks against American forces around Ste. Mère-Église the following day.[294] Quietly, however, it was already clear that a successful counterattack was no longer feasible on the Cotentin with the available troops. Instead, their mission became defensive as they awaited reinforcements. The *91. LL.D.* was to hold the west bank of the Merderet and *FJR 6* the high ground around St. Côme-du-Mont.[295]

Further north, the *709. I.D.*, with the rest of *GR 1058*, would also try to hold the line.[296] Here, the *II./1058* (*Maj.* Lewandowski), which had also sustained losses, was taken over for a few days by *Obstlt.* Hoffmann, an officer from the *709. I.D.*[297] The line was slowly pulled back to the north over the next few days.[298] During this period, *KG Hoffmann* (*709. I.D.*) was formed; it included the *II./1058* and held the front southwest of Montebourg. When the *77. I.D.* arrived on **11-12 June**, this battlegroup was dissolved and the elements belonging to the *91. LL.D.* returned to the division.[299] The first order of battle to show the return of the *II./1058* to the *91. LL.D.* is from **18 June**. This is also the first known organisational document after **10 June**.

Obst. Beigang no longer commanded the remnants of his regiment. Although not confirmed, he is thought to have committed suicide after witnessing its near annihilation.[300] Later in June, *Major* Lewandowski was listed as the regiment's new commander. He probably assumed this position soon after the death of *Obst.* Beigang, leaving his 2nd Battalion to *Obstlt.* Hoffmann. Meanwhile, the regimental headquarters appears to have been withdrawn.

Following the transition to defensive operations, elements of the division experienced heavy fighting on **8 June**. The 82nd AB met German resistance in the area of Le Port - Carquebut – Éturville, despite the latter town having been cleared by the day before. Left unoccupied, German troops had been able to reassemble in the area. The 82nd AB now finished the job and, after a brief engagement, about 120 Germans were taken prisoner.[301] These events may have been related to the surrender of a group of 60 German soldiers near Blosville. Tragically, there was a misunderstanding during the surrender, resulting in the death of *Oblt*. Richter.[302]

Further south that morning, the reinforced *FJR 6* was driven from St. Côme-du-Mont and the high ground to the south by the 101st AB. The regiment withdrew south and took up defensive positions around Carentan, where it continued to get support from the *III./1058* (*Maj.* Diekhoff).[303] Consequently, the final German bridgehead north of the Douve and Carentan collapsed. The withdrawal was complicated by the uncoordinated withdrawal of the *III./1058*, which became mixed up with other troops, breaking up the column. Having lost contact with its lead elements, the troops crossed the flooded terrain to the railway embankment in the wrong place and inadvertently led the rest of the regiment to do the same. As a result, instead of wading across, the men had to swim a considerable distance and left most of the weapons and equipment behind. Some men drowned with weapons they tried to save.[304]

The *8./AR 191* continued to provide valuable fire support during the withdrawal. The 4th Battery, on the other hand, abandoned its positions (west of Carentan) once again without orders and so failed to provide the necessary covering fire. On the highway, combat engineers from *Pi.Btl. 191* blew the bridge across the Douve to slow the American advance. Its destruction made it impossible to evacuate the vehicles and heavy equipment from the *II./FJR 6*.[305] Despite these challenges, the final units from *FJR 6* reached dry land at about 17:00. The defences around Carentan were hastily organised and the *III./1058* was sent southwest to cover the regiment's rear with the battalion's front facing towards Méautis. Scattered airborne forces were still in the area, firing on messengers and vehicles.

It was more difficult to get the *4./AR 191* to new positions, and it was several hours before the regiment managed to intercept the battery as it

---

The inundated fields along the Merderet and Douve rivers gave the 91. LL.D. its best terrain advantage to stop the American advance. By the evening of 8 June it had committed most of the GR 1057, reinforced by Pi.Btl.191 and KG Simon (243. I.D.) to hold the Merderet front. American pockets continued to prevent the division from building a continuous front and forced it to deploy manpower to contain them.

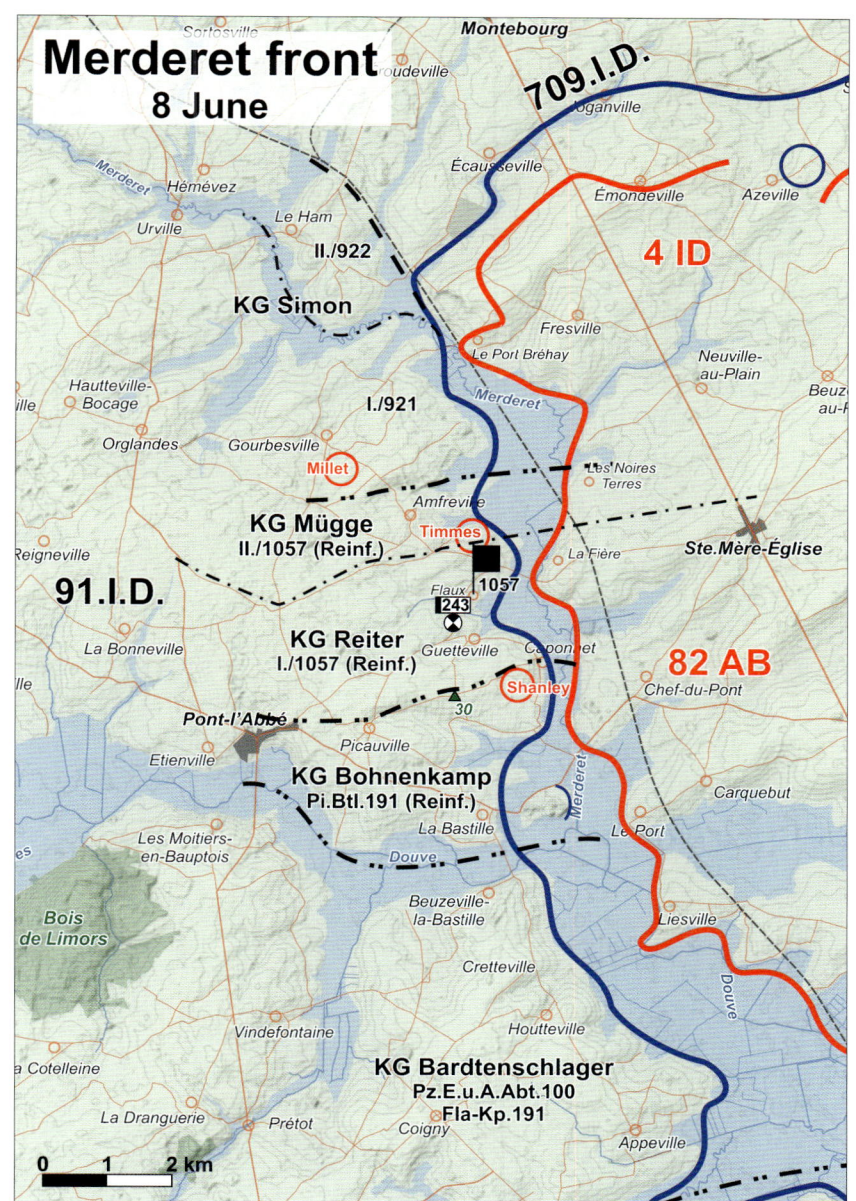

moved west between Baupte and St. Jores.[306] Communications between the headquarters of the *91. LL.D.* and *AR 191* that evening confirmed there were problems within the battery and that the commander had failed to exercise proper control of his men. The battery was ordered to gather and store its guns, equipment and horses under the protection of anti-tank positions from *Pz.Ers.u.Ausb.Abt. 100* (presumably in the Baupte area) and dig them in. Any remaining ammunition was to be turned over to the *I./AR 191*. As part of *KG Bardtenschlager* (the tank battalion commander), the gun crews were to be used as infantry to protect the defile at Baupte.[307] This plan appears to have been cancelled before it could be executed, and the battery remained part of *Artillerie-Gruppe Rock* (**10 June**), reportedly firing its last high-explosive shells on the afternoon of **11 June**. Out of ammunition, the battery returned to the division.[308] On the **20th**, it was under the *I./AR 191*, leaving only the 8th Battery with the *II./AR 191*.[309] This was still the case on **28 June**, although both the latter battery and battalion were not on the organisational documents at the time because they were away from the division.[310] These elements continued to fight on in the Carentan - Périers region well into **July**.[311]

On **8 June**, the bulk of the division held onto the Merderet front. *GR 1057*'s orders for the defence of this sector, later captured by US troops, provide insight into the German situation. Simply put, the regiment was to prevent the Americans from crossing the Merderet and eliminate all enemy troops in the rear areas. *GR 1057* held an area between Chef-du-Pont and Les Noires Terres (2 km northwest of Ste. Mère-Église). To its south was *KG Bohnenkamp*, its boundary with *GR 1057* going through Pont-l'Abbé, Picauville, the centre of Hill 30, to north of Chef-du-Pont. To the north was *KG Simon*. The boundary with this force was formed by the line Les Landes - Château d'Amfreville (known as the "Grey Castle" to the Americans) - Les Noires Terres.[312]

As for *GR 1057*, it sent its 1st Battalion (*KG Reiter*) to the right and its 2nd (*KG Mügge*) to the left (the 3rd Battalion's position is not known). The boundary between the battalions ran from the crossroads south of La Lande via La Moignerie, along the road to Les Aubris and finally to the northern outskirts of Ste. Mère-Église. The road was controlled by *KG Reiter*, which held the regiment's southern sector, including Cauquigny.[313]

KG Reiter consisted of the *I./1057*, a heavy infantry gun platoon, two light infantry gun platoons, a platoon of *7,5 cm Pak 40's* and two anti-tank sections. The organisation of *KG Mügge* was weaker with the *II./1057*, a platoon of light infantry guns, a *5 cm Pak 38* platoon and an anti-tank section.[314] All of the infantry guns and anti-tank units presumably came from the *13.* and the *14./1057*.

The fact that *Hptm.* Reiter was in charge of the 1st Battalion is interesting, as his parent battalion was the 3rd. The absence of *Maj.* Eitner, the actual commander of the 1st Battalion, is a mystery. According to several prisoners, the two battalions functioned as a single battlegroup under *Hptm.* Reiter — an arrangement that apparently started around **8 June**. Since the 3rd Battalion is not mentioned in the regimental orders, its position and role are not known.[315]

Artillery support was from the *I./AR 191*, which was to coordinate with the 13th Company. An unidentified bicycle company from the *243. I.D.* formed a regimental reserve and was 200 metres north of Gueutteville. The regimental command post was also close to the front, at Flaux (south of Cauquigny).[316]

The fighting west of the river on **8 June** is poorly documented. American sources refer to heavy fighting on and around Hill 30, as well as attacks against the pocket north of Cauquigny.[317]

By the end of the day, *AOK 7* notified *H.Gr. B* that its troops on the Cotentin had been forced onto the defensive.[318] That evening, *Gen.Lt.* Hellmich (commander of the *243. I.D.*) was put in charge of all forces on the Cotentin as *Gruppe Hellmich*.[319] This change did not affect the organisation of the troops. The *709. I.D.* was still responsible for the *Nordfront*, while the *91. LL.D.* defended the *Westfront* that stretched from west of Montebourg to Carentan, roughly following the Merderet and railway to Carentan.[320]

The night of **8-9 June** proved eventful for the three American pockets west of the river. The US troops on Hill 30 continued to hold out, while those under Colonel Millett were ordered to fall back to Timmes' orchard position north of Cauquigny. The attempt failed, and many men were captured (the colonel among them), although some made it across the Merderet. Other troops from the division moved in the opposite direction. Having learned of a sunken road crossing the river to Timmes' position, the 1/325th Glider Infantry Regiment (GIR) (82nd AB) was ordered to cross the river and attack Cauquigny from the rear. Several units were ambushed, and the attack was unsuccessful, suffering heavy casualties. For example, C/325 lost about half its strength. The position in the orchard was attacked several times in the morning without success.[321]

At 09:30 on **9 June**, it was reported that the *91. LL.D.* had ejected the enemy from Amfreville. The same report also mentions a route from La

Pécherie via La Pesquerie to Amfreville, but it fails to note its significance. It is likely a reference to Colonel Millett's group, which moved along this route to the edge of the flooded area that it ultimately crossed.[322] Although the night's fighting may have been perceived as a German success, the day was far from over. US troops needed to cross the river and the 82nd AB (with elements of the 325th GIR and 507th PIR) launched a frontal attack against Cauquigny across the heavily defended causeway. Despite serious losses, it pushed *GR 1057* back, established a bridgehead and made contact with the two surviving pockets. This American advance robbed the *91. LL.D.* of its terrain advantage and allowed the US 90th ID to pass through the 82nd AB and continue the attack to the west.[323]

At 17:15, the *LXXXIV. A.K.* notified *AOK 7* of the US attack across the flooded area west of Ste. Mère-Église. At the time, there was no mention of it being successful, but in the following hours the corps became increasingly concerned. At midnight, it reported that the enemy had crossed the Merderet and reached Pont-l'Abbé, although this was later changed to Picauville. Since American forces had also broken through across the Montebourg - Quinéville road, *Gen.* Marcks considered **10 June** to be decisive for the fate of *Festung Cherbourg*.[324]

As it turned out, US forces had yet to reach Picauville, let alone Pont-l'Abbé. A German report made just after midnight proved more accurate. In the *91. LL.D.* sector, the front stretched from Carentan west to Appeville, then north through Houtteville to Amfreville, Gourbesville and Urville, all of which were still in German hands.[325]

In the division's southern sector, *FJR 6* used the day to improve and reorganise its defences but saw little action. Around 16:00, it was informed that both the *II./914* with the *13./914 (352. I.D.)* and *Ost-Btl. 439* were subordinated to it. This meant the airborne regiment was also responsible for the area up to the Vire, where the troops were to hold the river's west bank. While this formally enlarged the *91. LL.D.* sector, *FJR 6* continued to operate largely independently. To help support the Vire front, the *8./AR 191*

By 10 June the division had become a peculiar mix of organic and attached troops. Significant support was received from the 243. I.D., but elements of the 77. I.D. also started to make an appearance. (T78 R672)

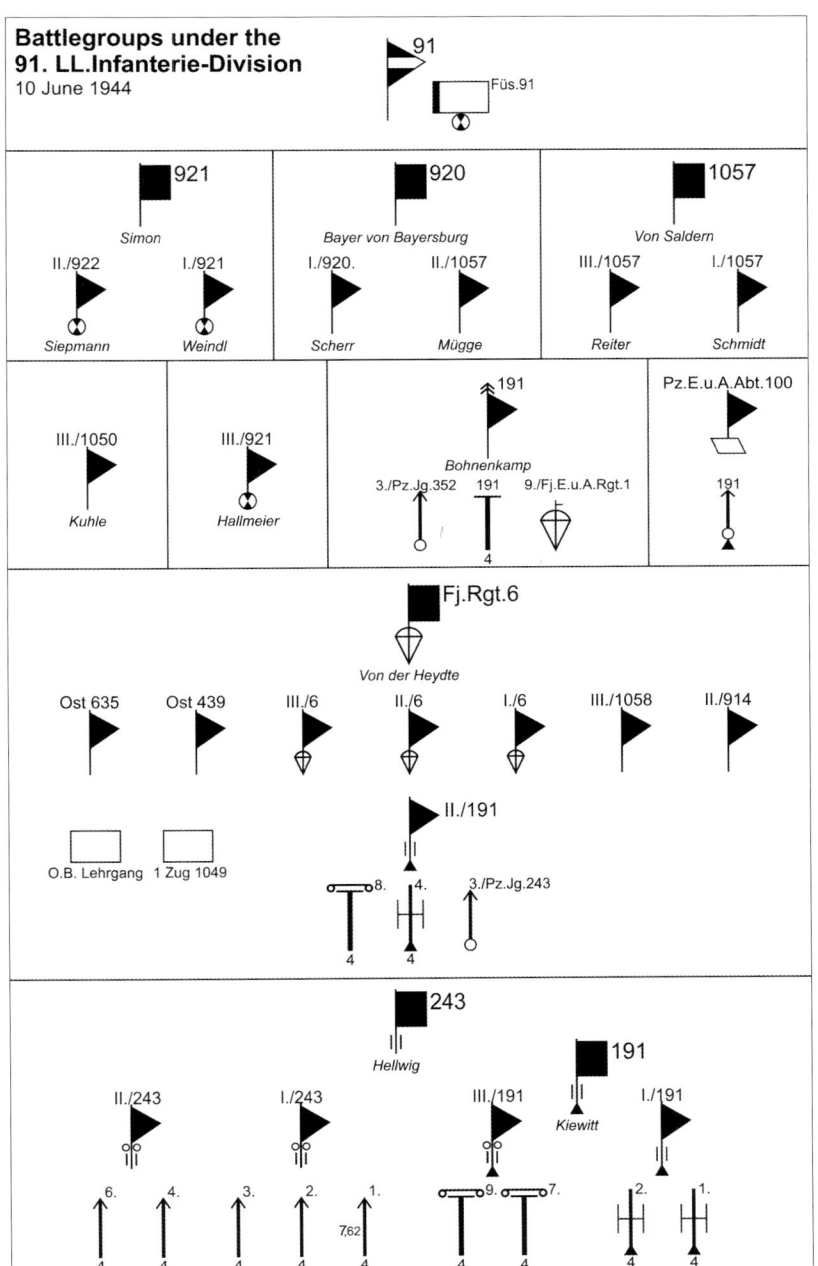

was ordered to take up positions to cover the area. The battery commander advised the regiment that he could not deliver accurate fire as there were no radios with which to communicate with the forward observer. Due in part to the inability to adequately support the new front with artillery fire, the decision was made to gradually pull back to Carentan.[326]

On **10 June**, the *LXXXIV. A.K.*'s primary objective was to prevent a breakthrough on the Montebourg front. Around Carentan, the *II. Fs.K.* would focus on keeping the Utah and Omaha beachheads from linking up, but this was less important than preventing an attack from the east (Merderet front) or southeast (Carentan - Vire River sector), thus cutting off the Cotentin.[327]

To support its mission, the *91. LL.D.* had numerous other elements attached to it (these were listed on a special organisational document).[328] These reinforcements were significant, since most of *GR 1058* was still not available — some of its units were in action with the *709. I.D.* southwest of Montebourg and others with *FJR 6*. The division had also suffered serious losses since the start of the invasion. A captured document gives the personnel strength of some of the divisional forces, which can be compared to the authorised strengths of a 25th wave division. The headquarters had a strength of 157 (84.9%), *GR 1057* had 2,126 (78.7%) and *GR 1058* 2,115 (78.3%). *AR 191* still had 1,036 personnel, while the strength of *Pz.Jg.Kp. 191*, *Pi.Btl. 191* and the signals battalion was 141 (82.9%), 424 (96.1%), and 304 (96.5%), respectively. The divisional support units had a combined strength of 507 men.[329]

Füs.Kp. 191 was still under divisional control and probably used as a reserve. Not counting *FJR 6*, which was defending the wider Carentan area, the division had three infantry regiments at the front. *GR 1057* was the only one organic to the division and had two battalions available (1st and 3rd), which were commanded by *Hptm.* Schmidt and *Hptm.* Reiter, respectively.[330]

Two regiments from the *243. I.D.* were also attached. *GR 920* (now led by *Obstlt.* Bayer von Bayersburg) had the *I./920* and the *II./1057* under its command. *GR 921* (*KG Simon*) also had infantry from two different

Leaving the heavily damaged town of Pont-l'Abbé, refugees make their way past an upside-down Kettenkrad and the body of a German soldier. The location is along the D70, just southeast of the town. (NARA)

One of the Sd.Kfz.7/2 of 3./Pz.Jg.Abt.352 was lost in Pont-l'Abbé. It met its end inside the town, at the crossroads of the D70 and D15. (NARA)

regiments: Its own *I./921* and the *II./922*. Two more battalions were attached to the division but these were not yet directed to a specific regiment: The *III./1050* (*77. I.D.*) and the *III./921*(-).[331]

Based on personal accounts, it appears that *GR 1057* (*KG von Saldern*) was used on the right, north of the Douve River, possibly with *KG Bohnenkamp* still on its right. It is also conceivable that the *III./921* relieved *KG Bohnenkamp* around this time, but this is not confirmed. *GR 921* (*KG Simon*) presumably held the left flank, with a battalion east of the Merderet around Le Ham. Since *GR 920* had assumed command of the *II./1057*, which was on the left flank on **8 June**, the regiment was likely moved to the centre of the front. Based on the area where the *III./1050* was later identified by Allied forces, it would seem this battalion had been inserted between *GR 1057* and *GR 920*.[332] On **10 June**, the 3rd Battalion may still have been in reserve, as it was only reported on **11 June** that the lead battalion of the *77. I.D.* had been committed to shield its approaching parent formation.[333]

Pz.Ers.u.Ausb.Abt. 100 (*KG Bardtenschlager*) was still south of the Douve. The battalion was reinforced by *Fla-Kp. 191* and was the left neighbour of *FJR 6*, which was furthest to the east, around Carentan.[334]

This regiment also had numerous attachments, including the *III./1058* and the *II./AR 191* with the 4th and 8th Batteries. Two *Ost-Bataillone* (*439* and *635*), as well as the *II./914* (*352. I.D.*) and the *13./914*, were also attached. Smaller forces in the area included the *3./Pz.Jg.Abt. 243*, a platoon from the *2./1049* and an unidentified officer candidate company.[335] On or around the evening of **9-10 June**, the *13./914* was attached to the *8./AR 191*; these units were assembled under the commander of the *II./AR 191* as *Artillerie-Gruppe Rock*.[336] The *4./AR 191* was not mentioned, but this may be an error as it should still have been available.

Pi.Btl. 191 still formed a battlegroup under its commander, *Hptm.* Bohnenkamp. Attached were six heavy AT guns from *Pz.Jg.Kp. 191* and the 3.7 cm *Flak* from the *3./Pz.Jg.Abt. 352*. Additional infantry was from an airborne training company, probably the *9./Fj.Ers.u.Ausb.Rgt. 1*.[337] The battlegroup was apparently still just north of the Douve, but because it was being formed around a specialised unit, it may have been relieved quickly. No dates for this have been found, and it is not clear how long it was operational.

Over-all command of the divisional artillery had been taken over by *AR 243*, which was in action with its own 1st and 2nd Battalions (the latter minus its 5th Battery). *AR 191* was attached to the regiment with its 1st and 3rd Battalions. Both battalions could field only two batteries each: The 1st, 2nd, 7th and 9th. All nine batteries were listed with four guns each.[338] As noted, the *3./AR 191* was lost on D-Day, and the 8th Battery was still in support of *FJR 6*.

On the morning of **10 June**, the 90th ID launched its offensive to secure the Douve line, running north-south between Terre de Beauval and St. Sauveur-le-Vicomte. After doing so, it was to turn north towards Cherbourg. The operation would be its baptism of fire. On the right (north) flank, the 357th IR attacked towards Amfreville but met heavy resistance and made little progress. On the left, the 358th IR had more success — until it reached an area 500 metres west of Picauville, where it met stiff opposition and dug in. After defeating a counterattack, it resumed the advance towards Pont-l'Abbé but then stalled and, in the early evening, the troops started to dig in.[339]

German reports were fairly accurate on **10 June**. At 11:00, the front ran from Beuzeville-la-Bastille via Picauville to Fresville (east of the river).[340] By 17:00, this line had been pushed back to Beuzeville-la-Bastille - Pont-l'Abbé - Gourbesville. The centre of gravity was identified as Pont-l'Abbé.[341] The other *91. LL.D.* sectors were not so quiet.

In the north, the *II./922* (*KG Simon*) still had a foothold east of the Merderet around Le Ham.[342] In the area of *FJR 6*, elements of the 101st AB (2/502nd PIR) spent much of the day trying to reach the last bridge on the highway before Carentan, but they were unable to cross. To the northeast, the 327th GIR crossed the Douve near Brévands and carried out a wide flanking move to approach Carentan from the east and make contact with V Corps, which was moving up from Isigny-sur-Mer. Both actions were successful, and Carentan was now cut off from the east.[343]

That afternoon, *Maj.* von der Heydte reorganised his forces. The reinforced regiment held a front from Le Port along the flooded area on the Taute River to the canal east of Carentan; it then went northwest around the town to the last bridge on the highway and, from there, west along the Douve to Le Moulinet. In the opposite direction, this line was held by the *III./1058* up to the Carentan - Cherbourg railway, the *III./FJR 6* to *L'Hôpital* (on the northwest outskirts of Carentan), the *II./FJR 6* to south of Carentan, *Ost-Btl. 635* south to St. Georges-de-Bohon and finally the *II./914*. *Ost-Btl. 439* was in reserve around Cantepie, and several of the regiment's specialised platoons and elements from the *77. I.D.* (1st Platoon of the *2./1049*) and the *243. I.D.* (*3./Pz.Jg.Abt. 243*) were also in reserve to the rear of the regiment. *Artillerie-Gruppe Rock* consisted of the *4.* and the *8./AR 191* and the *13./914*.[344]

In the afternoon, *Obst.* König, the new commander, arrived at divisional headquarters, now in Rauville-la-Place.[345] Previously, *Gen.* Marcks had expressed his appreciation for *Obst.* Klosterkemper's performance as acting commander and preferred to keep him in place, but the wheels had already been set in motion.[346] On **7 June**, *Obst.* König, recipient of the Oakleaves to the Knight's Cross, had just arrived in the Eifel to visit his family, when he was ordered to report to *H.Gr. B* in Paris.[347]

Although *Gen.* Marcks' fears of a decisive American breakthrough on **10 June** had failed to materialise, the situation facing *Obst.* König was far from encouraging. Since D-Day, the division had suffered serious losses while being constantly pushed back. Moreover, *AOK 7* assessed the division as having inadequate training for the hedgerow country in which it had recently arrived.[348] The division's left boundary was still on the Merderet River, but the Americans now had a firm bridgehead on the west bank. Further south, *FJR 6* had been driven back to Carentan and was under increasing pressure. There was little hope to salvage the situation without reinforcements.

The night of **10-11 June** saw bitter fighting around Pont-l'Abbé. Although it was reported that the lines on the Cotentin were holding, the town changed hands several times during the night. (Late in the afternoon, it was still in German hands.) At 18:00, strong enemy forces (358th IR) achieved a penetration at Pont-l'Abbé in the direction of Neuville (300 metres west of the town), but a rapid German counterattack forced them back. The main line of resistance was recaptured and contact made with strongpoints that had been cut off. Four officers and 78 men were taken prisoner and, at 19:00, the corps reported that the attack on the town had been defeated.[349] The Americans considered the town partially encircled.[350] Despite the German claim that the lines were holding, Amfreville had been lost in the morning to the 357th IR, which failed to clear the area of Les Landes during the day.[351]

There was also fighting in other areas on the division's front. In the north, the *II./922* (*KG Simon*) was pushed back across the Merderet after intense fighting, losing its final foothold east of the river.[352]

Further south, Carentan was under attack along the highway, which resulted in the Americans gaining a foothold northwest of the town. The *III./1058* and the remnants of *Ost-Btl. 439* counterattacked to support the *III./FJR 6*, but they were unable to drive the Americans back. Further east, elements of the 327th GIR advanced towards the town from the northeast on either side of the Bassin á Flot (the canal linking Carentan with the Douve River), but they were blocked by German fire.[353] That evening, *AOK 7* informed *H.Gr. B* of heavy fighting around the town, reporting that US troops had entered Carentan from the northwest and that, despite ammunition shortages, the Germans had rejected an ultimatum to surrender the town.[354] The report was inaccurate: US troops had not advanced that far, and the "ultimatum" was actually a request for a truce to evacuate casualties.[355]

Yet, the situation had become critical.[356] The German lines were now so fragile that new American attacks would inevitably lead to the loss of the town. Consequently, *Maj.* von der Heydte decided to evacuate it late in the afternoon.[357] His forces set up new defensive positions to the southwest, anchored on the high ground along the road to Périers (Hill 30). To give the regiment's organic troops some much needed rest, these new positions were initially occupied by other forces. The left flank was held by the *III./1058*, the centre by the *II./914* and the right by *Ost-Btl. 635*.[358]

Despite these setbacks, the priorities for the *LXXXIV. A.K.* had not changed: a) prevent the peninsula from being cut off by holding the centre and right flank; and b) prevent a thrust to Cherbourg on its left flank.[359] Troops were finally arriving to ease the situation. On the morning of **11 June**, it was reported that the *77. I.D.* had arrived in St. Sauveur-le-Vicomte; it was to be deployed during the night either side of the Merderet, to the left of the *91. LL.D.* On the other hand, the arrival of *KG 265*, another significant reinforcement, was delayed due to fuel shortages.[360] The battlegroup was to come to the aid of the *91. LL.D.* and push American forces back across the Merderet — an objective that would become considerably more difficult as time went on.[361]

While **12 June** was unusually quiet on the Cotentin, this was not the case for the *91. LL.D.*, which continued to face considerable pressure.[362] West of the Merderet, the 90th ID had been strengthened by the arrival of its 359th IR, which was inserted between the division's other regiments. Still, the 90th ID continued to make slow progress. The fighting ebbed and flowed, but Pont-l'Abbé finally fell that evening, having been subjected to heavy artillery fire, air attacks and armour.[363]

In the sector of *FJR 6*, it was simply a matter of time before Carentan was occupied by American forces. Due to communications problems with the *LXXXIV. A.K.*, it was not until 06:20 that *AOK 7* became aware that the town had been abandoned the night before.[364] The 101st AB had resumed its attack on the town in the morning. During the night, the 506th PIR had moved through the 502nd bridgehead and advanced south of the town. From there, it advanced into the town, while the 327th GIR attacked from the north. Resistance was limited to a German rearguard, and the regiments made contact around 07:30. From the east, the 3/501st PIR moved past the town, seized Hill 30, and linked up with the 506th. Attempts by the 501st on the left and the 506th on the right to push the front southwest were stopped.[365]

During the day, the *17. SS-Pz.Gren.Div.* took command of the Carentan area. The reinforced *FJR 6* — including the *III./1058* and the *II./AR 191*— was subordinated to it.[366] As of 12:00, all these troops were put under the command of the *II. Fs.K.*, which was itself reporting to the *LXXXIV. A.K.* The transfer of *FJR 6* to the *SS* division command reduced the *91. LL.D.* sector, which now stretched north from Baupte; more specifically, the dividing line ran from Le Plessis (*II. Fs.K.*), via Baupte (*91. LL.D.*) along the northern edge of the flooded plains around Carentan to the Canal de Carentan, then downstream to Le Moulin.[367]

After the changes had been made, the *III./1058* was released from its attachment to *FJR 6*. No date has been found for this and the charts of *AOK 7* for **22 June** still list it under *Fj.Rgt. 6* and the *SS* division.[368] On the organisational documents of the *91. LL.D.* it reappeared under *GR 1058* on **18 June**, but this might simply reflect the organic organisation.[369] On **28 June**, it was listed under *U.Gr. Lewandowski*, which was first listed on *AOK 7* maps on **22 June**.[370] As of noon on **12 June**, the Carentan area was no longer the responsibility of the *91. LL.D.*, and the battalion does not appear to have been in action, so this sector will not be discussed here further.

Although the divisional sector was reduced with the arrival of the *77. I.D.* and the *17. SS-Pz.Gren.Div.*, *91. LL.D.* was unable to master the situation. Early on **13 June**, American troops (508th PIR) launched a surprise attack across the Douve at Beuzeville-la-Bastille and rapidly advanced towards Baupte, opening a gap between the Douve River and the marshland southwest of Baupte (the Prairies Marécageuses de Gorges).[371] At 10:45, the *LXXXIV. A.K.* notified *AOK 7* of the breakthrough, stating — inaccurately as it turned out — that enemy armour had been seen, and forces to seal off the gap were not available. *KG 265* had not yet arrived and nothing could be taken from the *91. LL.D.*, which was fully committed north of the river. To the east, the *17. SS-Pz.Gren.Div.* was tied down in its own area. Nonetheless, the *7. Armee* ordered the gap be closed.[372] In response, a battalion from the *77. I.D.* (*II./1049*) was brought up by motor transport.[373] At 16:40, the corps reported that *KG 265* had been located and would be deployed that evening. The field army again ordered the gap closed and that a counterattack be conducted to push American forces back to the Douve. At 17:55, the corps reported the commitment of both *KG 265* and the *II./1049* (*Hptm.* Lausberg), although the latter had actually been intended for Cherbourg. Their mission was to hold Baupte and Les Moitiers-en-Bauptois, while advancing on the enemy.[374] The Americans preempted the Germans by entering Baupte. They cleared it by 20:15 and made contact with 101st AB.[375]

Obst. König later took responsibility for this disaster. Concerned by reports from *FJR 6* about the threat to Baupte and the only road linking the Carentan sector with that of the division, he decided to reduce the covering forces along the Douve River to reinforce the troops around Baupte.[376] Any hope of pushing the Americans back across the river soon evaporated and, instead, the division focussed on holding the line between the river and the marshland southwest of Baupte.

In the meantime, the fighting north of the Douve continued. In the morning, *AOK 7* noted a minor incursion west of Amfreville, against which countermeasures were in progress.[377] Here, the 357th IR continued to struggle and only managed to advance a few hundred metres, with the exception of the 3/357, which crossed the Amfreville - Gourbesville road to attack Gourbesville, but had failed to do so by nightfall. To the left (south), the 359th IR did not reach the Gourbesville - Pont-l'Abbé road, its initial objective, until the evening. Around Pont-l'Abbé, the 358th IR's attack was held up until noon and then made no progress. After four days of fighting, the 90th ID had barely accomplished its intermediate objective against the *91. LL.D.* Frustrated with the division's limited progress, VII Corps intervened. The divisional commander and two regimental commanders were sacked; the 82nd AB and the 9th ID would be brought up to take over the attacks on St. Sauveur-le-Vicomte and Ste. Colombe, respectively. Once these divisions had passed through the lines of the 90th, it would move north to guard the flank.[378]

As **14 June** dawned, *H.Gr. B* was still worried about the American bridgehead south of the Douve and about the *Westfront* as a whole. *Feldm.* Rommel observed that the centre of gravity had moved there from the *Nordfront*, so he ordered that all forces available in the north be used to prevent the Cotentin from being cut off.[379] In response to Rommel's orders, *AOK 7* informed the *LXXXIV. A.K.* that an enemy breakthrough to La Haye-du-Puits and Périers was to be prevented; the *77. I.D.* was to be withdrawn from either side of the Merderet and used to strengthen the *Westfront*. In case of an impending breakthrough around Valognes or the severing of the Cotentin, the troops in the north (*709. I.D., 243. I.D.* and *91. LL.D.*) were to move to *Festung Cherbourg*, either on orders of the corps or on the authority of *Gen.Lt.* Hellmich. The latter course of action was only to take place in the event of an emergency,[380]

Yet the Germans' concern for the situation south of the Douve was not entirely justified. At 15:10, the corps reported that *KG 265* had been committed and, at 18:40, that the front was stabilised as a result.[381] Both *KG 265* and the *II./1049* were reporting to the *91. LL.D.* and formed the right flank. *KG 265* would remain with the division. The *II./1049* had been earmarked to reinforce Cherbourg, but could not be withdrawn from the front. It remained with the division until the end of June, when it returned to the *77. I.D.*[382]

Despite *H.Gr. B*'s concerns, the greatest threat was north of the river. On the American's left (south), the 358th IR advanced 900 metres west of Pont-l'Abbé, before the 82nd AB began to move through around noon. The 325th GIR was committed on the left (south) and the 507th PIR on the right. After heavy fighting, the 325th GIR advanced 400 metres and the 507th PIR reached La Bonneville. To their right, the 39th IR (9th ID) moved north, opening a gap into which the 60th IR (9th ID) was inserted.[383] The regiment attacked at 10:00 and took Renouf at 20:00; continuing west, it reached the high ground north of La Bonneville.[384] On the right, the 90th ID, now primarily facing the *77. I.D.*, made slow progress.[385]

There are no German reports detailing the situation north of the Douve. The *7. Armee*'s daily report appears to have underestimated the situation, merely stating that the frontline now ran west and northwest of Pont-l'Abbé and from there as before.[386] It was noted later that evening, that the situation was deteriorating. With robust artillery support, the enemy consistently gained ground, while the German defenders sustained increasing losses and struggled to prevent further loss of ground.[387]

In a meeting that day, the *LXXXIV. A.K.* offered *Gen.* Dollmann, who was at the corps headquarters, a sober analysis. Although all gaps in the front had been temporarily sealed, the troops were worn out and had suffered unsustainable losses. They were still able to clean up minor incursions and fight off weak attacks, but success would not be forthcoming against a major enemy attack, which was considered likely in the centre of the corps (*91. LL.D.*). The situation had become more difficult due to the enemy's establishment of the Beuzeville bridgehead and a shortage of ammunition. Furthermore, the troops were scattered and operating under unfamiliar commanders from different units. *Gen.* Fahrmbacher considered it a miracle that the Americans had not yet broken through to Périers.[388]

German records highlight the division's poor condition. The fighting had been costly. By **12 June**, its losses had climbed to 2,212 men and, by the **14th**, *AOK 7* no longer considered it a division; it was now officially labelled as *Kampfgruppe 91.Inf.Div.* This was better than the *352.* and the *716. I.D.*, which were referred to as divisional detachments: *Div.Abt. 352* and *Div.Abt. 716*.[389]

That the division had not yet collapsed under pressure from VII Corps was largely due to the reinforcements it received from other divisions. Without clear records, it is difficult to determine the organisation. Until **10-11 June**, it is still possible to track the general organisation of the Merderet front, but after that date the situation is confusing.

The arrival of the *77. I.D.* further complicated matters. On the night of **11-12 June**, as it began to relieve the right flank of the *709. I.D.* (*KG Hoffmann*) and the left of the *91. LL.D.*, it freed up units for those two divisions. It is not known exactly which units were relieved on the left of the *91. LL.D.* The units that were relieved included *KG Simon* (*I./921* and *II./922*), the *II./921* (from the *709. I.D.* sector) and, at some point, elements of *KG Klosterkemper* (possibly just the *I./920*).[390]

This confusion was noticed by 90th ID (359th IR), which attempted to construct an overview of the German front west of the Merderet on **14 June**. From south to north, the Americans identified: The *III./921*;[391] followed by elements of *GR 1050* (presumably elements of its 3rd Battalion); elements of *GR 920*; yet more elements of *GR 1050*; *GR 921* (*KG Simon*), with elements of the *I./921*; two battalions of *GR 1057*; a battalion from *GR 921* (possibly the *II./921*); more elements of *GR 1057*; and the main body of KG 920. To an extent this makes sense, but it is possible that the overview was based

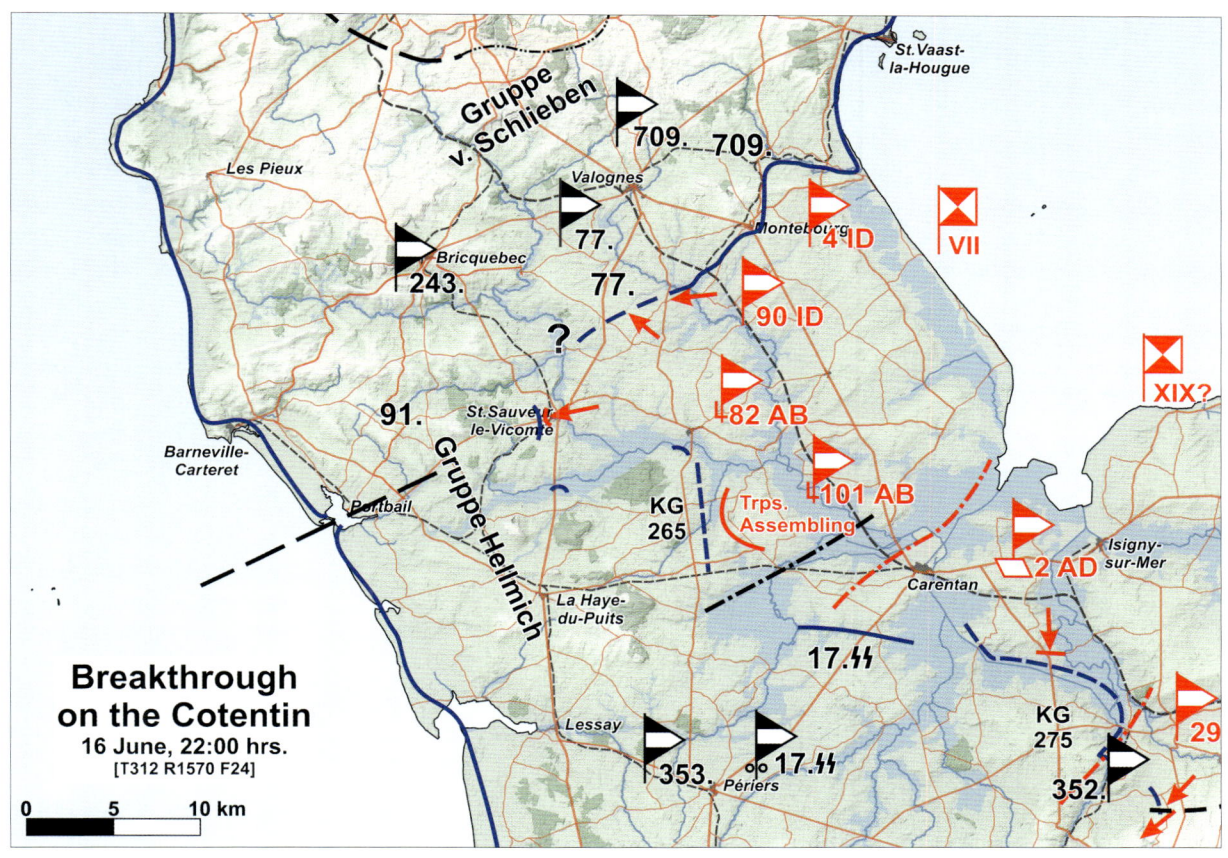

The situation along the Westfront continued to deteriorate. By 15 June it was apparent that the front would collapse, sooner rather than later. (T312 R1570 F21)

on outdated information. This is especially true for the north of the front, where the *77. I.D.* may have already relieved some units. When looking at the available information, some details can be noted. The *III./921* has indeed been linked to the south of the front, as were the *I.* and the *III./1057* (*KG von Saldern*). On **10** or **11 June**, the *II./1050* may have been north of this force, followed by *KG 920* with the *II./1057* and the *I./920* (probably in that order) and finally *KG Simon* (with the *I./921* and the *II./922*). It has been reported that both *KG Simon* and *KG 920* (*KG Klosterkemper*) were at some point relieved by the *77. I.D.*, but the dates are unclear, as is their composition. It is also not clear where these battlegroups were positioned. On **14-15 June**, elements from *KG Simon* (*I./921*) were in the area of Reigneville,[392] which suggests that the battlegroup was inserted there. This is supported by an order from **16 June** for *KG von Saldern* and *KG Simon* to make contact northeast of St. Sauveur-le-Vicomte.[393] The *II./1057* and the *II./922* are linked to an area next to the *77. I.D.*, which could suggest that they were not withdrawn with their battlegroups. In both cases, they were non-organic elements to the battlegroups they were attached to (*KG 921* and *KG 920*).[394]

15 June saw more heavy fighting on the division's front, but not for the troops west of the Beuzeville bridgehead. These forces were under the command of *Maj.* Eitner as *KG Eitner*. Their front ran along the low ground between the Baupte marshland and the Douve River. The right flank was held by the *II./895* and the left by the *II./1049*; from there, the *12./894* and remnants of *Pz.Ers.u.Ausb.Abt. 100* held the river front to the west and the crossing at Les Moitiers-en-Bauptois. Artillery support was provided by the *II./AR 177* for the *II./1049* and by the *I./AR 265* for the *II./895*. The *2./Pi.Btl. 265* and the *III./894* were held in reserve in the areas of Ste. Suzanne and La Poterie, respectively.[395]

During the day, despite significant fighting elsewhere, the greatest pressure against the *LXXXIV. A.K.* was on the *Westfront* of the Cotentin. Here, the situation was serious.[396] At 10:00, the *LXXXIV. A.K.* informed *AOK 7* that it was facing heavy enemy pressure in the Pont-l'Abbé sector, in the direction of La Bonneville. *AOK 7* ordered that the lines were to be held, while preparations were to be made for a withdrawal to Cherbourg. The *77. I.D.* would be the first option to close the gap east of St. Sauveur-le-Vicomte and would also allow the division to be rejoined by elements operating under the *91. LL.D.*[397] It was soon apparent that this was an unrealistic option, as most of the division's forces were already engaged elsewhere. Instead, the gap would have to be closed by units from both the *77. I.D.* and the *91. LL.D.* This new battlegroup would be led by *Obst.* König.[398]

At 13:00, the *7. Armee* informed *H.Gr. B* how *Gen.* Dollmann viewed the situation. He had just visited the *LXXXIV. A.K.* and echoed many of its conclusions. Without reinforcements, the troops would be unable to withstand the Allied offensive that was expected soon — from Carentan, west or north of Ste. Mère-Église. This sobering assessment was a result of diminishing combat strength, scattered formations and a dire shortage of ammunition. To secure the Cotentin and prevent a breakthrough, components of *Gruppe Hellmich* would be withdrawn, as no complete formations were available. To improve the command structure, it was decided to reorganise *Gruppe Hellmich*. Hellmich's forces in the east were split off as *Gruppe von Schlieben* and given responsibility for the *Nordfront* (Montebourg front). As a result, the sector of the new *Gruppe Hellmich* was reduced to the area between Urville and the marshland southwest of Baupte (the *Westfront*).[399]

At 21:00, it was reported that Orglandes had fallen. Half an hour later, the corps informed *AOK 7* that the situation east of St. Sauveur (north of the Douve) had become serious due to a total lack of ammunition, a problem which had grown over the preceding days.[400] In the eyes of the *7. Armee*, this confirmed the enemy's intention to cut off the Cotentin. If successful, this might trap German forces on the peninsula or even destroy them before they could reach Cherbourg. The field army requested the *Nordfront* be pulled back to Cherbourg and the *Westfront* to the south.[401]

Meanwhile, a new screening line was established north of the Douve. While not all reports agree on this line, it appears to have run north from 2 km west of Les Moitiers-en-Bauptois (south of the Douve), past the eastern edge of Crosville and La Bonneville to south of Hautteville and Orglandes, then east to the southeast edge of Gourbesville.[402] La Bonneville was a German strongpoint, which may explain why it may have held out despite being outflanked. The 9th ID had closed in on Reigneville (south of Hautteville) during the day.[403] The boundary between *Gruppe von Schlieben* and *Gruppe Hellmich* was changed to the line St. Jacques-de-Néhou - south of Hautteville-Bocage - Ste. Colombe - Orglandes - Ste. Mère-Église.[404] This boundary, now in part well west of the Merderet, also seems to represent the line between the *77. I.D.* and the *91. LL.D.*[405] The formation of these separate groups was apparently carried out during the night with its completion reported the next morning.[406]

Again, Allied records explain what happened on the **15th**. In the sector of the 82nd AB, the 325th GIR attacked at 05:00, reaching the creek southwest of La Bonneville (and east of Crosville) at 08:10. To its right the, 507th PIR also attacked at 05:00, but it was stopped by a German counterattack at 09:30, which restored the original German lines by 15:00. At that time, the 505th PIR moved through the regiment, reaching the creek north of Crosville at nightfall.[407] For the 9th ID, the 60th IR reached Reigneville-Bocage at 16:25. To its right, the 47th IR attacked the high ground west of Orglandes, which it reached at 20:00.[408]

Perhaps it was the American successes, combined with talk of creating a *Gruppe König*, that led the *91. LL.D.* to fall back to south of the Douve. *Obst.* König suggests he made the decision before St. Sauveur fell, which would point to **15 June**.[409]

Weakened by days of unrelenting attacks, the front finally collapsed on **16 June**. That morning, *AOK 7* still did not see a withdrawal to Cherbourg as necessary. The situation on the *Westfront* deteriorated rapidly and, at 10:35, the *LXXXIV. A.K.* informed *AOK 7* that (the new) *Gruppe Hellmich* had been adversely affected by a breakdown in the supply chain and worn out from fighting. A breakthrough to the west was to be expected with a collapse of the lines imminent.[410]

St.Sauveur-le-Vicomte was taken by the 82nd AB on 16 June, but not after it had been heavily damaged. The town formed a critical crossroads which blocked major roads leading into the Cotentin. Looking west, we see along the road to Portbail (D15) while the railway runs left to right. (NARA)

Men from the 82nd AB make their way through the rubble on the Rue du Vieux Château. Today little can be recognised as this area of the town received such heavy damaged that much of it had to be demolished later. (NARA)

On the heels of this catastrophic situation, an order arrived at the front that made things even worse: Hitler forbade *Bewegung Cherbourg* and, more importantly, ordered the troops to hold the lines unconditionally.[411]

About 13:00, the corps reported that the front between Étienville and Orglandes had been breached over a breadth of 5 km. The news was forwarded to *H.Gr. B* at once. The enemy was advancing on St. Sauveur-le-Vicomte and no reserves were available to challenge him, with the exception of two companies in the town. The only option was to pull out elements of the *77. I.D.* and move them into the threatened sector. Despite that, no immediate orders were forthcoming to the 7. Armee, as *Feldm.* Rommel was being briefed on the situation at the corps headquarters.[412]

At 15:35, the corps reported the town was lost.[413] With the collapse of the front to its south, the *77. I.D.* was forced to turn to the west with its right flank.[414] At the front, *Gen.* Hellmich did what little he could to restore the situation. At 16:11, he ordered *KG von Saldern* (*GR 1057*) to move at once and make contact with *KG Simon* (*GR 921, 243. I.D.*) at St. Clair (northeast of St. Sauveur); in turn, *KG Simon* was to move its left flank to La Basseour (a *Château*/farm complex north of Pigard). This line was to be held at all costs.[415] The orders suggest that *KG von Saldern* was still responsible for the right flank and *KG Simon* for the left.

Rommel could do little to help. Because of Hitler's order, he could only allow a few of the *77. I.D.*'s elements to be moved south. At 17:00, *AOK 7* received the latest report from the front: The enemy had reached the railway west of the town. In response, *KG 265* was ordered to secure a line 3 km to its south.[416] This meant it would cover the St. Sauveur-le-Vicomte - La Haye-du-Puits highway and the hills south of the Prairies Marécageuses. At 21:00, it was reported that an engineer platoon, possibly belonging to the headquarters company of *GR 896* (*265. I.D.*), had blocked the defile north of the Prairies in this sector. For additional support, *SS-Pz.Aufkl.Abt. 17* (*17.SS-Pz.Gren. Div.*) was also being brought up. No other reinforcements were available. A battalion each from the *77. I.D.* and the *353. I.D.* were not expected to arrive until the 20th. As a result, elements would have to be taken from *Gruppe Hellmich* to seal off the Cotentin.[417] The troops assembled in the area south of St. Sauveur later became *Untergruppe Jäger*.

At 17:45, the corps still hoped to stabilise the situation west of St. Sauveur by committing the *77. I.D.*, but Hitler's orders made this impossible. At 20:00, *Gen.* Fahrmbacher reported that the withdrawal by *Gruppe Hellmich* to the south would have to be carried out straightaway, as any delay would make a successful breakout impossible. All that was holding the front at St. Sauveur-le-Vicomte were two companies from the *91. LL.D.* and weak elements of the *243. I.D.*[418]

That evening, *AOK 7*, *H.Gr. B* and *Ob.West* discussed the situation. All options were restricted by Hitler's orders. And yet something had to be done to oppose the American advance at St. Sauveur. The Cotentin would fall faster without countermeasures, leaving neither troops in Cherbourg nor troops in the south to hold the Douve River and the marshland stretching west to the coast. Rommel therefore decided that the road from St. Sauveur to Cherbourg would have to be blocked by the *77. I.D.* immediately. Reserves could be moved at will (except for withdrawals), but all forces already engaged were to remain in place and hold the lines.[419] In view of the untenable situation, the orders were hardly realistic, but little else could be done.

That morning, the *LXXXIV. A.K.* had correctly concluded that the *Westfront* was on the verge of collapse. The remaining troops could offer only minor resistance against the VII Corps' continued advance. The 82nd AB's advance had resumed at 05:00, with the 325th GIR reaching the high ground overlooking St. Sauveur from the southeast by 09:30. Further north, the 505th PIR had also reached high ground by 11:30. Exploiting the confusion among the Germans, the 2/505 crossed the river and seized the town, followed by the rest of the regiment and the 508th PIR. By nightfall, the division had established a secure bridgehead with a depth of 1,800-2,800 metres.[420]

During the day, the 9th ID also established a bridgehead on the west bank of the Douve at Néhou. The 60th IR had attacked westwards, making good progress. By 21:00, the 2/60 had crossed the Douve River at Néhou and secured a foothold on the west bank. On its right, the 47th IR also gained significant ground, reaching Hautteville-Bocage at 16:20. The town was captured despite stiff German resistance, and the regiment crossed the St. Sauveur - Valognes road. On the division's right, the 39th IR attacked Orglandes, but it was unable to completely capture the town before dark.[421]

By the end of the day, *AOK 7* observed that the enemy breakthrough had given the Americans room to move at will to the west and north. Reserves to seal off the enemy advances were not available. A phase of the campaign had come to an end. Despite the collapse of the *Westfront*, *AOK 7* congratulated the troops and their commanders for having hitherto blocked the enemy from access to the west coast and Cherbourg; it noted that this had been achieved against an enemy greatly superior in manpower, weapons and equipment and despite heavy casualties.[422] That same day, *AOK 7* recommended that *Pi.Btl. 191* and its commander be mentioned in the Armed Force Daily Announcement.[423] Even for this major combat unit, German records say almost nothing about it after D-Day. This shows just how little is known about the division's combat history.

The chaos at the front can also be illustrated by the number of units encountered by the 82nd AB in a relatively narrow area north of the Douve on **15-16 June**. The division took prisoners from all infantry battalions. Those of *GR 1057* included seven men from the headquarters (and possibly the headquarters company), three from the 1st Battalion, two from the 2nd and seven from 3rd. The figures for *GR 1058* were 27 (1st Battalion), 10 (2nd), 3 (3rd), and 3 (13th Company.). Among the other divisional units were 16 men from *Fla-Kp. 191*, 9 from *Pz.Jg.Kp. 191*, 8 from *San.Kp. 191* and 6 from *AR 191*. Other prisoners included men from the *77.I.D.* (58), the *243. I.D.* (21) and *KG* 265 (four).[424]

On the night of **16-17 June**, German troops on the peninsula remained largely paralysed by Hitler's orders from the day before. At 10:35, on the **17**[th], *AOK 7* was finally informed of a new Hitler directive. *Gruppe von Schlieben* could conduct a fighting withdrawal, delaying the enemy, but this could only start under heavy enemy pressure.[425]

At 11:00, the corps reported fighting near St. Sauveur and stated that, as per its orders, the move south would only begin under pressure. At 14:30, it reported weak screening forces as holding the west of the town; but from there to Golleville (to the northeast) only a thin line of infantry was available. From that town to Le Ham, *Gruppe von Schlieben* only had a flimsy covering line.[426]

None of these forces, of course, were able to contest the advance of the VII Corps in a meaningful way. The push to the west coast had been taken over by the 9th ID, which launched its attack in the morning. To the south, the 47th IR moved through the 82nd AB bridgehead at St. Sauveur-le-Vicomte and advanced in the general direction of Portbail, capturing key hills and cutting important roads along the way. It was ordered to seal off the peninsula along the line St. Lô-d'Ourville - St. Sauveur-de-Pierrepont, and this was completed on the **18**[th]. Further north, the 60th IR began advancing to the west coast on the morning of the 17th. It moved along the road to Barneville, reaching the critical high ground overlooking the Barneville - Bricquebec highway by nightfall. Other forces moved directly to Barneville, reaching it on the morning of the **18**[th]. Together, the regiments had finally cut off the Cotentin Peninsula.[427] Putting up minor opposition, the German forces involved are difficult to identify.

Despite the rapid American advance to the west coast, only minor (organic) elements of the *91. LL.D.* were trapped. It seems that most troops had been engaged close to the Douve or had already moved south. On **21 June**, just 30 men were reported in *Festung Cherbourg*.[428] Far stronger formations had managed to escape and regroup to the south. A large number of men were captured, although it is not known how large this group was or when individual soldiers became POW's. An illustration of the number of prisoners can be found in the records of 82nd AB. Between **6** and **17 June**, it captured 615 men from the *91. LL.D.*, including 117 from *GR 1057* (4.3% of its authorised strength), 398 (14.7%) from *GR 1058*, 35 (20.6%) from *Pz. Jg.Kp. 191*, 18 from *Fla-Kp. 191* and 22 from *Pi.Btl. 191* (5%).[429]

The breakthrough marked the beginning of a new phase of the Normandy campaign in the American area of operations. While the US VII Corps turned its full attention to Cherbourg, the VIII Corps took over the American lines on the base of the peninsula. Over the next two weeks, except for fighting on **18-20 June**, this area south of the Douve was fairly quiet. The priority for the *LXXXIV. A.K.* was now to prevent an American breakthrough to the south; as a result, its depleted formations were reorganised and a new *Nordfront* established.[430] The *91. LL.D.*'s role in these activities is covered below.

Holding the *Nordfront*

The collapse of the *Westfront* and, with it, *Gruppe Hellmich*, required a major reorganisation south of the Douve. On the morning of the **18**[th], *Obst.* Klosterkemper, Hellmich's replacement, put his *243. I.D.* under the command of *Obst. König*, who was put in charge of the entire sector south of the Douve. The forces under his command were designated *Gruppe König*. The sector itself was referred to as the *Nordfront* of the *LXXXIV. A.K.*[431]

On **18 June**, the *91. LL.D.*'s headquarters was moved to Chau. Brocboeufs (northeast of La Haye-du-Puits).[432] Previously, it had moved to a location 3.5 km west of St. Sauveur-le-Vicomte, which put it in a good position to reach safety.[433]

Kampfgruppe 91. LL.I.D.
18 June 1944

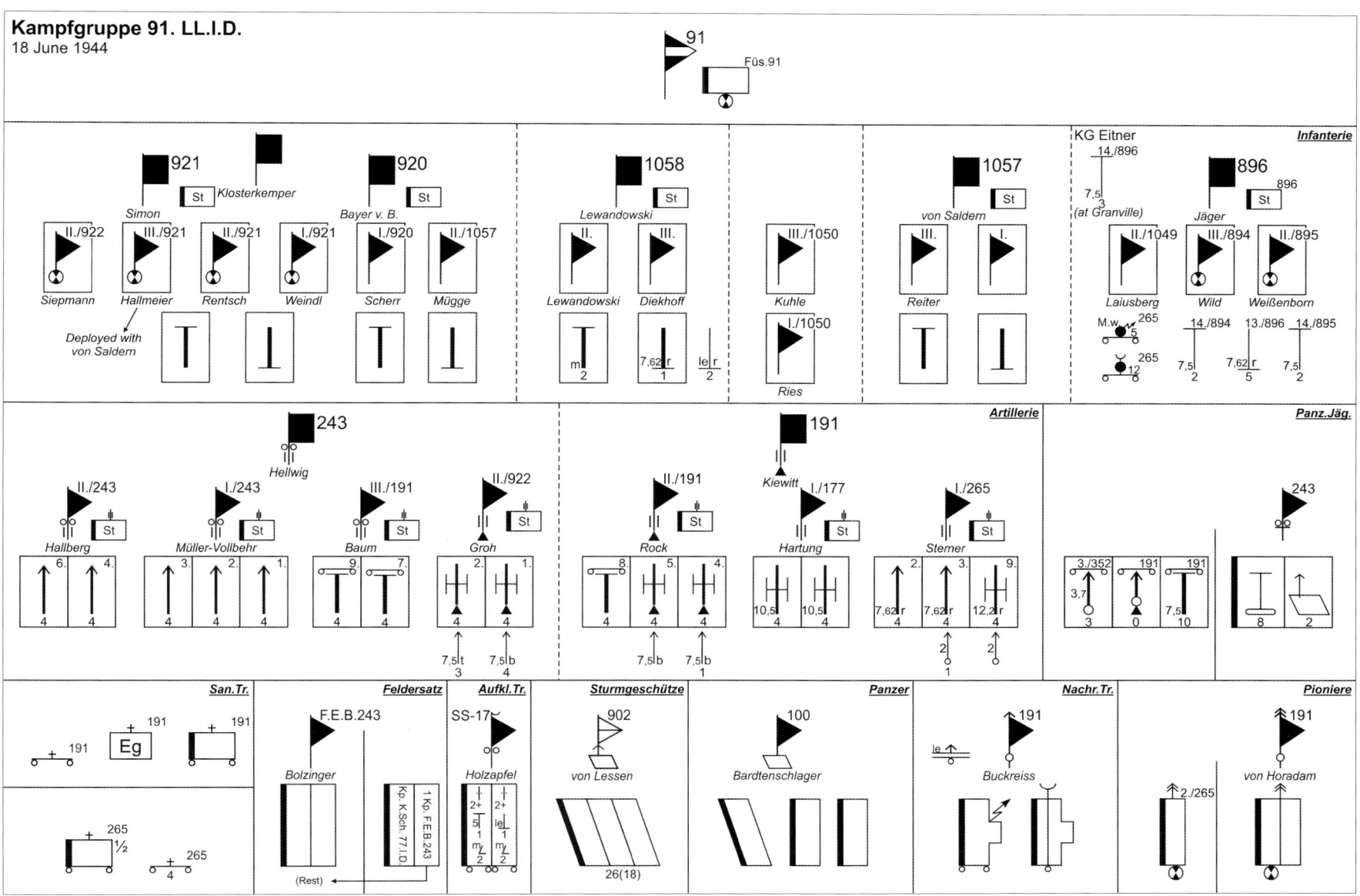

Much of the division was able to escape south before American forces cut the Cotentin in two on 17-18 June. As 'KG 91. LL.I.D.' the division (later Gruppe König) reorganised along the Douve – Prairies Marécageuses front. Holding this line was only possible with the support of a large number of attached elements. (T78 R672)

The composition of *Gruppe König* is confusing because its organisation changed over time. Fortunately, documents exist showing the units within the battlegroup from **18 June** until **28 June**.[434] The earliest report helps identify those troops that escaped the peninsula or were already south of the Douve. Unfortunately, it tells us very little about their condition.[435]

On **18 June**, König's infantry was divided among five forces of varying strength: *KG Klosterkemper, KG Eitner, KG von Saldern, KG Lewandowski* (the new commander of *GR 1058*) and a grouping of two battalions from the *77. I.D. Füs.Kp. 91* was under divisional control.[436] Appropriately, the *Kampfgruppen* under *Gruppe König* soon started to be referred to as *Untergruppen*, although this was not yet the case on the 18th.

The largest infantry force of *Gruppe König* was *KG Klosterkemper*, drawn principally from the *243. I.D.* and comprising two regimental-sized infantry groups. These were formed around the headquarters of *GR 920* and *921*, respectively. Six battalions were available, but how these were organised is not entirely clear. Based on the documents, it appears that *GR 920* consisted of the *I./920*, the *I./921* and the *II./1057*, as well as two regimental heavy weapons companies (probably the *13.* and the *14./920*). *GR 921* likely included the *II.* and the *III./921* and the *II./922* (*III./921* was with another battlegroup). Two heavy weapons companies were available, probably the *13.* and the *14./921*. The organisation of these two forces may reflect their composition in the final days of battle north of the Douve, although there is insufficient evidence to confirm this. *KG Klosterkemper* was supported by *AR 243* with four guns in each of its batteries. The 5th Battery and the entire 3rd Battalion were missing, although they later reappeared.[437] Even so, on **18 June**, the regiment had nine batteries, as the *I.* and the *III./AR 191* were attached, each with a headquarters battery and two gun batteries. The 1st Battalion provided the 1st and 2nd Batteries, while the 3rd Battalion had the 7th and 9th Batteries (each with four AT guns). The batteries of the 1st Battalion are interesting, because they were both listed with four mountain howitzers as well as other guns. The 1st Battery was shown with four Belgian 7.5 cm guns. The 2nd Battery had three Czech guns of similar calibre.[438] As already noted, these guns had been taken from the defences along the west coast. It would appear that the batteries tried to stay operational while waiting for ammunition. This is supported by an order from *AR 191* dated **24 June**, which instructed 1st, 2nd and 5th Batteries to move their howitzers to a rear area northwest of Coutances for maintenance. Only the 4th Battery could remain operational, because it still had a supply of ammunition.[439]

On **18 June**, *Gruppe König's* second largest infantry force was *KG Eitner*, essentially the reinforced core of *Kampfgruppe 265*. This group had two "organic" battalions: The *III./894* and the *II./895*, supported by heavy AT platoons from the 14th Companies of *GR 894, GR 895* and *GR 896*. The *14./896* had three guns, while the other two platoons both had two *Pak 40's*. The final unit was the *13./896*, with five Russian 7.62 cm infantry guns. Additionally, the *II./1049* was still part of *Maj.* Eitner's battlegroup, having stayed in the area since first going into action on **13 June**.[440]

KG von Saldern (*GR 1057*) had two organic battalions, the 1st and 3rd, plus two heavy weapons companies. It was supported by the *III./921*, while its own 2nd Battalion was with *KG Klosterkemper*.[441]

GR 1058 was listed with its 2nd and 3rd Battalions. The latter may have been with *FJR 6*, as the organisational document seems to show other organic elements, such as the *II./AR 191*, which had not yet returned. The regiment's heavy weapons companies were also included in the document. The 13th Company was listed with one Russian 7.62 cm infantry gun and two light infantry guns. The *14./1058* had two medium AT guns, probably *5 cm Pak 38's*.[442] The *I./1058* was not listed, probably due to losses sustained on **7 June** near Ste. Mère-Église.

The final infantry units of *Gruppe König* were the *I.* and the *III./1050*, although they were not listed as part of a regimental force.[443] The 3rd Battalion had been fighting with the *91. LL.D.* since its arrival and apparently retreated south with it. The *I./1050* was late arriving and unable to regroup with the *77. I.D.* before the peninsula was cut by American forces.[444]

The artillery not supporting *KG Klosterkemper* was assembled under *AR 191*. The 2nd Battalion was in command of the 4th, 5th and 8th Batteries.[445] Unfortunately, the entry on this battalion cannot be verified as all the units involved had been in action away from the division. The 5th Battery supported *GR 1058* on D-Day, spending some time fighting under the *709. I.D.*, while the battalion headquarters and the two other batteries were with *FJR 6*. In fact, the battalion headquarters was still expected to support *FJR 6* with its 8th Battery. This battery was listed with four AT guns and the other two batteries (4th and 5th) with Belgian 7.5 cm guns, although the information on the Belgian guns is unreliable. As noted, the 4th Battery retained two *10,5 cm Geb.H. 40's* instead of receiving replacements.[446] Records on **20** and **28 June** show the 5th Battery received four 7.5 cm guns, but their origin is not clear, suggesting they were German.[447] Other records indeed indicate these guns were *7,65 cm F.K.16 nA's*.[448] On **18 June**, two battalions under *AR 191* were from different divisions. The *I./AR 265* had three batteries of Russian guns. The number of 12.2 cm howitzers in the 9th Battery is not clear, but the 2nd and 3rd Batteries each had four 7.62 cm guns. Both the 3rd and 9th Batteries had a 2 cm *Flak* each. The third battalion, the *II./AR 177*, had two batteries, each with four 10.5 cm howitzers.[449] As of **19 June**, all artillery under *Gruppe König* was coordinated by the headquarters of *H.K.A.R. 1261*; it appears to have been responsible for the entire *Nordfront* and thus also coordinated *AR 353* and *AR zbV 621*.[450]

The **18 June** organisational documents also showed the wide variety of support units in *Gruppe König*, including the divisional anti-tank elements. *Pz. Jg.Kp. 191* had 10 motorised *Pak 40's*, but *Fla-Kp. 191* had lost all of its 2 cm *Flak*. Anti-aircraft guns were on hand with the *3./Pz.Jg.Abt. 352*, which still had three self-propelled 3.7 cm *Flak*. *Pz.Jg.Abt. 243* had two companies available: The 1st Company with eight *Marders* and the 2nd Company with two assault guns.[451] The 3rd Company was not listed, as it was still in action with the *17. SS-Pz.Gren.Div.*[452] Additional armoured support was from *Pz.Ers.u.Ausb.Abt. 100* with three companies, two shown as infantry companies and a third as a tank company. More significant was the armour of *Stu.Gesch.Brig. 902*, whose three batteries had 26 assault guns, although 18 were in need of repair. The engineer troops with *Gruppe König* were the expected units. *Pi.Btl. 191* still had two companies and the *2./Pi.Btl. 265* was also available.[453] *Pi.Btl. 243* had been in action around Montebourg and was unable to escape the Cotentin.[454] An interesting addition to *Gruppe König* was two reconnaissance companies of *SS-Pz.Aufkl.Abt. 17* (*17. SS-Pz.Gren.Div.*). Oddly, both were reported as merely having two machine guns and two medium mortars. One company had a light infantry gun and the other three heavy AT guns. Despite the previous losses, *Gruppe König* still had some replacement units. This included *Feld-Ers.Btl. 243*, apparently with three companies. The divisional combat school of the *77. I.D.*, at company strength, was also available to provide personnel.[455]

On **18 June**, the area most threatened was an isthmus running between the marshland southwest of St. Sauveur and the coast. Elsewhere, movement would be restricted by the terrain or face already established lines, such as *KG Eitner*. Remnants of the *243. I.D.* were reported to be defending a front running northwest from La Croix Blondel to Besneville, essentially blocking the St. Sauveur-le-Vicomte - Portbail road (D15) along the D903. *Gen.* Hellmich was no longer present; he had been killed by an Allied fighter-bomber attack on the **17th**.[456]

At 14:30, *AOK 7* issued new orders to the *LXXXIV. A.K.* The corps was to prevent the enemy from advancing in the direction of Périers and La Haye-du-Puits from the east and north. On its left, it would establish and defend a line stretching west from Les Moitiers-en-Bauptois to the coast.[457] This was already happening as the troops southwest of St. Sauveur-le-Vicomte held a line stretching west from Catteville, via Neuville-en-Beaumont and Canville-la-Rocque to St. Lô-d'Ourville on the coast, effectively sealing off the Cotentin. In addition, a blocking position (*Riegelstellung*) had been established running northwest from Canville to Besneville, which put the troops in an exposed position between American forces.[458] Indeed, on **19 June**, it was reported that a weak battlegroup under *Maj.* von Saldern had been surrounded south of Besneville. In fact, von Saldern and *Hptm.* Reiter were both taken prisoner near Neuville-en-Beaumont on the **18th**, making it a costly day for *GR 1057*.[459]

The lines were intact elsewhere along the *Nordfront*. The *U.Gr. Eitner* sector was held by three battalions, while to its left *SS-Pz.Aufkl.Abt. 17* and two companies were in position.[460] Reinforcements were on the way. On **11 June**, *Ost-Btl. Huber* and the *I./1050* (*77. I.D.*) had been ordered to move to the front from Bretagne, with *Ost-Btl. Huber* earmarked for the St. Sauveur-le-Vicomte defile and the *I./1050* ordered to reinforce its division around Valognes.[461] It took considerable time for these units to reach the front. Another eastern battalion, *Wolga-Tat.Inf.Btl. 627*, was ordered to move up from Bretagne on **18 June**;[462] as a result, it would be some time before it could join *Gruppe König*.

AOK 7 issued new orders at 02:45 on **19 June** to improve the defences south of the Douve. The forward edge of battle, stretching from northeast of Le Plessis (on the edge of the Prairies Marécageuses de Gorges), via Prétot and Les Moitiers-en-Bauptois along the Prairies Marécageuses southwest of St. Sauveur-le-Vicomte to Portbail, was to be improved by any means possible.[463] This would be the front line for *Gruppe König*.

The orders also called for defensive lines to be constructed to the rear. A second line would start at the northwest corner of the Prairies Marécageuses de Gorges and (including the Forêt de Mont-Castre) run to St. Germain-sur-Ay. This line was referred to as the *Waldbergstellung* and also as the *Mahlmann-*

Linie, its name derived from the commander of the *353. I.D.*, whose division was building it.[464] A blocking position would be created, beginning at the same northwest corner of the marshland and stretching northwest to Hill 131. Well to the rear, a third line was to be formed along the Sèves River to Lessay;[465] it was known as the *Wasserlinie*, although this term is not typically used in period records.[466]

That afternoon, *Gruppe König's* front was held by *U.Gr. Eitner* on the right, *U.Gr. Jäger* in the centre, and *U.Gr. Klosterkemper* on the left. The lines generally matched those ordered.[467]

U.Gr. Jäger was formed from the units sent to block the St. Sauveur-le-Vicomte - La Haye-du-Puits highway and the hills on either side. With *Maj.* Eitner commanding most of *KG 265*, the headquarters of *GR 896* was not required and was therefore available to *U.Gr. Jäger*. On **24 June**, it was composed of the *12./894* (minus one platoon), the engineer platoon from the headquarters company of *GR 896* and *SS-Pz.Aufkl.Abt. 17* (minus its 2nd Company).[468] Three days later, it was listed with the *11./894* (minus one platoon), instead of the *12./894*.[469] This was still being reported on **29 June**, but the situation map for **28 June** showed that *Ost-Btl. Huber* had taken over the front with the *SS* battalion returning to its division.[470]

While on the charts *KG Klosterkemper* was listed as a separate force alongside König's forces, this does not reflect the actual situation. It was finally correctly shown as subordinate to *Gruppe König* on the **24th**. At that time, it consisted of a platoon from the combined *GR 1057* and *1058*, and the intact *I./1050*, which had only recently arrived. These forces were apparently the only ones actually at the front, as the sector reserve consisted of *Stu.Gesch.Brig. 902* and the remnants of the *243. I.D.*[471] These forces did not change until **28 June**, when the *I./1050* was no longer listed, having been relieved by *Wolga-Tat.Inf. Btl. 627*.[472] At the front, however, there had been changes. As of **25 June**, *AOK 7* maps no longer showed *U.Gr. Klosterkemper* to the left of *Gruppe König*, but rather *U.Gr. Simon*, which indicates that *Obstlt.* Simon had been put in charge of the front.[473] The relief of the *I./1050* by the Volga Tatars was shown on **28 June** and, the next day, the *U.Gr. Simon* sector consisted of the eastern battalion on the left and the remnants of *GR 921* on the right.[474]

U.Gr. Eitner's composition has already been covered. Although its lines moved, its organisation did not change significantly until the creation of *U.Gr. Lewandowski*.

According to the new artillery commander, *Obst.* Triepel, *AR 191* was initially deployed in the area of Ste. Suzanne - Bois de Limors - Hill 131 - Lithaire. The artillery of both the *77.* and the *243. I.D.* was located in the area of La Haye-du-Puits - Denneville - Bretteville-sur-Ay. *AR zbV 621*, which could cover the entire *Gruppe König* sector, was positioned south of Mont-Castre and La Haye-du-Puits. Near the end of **June**, most of the artillery was pulled back south of Mont-Castre and south of the line La Haye-du-Puits - Bretteville-sur-Ay. Fire support was augmented by the arrival of *AR 353*, which also went into position south of Mont-Castre.[475]

Although *U.Gr. Eitner* had not seen much action after sealing off the Beuzeville bridgehead to its east, this was about to change. On the night of **18-19 June**, the 82nd AB launched a new attack to create a second bridgehead across the Douve south of Pont-l'Abbé and link up with the Beuzeville bridgehead to the east.[476] It took some time before German commanders understood the significance of these attacks. The left flank of the *Nordfront* received the most attention, at least initially. In the morning, it was reported that *Gruppe König* was in contact with the enemy along the line Canville-la-Rocque - Cussy - La Rue Baton.[477] At 14:00, the front of the entire battlegroup was reported to be unchanged.[478] This was certainly not true for *U.Gr. Eitner*.

At 14:00, *LXXXIV. A.K.* reported the enemy had attempted to cross the Douve at Les Moitiers-en-Bauptois at 23:30 (**18th**), and that a company was dispatched to deal with the threat.[479] The 82nd AB had staged a diversion in the woods west of Les Moitiers (Bois de Limors) in an effort to divert attention from the main attack. Around midnight, the 2/325 started to cross the Douve east of Les Moitiers. At about the same time, the 1/507 began an advance to Vindefontaine from the Beuzeville bridgehead, taking the town by 07:30 on the **19th**. The bridgehead was reinforced during the day by the 505th and 508th PIR, and the perimeter pushed south to 600 metres from Prétot.[480]

At 19:25, the corps was still only noting that reconnaissance across the Douve had occurred during the night. Finally, at 20:45, the events around Vindefontaine were confirmed, with *AOK 7* notifying *H.Gr. B* of a major incursion resulting in the loss of the town and the crossroads to the west. The situation at the Bois de Limors was still not known, the report noting that enemy troops had infiltrated the forest and that countermeasures were underway.[481] The field army, however, still considered the situation along the *Nordfront* as under control, albeit only if the enemy breach at Vindefontaine

Especially the outskirts of La Haye-du-Puits were heavily damaged. A large crater blocked the highway leading into the town from the north. Today the town's war memorial is located in the open space on the left of the photo. (NARA)

could be effectively contained. In other sectors, there were more reasons to be positive such as the escape by two battalions of the *77. I.D.* from the Cotentin and the arrival of the *I./1050* on the left flank. Moreover, minor enemy advances on the 18th had been cleaned up.[482]

Eliminating the 82nd AB's new bridgehead proved impossible. *U.Gr. Eitner* could only try to seal it off along the line Le Val - La Poterie - Hau. de Haut. The rest of the *Nordfront* remained unchanged.[483]

For *U.Gr. Eitner*, the fighting continued on **20 June**. At 09:00, the *LXXXIV. A.K.* reported renewed attacks against the right of the *Nordfront*. Prétot had already been captured by the Americans (3/508), and it would be difficult to restore the situation because there were no reserves. At this time, the front around the town was defended only by a few units from the *353. I.D.*: The headquarters and a company of *Pi.Btl.* 353, some assault guns and two platoons from *Pz.Jg.Abt.* 353. *AOK 7* ordered the lines to be held at any cost and directed the corps to commit *Ost-Btl. Huber* and the *353. I.D.*[484]

At 11:45, *Gruppe König* reported new lines. The front started at La Rivière on the northern edge of the Baupte marshes. From there, it continued north via Chaulieu to the southern edge of Les Sablons, then turned northwest via La Fèvrerie (south of Prétot) and La Guilloterie (west of Prétot) to La Cuiroterie. It continued north along the eastern edge of the Bois de Limors before turning southwest along the south of the Prairies Marécageuses. Via St. Sauveur-de-Pierrepont, Rue Bouille and La Groudière, it finally reached the coast.[485]

At 16:30, the corps reported that enemy troops had entered the Bois de Limors (3/505th PIR).[486] In its evening report, *AOK 7* stated that the fighting to clean up the enemy advances southwest of Vindefontaine had not yet been concluded.[487] The daily report was more positive, announcing that counterattacks had eliminated most of the advances. Prétot had been abandoned by the Americans at 16:00 after heavy German shelling and mortar fire. *KG Eitner*'s lines now ran from the northwest corner of the Baupte marshes, east past St. Jores, south past Prétot, and east past La Dranguerie to the centre of the Bois de Limors. US troops had already reached the western edge of the forest, although this was not reported in German records until **June 21**.[488] The German line was pulled back to 200 metres southwest of the woods to establish a more effective field of fire.[489]

Although an organisational document had already been compiled for **18 June**, the division apparently had cause to draw up another on the **20th**. This document is interesting as it only shows organic units and those subordinated directly to the division; as a result, it offers an overview of the reinforced division rather than of *Gruppe König*.[490] Simply put, it shows the division's organisation on D-Day, minus the destroyed 3. and 6./AR 191 but reinforced by a number of attached units. All units of *KG 265* are included, listed next to similar formations from the division. The *II./894* is also included, although it had not yet arrived.[491] In addition, *Stu.Gesch.Brig. 902* is listed with its three batteries, showing it was under the operational control of the division.[492]

The document gives no details as to the weapons or personnel strength of the elements, except the artillery. The *I./AR 191* had two Belgian 7.5 cm cannons in its 1st battery, two Czech guns of the same calibre in the 2nd battery and two mountain howitzers in the 4th Battery. Although the *II./AR 191* was listed, it was shown without a number of guns in the 8th Battery, probably because these were still operating away from the division. The 3rd Battalion had four unidentified 7.5 cm cannons in the 5th Battery and three 8.8 cm AT guns in both the 7th and 9th Batteries. The *I./AR 265* was also listed under *AR 191* — its batteries still at full strength with four Russian 7.62 cm cannons in the 2nd and 3rd Batteries and four Russian 12.2 cm howitzers in the 9th Battery. There were still two 2 cm *Flak* with the battalion headquarters.[493]

After **20 June**, activity on the *Gruppe König* front died down. König's force now faced the US VIII Corps, which had taken over the Carentan sector (101st AB) on **15 June** and along the *Nordfront* (82nd AB and the 90th ID) on **19 June**. The 82nd AB merely held its ground, its sector being reduced when its left flank was taken over by the 90th ID (358th and the 359th IR). On the right, the 47th IR had been relieved by the 357th IR on **18 June**, meaning it faced *Gruppe König's* left flank. 90th ID did not attempt any serious offensive operations either, so little changed until **3 July**, although the VIII Corps' right flank was taken over by the 79th ID on **30 June**.[494]

Throughout this period, activity against *Gruppe König* was generally limited to reconnaissance patrols and occasional local probing attacks. In addition, heavy air power, artillery and mortar fire was directed against the battlegroup.[495]

This period of relative calm gave both sides an opportunity to prepare for what was to come. It does not appear that the engineers under *Gruppe König* were part of a subordinate battlegroup, as was the case with *KG Bohnenkamp* on D-Day. Instead, they seem to have been used in standard engineering work to strengthen the defences. This is illustrated in a report from **21 June**, which stated that *Pi.Btl. 191* had prepared tree and wire obstacles south of the Bois de Limors and mined eight crossroads.[496]

The front of *Gruppe König* was still held by *U.Gr. Eitner* on the right, *U.Gr. Jäger* in the centre, and *U.Gr. Klosterkemper* on the left. *U.Gr. Eitner*'s area ran from St. Jores to the northern edge of the Bois de Limors; the next sector presumably continued from there to St. Nicolas-de-Pierrepont, as had been reported on the **20th**; the final sector covered the front to the coast.[497]

Several attacks hit the left of the battlegroup on **22 June**, as the 2/357th IR attempted to strengthen its position through *"an attack of a limited nature."* Movement in this area was restricted by the terrain, with the Olonde and Gorget Rivers forming natural obstacles, leaving only a narrow corridor in between. Straight across this bottleneck, between St. Lô-d'Ourville and Gare de Denneville, ran the Portbail - La Haye-du-Puits railway, which created another obstacle. Control of this corridor was naturally important to both sides. At 17:00, an attack was launched that reached Duprey (1 km southeast of St. Lô-d'Ourville, today Hau. Dupré). Although two enemy penetrations were eliminated by a German counterattack, the 90th ID still considered the attack a success, illustrating how perceptions differed. Late that evening, a probing attack was made towards the bridge at St. Nicolas-de-Pierrepont, but it was repulsed. The German main line of resistance was restored without change.[498]

On **23 June**, American troops advanced west out of the Bois de Limors and entered Varenguebec, before being pushed back again by a fresh German force.[499] The day before, *U.Gr. Lewandowski* (the commander of *GR 1058*) had appeared on the charts.[500] This force was positioned between *U.Gr. Jäger* and *U.Gr. Eitner*, and its arrival seems to have reduced the *U.Gr. Eitner* sector. Lewandowski's elements were formed from what remained of *GR 1057* and *1058*. On **23 June**, *AOK 7* charts listed the remnants of the division as the reserve for *U.Gr. Eitner*, but this information may have been overtaken by events. In any case, the precise composition of *U.Gr. Lewandowski* and when it joined the line is not known.[501]

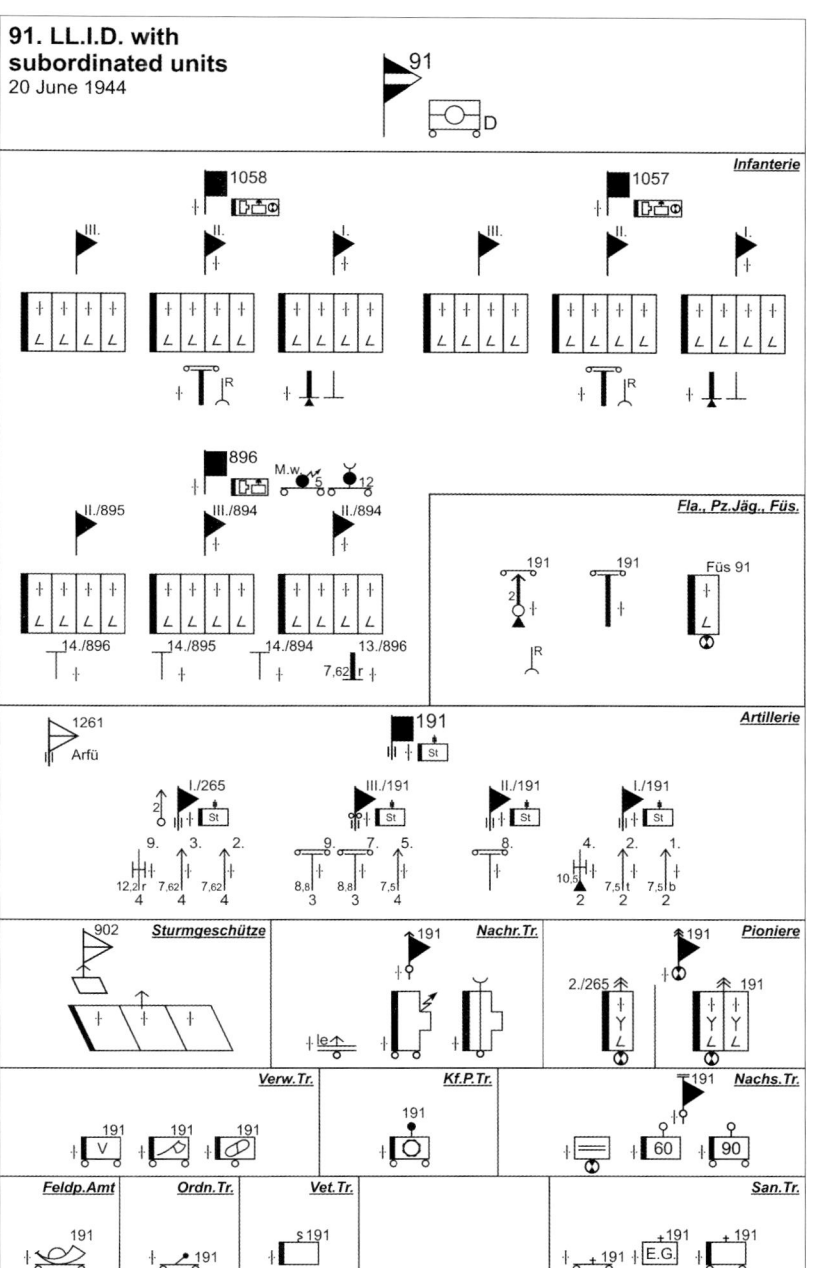

On 20 June the division drew up an Order of Battle of its organic units and attached units it regarded as such. KG 265 was included in full, as was Stu.Gesch.Brig. 902 and the staff of H.K.A.R. 1261 as the division's Artillerieführer (Arfü). (T78 R672)

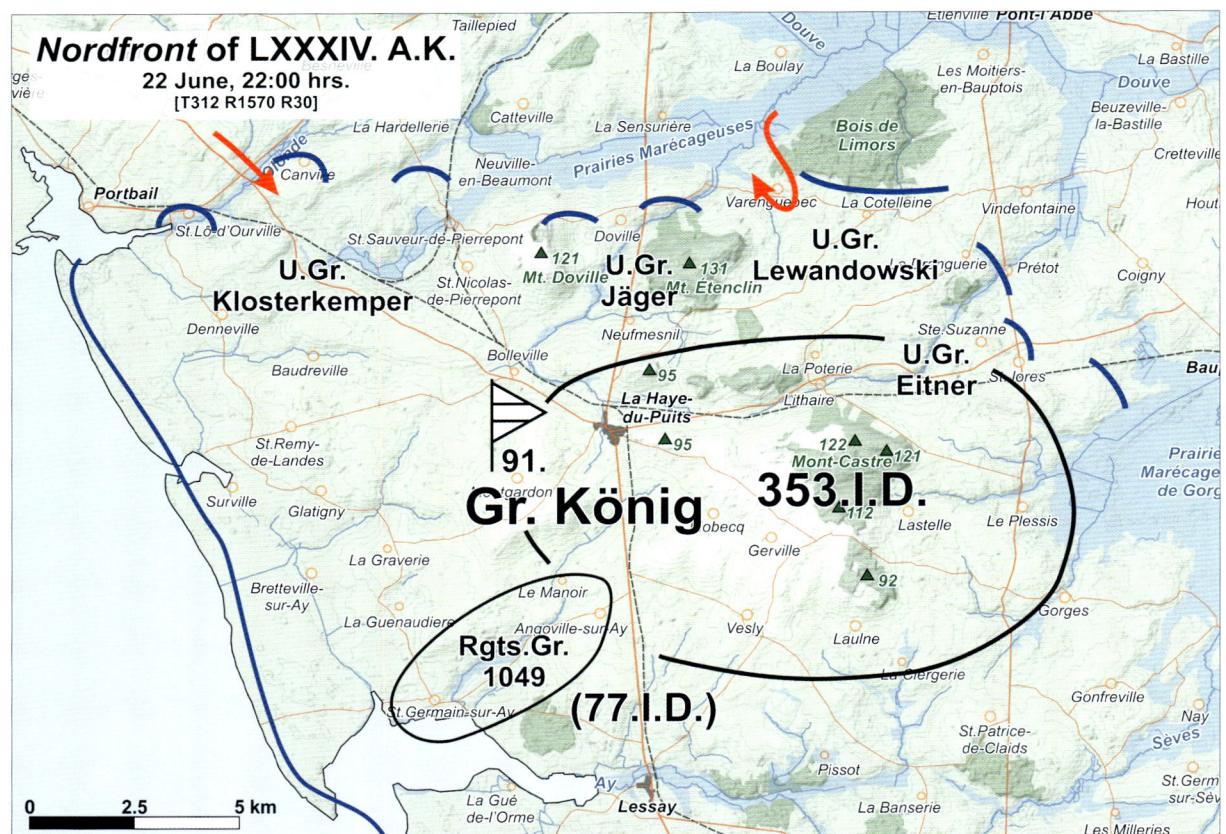

On 22 June U.Gr. Lewandowski appeared on the maps. It was formed from what remained of the division's infantry regiments, reinforced by elements of KG 265. Its arrival reduced the sectors of responsibility of U.Gr. Jäger and Eitner, and moved organic elements of the division back to the front. To the rear the 353. I.D. was arriving while the 77. I.D. reorganised. (T312 R1570 F30)

Also on the **23rd** the *LXXXIV. A.K.* recommended the *hessisch-nassauische 91. I.D.* (Hessia-Nassau) be mentioned in the Armed Forces Daily Announcement in recognition of its role in the fighting on the Cotentin.[502]

24 June was a quiet day. The most important change for the division was the movement of its headquarters from Vesly to La Caponnerie (northeast of Lessay).[503] On **25 June**, *Gruppe König's* front ran from La Rivière (today Villages des Mières) on the edge of the swamp via Les Sablons to La Cuiroterie and Le Becqueret, along the Prairies Marécageuses, via La Sangsurière to St. Sauveur-de-Pierrepont and then to La Groudière at the mouth of the Olonde River.[504]

This period of relative calm allowed the *LXXXIV. A.K.* to assess the strength of *Gruppe König*. On **27 June**, the corps reported its figures, including those of the *91. LL.D.*, to *AOK 7*. The division had incurred immense losses, amounting to 85% of its infantry, 21% of its artillery, 76% of its engineers and 48% of its anti-tank troops.[505]

It is possible to detail the losses further, albeit for a later date. A document provides this data for **1 July**, and a second document illustrates the situation of *Gruppe König* for **18-28 June**.[506] The latter document appears to show the condition on or around **28 June** and, together, the two documents provide the greatest insight on the state of *91. LL.D.* at the time of the American offensive in early **July**.[507] Still, because of changes in late **June** and early **July**, the documents will be examined separately. The **28 June** document includes the *243. I.D.*, as it was still part of *Gruppe König* but would become a separate

91. Luftlande-Infanterie-Division

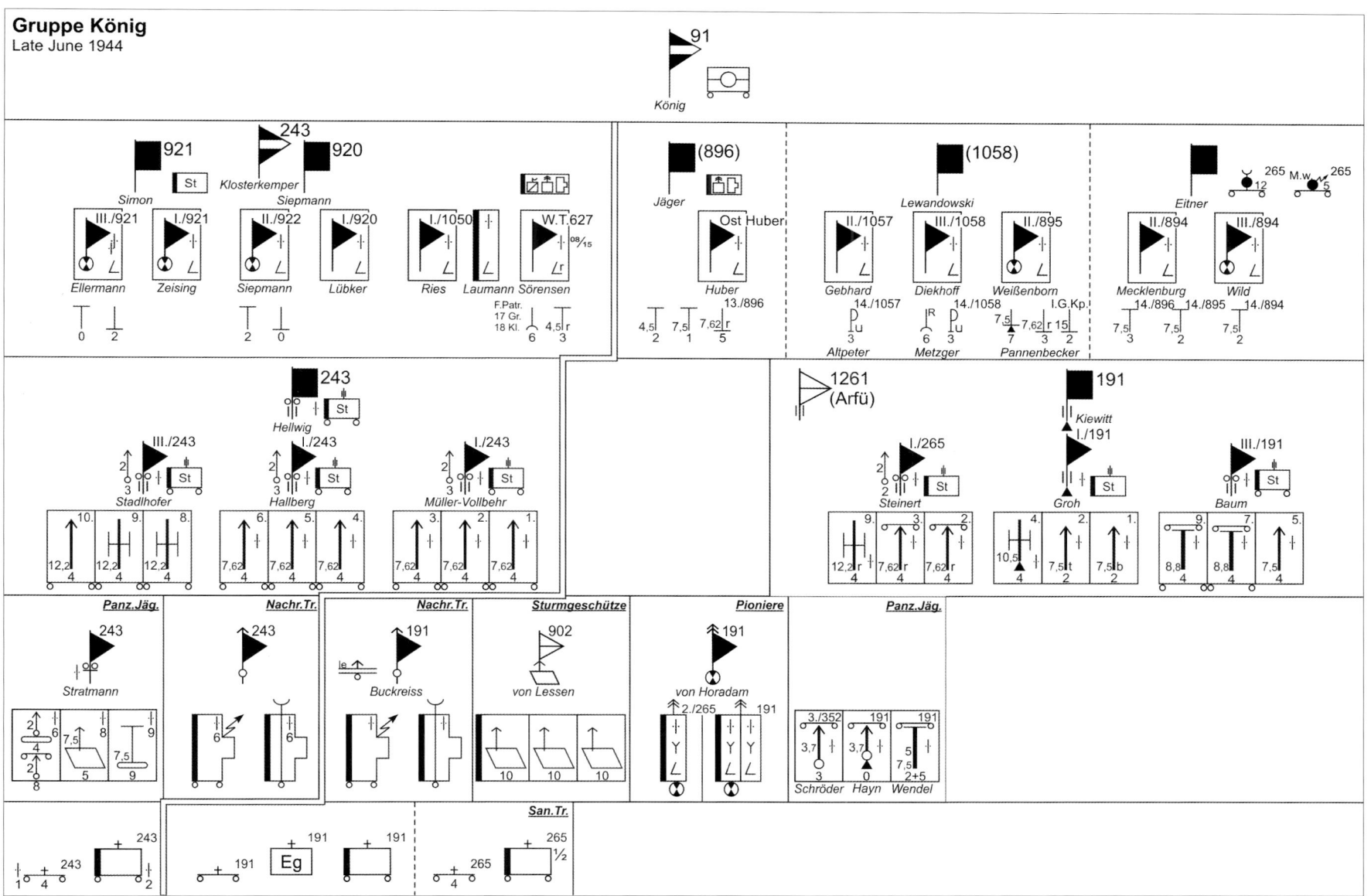

By the end of June Gruppe König still had not changed much compared to the 20th. Its Order of Battle however illustrates that it distinguished two main fighting forces: the 243. I.D. and the reinforced 91.LL.D. Within days Gruppe König would be dissolved with the two divisions assuming responsibility of their own sector on the front. (T78 R672)

element by the time of the American assault; as such, it will be covered in its own chapter. Conversely, as was the case on **20 June**, the elements of the *265. I.D.* and *Stu.Gesch.Brig. 902* were still listed with the *91. LL.D.*, rather than as separate formations of the *Gruppe*.

On **28 June**, the *91. LL.D.*, part of *Gruppe König*, had two regiment-sized forces, *U.Gr. Lewandowski* and *U.Gr. Eitner*, the latter still essentially consisting of *KG 265*. The *II./1049* (*77. I.D.*) had departed, as had the *II./895*.[508] The *II./894* had been brought up from Bretagne, and it relieved the *II./1049*.[509] Anti-tank support came from the heavy AT platoons of the 14th Companies of *GR 894, 895* and *896*. The latter had one AT gun; the others three each.[510]

U.Gr. Lewandowski (*GR 1058*) was in command of more than just organic troops. It had three battalions, all from different regiments: The *III./1058*, the *II./1057* and now also the *II./895*. This force was supported by all four heavy weapons companies from the *91. LL.D.*[511] According to an officer from the *13./1057*, the heavy weapons companies of the two regiments were combined.[512] A reason for this can be found by looking at their manpower versus weaponry. On **1 July**, the *13./1057* still had 55% of its personnel but few guns. In contrast, the *13./1058* had hardly lost a gun, but was down to 31% of it personnel. Despite the officer's claims, records only support a combined 13th Company with two heavy infantry guns, three Russian 7.62 cm infantry guns and seven 7.5 cm mountain infantry guns.[513] It appears that the two 14th Companies retained their separate identities and both are listed as having three *Püppchen*, while the *14./1058* also had three *Ofenrohre*.[514]

The third infantry force was *U.Gr. Jäger* which, while technically listed as a regiment, consisted of just the headquarters company of *GR 896* and *Ost-Btl. Huber*. In support was the *13./896* with five Russian 7.62 cm infantry guns. The eastern battalion appears to have had a *7,5 cm Pak 40* and an unspecified number of Russian 4.5 cm AT guns.[515]

The observant reader may have noticed how this overview of infantry formations has left out a number of the division's original infantry battalions. This is because the document only lists two: The *II./1057* and the *III./1058*. The others were apparently combat ineffective and not mentioned.

According to the organisational document, *Gruppe König's* artillery (including that of the *243. I.D.*) was still commanded by the headquarters of *H.K.A.R. 1261* (*Obst.* Triepel) as the battlegroup artillery officer. It had the status of a brigade headquarters. *AR 191* had its 1st and 3rd Battalions available in addition to the *I./AR 265*. All four headquarters still had a headquarters battery. The *I./AR 191* consisted of its 1st and 2nd Batteries and the attached 4th Battery. The first two were listed with two Belgian and two Czech cannons, respectively, while the 4th Battery still had two mountain howitzers. The *III./AR 191* also had three batteries — the attached 5th Battery and its organic 7th and 9th Batteries. The latter two both had three 8.8 cm AT guns; the 5th Battery was equipped with four 7.5 cm cannons. The 8th Battery had yet to return to the division from the Carentan area.[516] It was armed with four 8.8 cm AT guns on **14 July**, when the battery was reported as being attached to the *II./AR 191*. The *13./914* was probably still with the battalion since both light and heavy infantry guns were also reported.[517] The final battalion, the *I./AR 265*, was close to how it had left Bretagne: Two 2 cm *Flak* with the headquarters and 7.62cm cannons in the 2nd and 3rd Batteries. In the latter battery, these had been reduced to three pieces, while the attached 9th Battery still had four 12.2 cm howitzers. Among the remaining combat troops under the *91. LL.D.* were both organic and subordinated units. *Pi.Btl. 191* still had its two companies, but equipment numbers were not given. The *2./Pi.Btl. 265* was positioned next to this battalion and may well have been attached.[518]

Supporting the division were *Pz.Jg.Kp. 191*, *Fla-Kp. 191* and the *3./Pz.Jg.Abt. 352*. *Pz.Jg.Kp. 191* had three 5 cm and two *7,5 cm Pak 40's*, while the *3./Pz.Jg.Abt. 352* was down to just three of its original nine self-propelled 3.7 cm *Flak*. Armoured support was still provided by *Stu.Gesch.Brig. 902*, which was attached to the *91. LL.D.* in entirety; its three batteries still had 10 assault guns each, although it is not known if the headquarters had an assault gun.[519]

Reinforced by the *243. I.D.*, *Gruppe König* had a wide area to cover with these forces. On **29 June**, *AOK 7* recorded that the battlegroup held a 27 km frontline with four subordinate battlegroups. From left (west) to right these were *U.Gr. Simon, Jäger, Lewandowski* and *Eitner*. In addition to two "weak" battalions, the forces included *KG 265*, two eastern battalions (*Huber* and *Wolga-Tat.Inf.Btl. 627*) and two unidentified battalions from the *243. I.D.*[520] Situation maps identify the remnants of *GR 921* at the front, but the maps may actually be referring to the former *KG Simon*, which had included the *I./921* and the *II./922*. Since the division's other infantry battalions were not mentioned, these were probably in reserve.[521]

During the day, the *LXXXIV. A.K.* issued new orders for the reorganisation of its troops. *Gruppe König* was to be disbanded, with the *91. LL.D.* and the *243. I.D.* assuming command over the right and left of the *Nordfront*, respectively. This was to take effect on **1 July**. The *91. LL.D.* would remain in command of *KG 265*, while being reinforced by two batteries from *Stu.Gesch.Brig. 902*. The boundary between the two divisions would run from La Ronde-Haye (*91.*), via Millières (*91.*), Pissot (*243.*) and Varenguebec (*243.*) to the existing boundary between *U.Gr. Lewandowski* and *U.Gr. Jäger*; it then continued to Rauville-la-Place (*243.*). For the time being, *U.Gr. Jäger* would report to the *243.I.D.*, but the battlegroup would not exist much longer, as its sector was already destined to be taken over by *Ost-Regiments-Gruppe Bunjatschenko*. This would allow the headquarters of *U.Gr. Jäger* to be transferred to the *91. LL.D.*[522]

To the rear of the division, *AOK 7* also gave orders altering the situation on the *Mahlmann-Linie*. The army decided to pull out the *353. I.D.* so that it could relieve the *17. SS-Pz.Gren.Div.* Furthermore, the *77. I.D.* was given responsibility for the entire line, with its centre of gravity on the right, although the *353. I.D.* left some forces in position for the time being.[523]

To bolster the defences in western Normandy (*LXXXIV. A.K.* and *II. Fs.K.*), *AOK 7* would begin to strengthen several divisions with the five announced march battalions and their weapons. First priority was given to the *77. I.D.*, followed by the *91. LL.D.* and the *352. I.D.*[524] Once replenished, the *91. LL.D.* would relieve the unreliable Turkestan battalions.[525]

It was common practice for units to publish an order of battle on the first of the month, and the division issued one on **1 July**. It offers a sobering view of its organic units, although the divisional headquarters and mapping detachment were still at 97% strength and with two light MG's.[526]

For the infantry regiments it was much worse. The headquarters and headquarters company of *GR 1057* were down to 52.3% with no machine guns; its three battalions were at 32.65%, 41.15%, and 27.17%. The companies of the 1st and 3rd Battalions had lost their mortars and machine guns, while the two headquarters had one and two machine guns, respectively. In the 2nd Battalion, the 5th Company had two medium mortars and six light MG's. The other three companies had just two light MG's, and there were no machine guns with the headquarters. The 13th Company was at 55.3%, with two 7.5 cm mountain infantry guns, one Russian 7.62cm infantry gun and a single light MG. The 14th Company was down to 28.5% of its strength, with six *Ofenrohre*, one *5 cm Pak 38* and no machine guns. In all, the regiment had only 13 light MG's and two medium mortars.[527]

GR 1058's condition was similar. The headquarters and headquarters company were at 27.46% strength with no machine guns. The battalions were respectively at 28.25%, 31.25%, and 39% strength. Only the 2nd Battalion headquarters had a light MG; there were no mortars in any of the companies and neither the 1st Battalion nor the MG companies had machine guns. The 5th, 9th and 11th Companies still had five light MG's each, while the 6th, 7th and 10th Companies each had six light MG's. The 13th Company was at 30.95% strength and still armed with two heavy infantry guns, five 7.5 cm mountain infantry guns and three Russian 7.62cm infantry guns; there were no machine guns. Like the *14./1057*, the *14./1058* had no *7,5 cm Pak 40's*; its surviving weapons being nine *Ofenrohre*, two *5 cm Pak 38's*, and two light MG's. This gave the regiment a combined strength of 36 light MG's and no mortars.[528] The numbers and equipment of the regimental anti-tank companies differed from **28 June**. The *5 cm Pak 38's* appear to have been transferred from *Pz.Jg.Kp. 191*. An explanation has not been found for the disappearance of the *Püppchen* and arrival of the *Ofenrohre*.

The regimental headquarters and headquarters battery of *AR 191* had a strength of 88% but no machine guns. The 1st Battalion had a personnel strength of 84%. The 1st Battery still had with two mountain howitzers and 2nd Battery had three; both batteries had two light MG's. The document also shows two Belgian 7.5 cm guns with the 1st Battery and the same number of Czech 7.65 cm guns with the 2nd Battery. The 2nd Battalion had a strength of 74%, with one light MG in the headquarters battery. The battalion's 4th Battery was equipped with four mountain howitzers and two light MG's, while the 5th Battery had just half that number (this battery was also linked to four 7.5 cm guns, presumably German). The 3rd Battalion was in the best condition at 80% of its strength. The headquarters battery with two light MG's; its three batteries each had four anti-tank guns and three light MG's.[529]

The other combat units had been seriously weakened. *Füs.Kp. 91*, which was not listed on **28 June**, was at 40% strength with two MG's. *Pi.Btl. 191* was in a better shape with a personnel strength of 55%. The battalion had one light MG with the headquarters and both companies had four flamethrowers. The 2nd Company was down to three light MG's, but no figures are given for the 1st Company. *Pz.Jg.Kp. 191*, having lost the majority of its anti-tank guns, had

In anticipation of the US offensive towards the south, German forces prepared the terrain for defence. Fighting positions were built and minefields were laid. Many roads, crossroads, bridges and culverts were also mined or prepared for demolition. (NARA)

just two heavy AT guns and two light MG's; its personnel strength was at 35%. *Fla-Kp. 191* still had 53% of its personnel, but no *Flak* guns; instead, it had nine *Ofenrohre* and two light MG's. Personnel losses in the rest of the division (signals battalion and support troops) had been minimal, with strengths between 82-99%. The division's small arms were down to 4,658 K98k's, 23 K98k's with telescopes, 176 G41's, 55 G43's, 137 grenade launchers, 1,042 pistols, and 265 MP's.[530]

More insight into the division's personnel losses can be found in POW records. By the evening of **5 July**, 1,027 men from the division were prisoners in the UK. This date is still too early to include prisoners taken during the **July** offensive on the Cotentin. Because the division's organic components were not in heavy combat after the severing of the peninsula, most of these men must have been captured around or before that time. The largest group of prisoners was obviously from the infantry regiments: 233 men from *GR 1057* (8.3% of its authorised strength) and 634 from *GR 1058* (23.5%). In addition, 5 men from the divisional headquarters (2.7%) were captured, as well as 85 from *AR 191*, 16 from *Pi.Btl. 191* (3.6%), 30 from *Pz.Jg.Kp. 191* (17.6%), 14 from *Füs.Kp. 91* and 10 from the support troops.[531]

As ordered on **29 June**, the *Nordfront* of the *LXXXIV. A.K.* was divided into two main sectors on **1 July**, for which the *243. I.D.* (left) and the *91. LL.D.* (right) were responsible, the latter with the *77. I.D.* To the rear, the boundary between the two ran from Millières in the south, via Varenguebec, to Rauville-la-Place.[532] This put the critical St. Sauveur - La-Haye-du-Puits highway, Hill 121 (Mt. de Doville) and Hill 131 in the *243. I.D.* sector. The headquarters of the *91. LL.D.* was still at La Caponnerie.[533] Due to the order of **29 June**, the *91. LL.D.* front was held by *U.Gr. Lewandowski* (II./1057, III./1058 and II./895) on the left and *U.Gr. Mecklenburg* (II./894) on the right. *Maj.* Mecklenburg was in command of the II./894, having relieved *Maj.* Eitner. This put most of the *265. I.D.* under one of its own officers again.[534]

The records of the 82nd AB offer more details. As expected, the division identified *U.Gr. Lewandowski*, which defended the area south of the Bois de Limors. On the right (east), *GR 1057* was positioned around and east of La Cotellerie. The companies were the 5th Company (formed from remnants of other companies), the 11th Company and, possibly, the 12th Company. From the west of La Cotellerie to Varenguebec were the 7th, 11th and 12th Companies of *GR 1058*.[535]

The division would face the US VIII Corps on **3 July** with the strength and organisation described above. The 82nd AB attacked on the right (northwest) and the 90th ID on the left (southeast). The 325th GIR seized the eastern edge of the La Poterie ridge but not the town. Further west, in the eastern regiment's sector, the Americans took Hill 131 and the surrounding area.[536] The 90th ID attacked with two regiments abreast. On the right, the 359th IR, although engaged in heavy fighting around Prétot (1/359), was able to destroy a German battalion (possibly the *II./895*, which was in the Prétot area) and break through to the high ground north of Ste. Suzanne. The town itself was taken by the 2/359. On the left, the 358th IR captured St. Jores and Les Sablons and reached the railway. At the end of the day, the division had advanced 1,100 metres.[537]

The VIII Corps offensive prevented the *353. I.D.* from relieving the *17. SS-Pz.Gren.Div.* Instead, it was rushed back into combat as the front line was inexorably pushed back.[538] Its withdrawal had already put the *77. I.D.* behind the *91. LL.D.* and, that evening, the *77.I.D.* was ordered to take command of the *91. LL.D.'s* combat troops, while the headquarters, signals and supply troops were at the disposal of the *LXXXIV. A.K.*[539] Due to the position of the *77. I.D.* on the right of the *Mahlmann-Linie*, it could only take over those units that were nearby or to the rear. This meant that it took command of *KG 265*, while certain organic elements were subordinated to the *353. I.D.* in the centre or to the *243. I.D.* on the left.[540] The *91. LL.D.* would not become operational again until **17 July**. Until that time, its troops continued to fight with other divisions.

Sometime after the start of the **July** offensive, the artillery on the *Nordfront* was reorganised and moved south of the Sèves River. *AR 353*, as well as *AR 177* and *AR zbV 621* took up positions around Périers, while the newly arrived *Fs.Art.Abt. 5* (*5. Fj.Div.*) was deployed northeast of Périers. *AR 191* had moved to the left flank, roughly in the area Le Buisson - La Feuillie - La Martinerie (all southeast of Lessay). To its left, near the coast, was *AR 243* in the La Bourgogne - Pirou - Créances area.[541]

Some information on the losses of the division during the VIII Corps offensive have been discovered for **3-6 July**. At this time, the corps captured 59 men from *GR 1057*, 52 from *GR 1057*, 7 from the *II./AR 191* and 6 from *Pz.Jg.Kp. 191*.[542] These figures can be compared to men reported as POW's in the UK. Compared to **5 July**, the numbers had only increased by 68 to 1,095

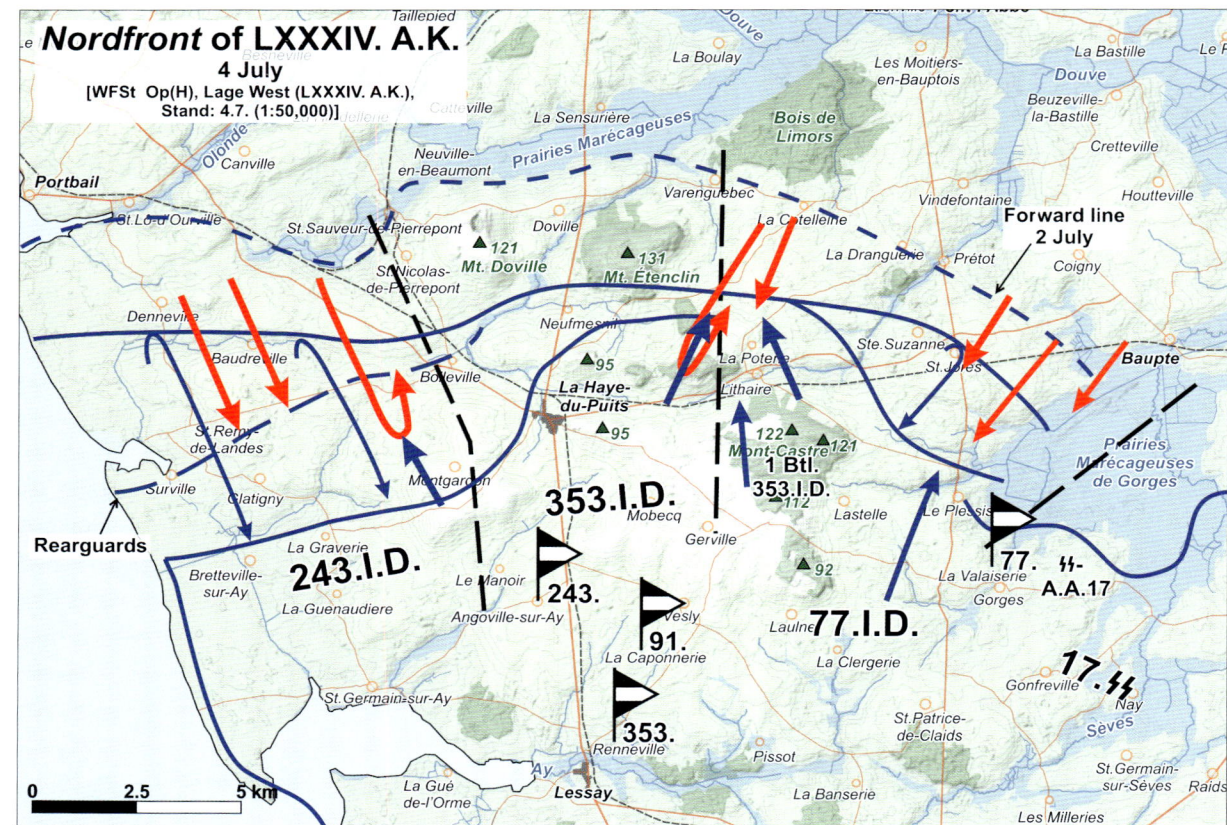

When VIII Corps started its offensive against the Nordfront on 3 July, the division's lines were pushed back. On the 4th the situation became so critical that the entire Nordfront had to be pulled back to the Mahlmann-Linie. The 77. I.D. headquarters took over the troops of the 91. LL.D., dissolving the division as a fighting force. (WFSt Op (H),Lage West, Stand: 4.7.44, 1:50.000)

by the **14th**. The number of prisoners from *GR 1057* had risen to 268 (+35) and from *GR 1058* to 655 (+21). For the divisional headquarters, *AR 191*, and *Fla-Kp. 191*, the new figures were 6 (+1), 94 (+9), and 2 (+2), respectively. No new prisoners were reported for *Pi.Btl. 191, Pz.Jg.Kp. 191, Füs.Kp. 91* or the support troops.[543] These minor increases suggest that the numbers for **14 July** might only have related to prisoners taken before the **July** offensive.

While some of the division's troops continued at the front, the headquarters and other units were sent to Lessay to establish and occupy a new defensive line — the so-called *Wasserlinie*. The headquarters was put in charge, but it lacked the forces to effectively carry this out. The divisional headquarters was in La Fresnerie (2 km west of Périers).[544] Fearing airborne landings on the night of **4-5 July** (possibly to destroy the bridges on the east of the Lande de Lessay), AOK 7 ordered *SS-Pz.Abt. 17*, reinforced with *SS-Pz. Aufkl.Abt. 17* (minus its 2nd Company), to move southeast of the threatened area (Lande de Bangard).[545] According to *Gen.* von Choltitz (commanding general of the *LXXXIV. A.K.*), *Obst.* König was the local area commander in case a threat emerged.[546] About the same time, the *2. SS-Pz.Div.* received orders to advance to Périers. AOK 7 ordered the elements from the *17. SS-Pz. Gren.Div.* to be included in a *Das Reich* battlegroup. This makes *Obst.* König's exact role confusing. Being in charge of construction of the *Wasserlinie*, it is likely he was also responsible for the general area south of the line.[547]

On **10 July**, the division's frontline troops were attached to the *353. I.D.*

Together, they occupied an 8 km front with a combined combat strength of just 1,250 men.[548] The idea was discussed as to whether to attach the artillery and transport capacity to the *5. Fj.Div.*, which was arriving without these elements. The remaining troops would then be attached to the *77. I.D.*, allowing the division to take responsibility for a larger area. *Obst.* König was considered for command of the *243. I.D.* but *Gen.* Pemsel did not think the change was necessary, so *Obst.* Klosterkemper stayed in charge.[549]

From **6-10 July**, the *Nordfront* was temporarily reinforced by a battlegroup from *Das Reich*. When this force was withdrawn, the front could no longer be held. Over the next few days, the troops moved south, reaching the *Wasserlinie* on the night of **13-14 July**, at which time the front was stable.[550] The following period of relative quiet allowed yet another reorganisation. The headquarters and support troops of the *77. I.D.* were withdrawn to St. Malo. On **17 July**, the *91. LL.D.* took command in the *77. I.D.* sector and moved its headquarters to Le Rouillais (1.5 km southwest of St. Sauveur-Lendelin).[551]

The *91. LL.D.* existed once again as a fighting force and, as a result, a new organisational document was drawn up that laid out its composition on **17 July**. As can be expected, the majority of its forces were taken from the *77. I.D.*[552]

The division's own infantry was apparently attached to the *243. I.D.*, although this was only reported on the **20th**. They were led by the headquarters of *GR 1058* (with its headquarters company) and consisted of the *III./1058* with four companies and the *II./1057* with its 5th and 9th Companies — all of which had belonged to *U.Gr. Lewandowski*. The heavy weapons were infantry guns organised in a mountain company, a platoon with heavy infantry guns and a platoon with Russian 7.62 cm guns.[553]

The infantry available to the *91. LL.D.* on **17 July** consisted of *GR 1050* and *FJR 15*. The grenadier regiment had few organic units. The infantry came from two battalions of *GR 1049*; the *I./1049* with three companies and the *III./1049* with four organic companies and one formed from *KG 265*. The 1st Battalion was supported by the 13th Companies of *GR 1049* and *GR 1050*, while the 3rd Battalion had the *14./1050* along with the 13th and 14th Companies of *GR 896*. *FJR 15* was listed with the typical organisation of an airborne regiment (regimental headquarters and headquarters company, three battalions with four companies each and three specialised companies: 13th through 15th Companies); moreover, it was reinforced by a company from *Fs.Pz.Jg.Abt. 5*.[554]

The division included a large number of reserve and emergency units, organised under the headquarters of *GR 1049*. These elements included remnants of *GR 1050*: The *II./1050* was present with four companies, along with a company from what remained of the *I./1050*. The *14./1049* was also listed, but it was not at company strength. Another headquarters merged into this ad hoc collection of troops was that of the battered *I./AR 177*. It was in charge of what was left of the battalion — barely battery strength — and also *Pz.Jg.Kp. 177*. The headquarters of *GR 896* was available, but it had no troops under its command. In contrast, the headquarters of *GR 1057* (*Mügge*) had three emergency companies, with men taken from the trains of *GR 1057, GR 1058* and *AR 191*. *Fla-Kp. 191* and *Pz.Jg.Kp. 191* were both listed as platoons and may have been attached to *GR 1057*.[555] *Fla-Kp. 191* had recently returned and, until the previous day, had been operating under the *353. I.D.*[556]

The operational artillery was under *AR 177* and consisted of the regiment's two remaining battalions and the *I./AR 265*, as well as the *I./AR 353* and *Fs.Art.Abt. 5* with two batteries. Attached to the *III./AR 177* were the *3./Pz.Jg.Abt. 352* and *Fla-Kp. 177*.[557]

Engineer units were plentiful. The *3./Pi.Btl. 319* was attached to *Pi. Btl. 177* and the *2./Pi.Btl. 265* to *Pi.Btl. 191*. In addition, *Bau-Pi.Btl. 94* was available with three companies and a support column, but it was most likely committed to building defensive positions rather than combat. The final reinforcement for *KG 91. I.D.* was *Stu.Gesch.Brig. 902* with two batteries.[558]

While the *Nordfront* had witnessed intense fighting, there had been significant activity in the east too. On the Carentan-Périers isthmus, the *2. SS-Pz.Div.* relieved much of the *17. SS-Pz.Gren.Div.*, taking command of the area on **11 July** and becoming the *91. LL.D.*'s new neighbour.[559] More units from *Das Reich* were on their way to the front. Once they arrived, the boundary between the two divisions would need to be redrawn and this was discussed by *AOK 7* on **18 July**.[560] Ultimately, no changes were made and the boundary was kept west of "Sèves Island".[561]

On **20 July**, *Kampfgruppe 91. I.D.* was again reorganised as illustrated on a new organisational document. *FJR 15* left, leaving only its anti-tank company with *GR 1050*. Compared to the situation on **17 July**, *GR 1050* had been broken up. The headquarters of *GR 1050* was now in charge of three company-sized formations: The *I./1050*, the *II./1049* and *GR 894*. Support was from an airborne AT company and the *14./895*.[562]

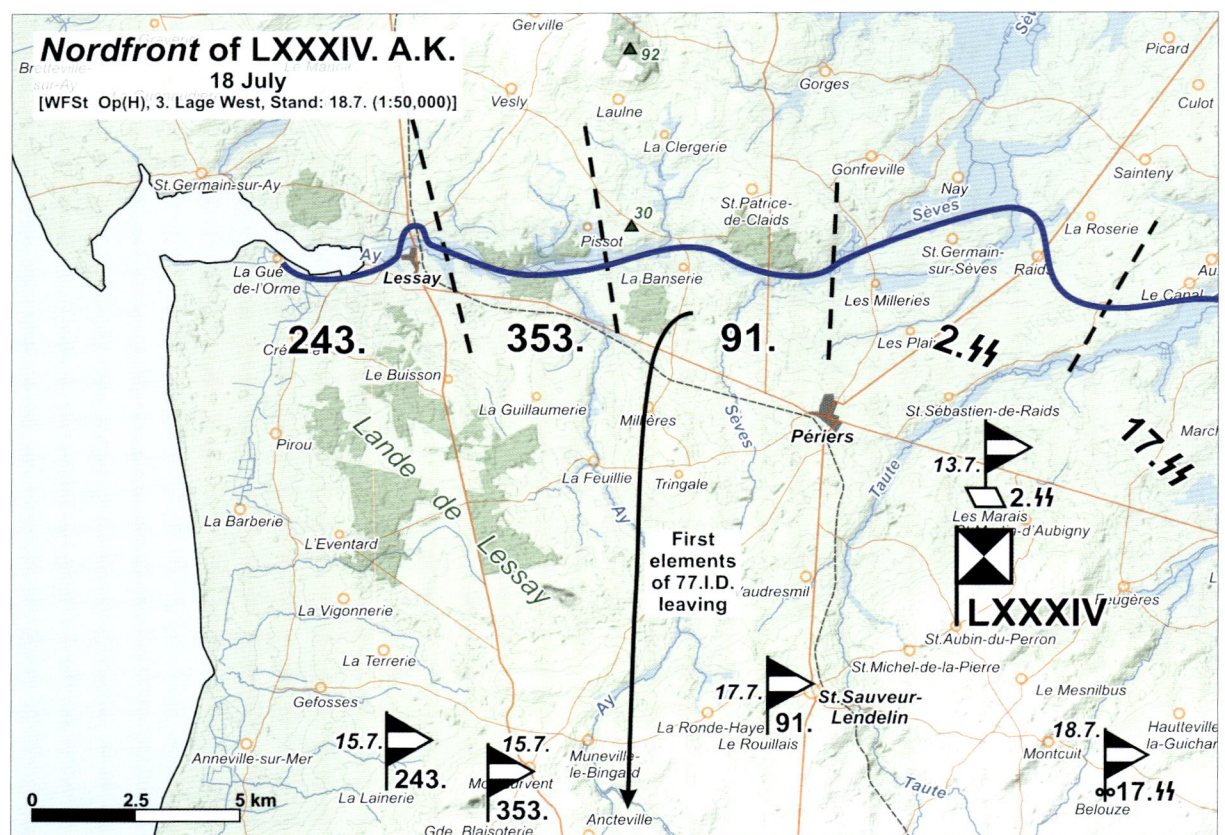

After more than a week of heavy fighting, the VIII Corps offensive forced the German lines back to the Wasserlinie. Now the 91. LL.D. headquarters relieved the 77. I.D., allowing the transfer of that division back to Bretagne for refitting. Yet, most of its troops remained, now subordinated to the 91. LL.D. (WFSt Op (H), 4. Lage West, 19.7.44, 1:50.000)

GR 1049 had been "reactivated" and comprised its 1st Battalion (two companies) and its 3rd Battalion (four companies). Attached to the regiment were the four heavy weapons companies from the *77. I.D.*, although the *14./1049* was only at platoon strength. The AT platoons from the *14./894* and the *14./896* from *KG 265* further reinforced the regiment.[563]

Support from *Stu.Gesch.Brig. 902* was unchanged: It had its headquarters and its 1st and 2nd Batteries. There were also no changes among the engineers. The emergency units were the same, except the battery from *AR 191* was no longer listed. Artillery formations changed little (*Fs.Art.Abt. 5* was no longer listed and the *13./896* was attached to the *I./AR 265*).[564]

On **21 July**, the *LXXXIV. A.K.* compiled an overview of its artillery elements, including their organisation and weaponry. *AR 191* was subordinated to the *353. I.D.* and still consisted of its 1st and 3rd Battalions. The 1st Battalion included the 1st, 2nd and 4th Batteries; the first two batteries with 7.5 cm cannons and the 4th Battery with four mountain howitzers. The 7.5 cm guns can be identified as *7,5 cm F.K. 235(b)'s* in the 1st Battery and *7,65 cm F.K. 17(t)'s* in the 2nd Battery. The 3rd Battalion was almost at original strength with its 7th through 9th Batteries on hand. This demonstrates that the 8th Battery had finally returned to its battalion. The 7th Battery was down one gun, and the other batteries still had four each. The *II./AR 191* was still operating on the Carentan - Périers front under *SS-Pz.Art.Rgt. 2* with a single battery from the *91. LL.D.* This battery was outfitted with four 7.5 cm cannons, probably *7,5 cm F.K.16 nA's*. Its presence suggests it was exchanged with the 8th Battery. In addition, there were four light and 2 heavy infantry guns with the *II./AR 191*, possibly from the *13./914*.[565]

The document also looks at the artillery operating under the *91. LL.D.* These elements were commanded by *AR 177* and included the same five battalions listed on the **17th**. *Fs.Art.Abt. 5*, which had not been on the organisational documents of the **20th**, was shown with three batteries and six guns. The batteries of *AR 177* itself remained strong, still possessing most of their original guns: The 4th Battery still had four; the 5th, 7th and 8th Batteries three each. The 9th Battery (combined *Fla-Kp. 177* and the *3./Pz.Jg.Abt. 352*) had two 3.7 cm *Flak's* and seven 2 cm *Flak's*. In the *I./AR 265*, no *Flak* were shown, but the 2nd and 3rd Batteries still had four guns, while the 9th Battery had three. The *I./AR 353* had 11 artillery pieces, with the 2nd Battery having three.[566]

On **21 July**, *AOK 7* decided to pull the entire *353. I.D.* (and two tank companies from *Das Reich*) from the *Nordfront*. To close the resulting gap, the *91. LL.D.* and the *243. I.D.* sectors were widened without either division receiving more troops The. *353. I.D.* was withdrawn on the night of **22 July**.[567] To do this, *GR 941* was relieved by the *II./1050* and *GR 1058* by the *III./921*. *GR 1058* was then transferred to the *353.I.D.* and used to relieve *GR 942*, which was to be transferred to its divisional assembly area.[568] In this manner, *GR 1058* left the *243. I.D.* and re-joined the *91. LL.D.* via the *353. I.D.*

On the **22nd**, *AOK 7* issued new orders for the *LXXXIV. A.K.* to reorganise its artillery. The corps was to release *Fs.Art.Abt. 5* from its attachment to the *91. LL.D.*, so the battalion could support *FJR 15*, which had been ordered to the *II. Fs.K.* This loss of artillery was probably why two light battalions from *AR 353* were to continue supporting the *Nordfront*. In addition, the *AR 191* headquarters was to transfer to the *5. Fj.Div.* and command the artillery in that area.[569]

The next day, the *LXXXIV. A.K.* updated *AOK 7* on the condition of its troops. Put simply, little remained of the original *91. LL.D.*, but despite its heavy losses it had a combat rating of III (*Kampfwert III*).[570] The many attachments to the division were largely responsible for this rating.[571]

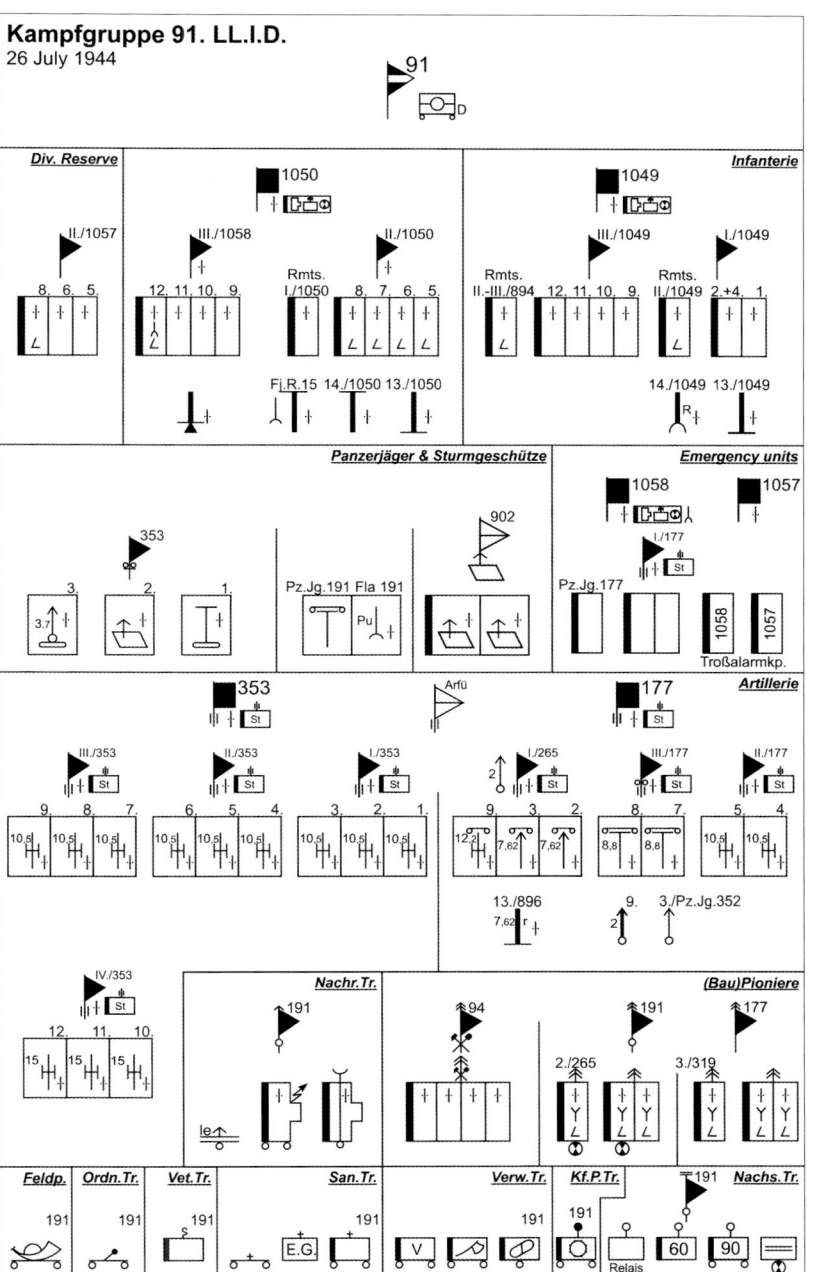

On 26 July, while Operation Cobra was starting to pick up momentum, the division drew up its final Order of Battle. As before, KG 91. LL.D. only still existed as a fighting due to numerous attached formations. (T78 R672)

The division still had two organic infantry battalions, but these were only cadre personnel. A third, strong battalion was with the *243. I.D.*; probably the *III./1058*. The division also had a second weaker battalion, the *II./1057*, but it is missing from the report. Five of the battalions operating under the *91. LL.D.* originated from the *77. I.D.*; of these, the *III./1049* and the *II./1050* were classified as average, the *I./1049* as weak and the last two were worn out (*II./1049* and *I./1050*). A battalion in similar condition was all that was left of *KG* 265.[572]

The anti-tank troops were also weak with just two heavy AT guns organic to the division. An additional five and three heavy AT guns were attached from *KG* 265 and the *5. Fj.Div.* (*1./Fs.Pz.Jg.Abt. 5*), respectively.[573]

As on the **21st**, none of the division's organic artillery was available. Three light and three 8.8 cm batteries had been dispatched to the *243. I.D.*, while another light battery was serving with *Das Reich*.[574]

Mobility of the division's organic units stood at 90% for horse-drawn and 60% for motorised units. Of the attached units, horse-drawn strength was at 75% and motorised at 50%.[575]

A final organisational document shows the division's organisation at the time of *Operation Cobra*. On **26 July**, *KG 91. I.D.* still consisted of a large number of sub-units with the bulk of its infantry from *GR 1049* and *1050*, albeit with a different organisation. Although the document shows weapon symbols, no numbers are given.[576]

GR 1049 was listed with its headquarters company, two infantry battalions and its two heavy weapons companies. The 14th Company was equipped with *Ofenrohre*, but the condition of the 13th Company is less clear. The 2nd Battalion, now reduced to company size, had returned to the regiment; however, it was the only formation listed with mortars. The remnants of *GR 894* were attached. This left *GR 1049* with eight infantry companies.[577]

The situation for *GR 1050* was somewhat better, and it resembled a regiment again in terms of its organisation. It had a regimental headquarters company, two infantry battalions and four heavy weapons companies. One of these battalions was the *II./1050*, which was no longer a divisional reserve. Each of its four companies had mortars (no numbers provided). What remained of the 1st Battalion, reduced to company size, was attached to the 2nd Battalion. It was supported by three heavy weapons companies: The 13. and the *14./1050* and the anti-tank company from the *5. Fj.Div.* The regiment's second battalion was the *III./1058*, which had returned from the *243. I.D.* It still had four companies and a mountain infantry gun company in support; the 12th Company had mortars and anti-tank weapons.[578]

The divisional reserve was the *II./1057*, which had also returned to divisional command, and it was composed of the 5th, 6th and 8th Companies (only the latter company was equipped with mortars.) The division's emergency troops (*Alarmeinheiten*) included the headquarters of *GR 1057* and *1058*; the headquarters company of *GR 1058* was also available. Furthermore, the emergency company that had been formed from e trains of both regiments still existed. The headquarters and headquarters battery of the of *I./AR 177* and two "companies" (remnants of its batteries) were also available. *Pz.Jg.Kp. 177* completed the emergency forces. The engineers matched the organisation document from the **20th** with the reinforced *Pi.Btl. 177* and *191*.[579]

Anti-tank and armoured support remained impressive, at least in numbers. *Pz.Jg.Abt. 353* was attached along with *Stu.Gesch.Brig. 902* with its two batteries. *Fla-Kp. 191* (with *Püppchen*) and *Pz.Jg.Kp. 191* were also available, albeit in platoon strength. For reasons unknown, the units of *Pz.Jg.Abt. 353* were depicted as platoons.[580]

The number of artillery units had increased and were commanded by an artillery headquarters, apparently still that of *Obst.* Triepel (*H.K.A.R. 1261*). The artillery was organised in two regiments: *AR 353* in its entirety and *AR 177*. The latter still consisted of the *II.* and the *III./AR 177* reinforced by the *I./AR 265*. Compared to the situation on **20 July**, *AR 177* had only relinquished command of the *I./AR 353*.[581]

While on the *Wasserlinie*, the division did not take part in any serious fighting. After the removal of the *353. I.D.*, the new boundary between the *91. LL.D.* and the *243. I.D.* ran from Orval (southwest of Coutances) via Bactol to Village ès Noels. To the east, the line with *Das Reich* ran from Courcy via St. Sauveur-de-Lendelin to west of Gorges.[582]

Attacks against the *Nordfront* of the *LXXXIV. A.K.* began at 06:30 on **26 July**, striking the *91. LL.D.* and *Das Reich*. Fighting was reported around La Banserie but most attacks were repulsed and the lines remained intact.[583] The boundary with the *243. I.D.* had changed and now ran south from Village ès Noels (north of the Ay) via the railway crossing east of Lessay, along the western edge of Montsurvent, to the eastern edge of Gratot and Bricqueville-

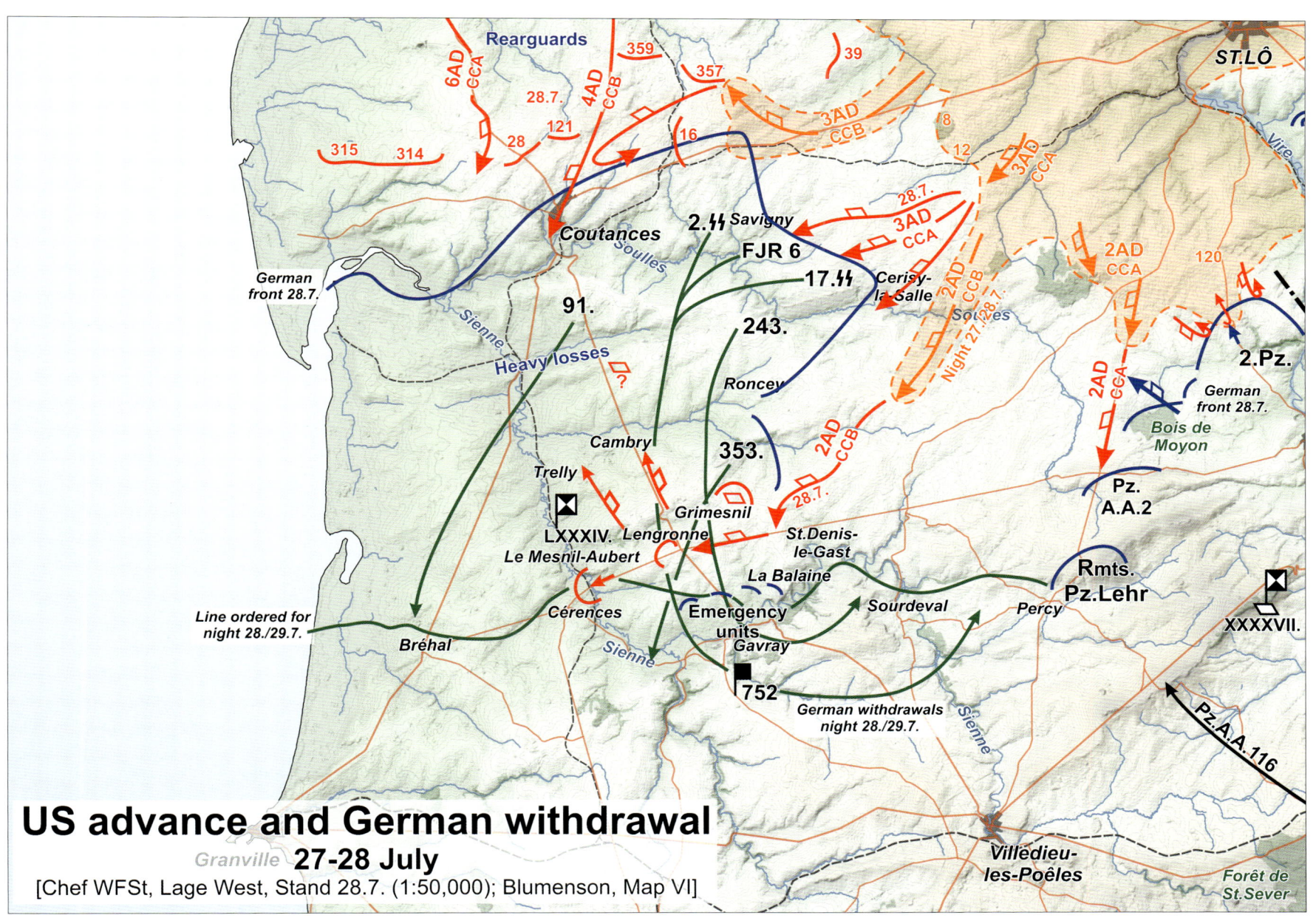

US advance and German withdrawal 27-28 July

[Chef WFSt, Lage West, Stand 28.7. (1:50,000); Blumenson, Map VI]

As American forces began to exploit their breakthrough west of St.Lô, the Germans attempted to save what was left of LXXXIV. A.K. and build new lines to stop the American advance. Being less mobile than its left neighbour (243. I.D.) the 91. LL.D. was left to hold the left wing, along the coast. (WFSt Op (H), Lage West, Stand 28.7.44, 1:50.000) la-Blouette. The boundary with *Das Reich* ran south from the road junction southwest of La Doderie via the western edge of Longuet (today Les Milleries) to Périers and then as before.[584]

Although the *Nordfront* had held, it became untenable as American forces broke through west of St. Lô, threatening to cut off the *Nordfront*. The next few days were characterised by withdrawals, makeshift defence lines and more withdrawals. The *243. I.D.* moved east, leaving the *91. LL.D.* to hold the left flank along the coast.[585] On the **26ᵗʰ**, the division, along with all forces on the left of the *LXXXIV. A.K.* (*Nordfront*), was ordered to withdraw to the south overnight (**26-27 July**). The new main line of resistance would be established from St.Sébastian-de-Raids in the east, via Millières to Pirou on the west coast (some 3-4 km south of the *Wasserlinie*). *AOK 7*'s desire to withdraw to a line even further south (west of St. Lô to Geffosses) and to populate the other line only with combat outposts, had already been rejected.[586]

The withdrawal generally proceeded according to plan.[587] As the situation continued to deteriorate on the **27ᵗʰ**, plans were adjusted accordingly. By early evening, the realisation dawned that establishing and holding the line Geffosses - St. Sauveur-Lendelin (4 km south of the previous line) was probably unrealistic. Instead, *Ob.West* ordered a withdrawal to a line running east from the river valley southwest of Coutances, via Coutances roughly to Dangy (15 km south of the lines ordered on the **26ᵗʰ**).[588]

On the morning of **28 July**, the command post of the *91. LL.D.* was at Orval, southwest of Coutances.[589] That evening, the division was still withdrawing to a line running northeast and north of Coutances to Tourville-sur-Sienne near the coast. The right-hand neighbour was a mixed force of *Götz von Berlichingen*, *Das Reich* and *FJR 6*.[590] The withdrawals continued, and the next morning it was reported that the *LXXXIV. A.K.* was pulling back to the line Percy - Sourdeval - west of Sourdeval - La Baleine - Gavray - Cérences - Bréhal - coast. The division would be responsible for the left flank, from Cérences to the coast, with the *353. I.D.* on its right.[591] Again, there was a considerable distance to be covered and, that evening, the division put up a weak security line stretching north from Cérences via Le Mesnil-Aubert to Trelly. The front here faced east. To defend the area from Trelly to the coast against attacks from the north, security forces were positioned in Quettreville, Hérenguerville and Montmartin-sur-Mer. The rest of the division was arriving in the area of Bréhal, while the artillery had taken up position in Muneville-sur-Mer. As this was taking place, Trelly and Les Mesnil-Aubert were already under attack.[592]

On the night of **29-30 July**, the *LXXXIV. A.K.* continued its efforts and build a blocking position from Bricqueville-sur-Mer (on the coast north of Bréhal) to Percy. The division defended the corps' left flank, which ran along various streams and rivers, primarily the Sienne. Towns in the area included Cérences and Ver. To the east, units from the *353. I.D.*, the *243. I.D.* and *Das Reich* were deployed to cover the line to Percy. The divisional command post was moved further south, to La Table, south of the Granville - Beauchamps road (D924). The infantry regiments had dwindled to 200 men, and the frontline was little more than individual scattered strongpoints. A battalion of eastern troops, probably *Georg.Inf.Btl. 797*, was deployed on the left. The division's right flank, around Ver, was held by a weak company of construction personnel and this sector was transferred to the division on the right.[593]

To secure his deep right flank against armour, *Obst.* König sent the *III./AR 191* to the crossroads at Le Repas (D924 & D35, north of Folligny) and ordered it to take up direct-fire positions with its 8.8 cm guns. In the morning, the last two assault guns were knocked out around Cérences. Enemy tanks were reported everywhere. Around noon, it was learned that the Americans had advanced even further, and were now south of La Haye-Pesnel. To prevent the division from being attacked from the rear, *Füs.Kp. 91* was rushed to the town with two infantry guns.[594]

Once again, there was no choice but to pull back. By afternoon, the front stood north of the Granville - Beauchamps road (D924, 8 km south of Cérences). There was no contact with friendly troops on the right. The situation grew even more dire when the eastern troops surrendered *en masse* around 13:00, leaving a 3 km gap on the left flank.[595]

The Allies continued to push ever closer to the divisional headquarters. As losses mounted, the order was given to assemble all troops on the high ground to the north.[596] *Obst.* König also ordered the naval installations at Granville be destroyed and the personnel withdrawn to Avranches. The naval radio station signed off at 20:34. The road to Granville was open to the Americans. The remnants of *Georg.Inf.Btl. 797*, 50 men, still held a line south of the town.[597]

At dusk, what was left of the division pulled out. The objective was to occupy the range of hills north of Avranches (10 km south of the D924) to block the roads leading into the town. This proved to be impossible as the Americans had already reached the hills and town itself.[598]

At 01:45 on **31 July**, H.Gr. B informed *Ob.West* that the Americans were in Avranches.[599] The gap to the east of the division proved to be a fatal weak point in the German defences. While trying to hold its front, the *91. LL.D.* had been outflanked by Combat Command B of 4th Armored Division, whose western column had advanced through Cérences, La Haye-Pesnel and Sartilly to Avranches, simply bypassing German troops on its flanks.[600]

The division was now cut off and isolated. Attempts to break out to the south were almost all unsuccessful. A bold course of action was taken. At low tide, under cover of darkness, the remnants of the division crossed the Baie du Mont-St. Michel at St. Léonard towards Le Rivage.[601] At 08:20, *Maj.* Seiffert (operations officer of the *77. I.D.*) informed the *XXV. A.K.* that *Obst.* König and several officers had successfully crossed the mud flats.[602]

After reaching Pontorson, what remained of the division was handed over to the headquarters of the *77. I.D.* (*Gruppe Bacherer*). The *91. LL.D.* headquarters was ordered to collect and assemble its rear area support troops, which had earlier been ordered south, and use them to build companies. The headquarters was tasked with blocking assignments and the construction of new positions.[603]

Meanwhile, some elements had crossed the American advance to Avranches and, on the morning of **31 July**, took up covering positions near Tirepied (4 km east of Avranches) facing north and west.[604] These may be the units that were later ordered to close gaps in the direction of Avranches in support of the *116. Pz.Div.*[605]

After his escape from Normandy, *Obst.* König was put in charge of the defence of Rennes, where a significant force was being assembled. The colonel arrived on the evening of **1 August**. By then, the initial American attacks on Rennes had been successfully turned back. After two more days of fighting, the force was ordered to pull out on the night of **3-4 August** and withdraw to St. Nazaire. *Obst.* König personally led the motorised units that reached St. Erblon on the 4th. Moving only at night, the troops reached Pléchâtel on **5 August** and the area north of Langon on the 6th. On the 7th, they reached the area west of Campbon and made contact with the *265. I.D.*. Finally, the troops reached Grière (northwest of Savenay) on the 8th. The horse-drawn units arrived the following night, and all forces were integrated into *Festung St. Nazaire*.[606]

The *91. LL.D.* was formally disbanded on **10 August**.[607] Administratively, the end came on **30 November** with a report on new assignments for the remaining units, which still included most of the support troops. Almost all of the division's surviving units (including the division headquarters and the entire *AR 191*) were used to rebuild the *344. I.D.*[608]

A small number of combat troops managed to escape Normandy and survive the journey to the German or Dutch border. Since the division no longer existed, their fate and operations during this chaotic period are beyond the scope of this book.[609]

Obst. König was briefly put in command of the *344. I.D.*[610] Although none of the infantry units from the *91. LL.D.* remained, *GR 1057* and *1058* were rebuilt and also incorporated into the *344. I.D.*. All of the other forces were renumbered to match their new division.[611] In April 1945, the division was trapped in the Kausche Pocket and captured by the Soviets.

Operation Cobra led to heavy German losses in men and equipment. With limited mobility, many infantry formations had little hope of escaping the rapid American advance. (NARA)

APPENDIX

The organisation of 7. Armee from D-Day to 24 July

Glossary
German Military Symbols
Comparative Table of Ranks
Terminology and Abbreviations

(Archives du Calvados 10Fi/2, photo 147)

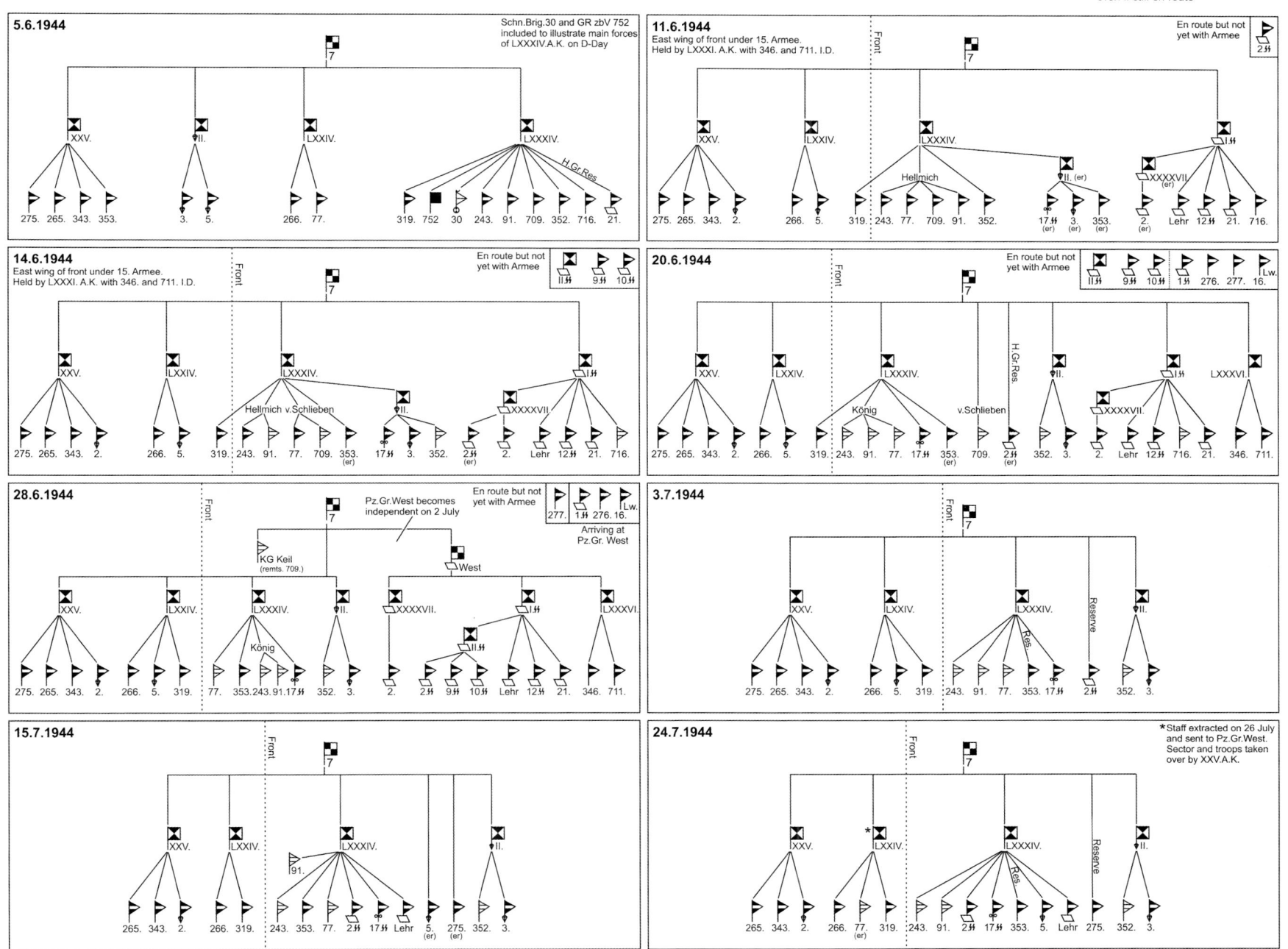

German military symbols (mid & late war)

Only most important (versions) shown
Symbols are commonly combined

Units (headquarters)

Symbol	German	English
	Heeresgruppen-kommando	(Field) Army HQ
	Armee Oberkommando	Field Army HQ
	Generalkommando	Corps HQ
	Divisionskommando	Division HQ
	Brigadestab	Brigade HQ
	Regimentsstab	Regimental HQ
	Abteilungsstab / Bataillonsstab	Battalion HQ
	Kompanie	Company (HQ)
	Zug	Platoon (HQ)

Branches

Symbol	German	English
	Infanterie	Infantry
	Panzer	Armoured trps.
	Sturmartillerie	Assault artillery
	Kradschützen	Motorcycle trps.
	Radfahreinheiten	Bicycle trps.
	Aufklärungstruppe	Reconnaissance trps.
	Kavallerie / Reiter	Cavalry / Mounted trps.
	Gebirgstruppen	Mountain trps.
	Fallschirm	Parachute / Airborne trps.
	Pioniere	(Combat) Engineers
	Festungspioniere	Fortress engineers
	Baupioniere	Construction trps.
	Artillerie	Artillery trps.
	Panzerjäger	Anti-tank trps.
	Flak	Anti-aircraft trps.
	Nebeltruppen	Smoke / Rocket launcher trps
	Nachrichtentruppen	Signals trps.
	Nachschubtruppen	Supply services
	Fahrtruppen	Transport troops
	Sanitätsdienste	Medical services
	Veterinärdienste	Veterinary services
	Feldpostdienste	Army postal services
	Feldgendarmerie	Military police

Battalions

Symbol	German	English
	Infanterie-Btl.	Infantry bn.
	Fallschirmjäger-Btl.	Parachute (infantry) bn.
	Panzergrenadier-Btl.	Armoured infantry bn.
	Artillerie-Abt.	Artillery bn.
	Pionier-Btl.	Engineer bn.
	Panzer-Abt.	Tank bn.
	Sturmgeschütz-Abt.	Assault gun bn.
	Panzerjäger-Abt.	Anti-tank bn.
	Flak-Abt.	Anti-aircraft bn.
	Aufklärungs-Abt.	Reconnaissance bn.
	Nachrichten-Abt.	Signals bn.
	Maschinengewehr-Btl.	Machine gun bn.
	Festungs-Pionier-Btl.	Fortress-engineer bn.
	Bau-Pionier-Btl.	Construction bn.
	Festungs-Stamm-Btl.	Fortress cadre bn.
	Panzeraufklärungs-Abt.	Armoured recon. bn.
	Werfer-Abt.	Rocket-launcher bn.
	Kdr.d.Div.Nachs. Tr. (Kodina)	Commander of the div. suppy troops

Mobility

Symbol	German	English
	Kraftrad	Motorcycle
	Rad	Bicycle
	teil motorisiert	partially motorised
	motorisiert	Motorised
	Halbketten	Halftrack
	selbstfahr / Ketten	Self-propelled (SP) / tracked
	Stellung	Position(al)
	unter Panzer / Beton (im Bau)	Under steel / concrete (under construction)
	Unter Panzer / Beton (fertig)	Under steel / concrete (finished)
	Panzer	Tank
	Sturmgeschütz	Assault gun
	Jagdpanzer	Tank destroyer
	Schützenpanzerwagen	Armoured personnel carrier
	Panzer-Spähwagen	Armoured recon car

Companies, batteries, columns and below

Symbol	German	English
	Infanteriekompanie	Infantry co.
	Reiterzug	Cavalry / Mounted pltn.
	Pionierkompanie	(Combat) Engineer co.
	Baupionierkompanie	Construction co.
	Stabsbatterie	HQ bttr.
	Panzerkompanie	Tank co.
	Kraftradmeldezug	Motorcycle messenger pltn.
	Radfahrzug	Bicycle pltn.
	Panzerjägerkompanie	Anti-tank co.
	Infanteriegeschüzkp.	Infantry-gun co.
	Flakbttr. / Flugabwehrkompanie	Flak battr. / Anti-aircraft co.
	Haubitzebatterie	Howitzer battr.
	Kanonenbatterie	Gun / Cannon battr.
	Werferbatterie	Rocket-launcher battr.
	Artillerievermessungstrupp	Artillery-survey section
	Funkkompanie	Wireless co.
	Fernsprechkompanie	Telephone co.
	Feldfernkabelkompanie	Field trunk cable co.
	Kraftfahrkp. 90 ton	Motor-transport co. (90-tonnes)
	Fahrschwadron 60 ton	Horse-drawn transport troop (60-tonnes)
	Kolonne (30 ton)	Horse-drawn transport column (30-tonnes)
	leichte Kol. (mot) (15 ton)	Light motor-transport column (15-tonnes)
	Nachschubzug	Supply pltn.
	Werkstattkp. (mot)	Workshop co. (mot.)
	Waffenmeisterzug	Ordnance-repair platoon (mot.)
	Bäckereikp. (t.mot)	Bakery co (part. mot.)
	Divisions-Verpflegungs-Amt (mot)	Divisional supply office (mot.)
	Verpflegungskp. (mot)	Supply co. (mot.)
	Schlächtereikp. (mot)	Butcher co. (mot.)
	Feldlazaret (mot)	Field hospital (mot.)
	Sanitätskompanie (mot)	Medical co. (mot.)
	Entgiftungszug	Decontamination pltn.
	Krankenkraftwagenzug	Ambulance pltn.
	Veterinärkompanie	Veterinary co.
	Feldgendarmerie-zug (t.mot)	Military police pltn. (part. mot.)
	Feldpostamt (mot)	Field post office (mot.)

Weapons & units details

Symbol	German	English
	Haubitze	Howitzer
	Panzerbüchse / Granatbüchse	Anti-tank rifle / converted to grenade launcher
8,8	Raketenpanzerbüchse	Anti-tank rocket launcher (Ofenrohr / Panzerschreck)
	Maschinengewehr	Machine gun
	Flammenwerfer	Flame thrower
	(Nebel)Werfer	Rocket launcher
	Granatwerfer	Mortar
	Pak	Anti-tank gun
	Infanterie-Geschütz	Infantry gun
	Kanone	Gun / Cannon
	Flak	Anti-aircraft gun
le	leicht	light
m	mittler	medium
s	schwer	heavy

Letters & abbreviations

	German	English
D	Divisions-	Divisional
E	Eisenbahn-	Railroad
K	Korps-	Corps
St	Stabs-	HQ

Country of origin

	German	English
b	belgisch	Belgian
e	englisch	British
f	französisch	French
h	holländisch	Dutch
i	italienisch	Italian
j	jugoschlawisch	Yugoslavian
p	polnisch	Polish
r	russisch	Russian / Soviet
t	Tschechisch	Czech

Comparative Table of Ranks

Heer	Waffen-SS	US Equivalent	UK Equivalent
Enlisted men			
*Soldat**	*Mann; Schütze*	Private	Private
*Obersoldat**	*Oberschütze*	Private First Class	Senior Private
Gefreiter	*Sturmmann*	Acting Corporal	Lance Corporal
Obergefreiter	*Rottenführer*	Corporal	Lance Corporal
Stabsgefreiter	-	Administrative Corporal	Lance Corporal
NCOs			
Unteroffizier	*Unterscharführer*	Sergeant	Corporal
Unterfeldwebel; Unterwachtmeister	*Scharführer*	Staff Sergeant	Sergeant
Feldwebel; Wachtmeister	*Oberscharführer*	Technical Sergeant	Staff Sergeant
Oberfeldwebel; Oberwachtmeister	*Hauptscharführer*	Master Sergeant	Sergeant Major
Stabsfeldwebel; Stabswachtmeister	*Sturmscharführer*	Sergeant Major	Regimental Sergeant Major
Officers			
Leutnant; Assistenzarzt; Veterinär	*Untersturmführer*	Second Lieutenant	Second Lieutenant
Oberleutnant; Oberarzt; Oberveterinär	*Obersturmführer*	First Lieutenant	Lieutenant
Hauptmann; Rittmeister; Stabsarzt; Stabsveterinär	*Hauptsturmführer*	Captain	Captain
Major; Oberstabsarzt; Oberstabsveterinär	*Sturmbannführer*	Major	Major
Oberstleutnant; Oberfeldarzt; Oberfeldveterinär	*Obersturmbannführer*	Lieutenant Colonel	Lieutenant Colonel
Oberst; Oberstarzt; Oberstveterinär	*Standartenführer*	Colonel	Colonel
-	*Oberführer*	-	Brigadier
Generalmajor	*Brigadeführer*	Brigadier General	-
Generalleutnant	*Gruppenführer*	Major General	Major-General
General (der Infanterie; der Artillerie; der Kavallerie; der Panzertruppen; der Pioniere)	*Obergruppenführer*	Lieutenant General	Lieutenant-General
Generaloberst	*Oberst-Gruppenführer*	General	General
Generalfeldmarschall	*Reichsführer-SS*	General of the Army	Field Marshal

*The basic private rank carried different names in the branches, e.g.: Infantry: *Schütze, Grenadier, Füsilier*; Engineers: *Pionier*; Cavalry: *Reiter*; Artillery: *Kanonnier*; Signal: *Funker* (wireless operator), *Fernsprecher* (telephonist); Anti-tank: *Panzerjäger*; Military-Police: *Feldgendarm*; Transport & logistics: *Fahrer*.

Specific ranks combine the role and branch, e.g.: Armoured Infantry: *Panzergrenadier*; Motorcycle: *Kradschütze*.

Terminology and Abbrevations

A

A.A.: *Artillerie-Abteilung*: Artillery battalion; *Aufklärungs-Abteilung*: Reconnaissance battalion
AB: Airborne (division)
Abt.: *Abteilung*: Battalion. Term used with artillery, (anti) tank and signals units. Can also refer to a detachment, when referring to training and replacement elements.
AD: Armored Division (US)
A.K.: *Armee-Korps*: Army corps
angegliedert: Semi-permanent attachment of a unit/formation to a larger formation it has no organic organisational ties with
AOK: *Armee-Oberkommando*: Field army headquarters
A.R. (AR): *Artillerie Regiment*: Artillery regiment
Arfü: *Artillerie-Führer*: Headquarters in overall control of all artillery in a sector, typically at division level
ARKO: *Artillerie-Kommandeur*: Headquarters in overall control of all artillery in a sector, typically above division level
Armee-Oberkommando: Field army headquarters
Art., *Artillerie*: Artillery
Arzt: Doctor, medical officer
Auf dem Kommandowege: Creation of a new element in the field (e.g. raised through "command channels")
Aufkl., *Aufklärung*: Reconnaissance
Ausb., *Ausbildung*: Training (e.g., *Pz.Ers.u.Ausb.Abt. 100*)
A.V.T.: *Artillerie-Vermessungstrupp*: Artillery survey section

B

(b), *belgisch*: Belgian
Bäck., *Bäckerei*: Bakery
Bataillon: Battalion. Term used with infantry and engineer formations
Batterie: Battery
Bau(truppen): Construction (troops)
Beamte: Civilian official in the military
Befehlshaber: Commander (general officer commanding above corps level)
Befh.: *Befehlshaber*
beh.: *behelfsmäßig*: Makeshift; ad hoc, field expedient
Beob.: *Beobachtung*: Observation (e.g., *Beobachtungs-Abteilung*)
(bew.): *beweglich*: Mobilised using means from the enhance mobility efforts (*Beweglichmachung*)
Beweglichmachung: Increasing the mobility of units over their TO/E authorisations
Bn: Battalion
bo.: *bodenständig*: Static, as in belonging to a sector. Not to be confused with immobile
Brig.: *Brigade*: Brigade
Brif.: *Brigadeführer*
Brigadeführer: A general officer; see "Comparative Table of Ranks"
Btl. (Btle.): *Bataillon(e)*; Battalion(s)
Bttr.: *Batterie*: Battery

C

Chef H. Rüst u. BdE, *Chef Heeresrüstung und Befehlshaber des Ersatzheeres*: Chief of Army Armaments and Commander-in-Chief of the Replacement Army
Closed formation: *geschlossen*: Commitment of a unit as a whole; in its entirety (not split up)
Co.: Company
CP: Command Post

D

Div.: *Division*: Division
d.R.: *der Reserve*: Used to indicate reserve officers (e.g.: *Maj.d.R.*)
DVL: *Deutsche Volksliste*: System to classify people in occupied territories based on their German descent

E

(E): *Eisenbahn*: Railway
(e): *englisch*: British
E.: *Ersatz*: Replacement
Eingegliedert: Officially incorporated into a larger formation. (e.g., *Ost-Btl. 649* was *eingegliedert* in *GR 729*)
Ers.: *Ersatz*: Replacement (e.g., *Pz.Ers.u.Ausb.Abt. 100*)

F

(f): *französisch*: French
FA: Field Artillery (Battalion)
Fallschirmjäger: Paratroop(er)
Faustpatrone: Single-shot handheld anti-tank weapon (superseded by the *Panzerfaust*)
F.E.B.: *Feldersatz-Bataillon*: Field Replacement Battalion
Feld: Field
Feldg(end).: *Feldgendarmerie*: Military Police
feldmässig: Field type (e.g., field-type fortifications)
Feldw., Feldwebel, Fldw.: A senior NCO; see "Comparative Table of Ranks"

Fernsprech: Telephone
Fest.: *Festung*: Fortress
F.H.: *Feldhaubitze*: Field howitzer
Fhr.: *Führer*: Leader or acting commander (e.g., *Zug-Führer*)
Fj.: *Fallschirmjäger*
FJR: *Fallschirmjäger-Regiment*
F.K.: *Feldkanone*: Field gun
Fla: *Flieger-Abwehr*: Anti-aircraft defence
Flak: *Flieger-* or *Flug-Abwehr-Kanone*: Anti-aircraft gun
FpA: *Feldpostamt*: Army Post Office
FpN: *Feldpostnummer*: Field Post Number
Fs.: *Fallschirm*: Parachute
Fu.: *Funk*: wireless
Führerreserve: Officer manpower reserve
Funk: Wireless
Füs.: *Füsilier*: Type of infantryman or unit (generally referring to light infantry)

G

Geb., Gebirgs-: Mountain (e.g., *Gebirgsgeschütz*)
Gef.Std.: *Gefechtsstand*: Headquarters of a combat formation/staff
Gefr.: *Gefreiter*: A senior enlisted soldier; see "Comparative Table of Ranks"
Gen.: *General*: A general officer; see "Comparative Table of Ranks"
Gen.Kdo.: *Generalkommando*: Corps headquarters
Gen.Lt.: *Generalleutnant*: A general officer; see "Comparative Table of Ranks"
Gen.Maj.: *Generalmajor*: A general officer; see "Comparative Table of Ranks"
Gen St.d.H.: *Generalstab des Heeres*: General Staff of the Army
gep.: *gepanzert*: armoured
GIR: Glider Infantry Regiment
Gliederung: (graphic representation of the) Order of Battle, organisation of units
GR: *Grenadier-Regiment*
Gren.: *Grenadier*: Infantry; infantryman (in general); *see also* "Comparative Table of Ranks"
groß: Large
Grundgliederung: Standard organisation (Order of Battle) of a specific type of formation (e.g., *Infanterie-Division 44*)
Gruppe: Group, section, squad
g.v.F.: *garnisonverwendungsfähig Feld*: Personnel suitable for garrison duty in the field
g.v.H.: *Heimat*: Personnel suitable for garrison duty in the homefront
Gruf.: *Gruppenführer*
Gruppenführer: A general officer; see "Comparative Table of Ranks"

H

(h): *hollandisch*: Dutch

Hafthohlladung: Magnetic anti-tank grenade
Hau., Haub.: *Haubitze*: Howitzer
Hauptkampffeld: Main Combat Area
Hauptkampflinie: Main Line of Resistance (MLR)
Hauptmann: A company-grade officer; see "Comparative Table of Ranks"
Hauptsturmführer: A company-grade officer; *see* "Comparative Table of Ranks"
Heer: Army (as a branch of service)
Heeresgruppe: (Field) Army Group
H.Gr.: *Heeresgruppe*
Hiwi: *Hilfswiliger*: Voluntary non-German personnel in military support service
H.K.A.A.: *Heeres-Küsten-Artillerie-Abteilung*: Army Coastal Artillery Battalion
H.K.A.R.: *Heeres-Küsten-Artillerie-Regiment*: Army Coastal Artillery Regiment
H.K.B.: *Heeres-Küsten-Batterie*: Army Coastal Artillery Battery
H.Kdo.: *Höheres Kommando*: Corps headquarters (generally with assigned or attached elements)
HKF: *Hauptkampffeld*
HKL: *Hauptkampflinie*
Hptm.: *Hauptmann*
HQ: Headquarters
Hstuf.: *Hauptsturmführer*

I

(i): *italienisch*: Italian
Ia: Chief of Operations (division or above)
Ib: Supply (Logistics) Officer (division or above)
Ic: Chief Intelligence Officer (division or above)
I.D.: *Infanterie-Division*: Infantry Division
ID: Infantry Division
i.G.: *im Generalstab*: Academy-trained General Staff Officer (e.g.: *Maj.i.G.*)
I.G.: *Infanterie-Geschütz*: Infantry gun
IIa: Officer for personnel matters of officers (division or above)
IIb: Officer for personnel matters of non-commissioned ranks (division or above)
I.K.H.: *Infanterie-Kanone-Haubitze*: Infantry-gun-howitzer
Inf.: *Infanterie*: Infantry
Instandsetzung: Maintenance (repair)
I.R.: *Infanterie-Regiment*: Infantry Regiment (later replaced with *Grenadier-Regiment*)
IR: Infantry Regiment
I-Staffel: *Instandsetzungsstaffel*: Maintenance Section
Ist-Stärke: Actual strength, as opposed to *Soll-Stärke*

J

(j): *jugoslavisch*: Yugoslavian

K

k.: *kurz*: Short
K.: *Kanone*: Cannon
Kampf: Combat
Kampfgruppe: Battlegroup
Kampfmittel-Staffel Section holding combat-related supplies and inventory (including ammunition and demolitions)
Kampfschule: Combat School
Kampfstärke: Combat strength (lit.); trench strength
Kampfzone: Battle zone
Kartenstelle: Mapping detachment
Kdr.: *Kommandeur*: Commander of formations (generally) of battalion through division level
Kdt.: *Kommandant*: Commander of specific entities. Localities such as a *Festung*, camp, road network, etc. Also used for vehicle commanders.
Kettenkrad: *Kettenkraftrad*: Motorcycle halftrack
Kf.: *Kraftfahr*: Motor vehicle (e.g. *Kraftfahrkompanie*)
Kfz.: *Kraftfahrzeug*: Motor vehicle
KG: *Kampfgruppe*
KM: *Kriegsmarine*: Navy
Kodina: *Kommander der Divisions-Nachschubtruppen*: Commander of divisional supply troops
Kompanie: Company
Kopfstärke: "Head-count"; see *Verpflegungsstärke*
Korps: Corps
Kp. (Kpn.): *Kompanie (Kompanien)*
Kps.: *Korps*
Kr.Kw.: *Krankenkraftwagen*: Ambulance
Krad: *Kraftrad*: Motorcycle
Kriegsgliederung: Existing organisation and strength of a formation; actual order of battle
Kriegsmarine: (German) Navy
Kriegstagebuch: War diary (daily logs)
KStN: *Kriegstärkenachweisung*: Table of Organisation and Equipment
KTB: *Kriegstagebuch*
k.v.: *kriegsverwendungsfähig*: Fit for active service
KVA: *Küstenverteidigungsabschnitt*: Coastal Defence Sector (usually defended by a single division)
KVG: *Küstenverteidigungsgruppe*: Coastal Defence Group (level below *KVA*)
KVU: *Küstenverteidigungsuntergruppe*: Coastal Defence Sub-group (level below *KVG*)
Kw.K.: *Kampfwagenkanone*: Main gun of an armoured vehicle

L

L: *Luftwaffe*
l.: *leichte*: Light; *lang*: Long
LAG: *Landesabwehrgeschütz*: Anti (sea) landing gun
landeseigen: Native
Lds.: *Landes*: Regional (e.g., *Landes-Bau-Pi.Btl.*)
le.: *Leichte*: Light
Lehr: Training, doctrine
Leutnant: A company-grade officer; *see* "Comparative Table of Ranks"
LL: *Luftlande*
Lt.: *Leutnant*
Luftlande: Airlanding (e.g., *91. Luftlande-Division*)
Luftwaffe: (German) Air Force
LW: *Luftwaffe*

M

M: *Marine*
m.: *mittler*: Medium
M.A.A.: *Marine-Artillerie-Abteilung*: Naval artillery battalion
m.d.F.b.: *mit der Führung beauftragt*: Temporarily placed in command, acting commander
M.K.B.: *Marine-Küsten-Batterie*: Navy coastal battery
MLR: Main Line of Resistance
Maj.: *Major*: A field-grade officer; *see* "Comparative Table of Ranks"
Marine: (German) Navy; naval
Melder: Messenger
MG: *Maschinen-Gewehr*: Machine gun
mittler: Medium
mot: *motorisiert*: Motorised
motZ: *motorisierter Zug*: Drawn by motor vehicle
MP: *Maschinenpistol*: Machine-pistol or sub-machine gun
MTW: *Mannschafttransportwagen*: Troop (personnel) carrier

N

nA: *neuer Art*: New style, type
Nachr.: *Nachrichten*: Signal's communications
Nachs.: *Nachschub*: Supply, logisitcs (broadest sense)
Nord: North

O

(o): *ortsfest*: Fixed, stationary, immobile
Ob.: *Oberbefehlshaber*: Commander-in-Chief; term used for field army commanders and up
Oberf: *Oberführer*

Oberführer: A general officer; *see* "Comparative Table of Ranks"
Obergruppenführer: A field-grade officer; *see* "Comparative Table of Ranks"
Oberleutnant: A company-grade officer; *see* "Comparative Table of Ranks"
Oberst: A field-grade officer; *see* "Comparative Table of Ranks"
Oberstgruf.: *Oberstgruppenführer*
Oberstgruppenführer: A general officer; *see* "Comparative Table of Ranks"
Oberstleutnant: A field-grade officer; *see* "Comparative Table of Ranks"
Obersturmbannführer: A field-grade officer; *see* "Comparative Table of Ranks"
Obersturmführer: A field-grade officer; *see* "Comparative Table of Ranks"
Obkdo.: *Oberkommando*: High Command (e.g. *AOK*, *OKH* and *OKW*)
Oblt.: *Oberleutnant*; Company-grade officer; *see* "Comparative Table of Ranks"
Obst.: *Oberst*
Obstlt.: *Oberstleutnant*
Ogruf.: *Obergruppenführer*
Ofenrohr: aka *Panzerschreck*: German type "bazooka"
Offz.: *Offizier*: officer
OKH: *Oberkommando des Heeres*: Army High Command
OKW: *Oberkommando der Wehrmacht*: High Command of the Armed Forces
O.Qu.: *Oberquartiermeister*: General staff officer in charge of supply and administration
Ord.Offz., (Ord.O.; O.O.): *Ordonnanzoffizier*: Special missions officer; officer assistant
Ost: East
Ost-Bataillon: Battalion formed using Slavic personnel from the Soviet Union
Osttruppen: Collective term for non-German units and personnel from the Soviet Union (excluding *Hiwi's*)
Ostubaf.: *Obersturmbannführer*
Ostuf.: *Obersturmführer*
OT: *Organisation Todt*
Otrag: *Organisation Todt Transportgruppe*

P

(p): *polnisch*: Polish
Pak: *Panzer-Abwehr-Kanone*: Anti-tank (AT) gun
Panzer: Tank; armour(ed)
Panzerfaust: Single-shot handheld anti-tank weapon
Panzerjäger: Anti-tank, term used for vehicles, units or soldiers
Panzerkampfwagen: Tank
Panzerschreck: aka *Ofenrohr*: German type "bazooka"
Panzer(späh)wagen: Armoured (reconnaissance/scout) car
Panzerzerstörer: Tank-destroyer, term used for units equipped with anti-tank rocket launchers
P.E., Personnal-Einheit: Unit with personnel only (no equipment)
PGR: *Panzer-Grenadier-Regiment*
Pi.: *Pionier*: engineer

PIR: Parachute Infantry Regiment
POL: Petroleum, oil, lubricants
Pz.: *Panzer*
Pz.Gren.: *Panzer-Grenadier*: Armoured (mechanised) infantry
Pz.Kpfw.: *Panzerkampfwagen*
Pz.Jg., Pzj.: *Panzerjäger*: Anti-tank vehicle, unit or soldier

Q

Quartiermeister: Quartermaster

R

(r): *russisch*: Russian (actually meaning from the USSR)
Rad: Bicycle
Radf., Radfahr-: Cyclist; bicycle-
Res., Reserve: Reserve
Reiter-: Mounted, cavalry (e.g., *Reiterzug*)
Riegelstellung: (Secondary) blocking position/line to prevent a breaktrough
Rgt.: *Regiment*: regiment
RSO: *Raupenschlepper Ost*: Fully tracked light truck / prime mover

S

s.: *schwer*: Heavy
San., Sanitäts: Medical
Schießbecher: Rifle grenade launcher
Schläct., Schlächterei: Butcher
Schlepper: Tractor (prime mover)
Schn., Schnelle: Fast (e.g., *Schnelle-Brigade*)
Schule: School
Schw., Schwadron: Company equivalent. Squadron (UK), Troop (US)
Sd.Fhr.: *Sonderführer*: Civilian specialist in a military role (translator, propaganda, etc.)
Sd.Kfz.: *Sonderkraftfahrzeug*
Selbstfahr(lafette): Self-propelled (gun carriage)
Sich., Sicherungs: Security (e.g., *Sicherungs-Rgt.*)
Sollgliederung: Theoretical (authorized) organisation of a formation
Soll-Stärke: Authorised strength, as opposed to *Ist-Stärke*
Sonderkraftfahrzeug: Special-purpose motor vehicle
Sonderstab: Special purpose staff
SP: Self-propelled
SPW: *Schützenpanzerwagen*: armoured halftrack for infantry
St., Stab: Staff
Staf.: *Standartenführer*:

Standartenführer: A field-grade officer; see "Comparative Table of Ranks"
Staffel: Section
ständig: Permanent (e.g., permanent fortifications)
St.P.: *Stützpunkt*: organised tactical locality, strong point. Term also used for resistance nests stronger than the *Widerstandsnest* (*Wn.*)
Stubaf.: *Sturmbannführer*
StuG., Stu.Gesch.: *Sturmgeschütz*
StuH., Stu.Haub.: *Sturmhaubitze*
Stu.K.: *Sturmkanone*: Main gun on an assault gun
Sturmbannführer: A field-grade officer; see "Comparative Table of Ranks"
Sturmgeschütz: Assault gun unit or vehicle
Sturmhaubitze: Assault gun armed with a howitzer
Süd: South

T

(t): *tschechisch*: Czech
(tmot): *teil motorisiert*: Partially motorised
Torn., Tornister: Backpack, term used for portable-wireless
Tr., Trupp: section, detachment
Tr.Üb.Pl.: *Truppenübungsplatz*: Troop training area/facility/camp
Troß(e): Trains, as in supply/baggage trains of a unit
Trupp: Section, team, squad
Truppen: Troops, forces
Turk-Bataillon: Type of battalion formed using Turcic personnel from the Soviet Union

U

U: *Unter*: Sub (e.g. UKG, *Unterkampfgruppe*)
u., und: and
Uffz., Unteroffizier: NCO or specific rank; see "Comparative Table of Ranks"
Untersturmbannführer: A field- grade officer; see "Comparative Table of Ranks"
Ustuf.: See *Untersturmführer*
Untersturmführer: A company grade officer; see "Comparative Table of Ranks"

V

(v): *verlegefähig*: Moveable, transportable
v.B.: *vordere Beobachter*: Forward observer
V.B.: *Verteidigungsbereich*
Verb.Kdo.: *Verbindungskommando*: Liaison section/ detail
Verpfl., Verpflegung: Supplies (of food)
Verpflegungsstärke: Rations strength
vers.: *Verstärkt*: Reinforced

Verteidigungsbereich: Defence sector (e.g., V.B. Cherbourg)
Verwaltungs-: Administrative
Vet., Veterinär: Veterinary-; veterinarian
V-weapons: *Vergeltungswaffen*: Reprisal weapons (V1, V2)

W

Wachtm.: *Wachtmeister*: Artillery rank equivalent to *Feldwebel*
Waffenmeisterei: Armoury, ordnance shop
Wehrkreis: Military district
Wehrmacht: German Armed Forces
Welle: Mobilisation wave (group of divisions formed around the same time with a similar organisation)
Werkstatt: Workshop
W.F.St.: *Wehrmachtführungsstab*: Armed Forces Operations Staff
wirtschaftlich: administrative
Wn.: *Wiederstandsnest*: Resistance nest

Z

Z.: *Zug*
z.b.V., zbV: *zur besondere Verwendung*: Special purpose
Zgkw.: *Zugkraftwagen*
Zug: Platoon; train (rail)
Zugkraftwagen: Prime mover, halftrack carrier
Zustandsbericht: Status report of a unit

Index

A
AIRCRAFT / GLIDERS
DFS 230: *160, 177*
GO 242: *160, 177*

M
MILITARY FORCES
Allied
British and Commonwealth
21st Army Group: *23*
Second Army: *23*

US
4th Armored Division: *153, 217*
4th Infantry Division: *181, 182*
9th Infantry Division: *134, 138, 139, 189, 190, 192, 195, 196*
39th Infantry Regiment (9th Infantry Division): *134, 190, 195*
47th Infantry Regiment (9th Infantry Division): *192, 195, 196, 202*
60th Field Artillery Battalion (9th Infantry Division): *134*
60th Infantry Regiment (9th Infantry Division): *134, 190, 192, 195, 196*
79th Infantry Division: *142, 202*
82nd Airborne Division: *128, 129, 142, 178, 179, 180, 181, 182, 184, 185, 189, 190, 192, 195, 196, 200, 202, 209*
90th Infantry Division: *128, 129, 142, 144, 148, 185, 187, 188, 189, 190, 202, 203, 209*
101st Airborne Division: *178, 183, 187, 189*
325th Glider Infantry Regiment (82nd Airborne Division): *184, 185, 190, 192, 195, 200, 209*
327th Glider Infantry Regiment (101st Airborne Division): *187, 188, 189*
357th Infantry Regiment: *142, 144, 187, 188, 189, 202, 203*
358th Infantry Regiment (90th Infantry Division): *142, 144, 187, 188, 189, 190, 202, 209*
359th Infantry Regiment: *142, 188, 189, 190, 202, 209*
501st Parachute Infantry Regiment (101st Airborne Division): *178, 189*
502nd Parachute Infantry Regiment (101st Airborne Division): *178, 187, 189*
505th Parachute Infantry Regiment (82nd Airborne Division): *178, 179, 180, 192, 195, 200, 202*
506th Parachute Infantry Regiment (101st Airborne Division): *178, 189*
507th Parachute Infantry Regiment (82nd Airborne Division): *178, 179, 185, 190, 192, 200*
508th Parachute Infantry Regiment (82nd Airborne Division): *129, 178, 179, 189, 195, 200*
Combat Command B (4th Armored Division): *217*
First US Army: *8, 23, 26*
Task Force Raff: *180*
V Corps: *8, 23, 26, 187*
VII Corps: *8, 23, 26, 189, 190, 195, 196*
VIII Corps: *8, 23, 26, 142, 144, 149, 196, 202, 209*
XIX Corps: *8, 23, 26*

German
Battalions / Squadrons / Separate Detachments
Abteilung Schmidt: *177, 179.* See also Artillerie-Regiment 191
Armee-Nachrichten-Abteilung 531: *54*
(Art.) Gruppe Schmidt. See Abteilung Schmidt
schwere Artillerie-Abteilung 456: *48, 54, 60, 63, 69*
Artillerie-Abteilung 656: *36, 52*
Artillerie-Abteilung 669: *45, 45, 46, 52*
Artillerie-Abteilung 1021: *66, 111, 117, 121, 167*
Artillerie-Abteilung 1025: *167*
Artillerie-Abteilung Römer: *44, 45, 46, 48*
Artillerie-Gruppe Rock: *184, 187, 188.* See also Artillerie-Regiment 191
Artillerie-Regiment 177. See also Panzerjäger-Abteilung 177
Aufklärungs-Abteilung 389: *56*
Aufklärungs-Abteilung 669: *45, 46*
Bataillon Siepmann. See Grenadier-Regiment 922
Bau-Pionier-Bataillon 59: *57, 58*
Bau-Pionier-Bataillon 94: *67, 69, 150, 211*
Bau-Pionier-Bataillon 158: *57, 58*
Bau-Pionier-Bataillon 802: *65, 67*
Bau-Pionier-Bataillon 803: *65, 67*
Divisions-Fusilier-Bataillon (Aufklärungs-Abteilung) 352: *61, 63, 67, 74, 75, 76*
Divisions-Nachrichten-Abteilung 301: *81*
Einheit Baumann: *118*
Eisenbahn-Artillerie-Abteilung 681: *56, 59, 63*
Eisenbahn-Artillerie-Abteilung 725: *75, 86*
Fallschirm-Artillerie-Abteilung 5: *209, 211, 212, 213*
Fallschirm-Panzerjäger-Abteilung: *41*
Fallschirm-Panzerjäger-Abteilung 5: *211, 214*
Fallschirm-Pionier-Bataillon: *41*
Feldersatz-Bataillon 177: *12, 119, 138*
Feldersatz-Bataillon 200: *76*
Feldersatz-Bataillon 243: *64, 72*
Feldersatz-Bataillon 352: *67, 75*
Festungs-Bau-Bataillon 11: *52*
Festungs-Bau-Bataillon 89: *40, 52.* See also Festungs-Bau-Bataillon 11
Festungs-Pionier-Bataillon 11: *59*
Festungs-Pionier-Bataillon 19: *57*
Fluganwärter-Bataillon II: *42, 62.* See also Flieger-Regiment 90
Fluganwärter-Bataillon V: *43, 48*
Fluganwärter-Bataillon VII: *43*
Füsilier-Bataillon 364: *110*
gemischte Flak-Abteilung 497: *75*
Georgisches-Infanterie-Bataillon 795: *57, 61, 66, 67, 70, 73, 176, 180, 182*
Georgisches-Infanterie-Bataillon 797: *48, 50, 52, 69, 70, 74, 216*
Georgisches-Infanterie-Bataillon 823: *57*
Gruppe Zerweck. See Heeres-Küsten-Artillerie-Abteilung 755
Heeres-Flak-Abteilung 305: *76*
Heeres-Küsten-Artillerie-Abteilung 404: *52, 59, 63*
Heeres-Küsten-Artillerie-Abteilung 755: *46, 59, 63*
Heeres-Küsten-Artillerie-Abteilung 832: *42, 52, 59, 60, 63.* See also Heeres-Küsten-Artillerie-Abteilung 1260
Heeres-Küsten-Artillerie-Abteilung 1260: *63, 75, 76.* See also Heeres-Küsten-Artillerie-Abteilung 832
Korps-Nachrichten-Abteilung 460: *43, 63, 84*
Landes-Bau-Pionier-Bataillon 17: *69*
Landesschützen-Bataillon 390: *54*
leichte Artillerie-Abteilung 90: *75*
leichte Beobachungs-Abteilung 33: *54, 54, 58, 66, 67, 69, 75*
leichte Flak-Abteilung 912: *124*
leichte Flak-Abteilung 996: *80*
Luftwaffen-Nachrichten-Abteilung 7: *41*
Marine-Artillerie-Abteilung 260: *34, 56, 56, 59*
Marine-Artillerie-Abteilung 608: *124*
Marschbataillon 158: *152*
Marschbataillon zbV 362: *140*
Maschinengewehr-Bataillon 17: *38, 40, 44, 45, 46, 47, 48, 51, 57, 61, 63, 67, 73, 106*

Nachrichten-Abteilung 177: *121, 123*
Nachrichten-Abteilung 191: *160, 169, 171*
Nachrichten-Abteilung 223: *67*
Nachrichten-Abteilung 352: *61, 67, 75*
Nachrichten-Abteilung 460: *43, 63, 67, 75, 78.* See also Korps-Nachrichten-Abteilung 460 (mot)
Nachrichten-Abteilung 716: *76*
Nachschub-Kolonnen-Abteilung Bauer zbV: *86.* See also Kommandeur der Korpsnachschubtruppen 460
Ost-Bataillon 439: *57, 57, 57, 61, 66, 67, 70, 75, 180, 185, 187, 187, 188*
Ost-Bataillon 441: *69, 74, 75, 76*
Ost-Bataillon 561: *69, 73*
Ost-Bataillon 602: *124, 152, 153*
Ost-Bataillon 627: *57*
Ost-Bataillon 630: *61, 65, 75*
Ost-Bataillon 635: *71, 175, 187, 187, 188*
Ost-Bataillon 642: *57, 61, 66, 67, 74, 75, 76*
Ost-Bataillon 643: *57.* See also Ost-Bataillon 627
Ost-Bataillon 649: *61, 222*
Ost-Bataillon Huber: *199, 200, 202, 206*
Ost-Reiter-Abteilung 281: *69, 71*
Panzer-Abteilung 206: *64, 69, 71, 72, 73*
Panzer-Abteilung 223: *44, 47*
Panzer-Aufklärungs-Abteilung 21: *76*
Panzer-Ersatz- und Ausbuildungs-Abteilung 100: *71, 72, 73, 172, 176, 177, 179, 182, 184, 187, 192, 199, 222*
Panzerjäger-Abteilung 22: *166*
Panzerjäger-Abteilung 177: *68, 115, 116, 117, 121, 133, 138, 140, 151, 156,*
Panzerjäger-Abteilung 189: *156*
Panzerjäger-Abteilung 200: *76, 118*
Panzerjäger-Abteilung 216: *38*
Panzerjäger-Abteilung 243: *67, 72, 177, 181, 187, 188, 199*
Panzerjäger-Abteilung 319: *37, 38*
Panzerjäger-Abteilung 323: *38, 39*
Panzerjäger-Abteilung 352: *67, 68, 74, 75, 150, 151, 176, 187, 199, 206, 211, 213*
Panzerjäger-Abteilung 353: *98, 142, 144, 202, 214*
Panzerjäger-Abteilung 355: *67, 116, 121.* See also Panzerjäger-Abteilung 177
Panzerjäger-Abteilung 356: *56, 57*
Panzerjäger-Abteilung 389: *55*
Panzerjäger-Abteilung 709: *73, 85*
Panzerjäger-Abteilung 716: *85*
Panzer-Pionier-Bataillon 220: *76*

Pionier-Bataillon 177: *68, 112, 118, 119, 120, 121, 133, 138, 140, 144, 149, 150, 151, 156, 211, 214*
Pionier-Bataillon 191: *150, 160, 169, 173, 175, 176, 177, 183, 186, 187, 196, 199, 203, 206, 207, 209, 210, 211*
Pionier-Bataillon 243: *64, 65, 67, 69, 71, 73, 199*
Pionier-Bataillon 265: *65, 192, 199, 206, 211*
Pionier-Bataillon 319: *37, 38, 39, 71, 150, 211*
Pionier-Bataillon 346: *61, 65*
Pionier-Bataillon 352: *57, 60, 63, 67, 68, 75*
Pionier-Bataillon 353: *142, 202*
Pionier-Bataillon 355: *67, 121*
Pionier-Bataillon 371: *57*
Pionier-Bataillon 389: *52, 53*
Pionier-Bataillon 709: *48, 51, 54*
Pionier-Bataillon 716: *46, 76*
Reserve-Radfahr-Abteilung 2: *48*
Reserve-Radfahr-Abteilung 11: *48*
Reserve-Radfahr-Abteilung 17: *48*
Schnelle Abteilung 11: *21, 25, 39, 40, 42, 43, 44, 46, 48, 49, 53, 55, 61, 63, 64, 67, 69, 72, 83, 108, 111, 121, 124, 127, 133, 134, 144, 147, 151, 167, 171, 182, 184, 187, 188, 190, 195, 199, 200, 202, 211, 213*
Schnelle Abteilung 17: *8, 9, 15, 17, 25, 26, 27, 28, 40, 44, 46, 47, 48, 49, 52, 54, 57, 61, 63, 64, 66, 67, 69, 73, 74, 116, 121, 127, 129, 132, 133, 135, 136, 138, 142, 147, 148, 149, 151, 153, 155, 169, 171, 177, 183, 185, 187, 189, 195, 196, 199, 203, 209, 211*
Schnelle Abteilung 513: *49*
Schnelle Abteilung 517: *49, 50, 54, 66*
Schnelle Abteilung 518: *49*
schwere Artillerie-Abteilung 457: *54, 58, 60*
schwere Artillerie-Abteilung 450: *48, 49, 52, 54*
schwere Artillerie-Abteilung 456: *48, 54, 56, 58, 60, 63, 75, 172*
schwere Artillerie-Abteilung 457: *48, 75*
schwere Artillerie-Abteilung 989: *67, 76*
schwere Stellungs-Werfer-Abteilung 103: *61, 64*
Sicherungs-Bataillon 521: *69*
Sicherungs-Bataillon 1220 (M): *153*
SS-Panzer-Abteilung 17: *210*
SS-Panzer-Aufklärungs-Abteilung 2: *144*
SS-Panzer-Aufklärungs-Abteilung 17: *142, 195, 199, 200, 210*
SS-Wehrgeologen-Bataillon: *124*
Sturm-Bataillon AOK 7: *71, 72, 73, 106, 129, 177, 181*
Sturmgeschütz-Abteilung 200: *76*
Sturmgeschutz-Abteilung 905: *50*
Wolga-Tatarisches-Infanterie-Bataillon 627: *124, 137, 138, 199, 200, 206*

Brigades

Artillerie-Brigade 1, gepanzert: *48, 51*
Schnelle Brigade 30: *23, 59, 75*
Schnelle Brigade West: *51*
Sturmgeschütz-Brigade 341: *152*
Sturmgeschütz-Brigade 902: *199, 200, 202, 206, 207, 211, 212, 214*

Companies / Batteries / Troops

Aufklärungs-Schwadron 84: *42, 47, 58, 78, 85*
Batterie Azeville: *180.* See also Heeres-Küsten-Artillerie-Regiment 1261
Batterie Graf Waldersee: *58.* See gepanzerte Geräte-Batterie 716
Batterie Reichenau. See gepanzerte Geräte-Batterie 709
Batterie Resi: *58, 63*
Divisions-Füsilier-Kompanie 91: *166, 176, 186, 198, 207, 209, 210, 216*
Eisenbahn-Batterie 722: *63, 63, 86, 86*
Festungs-Stamm-Kompanie LXXIV: *124*
Fla-Kompanie 177: *116, 150, 151, 211, 213*
Fla-Kompanie 191: *150, 176, 187, 196, 199, 206, 209, 210, 211, 214*
Fla-Kompanie 709: *69*
Fla-Kompanie 716: *69*
Fla-Kompanie 191: *165*
Geräte-Batterie Fort du Roule: *56*
Geräte-Batterie 709, gepanzert: *49, 54*
Geräte-Batterie 716, gepanzert: *9, 21, 23, 36, 37, 38, 40, 42, 44, 46, 47, 49, 52, 53, 54, 54, 56, 57, 58, 59, 61, 63, 64, 66, 68, 71, 74, 75, 76, 98, 99, 106, 121, 179, 190*
Geräte-Batterie Osteck: *56*
Gesteinsbohr-Kompanie 28: *59*
Heeres-Küsten-Artillerie-Batterie 1271: *124*
Heeres-Küstenbatterie 275: *19, 26, 27, 28, 38, 105, 106, 145*
Heeres-Küstenbatterie 315: *38*
Heeres-Küstenbatterie 316: *38*
Heeres-Küstenbatterie 317: *38*
Heeres-Küstenbatterie 318: *38, 165*
Kraftfahr-Kompanie 84: *42, 63, 78, 84, 86, 103*
Marine-Batterie Brommy: *34*
Marine-Batterie Gréville: *64*
Marine-Batterie Hamburg: *34*
Marine-Batterie Longues: *59*
Marine-Batterie Marcouf: *59, 64*
Marine-Batterie York: *34*
Marine-Batterie Fort du Roule

228

Ost-Batterie 582: *124*
Panzerjäger-Kompanie 177: *111, 115, 116, 123, 124, 133, 149, 151, 211, 214*
Panzerjäger-Kompanie 191: *150, 160, 165, 176, 186, 187, 196, 199, 206, 207, 209, 210, 211, 214*
Panzerjäger-Kompanie 352: *61, 111*
Panzerjäger-Kompanie 709: *67*
Panzerjäger-Kompanie (motZ) 352: *116*
Pionier-Kompanie 1021: *121*
Sanitäts-Kompanie 191: *196*
schwere Batterie 177 (Sf.): *124*
schwere Feld-Haubitze-Geräte-Batterie Weber: *124*. See also schwere Batterie 177
Stellungs-Batterie (Küste) 316: *46, 59*
Stellungs-Batterie (Küste) 317: *56*
Verpflegungs-Kompanie 191: *170*

Corps

Generalkommando LXXXIV. A.K.: *10, 32*
Höheres-Kommando zbV LX: *40, 41, 42*
Höheres-Kommando zbV XXXVII: *40, 41*
Höheres Kommando zbV XXXII: *34, 35*
Höheres Kommando zbV LX: *32, 84*
II. Fallschirm-Korps: *8, 19, 21, 23, 25, 26, 27, 28, 31, 81, 127, 186, 189, 207, 213*
I. SS-Panzer-Korps: *21, 31*
II. SS-Panzer-Korps: *21*
LXV. Armee-Korps zbV: *64*
LXVII. Reserve-Korps: *59*
LXXIV. Armee-Korps: *10, 17, 19, 23, 31, 69, 71, 80, 81, 108, 118, 123, 126, 127, 128, 152*
LXXXI. Armee-Korps: *21, 53, 63*
LXXXIV. Armee-Korps: *8, 9, 10, 17, 19, 23, 25, 26, 27, 28, 31, 32, 40, 42, 43, 46, 49, 52, 59, 61, 63, 64, 65, 66, 69, 70, 71, 72, 76, 78, 79, 80, 81, 82, 84, 86, 103, 105, 108, 110, 123, 126, 127, 129, 130, 132, 133, 135, 136, 137, 138, 142, 144, 145, 146, 147, 151, 158, 172, 175, 179, 180, 181, 186, 188, 189, 190, 192, 195, 196, 199, 200, 202, 204, 206, 207, 209, 210, 212, 213, 214, 216, 259*
LXXXV. Armee-Korps: *81*
LXXXVI. Armee-Korps: *21*
LXXXVII. Armee-Korps: *34, 45, 52, 53*
Panzergruppe Eberbach: *28*
XXV. Armee-Korps: *10, 17, 19, 23, 34, 44, 47, 50, 51, 71, 80, 105, 126, 126, 136, 152, 171, 217*
XXXXIII. Armee-Korps: *34*
XXXXVII. Panzer-Korps: *21, 25, 27, 28*

Divisions

1. Fallschimjäger-Division: *51*
1. SS-Panzer-Division "Leibstandarte SS Adolf Hitler": *28*
2. Fallschimjäger-Division: *19, 71, 72, 152, 153, 171*
2. Panzer-Division: *38*
2. SS-Panzer-Division "Das Reich": *9, 26, 27, 27, 44, 144, 145, 146, 147, 210, 211, 213, 214, 216*
3. Fallschimjäger-Division: *19, 25, 127*
5. Fallschirmjäger-Division: *9, 19, 26, 27, 28, 119, 127, 144, 145, 146, 147, 151, 152, 153, 209, 211, 213, 214*
6. Infanterie-Division: *34, 35*
6. Panzer-Division: *44*
7. Flieger-Division: *40, 41, 43, 44, 51*
10. SS-Panzer-Division "Frundsberg": *28, 31*
12. SS-Panzer-Division "Hitlerjugend": *21, 31, 72*
16. Panzer-Division: *49*
17. SS-Panzergrenadier-Division "Götz von Berlichingen": *8, 8, 9, 25, 26, 27, 127, 142, 147, 177, 189, 199, 207, 209, 210, 211, 216*
19. Panzer-Division: *55*
21. Panzer-Division: *21, 23, 51, 69, 70, 71, 72, 75, 76, 118, 123*
22. Infanterie-Division: *166*
24. Panzer-Division: *40, 52*
57. Infanterie-Division: *34, 35*
76. Infanterie-Division: *49*
77. Infanterie-Division: *9, 17, 26, 66, 67, 69, 91, 98, 99, 105, 106, 108, 110, 111, 112, 116, 120, 121, 123, 126, 127, 130, 131, 132, 133, 135, 136, 138, 139, 140, 142, 143, 144, 145, 146, 147, 148, 149, 150, 151, 152, 153, 156, 158, 166, 168, 182, 187, 188, 189, 190, 191, 192, 195, 198, 199, 200, 202, 206, 207, 209, 211, 212, 217*
83. Infanterie-Division: *36, 37, 38*
84. Infanterie-Division: *28, 31, 108, 111, 168*
85. Infanterie-Division: *108, 111*
89. Infanterie-Division: *31, 108, 156*
91. Infanterie-Division (91. Luftlande-Infanterie-Division): *9, 23, 24, 26, 27, 71, 72, 73, 75, 91, 99, 106, 108, 116, 128, 129, 130, 135, 136, 137, 139, 140, 142, 143, 145, 147, 148, 149, 150, 151, 158, 160, 161, 166, 167, 168, 178, 179, 181, 182, 184, 185, 186, 187, 188, 189, 190, 192, 195, 196, 198, 204, 206, 207, 209, 211, 212, 213, 214, 216, 217*
92. Infanterie-Division: *108, 111, 112, 168*
101. Infanterie-Division: *126*
113. Infanterie-Division: *49*
116. Panzer-Division "Windhund": *28, 217*
158. Reserve-Division: *152*
161. Infanterie-Division: *110, 121*
165. (Reserve-)Division: *44, 45, 46, 48, 52*
182. Reserve-Division: *46*
223. Infanterie-Division: *60, 61, 63*
225. Infanterie-Division: *34, 35*
242. Infanterie-Division: *54, 55, 56*
243. Infanterie-Division: *9, 23, 24, 26, 27, 28, 54, 56, 64, 66, 67, 68, 69, 71, 72, 73, 75, 89, 97, 98, 104, 105, 106, 128, 130, 135, 136, 137, 138, 140, 142, 175, 176, 181, 184, 186, 188, 190, 195, 196, 198, 199, 200, 204, 206, 207, 209, 211, 213, 214, 216*
264. Infanterie-Division: *126*
265. Infanterie-Division: *19, 65, 89, 98, 102, 106, 106, 137, 153, 195, 206, 209, 217*
266. Infanterie-Division: *17, 106, 123, 126, 152, 153*
271. Infanterie-Division: *31*
275. Infanterie-Division: *19, 27, 28, 106, 145*
277. Infanterie-Division: *31*
282. Infanterie-Division: *46, 48*
285. Infanterie-Division: *126*
305. Infanterie-Division: *49*
319. Infanterie-Division: *23, 35, 36, 37, 38, 39, 57, 82*
320. Infanterie-Division: *38, 39, 40, 42, 42, 43, 44, 45, 46, 52, 85*
321. Infanterie-Division: *61, 63*
323. Infanterie-Division: *35, 38, 39, 40, 81*
331. Infanterie-Division: *28*
334. Infanterie-Division: *52*
343. Infanterie-Division: *19, 52, 81, 106*
344. Infanterie-Division: *217*
346. Infanterie-Division: *45, 52, 59, 65, 75, 104, 124*
348. Infanterie-Division: *44*
352. Infanterie-Division: *9, 21, 23, 25, 27, 56, 57, 60, 61, 63, 66, 67, 68, 71, 74, 75, 76, 98, 99, 105, 106, 111, 116, 145, 147, 180, 185, 187, 190, 207*
353. Infanterie-Division: *9, 19, 26, 27, 28, 31, 66, 91, 97, 98, 99, 105, 106, 140, 142, 143, 144, 146, 147, 151, 195, 200, 202, 207, 209, 210, 211, 213, 214, 216*
355. Infanterie-Division: *67, 110, 116, 121, 160*
356. Infanterie-Division: *56*
363. Infanterie-Division: *28, 31*
364. Infanterie-Division: *110, 121*
370. Infanterie-Division: *40, 42*
371. Infanterie-Division: *42, 49*
384. Infanterie-Division: *54*
389. Infanterie-Division: *49, 51, 52, 54, 55, 56*

709. Infanterie-Division: *9, 23, 26, 45, 46, 47, 48, 52, 53, 54, 56, 57, 59, 60, 63, 64, 66, 68, 69, 71, 72, 73, 81, 82, 84, 85, 89, 98, 99, 102, 103, 105, 106, 110, 127, 128, 130, 132, 135, 136, 139, 175, 179, 180, 181, 182, 184, 186, 190, 198*
711. Infanterie-Division: *38, 39, 71*
716. Infanterie-Division: *9, 21, 23, 36, 37, 38, 40, 42, 44, 46, 47, 52, 53, 54, 56, 57, 58, 59, 61, 63, 64, 66, 71, 74, 75, 76, 85, 98, 99, 106, 121, 179, 190*
Division Nummer 172: *160, 162*
Division Nummer 462: *160, 162*
Divisions-Abteilung 352: *190*. See also 352. Infanterie-Division
Divisions-Abteilung 716. See also 716. Infanterie-Division
Divisions-Kommando zbV 136: *124, 126*
Panzer-Lehr-Division: *21, 26, 27, 28*

Field Armies
1. Fallschirm-Armee: *15*
5. Panzer Armee: *15, 21, 28, 31*. See also Panzergruppe West
6. Armee: *49*
7. Armee: *10, 17, 19, 21, 23, 24, 25, 26, 28, 31, 34, 36, 42, 43, 47, 48, 49, 50, 52, 54, 55, 56, 57, 59, 61, 62, 65, 66, 67, 69, 70, 71, 72, 75, 81, 82, 86, 91, 98, 99, 100, 104, 105, 106, 108, 110, 116, 118, 119, 121, 123, 126, 127, 129, 130, 132, 133, 135, 136, 137, 138, 144, 145, 146, 147, 152, 153, 156, 158, 160, 161, 162, 169, 171, 176, 177, 178, 179, 181, 182, 184, 185, 188, 189, 190, 192, 195, 196, 199, 200, 202, 203, 204, 206, 207, 210, 211, 213, 216*. See also Armee-Oberkommando 7
15. Armee: *17, 21, 34, 38, 39, 40, 42, 48, 50, 51, 52, 65, 71, 75, 108, 119, 126*
19. Armee: *15*
Armee-Gruppe Marcks: *26*
Armee-Oberkommando 1: *59, 75, 126*
Armee-Oberkommando 7: *10, 17, 19, 21, 23, 24, 25, 26, 28, 31, 34, 36, 42, 43, 47, 48, 49, 50, 52, 54, 55, 56, 57, 59, 61, 62, 65, 66, 67, 69, 70, 71, 72, 73, 75, 81, 82, 86, 91, 98, 100, 104, 105, 108, 110, 116, 118, 119, 123, 126, 127, 129, 130, 132, 135, 136, 137, 138, 140, 144, 145, 146, 147, 152, 153, 156, 158, 160, 161, 162, 169, 171, 176, 177, 178, 179, 181, 182, 184, 185, 188, 189, 190, 192, 195, 196, 199, 200, 202, 203, 204, 206, 207, 210, 211, 213, 216*. See also 7. Armee
Armee-Oberkommando 9: *34, 35, 36*
Armee-Oberkommando 19: *56, 59, 126*
Panzergruppe West: *15, 17, 25*. Also see 5. Panzer-Armee

High Commands
Armeegruppe G: *15*
Heeresgruppe A: *34*
Heeresgruppe B: *10, 15, 17, 19, 21, 23, 25, 65, 70, 71, 72, 104, 126, 127, 130, 132, 133, 135, 136, 137, 144, 145, 147, 153, 179, 181, 184, 188, 190, 192, 195, 200, 217*
Heeresgruppe D: *15, 21, 34, 36, 98, 100, 132*
Heeresgruppe zur besonderen Verwendung: *1*. See Sonderstab Rommel
Heeresgruppe Nordukraine: *21*
Heeresgruppe Süd: *46*
Heeresgruppe Südwest: *51*
Marine-Gruppe West: *59*
Oberbefehlshaber Südost: *178*
Oberbefehlshaber Südwest: *178*
Oberbefehlshaber West: *10, 15, 17, 40, 42, 43, 44, 48, 52, 53, 54, 56, 59, 61, 63, 64, 66, 75, 81, 82, 83, 96, 99, 100, 104, 111, 112, 118, 119, 126, 136, 151, 160, 169, 177, 178, 195, 216, 217*
Oberkommando der Wehrmacht: *10, 15, 17, 59, 64, 82, 83, 136, 137, 177, 178*
Oberkommando der Wehrmacht (OKW): *225*
Oberkommando des Heeres: *10, 36, 38, 43, 52, 53, 55, 63, 80, 83, 84, 91, 96, 102, 111, 116, 118, 120, 137, 152, 158, 169*
Oberkommando des Heeres (OKH): *225*
Replacement Army: *38, 52, 222*
Sonderstab Rommel: *17*. See Heeresgruppe zur besonderen Verwendung
Wehrkreis I: *32*
Wehrkreis Prag: *32*
Wehrmachtbefehlshaber Niederlande: *17*

Kampfgruppen (Battlegroups)
Gruppe Hellmich: *23, 25, 26, 130, 131, 132, 133, 136, 184, 192, 195, 196*
Gruppe König: *12, 26, 140, 142, 192, 196, 198, 199, 200, 202, 203, 204, 206, 207*
Gruppe von Schlieben: *26, 130, 131, 132, 133, 135, 136, 192, 196*
Kampfgruppe 77: *134*
Kampfgruppe 265: *106, 129, 148, 151, 188, 189, 190, 195, 196, 198, 200, 202, 206, 207, 209, 211, 212, 214*
Kampfgruppe 275: *26*
Kampfgruppe 920: *190, 191*. See also Grenadier-Regiment 920
Kampfgruppe Bacherer: *129, 133*. See also Grenadier-Regiment 1049
Kampfgruppe Bardtenschlager: *177, 184, 187*. See also Panzer-Ersatz-und- Ausbildungs-Abt. 100
Kampfgruppe Bohnenkamp: *175, 176, 177, 184, 187, 202*. See also Pionier-Bataillon 191
Kampfgruppe Brandt: *128, 129, 133*. See also Grenadier-Regiment 1050
Kampfgruppe Diekhoff: *175, 176, 177*. See also Grenadier-Regiment 1058
Kampfgruppe Dobeneck: *28*
Kampfgruppe Eitner: *129, 138, 142, 175, 176, 177, 191, 198, 199, 200, 202, 203, 206*. See also Grenadier-Regiment 894
Kampfgruppe Hauser: *28*
Kampfgruppe Heintz: *26*
Kampfgruppe Hoffmann: *128, 129, 182, 190*. See also 709. Infanterie-Division
Kampfgruppe Kiewitt: *175, 176, 177*. See also Artillerie-Regiment 191
Kampfgruppe Klosterkemper: *190, 191, 198, 200*. See also Grenadier-Regiment 920
Kampfgruppe Lausberg: *142, 143*. See also Grenadier-Regiment 1050
Kampfgruppe Lewandowski: *175, 198*. See also Grenadier-Regiment 1058
Kampfgruppe Lüder: *28*
Kampfgruppe Moch: *175, 177*. See also Grenadier-Regiment 1058
Kampfgruppe Mügge: *176, 177, 184*. See also Grenadier-Regiment 1057
Kampfgruppe Müller: *181*. See also Grenadier-Regiment 922
Kampfgruppe Normandie: *56, 57, 58, 61*
Kampfgruppe Reiter: *176, 177, 184*. See also Grenadier-Regiment 1057
Kampfgruppe Richter: *175, 176, 177, 180, 182*. See also Grenadier-Regiment 1058
Kampfgruppe Schiller: *28*
Kampfgruppe Simon: *129, 130, 181, 186, 187, 188, 190, 190, 191, 195, 206*. See also Grenadier-Regiment 921
Kampfgruppe von Saldern: *187, 191, 195, 198*. See also Grenadier-Regiment 1057
Kampfgruppe Wittner. See Kampfgruppe Reiter
Nordgruppe (Schlieben): *26, 131, 133, 135, 136*
Südgruppe (Hellmich): *26, 131, 135, 136*
Untergruppe Eitner: *206*
Untergruppe Jäger: *195, 200, 203, 206, 207*
Untergruppe Klosterkemper: *138, 200, 203*. See also 243. Infanterie-Division
Untergruppe Lewandowski: *189, 200, 203, 206, 207, 209, 211*
Untergruppe Mecklenburg: *209*
Untergruppe Simon: *200, 206*

Miscellaneous: *61*
Artillerie Kommandeur 118 (Arko 118): *42, 52, 66, 78, 81*
Artillerie Kommandeur 474 (Arko 474): *71, 75, 78, 81*
Artillerie Kommandeur 484 (Arko 484): *81*
Artillerie Kommandeur 486 (Arko 486): *81*
Baustoff-Kolonne 429: *59*
Einsatzverband 390: *54, 58, 62, 63*
Feldgendarmerie-Trupp 177: *120*
Feldgendarmerie-Trupp 460: *78*
Feldkommandantur 723: *43*
Feldkommandantur 916: *43*
Festungs-Pionier-Abschnitts-Gruppe Beger: *65, 67*
Festungs-Pionier-Abschnitts-Gruppe I/11: *40*
Festungs-Pionier-Abschnitts-Gruppe II/11: *40, 57*
Festungs-Pionier-Abschnitts-Gruppe II/14: *57*
Festungs-Pionier-Gruppe 107: *67, 69.* See also Festungs-Pionier-Abschnitts-Gruppe Beger
Festungs-Pionier-Kommandeur XIV: *44*
Festungs-Pionier-Kommandeur XIX: *61*
Festungs-Pionier-Stab 9: *57*
Festungs-Pionier-Stab 11: *40, 42, 52, 57, 61, 63, 83*
Festungs-Pionier-Stab 19: *57, 57*
Festungs-Stamm-Abteilung LXXXIV: *52, 84*
Festungs-Stamm-Reserve Ob.West: *140*
Höheres Artillerie-Kommando 309: *86*
Kommandeur der Korps-Nachschubtruppen 460: *78, 86*
Kraftfahr-Abteilung LXXIV: *127*
Luftlandegeschwader 1: *177*
Luftlandegeschwader 2: *177*
Organisation Todt: *40, 47, 103, 225*
Übungsverband Le Havre: *38*

Regiments
Artillerie-Regiment 1, gepanzert: *44, 48*
Artillerie-Regiment 157: *34*
Artillerie-Regiment 177: *69, 111, 116, 121, 123, 124, 126, 129, 133, 134, 138, 139, 149, 150, 151, 192, 199, 209, 211, 213, 214*
Artillerie-Regiment 183: *36*
Artillerie-Regiment 191: *71, 73, 150, 160, 167, 168, 169, 171, 173, 175, 176, 177, 179, 180, 183, 184, 185, 186, 187, 188, 189, 196, 198, 199, 200, 202, 206, 207, 209, 210, 211, 212, 213, 216, 217*
Artillerie-Regiment 216: *34, 35, 36, 38*
Artillerie-Regiment 225: *34, 35*
Artillerie-Regiment 242: *56*
Artillerie-Regiment 243: *64, 67, 72, 187, 198, 209*
Artillerie-Regiment 265: *150, 151, 192, 199, 202, 206, 211, 212, 213, 214*
Artillerie-Regiment 319: *23, 35, 36, 37, 38, 39, 42, 44, 57, 32, 85*
Artillerie-Regiment 320: *38, 41, 42, 43, 45, 46*
Artillerie-Regiment 321: *63*
Artillerie-Regiment 323: *35, 38, 39, 40, 81*
Artillerie-Regiment 352: *61, 63, 66, 67, 75, 76*
Artillerie-Regiment 353: *142, 150, 151, 199, 200, 209, 211, 213, 214*
Artillerie-Regiment 355: *67, 111, 121*
Artillerie-Regiment 384: *54, 56*
Artillerie-Regiment 389: *51, 55, 61*
Artillerie-Regiment 656: *52, 53, 59*
Artillerie-Regiment 669: *52, 56, 63.* See also Artillerie-Regiment 709; See also Artillerie-Regiment 1709
Artillerie-Regiment 709: *52, 63*
Artillerie-Regiment 716: *52, 63.* See also Artillerie-Regiment 1716
Artillerie-Regiment 725: *86*
Artillerie-Regiment 1709: *63, 67, 75, 83.* See also Artillerie-Regiment 709; See also Artillerie-Regiment 669
Artillerie-Regiment 1716: *63, 75, 76.* See also Artillerie-Regiment 716
Artillerie-Regiment zbV 621: *48, 51, 54, 58, 59, 60, 66, 69, 72, 75, 172, 199, 200*
Fallschirm-Artillerie-Regiment 1: *41, 43*
Fallschirm-Artillerie-Regiment 2: *153*
Fallschirm-Artillerie-Regiment 5: *150, 151*
Fallschirmjäger-Ersatz- und Ausbildungs-Regiment 1 (Fj.Ers.u.Ausb.Rgt. 1: *75, 176, 187*
Fallschirmjäger-Ersatz- und Ausbildungs-Regiment 2: *152*
Fallschirmjäger-Regiment 1: *41*
Fallschirmjäger-Regiment 3: *41, 42*
Fallschirmjäger-Regiment 4: *41, 42, 43*
Fallschirmjäger-Regiment 5: *41, 42, 43*
Fallschirmjäger-Regiment 6: *9, 11, 23, 26, 72, 73, 147, 158, 171, 172, 175, 177, 178, 179, 180, 181, 182, 183, 185, 186, 187, 188, 189, 198, 216*
Fallschirmjäger-Regiment 7: *153*
Fallschirmjäger-Regiment 13: *129*
Fallschirmjäger-Regiment 15: *26, 144, 145, 146, 147, 148, 149, 150, 151, 211, 213*
Flak-Regiment 30: *172*
Flak-Regiment 155: *63*
Flieger-Regiment 32 (Luftwaffe): *75*
Flieger-Regiment 90: *62.* See also Fluganwarter-Bataillon II
(Gebirgs) Artillerie-Regiment 191: *166, 167.* See also Artillerie-Regiment 191
Grenadier-Regiment 336: *67, 110, 121.* See also Grenadier-Regiment 1050
Grenadier-Regiment 534: *54*
Grenadier-Regiment 535: *54, 57*
Grenadier-Regiment 536: *54*
Grenadier-Regiment 544: *51*
Grenadier-Regiment 546: *51*
Grenadier-Regiment 586: *45*
Grenadier-Regiment 589: *63.* See also Grenadier-Regiment 915
Grenadier-Regiment 726: *46, 48, 52, 57, 58, 63, 67, 69, 74, 75, 76*
Grenadier-Regiment 729: *45, 46, 47, 57, 66*
Grenadier-Regiment 736: *47, 53, 76*
Grenadier-Regiment 739: *45, 45, 46, 48, 52, 55, 73, 75*
Grenadier-Regiment 857: *124*
Grenadier-Regiment 894: *137, 138, 142, 149, 150, 151, 192, 198, 200, 202, 206, 209, 211, 212, 214*
Grenadier-Regiment 895: *149, 151, 192, 198, 206, 209, 211*
Grenadier-Regiment 896: *149, 150, 151, 195, 198, 200, 206, 211, 212*
Grenadier-Regiment 897: *152*
Grenadier-Regiment 914: *60, 61, 63, 67, 75, 180, 185, 187, 188, 206, 213.* See also Infanterie-Regiment 869
Grenadier-Regiment 915: *60, 61, 63, 63, 63, 67, 74, 74, 74, 74, 75.* See also Infanterie-Regiment 871; See also Grenadier-Regiment 589
Grenadier-Regiment 916: *60, 61, 63, 67, 74, 75, 76.* See also Infanterie-Regiment 546
Grenadier-Regiment 919: *56, 57, 58, 59, 61, 66, 73, 176, 179, 180*
Grenadier-Regiment 920: *56, 61, 63, 64, 69, 71, 72, 130, 186, 187, 190, 191, 198*
Grenadier-Regiment 921: *11, 64, 68, 69, 71, 72, 130, 181, 186, 187, 190, 191, 195, 198, 200, 206, 213*
Grenadier-Regiment 922: *56, 58, 61, 63, 64, 67, 69, 71, 72, 130, 133, 135, 187, 188, 190, 191, 198, 206*
Grenadier-Regiment 941: *144, 213*
Grenadier-Regiment 942: *142, 143, 213*
Grenadier-Regiment 1021: *64, 66, 67, 108, 110, 120, 121*
Grenadier-Regiment 1025: *158, 160, 162, 167, 170.* See also Grenadier-Regiment 1057
Grenadier-Regiment 1032: *110, 158, 162*
Grenadier-Regiment 1049: *110, 113, 114, 115, 116, 119, 120, 121, 123, 124, 126, 128, 129, 130, 133, 134, 136, 137, 138, 139, 140, 142, 144, 146, 147, 148, 149, 150, 151, 187, 188, 189, 190, 192, 198, 206, 211, 212, 214*

Grenadier-Regiment 1050: *110, 113, 114, 115, 116, 120, 121, 123, 124, 126, 127, 128, 129, 130, 133, 134, 135, 136, 137, 138, 140, 142, 143, 144, 146, 148, 149, 150, 151, 152, 187, 190, 191, 198, 199, 200, 202, 211, 213, 214*

Grenadier-Regiment 1057: *71, 73, 130, 150, 161, 162, 163, 164, 165, 171, 172, 175, 176, 177, 179, 181, 182, 184, 185, 186, 187, 190, 191, 195, 196, 198, 199, 200, 203, 206, 207, 209, 210, 211, 214, 217*

Grenadier-Regiment 1058: *71, 73, 151, 162, 163, 164, 170, 171, 175, 177, 179, 180, 181, 182, 183, 186, 187, 188, 189, 196, 198, 203, 206, 207, 209, 210, 211, 213, 214*

Grenadier-Regiment Reithinger: *46, 48*
Grenadier-Regiment zbV 752: *23, 69, 106, 127, 175, 191*
Heeres-Küsten-Artillerie-Regiment 644: *46, 59, 63*
Heeres-Küsten-Artillerie-Regiment 645: *52, 59, 63, 63*. See also Heeres-Küsten-Artillerie-Regiment 1262
Heeres-Küsten-Artillerie-Regiment 760: *59*. See also Heeres-Küsten-Artillerie-Regiment 645
Heeres-Küsten-Artillerie-Regiment 761: *59*. See also Heeres-Küsten-Artillerie-Regiment 645
Heeres-Küsten-Artillerie-Regiment 762: *59*. See also Heeres-Küsten-Artillerie-Regiment 644
Heeres-Küsten-Artillerie-Regiment 1261: *63, 81, 177, 180, 199, 206, 214*. See also Heeres-Küsten-Artillerie-Regiment 644
Heeres-Küsten-Artillerie-Regiment 1262: *63, 71, 124*. See also Heeres-Küsten-Artillerie-Regiment 645
Infanterie-Regiment 79: *34, 169*
Infanterie-Regiment 199: *34*
Infanterie-Regiment 217: *34*
Infanterie-Regiment 251: *36*
Infanterie-Regiment 257: *36*
Infanterie-Regiment 277: *31, 36, 37*
Infanterie-Regiment 333: *34*
Infanterie-Regiment 348: *34, 38*
Infanterie-Regiment 376: *34*
Infanterie-Regiment 377: *34*
Infanterie-Regiment 396: *34*
Infanterie-Regiment 398: *34, 196*
Infanterie-Regiment 536: *54*
Infanterie-Regiment 544: *52, 54*
Infanterie-Regiment 546: *55, 56, 61*
Infanterie-Regiment 582: *35, 36, 37, 57*
Infanterie-Regiment 583: *35, 37, 38, 57*
Infanterie-Regiment 584: *35, 37, 39*
Infanterie-Regiment 585: *38, 39, 40, 42, 43, 44, 45*
Infanterie-Regiment 586: *38, 40, 41, 42, 43, 44, 45, 46*
Infanterie-Regiment 587: *39, 40, 44, 45, 46*

Infanterie-Regiment 591: *35*
Infanterie-Regiment 593: *35, 39*
Infanterie-Regiment 594: *35*
Infanterie-Regiment 726: *36, 46, 48, 52, 53, 57, 67, 69, 74, 75, 76*
Infanterie-Regiment 729: *45, 46, 47, 48, 48, 50, 52, 53, 55, 56, 66, 67*
Infanterie-Regiment 731: *38*
Infanterie-Regiment 736: *36, 46, 48, 50, 51, 52, 57, 61, 63, 67, 69, 76*
Infanterie-Regiment 739: *46, 48, 50, 54, 57, 61, 63, 66, 67*
Infanterie-Regiment 744: *38*
Infanterie-Regiment 869: *56, 57, 61*
Infanterie-Regiment 871: *56, 57, 61*
Infanterie-Regiment 973: *110*. See also Grenadier-Regiment 1050
Infanterie-Regiment Reithinger: *44*
Luft-Nachrichten-Regiment 53: *43*
Panzer-Artillerie-Regiment 89: *52, 52*
Panzer-Artillerie-Regiment 155: *76*
Panzer-Grenadier-Regiment 21: *52, 52*
Panzer-Grenadier-Regiment 125: *76*
Panzer-Grenadier-Regiment 192: *76*
Panzer-Regiment 100: *47, 50, 58, 61, 76*
Panzer-Regiment 202: *44*
Regiment Krug: *47*
Regiment Rohrbach: *47*
Reserve-Radfahr-Regiment 30: *48*
schweres Stellungs-Werfer-Regiment 101: *64, 67, 71, 72, 73, 75*. See also schwere Werfer-Abteilung 103
Sicherungs-Regiment 5: *50*
Sicherungs-Regiment 195: *62, 63, 65*
SS-Panzer-Artillerie-Regiment 2: *212*
SS-Panzer-Grenadier-Regiment 3 "Deutschland": *144*
SS-Panzer-Grenadier-Regiment 4 "Der Führer": *44, 144*

Italian
1st Italian Naval Infantry Division: *126*

MILITARY OPERATIONS, PLACES AND LINES

Atlantikwall: *43, 44, 50, 59, 63, 64, 82, 105*
Beuzeville bridgehead: *190, 191, 200*
Bewegung Cherbourg: *132, 133, 195*
Bewegung Leonore: *171*
Caumont Gap: *21*
D-Day: *7, 8, 9, 10, 15, 17, 19, 21, 23, 25, 26, 32, 35, 46, 69, 75, 76, 78, 80, 84, 85, 86, 89, 98, 99, 100, 106, 108, 110, 112, 115, 118, 119, 123, 150, 158, 160, 161, 162, 163, 164, 169, 175, 176, 177, 179, 180, 187, 188, 196, 198, 202*
Epsom Offensive: *21*
Falaise Pocket: *9, 23*
Festung Cherbourg: *26, 68, 69, 72, 72, 81, 82, 130, 136, 172, 185, 190, 196*
Festung St. Malo: *123, 124, 126, 152, 153, 156*
Festung St. Nazaire: *217*
Mahlmann-Linie: *26, 140, 142, 143, 199, 207, 209*
Merderet bridgehead: *128, 129*
Nordfront: *8, 26, 27, 136, 142, 144, 145, 146, 147, 151, 184, 190, 192, 196, 199, 200, 202, 207, 209, 211, 213, 214, 216*
Omaha Beach: *8, 26, 186*
Operation Barbarossa: *34*
Operation Cobra: *8, 9, 27, 151, 214*
Unternehmen Fichte: *158*
Unternehmen Lüttich: *28*
Unternehmen Tanne: *158*
Utah Beach: *6, 26, 66, 86, 176, 178*
Verteidigungsbereich Brest: *82*
Verteidigungsbereich Cherbourg: *82*
Verteidigungsbereich Lorient: *82*
Verteidigungsbereich St. Nazaire: *82*
Wasserlinie: *8, 26, 140, 147, 148, 200, 210, 211, 214, 216*
Westfront: *17, 26, 130, 131, 184, 190, 192, 195, 196*

MISCELLANEOUS

Armed Forces Daily Announcement (Wehrmachtsbericht): *144, 147, 196, 204*
Band of Brothers: *179*
Knight's Cross: *135, 146, 188*
Nationalsozialistischer-Führungsoffizier (NSFO): *80*
U-Boot: *82*
ULTRA: *11, 23, 75, 138*

P

PLACE NAMES

Abbaye de Blanchelande: *146*
Agneaux: *75*
Airel: *38, 46, 59, 62, 63, 67*
Alderney: *37, 38, 39*
Alençon: *43*
Amblie: *67*
Amfreville: *74, 75, 76, 178, 179, 184, 185, 187, 188, 189*
Angers: *52, 53, 63, 68, 121*
Angoville: *76, 137, 147, 176*
Anisy: *69*
Appeville: *73, 185*
Argentan: *28, 36, 40, 48, 49, 140*
Arromanches: *21, 34*
Asnelles-sur-Mer: *75, 76*
Asnières-en-Bessin: *76*
Aubigny: *76*
Audouville-la-Hubert: *61*
Audrieu: *121*
Aumeville: *73*
Aunay-sur-Odon: *43*
Avranches: *27, 28, 42, 43, 70, 152, 153, 175, 216, 217*
Ay River: *6, 8, 140, 199, 200, 214*
Azeville: *46*
Bactol: *214*
Bagnoles-de-l'Orne: *36*
Baie de la Fresnaye: *124*
Baie de St. Brieuc: *123*
Baie du Mont-St. Michel: *126, 217*
Balleroy: *25, 43, 44, 49, 69*
Banc de Madeleine: *86*
Barfleur: *5, 40, 67*
Barneville: *5, 23, 69, 72, 133, 134, 138, 171, 196*
Baron-sur-Odon: *121*
Basse Addeville: *182*
Bassin á Flot: *188*
Baumholder Training Area: *158, 160, 170, 177*
Baupte River: *8, 58, 72, 73, 129, 142, 147, 176, 177, 184, 189, 191, 192, 202*
Bayeux: *21, 25, 46, 52, 53, 57, 58, 61, 66, 67, 69, 70, 75, 76, 86, 121*
Bay of Biscay: *21*
Beauchamps: *216*
Beau Coudray: *142, 144, 147*
Beaumont-Hague: *56, 57, 63, 73, 182, 199*
Belle Eneau: *182*

Bellengreville: *69, 121*
Bénouville: *50*
Besneville: *72, 133, 171, 175, 176, 199*
Beuville: *76*
Beuzeville-au-Plain: *57, 66, 73*
Beuzeville-la-Bastille: *176, 187, 189*
Bitsch (Bitche) Training Area: *170*
Blainville-sur-Mer: *69*
Blanchelande: *43, 48*
Blandamour: *73, 171*
Blosville: *58, 69, 183*
Bois de la Poterie: *143, 144*
Bois de Limors: *6, 200, 202, 203, 209*
Bois d'Étenclin: *73, 171*
Bolleville: *54*
Bout de Ville: *123*
Brécey: *21, 43*
Brécourt: *177, 179*
Bréhal: *66, 74, 216*
Brest: *17, 40, 153*
Bretagne: *10, 17, 19, 21, 23, 26, 40, 42, 44, 47, 51, 52, 56, 57, 58, 61, 63, 64, 65, 66, 68, 69, 71, 72, 81, 108, 116, 118, 119, 123, 126, 127, 128, 137, 145, 147, 151, 152, 199, 206*
Bretteville: *43, 66, 121, 200*
Bretteville-l'Orgueilleuse: *67*
Brévands: *180, 187*
Bréville: *123*
Bricquebec: *5, 48, 50, 54, 55, 57, 63, 66, 67, 69, 73, 133, 134, 136, 176, 196*
Bricqueville-la-Blouette: *214*
Bricqueville-sur-Mer: *45, 216*
Briouze: *28, 76*
Brix: *39, 40, 43, 62, 172, 175*
Brouay: *121*
Cabourg: *75*
Caen: *17, 21, 23, 25, 28, 40, 42, 43, 46, 53, 54, 57, 61, 66, 67, 69, 70, 76, 108, 110, 121, 123*
Cagny: *76, 121, 123*
Cairon: *121*
Calvados: *9, 21, 23, 34, 36, 38, 40, 42, 43, 46, 48, 51, 53, 54, 59, 60, 61, 63, 65, 67, 69, 70, 71, 74, 75, 76, 81, 86*
Campbon: *217*
Camp d'Avours: *42*
Canal du Couesnon: *69*
Canal du Port de Carentan: *57*
Cancale: *123, 124, 124, 124, 124, 124, 126*
Canisy: *44, 51, 61*

Canteloup: *54*
Cantepie: *187*
Canvale: *126*
Canville-la-Rocque: *199, 200*
Cap de Carteret: *69, 70, 71*
Cap de Flamanville: *56*
Cap de la Hague: *6, 71*
Carcagny: *69*
Carentan: *5, 6, 8, 9, 21, 26, 27, 37, 38, 44, 50, 51, 54, 56, 57, 58, 61, 63, 64, 66, 72, 73, 129, 142, 147, 172, 175, 176, 177, 179, 180, 183, 184, 185, 186, 187, 188, 189, 192, 206, 211, 212*
Carpiquet: *43, 61, 121*
Carquebut: *182*
Carrefour St. Jores: *142*
Carteret: *5, 42, 46, 61*
Câtelet: *73*
Catteville: *199*
Catz: *75*
Caudard: *72*
Caumont: *21, 43, 44, 67, 75*
Cauquigny: *179, 182, 184, 185*
Cérences: *45, 48, 69, 216, 217*
Cerisy-la-Forêt: *63*
Cézembre: *155*
Chambert: *72*
Champ Moqtet: *72. See also La Chalerie*
Channel Coast: *32, 34, 35*
Channel Islands: *17, 23, 32, 34, 35, 36, 37, 38, 39, 40, 44, 56, 57, 58*
Château Brocboeufs: *73, 171*
Château Castillon: *67, 75*
Château d'Amfreville: *184*
Château d'Auxais: *61*
Château de Broglie: *31*
Château de Courcy: *58*
Château de Juaye: *67*
Château de Jucoville: *75*
Château de l'Ermitage: *48*
Château de Pépinvast: *46*
Château de Tourville: *46*
Château Digosville: *61*
Château du Bigard: *73*
Châteaudun: *41, 42, 43*
Château Franquetot: *69*
Château Frêsne: *123*
Château de Bernaville: *73, 171*
Château Jucoville: *61*
Château Les Désert: *64*

Château Malassis: *72*
Châteauneuf-d'Ille-et-Vilaine: *153*
Château Rupalet: *64*
Château Brocboeufs: *196*
Château de Bernaville: *179*
Château Perron: *64*
Chaulieu: *202*
Chef-du-Pont: *175, 176, 179, 184*
Cherbourg: *5, 6, 8, 23, 26, 34, 42, 43, 44, 45, 46, 48, 48, 50, 52, 54, 56, 57, 61, 62, 63, 66, 73, 78, 82, 83, 84, 86, 86, 127, 129, 129, 130, 131, 132, 133, 135, 136, 137, 149, 175, 187, 188, 189, 190, 192, 192, 195, 196, 226*
Cherbourg Peninsula: *5*
Chérencé-le-Roussel: *28*
Cherrueix: *126*
Cité (St. Malo Citadel): *155*
Clécy: *76*
Coëtquidan Training Area: *75*
Coigny: *47, 61*
Colleville-sur-Mer: *67*
Colleville-sur-Orne: *76*
Colombelles: *76*
Colombières: *55, 64, 69*
Colombiers-sur-Seulles: *67*
Colomby: *72, 133*
Condé-sur-Noireau: *36, 76*
Cormelles-le-Royal: *67, 121*
Cosniam: *72. See also* La Maison Quoniam
Cotentin: *5, 6, 7, 8, 9, 23, 24, 25, 26, 34, 38, 40, 42, 44, 45, 46, 48, 50, 52, 54, 56, 57, 58, 59, 61, 62, 63, 64, 65, 67, 68, 69, 70, 71, 72, 73, 74, 75, 81, 86, 89, 106, 110, 116, 127, 130, 131, 132, 133, 135, 136, 137, 138, 139, 169, 171, 172, 182, 184, 186, 188, 190, 192, 195, 196, 199, 202, 204, 209*
Courcy: *58, 147, 214*
Coutances: *5, 23, 37, 40, 41, 42, 44, 49, 70, 71, 74, 127, 128, 142, 147, 198, 214, 216*
Créances: *209*
Crépon: *75, 76*
Cresserons: *69, 76*
Cricqueville-en-Bessin: *75*
Crosville: *131, 192*
Cuilberville: *36*
Cussy: *67, 200*
Cuve: *147*
Cuverville: *123*
Dahoët: *123*
Dangy: *216*

Dax: *21*
D-Day Beaches
Utah Beach: *6, 66, 86, 176, 178*
Digosville: *46*
Dinan: *116, 123, 153*
Dinan: *153*
Dinard: *123, 124, 153, 155*
Dives River: *28, 31, 31, 70*
Dives-sur-Mer: *34*
Dol-de-Bretagne: *123, 126, 152, 153*
Domfront: *36, 48, 86*
Douer River: *69, 126*
Douve River: *6, 26, 38, 58, 74, 128, 129, 131, 137, 138, 139, 176, 177, 179, 180, 183, 187, 188, 189, 190, 191, 192, 195, 196, 198, 199, 200*
Ducey: *43, 153*
Duprey: *203*
Émondeville: *63, 180*
Épinay-sur-Odon: *123*
Équeurdreville: *56*
Éroudeville: *128*
Erquy: *118, 124, 126*
Étienville: *58, 61, 132, 195*
Étoupeville: *72*
Étréham: *67, 76*
Éturville: *182*
Évran: *123*
Évrecy: *49*
Falaise: *9, 23, 28, 36, 40, 52, 64, 66, 76, 123*
Fauville: *56*
Feugères: *57*
Fierville-la-Campagne: *76*
Fierville-les-Mines: *133*
Flamanville: *56, 69, 71, 72*
Flaux: *184*
Flers: *28, 48*
Florimond: *146*
Flottemanville: *54, 57*
Folligny: *216*
Fontaine-Henry: *121*
Fontenay-le-Pesnel: *66, 121*
Fontenay-sur-Mer: *58*
Forêt de Cerisy: *66*
Forêt de Mont-Castre: *6, 73, 142, 143, 144, 199*
Formigny: *76*
Fort du Roule: *56*
Fougères: *38, 43, 48*

Francquetot: *73*
Franquetot: *69*
Fresné-la-Mère: *76*
Fresville: *176, 187*
Frimot: *72*
Gare de Denneville: *203*
Gavray: *69, 216*
Geffosses: *216*
Gerville-la-Forêt: *73*
Girard: *176*
Gironde River: *40*
Golleville: *196*
Gonfréville: *147*
Gorges: *6, 8, 26, 64, 72, 142, 147, 199, 214*
Gorin-l'Epinay-Tesson: *57*
Gouet River: *123*
Gourbesville: *129, 131, 179, 185, 187, 189, 192*
Gouttière: *133*
Gouville-sur-Mer: *74*
Grandcamp: *75*
Granville: *17, 23, 35, 37, 42, 43, 69, 71, 74, 127, 216*
Grasville: *46*
Gratot: *214*
Graye-sur-Mer: *76*
Gréville: *64*
Grière: *217*
Grosville: *73*
Grouville-la-Fontaine: *57*
Gruchy: *147*
Guernsey: *36, 37, 57*
Gueutteville: *184*
Guilberville: *86*
Guingamp: *124*
Hainneville: *68, 73, 75*
Halte la Guillaumerie: *144*
Hamars: *123*
Hameau aux Petits: *72*
Hameau ès Galle: *73*
Hameau de Haut: *202*
Hameau Dupré. *See* St. Lô-d'Ourville
Hameau Gaillot: *133*
Hameau le Haquais: *72*
Hameau Quettier: *133*
Hatainville: *67, 72*
Haut Gue: *137*
Haut Mesnil: *67*
Hautteville: *192, 195*

Helleville: *73*
Hémevez: *42*
Hénansal: *123*
Hérenguerville: *216*
Hérouville-St. Clair: *76*
Hiesville: *176, 180*
Hill 20: *180*
Hill 30: *147, 179, 182, 184, 188, 189*
Hill 41: *144*
Hill 92: *147*
Hill 112: *123, 144*
Hill 121: *6, 144, 169, 172, 175, 176, 209*
Hill 122: *144, 144, 144, 144*
Hill 131: *6, 146, 169, 172, 175, 176, 200, 209*
Hill 145: *134, 138*
Hillion: *126*
Holdy: *177*
Houesville: *47, 180, 182*
Houtteville: *185*
Isigny-sur-Mer: *38, 46, 52, 57, 58, 61, 66, 68, 75, 187*
Jersey: *36, 37, 57*
Jobourg Peninsula: *6, 45, 46, 48, 61, 67, 70, 72, 73*
Jort: *76*
Josefsberg: *153*
Juaye: *67, 76*
La Baleine: *27, 216*
La Banserie: *214*
La Barrière-du-Lude: *73*
La Basseour: *195*
La Bouillie: *124*
La Bourgogne: *209*
La Butte: *143, 144*
La Cambe: *60, 61, 75, 76*
La Caponnerie: *204, 209*
La Chalerie: *72. See also* Champ Moqtet
La Commanderie: *73*
La Coquerie: *64, 175*
La Cotellerie: *209*
La Croix: *123, 133, 199*
La Cuiroterie: *202, 204*
La Doderie: *216*
La Dranguerie: *202*
La Ferté-Macé: *40*
La Feuillie: *209*
La Fèvrerie: *202*
La Fière: *179, 182*
La Fresnerie: *210*

La Glacerie: *54, 75*
La Groudière: *202, 204*
La Guilloterie: *202*
La Guimorais: *124*
La Haye-du-Puits: *5, 6, 37, 39, 40, 42, 43, 46, 48, 51, 52, 53, 54, 56, 58, 62, 64, 66, 67, 71, 72, 73, 127, 128, 130, 133, 134, 140, 142, 144, 146, 171, 172, 175, 176, 177, 190, 195, 196, 199, 200, 203, 209*
La Haye-Pesnel: *216, 217*
La Jardinerie: *73, 171, 175*
La Lande: *128, 184*
La Ligue: *73, 171*
La Madeleine: *58*
La Maison Quoniam: *72. See also* Cosniam
La Manche: *5–12*
La Martinerie: *209*
La Massuère: *124*
Lamballe: *123*
La Meauffe: *86*
La Moignerie: *184*
La Motinerie: *74*
Lande de Bangard: *210*
Lande de Lessay: *5, 59, 210*
Landigou: *28*
Langon: *217*
La Noé: *67, 76*
Lantheuil: *66, 121*
Lanvallay: *123*
La Pasquerie: *73*
La Pécherie: *184*
La Pernelle: *60, 69*
La Pesquerie: *185*
La Poterie: *6, 143, 144, 192, 202, 209*
La Poterie Ridge: *6*
La Rivagerie: *144*
La Rivière: *202, 204*
La Roche à Coucou: *71, 71*
La Rochelle: *83, 152*
La Ronde-Haye: *207*
La Rue Baton: *200*
La Sangsurière: *204*
Lasson: *121*
Lastelle: *142*
La Table: *216*
La Tourelle: *146, 147*
Laulne: *133, 146, 147*
La Valaisserie: *137*

l'Avenel: *46*
La Vilette: *144*
La Ville Garnier: *124*
Le Becqueret: *204*
Le Bigard: *57, 63, 67, 73*
Lébisey: *123*
Le Buisson: *209*
Le Carrefour: *133*
Le Dézert: *43, 50, 56, 63, 64, 67, 84*
Le Fresne: *148*
Le Fry: *144*
Le Gardin: *73*
Le Ham: *49, 54, 66, 128, 129, 179, 187, 196*
Le Haut Gaillon: *73*
Le Haut-Geley: *171, 175*
Le Havre: *43*
Le Hequet: *176, 177*
Le Hommet: *142, 147*
Le Mans: *62, 116*
Le Melleret: *176*
Le Mesnil: *57, 67, 69, 75, 76, 216*
Le Molay: *53, 58, 61, 62, 65*
Le Moulin: *189*
Le Moulinet: *187*
Le Parc de la Mare: *76*
l'Epinay-Tesson: *57, 67*
Le Plessis: *144, 189, 199*
Le Poiré: *128*
Le Pont aux Moines: *72, 133*
Le Port: *124, 182, 187*
Le Port St. Hubert: *124*
Le Repas: *216*
Le Rivage: *217*
Le Rouillais: *211*
Le Rozel: *72*
Les Aubris: *184*
Les Carrières: *177*
Les Courts: *69*
Les Droueries: *182*
Les Fosses: *133*
Les Fresnaies: *176*
Les Landes: *128, 184, 188*
Les Mesnil-Aubert: *216*
Les Milleries. *See* Longuet
Les Moitiers-en-Bauptois: *189, 192, 199, 200*
Les Noires Terres: *184*
Les Oubeaux: *64*

Les Perques: *134*
Les Pieux: *48, 49, 54, 56, 71, 72, 73*
Les Rivières: *143*
Les Rosaires: *123*
Les Sablons: *202, 204, 209*
Les Salines: *45*
Lessay: *5, 8, 26, 42, 43, 48, 58, 59, 64, 66, 72, 73, 127, 133, 137, 140, 142, 175, 177, 200, 204, 209, 210, 214*
Lestre: *46, 73*
Les Verges: *74*
Les Veys: *75*
L'Étang-Bertrand: *133, 134, 136*
Le Temple: *148*
Le Val: *146, 202*
Le Valdecie: *138*
Le Valhue: *134*
Le Vast: *46, 60, 66, 73*
Le Vivier-sur-Mer: *126*
Le Vrétot: *72*
l'Hioval: *124*
l'Hôpital: *124*
l'Hôtellerie: *73*
Lison: *46*
Lithaire: *46, 143, 200*
Littry: *67, 69, 75*
Loire River: *17*
Longuet: *216*
Lorient: *19, 171*
L'Ossière: *73, 171, 177*
Luçon: *152*
Magneville: *133*
Maison Bosquet: *134*
Maisons: *57, 76*
Manche: *5, 34, 35, 37, 42, 47, 69, 71, 74, 75, 81, 127, 151, 175*
Marchésieux: *56*
Marigny: *37, 56*
Martragny: *66, 121*
Mathieu: *76*
Matignon: *123, 124*
Mauger: *72*
Maupertus: *5*
Mayenne: *44*
May-sur-Orne: *67, 76, 121*
Méautis: *61, 183*
Merderet River: *6, 24, 26, 127, 128, 129, 130, 176, 177, 178, 179, 180, 181, 182, 184, 185, 186, 187, 188, 190, 192*
Merdrignac: *152*

Merville: *75*
Mesnil-au-Val: *54, 61*
Mestry: *67, 75*
Michauderie: *60*
Miniac-Morvan: *123, 127, 153*
Mobecq: *143, 144, 146*
Mont-Castre: *6, 73, 142, 144, 146, 147, 199, 200*
Mont du Tot: *146*
Montebourg: *5, 6, 26, 40, 44, 45, 46, 48, 50, 53, 55, 56, 57, 58, 60, 66, 72, 73, 127, 128, 129, 133, 136, 175, 177, 179, 180, 182, 184, 185, 186, 192, 199*
Montfiquet: *67*
Montgardon Ridge: *6*
Montmartin-sur-Mer: *69, 216*
Mont-St. Michel: *34, 35, 45, 70, 126, 151*
Montsurvent: *64, 214*
Mortain: *36, 48, 86*
Mouen: *66, 121*
Moult: *123*
Mt. de Doville: *169, 172, 209. See also* Hill 121
Mt. Étenclin: *169, 172. See also* Hill 131
Muneville-le-Bingard-Millières: *147*
Muneville-sur-Mer: *216*
N13 Highway: *5, 123, 175*
Nacqueville: *57, 69*
Nantes: *171*
Négreville: *69, 172*
Néhou: *128, 131, 133, 134, 136, 192, 195*
Neufmesnil: *46*
Neuilly-la-Forêt: *67, 75*
Neuville-au-Plain: *180, 181, 182, 188, 199*
Noirpalu: *148*
Normandy Peninsula: *5*
Noyers-Bocage: *49, 121*
Octeville: *46, 57, 66, 73*
Ollande River: *135*
Olonde River: *203, 204*
Orglandes: *24, 61, 130, 131, 132, 133, 192, 195*
Orne River: *21, 28, 31, 44, 61, 76, 123*
Orval: *214, 216*
Ouistreham: *76*
Paramé: *124*
Paris: *5, 123, 156, 188*
Pas-de-Calais: *41*
Pépinvast: *46, 69*
Percy: *49, 66, 216*
Périers: *5, 8, 9, 26, 27, 38, 42, 44, 46, 48, 54, 55, 64, 72, 73, 129,*

130, 133, 142, 144, 147, 177, 180, 184, 188, 190, 199, 209, 210, 211, 212, 216
Picauville: *175, 179, 184, 185, 187*
Pierreville: *71*
Pigard: *195*
Pirou: *209, 216*
Pissot: *147, 207*
Plancoët: *123*
Pléchâtel: *217*
Pléhérel: *124*
Pléneuf: *123, 124*
Plérin: *123*
Pleslin: *124*
Pleurtuit: *124, 153*
Plouescat: *17*
Pointe de la Garde Guérin: *153*
Pointe de l'Assiette: *123*
Pointe de la Varde: *124*
Pointe de Pléneuf: *123*
Pointe de Pordic: *123*
Pointe du Hoc: *75*
Pointe du Pornic: *123*
Pointe et Raz de la Percée,: *35*
Pontaubault: *17, 69, 126, 153*
Pontchâteau: *171*
Pont-Hébert: *62*
Pont-l'Abbé: *6, 64, 72, 74, 132, 150, 176, 179, 184, 185, 187, 188, 189, 190, 192, 200*
Pontorson: *69, 126, 127, 151, 152, 153, 217*
Portbail: *5, 35, 71, 72, 73, 133, 175, 196, 199, 203*
Port en Bessin: *34, 59*
Prairies Marécageuses: *6, 26, 58, 71, 176, 195, 197, 199, 202, 204*
Prairies Marécageuses de Gorges: *6, 8, 26, 142, 189, 199*
Prétot: *129, 199, 200, 202, 209*
Pte. des Tablettes: *123*
Putanges: *28, 76*
Putot-en-Bessin: *66, 121*
Queron: *69*
Querqueville: *42, 69*
Quettehou: *60, 61, 66*
Quettetot: *69*
Quetteville: *73*
Quettreville: *216*
Quiberon: *40*
Quimper: *19*
Quinéville: *6, 59, 60, 185*
Raids: *180*

Rance River: *124, 153, 155*
Ranville: *74, 123*
Rauville-la-Place: *177, 188, 207, 209*
Rauville-le-Bigot: *49*
Ravenoville: *50*
Redon: *171*
Reigneville: *61, 191, 192*
Reims: *177*
Rennes: *44, 48, 51, 152, 153, 171, 217*
Renouf: *190*
Reviers: *67, 76*
Roncey: *27*
Rots: *67, 121*
Rue Bouille: *202*
Ruffosses: *48*
Ruisseau de Bachelet: *123*
Ryes: *67, 76*
Sainteny: *42, 54, 56, 61, 64, 67, 177*
Sartilly: *217*
Saussetour: *176*
Savenay: *217*
Scye River: *134*
Seine River: *21, 34*
Sélune River: *17, 69, 123, 126, 153*
Sèves River: *6, 8, 26, 140, 147, 200, 209*
Sideville: *51*
Sienne River: *216*
Soissons: *133*
Sommervieu: *54*
Sortosville: *69*
Sottevast: *5*
Sotteville: *63, 73*
Soulles River: *128*
Sourdeval: *28, 216*
St. Alban: *124*
St. André-sur-Orne: *76, 121, 123*
St. Anne: *171, 176*
St. Aubin-d'Arquenay: *50, 57*
St. Aubin-du-Perron: *142*
St. Aubin-sur-Mer: *75, 76*
St. Briac: *124*
St. Brieuc: *17, 123*
St. Cast-le-Guildo: *126*
St. Clément: *75*
Ste. Colombe: *131, 139, 189, 192*
St. Côme-du-Mont: *38, 44, 64, 73, 171, 175, 178, 180, 182, 183*
St. Coulomb: *124, 126*

St. Croix-Hague: *39, 46, 48, 51, 54, 57, 63, 73*
St. Croix-sur-Orne: *28*
St. Cyr: *73, 128, 171, 175*
Ste. Colombe: *131, 139, 192*
Ste. Croix-sur-Mer: *74, 76*
Ste. Marie-du-Mont: *57, 58, 67, 72, 175, 176, 177, 179, 180*
Ste. Mère-Église: *5, 54, 56, 58, 61, 72, 73, 131, 170, 175, 177, 178, 179, 180, 181, 182, 184, 185, 192, 198*
St. Erblon: *217*
Ste. Suzanne: *142, 192, 200, 209*
St. Fromond: *42, 46, 49, 57*
St. Georges-de-Bohon: *61, 187*
St. Germain-de-Tallevende: *75, 86*
St. Germain-de-Tournebut: *57*
St. Germain-sur-Ay: *137, 147, 199*
St. Germain-sur-Sèves: *8, 147*
St. Hélen: *123*
St. Hilaire-du-Harcouët: *40, 43, 48*
St. Jacques-de-Néhou: *128, 131, 133, 134, 136, 192*
St. Jacut-de-la-Mer: *124*
St. Jean-de-Daye: *40, 51, 56, 64*
St. Joan-de-Guérets: *153*
St. Jores: *61, 73, 142, 143, 144, 184, 202, 203, 209*
St. Jouan-des-Guérets: *124*
St. Laurent-sur-Mer: *69*
St.Léonard: *217*
St. Lô: *8, 19, 21, 26, 27, 35, 37, 42, 43, 44, 54, 57, 60, 61, 63, 65, 70, 72, 75, 80, 81, 84, 86, 127, 216*
St. Lô d'Ourville: *133, 135, 196, 199, 203*
St. Lunaire: *153*
St. Malo: *17, 43, 57, 69, 74, 108, 123, 124, 127, 128, 129, 130, 137, 147, 148, 152, 153, 155, 156, 211*
St. Marcouf: *42*
St. Martin-d'Audouville: *56, 56, 57*
St. Martin-de-Blagny: *75*
St. Martin-de-Fontenay: *67, 121*
St. Martin-des-Besaces: *49, 66*
St. Méloir-des-Ondes: *153*
St. Nazaire: *17, 40, 171, 217*
St. Nicolas: *71, 133, 203*
St. Paul-du-Vernay: *67, 76*
St. Pierre: *76*
St. Pierre-Église: *46, 62, 65, 67*
St. Pierre-sur-Dives: *76*
St. Pois: *28*
Strasbourg: *177*
St. Sauveur-Lendelin: *42, 44, 46, 64, 72, 74, 147, 148, 211, 216*

St. Sauveur-le-Vicomte: *5, 26, 40, 54, 55, 58, 61, 64, 67, 69, 72, 73, 74, 75, 127, 128, 130, 131, 132, 133, 136, 171, 172, 175, 176, 177, 187, 188, 189, 191, 192, 195, 196, 199, 200, 209*
St. Sébastien-de-Raids: *142, 216*
St. Servan: *124*
St. Sever: *36*
St. Sylvain: *67, 121*
St. Vaast-la-Hougue: *5, 40, 50, 58, 61*
St. Vigor-le-Grand: *57*
Sully: *76*
Surtainville Bight: *72, 73*
Tailleville: *76*
Taute River: *6, 8, 26, 187*
Terfouru: *67*
Terre de Beauval: *187*
Tessy-sur-Vire: *42, 66*
Teurteville: *75*
Teurthéville-Bocage: *61, 67*
Teurthéville-Hague: *52*
Théville: *5, 42*
Thiéville: *76*
Thury-Harcourt: *34, 66, 76, 123*
Tilly: *73*
Tilly-sur-Seulles: *55, 67, 75, 76*
Tinchebray-Bocage: *28*
Tirepied: *217*
Tocqueville: *52, 53, 57, 67, 73*
Tollevast: *52*
Tombelaine: *69, 126*
Tonneville: *57*
Torigni-sur-Vire: *40, 41, 42, 43, 44, 51, 55, 63, 75, 84, 86*
Tourlaville: *43, 69*
Tournières: *67*
Tourteville: *75*
Tourville-sur-Sienne: *216*
Tréauville: *72*
Trelly: *216*
Tressaint: *123, 152*
Trévières: *60, 66, 67, 75*
Tribehou: *61*
Troarn: *67, 121, 123*
Turqueville: *73, 176, 180*
Urville: *54, 123, 185, 192*
Valognes: *5, 46, 51, 57, 66, 73, 75, 81, 84, 127, 128, 130, 136, 171, 175, 179, 190, 195, 199*
Varenguebec: *143, 203, 207, 209*
Vauville: *71, 72, 73*

237

Ver: *216*
Verson: *76*
Vesly: *147, 204*
Vierville: *182*
Vieux: *69, 121*
Vildé la Marine: *124, 126*
Village ès Noels: *214*
Villages des Mières. *See* La Rivière
Villedieu-les-Poêles: *28, 40, 41, 44, 127, 148*
Villers-Bocage: *43, 49, 62, 86*
Villot: *135*
Vimont: *76*
Vindefontaine: *56, 64, 200, 202*
Vire: *25, 28, 38, 40, 44, 70, 75, 86, 185, 186*
Vire Estuary: *6, 8, 35, 37*
Vire River: *8, 9, 20, 23, 25, 26, 34, 37, 38, 58, 70, 185, 186*
Wahn: *171*
Waldbergstellung: *199*. *See also* Mahlmann-Linie
Westwall: *39, 43*
Yffiniac: *123, 123, 123, 123, 123, 126*

PROPER NAMES

Bacherer, Rudolf: *108, 113, 128, 134, 135, 136, 137, 147, 151, 152, 153, 155, 217*
Bartuzat: *175, 178*
Baumann: *118*
Bayer von Bayersburg: *186*
Behlendorff, Hans: *34*
Beigang: *161, 181, 182*
Benzmann: *84*
Bernhardt: *40*
Beust, Henning von: *137*
Bickel: *179*
Bittrich, Wilhelm: *21*
Blaskowitz, Johannes: *15, 15*
Blumentritt, Günther: *15, 48, 50, 82, 132*
Bohnenkamp: *169, 187*
Bradley, Omar: *23*
Brandt: *113, 128, 134, 137*
Buckreihs: *171*
Burkhard: *119, 120*
Choltitz, Dietrich von: *23, 81, 137, 145, 210*
Criegern, Friedrich von: *23, 31, 181*
Dempsey, Miles: *23*
Diekhoff: *183*
Dietrich Sepp: *21*

Dollmann, Friedrich: *17, 21, 66, 72, 130, 132, 155, 190, 192*
Dropmann: *143, 146*
Eitner: *172, 184, 191, 198, 200, 209*
Elfeldt, Otto: *23, 31*
Evers: *175*
Fahrmbacher, Wilhelm: *17, 23, 132, 136, 137, 153, 190, 195*
Falley, Wilhelm: *158, 178*
Förster: *180*
Gersdorff, Rudolf-Christoph Freiherr von: *17*
Guderian, Heinz: *96*
Gärtner: *128*
Hamann: *81*
Harrison, Gordon A., author: *6, 138*
Hausser, Paul: *17, 21, 23*
Hayn: *23, 31, 132*
Hellmich, Heinz: *23, 24, 25, 26, 130, 131, 133, 137, 184, 190, 195, 196, 199*
Hellwig: *61*
Hitler, Adolf: *17, 23, 36, 38, 39, 40, 43, 55, 59, 63, 66, 71, 81, 132, 133, 135, 136, 137, 145, 147, 195, 196*
Hoffmann: *182*
Hümmerich: *85*
Indlekofer: *129, 135, 142*
Jühne: *78*
Jäger: *153*
Karsten: *146*
Kattermann: *166*
Keil: *179, 180*
Keitel, Wilhelm: *137*
Kiewitt: *166*
Klosterkemper, Bernard: *178, 188, 196, 211*
Kluge, Günther von: *15, 17, 23, 152*
Koch-Erpach, Rudolf: *32*
Kohtz: *83*
Konrad: *120*
Kruse, Hermann: *42, 52, 81*
Kuhle: *127, 130*
König, Eugen: *26, 153, 158, 177, 188, 189, 192, 196, 210, 211, 216, 217*
Lausberg: *128, 130, 142, 189*
Lefèvre, Eric, author: *7*
Lewandowski: *182, 203*
Marcks, Erich: *17, 23, 24, 25, 26, 34, 127, 171, 172, 180, 185, 188*
Marnitz: *44*
Mayer-Krapoll: *61*
Mecklenburg: *209*
Meindl, Eugen: *19, 23*
Mertz: *81*

Moch: *180*
Model, Walter: *15, 17, 126*
Montgomery, Bernard Law: *23*
Nake, Albin: *46*
Ortner, Bruno: *108, 121, 158*
Overmans, Rüdiger, author: *100*
Pemsel: *17, 130, 132, 211*
Poppe, Walter: *67, 108, 121*
Reiter: *83, 184, 186, 199*
Richter: *175, 183*
Ries: *127, 130*
Rogge: *144*
Rohr von: *50, 80, 81*
Rolf, Rudi, author: *124*
Rommel, Erwin: *15, 17, 23, 66, 69, 70, 72, 119, 126, 127, 130, 132, 133, 135, 136, 137, 145, 190, 195*
Rundstedt, Gerd von: *15, 59, 132, 133, 137*
Saldern von: *161, 199*
Sattler, Robert: *66, 81, 83*
Schacky auf Schönfeld, Sigmund von: *44*
Schlieben, Karl-Wilhelm von: *24, 26, 81, 130, 131, 135, 137, 180, 181, 182*
Schmidt: *177, 186*
Schweppenburg, Leo Freiherr Geyr von: *17*
Seifert: *81, 118*
Siepmann: *130*
Simon: *200*
Spang, Willibald: *153*
Speidel, Hans: *132*
Stegmann, Rudolf: *26, 108, 113, 121, 133, 134, 136, 137, 155*
Steinmüller: *146*
Stoltenburg: *117, 133, 153*
Straube, Erich: *17*
Tessin, Georg, author: *11, 84, 166*
Theissen, Edgar: *137*
Triepel: *200, 206, 214*
Viebahn, Max von: *32, 34, 36*
Viebig: *31, 132*
Wetzel, Wilhelm: *34*
Weustermann: *134*
Witt: *21*
Witte: *175*
Wittenberg: *151*
Zangen, Gustav von: *34*
Zerweck: *59*
Zetterling, Niklas, author: *7, 9, 117, 161*

V

VEHICLES

Prime Movers
Kfz. 12 (mittlerer geländegängiger Personenkraftwagen mit Zugvorrichtung): *170*
Sd.Kfz. 7 (mittlerer Zugkraftwagen 8t / medium prime mover, 8-tonne): *118, 170*
Sd.Kfz. 8 (schwerer Zugkraftwagen 12t / heavy prime mover, 12-tonne): *118*

Support Vehicles
Kfz. 1 (Volkswagen Kübelwagen): *162, 170*
Kfz. 2 (Funkkraftwagen / radio vehicle): *166, 170*
Kfz. 3 (leichter Meßtruppkraftwagen / light surveying vehicle): *170*
Kfz. 4 (Truppenluftschuftkraftwagen / troop air defence vehicle): *170*
Kfz. 15 (signals support vehicle): *170*
Kfz. 17 (signals support vehicle): *170*
Kfz. 31 (Krankenkraftwagen / field ambulance): *170*
Kfz. 42 (Sammlerkraftwagen a / battery vehicle): *170*
Kfz. 100 (Drehkrankraftwagen (Hebekraft 3t) / rotating crane vehile with 3-tonne lift capacity): *170*
Raupenschlepper Ost: *93, 103, 115, 117, 120, 164, 165, 166, 170, 225*
Sd.Anh. 23 (Anhänger (1 achs.) für Sammlerladegerät D / 1-axle battey-charging trailer: *170*
Sd.Anh. 24 (schwerer Maschinensatz A als Anhänger (1 achs.) fahrbar / single-axle generator trailer): *170*
Sd.Anh. 32 (Anhänger (1 achs.) für Munition / 1-axle ammunition trailer): *170*
Sd.Kfz. 2 (Kettenkraftrad / Kettenkrad / halftrack motor-cycle): *103, 115, 117, 120, 160, 162, 163, 164, 165, 166, 170, 175, 177*
Sd.Kfz. 3 (Maultier / "mule" halftrack vehicle): *103, 120, 170*
Volkswagen Schwimmwagen, Typ 166: *119, 120, 128, 162, 170*

W

WEAPONS

GERMAN

Anti-aircraft Weapons
2 cm Flak 30: *124*
2 cm Flak 38: *116, 124*
2 cm Flakvierling 38: *126*
3,7 cm Flak (18 / 36/ 37 / 43): *142*
7,5 cm Flak M 35(d): *126*
7,5 cm Flak M 35(h): *126*

Anti-tank Guns
3,7 cm Pak: *85, 96*
4,5 cm Pak 184/1(r): *124*
5 cm Pak 38: *115, 117, 119, 151, 164, 184, 198, 206, 207*
7,5 cm Pak 40: *85, 98, 111, 115, 116, 117, 120, 121, 123, 126, 139, 164, 165, 184, 198, 199, 206, 207*
7,5 cm Pak 97/38: *85*
8,8 cm Pak 43: *118, 168*
8,8 cm Pak 43/41: *118, 168*
8,8 cm Raketenwerfer 43 (Puppchen): *150, 206, 207, 214*

Anti-tank Weapons
Faustpatrone(n). *See* Panzerfaust
Panzerfaust: *114, 117, 143*
Panzerschreck: *see* Raketenpanzerbüchse 54
Raketenpanzerbüchse 54 (Ofenrohr): *93, 96, 111, 114, 115, 128, 149, 150, 160, 164, 206, 207, 209, 214*

Armour
Panzerjäger Marder: *142, 199*
Panzerkampfwagen 17R/18R 730(f): *172*
Sturmgeschütz: *69*

Artillery
7,5 cm Feld-Kanone 16 neuer Art (7,5 cm FK 16 nA): *139, 169, 199, 213*
7,5 cm Feld-Kanone 235 (b) (7,5 cm F.K. 235(b)): *169, 172, 198, 202, 207, 212*
7,5 cm Gebirgs-Infanterie-Geschütz 18 (7,5 cm GebIG 18): *160, 163*
7,5 cm Gebirgs-Geschütz 36 (7,5 cm GebG 36): *164, 167*
7,5 cm leichtes Infanterie-Geschütz 18 (7,5 cm le.IG 18): *95, 115, 163*
7,62 cm Infanterie-Kanonen-Haubitze 290 (r) (I.K.H. 290 (r)): *113, 114, 163, 164, 198, 199, 202, 207, 211*
7,65 cm Feldkanone 17(t) (7,65 cm F.K 17(t)): *169, 207*
10,5 cm Gebirgs-Haubitze 40 (10,5 cm GebH 40): *167, 169, 198*
10 cm leichte Feld-Haubitze 316 (j) (l.F.H. 316(j)): *124*
10,5 cm leichte Feld-Haubitze (le.F.H.18/40): *111, 117, 138, 139, 167, 177*
12,2 cm Küstenkanone 393(r) (12,2 cm KstK 393(r)): *63, 199, 202*
15 cm schwere Feld-Haubitze 13 (s.F.H. 13): *124*
15 cm schwere Feld-Haubitze 18 (s.F.H. 18): *112, 118, 160*
15 cm schweres Infanterie-Geschütz 33 (s.I.G. 33): *113, 163, 164*
17 cm Kanone 18 in Mörserlafette (17 cm K 18 in MrsLaf): *63*
24 cm "Theodor Bruno" Kanone (Eisenbahn): *86*
28 cm "Neue Bruno" Kanone (Eisenbahn): *86*
Gebirgs-Haubitze 36: *167*

Machine Guns
Maschinengewehr 34 (MG 34): *162*
Maschinengewehr 42 (MG 42): *85, 114, 117, 118, 119, 120, 162, 166*

Mortars
8,1 cm Gr.W. 34: *161*

Rifles
Karabiner 98k: *93, 113, 114, 118, 120, 164*
Selbstladegewehr 41: *93, 113, 162*
Selbstladegewehr 43: *93, 113*

Rocket Artillery
28/32 cm Nebelwerfer 41 (28/32 cm schweres Wurfgerät): *119*
schweres Wurfgerät (40 and 41): *119*

US
M4 (Sherman): *143*

Endnotes

Introduction

1. While purists may argue that the term "units" applies only to company and smaller elements, it will be used here in the generally understood sense of all elements of a military organisation. A formation is understood to be a battalion-sized organisation or higher.
2. Also referred to as "separate" or "General Headquarters" formations. These are elements that are not specifically assigned to divisions or corps or even field armies but are designated to support those types of formations
3. This includes four assault-gun brigades, *Sturmpanzer-Abt. 217*, and several others.
4. For those not versed in Roman numerals, the Arabic equivalent will be indicated upon first reference, although standard usage dictates the use of Roman numerals for corps, e.g. in this case, LXXXIV Army Corps.
5. E.g.: *352. I.D.; 716. I.D.; 21. Pz.-Div.; s.Brig. 30;* and *H.K.A.A. 1260.*
6. Units that exclusively fought here and/or further east include the *II. Fs.K.*, the *Panzer-Lehr Division, KG Heintz (275. I.D.), Pi.Btl. Angers, Fs.Aufkl.-Abt. 12* and several artillery formations.
7. These archives are abbreviated in the endnotes as "NARA", "BAMA", "CAMO", and "UKNA", respectively.
8. The secret recordings are listed as "C.S.D.I.C. (UK) S.R. Report S.R.M." or "C.S.D.I.C.(UK) GRG.G." in the endnotes.
9. They are listed as "PWIS(H)" or "C.D.I.S.C.(UK) S.I.R." in the endnotes. PWIS(H) stands for "Prisoner of War Interrogation Section (Home)" and C.S.D.I.C. stands for "Combined Services Detailed Interrogation Centre".
10. E.g.: Paul Carell's influential *"They"re Coming"* suffers serious reliability issues. Upon closer examination, it is apparent that some content was based on records or accounts. Such details have been used in this book in a more accurate and specific context.
11. E.g.: Ambrose, S.E. (1994), *D-Day - June 6, 1944: The Climactic Battle of World War II.*
12. The Foreign Military Studies were a post-war program of the Historical Division, United States Army, Europe. High ranking German officers in Allied captivity were encouraged to answer questions and write monographs about their experiences. With a few exceptions, the original German texts have been used in this work to avoid translation issues. The language versions used are identified in the endnotes.

Part 1: German Chain of Command

German Command Structure in Normandy

1. Tessin, G. (1977), *1.Band*, p.5
2. Tessin, G. (1977), *Ibid*, p.5
3. Tessin, G. (1980), *14.Band*, p.91; OKH/GenStdH/Op.Abt., Schematische Kriegsgliederung of 15 May 1944 [T78 R708 H22/339b]; **Schramm, P.E. (1961)**, *Kriegstagebuch des Oberkommandos der Wehrmacht (Wehrmachtführungsstab), Band IV: 1.Januar 1944 - 22. Mai 1945*, Frankfurt am Main: Bernard und Graefe Verlag, p.300-301
4. *Panzergruppe West* became famous after the war as *"Panzer-Reserve"*. The force included, among other units, the *I. SS-Pz.K.*, the *1. SS-* and the *12. SS-Pz.Div.*, the *17. SS-Pz.Gr.Div.* and the *Pz.Lehr-Div.* The *2.*, *21.* and *116. Pz.Div.* had been tactically subordinated to *H.Gr. B.* in early May. [Pz.Gr. West, Ia Nr.89/44 g.Kch., 2.5.44 in CAMO, Bestand 500, Findbuch 12450, Akte 115]
5. OKH/GenStdH/Op.Abt., Schematische Kriegsgliederung of 15 May 1944 [T78 R708 H22/339b]; WFSt. Op. (H), Lage West, Stand: 5.6.44 (1.000.000) [NARA, via www.wwii-photos-maps.com]
6. *H.Gr. D (Ob.West), Kriegstagebuch (Text) 1.8. - 31.8.44*, p.457 [T311 R16 F7017153] The official date for this change was apparently 16.8.44. See German general staff officers files, index cards of *Gen.Feldm.* von Kluge [T78 R888 H6/26]
7. Volksbund; **Schramm, P.E.(1961)**, p.60-62 & 345
8. See German general staff officers files, index cards of *Gen. Feldm.* Model [T78 R890 H6/26] and *Gen.Feldm.* von Rundstedt [T78 R892 H6/26]
9. The respective Chiefs of Staff are mentioned as they feature prominently in original records. For easier reading they will be referred to as *"Chef"* followed by the formation involved. E.g.: Chef Ob.West.
10. *AOK 7*, Kriegsgliederung *7. Armee*, Stand 18.5.44, *Kriegsgliederung AOK 7, Stand: 25.5.1944* [T312 R1566 F209]
11. WFSt. Op. (H), Lage West, Stand: 5.6.44 (1.000.000) [NARA, via www.wwii-photos-maps.com]; **Tessin, G. (1980)**, *14.Band*, p.23
12. *AOK 7 Ia, AOK 7 Kriegstagebuch Ia - 6 June 1944-25 July 1944*, p.125 (a chronological overview of the direct communication of *AOK 7* Ia) [T312 R1569 F345] — Hereafter referred to as: *AOK 7 Ia, KTB 6.6.-25.7.44*
13. *H.Gr. D (Ob.West), Kriegstagebuch (Text) 1.8. - 31.8.44*, p.457 [T311 R16 F7017153] The official date for this change was apparently 16.8.44. See German general staff officers files, index cards of *Gen.Feldm.* von Kluge [T78 R888 H6/26] and *Gen.Feldm.* Model [T78 R890 H6/26]
14. OKW/WFSt/Op. Nr.662642/43 g.K. Chefs., 6.11.43 [in **Hubatsch, W. (reprint 2005b)**, *Kriegstagebuch des Oberkommandos der Wehrmacht (Wehrmachtführungsstab), Band III: 1. Januar 1943 - 31. Dezember 1943*, Augsburg: Verlagsgruppe Weltbild GmbH, p.1466-1447]
15. Schramm, P.E. (1961), p.276-277 & 300
16. *AOK 7*, Ia Nr.275/44 g.K., 15.1.44 [T312 R1564 F457]; **Tessin, G. (1980)**, *14.Band*, p.23
17. Der Oberbefehlshaber West, Ia Nr.4591/44 g., 6.6.44 [T311 R25 F7029343]
18. Pz.AOK5 Ia, *Kriegstagebuch Panzer-Armeeoberkommando 5, I.Teil*, 10.6.44-8.8.44 [T313 R420 F8713531]
19. Okdo.d.H.Gr. B, Ia Nr.4276/44 g.K., 1.7.44 [T311 R3 F7003756]; *AOK 7 Ia, AOK 7 Kriegstagebuch Ia, 6 June 1944-16 August 1944*, p.105-6 [T312 R1569 F108-9] — Hereafter referred to as: *AOK 7 Ia, KTB 6.6.-16.8.44*
20. *AOK 7*, Ia Nr.3476/44 g.K., 28.6.44 [T312 R1565 F1407]; Armeearzt 7 Ia Nr.1040/44 g., *Sanitätstaktische Lage am 28.6.1944.* [T312 R1571 F833]
21. German general staff officers files, index cards of *Gen.Maj.* von Gersdorff [T78 R885 H6/26]; Kartei von Inf.-Kommandeuren, index card of *Gen.Lt.* Pemsel [T78 R908 H6/354]
22. *AOK 7* Ia, Anlage zum K.T.B. Führungsabtl. *AOK 7*, Lage-Karten A.O.K.7 vom 6.1.-5.6.44, *Stand: 6.1.44* [T312 R1570 F4]
23. *AOK 7*, Ia Nr.1644/44 g.K. II.Ang., 14.3.44, p.1 [T312 R1565 F274]; *AOK 7*, Ia Nr.91/44 g., 2.4.44 [T312 R1565 F393]
24. *AOK 7* Ia, Anlage zum K.T.B. Führungsabtl. *AOK 7*, Lage-Karten A.O.K.7 vom 6.1.-5.6.44, *Stand: 5.6.44* [T312 R1570 F9-10, original in BaMa RH 20-7/138K] — Hereafter referred to as: *AOK 7*, Situation map, 5.6.44; *AOK 7*, Kriegsgliederung *7. Armee*, Stand 18.5.44, *Kriegsgliederung AOK 7, Stand: 25.5.1944* [T312 R1566 F209]
25. *AOK 7*, Situation map, 5.6.44; *AOK 7*, Kriegsgliederung *7. Armee*, Stand 18.5.44, *Kriegsgliederung AOK 7, Stand: 25.5.1944* [T312 R1566 F209]
26. *AOK 7*, Ia Nr.2355/44 g.K., 2.5.44, p.3 [T312 R1565 F590]
27. *AOK 7*, Situation map, 5.6.44; *AOK 7*, Kriegsgliederung *7. Armee*, Stand 18.5.44, *Kriegsgliederung AOK 7, Stand: 25.5.1944* [T312 R1566 F209]
28. *AOK 7*, Kriegsgliederung *7. Armee*, Stand 18.5.44, *Gen.Kdo.II. Fallsch.-Korps u. Korps-Truppen, Stand vom 17.5.44* [T312 R1566 F233]
29. *AOK 7*, Ia Nr.2471/44 g.K., 10.5.44 [T312 R1565 F684]
30. *AOK 7* Ia, *KTB 6.6.-25.7.44*, p.17 [T312 R1569 F235]
31. Gen.Kdo.*XXV. A.K.*, *KTB Nr.15(II)* [T314 R747 F273]
32. Obkdo.H.Gr. B, Ia Nr.5615/44 g.K., 5.8.44 [T311 R4 F7003887]
33. *AOK 7*, *KTB 6.6.-25.7.44*, p.12 [T312 R1569 F230]
34. *AOK 7*, Ia Nr.?/44 g.K., p.1 [T312 R1565 F867]
35. *AOK 7* Ia, *KTB 6.6.-25.7.44*, p.18 [T312 R1569 F236]; *AOK 7* Ia Nr.2889/44 g.K., 8.6.44 [T312 R1565 F893]
36. *AOK 7*, Ia Nr.2856/44 g.K., 7.6.44 [T312 R1565 F885]
37. *AOK 7*, Ia Nr.1273/44 g., 10.6.44 [T312 R1565 F923]
38. See *KTB Pz.Gruppe West* for details and information about the rebuilding of the staff [Pz.AOK5 Ia, *Kriegstagebuch Panzer-Armeeoberkommando 5, I.Teil*, 10.6.44-8.8.44 in T313 R420 F8713531]
39. Pz.AOK5 Ia, *Kriegstagebuch Panzer-Armeeoberkommando 5, I.Teil*, 10.6.44-8.8.44 [T313 R420 F8713531]
40. Obko.d.H.Gr. B, Ia Nr.3233/44 g.K., 10.6.44, p.2 [T311 R3 F7002364] *AOK 7* had already requested *H.Gr. B* for assistance from *Gen.Kdo. XXXXVII. Pz.K.* on D-Day. [*AOK 7* Ia, *KTB 6.6.-25.7.44*, p.13 in T312 R1569 F231]
41. Ob.West Ia Nr.4684/44 g.K., p.1, 16.6.44 [T311 R25 F7029597];

AOK 7 Ia, Anlage zum *KTB* Führungsabteilung, Lagenkarten A.O.K.7 vom 6.6.44-30.6.44, *Stand: 13.6.44, 22 Uhr* [T312 R1570 F21]

42. *AOK 7* Ia, *KTB 6.6.-25.7.44*, p.55 [T312 R1569 F274]; *AOK 7* Ia, Anlage zum *KTB* Führungsabteilung, Lagenkarten A.O.K.7 vom 6.6.44-30.6.44, *Stand: 28.6.44, 22 Uhr* [T312 R1570 F28]; *Ob.West*, Ia Nr.4640/44 g.K., 16.6.44 [T311 R25 F7029606]

43. *AOK 7* Ia, Anlage zum *KTB* Führungsabteilung, Lagenkarten A.O.K.7 vom 6.6.44-30.6.44, *Stand: 11.6.44, 22 Uhr* [T312 R1570 F19]

44. *AOK 7* Ia, Anlage zum *KTB* Führungsabteilung, Lagenkarten A.O.K.7 vom 6.6.44-30.6.44, *Stand: 20.6.44, 22 Uhr* [T312 R1570 F28]

45. *Pz.AOK5* Ia, *Kriegstagebuch Panzer-Armeeoberkommando 5, I.Teil*, 10.6.44-8.8.44 [T313 R420 F8713532]

46. *AOK 7* Ia, *Kriegstagebuch der Führungsabteilung AOK 7 für die Zeit vom 1.Jan. - 30.Juni 1944* [T312 R1564 F371] — Hereafter referred to as: AOK 7 Ia, KTB 1.1.-30.6.1944; *AOK 7, Ia Nr.3487/44 g.K.*, 28.6.44, p.1 [T312 R1565 F1414]

47. *AOK 7* Ia, *KTB 1.1.-30.6.1944* [T312 R1564 F363-72]; **D'Este, C. (1983, reprint 2001)**, Decision in Normandy, London: Penguin books, p.231-245

48. *AOK 7*, Ia Nr.3481/44 g.K., 28.6.44 [T312 R1565 F1405]

49. *AOK 7* Ia, *KTB 6.6.-25.7.44*, p.81 [T312 R1569 F301]; *AOK 7*, Ia Nr.3476/44 g.K., 28.6.44 [T312 R1565 F1407]

50. *Pz.AOK5* Ia, *Kriegstagebuch Panzer-Armeeoberkommando 5, I.Teil*, 10.6.44-8.8.44, 29.6.44 [T313 R420 F8713536]

51. *AOK 7*, Kriegsgliederungen zum *KTB* der Führungsabteilung *AOK 7* ab 6.6.44 bis 30.6.44, *Stand: 28.6.44* [T312 R1566 F21] – Collection hereafter referred to as: Kriegsgliederungen z. KTB 6.-29.6.44; *Pz.AOK5* Ia, *Kriegstagebuch Panzer-Armeeoberkommando 5, I.Teil*, 10.6.44-8.8.44 [T313 R420 F8713534]

52. *AOK 7*, Ia Nr.3476/44 g.K., 28.6.44 [T312 R1565 F1407]; *AOK 7* Ia, *KTB 6.6.-16.8.44*, p.105 [T312 R1569 F108]

53. Gen.Kdo.*LXXXIV. A.K.*, Kriegstagebuch vom 1. Juli bis 31. Dez. 43 des Gen.Kdo.LXXXIV. A.K., Ia [T314 R1603 F964]

54. For a testament to his character see Keil, G. (**1948a**), (Engl.), p.36-39 and Pemsel [**Pemsel, M.J. (1949b)**, (Germ.), p.9-10]. Both von Rundstedt and Dollmann regarded him as suitable to command a field army, regardless of his prosthetic leg. [T78 R890]

55. **Criegern, F. von (1948)**, MS # B-784 (Germ.), *Teil I, Die Kämpfe des LXXXIV. A.K. in der Normandie von der alliierten Landung bis 17.6.44*, p.25; **Fahrmbacher, W.K. (1946)**, MS # B-371 (Germ.), *Bretagne 6.6.44-10.6.44 und Normandie 12.6.44-25.6.44*, p.27

56. *AOK 7* Ia, *KTB 6.6.-25.7.44*, p.32 [T312 R1569 F251]; *AOK 7*, Ia Nr.3065/44 g.K., 13.6.44, p.2 [T312 R1565 F1004]

57. *AOK 7* Ia, *KTB 6.6.-25.7.44*, p.51 [T312 R1569 F270]

58. See chapter "77. Infanterie-Division"

59. **Criegern, F. von (1948)**, *Teil I*, p.36; *AOK 7* Ia, *KTB 6.6.-25.7.44*, p.51 [T312 R1569 F270]; **Choltitz, D. von (1947)**, MS # B-418 (Germ.), *Kämpfe des LXXXIV. A.K. in der Normandie vom 18.6.144 ab*, p.3.

60. German general staff officers files, index cards of *Gen. Lt.* Elfeldt [T78 R885 H6/26] Elfeldt was informed of his new assignment at *Ob.West* on 28 July. The next day, he arrived at *AOK 7*, but objected to taking over the corps because of the confusing situation at the front. He was given until noon on the 30th to familiarise himself with the conditions. [C.S.D.I.C.(UK) GRG.G.178, App. p.2-3 in UKNA, WO 208/4363; C.S.D.I.C.(UK) GRG.G.185, App. p.1-3 in UKNA, WO 208/4363,; H.Gr. D (*Ob. West*), Kriegstagebuch (Text) 1.-31.7.44, 30.7.44, p.308 in T311 R16 F7016904]

61. **Elfeldt, O. (1946)**, MS # A-968 (Engl.), *LXXXIV Corps, 28 July to 20 August 1944*, p.3 & 11; C.S.D.I.C. (UK) GRG.G.185, App. p.2-3 [UKNA, WO 208/4363] Von Kluge has been accused of being responsible for these orders, but to von Choltitz he insisted that he had wanted to keep him in place. [**Hausser, P. (1945)**, p.11]

62. **Elfeldt, O. (1946)**, p.11-16

63. **Tessin, G. (1972)**, *6.Band*, p.75

64. See **Choltitz, D. von (1947)**; **Criegern, F. von (1948)**; **Elfeldt, O. (1946)**; **Fahrmbacher, W.K. (1946)**, MS # B-731

65. *AOK 7*, Situation maps, 5.6.44; *AOK 7* Ia, Kriegsgliederung *7. Armee, Stand 18.5.44, Kriegsgliederung AOK 7, Stand: 18.5.1944* [T312 R1566 F208]; *AOK 7* Ia, Kriegsgliederung *7. Armee*, Stand 18.5.44, *LXXXIV.Armee-Korps, Stand: 1.4.44* [T312 R1566 F213]; Armeeintendant der *7. Armee* S I,2 Nr.245/44 g.K., 5.6.44 [T312 R1571 F614]; *AOK 7* Ia, Nr.2314/44 g.K., 30.4.44, p.1 [T312 R1565 F567]; OKH/GenStdH/Op.Abt.IIIb Prüf Nr.92293, *Lage West, Stand: 5.6.44* g.K.Chefs. (1.000.000) [NARA, via www.wwii-photos-maps.com]

66. *AOK 7*, Ia Nr.2363/44 g.K., 1.5.44, p.2 [T312 R1565 F579]

67. *AOK 7*, Ia Nr.2528/44 g.K., *Bericht über die Reise des Herrn Oberbefehlshsbers in den Bereich des LXXXIV. A.K. v. 10. - 12. Mai 44.*, 13.5.44, p.1-2 [T312 R1565 F64-75]

68. Gen.Kdo.LXXXIV. A.K., Ia Nr.1168/44, 12.5.44 [T312 R1565 F682] (document incorrectly dated 12.4.44)

69. **Schlieben, K.W. von (1948)**, MS # B-845 (Germ.) *Die deutsche 709. Infanterie-Division vor und während der anglo-amerikanischen Invasion vom 6. Juni 1944.*, p28-29; **Mauer, E. (1946)**, MS # D-382 (Engl.), *Operations against American Army troops (from 5 June approximately 30 June 1944*, p.13

70. **Schlieben, K.W. von (1948)**, p.28-29

71. *Ibid.*, p.29

72. see **Mauer, E. (1946)**, (Engl.) p.17

73. *AOK 7* Ia, Anlage zum *KTB* Führungsabteilung, Lagenkarten A.O.K.7 vom 6.6.44-30.6.44, *Stand: 8.6.44, 22 Uhr* [T312 R1570 F17]

74. *AOK 7*, Ia Nr.2870/44 g.K., 7.6.44, p.1 [T312 R1565 F883]

75. This was also practical because it would take time before a corps would be fully operational. Another example of this is the role of the *I. SS-Pz.K.* in the east of the *Invasionsfront*. [*AOK 7*, Kriegsgliederungen zum *KTB* der Führungsabteilung *AOK 7* ab 6.6.44 bis 30.6.44, Stand: 28.6. 17 Uhr in T312 R1566 F23]

76. *AOK 7* Ia, *KTB 1.1.-30.6.1944* [T312 R1564 F284]; Okdo.d.*H.Gr. B*, Ia Nr.3233/44 g.K., 10.6.44, p.2 [T311 R3 F7002364]; *AOK 7*, Ia Nr.3023/44 g.K., 12.6.44 [T312 R1565 F992]; *AOK 7*, Kriegsgliederungen z. *KTB* 6.-29.6.44, Stand: 15.6.44, 12 Uhr [T312 R1566 F6]; *AOK 7* Ia, Anlage zum *KTB* Führungsabteilung, Lagenkarten A.O.K.7 vom 6.6.44-30.6.44 [T312 R1570 F19-20]

77. *AOK 7*, IaNr.2856/44 g.K., 7.6.44 [T312 R1565 F885]

78. *AOK 7* Ia, Anlage zum *KTB* Führungsabteilung, Lagenkarten A.O.K.7 vom 6.6.44-30.6.44, *Stand: 13.6.44, 22 Uhr* [T312 R1570 F21]

79. *AOK 7* Ia, *KTB 1.1.-30.6.1944* [T312 R1564 F333]

80. WFSt. Op.(H), Situation maps (Lage West) for the period of 12 Jun to 26 Jul 44 (1:200:000) [NARA, via www.wwii-photos-maps.com]; *AOK 7*, Ia Nr.3238/44 g.K., 19.6.44, p.2 [T312 R1565 F1133]

81. Gen.Kdo.*LXXXIV. A.K.*, Ia Nr.1273/44 g.K., 8.6.44, p.3 [T312 R1565 F939]; **Criegern, F. von (1948)**, *Teil I*, p.21

82. *AOK 7* Ia, *KTB 6.6.-25.7.44*, p.23 [T312 R1569 F241]

83. *Ibid.*, p.30 [T312 R1569 F248]

84. *Ibid.*, p.29 [T312 R1569 F247]

85. *Gen.* Fahrmbacher nonetheless refers to the corps as *Armee-Gruppe Fahrmbacher* which appears to have been an unofficial designation, but does reflect the reality of him being in command of two corps. [**Fahrmbacher, W. (1946)**, p.27 & Anl.12]

86. **Harrison, G.A. (1951, reprint 1984)**, Cross-Channel Attack, Office of the Chief of Military History United States Army: Washington D.C., Chapter VIII.-X.; *AOK 7* Ia, *AOK 7* Ia, *KTB 6.6.-16.8.44*, p.1-36 [T312 R1569 F19-41]; *AOK 7* Ia, *KTB 6.6.-25.7.44*, p.1-40 [T312 R1569 F219-59]

87. *AOK 7*, Ia Nr.3113/44 g.K., p.3 [T312 R1565 F1042]; **Criegern, F. von (1948)**, *Teil I*, p.30

88. *AOK 7*, Ia Nr.3113/44 g.K., p.3 [T312 R1565 F1042]; Captured *Korpsbefehl* of Gen.Kdo.*LXXXIV. A.K.*, 15.6.44. Copied and translated in Annex 1 to G-2 Periodic Report Nr.9, HQ First US Army, 19 June 1944 [Available at: https://firstdivisionmuseum.nmtvault.com/jsp/viewer.jsp?doc_id=iwfd0000%2F20141124%2F165&page_name=798, accessed on 4 Aug. 2018] — Hereafter referred to as: Gen.Kdo.LXXXIV. A.K., Korpsbefehl, 15.6.44

89. **Criegern, F. von (1948)**, *Teil I*, p.30; Gen.Kdo.*LXXXIV. A.K.*, *Korpsbefehl*, 15.6.44. According to von Criegern, this was discussed with *Gen.* Dollmann on 14 June and forwarded to the *77. I.D.* Although the plan is not specifically mentioned in the *AOK 7* report of the meeting, the report does not contradict it either.

90. *AOK 7* Ia, *KTB 6.6.-25.7.44*, p.41 [T312 R1569 F260]

91. *Ibid.*, p.52 [T312 R1569 F271]

92. *Ibid.*, p.54 [T312 R1569 F273]

93. *AOK 7* Ia, *KTB 1.1.-30.6.1944* [T312 R1564 F333-4]; *AOK 7*, Ia Nr.3241/44 g.K., 20.6.44, p.2 [T312 R1565 F1175]; *AOK 7* Ia, Anlage zum *KTB* Führungsabteilung, Lagenkarten A.O.K.7 vom 6.6.44-30.6.44, *Lage Normandie, Stand: 23.6.44, 22:00* [T312 R1570 F32]; *AOK 7*, Kriegsgliederungen z. *KTB* 6.-29.6.44, *Stand: 23.6. 14 Uhr*, 23.6.44

94. **Nauroth, H.S. & B. Steinberg (2017)**, *Die Geschichte der 91. Luftlande-Division - Rekonstruktion eines Großverbands der Deutschen Wehrmacht*, Hamburg: tradition GmbH, p.118-119

95. The goals of the July (pre-Cobra) offensives of First US Army are still debated. Post-war, these have typically been presented, from a US perspective, as having been limited to capturing St. Lô and gaining ground for a later breakout. From a British perspective these offensives are seen as a breakout attempt by First Army, downplayed after its failure.

96. Blumenson, M. (1961, 1993 reprint), *Breakout and Pursuit*, Center of Military History, United States Army, Washington D.C., Chapter IV.-VII. & Map 3-5 & Map II
97. This period (3-15 Jul 44) is covered by: *AOK 7* Ia, *KTB 6.6.-16.8.44*, p.107-161 [T312 R1569 F110-65]; *AOK 7* Ia, *KTB 6.6.-25.7.44*, p.90-121 [T312 R1569 F310-41]
98. *AOK 7* Ia, *KTB 6.6.-25.7.44*, p.106 [T312 R1569 F326]
99. This period (7-24 Jul 44) is covered by: *AOK 7* Ia, *KTB 6.6.-16.8.44*, p.125-189 [T312 R1569 F128-93]; *AOK 7* Ia, *KTB 6.6.-25.7.44*, p.101-130 [T312 R1569 F321-50]
100. *AOK 7* Ia, *KTB 6.6.-16.8.44*, p.180-187 [T312 R1569 F184-91]
101. *AOK 7* Ia, *KTB 6.6.-16.8.44*, p.187-193 [T312 R1569 F191-7]; Daily reports of *H.Gr. B.* (*Tagesmeldungen*) for 26.-31.7. and 1.8.44 [T311 R3 F7002625-69]; **Blumenson, M. (1961, 1993 reprint)**, *Breakout and pursuit*, Center of Military History, United States Army, Washington D.C., Chapter XII.-XVI.; Telephone conversation between *Feldm.* v. Kluge and *Gen.Lt.* Speidel at 09:20 on 31.7.44 [T312 R1569 F631]; **König, E. (1946)**, MS # B-010 (Germ.), *Kämpfe in der Normandie*, p.7-10; **Hausser, P. (1945)**, MS # A-907 (Germ.), *Seventh Army 29 June-20 August 1944*, p.11-12; **Criegern, F. von (1948)**, MS B-784 (Germ.), *Teil II, Die Kämpfe des LXXXIV. A.K. in der Normandie vom 30.7.-20.8.44*, p.37-41; **Mahlmann, P. (1946b)**, MS # A-984 (Engl.), *353.Inf.Div. (24 July-10 September 1944), Report of the Commander*
102. See chapter *"91. Luftlande-Infanterie-Division"*
103. WFSt. Op.(H), Situation maps (Lage West) for the period 25-31 July 1944 (1:50.000 and 1:200.000) [NARA, via www.wwii-photos-maps.com]; Report from *LXXXIV. A.K.* on 2.8.44 at 04:00 [UKNA, HWHW 5/550, CX/MSS/T265/110]; Okdo.d.*H.Gr. B*, Ia Nr.5277/44 g.K., 29.7.44, p.1-2 & 5 [T311 R3 F7002637-8 & 41]; Okdo.d.*H.Gr. B*, Ia Nr.5313/44 g.K., 30.7.44, p.1, 4-5 [T311 R3 F7002644 & 7-8]; Okdo.d.*H.Gr. B*, Ia Nr.5339/44 g.K., 31.7.44, p.2 [T311 R3 F7002651]
104. The fighting in August is fairly well covered by the records of *H.Gr. B* [T311 R3 and R4] and *AOK 7* [T312 R1568 and R1569]. Among other information, these sources contain both orders and situation reports. Additional reports and orders, including details on lines and boundaries of the corps, can be found in the ULTRA records [UKNA, HW 5/547-5/567]. Situation maps (Lage West) also provide information on how the fighting developed and the movements of German formations.
105. Okdo.d.*H.Gr. B*, Ia Nr.5322/44 g.K., 30.7.44, p.3 [T311 R4 F7004678] ; *AOK 7*, Ia 432/44, 31.7.44 (16:00) [UKNA, HW 5/548, CX/MSS/T263/43, XL 4338]; Okdo.d.*H.Gr. B*, Ia Nr.5434/44 g.K., 2.8.44, p.5 [T311 R3 F7002669]; *AOK 7*, Ia Nr.498/44 g., 3.8.44 [T312 R1569 F360]; *AOK 7*, Ia Nr.512/44 g., 3.8.44, p.2 [T312 R1569 F373]; *AOK 7*, Ia Nr.532/44 g., 4.8.44, p.2 [T312 R1569 F385]; WFSt. Op.(H), Situation maps (Lage West) for the period 26 Jul - 1 Aug 44 (1:80.000 and 1:200.000) [NARA, via www.wwii-photos-maps.com]; **Criegern, F. von (1948)**, *Teil II*, p.37-41; **Mahlmann, P. (1946c)**, (Engl.), *353.Inf.Div. (11 - 21 Aug 44), Report of the Commander*, p.9-12
106. *AOK 7* Vorg.Gef.Std., Ia Nr.687/44 g.K. [T312 R1569 F458]; Okdo.d.*H.Gr. B*, Ia Nr.6162/44 g.K., 16.8.44, p.4 [T311 R3 F7002771]; **Mahlmann P. (1946b); Mahlmann P. (1946c)**
107. Okdo.d.*H.Gr. B*, Ia Nr.5421/44 g.K., 1.8.44, p.2 [T311 R4 F7004661]; Report from *LXXXIV. A.K.*, 2.8.44 at 04:00 [UKNA, HW 5/550, CX/MSS/T265/110, XL 4639]
108. WFSt. Op.(H), *3.Lage West, Chef WFSt*, 3.8.44 (1:200.000) [NARA, via www.wwii-photos-maps.com]; *AOK 7*, Ia Nr.512/44 g., 3.8.44, p.2 [T312 R1569 F373]
109. Okdo.d.*H.Gr. B*, Ia Nr.5434/44 g.K., 2.8.44, p.1-2 & 5 [T311 R3 F7002664-5 & 9]; Okdo.d.*H.Gr. B*, Ia Nr.5486/44 g.K., 3.8.44, p.2 & 6 [T311 R3 F7002673 & 7]; Okdo.d.*H.Gr. B*, Ia Nr.5517/44 g.K., 3.8.44; Okdo.d.*H.Gr. B*, Ia Nr.5548/44 g.K., 4.8.44, p.1-2 & 5 [T311 R3 F7002684-5 & 8]; Okdo.d.*H.Gr. B*, Ia Nr.5590/44 g.K., 5.8.44, p.1 & 4 [T311 R3 F7002692 & 5]; Okdo.d.*H.Gr. B*, Ia Nr.5630/44 g.K., 6.8.44, p.2 & 5 [T311 R3 F7002700 & 3]; Okdo.d.*H.Gr. B*, Ia Nr.5680/44 g.K., 7.8.44, p.1 & 4 [T311 R3 F7002704 & 7]
110. Situation maps (4-7 August) put the *363.I.D.* under the command of the *II. Fs.K.*, but this conflicts with period reports that clearly link the division to the *LXXXIV. A.K.*
111. WFSt. Op.(H), Situation maps (Lage West) for the period of 1-5 Aug 44 (1:80.000 and 1:200.000) [NARA, via www.wwii-photos-maps.com]; Okdo.d.*H.Gr. B*, Ia Nr.5486/44 g.K., 3.8.44, p.6 [T311 R3 F7002677]; *AOK 7* Ia, *KTB 6.6.-16.8.44*, 4.-5.8.44 [T312 R1569 F198-201]; Report from *LXXXIV. A.K.* on 5.8.44 at 05:15 [UKNA, HW 5/554]; Report from *LXXXIV. A.K.*, 5.8.44 at 05:30 [UKNA, HW 5/552, CX/MSS/T267/30, XL 4805]
112. WFSt. Op.(H), Situation maps (Lage West) for the period 5-7 Aug 44 (1:80.000 and 1:200.000) [NARA, via www.wwii-photos-maps.com]; *AOK 7* Ia Nr.562/44 g. II.Ang., 6.8.44 [T312 R1569 F399]; **Criegern, F. von (1948)**, *Teil II*, p.41-45; **Mahlmann, P. (1946b)**, Engl., App.15, 17-20; Okdo.d.*H.Gr. B*, Ia Nr.5630/44 g.K., 6.8.44, p.2 [T311 R3 F7002700]; **Dettling. A. (1946)**, MS # B-163 (Engl.), *Report on the participation of the 363. Inf .Div. in the campaign in Northern France*, p.2
113. LSSAH: "Leibstandarte *SS* Adolf Hitler"
114. WFSt. Op.(H), Situation maps (Lage West) for the period 7-10 Aug 44 [NARA, via www.wwii-photos-maps.com]; Okdo.d.*H.Gr. B*, Ia Nr.5731/44 g.K., 8.8.44, p.1-2 & 4 [T311 R3 F7002713-4 & 6]; Okdo.d.*H.Gr. B*, Ia Nr.4785/44 g.K., 9.8.44, p.2 & 4 [T311 R3 F7002724 & 6]; *AOK 7*, Ia Nr.656/44 g., 9.8.44, p.1 [T312 R1569 F441]; Okdo.d.*H.Gr. B*, Ia Nr.5843/44 g.K., 10.8.44, p.1-2 & 4-5 [T311 R3 F7002733-4 & 6-7]; *AOK 7* Nr.Ia 674/44 g., 10.8.44, p.1 [T312 R1569 F449]; *AOK 7*, Ia Nr.686/44 g., 10.8.44, p.2 [T312 R1569 F456]; **Mahlmann, P. (1946c)**, Engl., p.17, 23-24, 26 & App. 9-10
115. In the Foreign Military Studies this period (at corps level and below) is covered by: **Criegern, F. von (1948)**, *Teil II*, p.41-56; **Elfeldt, O. (1946)**, p.13-16; **Mahlmann, P. (1946b)**, Engl., p.11-15 & App.17; **Mahlmann, P. (1946c)**, Engl., p.16-27. A lot of information can be found in the records of *AOK 7* and *H.Gr. B*: *AOK 7* Ia, *KTB 6.6.-16.8.44*, period of 4.-16.8.44 [T312 R1569 F198-215]; *AOK 7* periodic reports, orders and other communications for the period 1.-19.8.44 [T312 R1569 F354-565]; *H.Gr. B*, daily reports for 1.-20.8.44 [T311 R3 F7002664-796]. For an overview of the Allied operations see **Blumenson, M. (1961, 1993 reprint)**, Chapter XXII.-XXVII. & Map IX
116. This period is covered in the daily reports of *H.Gr. B.* (*Tagesmeldungen*) for 10-19 Aug 44 [T311 R3 F7002744-92]; WFSt. Op.(H), Situation maps for 10-19 Aug 44 provide a useful graphic overview. [NARA, via www.wwii-photos-maps.com] At corps and army level more details can be found in ULTRA records: Report Flivo *AOK 7* on 11.8. at 06:00 [UKNA, HW 5/558, CX/MSS/T273/108, XL 5728/XL 5736]; Report Flivo *LXXXIV. A.K.* on 11.8. at 09:00 [UKNA, HW 5/558, CX/MSS/T273/121, XL 5739]; Report *LXXXIV. A.K.* on 12.8. at 07:30 [UKNA,HW 5/559, CX/MSS/T274/47, XL 5846]; Report Flivo *LXXXIV. A.K.* on 13.8. at 05:00 [UKNA, HW 5/560, CX/MSS/T275/134, XL 6100]; Message *LXXXIV. A.K.* on 15.8. at 00:45 [UKNA, HW 5/562, CX/MSS/T277/134, XL 6438]; Message *LXXXIV. A.K.* on 15.8. at 01:00 [UKNA, HW 5/562, CX/MSS/T277/73, XL 6381]; Report *AOK 7* on 16.8. at 11:00 [UKNA, HW 5/564, CX/MSS/T279/113, XL 6792]; Okdo.d.*H.Gr. B*. Ia Nr.6188/44 g.K., 16.8.44 (at 12:30) [UKNA, HW 5/565, CX/MSS/T280/52, XL 6938]; Report *LXXXIV. A.K.* on 16.8. at 13:00 [UKNA, HW 5/564, CX/MSS/T279/38, XL 6735]; Report Flivo *LXXXIV. A.K.* on 16.8. at 19:00 [UKNA, HW 5/564, CX/MSS/T279/32, XL 6732]; Report *LXXXIV. A.K.* on 17.8. at 08:00 [UKNA, HW 5/564, CX/MSS/T279/162, XL 6830]; Message Pz.AOK 5 on 17.8. at 14:30 [UKNA, HW 5/566, CX/MSS/T281/25, XL7066]. Additional documents: Okdo.d.*H.Gr. B*, Ia Nr.6023/44 g.K., 13.8.44 [T311 R4 F7003942]
117. Personal accounts from the pocket can be found in: **Criegern, F. von (1948)**, *Teil II*, p.53-54; **Dettling. A. (1946)**, p.6-10; **Elfeldt, O. (1946)**, p.13-15; **Mahlmann, P. (1946c)**, Engl., p.21; **Meindl, E. (1946)**, MS # A-923, (Engl.), *The part played by the II. Paratroop Corps in Northern France, 20 July till 14 September 1944*, p.25-42; **Neitzel, H. (1947)**, MS # B-536 (Engl.), *89th Infantry Division in Engagements on the Invasion Front and during the Retreat to the Westwall*, p.1-5; **Straube, E. (1948)**, MS # B-824 (Engl.), *The LXXIV Infantry Corps in Brittany, May - Sep.* 1944, p.29-38; **Viebig, W. (1946)**, MS # B-610 (Engl.), *Commitment and battles of the 277th I.D. in the time from 13 Aug. - 1 Sep. 1944*, p.6-16; C.S.D.I.C. (UK) S.I.R. 876, p.1 [NARA, RG 165, Box 661]; C.S.D.I.C. (UK) S.R. Report, S.R.M.817 [UKNA, WO 208/4139]
118. Okdo.d.*H.Gr. B*, Ia Nr.6162/44 g.K., 16.8.44, p.4 [T311 R3 F7002771]; Report *LXXXIV. A.K.* on 16.8.44 at 13:00 [UKNA, HW 5/564, CX/MSS/T279/38, XL 6735]
119. WFSt. Op.(H), Situation maps (Lage West) for 18-19 Aug 44 (1:500.000) [NARA, via www.wwii-photos-maps.com]; Okdo.d.*H.Gr. B*, Ia Nr.6162/44 g.K., 16.8.44, p.4 [T311 R3 F7002771]; *AOK 7*, Ia Nr.851/44 g.K., 17.8.44 [T312 R1569 F545]; Note from *LXXIV. A.K.*, 16.8.44 at 13:00 [UKNA, HW 5/564, CM/MSS/T279/38, XL 6735]; **Criegern, F. von (1948)**, *Teil II*, p.52-53; **Leleu, J.L. (1999)**, *10. SS-Panzer-Division "Frundsberg"*, Bayeux: Editions Heimdal, p.140-145
120. *AOK 7* Ia Nr.851/44 g.K., 17.8.44 [T312 R1569 F545]; **Mahlmann, P. (1946c)**, Engl., p.21
121. **Criegern, F. von (1948)**, p.54-55; **Elfeldt, O. (1946)**, p.14-15; **Meyer, H. (1982)**, *Kriegsgeschichte der 12. SS-Panzerdivision „Hitlerjugend", Band I*, Osnabrück: Munin Verlag GmbH, p.343-344; **Neitzel, H. (1947)**, p.3-4; C.S.D.I.C. (UK) S.R. Report, S.R.M.817 [UKNA, WO 208/4139]; C.S.D.I.C. (UK) S.I.R.876, p.1 [NARA, RG 165, Box 661]
122. **Meyer, H. (1982)**, p.343-344; **Neitzel, H. (1947)**, p.3-4; **Keppler, G. (1947)**, MS # B-623 (Engl.), *Fighting of the I SS-Panzer-Corps in Northern France (from 16 August to 18 October 1944)*, p.2
123. **Neitzel, H. (1947)**, p.3-4; Message sent to *AOK 7* by *II. Fs.K.*

at 21:25 on 18.8., and received by *AOK 7* at 03:43 on 19.8.44. [T312 R1569 F554]; **Elfeldt, O. (1946)**, p.14-15; **Leleu, J.-L. (1999)**, *10. SS-Panzer-Division "Frundsberg"*, Bayeux: Editions Heimdal, p.140-145; Report from LXXXIV. A.K. on 19.8.44 at 08:30 [UKNA, HW 5/566, CX/MSS/T281/90, XL 7113]

124. **Neitzel, H. (1947)**, p.3-4

125. **Elfeldt, O. (1946)**, p.15; **Viebig, W. (1946)**, p.10; **Straube, E. (1946)**, p.35; For divisions with the LXXIV. A.K. see message of *Gen.Kdo.LXXIV. A.K.* to *AOK 7* at 11:30 on 19.8.44 [T312 R1569 F560-1]

126. **Criegern, F. von (1948)**, *Teil II*, p.56; **Elfeldt, O. (1946)**, p.14; **Hausser, P. (1945)**, p.14-15; Okdo.d.*H.Gr. B*, Ia Nr.6310/44 g.K., 20.8.44, p.1 & 4 [T311 R3 F7002788 & 91]; Okdo.d.*H.Gr. B*, Ia Nr.6350/44 g.K., p.1 & 4 [T311 R3 F7002793 & 6]

127. **Elfeldt, O. (1946)**, p.15; C.S.D.I.C. (UK) GRG.G.178, Appendix p.2 [UKNA, WO 208/4363]; C.S.D.I.C. (UK) S.R. Report, S.R.M.817 [UKNA, WO 208/4139]

128. **Leleu, J.L. (1999)**, p.140-145

129. The commander of the *277. I.D.*, *Obst*. Viebig, refutes that a proper relief took place. [**Viebig, W. (1946)**, p.10]

130. **Elfeldt, O. (1946)**, p.15-16; **Criegern, F. von (1948)**, *Teil II*, p.56; C.S.D.I.C. (UK). GRG.G.178, Appendix p.1-2 [UKNA, WO 208/4363]

131. **Criegern, F. von (1948)**, *Teil II*, p.55-56; **Elfeldt, O. (1946)**, 15-16; **Tessin, G. (1976)**, *6.Band*, p.75

LXXXIV. Armee-Korps: Normandy from 1941 to D-Day

1. LXXXIV. Armee-Korps: Normandy from 1941 to D-Day
Tessin, G. (1965), *5.Band*, p.232; H.Kdo.LX, *Tätigkeitsbericht des H.Kommandos LX für den Monat April 1941*, p.1 [T314 R1603 F3] — Hereafter referred to as: H.Kdo.LX, *Tätigkeitsbericht April 1941*

2. **Tessin, G. (1977)**, *1.Band*, p.15

3. **Tessin, G. (1965)**, *5.Band*, p.232

4. German general staff officers files, index cards of *Gen.d.Kav. Koch-Erpach* [T78 R888 H6/26]

5. H.Kdo.LX, *Tätigkeitsbericht April 1941*, p.2 [T314 R1603 F4]

6. H.Kdo.LX, *Tätigkeitsbericht des H.Kommandos LX für Monat Dezember 1941*, p.2 [T314 R1603 F37]

7. H.Kdo.LX, *Tätigkeitsbericht des H.Kommandos LX für Monat Januar 1942*, p.3 [T314 R1603 F187] — Hereafter referred to as: H.Kdo.LX, *Tätigkeitsbericht Januar 1942*; Gen.Kdo.LXXXIV. A.K., *KTB Ia 1.1.-30.6.43* [T314 R1603 F890]

8. Gen.Kdo.LXXXIV. A.K., *Veränderungen zur Kriegsrangliste sämtlicher Offiziere und Beamten im Offizierrang des Stabes/ Generalkommando LXXXIV. A.K., Monat August 1943* [T314 R1604 F879]

9. Gen.Kdo.LXXXIV. A.K., *Kriegstagebuch vom 1. Juli bis 31. Dez. 43 des Gen.Kdo.LXXXIV. A.K., Ia* [T314 R1603 F968 & 989]

10. H.Kdo.LX, *Tätigkeitsbericht April 1941*, p.1-2 [T314 R1603 F3-4]

11. GenStdH Op.Abt. III/Prüf Nr.illegible, *Schematische Kriegsgliederung, Stand: 5.4.41* [T78 R708 H22/337a]; GenStdH Op.Abt. III/Prüf Nr.13928, *Schematische Kriegsgliederung, Stand: 23.4.41* [T78 H22/337a]

12. GenStdH Op.Abt. III/Prüf Nr.15759, *Schematische Kriegsgliederung, Stand: B-Tag 1941* [T78 R708 H22/337a] B-Tag stands for the launch of Operation Barbarossa, the invasion of the Soviet Union on 22.6.41

13. H.Kdo.LX, *Tätigkeitsbericht des H.Kommandos LX für Monat Juli 1941*, p.5 [T314 R1603 F22]

14. H.Kdo.LX, *Anl.1 zum Tätigkeitsbericht des H.Kdos.LX für den Monat April 1941*, p.1 [T314 R1603 F42] — Hereafter referred to as: H.Kdo.LX, *Anl.1 z. Tätigkeitsbericht April 1941*

15. Ob.West, Anlagenband zur Gesichte des *Oberbefehlshaber West*, I.Teil, Anl.2, Gliederung im Westen in großen (April 1941) [T311 R25 F7030169]; *Ibid.*, Anl.2a, Lage West, Stand: 18.12.1941 [T311 R25 F7030170]; Gen.Kdo.XXXXIII. A.K. Abt. T a Nr.64/41 g.K., 20.4.41 [T314 R1603 F54]; Anl. zu Gen.Kdo.XXXXIII. A.K. Abt. T Ia Nr.64/41 g.K. II.Ang., 26.4.41 [T314 R1603 F57]

16. H.Kdo.LX, *Tätigkeitsbericht April 1941*, p.1-5 [T314 R1603 F3-7]; Anl.1 z. Tätigkeitsbericht des H.Kdos.LX für den Monat April 1941, p.5-12 [T314 R1603 F46-53]

17. H.Kdo.LX, *Anl.1 z. Tätigkeitsbericht April 1941*, p.9 [T314 R1603 F50]; **Tessin, G. (1973)**, *8.Band*, p.117

18. H.Kdo.LX, *Anl.1 z. Tätigkeitsbericht April 1941*, p.10 [T314 R1603 F51]; **Tessin, G. (1973)**, *5.Band*, p.211

19. H.Kdo.LX, *Anl.1 z. Tätigkeitsbericht April 1941*, p.11 [T314 R1603 F52]; GenStdH Op.Abt. III/Prüf Nr.illegible, *Schematische Kriegsgliederung, Stand: 18.3.41* [T78 R708 H22/337a]; GenStdH Op.Abt. III/Prüf Nr.illegible, *Schematische Kriegsgliederung, Stand: 27.3.41* [T78 R708 H22/337a]; **Tessin, G. (1973)**, *8.Band*, p.77

20. H.Kdo.LX, *Tätigkeitsbericht April 1941*, p.3 [T314 R1603 F5]; **Tessin, G.**, *9.Band*, p.150

21. H.Kdo.LX, *Tätigkeitsbericht April 1941*, p.3 [T314 R1603 F5]; **Tessin, G.**, *9.Band*, p.135

22. H.Kdo.LX, *Tätigkeitsbericht April 1941*, p.3 [T314 R1603 F5]

23. *Ibid.*, p.5 [T314 R1603 F7]; Gen.Kdo.XXXII.A.K. Abt.T, Abt. Ia Nr.64/41 g.K., II.Ang., Korps-Befehls, 26.4.41, p.2 [T314 R1603 F55]

24. Gen.Kdo.XXXXIII. A.K. Abt.T, *Tätigkeitsbericht des Gen.Kdo. XXXXIII. A.K. Abt.T für Monat Mai 1941*, p.4 [T314 R1603 F10]; Gen.Kdo.XXXXIII.A.K.(T), *Tätigkeitsbericht des Gen.Kdos.XXXXIII.A.K.(T) Monat Juni 1941*, p.1 [T314 R1603 F14]] — Hereafter referred to as: Gen.Kdo.XXXXII.A.K. Abt.T, *Tätigkeitsbericht Juni 1941*; Gen.Kdo.XXXXIII. A.K., Abt. Ia Nr.201/41 g.K., 31.5.41, p.2 [T314 R1603 F85]; **Tessin, G. (1972)**, *6.Band*, p.68

25. Gen.Kdo.XXXXIII.A.K.(T), *Tätigkeitsbericht Juni 1941*, p.1 [T314 R1603 F14]; Gen.Kdo.XXXXIII. A.K. Abt. Ia Nr.186/41 g.K., 29.5.41, p.1 [T314 R1603 F82]; Gen.Kdo.XXXXIII. A.K. Abt.T, Abt. Ia Nr.201/41 g.K., 31.5.41, p.1 [T314 R1603 F84]

26. Gen.Kdo.XXXXIII. A.K. Abt.T, *Tätigkeitsbericht des Gen.Kdo. XXXXIII. A.K. Abt.T für Monat Mai 1941*, p.4 [T314 R1603 F13]; Gen.Kdo.XXXXIII. A.K. Abt. Ia Nr.216/41 g.K., 2.6.41, p.1 [T314 R1603 F86]

27. Gen.Kdo.XXXXIII.A.K.(T), *Tätigkeitsbericht Juni 1941*, p.1 [T314 R1603 F14]

28. Gen.Kdo.XXXXIII. A.K.T, Abt. Ia Nr.266/41 g.K., 19.6.41, p.1 [T314 R1603 F93]

29. Gen.Kdo.XXXXIII.(A.K.(T), *Tätigkeitsbericht Juni 1941*, p.1-2 [T314 R1603 F14-5]

30. Gen.Kdo.XXXXIII. A.K. Abt.T, Abt. Ia Nr.266/41 g.K., 19.6.41, p.1 [T314 R1603 F93]; **Tessin, G. (1975)**, *12.Band*, p.183

31. This battalion´s arrival has not been found in the corps records, suggesting it arrived before April 1941.

32. Gen.Kdo.XXXXIII.A.K.(T), *Tätigkeitsbericht Juni 1941*, p.2 [T314 R1603 F15]

33. *Ibid.*

34. Gen.Kdol.XXXXIII.A.K.T., Abt. Ia Nr.304/41 g.K., 26.6.41 [T314 R1603 F99]

35. Gen.Kdo.XXXXIII.A.K.(T), *Tätigkeitsbericht Juni 1941*, p.2 [T314 R1603 F15]

36. H.Kdo.LX, *Tätigkeitsbericht des H.Kommandos LX für Monat Juli 1941*, p.1 [T314 R1603 F18]

37. H.Kdo.LX, *Tätigkeitsbericht des H.Kommandos LX für Monat August 1941*, p.1 [T314 R1603 F23]

38. Anl.4 zum Tätigkeitsbericht des H.Kommandos LX für November 1941, Kriegsgliederung 83.Inf.Div., Stand v. 1.11.1941 [T314 R1603 F158]; *Ibid.*, Kriegsgliederung 323.Inf.Div., Stand v. 1.11.1941 [T314 R1603 F159]

39. *Chef H. Rüst u. BdE*: Chef Heeresrüstung und Befehlshaber des Ersatzheeres, Chief of Army Equipment and Commander of the Replacement Army

40. H.Kdo.LX, *Tätigkeitsbericht des H.Kommandos LX für Monat September 1941*, p.1 [T314 R1603 F26]

41. Notetat: a temporarily reduced *Soll-Stärke* (authorised strength).

42. *Ibid.*, p.1 & 3 [T314 R1603 F26 & 28]

43. H.Kdo.LX, *Tätigkeitsbericht des H.Kommandos LX für Monat Oktober 1941*, p.1 [T314 R1603 F30] — Hereafter referred to as: H.Kdo.LX, *Tätigkeitsbericht Oktober 1941*

44. H.Kdo. LX, Abt. Ia Nr.4065/41 g., Ia - Mitteilung Nr.14, 9.11.41, p.1-2 [T314 R1603 F145-146]

45. H.Kdo.LX, *Tätigkeitsbericht Oktober 1941*, p.1 [T314 R1603 F30]

46. H.Kdo.LX, Abt. Ia Nr.653/41 g.K., 10.10.41, p.5 [T314 R1603 F141]

47. H.Kdo.LX, *Tätigkeitsbericht Oktober 1941*, p.2 [T314 R1603 F31]; H.Kdo.LX, Abt. Ia Nr.653/41 g.K., 10.10.41, p.5 [T314 R1603 F141]; H.Kdo.LX, Abt. Ia Nr.683/41 g.K., 16.10.41, p.1 [T314 R1603 F142]

48. H.Kdo.LX, *Tätigkeitsbericht des H.Kommandos LX für Monat November 1941*, p.1-2 [T314 R1603 F34-5]; *H.Kdo. LX*, Abt. Ia Nr.4065/41 g., Ia - Mitteilung Nr.14, 9.11.41, p.1 [T314 R1603 F145]; **Tessin, G. (1975)**, *12.Band*, p.169

49. *H.Kdo. LX*, Abt. Ia Nr.4065/41 g., Ia - Mitteilung Nr.14, 9.11.41, p.1 [T314 R1603 F145]; for the previous situation see the situation map of July 1941 [T314 R1603 F115]

50. H.Kdo.LX, *Tätigkeitsbericht des H.Kommandos LX für Monat Dezember 1941*, p.1 [T314 R1603 F36]

51. *Ibid.*, p.1-2 [T314 R1603 F36-37]; H.Kdo.LX, *Tätigkeitsbericht Januar 1942*, p.1 [T314 R1603 F185]; **Tessin, G. (1974)**, *9.Band*, p.138

52. H.Kdo.LX, *Tätigkeitsbericht Januar 1942*, p.1 [T314 R1603 F185]; Anl. zu Gen.Kdo.LXXXIV. A.K. (sic) Ia Nr.24.42 g.K., 4.1.42 [T314 R1603 F247-250]

53. *H.Kdo. LX*, Abt. Ia Nr.24/42 g.K., 4.1.42, p.2 [T314 R1603 F245]
54. H.Kdo.LX, *Tätigkeitsbericht Januar 1942*, p.1-2 [T314 R1603 F185-6]
55. *Ibid.*, p.2 [T314 R1603 F186]
56. *Ibid.*, p.1 [T314 R1603 F185]
57. H.Kdo.LX, *Tätigkeitsbericht des H.Kdos. LX für den Monat Februar 1942*, p.1 [T314 R1603 F189] — Hereafter referred to as: H.Kdo.LX, *Tätigkeitsbericht Februar 1942*
58. *Westwall:* The German defence line opposite the Maginot Line at the outbreak of the war. Often referred to as the Siegfried Line.
59. OKW/WFSt/Abt. L (I Op) Nr.003022/41 g.K., 14.12.41 [copied and translated in **Rolf, R. (2014)**, *Atlantikwall - Batteries and Bunkers*, Middelburg: PRAK publishing, p.149]
60. *Ibid.*
61. *Ibid.*
62. H.Kdo.LX, *Tätigkeitsbericht Februar 1942*, p.1 [T314 R1603 F189]
63. *Ibid.*, p.1-2 [T314 R1603 F189-90]
64. *Ibid.*, p.2 [T314 R1603 F190]; **Tessin, G. (1977)**, *1.Band*, p.61
65. H.Kdo.LX, *Tätigkeitsbericht Februar 1942*, p.2 [T314 R1603 F190]
66. H.Kdo.LX, *Tätigkeitsbericht des H.Kdos LX für den Monat März 1942*, p.1 [T314 R1603 F192] — Hereafter referred to as: H.Kdo.LX, *Tätigkeitsbericht März 1942*
67. H.Kdo.LX, situation map, *Stand 13. April 1942* [T314 R1603 F259]
68. H.Kdo.LX, *Tätigkeitsbericht März 1942*, p.2 [T314 R1603 F193]
69. *Ibid.*, p.1-2 [T314 R1603 F192-3]
70. *Ibid.*, p.2 [T314 R1603 F193]; Der Führer und Oberste Befehlshaber der Wehrmacht, *OKW/WFst/Op. Nr.001031/42 g.K., Weisung Nr.40 für die Kriegführung*, 23.3.42 [T1022 R2231, frame numbers not available]
71. H.Kdo.LX, *Tätigkeitsbericht März 1942*, p.2-3 [T314 R1603 F193-4]
72. **Tessin, G. (1977)**, *1.Band*, p.355; **Tessin, G. (1965)**, *2.Band*, p.63
73. H.Kdo.LX, *Tätigkeitsbericht des H.Kdos. LX für den Monat April 1942*, p.1 [T314 R1603 F196]
74. *Ibid.*; H.Kdo.LX, *Tätigkeitsbericht des H.Kdos LX für den Monat Mai 1942*, p.1 [T314 R1603 F204] — Hereafter referred to as: H.Kdo.LX, *Tätigkeitsbericht Mai 1942*
75. H.Kdo.LX, *Tätigkeitsbericht Mai 1942*, p.1 [T314 R1603 F204]
76. *Ibid.*
77. *Ibid.*, p.5 [T314 R1603 F208]
78. In period German writing the "I" often resembled a "J". As a result postwar publications commonly refer to KVA "I" as KVA "J". This book does the same, even though it is technically incorrect.
79. **Rolf, R. (2014)**, p.150
80. Gen.Kdo.*LXXXIV. A.K.* Ia, *Tätigkeitsbericht Mai 1942*, p.1 [T314 R1603 F205]
81. *Ibid.*, p.1 & 6 [T314 R1603 F210 & 215]
82. Gen.Kdo.*LXXXIV. A.K.*, Situation map, *Gen.Kdo.LXXXIV. A.K., Stand: 31.8.42* [T314 R1603 F320]
83. Gen.Kdo.*LXXXIV. A.K.* Ia, *Tätigkeitsbericht des Gen.Kdo.LXXXIV. A.K. für den Monat Juni 1942*, p.1 [T314 R1603 F210] — Hereafter referred to as: Gen.Kdo.*LXXXIV. A.K.* Ia, *Tätigkeitsbericht Juni 1942*
84. Gen.Kdo.*LXXXIV. A.K.* Ia Nr.167/43 g.K., 14.2.43, p.2 [T314 R1604 F158]
85. Gen.Kdo.*LXXXIV. A.K.* Ia, *Tätigkeitsbericht Juni 1942*, p.1-2 [T314 R1603 F210-211]
86. *Ibid., p.2* [T314 R1603 F211]
87. *Ibid.*, p.2-3 [T314 R1603 F211-2]
88. *Ibid.*, p.3 [T314 R1603 F212]
89. Gen.Kdo.*LXXXIV. A.K.* Ia, *Tätigkeitsbericht des Gen.Kdo.LXXXIV. A.K. für Monat Juli 1942*, p.1-2 [T314 R1603 F217-8] — Hereafter referred to as: Gen.Kdo.*LXXXIV. A.K.* Ia, *Tätigkeitsbericht Juli 1942*
90. *Ibid.*, p.2-3 [T314 R1603 F218-9]
91. *Fluganwärter:* pilot candidate
92. *Ibid.*, p.3 [T312 R1603 F219]
93. Gen.Kdo.*LXXXIV. A.K.* Ia, *Tätigkeitsbericht des Gen.Kdo.LXXXIV. A.K. für den Monat September 1942*, p.3 [T314 R1603 F232] — Hereafter referred to as: Gen.Kdo.*LXXXIV. A.K.* Ia, *Tätigkeitsbericht September 1942*
94. Gen.Kdo.*LXXXIV. A.K.* Ia, *Tätigkeitsbericht Juli 1942*, p.4 [T314 R1603 F220]
95. Gen.Kdo.*LXXXIV. A.K.* Ia, *Tätigkeitsbericht des Gen.Kdo.LXXXIV. A.K. für Monat August 1942*, p.1 [T314 R1603 F225]
96. **Tessin, G. (1977)**, *1.Band*, p.55; Gen.Kdo.*LXXXIV. A.K.* Ia, *Tätigkeitsbericht Juli 1942*, p.5 [T314 R1603 F221]
97. Gen.Kdo.*LXXXIV. A.K.* Ia, *Tätigkeitsbericht Juli 1942*, p.5 [T314 R1603 F221]; **Tessin, G. (1977)**, *1.Band*, p.55
98. Gen.Kdo.*LXXXIV. A.K.*, IIa/IIb, *Tätigkeitsbericht IIa/IIb für den Monat Oktober 1942*, 31.10.42 [T314 R1603 F600]; Chef d Gen. St.d.*LXXXIV. A.K.*, Ia Nr.2832/42, 4.12.42 [T314 R1603 F726]
99. Gen.Kdo.*LXXXIV. A.K.* Ia, *Tätigkeitsbericht des Gen.Kdo.LXXXIV. A.K. für Monat August 1942*, p.1 [T314 R1603 F225]
100. Gen.Kdo.*LXXXIV. A.K.* Ia, *Tätigkeitsbericht September 1942*, p.2 [T314 R1603 F231]; Gen.Kdo.*LXXXIV. A.K.*, *Kriegstagebuch des Gen.Kdo.LXXXIV. A.K., Ia, vom 1.Okt. 1942 bis 31 Dez. 42* [T314 R1603 F351] — Hereafter referred to as Gen.Kdo. *LXXXIV. A.K., KTB Ia vom 1.10-31.12.42*
101. For the outlines of the project as given by the *OKW* see T312 R519 F8119505-15.
102. Rolf, R. (2014), p.197-201 & 212; Gen.Kdo.*LXXXIV. A.K.* Ia, *Tätigkeitsbericht September 1942*, p.4 [T314 R1603 F233]
103. After consulting with *Einsatzgruppe West* of *Organisation Todt*, *Ob.West* concluded that only 40% of the programme could be completed by this date. The planning, construction and associated problems of the *Atlantikwall* will be explored in a future volume.
104. **Rolf, R. (2014)**, p.211
105. Gen.Kdo.*LXXXIV. A.K.* Ia, *Tätigkeitsbericht September 1942*, p.4 [T314 R1603 F233]
106. *Ibid.*; Gen.Kdo.*LXXXIV. A.K.* Ia Nr.2145/42 g.K., 2.10.42, p.1 & Anl. [T314 R1603 F438-9]
107. Gen.Kdo.*LXXXIV. A.K.* Ia, *Tätigkeitsbericht September 1942*, p.5 [T314 R1603 F234]
108. Althought these were not the official designations of the respective *SS* formations at the time, these were in effect at the time of the fighting in Normandy. *SS* formations underwent frequent redesignations, and it will be easier for the reader to keep track this way.
109. *Ibid.*, p.3 [T314 R1603 F232]
110. Gen.Kdo.*LXXXIV. A.K.*, *KTB Ia vom 1.10-31.12.42* [T314 R1603 F351]
111. Gen.Kdo.*LXXXIV. A.K.* Ia, *Tätigkeitsbericht September 1942*, p.3 [T314 R1603 F232]
112. Gen.Kdo.*LXXXIV. A.K.*, *KTB Ia vom 1.10-31.12.42* [T314 R1603 F352]; AOK 7, Ia Nr.4458/42 g.K., 9.10.42 [T314 R1603 F480]; *AOK 7*, Ia Nr.4457/42 g.K., 9.10.42 [T314 R1603 F481]; Gen.Kdo.*LXXXIV. A.K.*, *KTB Ia vom 1.10-31.12.42* [T314 R1603 F356]
113. Gen.Kdo.*LXXXIV. A.K.*, *KTB Ia vom 1.10-31.12.42* [T314 R1603 F352 & 354]; Map with the planned locations of the *165. Division* [T314 R1603 F482]
114. **Tessin, G. (1973)**, *7.Band*, p.144; Gen.Kdo.*LXXXIV. A.K.*, Ia Nr.2239/42 g.K., 10.10.42 [T314 R1603 F483]; 165.Division, *Tätigkeitsbericht der 165.Division, 9.10.1942-30.11.1942*, p.1-4 [T315 R1475 F75]
115. Gen.Kdo.*LXXXIV. A.K.*, *KTB Ia vom 1.10-31.12.42* [T314 R1603 F352 & 56]
116. AOK 7, Ia Nr.4464/42 g.K., 10.10.42 [T314 R1603 F484]
117. Gen.Kdo.*LXXXIV. A.K.*, *KTB Ia vom 1.10-31.12.42* [T314 R1603 F356]; Gen.Kdo.*LXXXIV. A.K.*, Ia Nr.2230/42 g.K., 12.10.42 [T314 R1603 F493]
118. On 15 October 1942, *OKH* changed the names of all infantry regiments to "Grenadier Regiment". The abbreviation *Gren.Rgt.* and *GR* will be used from that date forward.
119. Gen.Kdo.*LXXXIV. A.K.*, *KTB Ia vom 1.10-31.12.42* [T314 R1603 F362 & 364]
120. *Ibid.* [T314 R1603 F372]
121. Gen.Kdo.*LXXXIV. A.K.*, Ia Nr.2420/42 g.K., 28.10.42 [T314 R1603 F550]
122. Gen.Kdo.*LXXXIV. A.K.*, *KTB Ia vom 1.10-31.12.42* [T314 R1603 F374, 380-94, 96]
123. *Ibid.* [T314 R1603 F382, 86, 88, 90]
124. Gen.Kdo.*XXV. A.K.*, Abt. Ia Nr.3303/42 g., *Korps-Befehl Nr.44*, 25.11.42 [T314 R743 F201]
125. Gen.Kdo.*LXXXIV. A.K.*, *KTB Ia vom 1.10-31.12.42* [T314 R1603 F398]
126. *Ibid.* [T314 R1603 F410]
127. *Ibid.* [T314 R1603 F390, 392, 394]
128. Gen.Kdo.*LXXXIV. A.K.*, Ia-Tagesmeldung, 23.11.42 [T314 R1603 F700]
129. Gen.Kdo.*LXXXIV. A.K.*, *KTB Ia vom 1.10-31.12.42* [T314 R1603 F380 & 388]
130. Gen.Kdo.*LXXXIV. A.K.*, Ia-Tagesmeldung, 18.11.42 [T314 R1603 F695]
131. Gen.Kdo.*LXXXIV. A.K.*, *KTB Ia vom 1.10-31.12.42* [T314 R1603 F396]; AOK 7, Ia Nr.5221/42 g.K., 22.11.43 [T314 R1603 F654]; **Tessin, G. (1975)**, *12.Band*, p.163
132. AOK 7, Ia Nr.5233/42 g.K., 23.11.42 [T314 R1603 F653]; Karte d. neuen Korpsgrenze zwischen *LXXXVII. A.K. u. LXXXIV. A.K.* [T314 R1603 F655]; Gen.Kdo.*LXXXIV. A.K.*, Ia Nr.2739/42 g.K., 27.11.42, p.1 [T314 R1603 F663]
133. Gen.Kdo.*LXXXIV. A.K.*, *KTB Ia vom 1.10-31.12.42* [T314 R1603 F396 & 398]; Gen.Kdo.*LXXXIV. A.K.*, Ia Nr.9388/42 g., 27.11.42, p.1-2 & Anl. [T314 R1603 F660-2]; Gen.Kdo.*LXXXIV. A.K.*, Ia Nr.2739/42

g.K., 27.11.42 [T314 R1603 F663-5]
134. Gen.Kdo.*LXXXIV. A.K.*, Ia Nr.2739/42 g.K., 27.11.42, p.1 [T314 R1603 F663]
135. Gen.Kdo.*LXXXIV. A.K.*, Ia Nr.2739/42 g.K., 27.11.42 [T314 R1603 F663-4]
136. Gen.Kdo.*LXXXIV. A.K.*, *KTB Ia vom 1.10-31.12.42* [T314 R1603 F398]; Gen.Kdo.*LXXXIV. A.K.*, Ia Nr.2739/42 g.K., 27.11.42, p.1. -2 [T314 R1603 F663-4]
137. Gen.Kdo.*LXXXIV. A.K.*, Ia Nr.2739/42 g.K., 27.11.42, p.2 [T314 R1603 F664]
138. Gen.Kdo.*LXXXIV. A.K.*, *KTB Ia vom 1.10-31.12.42* [T314 R1603 F400]
139. Gen.Kdo.*LXXXIV. A.K.*, Ia Nr.2794/42 g.K., 30.11.42 [T314 R1603 F674]; Gen.Kdo.*LXXXIV. A.K.*, Ia Nr.2802/42 g.K., 30.11.42 [T314 R1603 F675-6]
140. Gen.Kdo.*LXXXIV. A.K.*, *KTB Ia vom 1.10-31.12.42* [T314 R1603 F400]
141. *Ibid*. [T314 R1603 F406]
142. Gen.Kdo.*LXXXIV. A.K.*, *KTB Ia vom 1.10-31.12.42* [T314 R1603 F416]; Gen.Kdo.*LXXXIV. A.K.*, *Kriegstagebuch vom 1. Jan. bis 30. Juni 1943 des Gen.Kdo.LXXXIV. A.K. Ia* [T314 R1603 F840] — Hereafter referred to as Gen.Kdo.*LXXXIV. A.K.*, *KTB Ia 1.1.-30.6.43*
143. Gen.Kdo.*LXXXIV. A.K.*, Ia-Tagesmeldung, 6.12.42 [T314 R1603 F796]
144. Gen.Kdo.*LXXXIV. A.K.*, *KTB Ia vom 1.10-31.12.42* [T314 R1603 F404]
145. Gen.Kdo.*LXXXIV. A.K.*, Ia-Tagesmeldung, 2.12.42 [T314 R1603 F792]
146. Gen.Kdo.*LXXXIV. A.K.*, *KTB Ia vom 1.10-31.12.42* [T314 R1603 F404]; Gen.Kdo.*LXXXIV. A.K.*, Ia-Tagesmeldung, 4.12.42 [T314 R1603 F794]; Gen.Kdo.*LXXXIV. A.K.*, Ia-Tagesmeldung, 6.12.42 [T314 R1603 F796]
147. Gen.Kdo.*LXXXIV. A.K.*, Ia-Tagesmeldung, 5.12.42 [T314 R1603 F795]; Gen.Kdo.*LXXXIV. A.K.*, *KTB Ia vom 1.10-31.12.42* [T314 R1603 F408]
148. Gen.Kdo.*LXXXIV. A.K.*, Ia-Tagesmeldung, 7.12.42 [T314 R1603 F797]
149. Gen.Kdo.*LXXXIV. A.K.*, *KTB Ia vom 1.10-31.12.42* [T314 R1603 F408]
150. Gen.Kdo.*LXXXIV. A.K.*, Ia-Tagesmeldung, 8.12.42 [T314 R1603 F798]
151. Gen.Kdo.*LXXXIV. A.K.*, Ia-Tagesmeldung, 10.12.42 [T314 R1603 F800]
152. Gen.Kdo.*LXXXIV. A.K.*, *KTB Ia vom 1.10-31.12.42* [T314 R1603 F408] The corps records do not mention its exact arrival. According to Tessin it was created on 1 September 1942. [**Tessin, G. (1975)**, *12.Band*, p.27]
153. Gen.Kdo.*LXXXIV. A.K.*, *KTB Ia vom 1.10-31.12.42* [T314 R1603 F418]
154. Gen.Kdo.*LXXXIV. A.K.*, *KTB Ia 1.1.-30.6.43* [T314 R1603 F842 & 844]
155. *Ibid*. [T314 R1603 F838]; Gen.Kdo.*LXXXIV. A.K.*, Ia-Tagesmeldung, 3.1.43 [T314 R1604 F91]; Gen.Kdo.*LXXXIV. A.K.*, Ia-Tagesmeldung, 7.1.43 [T314 R1604 F87]
156. Gen.Kdo.*LXXXIV. A.K.*, Ia-Tagesmeldung, 4.1.43 [T314 R1604 F90]
157. Gen.Kdo.*LXXXIV. A.K.*, Ia-Tagesmeldung, 5.1.43 [T314 R1604 F89]
158. Gen.Kdo.*LXXXIV. A.K.*, Ia-Tagesmeldung, 17.1.43 [T314 R1604 F77]
159. Gen.Kdo.*LXXXIV. A.K.*, Ia-Tagesmeldung, 27.1.43 [T314 R1604 F67]; Gen.Kdo.*LXXXIV. A.K.*, *KTB Ia vom 1.1.-30.6.43* [T314 R1603 F850]
160. Gen.Kdo.*LXXXIV. A.K.*, *KTB Ia vom 1.1.-30.6.43* [T314 R1603 F850]
161. Gen.Kdo.*LXXXIV. A.K.*, Ia-Tagesmeldung, 8.1.43 [T314 R1604 F86]; Gen.Kdo.*LXXXIV. A.K.*, Ia-Tagesmeldung, 17.1.43 [T314 R1604 F77]
162. Gen.Kdo.*LXXXIV. A.K.*, Ia-Tagesmeldung, 16.1.43 [T314 R1604 F78]
163. Gen.Kdo.*LXXXIV. A.K.*, Ia-Tagesmeldung, 19.1.43 [T314 R1604 F75]
164. *Turk-Bataillon:* Type of battalion formed with non-Slavic troops from the Soviet Union, part of the *Osttruppen*.
165. A.O.K.7, Ia Nr.380/43 g.K., 31.1.43, p.1-2 [T314 R1604 F54-55]
166. Gen.Kdo.*LXXXIV. A.K.*, Ia Nr.235/43 g.K., 31.1.43, p.1-2 [T314 R1604 F57-58]
167. Gen.Kdo.*LXXXIV. A.K.*, Ia-Tagesmeldung, 19.2.43 [T314 R1604 F214]; Gen.Kdo.*LXXXIV. A.K.*, *KTB Ia vom 1.1.-30.6.43* [T314 R1603 F866]; Gen.Kdo.*LXXXIV. A.K.*, Ia-Tagesmeldung, 23.2.43 [T314 R1604 F210]
168. Gen.Kdo.*LXXXIV. A.K.*, Ia-Tagesmeldung, 24.2.43 [T314 R1604 F209]
169. Gen.Kdo.*LXXXIV. A.K.*, Ia-Tagesmeldung, 18.2.43 [T314 R1604 F205]; Also see Gen.Kdo.*LXXXIV. A.K.*, Ia Nr.167/43 g.K., 14.2.43, p.2 [T314 R1604 F158]
170. Gen.Kdo.*LXXXIV. A.K.*, *KTB Ia vom 1.1.-30.6.43* [T314 R1603 F854]
171. *Ibid.*; Gen.Kdo.*LXXXIV. A.K.*, Ia-Tagesmeldung, 2.2.43 [T314 R1604 F231]
172. Gen.Kdo.*LXXXIV. A.K.*, *KTB Ia vom 1.1.-30.6.43* [T314 R1603 F858]; AOK 7, Ia Nr.592/43 g.K., 11.2.43 [T314 R1604 F145]
173. Gen.Kdo.*LXXXIV. A.K.*, Ia Nr.317/43 g.K., 12.2.43 [T314 R1604 F146]
174. The *Oberst's* position was complicated; this is explained in the chapter *"Generalkommando LXXXIV. A.K. and Korpstruppen"*.
175. Gen.Kdo.*LXXXIV. A.K.*, Ia Nr.1349/43 (664) g., 14.2.43 [T314 R1604 F156]
176. Gen.Kdo.*LXXXIV. A.K.*, Ia-Tagesmeldung, 17.2.43 [T314 R1604 F216]
177. Gen.Kdo.*LXXXIV. A.K.*, Ia Nr.344/43 g.K., 15.2.43 [T314 R1604 F160]
178. Gen.Kdo.*LXXXIV. A.K.*, Ia-Tagesmeldung, 16.2.43 [T314 R1604 F217]
179. Gen.Kdo.*LXXXIV. A.K.*, *KTB Ia vom 1.1.-30.6.43* [T314 R1603 F864]
180. Gen.Kdo.*LXXXIV. A.K.*, Ia-Tagesmeldung, 17.2.43 [T314 R1604 F216]
181. Gen.Kdo.*LXXXIV. A.K.*, Ia Nr.432/43 g.K., 25.2.43 [T314 R1604 F181]
182. Gen.Kdo.*LXXXIV. A.K.*, *KTB Ia vom 1.1.-30.6.43* [T314 R1603 F856]; AOK 7, Ia Nr.513/43 g., 7.2.43 [T314 R1604 F121]
183. Gen.Kdo.*LXXXIV. A.K.*, *KTB Ia vom 1.1.-30.6.43* [T314 R1603 F864]; Gen.Kdo.*LXXXIV. A.K.*, Ia-Tagesmeldung, 17.2.43 [T314 R1604 F216]; Gen.Kdo.*LXXXIV. A.K.*, Ia-Tagesmeldung, 23.2.43 [T314 R1604 F210]
184. Gen.Kdo.*LXXXIV. A.K.*, Ia-Tagesmeldung, 20.2.43 [T314 R1604 F213]; Gen.Kdo.*LXXXIV. A.K.*, Ia-Tagesmeldung, 22.2.43 [T314 R1604 F211]
185. Gen.Kdo.*LXXXIV. A.K.*, Ia-Tagesmeldung, 23.2.43 [T314 R1604 F210]; Gen.Kdo.*LXXXIV. A.K.*, *KTB Ia vom 1.1.-30.6.43* [T314 R1603 F862]; AOK 7 /Stoart/Ia Nr.652/43 g., 15.2.43 [T314 R1604 F162]
186. AOK 7, Ia Nr.661/43 g.K., 17.2.43 [T314 R1604 F164];
187. Gen.Kdo.*LXXXIV. A.K.*, Ia Nr.353/43 g.K., 19.2.43, p.2 [T314 R1604 F167]; Gen.Kdo.*LXXXIV. A.K.* Ia 358/43 g.K., 17.2.43 [T314 R1604 F164]
188. Gen.Kdo.*LXXXIV. A.K.*, Ia Nr.353/43 g.K., 19.2.43, p.2 [T314 R1604 F167]
189. Gen.Kdo.*LXXXIV. A.K.*, Ia-Tagesmeldung, 24.2.43 [T314 R1604 F209]; Gen.Kdo.*LXXXIV. A.K.*, Ia-Tagesmeldung, 25.2.43 [T314 R1604 F208]
190. Gen.Kdo.*LXXXIV. A.K.*, Ia-Tagesmeldung, 24.2.43 [T314 R1604 F209]
191. Gen.Kdo.*LXXXIV. A.K.*, *KTB Ia vom 1.1.-30.6.43* [T314 R1603 F854]; AOK 7, Ia Nr.468/43 g.K., 3.2.43, p.1-2 [T314 R1604 F117-8]
192. AOK 7, Ia Nr.468/43 g.K., 3.2.43, p.2 [T314 R1604 F118]
193. Gen.Kdo.*LXXXIV. A.K.*, Ia Nr.272/43 g.K. & Anlage: *Vorschlag des Gen.Kdo.LXXXIV. A.K für Unterbringung der gepz.Artl.Brig.1 u. der Aufzufrischenden Ostdiv. A u. B*, 9.2.43 [T314 R1604 F131-2]
194. Gen.Kdo.*LXXXIV. A.K.*, Ia-Tagesmeldung, 17.2.43 [T314 R1604 F216]; Gen.Kdo.*LXXXIV. A.K.*, *KTB Ia vom 1.1.-30.6.43* [T314 R1603 F864]
195. Gen.Kdo.*LXXXIV. A.K.*, *KTB Ia vom 1.1.-30.6.43* [T314 R1603 F860]
196. Gen.Kdo.*LXXXIV. A.K.*, Ia Nr.3040/42 g.K., 27.12.42 [T314 R1603 F782]; Gen.Kdo.*LXXXIV. A.K.*, *KTB Ia vom 1.10-31.12.42* [T314 R1603 F418]; Gen.Kdo.*LXXXIV. A.K.*, Ia Nr.3058/42 g.K., *Korps - Befehl Nr.9*, 30.12.42 [T314 R1603 F786]; Gen.Kdo.*LXXXIV. A.K.*, *Artillerie-Karte Gen.Kdo.LXXXIV. A.K., Stand: 1.3.43* [T314 R1603 F266]. It had been intended to provide cadre troops for batteries from two artillery battalions, but these were ordered to return to the battalion on 31 January 1943. [Anl. z. Gen.Kdo.*LXXXIV. AK*K. Ia Nr 3070/42 g.K., 27.12.42, *Verlegung der Div.- und Korpsreserven sowie der Kraftfahr-Kompanie* in T314 R1603 F783; Gen.Kdo.*LXXXIV. A.K.*, Ia 928/43 (461) g., 31.1.43 in T314 R1604 F62]
197. Gen.Kdo.*LXXXIV. A.K.*, Ia Nr.2893/43 (1450) g., 8.4.43 [T314 R1604 F375]; Gen.Kdo.*LXXXIV. A.K.*, *KTB Ia vom 1.1.-30.6.43* [T314 R1603 F860, 862, 914 & 916]; Gen.Kdo.*LXXXIV. A.K.*, *Kriegstagebuch vom 1. Juli bis 31. Dez. 43 des Gen.Kdo.LXXXIV. A.K., Ia* [T314 R1603 F962]
198. Gen.Kdo.*LXXXIV. A.K.*, *KTB Ia vom 1.1.-30.6.43* [T314 R1603 F858]
199. AOK 7, Ia Nr.778/43 g.K., 24.2.43 [T314 R1604 F189]; AOK 7, Nr.778/43 g.K., 24.2.43, p1 [T314 R1604 F189]
200. AOK 7, Ia Nr.778/43 g.K., 24.2.43 [T314 R1604 F189]
201. Anl. zu Gen.Kdo.*LXXXIV. A.K.*, Ia Nr.449/43 g.K., *Unterbringung der Kampfgruppe bzw. Volldivision*, 28.2.43

[T314 R1604 F204]
202. Gen.Kdo.*LXXXIV. A.K.*, *KTB Ia vom 1.1.-30.6.43* [T314 R1603 F874]
203. Gen.Kdo.*LXXXIV. A.K.*, Ia-Tagesmeldung, 31.3.43 [T314 R1604 F322]
204. Tessin, G. (1975), *11.Band,* p.41, 51 & 53; Gen.Kdo. *LXXXIV. A.K.*, Ia-Tagesmeldung, 17.3.43 [T314 R1604 F336]; Feldpostübersicht
205. Gen.Kdo.*LXXXIV. A.K.*, Ia-Tagesmeldung, 17.3.43 [T314 R1604 F336]
206. Gen.Kdo.*LXXXIV. A.K.*, *KTB Ia vom 1.1.-30.6.43* [T314 R1603 F876]
207. *Ibid.* [T314 R1603 F878]; Gen.Kdo.*LXXXIV. A.K.*, Ia-Tagesmeldung, 3.3.43 [T314 R1604 F350]
208. Gen.Kdo.*LXXXIV. A.K.*, Ia-Tagesmeldung, 9.3.43 [T314 R1604 F344]
209. Gen.Kdo.*LXXXIV. A.K.*, Ia Nr.576/43 g.K., 13.3.43; Gen.Kdo. *LXXXIV. A.K.*, Ia-Tagesmeldung, 13.3.43 [T314 R1604 F340]; Sich. Rgt.5, Ia Nr.27/43 g.K., *Kriegsgliederung des Sich.Rgt.5, Stand vom 5.3.1943*, 4.3.43 [T314 R1604 F279]
210. *AOK 7* Ia, *Kriegstagebuch der Führungsabteilung AOK 7 für die Zeit vom 1.1.-30.6.43* [T312 R1553 F358] — Hereafter referred to as: AOK 7 Ia, KTB 1.1.-30.6.1944
211. Gen.Kdo.*LXXXIV. A.K.*, *KTB Ia vom 1.1.-30.6.43* [T314 R1603 F888]
212. Gen.Kdo.*LXXXIV. A.K.*, Ia-Tagesmeldung, 22.3.43 [T314 R1604 F331]
213. Gen.Kdo.*LXXXIV. A.K.*, Ia Nr.2776/43 (1379) g., 3.4.43 [T314 R1604 F372]; Gen.Kdo.*LXXXIV. A.K.*, Ia-Tagesmeldung, 10.4.43 [T314 R1604 F448]; Gen.Kdo.*LXXXIV. A.K.*, Ia-Tagesmeldung, 9.4.43 [T314 R1604 F449]; Gen.Kdo.*LXXXIV. A.K.*, *Lagenkarte Gen. Kdo.LXXXIV. A.K., Stand: 5.5.43* [T314 R1604 F481]
214. Gen.Kdo.*LXXXIV. A.K.*, Ia-Tagesmeldung, 10.4.43 [T314 R1604 F448]
215. Gen.Kdo.*LXXXIV. A.K.*, *KTB Ia vom 1.1.-30.6.43* [T314 R1603 F894]
216. Gen.Kdo.*LXXXIV. A.K.*, Ia-Tagesmeldung, 22.4.43 [T314 R1604 F427]; Gen.Kdo.*LXXXIV. A.K.*, Ia-Tagesmeldung, 27.4.43 [T314 R1604 F421]
217. Gen.Kdo.*LXXXIV. A.K.*, Ia Nr.3786/44 (1901) g.II.Ang. 8.5.43 [T314 R1604 F485]
218. Gen.Kdo.*LXXXIV. A.K.*, *KTB Ia vom 1.1.-30.6.43* [T314 R1603 F900]
219. *Ibid.* [T314 R1603 F904]
220. Gen.Kdo.*LXXXIV. A.K.*, Ia-Tagesmeldung, 5.4.43 [T314 R1604 F453] In some records *schnelle Brig. West* was called *schnelle Division West*.
221. AOK 7, Ia Nr.1582/43 g.K., 2.4.43 [T314 R1604 F370]; AOK 7, *Kriegsgliederung 7. Armee*, Stand: 15.4.43, *Verst. Schn. Brigade West, Stand: 1.4.43* [T312 R1553 F587]
222. Gen.Kdo.*LXXXIV. A.K.*, *KTB Ia vom 1.1.-30.6.43* [T314 R1603 F894 & 900]
223. Gen.Kdo.*LXXXIV. A.K.*, Ia-Tagesmeldung, 25.4.43 [T314 R1604 F423]; Gen.Kdo.*LXXXIV. A.K.*, Ia-Tagesmeldung, 30.4.43 [T314 R1604 F417]; OKH/GenStdH/Op Abt (II), Nr.5731/43 g.K., 31.5.43, p.2 [T78 R314 F6267964]; Gen.Kdo.*LXXXIV. A.K.*, Ia-Tagesmeldung, 20.5.43 [T314 R1604 F532]
224. OKH/GenStdH/Op Abt (II) Nr.5428/43 g.K., 21.5.43, p.1 [T78 R314 F6267922]. The divisions' others locations can be found on the situation map of 5 June. [Gen.Kdo.*LXXXIV. A.K.*, *Lagenkarte Gen.Kdo.LXXXIV. A.K., Stand: 5.6.43* in T314 R1604 F565]
225. Gen.Kdo.*LXXXIV. A.K.*, *KTB Ia vom 1.1.-30.6.43* [T314 R1603 F916] & 918]; OKH/GenStdH/Op Abt (II) Nr.5697/43 g.K., 30.5.43, p.1 [T78 R314 F6267959]
226. Gen.Kdo.*LXXXIV. A.K.*, *KTB Ia vom 1.1.-30.6.43* [T314 R1603 F908]
227. *Ibid.* [T314 R1603 F910]
228. *Ibid.* [T314 R1603 F916]; Gen.Kdo.*LXXXIV. A.K.*, Ia-Tagesmeldung, 29.5.43 [T314 R1604 F523]
229. Gen.Kdo.*LXXXIV. A.K.*, *KTB Ia vom 1.1.-30.6.43* [T314 R1603 F918 & 922]; Gen.Kdo.*LXXXIV. A.K.*, Ia-Tagesmeldung, 2.6.43 [T314 R1604 F632]
230. Gen.Kdo.*LXXXIV. A.K.*, Abt.Ia Nr.854/43 g.K., 17.4.43, p.1-2 [T314 R1604 F393-4]
231. Gen.Kdo.*LXXXIV. A.K.*, *KTB Ia vom 1.1.-30.6.43* [T314 R1603 F908 & 22]
232. Gen.Kdo.*LXXXIV. A.K.*, Ia Nr.1171/43 g.K., 5.6.43 [T314 R1604 F564]
233. AOK 7 Ia/Stoart Nr.638/43 g., 15.6.43 [T314 R1604 F575]
234. Gen.Kdo.*LXXXIV. A.K.*, Ia-Tagesmeldung, 5.6.43 [T314 R1604 F629]
235. Gen.Kdo.*LXXXIV. A.K.*, Ia-Tagesmeldung, 17.6.43 [T314 R1604 F617]
236. Gen.Kdo.*LXXXIV. A.K.*, Ia-Tagesmeldung, 8.6.43 [T314 R1604 F626]
237. Gen.Kdo.*LXXXIV. A.K.*, *KTB Ia vom 1.1.-30.6.43* [T314 R1603 F934]
238. Tessin, G. (1977), *1.Band,* p.212
239. Gen.Kdo.*LXXXIV. A.K.*, *I* Ia-Tagesmeldung, 13.8.43 [T314 R1604 F854]; Gen.Kdo.*LXXXIV. A.K.*, Ia-Tagesmeldung, 1.6.43 [T314 R1604 F633]
240. BvTO b. AOK 7, (illegible) Nr.13/44 g.K., *Tätigkeitsbericht für die Zeit vom 1. Juli bis 31. Dezember 1943*, 2.1.44, p.13 [T312 R1563 F15]; Gen.Kdo.*LXXXIV. A.K.*, Ia Nr.1269/43 g.K., 28.6.43, p.1-6 [T314 R1604 F590-5]
241. Gen.Kdo.*LXXXIV. A.K.*, Ia Nr.1269/43 g.K., 28.6.43, p.1-3 [T314 R1604 F590-2]
242. *Ibid.*, p.3-4 [T314 R1604 F592-3]
243. *Ibid.*, p.5 [T314 R1604 F594]
244. Gen.Kdo.*LXXXIV. A.K.*, Ia-Tagesmeldung, 6.7.43 [T314 R1604 F766]
245. Gen.Kdo.*LXXXIV. A.K.*, Ia-Tagesmeldung, 17.7.43 [T314 R1604 F755]
246. Gen.Kdo.*LXXXIV. A.K.*, Ia-Tagesmeldung, 27.3.43 [T314 R1604 F745]; Gen.Kdo.*LXXXIV. A.K.*, Ia-Tagesmeldung, 28.7.43 [T314 R1604 F744]
247. Gen.Kdo.*LXXXIV. A.K.*, Ia Nr.5777/43 (2973) g., 11.7.43 [T314 R1604 F683]. The actual order (OKH/GenStdH/Org.Abt.I Nr.2663/43 g.K. v.28.6.43) had already been issued on 28 June.
248. Gen.Kdo.*LXXXIV. A.K.*, Ia Nr.5968/43 (3062) g., 17.7.43 [T314 R1604 F701]
249. Gen.Kdo.*LXXXIV. A.K.*, Ia-Tagesmeldung, 22.7.43 [T314 R1604 F750]; Gen.Kdo.*LXXXIV. A.K.*, Ia-Tagesmeldung, 24.7.43 [T314 R1604 F748]
250. Gen.Kdo.*LXXXIV. A.K.*, *Kriegstagebuch vom 1. Juli bis 31. Dez. 43 des Gen.Kdo.LXXXIV. A.K., Ia* [T314 R1603 F962] — Hereafter referred to as: Gen.Kdo.*LXXXIV. A.K.*, KTB Ia 1.7.-31.12.43
251. Gen.Kdo.*LXXXIV. A.K.*, *KTB Ia 1.7.-31.12.43* [T314 R1603 F964]; Gen.Kdo.*LXXXIV. A.K.*, Ia-Tagesmeldung, 6.8.43 [T314 R1604 F861]; Gen.Kdo.*LXXXIV. A.K.*, Ia-Tagesmeldung, 5.8.43 [T314 R1604 F862]
252. Gen.Kdo.*LXXXIV. A.K.*, Ia-Tagesmeldung, 6.8.43 [T314 R1604 F861]; Gen.Kdo.*LXXXIV. A.K.*, Ia-Tagesmeldung, 7.8.43 [T314 R1604 F860]
253. Gen.Kdo.*LXXXIV. A.K.*, Ia-Tagesmeldung, 21.8.43 [T314 R1604 F846]; Gen.Kdo.*LXXXIV. A.K.*, Ia Nr.1537/43 g.K., 19.8.43, p.3 [T314 R1604 F824]
254. Gen.Kdo.*LXXXIV. A.K.*, Ia-Tagesmeldung, 23.8.43 [T314 R1604 F844]; Gen.Kdo.*LXXXIV. A.K.*, Ia-Tagesmeldung, 28.8.43 [T314 R1604 F839]
255. Gen.Kdo.*LXXXIV. A.K.*, Ia Nr.1523/43 g.K. II.Ang., 18.8.43, p.2 [T314 R1604 F821]; Gen.Kdo.*LXXXIV. A.K.*, Ia Nr.1537/43 g.K., 19.8.43 [T314 R1604 F822]; Gen.Kdo.*LXXXIV. A.K.*, Ia-Tagesmeldung, 21.8.43 [T314 R1604 F846]; Gen.Kdo.*LXXXIV. A.K.*, Ia-Tagesmeldung, 23.8.43 [T314 R1604 F844]; Gen.Kdo.*LXXXIV. A.K.*, KTB Ia 1.7.-31.12.43 [T314 R1603 F970-1]
256. Gen.Kdo.*LXXXIV. A.K.*, Ia Nr.1523/43 g.K. II.Ang., 18.8.43, p.2 [T314 R1604 F821]; Gen.Kdo.*LXXXIV. A.K.*, Ia-Tagesmeldung, 20.8.43 [T314 R1604 F847]
257. Gen.Kdo.*LXXXIV. A.K.*, Ia Nr.1523/43 g.K. II.Ang., 18.8.43, p.1-2 [T314 R1604 F820-1]; Gen.Kdo.*LXXXIV. A.K.*, Ia Nr.1537/43 g.K., 19.8.43 [T314 R1604 F822]
258. AOK 7/O.Qu., Kriegstagebuch Nr.42, 1. August 1943 - 31. August 1943 [T312 R1562 F266]; Gen.Kdo.*LXXXIV. A.K.*, KTB Ia 1.7.-31.12.43 [T314 R1603 F970-1]
259. Gen.Kdo.*LXXXIV. A.K.*, Ia-Tagesmeldung, 22.8.43 [T314 R1604 F845]; Gen.Kdo.*LXXXIV. A.K.*, Ia-Tagesmeldung, 31.8.43 [T314 R1604 F837]
260. *V-Waffen* or *Vergeltungswaffen*: Reprisal Weapons, the famous V-1, V-2 and V-3. In Normandy the V-1 is primarily associated with the Cotentin and the V-2 with the Calvados.
261. Gen.Kdo.*LXXXIV. A.K.*, KTB Ia 1.7.-31.12.43 [T314 R1603 F970-1 & 973]; **Tessin, G. (1975)**, *10.Band,* p.34
262. Gen.Kdo.*LXXXIV. A.K.*, Ia Nr.1537/43 g.K., 19.8.43, p.1 [T314 R1604 F822] The artillery battalion was initially identified as *I./AR 384*.
263. Gen.Kdo.*LXXXIV. A.K.*, Ia-Tagesmeldung, 26.8.43 [T314 R1604 F841]
264. Gen.Kdo.*LXXXIV. A.K.*, Ia Nr.1559/43 g.K., 21.8.43, p.2 [T314 R1604 F829]; Gen.Kdo.*LXXXIV. A.K.*, Ia-Tagesmeldung, 23.8.43 [T314 R1604 F844]
265. Gen.Kdo.*LXXXIV. A.K.*, Ia-Tagesmeldung, 25.8.43 [T314 R1604 F842]
266. Gen.Kdo.*LXXXIV. A.K.*, Ia Nr.1621/43 g.K., 31.8.43 [T314 R1604 F836]
267. Gen.Kdo.*LXXXIV. A.K.*, Ia-Tagesmeldung, 27.9.43 [T314 R1604 F966]
268. AOK 7 Ia Nr. 4621/43 g.K., 13.9.43 [T314 R1604 F920]; Gen.

Kdo.*LXXXIV. A.K.*, Ia Nr.1704 g.K., 14.9.43 [T314 R1604 F921-2]
269. Gen.Kdo.*LXXXIV. A.K.*, Ia-Tagesmeldung, 16.9.43 [T314 R1604 F977]
270. Gen.Kdo.*LXXXIV. A.K.*, Ia Nr.1704 g.K., 14.9.43, p.1 [T314 R1604 F921]
271. Gen.Kdo.*LXXXIV. A.K.*, Ia Nr.1635 g.K., 4.9.43 [T314 R1604 F884]; Gen.Kdo.*LXXXIV. A.K.*, Ia-Tagesmeldung, 13.9.43 [T314 R1604 F980]
272. Gen.Kdo.*LXXXIV. A.K.*, Ia Nr.1664/43 g.K., 8.9.43 [T314 R1604 F910]; Gen.Kdo.*LXXXIV. A.K.*, Ia-Tagesmeldung, 18.9.43 [T314 R1604 F975]; Gen.Kdo.*LXXXIV. A.K.*, Ia-Tagesmeldung, 25.9.43 [T314 R1604 F968]
273. Gen.Kdo.*LXXXIV. A.K.*, Ia Nr.1635 g.K., 4.9.43 [T314 R1604 F884]; Gen.Kdo.*LXXXIV. A.K.*, Ia Nr.1664/43 g.K., 8.9.43 [T314 R1604 F910]
274. Gen.Kdo.*LXXXIV. A.K.*, Ia-Tagesmeldung, 11.9.43 [T314 R1604 F982]
275. Gen.Kdo.*LXXXIV. A.K.*, Ia Nr.1654/43 g.K., 6.9.43 [T314 R1604 F902]
276. Gen.Kdo.*LXXXIV. A.K.* Ia, Nr.1734/43 g.K., 18.9.43 [T314 R1604 F924]. To prevent confusion, the new 8./AR 389 and the III./546 were identified by adding "*neu*" (new) to their designations. The original units were called "*alt*" (old/former).
277. Gen.Kdo.*LXXXIV. A.K.*, Ia Nr.1908/43 g.K., 23.10.43 [T314 R1604 F1063]
278. Gen.Kdo.*LXXXIV. A.K.*, Ia Nr.1726/43 g.K.II.Ang., 17.9.43 [T314 R1604 F923]. The III./AR 389 was to stay in France only as long as the 709. I.D. had not received an additional artillery battalion. Gen.Kdo.*LXXXIV. A.K.* Ia, Nr.1734/43 g.K., 18.9.43 [T314 R1604 F924]
279. Gen.Kdo.*LXXXIV. A.K.* Ia, Nr.1734/43 g.K., 18.9.43 [T314 R1604 F924]
280. Gen.Kdo.*LXXXIV. A.K.* Ia, Nr.1735/43 g.K., 18.9.43 [T314 R1604 F925]
281. AOK 7, Ia Nr.4738/43 g.K., 19.9.43 [T314 R1604 F931]
282. Gen.Kdo.*LXXXIV. A.K.*, Ia-Tagesmeldung, 26.9.43 [T314 R1604 F967]
283. Gen.Kdo.*LXXXIV. A.K.*, Ia-Tagesmeldung, 25.9.43 [T314 R1604 F968]
284. AOK 7, Ia Nr.4900/43 g.K., p.1-3 [T314 R1604 F944-6]
285. Gen.Kdo.*LXXXIV. A.K.*, Ia Nr.1784/43 g.K., 26.9.43, p.1 [T314 R1604 F953]; List with changes to the staff of Gen.Kdo.*LXXXIV. A.K.* in September 1943 [T314 R1604 F1003]; List with changes to the staff of Gen.Kdo.*LXXXIV. A.K.* in December 1943 [T314 R1604 F1349]
286. Gen.Kdo.*LXXXIV. A.K.*, Ia-Tagesmeldung, 2.10.43 [T314 R1604 F1113]; Anlage zu *243. I.D.*, Ia Nr.242/43 g.K., (Kriegsgliederung) *243.Inf.Div., Stand vom 1.11.43*, 4.11.1943 [T314 R745 F180]
287. Gen.Kdo.*LXXXIV. A.K.*, Ia-Tagesmeldung, 2.10.43 [T314 R1604 F1113]
288. Gen.Kdo.*LXXXIV. A.K.*, Ia Nr.8301/43 (4231) g.II.Ang., 3.10.43 [T314 R1604 F1012]
289. Gen.Kdo.*LXXXIV. A.K.*, Ia Nr.8412/43 (4276) g., 5.10.43 [T314 R1604 F1019]
290. Gen.Kdo.*LXXXIV. A.K.*, Ia/Nr.1811/43 g.K., 3.10.43, p.1 [T314 R1604 F1017]
291. Gen.Kdo.*LXXXIV. A.K.*, Ia Nr.8412/43 (4276) g., 5.10.43 [T314 R1604 F1019]
292. Gen.Kdo.*LXXXIV. A.K.*, Ia-Tagesmeldung, 6.10.43 [T314 R1604 F1109]; Gen.Kdo.*LXXXIV. A.K.*, Ia/Art. Nr.1811/43 g.K., 2.10.43, p.1 [T314 R1604 F1017]; Gen.Kdo.*LXXXIV. A.K.*, Ia-Tagesmeldung, 7.10.43 [T314 R1604 F1108]
293. Gen.Kdo.*LXXXIV. A.K.*, Ia/Art. Nr.1811/43 g.K., 2.10.43, p.2 [T314 R1604 F1018]
294. Gen.Kdo.*LXXXIV. A.K.*, Ia-Tagesmeldung, 10.43 [T314 R1604 F1103]
295. Gen.Kdo.*LXXXIV. A.K.*, Ia-Tagesmeldung, 22.10.43 [T314 R1604 F1092]
296. *Etatisierung:* Formal establishment of a formation that had previously existed without official approval; it was formally added to the budgeting process.
297. AOK 7 IIa Az. Nr.13/43, 21.10.43 [T314 R1604 F1061] For the *716. I.D.* these presumably included *Geräte-Batterie Franziska, Graf Waldersee, Resi* and *Vera*. The *709. I.D.* listed *Ger. Bttr. Cosqueville* (later *Thüringen*), *Reichenau* and *Westeck* (aka *Westmark*). The status of *Ger.Bttr. Brasilia* (716. I.D.), *Osteck* (aka *Ostmark*), and *Fort du Roule* (later *Hessen*) is unclear, but all three were presumably formally established as well.
298. Gen.Kdo.*LXXXIV. A.K.*, Ia-Tagesmeldung, 6.10.43 [T314 R1604 F1109]; Gen.Kdo.*LXXXIV. A.K.* Ia Nr.8301/43 (4231) g. II.Ang., 3.10.43 [T314 R1604 F1012]; Gen.Kdo.*LXXXIV. A.K.*, Ia-Tagesmeldung, 9.10.43 [T314 R1604 F1106]
299. Gen.Kdo.*LXXXIV. A.K.*, Ia Nr.1845/43 g.K., *Korpsbefehl Nr.6*, 11.10.43 [T314 R1604 F1051]; Gen.Kdo.*LXXXIV. A.K.*, Ia Nr.1944/43 g.K., 30.10.43, p.1 [T314 R1604 F1079]
300. *Ost-Bataillon:* Battalion formed with Slavic personnel from the Soviet Union.
301. Gen.Kdo.*LXXXIV. A.K.*, Ia Nr.1873/43 g.K., *Korpsbefehl Nr.7*, 17.10.43 [T314 R1604 F1058]
302. Gen.Kdo.*LXXXIV. A.K.*, Ia Nr.1873/43 g.K., *Korpsbefehl Nr.7*, 17.10.43 [T314 R1604 F1058]
303. Gen.Kdo.*LXXXIV. A.K.*, Ia-Tagesmeldung, 17.10.43 [T314 R1604 F1098]
304. Gen.Kdo.*LXXXIV. A.K.*, Ia-Tagesmeldung, 19.10.43 [T314 R1604 F1096]
305. Gen.Kdo.*LXXXIV. A.K.*, Ia-Tagesmeldung, 25.10.43 [T314 R1604 F1089]
306. Gen.Kdo.*LXXXIV. A.K.*, Ia-Tagesmeldung, 24.10.43 [T314 R1604 F1090]
307. Gen.Kdo.*LXXXIV. A.K.*, Ia-Tagesmeldung, 26.10.43 [T314 R1604 F1088]
308. Gen.Kdo.*LXXXIV. A.K.*, Ia-Tagesmeldung, 21.10.43, p.1-2 [T314 R1604 F1093-4]
309. *Osttruppen:* Collective term for non-German units and personnel from the Soviet Union (excluding *Hilfswillige* (Hiwi's).
310. Gen.Kdo.*LXXXIV. A.K.*, Ia-Tagesmeldung, 13.10.43 [T314 R1604 F1102]
311. Gen.Kdo.*LXXXIV. A.K.*, Ia-Tagesmeldung, 14.10.43 [T314 R1604 F1101]
312. Gen.Kdo.*LXXXIV. A.K.*, Ia-Tagesmeldung, 22.10.43 [T314 R1604 F1092]
313. Gen.Kdo.*LXXXIV. A.K.*, Ia-Tagesmeldung, 31.10.43 [T314 R1604 F1083]
314. Gen.Kdo.*LXXXIV. A.K.*, Ia-Tagesmeldung, 1.11.43 [T314 R1604 F1238]
315. Gen.Kdo.*LXXXIV. A.K.*, Ia-Tagesmeldung, 3.10.43 [T314 R1604 F1112]; Gen.Kdo.*LXXXIV. A.K.*, Ia-Tagesmeldung, 5.10.43 [T314 R1604 F1110]
316. Gen.Kdo.*LXXXIV. A.K.*, Ia-Tagesmeldung, 4.10.43 [T314 R1604 F1111]
317. Gen.Kdo.*LXXXIV. A.K.*, Ia Nr.8330/43 (4240) g., 3.10.43, p.1-2 [T314 R1604 F1015-6]
318. Gen.Kdo.*LXXXIV. A.K.*, Ia-Tagesmeldung, 13.10.43 [T314 R1604 F1102]
319. Gen.Kdo.*LXXXIV. A.K.*, Ia-Tagesmeldung, 8.10.43 [T314 R1604 F1107]; Gen.Kdo.*LXXXIV. A.K.*, Ia-Tagesmeldung, 6.10.43 [T314 R1604 F1109]
320. Gen.Kdo.*LXXXIV. A.K.*, Ia Nr.1781/43 g.K. II.Ang., 26.9.43 [T314 R1604 F952]
321. Gen.Kdo.*LXXXIV. A.K.*, Ia-Tagesmeldung, 23.10.43 [T314 R1604 F1091]; *Ob.West/Okdo.d.H.Gr. D, II. Ausfertigung Ia, K.T.B. vom 1.10 - 31.10.43*, p.86 [T311 R20 F7023303]
322. Gen.Kdo.*LXXXIV. A.K.*, Ia Nr.8258/43 (4218) g., 3.10.43, p.1-2 [T314 R1604 F1013-4]; **Tessin G. (1972)**, *5.Band*, p.273
323. Gen.Kdo.*LXXXIV. A.K.*, Ia-Tagesmeldung, 8.10.43 [T314 R1604 F1107]
324. AOK 7, *Kriegsgliederung 7. Armee, Stand: 20.10.43, Kriegsgliederung der Festungspionierestäbe und Baubataillone im Bereich des A.O.K.7, Stand vom 10.9.43* [T312 R1559 F663]
325. Gen.Kdo.*LXXXIV. A.K.*, Ia Nr.8258/43 (4218) g., 3.10.43, p.1-2 [T314 R1604 F1013-4]; Gen.Kdo.*LXXXIV. A.K.*, Ia-Tagesmeldung, 15.10.43 [T314 R1604 F1100]
326. Gen.Kdo.*LXXXIV. A.K.*, Ia-Tagesmeldung, 12.10.43 [T314 R1604 F1103]; Gen.Kdo.*LXXXIV. A.K.*, Ia-Tagesmeldung, 24.10.43 [T314 R1604 F1090]
327. Gen.Kdo.*LXXXIV. A.K.*, Ia Nr.1831/43 g.K., 9.10.43, p.1 [T314 R1604 F1035]
328. *Ibid.*, p.2 [T314 R1604 F1036]
329. *Ibid.*, p.2-3 & Anlage [T314 R1604 F1036-8]
330. Gen.Kdo.*LXXXIV. A.K.*, Ia Nr.1836/43 g.K., 9.10.43, p.1-4 [T314 R1604 F1042-5]
331. Gen.Kdo.*LXXXIV. A.K.*, Ia Nr.1835/43 g.K., 9.10.43, p.1-2 [T314 R1604 F1039-40]; Gen.Kdo.*LXXXIV. A.K.*, Ia Nr.1836/43 g.K., 9.10.43, p.2 [T314 R1604 F1043]
332. Gen.Kdo.*LXXXIV. A.K.*, Ia Nr.1845/43 g.K., 11.10.43 [T314 R1604 F1051]; Gen.Kdo.*LXXXIV. A.K.*, Ia/Art. Nr.8901/43 g., 21.10.43 [T314 R1604 F1060]
333. Gen.Kdo.*LXXXIV. A.K.*, Ia Art Nr.9135/43 g., 30.10.43 [T314 R1604 F1082]
334. *Arfü (Artillerie-Führer):* Officer and staff in over-all control of the artillery in a sector, typically at division level
335. Gen.Kdo.*LXXXIV. A.K.*, Ia Art. Nr.9154/43 g., 30.10.43 [T314 R1604 F1081]
336. Der *Oberbefehlshaber West*, Ia Nr.550/43 g.K. Ch., 28.10.1943 [T78 R311 F6263267-9]
337. Ibid. [T78 R311 F6263228-76]
338. Gen.Kdo.*LXXXIV. A.K.* Ia Art. Nr.1949/43 g.K., 6.11.43, p.1-4

247

[T314 R1604 F1152-5]
339. *AOK 7*, Ia Nr.5527/43 g.K., 6.11.43 [T314 R1604 F1151]
340. Gen.Kdo.*LXXXIV. A.K.*, Ia Nr.2280/43 g.K., 28.12.43, p.3-4 [T314 R15604 F1293-4]; **Rolf, R. (2014)**, p.414
341. Gen.Kdo.*LXXXIV. A.K.* Ia/Art. Nr.1926/43 g.K., 28.10.43 [T314 R1604 F1068]
342. Gen.Kdo.*LXXXIV. A.K.* Ia Art. Nr.9425/43 (4774) g., 8.11.43 [T314 R1604 F1166
343. Gen.Kdo.*LXXXIV. A.K.*, Ia-Tagesmeldung, 12.11.43 [T314 R1604 F1227]
344. Gen.Kdo.*LXXXIV. A.K.*, Ia-Tagesmeldung, 11.11.43 [T314 R1604 F1228]
345. Gen.Kdo.*LXXXIV. A.K.*, Ia Nr.9533/43 (4840) g., 11.11.43 [T314 R1604 F1173]
346. Gen.Kdo.*LXXXIV. A.K.*, Ia-Tagesmeldung, 2.11.43 [T314 R1604 F1237]; Gen.Kdo.*LXXXIV. A.K.*, Ia-Tagesmeldung, 8.11.43 [T314 R1604 F1231]
347. A.O.K.7, Ia Nr.5711/43 g.K., 9.11.43 [T314 R745 F111-13]; Gen.Kdo.*LXXXIV. A.K.*, Ia Nr.1993/43 g.K., 10.11.43, p.1 [T314 R1604 F1171]
348. Gen.Kdo.*LXXXIV. A.K.*, Ia-Tagesmeldung, 8.11.43 [T314 R1604 F1231]
349. Gen.Kdo.*LXXXIV. A.K.*, Ia-Tagesmeldung, 16.11.43 [T314 R1604 F1223]
350. Gen.Kdo.*LXXXIV. A.K.*, Ia-Tagesmeldung, 20.11.43 [T314 R1604 F1219]; Gen.Kdo.*LXXXIV. A.K.* Ia, *Kriegstagebuch vom 1.Juli bis 31.Dez.43 des Gen.Kdo.LXXXIV. A.K.* [T314 R1603 F1012]
351. Gen.Kdo.*LXXXIV. A.K.*, Ia-Tagesmeldung, 20.11.43 [T314 R1604 F1219]
352. Gen.Kdo.*LXXXIV. A.K.*, Ia Nr.2075/43 g.K., 27.11.43 [F1203]; Gen.Kdo.*LXXXIV. A.K.*, Ia Nr.9909/43 (5038) g., 27.11.43 [T314 R1604 F1202]
353. Gen.Kdo.*LXXXIV. A.K.*, Ia-Tagesmeldung, 29.11.43 [T314 R1604 F1210]
354. Gen.Kdo.*LXXXIV. A.K.*, Ia Nr.1955/43 g.K., 3.11.43 [T314 R1604 F1141]; Gen.Kdo.*LXXXIV. A.K.*, Ia-Tagesmeldung, 12.11.43 [T314 R1604 F1227]
355. *AOK 7*, Ia Nr.5579/43 g., 2.11.43 [T312 R1559 F6]
356. Gen.Kdo.*LXXXIV. A.K.*, Ia Nr.938/43 (4757) g., 6.11.43 [T314 R1604 F1161]
357. Gen.Kdo.*LXXXIV. A.K.*, Ia-Tagesmeldung, 12.11.43 [T314 R1604 F1227]
358. Gen.Kdo.*LXXXIV. A.K.*, Ia Nr.9826/43 (4993) g., 24.11.43 [T314 R1604 F1192]
359. Gen.Kdo.*LXXXIV. A.K.*, Ia-Tagesmeldung, 11.11.43 [T314 R1604 F1228]
360. Gen.Kdo.*LXXXIV. A.K.*, Ia-Tagesmeldung, 12.11.43 [T314 R1604 F1227]; Gen.Kdo.*LXXXIV. A.K.*, Ia-Tagesmeldung, 13.11.43 [T314 R1604 F1226]
361. Gen.Kdo.*LXXXIV. A.K.*, Ia-Tagesmeldung, 27.11.43 [T314 R1604 F1212]
362. Gen.Kdo.*LXXXIV. A.K.*, Ia 9898 (5030) g., 30.11.43 [T314 R1604 F1207]
363. *Hauptkampffeld:* main battle area; *2.Stellung:* Second Defence Line (Position), a line some distance inland protecting key locations.

364. Gen.Kdo.*LXXXIV. A.K.*, Ia Nr.2004/43 g.K., 17.11.43, p.1-2 [T314 R1604 F1179-80]
365. *Ibid.*, p.3-4 [T314 R1604 F1181-2]
366. PWIS(H)/LDC/170, 24 Jul 1944, p.1 [UKNA, WO 208/3646]
367. *AOK 7* Ia, *Vortragsnotiz, Kräfteeinsatz für Ausbau im Abschnitt LXXXIV. A.K.*, 4.11.43 [T312 R1559 F20]
368. *AOK 7* (Maj.i.G. Johannes), Anl.1 z. Ia Nr.6001/43 g., 22.11.43, p.1 [T312 R1559 F162]
369. Gen.Kdo.*LXXXIV. A.K.*, Ia Nr.9918/43 (5040) g., 26.11.43 [T314 R1604 F1200]; Gen.Kdo.*LXXXIV. A.K.*, Ia-Tagesmeldung, 4.12.43 [T314 R1604 F1334]; Gen.Kdo.*LXXXIV. A.K.*, Ia-Tagesmeldung, 3.12.43 [T314 R1604 F1335]
370. Gen.Kdo.*LXXXIV. A.K.*, Ia Nr.9926/43 (5041), 26.11.43 [T314 R1604 F1201]; **Tessin, G. (1965)**, *2.Band*, p.142; Gen.Kdo.*LXXXIV. A.K.*, Ia Nr.167/44 g., 14.2.43, p.2 [T314 R1604 F158] No records have been found to show that *Fluganwärter-Btl. II* ever left the Cotentin after arriving in June 1942, although this was planned in February 1943.
371. Gen.Kdo.*LXXXIV. A.K.*, Ia Nr.1985/43 g.K., 12.11.43, p.1-3 [T314 R1604 F1175-7]; Gen.Kdo.*LXXXIV. A.K.*, Ia Nr.2058/43 g.K., 30.11.43 [T314 R1604 F1208]
372. *AOK 7*, Ia Nr.6132/43 g., 30.11.43 [T312 R1559 F259]
373. Gen.Kdo.*LXXXIV. A.K.*, Ia-Tagesmeldung, 4.12.43 [T314 R1604 F1334]
374. Gen.Kdo.*LXXXIV. A.K.*, Ia-Tagesmeldung, 2.12.43 [T314 R1604 F1336]
375. Gen.Kdo.*LXXXIV. A.K.*, Ia-Tagesmeldung, 1.12.43 [T314 R1604 F1337]
376. Gen.Kdo.*LXXXIV. A.K.*, Ia-Tagesmeldung, 3.12.43 [T314 R1604 F1335]; Gen.Kdo.*LXXXIV. A.K.*, Ia-Tagesmeldung, 4.12.43 [T314 R1604 F1334]
377. Gen.Kdo.*LXXXIV. A.K.*, Ia-Tagesmeldung, 5.12.43 [T314 R1604 F1333]
378. *AOK 7*, Ia Nr.6217/43 g., 4.12.43 [T312 R1559 F311]; *AOK 7*, Ia Nr.6331/43 g., 9.12.43 [T312 R1559 F336]
379. *AOK 7*, Ia Nr.6286/43 g., 7.12.43 [T312 R1559 F326]
380. *AOK 7*, Ia Nr.6518/43 g., 19.12.43 [T312 R1559 F396]
381. *AOK 7*, Ia Nr.6518/43 g., 19.12.43 [T312 R1559 F396]
382. Gen.Kdo.*LXXXIV. A.K.*, Ia-Tagesmeldung, 5.12.43 [T314 R1604 F1333]; Gen.Kdo.*LXXXIV. A.K.*, Ia-Tagesmeldung, 6.12.43 [T314 R1604 F1332]
383. Gen.Kdo.*LXXXIV. A.K.*, Ia-Tagesmeldung, 13.12.43 [T314 R1604 F1325]
384. Gen.Kdo.*LXXXIV. A.K.*, Ia-Tagesmeldung, 18.12.43 [T314 R1604 F1320]
385. Gen.Kdo.*LXXXIV. A.K.* Ia, *Kriegstagebuch vom 1.Juli bis 31.Dez.43 des Gen.Kdo.LXXXIV. A.K.* [T314 R1603 F1022]
386. Gen.Kdo.*LXXXIV. A.K.* Ia/Art. Nr.1655/43 g.K., 6.9.43, p.1-2 [T314 R1604 F900-1]
387. Gen.Kdo.*LXXXIV. A.K.*, Ia-Tagesmeldung, 1.12.43 [T314 R1604 F1337]; Gen.Kdo.*LXXXIV. A.K.*, Ia-Tagesmeldung, 2.12.43 [T314 R1604 F1336]; *AOK 7*, Ia Nr.6197/43 g., 3.12.43 [T312 R1559 F309]; Gen.Kdo.*LXXXIV. A.K.*, Ia-Tagesmeldung, 3.12.43 [T314 R1604 F1335]; Gen.Kdo.*LXXXIV. A.K.*, Ia-Tagesmeldung, 4.12.43 [T314 R1604 F1334]

388. *AOK 7*, Ia Nr.6518/43 g., 19.12.43 [T312 R1559 F396]
389. Gen.Kdo.*LXXXIV. A.K.*, Ia-Tagesmeldung, 17.12.43 [T314 R1604 F1321]
390. Gen.Kdo.*LXXXIV. A.K.*, Ia-Tagesmeldung, 22.12.43 [T314 R1604 F1316]; *OKW*/WFSt/Op. Nr.662890/43 g.K. Chefs., 1.12.43 in **Hubatsch, W. (reprint 2005b)**, *Kriegstagebuch des Oberkommandos der Wehrmacht (Wehrmachtführungsstab), Band III: 1. Januar 1943 - 31. Dezember 1943,* Augsburg: Verlagsgruppe Weltbild GmbH, p.1473; **Hubatsch, W. (reprint 2005b)**, p.1250 & 1357
391. Anl. 4 zu *OKH*/GenStdH/Org.Abt.Nr.I/5700/43 g.K., *Artillerie im Bereich A.O.K.7*, 19.12.43, p.1 [T78 R528 F888]
392. *Ibid.*, p.5 [T78 R528 F892]
393. Rolf, R. (2014), p.295; Gen.Kdo.*LXXXIV. A.K.*, Ia Nr.2271/43 g.K., 27.12.43, p.1 [T314 R1604 F1290]
394. *OKW*, Gen. d. Pi. u. Fest., Abt.L (A O) Az.39 Artl. Nr.1800/43 g.K., *Zusammenfassung der grundsätzlichen Verfügungen über ständigen Ausbau der Artillerie*, 10.10.43, p.1-2 [T312 R519 F8119317-8]
395. Gen.Kdo.*LXXXIV. A.K.*, Ia Nr.2271/43 g.K., 27.12.43 [T314 R1604 F1290-1]
396. *Gen.Kdo. LXV.A.K. zbV* was raised in November 1943 for the operation of *V*-Weapons. As such the corps operated over a vast sector of *Ob.West*. Locally, its construction work was supervised by special staffs such as *Gen.Maj.* Hellwig. [*OKH* Chef H Rüst und BdE, AmA Ia(I) Nr.6482/43 g.K., 28.11.43 in T78 R849 H36/159]
397. Gen.Kdo.*LXXXIV. A.K.*, Ia Nr.2271/43 g.K., 27.12.43 [T314 R1604 F1290-1]
398. Gen.Kdo.*LXXXIV. A.K.*, Ia Nr.2280/43 g.K., 28.12.43, p.3-4 [T314 R1604 F1294-5]
399. Rolf, R. (2014), p.295; *AOK 7* Fest.Pi./Ia Nr.331/44 g.K., 17.1.44 [T312 R1564 F465-6]
400. *AOK 7* Fest.Pi./Ia Nr.331/44 g.K., 17.1.44, p.1-2 [T312 R1564 F465-7]
401. Gen.Kdo.*LXXXIV. A.K.*, Ia Nr.098/43 g.K. Chefs., 1.1.44 & Anlage [T312 R1564 F399-400]; *AOK 7*, Ia Nr.38/44 g.K., 3.1.44 [T312 R1564 F401]
402. *AOK 7*, Ia Nr.133/44 g., 7.1.44 [T312 R1564 F414]
403. *AOK 7*, Ia Nr.106/44 g., 6.1.44 [T312 R1564 F410]; *AOK 7*, Ia Nr.642/44 g., 1.2.44, p.1 [T312 R1565 F4]
404. *AOK 7*, Ia Nr.194/44 g.K., 10.1.44 [T312 R1564 F429]
405. *AOK 7*, Ia Nr.365/44 g.K., 18.1.44 [T312 R1564 F472]; *AOK 7*, Ia Nr.382/44 g., 19.1.44 [T312 R1564 F474]; *AOK 7*, Ia Nr.433/44 g., 21.1.44, p.2 [T312 R1564 F484]
406. *AOK 7*, Ia Nr.453/44 g., 22.1.44 [T312 R1564 F496]; *AOK 7*, Ia Nr.473/44 g., 23.1.44 [T312 R1564 F502]
407. *AOK 7*, Ia Nr.473/44 g., 23.1.44 [T312 R1564 F502]
408. *AOK 7*, Ia Nr.494/44 g., 24.1.44 [T312 R1564 F523]
409. Gen.Kdo.*LXXXIV. A.K.*, Ia 9898 (5030) g., 30.11.43 [T314 R1604 F1207]; *AOK 7*, Ia Nr.48/44 g., 3.1.44 [T312 R1564 F395]; *AOK 7*, Ia Nr.66/44 g., 4.1.44 [T312 R1564 F403]
410. *AOK 7*, Ia Nr.225/44 g., 11.1.44 [T312 R1564 F432]
411. *AOK 7*, Ia Nr.343/44 g., 17.1.44 [T312 R1564 F463]
412. *AOK 7*, Ia Nr.106/44 g., 6.1.44 [T312 R1564 F410]
413. *AOK 7*, Ia Nr.6574/43 g., 23.12.43 [T312 R1559 F433]; Gen.Kdo.*XXV. A.K.*, *Kriegstagebuch Nr.11 Gen.Kdo.XXV. A.K.*

Führungsabteilung (Ia) 1.10.43 - 31.12.43 [T314 R745 F37] — Hereafter referred to as: Gen.Kdo.*XXV. A.K.* Ia, *KTB Nr.11. Fest. Pi.Abschn.Gr. Beger* (also *Sonderstab Beger*) was created in late 1943 and operated under a number of cover names and eventually became *Fest.Pi.Stab 36*. This will be looked at in a future volume.

414. *AOK 7* Ia, Vortragsnotiz, Kräfteeinsatz für Ausbau im Abschnitt LXXXIV. A.K., 4.11.43 [T312 R1559 F20]; *AOK 7*, Ia Nr.155/44 g., 8.1.44, p.1 [T312 R1564 F421]

415. *AOK 7*, Ia Nr.382/44 g., 19.1.44 [T312 R1564 F474]; *AOK 7*, Ia Nr.155/44 g., 8.1.44, p.1 [T312 R1564 F421]; *AOK 7*, Ia Nr.169/44 g., 9.1.44 [T312 R1564 F426]

416. *AOK 7*, Ia Nr.826/44 g., 20.5.44 [T312 R1565 F738]

417. *AOK 7*, Ia Nr.155/44 g., 8.1.44, p.1 [T312 R1564 F421]

418. *AOK 7*, Ia Nr.382/44 g., 19.1.44 [T312 R1564 F474]

419. *AOK 7*, Ia Nr.155/44 g., 8.1.44, p.1 [T312 R1564 F421]

420. *Wehrmachtgerichtlich verurteilte Zuchthäusler*: German soldiers imprisoned after being convicted by military courts. They would have been guarded by the *II./Sich.Rgt. 195*.

421. Gen.Kdo.*LXXXIV. A.K.* Ia 9856/43 (5008) g., 25.11.43; *AOK 7* Ia, Ferngespräche Ia, 23.12.43 [T312 R1559 F416]; *AOK 7*, Ia Nr.155/44 g., 8.1.44, p.1 [T312 R1564 F421]; *AOK 7*, Abt. Ia, *Ferngespräche Chef d.G.*, 7.1.44 [T312 R1564 F416]; *AOK 7*, Invertergespräch Chef d.Gen.Stab *AOK 7* mit Komm.General *LXXXIV. A.K.*, 9.1.44 [T312 R1564 F427]

422. *AOK 7* Ia, *Besprechung O.B. H.Gr. B mit O.B. am 9.3.44*, 9.3.44, p.1 [T312 R1565 F238]; *Besprechungspunkte für Generalfeldmarschall Rommel*, 9.3.44 [T312 R1565 F240]

423. *AOK 7*, Ia Nr.267/44 g., 13.1.44 [T312 R1564 F446]

424. C.S.D.I.C. (UK) S.I.R.395, p.2-4, Annex 1-5 [NARA, RG 165, Box 660]

425. *AOK 7*, Ia Nr.106/44 g., 6.1.44 [T312 R1564 F410]; *AOK 7*, Ia Nr.133/44 g., 7.1.44 [T312 R1564 F414]

426. *AOK 7*, Ia Nr.382/44 g., 19.1.44 [T312 R1564 F474]; *AOK 7* Ia, Anlage zum K.T.B. Führungsabtl. *AOK 7* Ia, Lage-Karten A.O.K.7 vom 6.1.-5.6.44, Stand: 15.2.44 [T312 R1570 F3]

427. *AOK 7*, Ia Nr.153/44 g., 8.1.44 [T312 R1564 F418]

428. *AOK 7*, Ia Nr.519/44 g.K., 26.1.44, p.1 [T312 R1564 F530]

429. *AOK 7*, Ia Nr.153/44 g., 8.1.44 [T312 R1564 F418]

430. *AOK 7*, Ia Nr.169/44 g., 9.1.44 [T312 R1564 F426]

431. *AOK 7*, Ia Nr.343/44 g., 17.1.44 [T312 R1564 F463]; *AOK 7*, Ia Nr.382/44 g., 19.1.44 [T312 R1564 F474]

432. *AOK 7*, Ia Nr.433/44 g., 21.1.44, p.1 [T312 R1564 F482]

433. *AOK 7*, Ia Nr.273/44 g., 15.1.44 [T312 R1564 F455-8]

434. AKA *Feste Plätze* (strongpoints), these were locations of significant military value (usually transportation nodal points, which were not to be surrendered). If necessary, they were to allow themselves to be surrounded in an effort to tie up as many enemy forces as possible.

435. *AOK 7*, Ia Nr.735/44 g., 4.2.44 [T312 R1565 F31-6]

436. Schramm, P.E. (1961), *Kriegstagebuch des Oberkommandos der Wehrmacht (Wehrmachtführungsstab), Band IV: 1.Januar 1944 - 22. Mai 1945*, Frankfurt am Main: Bernard und Graefe Verlag, p.266; *AOK 7* Ia, *KTB* 1.1.-30.6.1944 [T312 R1564 F169-70]

437. *AOK 7*, Ia Nr.735/44 g.K., 4.2.44 [T312 R1565 F31-6]; *AOK 7* Ia, *KTB* 1.1.-30.6.1944 [T312 R1564 F182]

438. German general staff officers files, index cards of *Gen.Maj.* Sattler [T78 R892 H6/26]; Kartei von Inf.-Kommandeuren, index card of *Gen.Maj.* Sattler [T78 R908 H6/354]; C.S.D.I.C. (UK) S.*IR* 526, 9 Jul 44, p.1 [NARA, RG 165, Box 659]; **Schlieben, K.W. von (1948)**, MS # B-845 (Germ.), *Die deutsche 709. Infanterie-Division vor und während der anglo-amerikanischen Invasion vom 6. Juni 1944*, p.5; C.S.D.I.C. (UK) GRG.G. 152, p.2 [UKNA, WO 208/4363]

439. *AOK 7*, Ferngespräche Oberst i.G. Helmdach, 3.2.44 [T312 R1565 F26]

440. Der Oberbefehlshaber der 7. Armee Ia Nr.765/44 g.K., 6.2.44, p.1-2 [T312 R1565 F41-2]

441. *AOK 7*, Ia Nr.881/44 g., 11.2.44, p.1 [T312 R1565 F89]

442. *AOK 7*, Ia Nr.759/44 g., 5.2.44 [T312 R1565 F38]; *AOK 7*, Ia Nr.861/44 g., 10.2.44 [T312 R1565 F87]

443. *AOK 7*, Ia Nr.861/44 g., 10.2.44 [T312 R1565 F87]

444. *AOK 7*, Ia Nr.881/44 g., 11.2.44, p.1 [T312 R1565 F89]; *AOK 7*, Ia Nr.904/44 g., 12.2.44 [T312 R1565 F102]

445. *AOK 7*, Ia Nr.1038/44 g., 17.2.44 [T312 R1565 F132]

446. *AOK 7*, Ia Nr.716/44 g., 3.2.44 [T312 R1565 F23]

447. *AOK 7*, Ia Nr.832/44 g., 8.2.44 [T312 R1565 F63]; *AOK 7*, Ia Nr.881/44 g., 11.2.44, p.1 [T312 R1565 F89]

448. *AOK 7*, Ia Nr.925/44 g., 13.2.44 [T312 R1565 F106]

449. *AOK 7*, Ia Nr.777/44 g., 6.2.44 [T312 R1565 F40]

450. *AOK 7*, Ia Nr.795/44 g., 7.2.44 [T312 R1565 F57]

451. *AOK 7*, Ia Nr.832/44 g., 8.2.44 [T312 R1565 F63]

452. *AOK 7*, Ia Nr.839/44 g., 9.2.44 [T312 R1565 F67]

453. *AOK 7*, Ia Nr.1288/44 g., 27.2.44, p.1 [T312 R1565 F180]

454. *AOK 7*, Ia Nr.656/44 g., 1.2.44 [T312 R1565 F3]; *AOK 7*, Ia Nr.1061/44 g., 18.2.44 [T312 R1565 F137]

455. *AOK 7*, Ia Nr.692/44 g., 2.2.44 [T312 R1565 F10]

456. *AOK 7*, Ia Nr.1288/44 g., 27.2.44, p.1 [T312 R1565 F180]

457. *AOK 7*, Ia Nr.9854/44 g.K., p.1-2 [T312 R1565 F114-5]

458. *AOK 7*, Ia Nr.904/44 g., 12.2.44 [T312 R1565 F102]; *AOK 7*, Ia Nr.925/44 g., 13.2.44 [T312 R1565 F106]

459. *AOK 7*, Ia Nr.1224/44 g., 24.2.44 [T312 R1565 F169]

460. *AOK 7*, Ferngespräche Oberst i.G. Helmdach, 3.2.44, p.2 [T312 R1565 F27]

461. *AOK 7* Ia, *KTB* 1.1.-30.6.1944 [T312 R1564 F185]

462. *Ibid.* [T312 R1564 F199]

463. Armee-Ober-Kommando 7 Ia Nr.433/44 g., 21.1.44, p.2 [T312 R1564 F484]; *AOK 7*, Kriegsgliederung *7. Armee*, Stand 12.3.44, Kriegsgliederung der Fest.Pi.Stäbe, Fest.Pi.Btl. und Bau-Pi. Btl. im Bereich des A.O.K.7, Stand 11.2.1944 [T312 R1566 F168]

464. *AOK 7*, Ia Nr.1517/44 g., 7.3.44 [T312 R1565 F221]; *AOK 7*, Ia Nr.1649/44 g., 11.3.44 [T312 R1565 F253]

465. *AOK 7*, Ia Nr.1406/44 g.K., 2.3.44 [T312 R1565 F204]

466. *AOK 7*, Ia Nr.1825/44 g., 19.3.44 [T312 R1565 F306]; *AOK 7*, Ia Nr.1714/44 g.K., 16.3.44 [T312 R1565 F295] The new positions of the division's units, including those on the coast, were not reported but can be found on a number of situation maps.

467. AOK 7 Ia, Anlage zum K.T.B. Führungsabt. AOK 7 Ia, Lage-Karten AOK 7 vom 6.1.-5.6.44, Stand: 8.4.44 [T312 R1570 F5]

468. *AOK 7*, Ia Nr.1406/44 g.K., 2.3.44 [T312 R1565 F204]; *AOK 7*, Ia Nr.1476/44 g., 5.3.44 [T312 R1565 F213]

469. *AOK 7*, Ia Nr.1891/44 g., 22.3.44, p.1 [T312 R1565 F320]; *AOK 7*, Ia Nr.1926/44 g., 24.3.44 [T312 R1565 F335]

470. Example: *AOK 7* Ia, *AOK 7 Kriegstagebuch Ia - 6 Jun 1944 - 25 Jul 1944*, p.24 [T312 R1569 F242]

471. *AOK 7*, Ia Nr.1406/44 g.K., 2.3.44 [T312 R1565 F204]; *AOK 7*, Ia Nr.1517/44 g., 7.3.44 [T312 R1565 F221]; *AOK 7*, Ia Nr.1910/44 g., 23.3.44 [T312 R1565 F328]

472. *AOK 7*, Ia Nr.1565/44 g., 8.3.44 [T312 R1565 F235]; *AOK 7*, Ia Nr.1755/44 g., 16.3.44 [T312 R1565 F294]

473. *AOK 7*, Ia Nr.1592/44 g., 9.3.44 [T312 R1565 F237]

474. *AOK 7*, Ia Nr.1891/44 g., 22.3.44, p.1 [T312 R1565 F320]; *AOK 7*, Ia Nr.1910/44 g., 23.3.44 [T312 R1565 F328]

475. *AOK 7*, Ia Nr.1592/44 g., 9.3.44 [T312 R1565 F237]

476. *AOK 7*, Ia Nr.91/44 g., 2.4.44 [T312 R1565 F393]; *AOK 7*, Ia Nr.1930/44 g., 24.3.44 [T312 R1565 F347]

477. *AOK 7*, Ia Nr.316/44 g., 16.4.44 [T312 R1565 F497]; *AOK 7*, Ia Nr.332/44 g., 17.4.44 [T312 R1565 F499]

478. *AOK 7*, Ia Nr.1891/44 g., 22.3.44, p.1 [T312 R1565 F320]

479. *AOK 7*, Besprechung auf Grund der Anwesenheit des Generalfeldmarschalls Rommel am 14.4., 15.4.44, p.1 [T312 R1565 F486]

480. *AOK 7*, Ia Nr.457/44 g., 25.4.44, p.1 [T312 R1565 F543]

481. *AOK 7*, Ia Nr.503/44 g., 28.4.44 [T312 R1565 F552]

482. *AOK 7*, Ia Nr.122/44 g., 4.4.44 [T312 R1565 F417]; *AOK 7*, Ia Nr.2152/44 g.K., 11.4.44, p.1 [T312 R1565 F467]

483. *AOK 7*, Ia Nr.2152/44 g.K., 11.4.44, p.1 [T312 R1565 F467]

484. *AOK 7*, Ia Nr.409/44 g., 22.4.44 [T312 R1565 F526]

485. *AOK 7*, Ia Nr.138/44 g., 5.4.44 [T312 R1565 F442]

486. *AOK 7*, Ia Nr.187/44 g., 8.4.44 [T312 R1565 F451]

487. *AOK 7*, Ia Nr.389/44 g., 20.4.44 [T312 R1565 F516]

488. *AOK 7*, Ia Nr.454/44 g., 25.4.44 [T312 R1565 F539]

489. *AOK 7*, Ia Nr.2152/44 g.K., 11.4.44, p.1 [T312 R1565 F467]; *AOK 7*, Ia Nr.2168/44 g., 13.4.44 [T312 R1565 F482]

490. *AOK 7*, Ia Nr.389/44 g., 20.4.44 [T312 R1565 F516]

491. *AOK 7*, Ia Nr.399/44 g., 21.4.44, p.1 [T312 R1565 F521]

492. *AOK 7*, Ia Nr.518/44 g., 29.4.44 [T312 R1565 F564]; *AOK 7*, Ia Nr.610/44 g., 6.5.44 [T312 R1565 F628]; *AOK 7* Ia, *KTB* 1.1.-30.6.1944 [T312 R1565 F240]

493. The *21. Pz.Div.* arrived in the *7. Armee* sector and took over responsibility for much of the areas previously held by the *155.* and the *179. Res.Pz.Div.*

494. *AOK 7*, Ia Nr.473/44 g., 26.4.44 [T312 R1565 F546]; *AOK 7*, Ia Nr.536/44 g., 30.4.44 [T312 R1565 F564]

495. *AOK 7*, Ia Nr.2361/44 g.K., copied as Gen.Kdo.*XXV. A.K.*, Ia Nr.533/33 g.K., 1.5.44 [T314 R746 F379]

496. *AOK 7* Ia Nr.2363/44 g.K., 1.5.44, p.1 [T312 R1565 F578]

497. *Grossverband*, literally "large formation". The term is usually used to describe larger formations, such as divisions.

498. *Ibid.*, p.2 [T312 R1565 F579]

499. *Ibid.*; *AOK 7*, Ia Nr.2357/44 g.K., 2.5.44 [T312 R1565 F592]

500. *AOK 7*, Ia Nr.575/44 g., 3.5.44 [T312 R1565 F596]; *AOK 7*, Ia Nr.586/44 g., 4.5.44, p.1-2 [T312 R1565 F619-620]

501. *AOK 7*, Ia Nr.599/44 g., 5.5.44 [T312 R1565 F624]; *AOK 7*, Ia Nr.610/44 g., 6.5.44 [T312 R1565 F628]; BvTO b. *AOK 7*, Anl.15 zum Tätigkeitsbericht BvTO *AOK 7*, Zusammenstellung der in der Zeit vom 1.4. - 30.6.44 im bearbeiten und durchgeführten grösseren Einzeltransporte., p.1 [T312 R1571 F986]

502. *AOK 7*, Ia Nr.599/44 g., 5.5.44 [T312 R1565 F624]
503. *AOK 7*, Ia Nr.641/44 g., 8.5.44, p.1 [T312 R1565 F658]
504. *AOK 7*, Ia Nr.2528/44 g., 13.5.44, p.7 [T312 R1565 F680]
505. *AOK 7*, Invertergespräch Ia/*AOK 7* mit Ia/*H.Gr. B*, 5.5.44 [T312 R1565 F626]
506. *AOK 7*, Ia Nr.2404/44 g.K., 6.5.44 [T312 R1565 F630]
507. *AOK 7*, Ferngespräch Ia mit Chef Gen.Kdo.*LXXXIV. A.K.* um 20.15 Uhr., 6.5.44 [T312 R1565 F629]
508. *AOK 7*, Ia Nr.2347/44 g.K., 2.5.44 [T312 R1565 F667]
509. *AOK 7*, Ferngespräch Ia mit Chef Gen.Kdo.*LXXXIV. A.K.* um 20.15 Uhr., 6.5.44 [T312 R1565 F629]
510. *AOK 7*, Ia Nr.2430/44 g.K., 7.5.44, p.1 [T312 R1565 F634]
511. *Ibid.*, Ia Nr.2430/44 g.K., 7.5.44, p.1-2 [T312 R1565 F634-5]
512. *Ibid.*, Ia Nr.2430/44 g.K., 7.5.44, p.1 [T312 R1565 F634]
513. *Ibid.*, p.2 [T312 R1565 F635]
514. *Ibid.*
515. *AOK 7*, Ia Nr.2430/44 g.K.II.Ang., 8.5.44 [T312 R1565 F636]
516. *AOK 7*, Ia Nr.2347/44 g.K., 1.5.44 [T312 R1565 F580-1]; *AOK 7*, Ia Nr.599/44 g., 5.5.44 [T312 R1565 F624]; *AOK 7*, Ia Nr.680/44 g., 10.5.44, p.1 [T312 R1565 F670]
517. *AOK 7*, Ia Nr.2430/44 g.K.II.Ang., 8.5.44 [T312 R1565 F636]
518. *AOK 7*, Ia Nr.2431/44 g.K., 8.5.44, p.1 [T312 R1565 F662]
519. *Ibid.*, p.1-2 [T312 R1565 F662-3]
520. *Ibid.*
521. *AOK 7* Ia, *Invertergespräch Ia mit Chef LXXXIV. A.K.*, 9.5.44 [T312 R1565 F666]
522. *AOK 7*, Ia Nr.2471/44 g.K., 10.5.44 [T312 R1565 F685]
523. *AOK 7*, Ia Nr.2528/44 g.K., 13.5.44 [T312 R1565 F674-82]; *H.Gr. B.*, War Journal *H.Gr. B*, 15 Jan - 5 Jun 1944, p.244, 247 & 250 [CAMO, Bestand 500, Findbuch 12465, Akte 19]
524. *AOK 7*, Ia Nr.2528/44 g.K., 13.5.44 [T312 R1565 F674-82], p.1& 7 [T312 R1565 F674 & 80]
525. *Ibid.*, p.7-8 [T312 R1565 F680-1]; *H.Gr. B.*, War Journal *H.Gr. B*, 15 Jan - 5 Jun 1944, p.252 [CAMO, Bestand 500, Findbuch 12465, Akte 19]: It would consist of the division's armoured reconnaissance battalion, a mechanised infantry battalion, a SP artillery battalion, an assault-gun battery and an armoured engineer company. This force would be led by the commander of *Pz.Gren.Rgt.125*.
526. *AOK 7*, Ia Nr.25386/44 g.K., 13.5.44, p.1-2 [T312 R1565 F693-4]
527. *AOK 7*, Ia Nr.25386/44 g.K., 13.5.44, p.2 [T312 R1565 F694]; C.S.D.I.C. (UK) S.IR 485, 3 Jul 44, p.2 [NARA, RG 165, Box 659, Folder 2]
528. *AOK 7*, Ia Nr.25386/44 g.K., 13.5.44, p.2 [T312 R1565 F694]
529. *AOK 7*, Ia Nr.773/44 g., 15.5.44 [T312 R1565 F705]
530. *AOK 7*, Ia Nr.834/44 g., 19.5.44 [T312 R1565 F731]
531. *AOK 7*, Ia Nr.696/44 g., p.1, 11.5.44 [T312 R1565 F687]
532. *AOK 7*, Ia Nr.25386/44 g.K., 13.5.44, p.2 [T312 R1565 F694]
533. *AOK 7*, Ia Nr.885/44 g., 22.5.44 [T312 R1565 F744]
534. *AOK 7*, Ia Nr.680/44 g., 10.5.44, p.2 [T312 R1565 F671]
535. *AOK 7*, Ia Nr.2538/44 g., 13.5.44, p.2 [T312 R1565 F694]
536. *AOK 7*, Ia Nr.795/44 g., 7.2.44 [T312 R1565 F57]
537. *AOK 7*, Ia Nr.561/44 g., 2.5.44 [T312 R1565 F585]
538. *AOK 7*, Ia Nr.714/44 g., 12.5.44 p.2 [T312 R1565 F690]; *AOK 7*, Ia Nr.2538/44 g., 13.5.1941944, p.2 [T312 R1565 F694]
539. *AOK 7*, Ia Nr.680/44 g., 10.5.44, p.2 [T312 R1565 F671]
540. *AOK 7*, Ia Nr.714/44 g., 12.5.44 [T312 R1565 F689]; *AOK 7*, Ia Nr.2538/44 g., 13.5.1941944, p.2 [T312 R1565 F694]; *AOK 7*, Ia Nr.2567/44 g.K., 16.5.44, p.1 [T312 R1565 F710]; *AOK 7 BvTO*, Anl.15 zum Tätigkeitsbericht BvTO *AOK 7, Zusammenstellung der in der Zeit vom 1.4. - 30.6.44 im Armeebereich durchgeführten Bewegungen.*, p.1 [T312 R1571 F982]
541. *AOK 7*, Ia Nr.2567/44 g.K., 16.5.44, p.1 [T312 R1565 F710]; *AOK 7*, Ia Nr.854/44 g., 20.5.44 [T312 R1565 F737]
542. *AOK 7*, Ia Nr.680/44 g., p.1, 10.5.44 [T312 R1565 F672]; *AOK 7*, Ia Nr.696/44 g., p.1, 11.5.44 [T312 R1565 F687]; *AOK 7*, Ia Nr.714/44 g., 12.5.44 [T312 R1565 F689]; *AOK 7*, Ia Nr.25386/44 g.K., 13.5.44, p.1 [T312 R1565 F693]; *AOK 7*, Ia Nr.2546/44 g.K., 14.5.44 [T312 R1565 F700]; *AOK 7*, Ia Nr.773/44 g., 15.5.44 [T312 R1565 F705]
543. *AOK 7*, Ia Nr.2546/44 g.K., 14.5.44 [T312 R1565 F700]
544. *AOK 7*, Ia Nr.2567/44 g.K., 16.5.44, p.1 [T312 R1565 F710]
545. *AOK 7*, Ia Nr.2546/44 g.K., 14.5.44 [T312 R1565 F700]
546. *AOK 7*, Ia Nr.2567/44 g.K., 16.5.44, p.1 [T312 R1565 F710]
547. *Ibid.*, 16.5.44 [T312 R1565 F711]
548. *AOK 7*, Ia Nr.680/44 g., 10.5.44, p.1 [T312 R1565 F670]
549. *AOK 7*, Ia Nr.696/44 g., 11.5.44, p.1 [T312 R1565 F687]; *AOK 7*, Ia Nr.2546/44 g.K., 14.5.44 [T312 R1565 F700]; *AOK 7*, Ia Nr.773/44 g., 15.5.44 [T312 R1565 F705]
550. *AOK 7*, Ia Nr.680/44 g., 10.5.44, p.2 [T312 R1565 F671]
551. *AOK 7*, Ia Nr.696/44 g., 11.5.44 p.1 [T312 R1565 F687]
552. *AOK 7*, Ia Nr.575/44 g., 3.5.44 [T312 R1565 F596]
553. *AOK 7*, Ia Nr.25386/44 g.K., 13.5.44, p.2 [T312 R1565 F694]; *AOK 7*, Ia Nr.798/44 g., 17.5.44 [T312 R1565 F714]; *AOK 7*, Ia Nr.809/44 g., 18.5.44 [T312 R1565 F723]; *AOK 7*, Ia Nr.834/44 g., 19.5.44 [T312 R1565 F731]
554. *AOK 7*, Ia Nr.610/44 g., 6.5.44 [T312 R1565 F628]
555. *AOK 7*, Ia Nr.885/44 g., 22.5.44 [T312 R1565 F744]; Mistakenly written as "Henneville".
556. *AOK 7*, Ia Nr.971/44 g., 26.5.44 [T312 R1565 F773]; *AOK 7*, Ia Nr.1005/44 g., 29.5.44, p.1 [T312 R1565 F782]
557. *AOK 7*, Ia Nr.2567/44 g.K., 16.5.44, p.1 [T312 R1565 F710]
558. *AOK 7*, Ia Nr.798/44 g., 17.5.44 [T312 R1565 F714]
559. *AOK 7*, Ia Nr.809/44 g., 18.5.44 [T312 R1565 F723]
560. *AOK 7*, Ia Nr.2640/44 g.K., 21.5.44, p.1 [T312 R1565 F741]
561. *AOK 7*, Ia Nr.548/44 g., 1.5.44 [T312 R1565 F573]
562. *AOK 7*, Ia Nr.575/44 g., 3.5.44 [T312 R1565 F596]
563. *AOK 7*, Ia Nr.988/44 g., 27.5.44 [T312 R1565 F777]
564. *AOK 7*, Ia Nr.1005/44 g., 29.5.44, p.1 [T312 R1565 F782]
565. *AOK 7*, Ia Nr.988/44 g., 27.5.44 [T312 R1565 F777]; *AOK 7*, Ia Nr.1005/44 g., 29.5.44, p.1 [T312 R1565 F782]
566. *AOK 7*, Ia Nr.641/44 g., 8.5.44, p.1 [T312 R1565 F658]; *AOK 7*, Ia Nr.798/44 g., 17.5.44 [T312 R1565 F714]; *AOK 7*, Ia Nr.854/44 g., 20.5.44 [T312 R1565 F737]
567. *AOK 7*, Ia Nr.2546/44 g.K., 14.5.44 [T312 R1565 F700]
568. *AOK 7*, Ia Nr.641/44 g., 8.5.44, p.1 [T312 R1565 F658]
569. *AOK 7*, Ia Nr.824/44 g., 18.5.44, p.1, 3-4 [T312 R1565 F716, 718-9]; *AOK 7*, Ia Nr.826/44 g., 20.5.44 [T312 R1565 F738]
570. *AOK 7*, Ia Nr.1025/44 g., 29.5.44 [T312 R1565 F797]
571. *AOK 7*, Ia Nr.1035/44 g., 30.5.44 [T312 R1565 F800]
572. *AOK 7*, Ia Nr.610/44 g., 6.5.44 [T312 R1565 F628]
573. *AOK 7*, Ia Nr.1005/44 g., 29.5.44, p.1 [T312 R1565 F782]
574. *AOK 7*, Ia Nr.1035/44 g., 30.5.44 [T312 R1565 F800]
575. *AOK 7* Ia, Anlage zum K.T.B. Führungsabtl. *AOK 7* Ia, *Lage-Karten A.O.K.7 vom 6.1.-5.6.44, Stand: 22.5.44* [T312 R1570 F7-8]; *AOK 7* Ia, Anlage zum K.T.B. Führungsabtl. *AOK 7* Ia, *Lage-Karten A.O.K.7 vom 6.1.-5.6.44, Stand: 5.6.44* [T312 R1570 F9-10, original in BaMa RH 20-7/138K] — Hereafter referred to as: *AOK 7*, Situation map, 5.6.44
576. *AOK 7*, Ia Nr.25386/44 g.K., 13.5.44, p.1 [T312 R1565 F693]
577. Anlage zu *AOK 7*, Ia Nr.2710/44 g.K., p.1, 28.5.44 [T312 R1565 F794]
578. *AOK 7*, Ia Nr.1093/44 g., 2.6.44 [T312 R1565 F827]
579. *AOK 7*, Ia Nr.1146/44 g., 5.6.44 [T312 R1565 F851]
580. *AOK 7*, Ia Nr.1093/44 g., 2.6.44 [T312 R1565 F827]
581. *AOK 7*, Ia Nr.1134/44 g., 4.6.44 [T312 R1565 F839]
582. Most locations are based on the *AOK 7* situation map for **5 June 1944.**
583. *AOK 7*, Situation map, 5.6.44; *AOK 7*, Ia Nr.1038/44 g., 17.2.44 [T312 R1565 F132]
584. *AOK 7*, Situation map, 5.6.44
585. *AOK 7*, Situation map, 5.6.44; **Historical Section (G.S.), Army Headquarters (1951)**, *Report No. 41, The German Defences in the Courseulles St.Auvin Area of the Normandy Coast - Information from German sources*, App. C & D — Hereafter referred to as: Historical Section (G.S.), (1951). Many locations are based on the *AOK 7* situation map, but the other map covers the *716. I.D.* sector in more detail. It seems to be up to date for this division, but for some other units the situation seems closer to mid-May.
586. *AOK 7*, Situation map, 5.6.44; **Historical Section (G.S.), (1951)**
587. The 5 June 1944 map shows the *I./AR 1716* at Colomby. [*AOK 7*, Situation map, 5.6.44]
588. The map of the *716. I.D.* sector in Report No.41 does not yet show it there. [Historical Section (G.S.), (1951)]
589. *AOK 7*, Situation map, 5.6.44; **Perrigault, J.C. (2002)**, *21. Panzer-Division*, Bayeux: Editions Heimdal, p.230-232; *AOK 7*, Ia Nr.2538/44 g., 13.5.1941944, p.2 [T312 R1565 F694]; **Historical Section (G.S.), (1951)**, App. C & D. It is Perrigault who made the claim about Cagny.

Generalkommando LXXXIV. A.K. and Korpstruppen

1. For examples see Anl. zu *OKH/GenStdH/Org.Abt. Nr.I/4500/43 g.K., 4.10.43, Kriegsgliederung des Feldheeres (Sollgliederung) - Band I: Kommandobehörden u. Divisionsverbände, Stand: September 1943* [T78 R408 F6377862-8]
2. *Kopfstärke*: "headcount". Presumably same as *Verpflegungsstärke* (rations count): Number of men that have to be fed.
3. *AOK 7*, Kriegsgliederung 7. Armee, Stand 18.5.44, LXXXIV. Armee-Korps, Stand: 1.4.44 [T312 R1566 F213]
4. *K.St.N. (Heer) Nr.12, Generakommando*, 1.3.42 [T78 R391 F6358781-91]
5. *Ordonnanzoffizier*: Junior officer supporting a senior officer,

also referred to a Special Missions (Duties) Officer in English language sources. Commonly abbreviated to O.O. or with a number when serving in a particular role, e.g.: O2.

6. OKH/GenStdH/Org.Abt. Nr.II/12550/43 g.K., 3.11.43 [T78 R527 F528-30]

7. *IIa*: Officer for personnel matters concerning officers. *IIb*: Officer for personnel matters concerning NCO's and men.

8. *I K.St.N. (Heer) Nr.12, Generalkommando,* 1.3.42 [T78 R391 F6358790]

9. Gen.Kdo.*LXXXIV. A.K., Gefechts- und Verpflegungstärken des Generalkommando LXXXIV. A.K. Dezember 1943* [T314 R1604 F1350]

10. *K.St.N. (Heer) Nr.12, Generalkommando,* 1.3.42 [T78 R391 F6358787]

11. Gen.Kdo.*LXXXIV. A.K., Gefechts- und Verpflegungstärken des Generalkommando LXXXIV. A.K. Dezember 1943* [T314 R1604 F1350]

12. CX/MSS/R.224 (C), 24 Jun 44, p.36 [UKNA, HW 5/510]

13. Gen.Kdo.*LXXXIV. A.K.* Ia, *Tätigkeitsbericht der Gen.Kdo.LXXXIV. A.K. für den Monat Juni 1942*, p.1 [T314 R1603 F210]

14. See Gliederungen in T312 R1547, R1553, R1559 & R1566

15. *AOK 7, Kriegsgliederung 7. Armee,* Stand 18.5.44, *LXXXIV. Armee-Korps, Stand: 1.4.44* [T312 R1566 F213]

16. German general staff officers files, index cards of *Gen.Maj.* Kruse [T78 R888 H6/26]

17. German general staff officers files, index cards of Personnel file of *Obst.* Hamann [T78 R885 H6/26]

18. *AOK 7, Kriegsgliederung 7. Armee,* Stand: 10.9.43, *LXXIV. Armee-Korps, Stand: 5.8.43* [T312 R1559 F612]; German general staff officers files, index cards of *Gen.Maj.* Kruse [T78 R888 H6/26]

19. H.Kdo.*LX, Tätigkeitsbericht des H.Kdos. LX für den Monat Februar 1942*, p.3 [T314 R1603 F191]

20. H.Kdo.*LX,* Anl. 3 zum Tätigkeitsbericht des H.Kdos.LX für März 1942 [T314 R1603 F258]

21. Gen.Kdo.*LXXXIV. A.K., Kriegsrangliste sämtlicher Offizier und Beamten im Offizierrang des Generalkommandos LXXXIV. A.K.,* p.2 [T314 R1603 F602]

22. *AOK 7,* Ia Nr.153/44 g., 8.1.44 [T312 R1564 F418]; *AOK 7* Ia, Anlage zum K.T.B. Führungsabt. AOK 7 Ia, *Lage-Karten A.O.K.7 vom 6.1.-5.6.44, Stand: 5.6.44* [T312 R1570 F9-10, original in BaMa RH 20-7/138K] — Hereafter referred to as: *AOK 7,* Situation map, 5.6.44. For additional information see chapter *"709. Infanterie-Division".*

23. OKW, Abwicklungsstab Rudolstadt, Ob.West, Oblt. Becker, *Vorläufiger Gefechtsbericht der 709. I.D. über die Kämpfe von 6. bis 30.6.1944,* p.2 [T78 R672 H41/61a] — Hereafter referred to as: **Becker,** *Vorläufiger Gefechtsbericht der 709. I.D.;* **Schlieben, K.W. von (1948),** MS # B-845 (Engl.), *Die deutsche 709.Infanterie - Division vor und während der anglo-amerikanischen Invasion vom 6. Juni 1944,* App.H, Supplementary Information, p.160

24. **Triepel, G. (1946),** MS # B-260 (Germ.), *I.Abschnitt, Cotentin (6.Juni - 18.Juni 1944),* p.11

25. *AOK 7* Ia, *AOK 7 Kriegstagebuch Ia - 6 Jun 1944 - 25 Jul 1944,* p.67 [T312 R1569 F287] — Hereafter referred to as: *AOK 7* Ia, *KTB 6.6.-25.7.44*

26. *AOK 7, Kriegsgliederungen zum KTB der Führungsabteilung AOK 7 ab 6.6.44 bis 30.6.44, Stand: 22.6.44, 14 Uhr* [T312 R1566 F13]

27. German general staff officers files, index cards of *Obst.* Hamann and *Obst.* Seifert [T78 R885 H6/26]

28. **Tessin, G. (1972),** *6.Band,* p.274

29. *AOK 7,* Ia Nr.25386/44 g.K., 13.5.44, p.1 [T312 R1565 F693]

30. *AOK 7, Kriegsgliederung 7. Armee,* Stand 18.5.44, *LXXIV. Armee-Korps, Stand: 1.4.44* [T312 R1566 F222]

31. *AOK 7* Ia, *KTB 6.6.-25.7.44,* p.67 [T312 R1569 F287]; **Tessin, G. (1975),** p.256

32. *AOK 7, Kriegsgliederung 7. Armee,* Stand 18.5.44, *LXXXIV. Armee-Korps, Stand: 1.4.44* [T312 R1566 F213]

33. German general staff officers files, index cards of *Gen.Maj.* Sattler [T78 R892 H6/26]

34. *AOK 7, Kriegsgliederung 7. Armee,* Stand 18.5.44, *LXXXIV. Armee-Korps, Stand: 1.4.44* [T312 R1566 F213]

35. *Ob.West* Ia Nr.4876/44 g.K., 23.6.44 [T311 R25 F7029784]; *AOK 7,* Ia Nr.3349/44 g.K., 23.6.44 [T312 R1565 F1265]; German general staff officers files, index cards of *Gen.Maj.* Sattler [T78 R892 H6/26]

36. **Historical Division, Department of the Army (1948),** *Utah Beach to Cherbourg (6 June-27 June 1944),* United States Army, Washington, D.C., p.195-197

37. *AOK 7* Ia, *Kriegstagebuch der Führungsabteilung AOK 7 für die Zeit vom 1.Jan. - 30.Juni 1944* [T312 R1564 F169-70] — Hereafter referred to as: *AOK 7* Ia, *KTB 1.1.-30.6.1944*

38. Gen.Kdo.*LXXXIV. A.K.* Ia, *Tätigkeitsbericht des Gen.Kdo.LXXXIV. A.K. für den Monat September 1942,* p.4 [T314 R1603 F233]; Gen.Kdo.*LXXXIV. A.K., KTB Ia vom 1.10-31.12.42* [T314 R1603 F362 & 408]

39. Gen.Kdo.*LXXXIV. A.K.,* Ia Nr.1349/43 (664) g., 14.2.43 [T314 R1604 F156]

40. *AOK 7* Ia, *KTB 1.1.-30.6.1944* [T312 R1553 F353]

41. *Ibid.* [T312 R1553 F356]

42. Gen.Kdo.*LXXXIV. A.K., KTB Ia 1.1.-30.6.43* [T314 R1603 F900]

43. *AOK 7,* Ia Nr.3786/44 (1901) g.II.Ang. 8.5.43 [T314 R1604 F485]

44. *AOK 7* Ia, *KTB 1.1.-30.6.1944* [T312 R1553 F357]

45. Gen.Kdo.*LXXXIV. A.K.,* Ia Nr.1667/43 (811) g., 2.3.44 [T314 R1604 F251-252]

46. OKW Az. 2 f 46 10 Wz (I) Nr.2054/43 g., 17.6.1943 [T314 R1604 F710]

47. Gen.Kdo.*LXXXIV. A.K.,* Ia Nr.1667/43 (811) g., Anl.1: K.St.N. für den Stab des Kommandanten des Vert. Bereichs Cherbourg., 2.3.1943 [T314 R1604 F252]; for reference see: *Vorläufige K.St.N., Wehrmacht, Nr.94q (W), Kommandant des Verteidigungsbereiches Piräus,* 1.8.43 [T378 R391 F6359006-7]; OKW Az. 2 f 46 10 Wz (I) Nr.2054/43 g., 17.6.1943 [T314 R1604 F710]

48. For reference see: *Vorläufige K.St.N., Wehrmacht, Nr.94q (W), Kommandant des Verteidigungsbereiches Piräus,* 1.8.43 [T378 R391 F6359006-7]

49. Gen.Kdo.*LXXXIV. A.K.,* Ia Nr.1667/43 (811) g., 2.3.44 [T314 R1604 F251-252]

50. OKW Az. 2 f 46 10 Wz (I) Nr.2054/43 g., 17.6.1943 [T314 R1604 F710]

51. Gen.Kdo.*LXXXIV. A.K.,* Ia Nr.1667/43 (811) g., Anl.1: K.St.N. für den Stab des Kommandanten des Vert. Bereichs Cherbourg., 2.3.1943 [T314 R1604 F252]; for reference see: *Vorläufige K.St.N., Wehrmacht, Nr.94q (W), Kommandant des Verteidigungsbereiches Piräus,* 1.8.43 [T78 R391 F6359006-7]

52. Gen.Kdo.*LXXXIV. A.K.,* Ia Nr.1667/43 (811) g., Anl.1: K.St.N. für den Stab des Kommandanten des Vert. Bereichs Cherbourg., 2.3.1943 [T314 R1604 F252]

53. See: *Vorläufige K.St.N., Wehrmacht, Nr.94q (W), Kommandant des Verteidigungsbereiches Piräus,* 1.8.43 [T378 R391 F6359006-7]

54. *Funktrupp 80Mw:* Wireless section operating the medium wave (*Mittelwelle*) Fu.12, which consisted of the "80 Watt Sender a" (an 80W transmitter) combined with a receiver (*Torn. Empfänger b* or *c*). *Tornisterfunktrupp:* Portable wireless operating section; *Fernsprech-Betriebstrupp:* Telephone operating section; *Feldkabeltrupp:* (Telephone) cable laying section; *Fernsprech-Instandhaltungstrupp:* Telephone maintenance section.

55. *Ob.West (Okdo.d.H.Gr. D),* Ia Nr.2581/44 g.K., 27.3.44, p.1 & Anl. [T78 R311 F8262788-93]

56. OKH/GenStdH/Org.Abt. Nr.II/45744/44 g.K., 22.4.44 [T78 R533 F1025-29]

57. *Ibid.* [T78 R533 F1027-9]

58. *Ibid.*

59. *Sachbearbeiter:* Subject matter expert within a specific field.

60. *Ibid.*

61. *Ob.West (Okdo.d.H.Gr. D),* Ia Nr.2581/44 g.K., 27.3.44, p.1 & Anl. [T78 R311 F8262788-93]

62. OKH/GenStdH/Org.Abt. Nr.II/45744/44 g.K., 22.4.44 [T78 R533 F1028]

63. *Ibid.*

64. OKH/GenStdH/Org.Abt. I/II/35846/44 g., 26.7.44 [T78 R418 F6387146]

65. C.S.D.I.C. (UK) S.IR 483, p.1 [NARA, RG 165, Box 659, Folder 2]; C.S.D.I.C. (UK) S.IR 528, p.1-2 [NARA, RG 165, Box 659, Folder 2]

66. C.S.D.I.C. (UK) S.IR 483, p.1 [NARA, RG 165, Box 659]; **Becker,** *Vorläufiger Gefechtsbericht der 709. I.D.,* p.2 [T78 R672 H41/61a]; *AOK 7,* Situation map, 5.6.44

67. C.S.D.I.C. (UK) S.IR 483, p.1 [NARA, RG 165, Box 659, Folder 2]; PWIS(H)/LF/219, 3 Jul 44 [UKNA, WO 208/3631]

68. PWIS(H)/LF/219, 3 Jul 44 [UKNA, WO 208/3631]

69. **Tessin, G. (1975),** *10.Band,* p.222

70. Feldpostübersicht

71. **Tessin, G. (1975),** *10.Band,* p.222

72. Feldpostübersicht

73. *AOK 7, Kriegsgliederung 7. Armee,* Stand 18.5.44, *LXXXIV. Armee-Korps, Stand: 1.4.44* [T312 R1566 F213]

74. *AOK 7,* Ia/ANF(I) Nr.1426/44 g., 21.4.44 [T312 R1566 F639]

75. PWIS(H)/LF/254, 6 Jul 44 [UKNA, WO 208/3631]; PWIS(H)/KP/102, 4 Jul 44 [UKNA, WO 208/3624]

76. *AOK 7, Kriegsgliederung 7. Armee,* Stand 18.5.44, *LXXXIV. Armee-Korps, Stand: 1.4.44* [T312 R1566 F213]

77. PWIS(H)/LF/254, 6 Jul 44 [UKNA, WO 208/3631]; PWIS(H)/KP/102, 4 Jul 44 [UKNA, WO 208/3624]

78. *AOK 7, Kriegsgliederung 7. Armee,* Stand 18.5.44, *LXXXIV. Armee-Korps, Stand: 1.4.44* [T312 R1566 F213]

79. *AOK 7,* Ia Nr.798/44 g., 17.5.44 [T312 R1565 F714]

80. PWIS(H)/LF/254, 6 Jul 44 [UKNA, WO 208/3631]; PWIS(H)/KP/102, 4 Jul 44 [UKNA, WO 208/3624]
81. Armee-Ober-Kommando Ia Nr.1224/44 g., 24.2.44 [T312 R1565 F169]
82. Gen.Kdo.*LXXXIV. A.K.* Ia, *Tätigkeitsbericht des Gen.Kdo. LXXXIV. A.K. für den Monat Juni 1942*, p.3 [T314 R1603 F212]] — Hereafter referred to as: Gen.Kdo.*LXXXIV. A.K.* Ia, *Tätigkeitsbericht Juni 1942*
83. PWIS(H)/LF/452, 7 Aug 44, p.1 [UKNA, WO 208/3634]
84. Gen.Kdo.*LXXXIV. A.K.* Ia, *Tätigkeitsbericht Juni 1942*, p.3 [T314 R1603 F212]; PWIS(H)/LF/452, 7 Aug 44 [UKNA, WO 208/3634]
85. AOK 7, Kriegsgliederung *7. Armee*, Stand 18.5.44, *LXXXIV. Armee-Korps, Stand: 1.4.44* [T312 R1566 F213]
86. PWIS(H)/LF/452, 7 Aug 44, p.1 [UKNA, WO 208/3634]
87. Gen.Kdo.*LXXXIV. A.K.*, *Gefechts- und Verpflegungstärken des Gen.Kdo.LXXXIV. A.K.*, data for 21.11.42 [T314 R1603 F723]
88. PWIS(H)/LF/452, 7 Aug 44, p.2 [UKNA, WO 208/3634]
89. Gen.Kdo.*LXXXIV. A.K.* Ia, *Tätigkeitsbericht Juni 1942*, p.3 [T314 R1603 F212]
90. s. MG: *schweres Maschinengewehr*, heavy machine gun. *le. MG*: *leichtes Maschinengewehr*, light machine gun. The *Wehrmacht* did not identify machine guns based on calibre but rather on how they were deployed. Heavy machine guns were those mounted on tripods and used for long range and sustained fire, while light machine guns were used in a mobile fashion, typically with a bipod.
91. AOK 7, Kriegsgliederung *7. Armee*, Stand 10.4.44, *LXXXIV. Armee-Korps, Stand: 1.2.44* [T312 R1566 F191] The situation on 1 February was still part of the overview of 10 April. The *Gliederung* of 1 April was used in the situation report for 18 May and no longer listed the Schwadron; AOK 7, Anl.1 zu AOK 7, O.Qu./Qu.1 Nr.1271/43 g.K/v.8.11.43, *Übersicht über vorhandene s.Pak* [T312 R1562 F830]
92. Attachment to Gen.Kdo.*LXXXIV. A.K.* Abt.Qu//IIa/IIb/Ia Nr.1520/43 (1780) g., 28.4.43, *Kriegsgliederung der Aufkl. Schw.84* [T314 R1604 F415]
93. C.S.D.I.C. (UK) S.*IR* 354 [NARA, RG 165, Box 660, Folder 4]
94. An acting commander had essentially the same authority as an officially designated one, except in certain administrative areas, especially with regard to military justice. It was in essence a temporary position until a regular commander could be designated.
95. *Ibid.*; Anl. 3 zum Tätigkeitsbericht des Gen.Kdos.*LXXXIV. A.K.* für Juni 1942, Personalveränderungen Stab/Gen.Kdo.*LXXXIV. A.K.*, *Monat June 1942* [T314 R1603 F295]
96. C.S.D.I.C. (UK) S.*IR* 354 [NARA, RG 165, Box 660, Folder 4]; PWIS(H)/82, 12 Jun 44 [UKNA, WO 208/3621]; PWIS(H)/85, PW captured on 7 Jun 44 [UKNA, WO 208/3621]; Gen.Kdo.*LXXXIV. A.K.*, Ia Nr.2127/43 g.K., 14.12.43, p.1 [T314 R1604 F1281]
97. AOK 7, Kriegsgliederung *7. Armee*, Stand 10.4.44, *LXXXIV. Armee-Korps, Stand: 1.2.44* [T312 R1566 F191]
98. See T312 R1553 & T312 R1559; Kriegsgliederung *7. Armee*, Stand: 12.1.44, *LXXXIV.Armee-Korps, Stand: 1.12.43* [T312 R1566 F49]
99. Tessin, G. (1975), *10.Band*, p.222; AOK 7/O.Qu., *Kriegstagebuch A.O.K.7/O.Qu. Nr.42 (1.-31.8.43)* [T312 F257]; AOK 7, Kriegsgliederung *7. Armee*, Stand: 4.2.43, *VeRSOrgungstruppen der 7. Armee, Stand vom 15.1.43* [T312 R1553 F460]; Feldpostübersicht; Gen.Kdo.*LXXXIV. A.K.*, *Kriegstagebuch vom 1. Jan. bis 30. Juni 1943 des Gen.Kdo.LXXXIV. A.K. Ia* [T314 R1603 F914]
100. AOK 7, Kriegsgliederung *7. Armee*, Stand: 28.6.43, *VeRSOrgungstruppen der 7. Armee, Stand vom 12.6.43* [T312 R1553 F641]; AOK 7, Kriegsgliederung *7. Armee*, Stand: 28.6.43, *LXXXIV.Armee-Korps, Stand: 1.6.43* [T312 R1553 F657] Oddly, the columns were consistently listed as motor transport columns under LXXXIV. A.K.
101. Tessin, G. (1975), *10.Band,* p.222
102. AOK 7, Kriegsgliederung *7. Armee*, Stand 10.4.44, *LXXXIV.Armee-Korps, Stand: 1.2.44* [T312 R1566 F191]; AOK 7, Kriegsgliederung *7. Armee*, Stand 18.5.44, *LXXXIV.Armee-Korps, Stand: 1.4.44* [T312 R1566 F213]
103. *Feldpostübersicht*
104. Gen.Kdo.*LXXXIV. A.K.* Ia, *Kriegstagebuch vom 1.Juli bis 31.Dez.43 des Gen.Kdo.LXXXIV. A.K.* [T314 R1603 F1013]; Gen.Kdo.*LXXXIV. A.K.*, Ia-Tagesmeldung, 23.11.43 [T314 R1604 F1216]; Gen.Kdo.*LXXXIV. A.K.*, Ia-Tagesmeldung, 27.11.43 [T314 R1604 F1212]
105. AOK 7, Kriegsgliederung *7. Armee*, Stand 18.5.44, *LXXXIV. Armee-Korps, Stand: 1.4.44* [T312 R1566 F213]
106. *Ibid.*
107. First mention in *LXXXIV. A.K.* records in Gen.Kdo.*LXXXIV. A.K.* Ia, *Tätigkeitsbericht des Gen.Kdo.LXXXIV. A.K. für Monat August 1942*, p.3 [T314 R1603 F227]; Gen.Kdo.*LXXXIV. A.K.* Ia/Art. Nr.1655/43 g.K., 6.9.43, p.1-2 [T314 R1604 F900-1]
108. Gen.Kdo.*LXXXIV. A.K.*, Ia-Tagesmeldung, 23.12.43 [T314 R1604 F1315]
109. AOK 7, Ia Nr.1035/44 g., 30.5.44 [T312 R1565 F800]
110. Seekdt. Normandie, 6 June 44 [UKNA, HW 5/494, CX/MSS/T207/101, KV 6676]
111. *Harko: Höherer Artillerie-Kommandeur.* Commander and staff to coordinate artillery, typically at field-army level.
112. Post by Uwe Kleinert at https://forum.axishistory.com/viewtopic.php?p=1905415# p1905415, accessed 2 November 2019. The same discussion includes additional information and photos.

Part 2: Heer Infantry Formations

Heer Infantry Formations: An Introduction

1. Anl. zu. *OKH*/GenStdH/Org.Abt. (I) Nr.400/41 g.K., 19.2.41, *Kriegsgliederung des Feldheeres, Stand: 10.Febr.1941* [T78 R404 F6374291-364] — Hereafter referred to as: *OKH, Kriegsgliederung des Feldheeres, Stand: 10.Febr.1941; OKH/*GenStdH/Org.Abt., *Zwischengliederung, Band II: 1942* [T78 R405]
2. *OKH, Kriegsgliederung des Feldheeres, Stand: 10.Febr.1941* [T78 R404 F6374291-364]
3. *OKH/*Chef GenStdH/Org.Abt. (I) Nr.I/3197/43 g.K., 5.8.1943 [BaMa, RH 2/1108, fiche 2-3]
4. *OKH/*GenStdH/Org.Abt. (I), Nr.I/3197/43 g.K.II.Ang., 2.10.43, p.1 [T78 R527 F115]
5. *Ibid.*, Anl.1 [T78 R527 F117]
6. Anl.2 zu Chef H Rüst u BdE/AHA/I(a) Nr.5541/43 g.K, 14.10.43, p.1-3 [T78 R850 H36/158]
7. *OKH/*GenStdH/Org.Abt. Nr.I/16000/44 g.K., 4.3.44 and attachments [T78 R398 H1/37]; *OKH/*GenStdH/Org.Abt. Nr.I/16000/44 g.K., 20.5.44, p.3 [T78 R410 F6378460]
8. *OKH/*GenStdH/Org.Abt. Nr.I/16000/44 g.K., 4.3.44 and attachments [T78 R398 H1/37]
9. *OKH/*GenStdH/Org.Abt. Nr.I/16000/44 g.K., 20.5.44 [T78 R410 F6378458-60]
10. AOK 7 Ia, *Kriegstagebuch der Führungsabteilung AOK 7 für die Zeit vom 1.Jan. - 30.Juni 1944* [T312 R1564 F270-1] — Hereafter referred to as: AOK 7 Ia, *KTB 1.1.-30.6.1944*
11. *OKH/*GenStdH/Org.Abt. Nr.I/16000/44 g.K., 20.5.44, p.1-2 [T78 R410 F6378458-9]
12. *OKH/*GenStdH/Org.Abt. Nr.I/16000/44 g.K., 20.5.44, p.2 [T78 R410 F6378459]; Anlage 2 zu *OKH/*GenStdH/Org.Abt. Nr.I/1600/44.g.K., 20.5.44 [T78 R410 F6378462-3]
13. Readers who want more detail can find a good selection of the *KStN*'s of the "*Inf.Div.44*" in CAMO, Bestand 500, Findbuch 12451, Akte 142, while NARA T78 R398 H1/37 provides an excellent overview of this type of division. More *KStN*'s can be found in T78 R391-397.
14. *K.St.N. (Heer) Nr.21 n, Kommando einer Infanteriedivision 44,* 1.4.44 [CAMO, Bestand 500, Findbuch 12451, Akte 142]
15. *Ibid.*
16. *Ibid.*
17. *Ibid.*
18. Anl.1 zu *OKH/*GenStdH/Org.Abt. Nr.I./16900/44 g.K., *Grundgliederung der Inf.Div.44 mit Stärkeberechnung*, 20.5.44, p.2 [T78 R410 F6378466]
19. *K.St.N. (Heer) Nr.101 n, Stab eines Infanterieregiments (n.A.),* 1.12.43 [CAMO, Bestand 500, Findbuch 12451, Akte 142]
20. *K.St.N. (Heer) Nr.130 n, Stabskompanie eines Infanterieregiments (n.A.),* 1.4.44 [CAMO, Bestand 500, Findbuch 12451, Akte 142]
21. Anl.1 zu *OKH/*GenStdH/Org.Abt. Nr.I./16900/44 g.K., *Grundgliederung der Inf.Div.44 mit Stärkeberechnung*, 20.5.44, p.2 [T78 R410 F6378466]
22. *K.St.N. (Heer) Nr.111 n, Stab eines Infanteriebataillons (n.A.),* 1.12.43 [CAMO, Bestand 500, Findbuch 12451, Akte 142]
23. Anl.1 zu *OKH/*GenStdH/Org.Abt. Nr.I/3197/43 g.K., *Inf.Div. (n.A.)*, 24.6.43 [T78 R399 F6368965]
24. Anl.1 zu *OKH/*GenStdH/Org.Abt. Nr.I./16900/44 g.K., *Grundgliederung der Inf.Div.44 mit Stärkeberechnung*, 20.5.44, p.2 [T78 R410 F6378466]
25. *K.St.N. (Heer) Nr.131 n, Schützenkompanie (n.A.),* 1.5.44 [CAMO, Bestand 500, Findbuch 12451, Akte 142]
26. Such details are not mentioned in the *KStN* but are evident from POW interviews and supported by the number of small arms in a division. The number of self-loading rifles would allow for considerably more of those weapons in the sections, but this was never mentioned by prisoners, suggesting they were used elsewhere.

27. Anl zu *OKH*/GenStdH/Org.Abt. Nr.I/3197/43 g.K., *Inf.Div. (n.A.)*, 24.6.43 [T78 R399 F6368965]
28. Anl.1 zu *OKH*/GenStdH/Org.Abt. Nr.I./16900/44 g.K., *Grundgliederung der Inf.Div.44 mit Stärkeberechnung*, 20.5.44 [T78 R410 F6378466
29. *K.St.N. (Heer) Nr.151 n, Schwere Kompanie eines Infanteriebataillons (n.A.)*, 1.5.44 [CAMO, Bestand 500, Findbuch 12451, Akte 142]
30. *RSO*: Raupenschlepper Ost, lit. Caterpillar Tractor East.
31. Anl.1 zu *OKH*/GenStdH/Org.Abt. Nr.I./16900/44 g.K., 20.5.44, p.3 [T78 R410 F6378467]; *K.St.N. (Heer)* 188a n, *Teileinheit, Führer einer Infanteriepanzerjägerkompanie (tmot) (n.A.)*, 1.12.43 [CAMO, Bestand 500, Findbuch 12451, Akte 142]; *K.St.N. (Heer) Nr.188f n, Infanteriepanzerjägerzug (zu 3 Geschützen 7.5cm Pak (mot) (n.A.)*, 1.12.43 [CAMO, Bestand 500, Findbuch 12451, Akte 142]; *K.St.N. (Heer) Nr.154 b, Panzerzerstörerzug einer Infanterie-Panzerjägerkompanie*, 1.2.44 [CAMO, Bestand 500, Findbuch 12451, Akte 142]
32. *K.St.N. (Heer) Nr.188f n, Infanteriepanzerjägerzug (zu 3 Geschützen 7.5cm Pak (mot) (n.A.)*, 1.12.43 [CAMO, Bestand 500, Findbuch 12451, Akte 142]
33. *K.St.N. (Heer) Nr.154 b, Panzerzerstörerzug einer Infanterie-Panzerjägerkompanie*, 1.2.44 [CAMO, Bestand 500, Findbuch 12451, Akte 142]
34. Anl.1 zu *OKH*/GenStdH/Org.Abt. Nr.I./16900/44 g.K., *Grundgliederung der Inf.Div.44 mit Stärkeberechnung*, 20.5.44, p.2 [T78 R410 F6378466]
35. *K.St.N. (Heer) Nr.149 n, Schützenkompanie (auf Fahrrädern) (n.A.)*, 1.5.44 [CAMO, Bestand 500, Findbuch 12451, Akte 142]
36. *K.St.N. (Heer) Nr.401, Stab und Stabsbatterie eines Artillerie regiments einer Infanteriedivision 44*, 1.3.44 [CAMO, Bestand 500, Findbuch 12451, Akte 142]
37. *K.St.N. (Heer) Nr.403, Stab und Stabsbatterie einer Artillerieabteilung einer Infanteriedivision 44*, 1.3.44 [CAMO, Bestand 500, Findbuch 12451, Akte 142]
38. *Ibid.*
39. *K.St.N. (Heer) Nr.433, Batterie leichte Feldhaubitzen (zu 4 geschützen) einer Infanteriedivision 44*, 1.3.44 [CAMO, Bestand 500, Findbuch 12451, Akte 142]
40. Anl.1 zu *OKH*/GenStdH/Org.Abt. Nr.I./16900/44 g.K., *Grundgliederung der Inf.Div.44 mit Stärkeberechnung*, 20.5.44, p.2 [T78 R410 F6378466]
41. *K.St.N. (Heer) Nr.702 n, Stab eines Pionierbataillons (n.A.)*, 1.4.44 [CAMO, Bestand 500, Findbuch 12451, Akte 142]
42. *K.St.N. (Heer) Nr.711 n, Pionierkompanie (n.A.)*, 1.4.44 [CAMO, Bestand 500, Findbuch 12451, Akte 142]
43. Anl.1 zu *OKH*/GenStdH/Org.Abt. Nr.I./16900/44 g.K., *Grundgliederung der Inf.Div.44 mit Stärkeberechnung*, 20.5.44, p.2 [T78 R410 F6378466]
44. *K.St.N. (Heer) Nr.711 n, Pionierkompanie (n.A.)*, 1.4.44 [CAMO, Bestand 500, Findbuch 12451, Akte 142]; *K.St.N. (Heer) Nr.723 n, Pionierkompanie (n.A.) (auf Fahrrädern)*, 1.4.44 [CAMO, Bestand 500, Findbuch 12451, Akte 142]
45. Anl.1 zu *OKH*/GenStdH/Org.Abt. Nr.I./16900/44 g.K., *Grundgliederung der Inf.Div.44 mit Stärkeberechnung*, 20.5.44, p.2 [T78 R410 F6378466]

46. *K.St.N. (Heer) Nr.125 a, Feldersatzbataillon einer Infanteriedivision 44*, 1.4.44 [CAMO, Bestand 500, Findbuch 12451, Akte 142]
47. *Ibid.*
48. *Ibid.*
49. *Ibid.*
50. *OKH*/GenStdH/Org.Abt. Nr.I/2197/43 g.K., 15.7.43, p.1-4 [T78 R398 H1/39]
51. Müller, P. & W. Zimmermann, (2007), *Sturmgeschütz III, Rückgrat der Infanterie, Band 1, Geschichte: Entwicklung, Fertigung, Einsatz*, History Facts, p.200. The book quotes from: *Der Generalinspekteur der Panzertruppen 6980/44, Verwendung von Panzerjäger-Sturmgeschütz-Abteilungen*, 2.6.44
52. Example for the 349., 352. and 353. *I.D.* (21.Welle): *OKH*/GenStdH/Org.Abt. Nr.I/4367/43 g.K. II.Ang., 5.11.43, p.1 [T78 R527 F559]; Example for the 25th wave: *OKH*/Ch H Rüst u BdE AHA/Ia(I) Nr.377/44 g.K., 15.1.44, p.1 [T78 R848 H36/153]
In January 1944 it was announced that 21st and 22nd wave divisions would only receive 22 s.Pak (motZ), allowing the formation of just a divisional AT company, regimental AT platoons and a spare gun in the field-replacement battalion. This was still an improvement from the minimum of 18 guns from June 1943. [*OKH*/GenStdH/ Org.Abt. Nr.I.15229/44 g.K., 19.1.44 in T78 R848 H36/153]
53. *OKH*/ Ch H Rüst u BdE/ AHA Ia (I) Nr.214/44 g. Kdos., 11.1.44 [T78 R848 H36/153]
54. *OKH*/GenStdH/Org.Abt. Nr.I/15461/44 g.K., 25.3.44 [T78 R398 H1/39]; *OKH*/GenStdH/Org/Abt/ Nr.I/15461/44 g.K.II.Ang., 30.3.44 [T78 R398 H1/39]
55. *OKH*/GenStdH/Org.Abt. Nr.I/15461/44 g.K., 25.3.44, p.1 [T78 R398 H1/39]; *OKH*/GenStdH/Org.Abt. Nr.I.15229/44 g.K., 19.1.44 [T78 R848 H36/153]
56. Light Pak (1944): < 5cm; Medium Pak (1944): *5 cm Pak 38* or *7,5 cm Pak 97/38*; Heavy Pak (1944): 7.5 cm and heavier.
57. *OKH*/GenStdH/Org.Abt. Nr.I/15461/44 g.K., 25.3.44, p.1-3 [T78 R398 H1/39]
58. *Ibid.*, p.3
59. Anl.1 zu *OKH*/GenStdH/Org.Abt. Nr.I/16900/44 g.K., 20.5.44, p.2 [T78 R410 F6378466]
60. *Ibid.* [T78 R410 F6378466-8]
61. *K.St.N. (Heer) Nr.1106, Stab und Stabskompanie einer Panzerjägerabteilung (gem.)*, 1.2.44 [CAMO, Bestand 500, Findbuch 12451, Akte 142]
62. Anl. 1 zu *OKH*/GenStdH/Org.Abt. Nr.I/16900/44 g.K., 20.5.44, p.2 & 4 [T78 R410 F6378466 & 8]; *K.St.N. (Heer) 1140 n, Panzerjägerkompanie (n,A,) (zu 12 Geschützen 7.5cm Pak)*, 1.10.43 [T78 R393 F6361777-9]
63. Anl.1 zu *OKH*/GenStdH/Org.Abt. Nr.I/16900/44 g.K., 20.5.44, p.4 [T78 R410 F6378468]
64. *K.St.N. (Heer) 1140, schwere Panzerjägerkompanie (9 oder 12 Geschütze) (motZ)*, 1.11.43 [T78 R393 F6361770-3]
65. Anl.1 zu *OKH*/GenStdH/Org.Abt. Nr.I/16900/44 g.K., 20.5.44, p.4 [T78 R410 F6378468]
66. *K.St.N. (Heer) 191, Gebirgs-Fliegerabwehrkompanie (zu 12 Geschützen 2cm Geb.Flak) (mot Z)*, 1.3.44 [T78 R391 F6359724-7]; *K.St.N. (Heer) 192, Fliegerabwehrkompanie (zu 12 Geschützen

2cm Flak) (Sfl)*, 1.4.44 [T78 R391 F6359728-30]; *K.St.N. (Heer) 198, Fliegerabwehrkompanie (zu 9 Geschützen 3,7cm Flak) (mot Z)*, 1.4.44 [T78 R391 F6359735-8]. *KStN 191*: 34 NCO's, 111 men; *KStN 192*: 34, 112; *KStN 198*: 29, 116.
67. Anl. 1 zu *OKH*/GenStdH/Org.Abt. Nr.I/16900/44 g.K., 20.5.44, p.2 & 4 [T78 R410 F6378466 & 8]
68. Self-propelled 7.5 or 7.62 cm Pak mounted on the chassis of a *Pz.Kpfw. II* (Marder II) were designated as the *Sd.Kfz.131* or *132* and those on a *Pz.Kpfw. 38(t)* (Marder III) as *Sd.Kfz. 138* or *139*.
69. *K.St.N. (Heer) Nr.1148 d, schnelle Panzerjägerkompanie (14 Gesch. 7.5 oder 7.62cm Pak (Sf)*, 1.11.1943 [T78 R393 F6361806-9]; *OKH*/Ch H Rüst u BdE AHA Ia(I) Nr.214/44 g.K., 11.1.44 [T78 R848 H36/153]; *OKH*/Ch H Rüst u BdE AHA Ia(I) Nr.3490/43 g.K., 13.7.43 [T78 R850 H36/157]
70. Anl. 1 zu *OKH*/GenStdH/Org.Abt. Nr.I/16900/44 g.K., 20.5.44, p.2 & 4 [T78 R410 F6378466 & 8]
71. *K.St.N. (Heer) Nr.1149, Sturmgeschützabteilung (in Panzer-Jager-Abteilung) (10 oder 14 Geschütze)*, 1.2.44 [T78 R393 F6361812-7]
72. On 1 April 1943. the *Schnelle Truppen* branch was dissolved and the *Panzertruppen* branch created (more or less) to replace it. [*OKH*/Ch H Rüst u BdE/HPA/GenStdH/Org.Abt, (II) Nr.16840/43 g., 24.4.43 in T78 R298 H1/36]
73. For examples of *StuG* in tank regiments and battalions in *Pz.Gren.* and *Pz.Div.* see: *OKH*/GenStdH/Org.Abt.(I), *Kriegsgliederung des Feldheeres (ohne Heerestruppen), Stand: Sommer-Sept.1943* [T78 R407 F6376378-477]; for comparison see: Anl. zu *OKH*/GenStdH/Org.Abt.(I) Nr.5000/42 g.K., 10.42, *Kriegsgliederung des Feldheeres, Stand: 15 Okt. 1942 bis Sommer 1943* [T78 R406 F6376043-96]
74. *OKH*/Ch H Rüst u BdE/HPA/GenStdH/Org.Abt, (II) Nr.16840/43 g., 24.4.43. The first "infantry" divisions to start the conversion to assault guns were the *3. Geb., 5. Jäg. and 28. Jäg.Div.*, followed by the *1. Inf., 21. Inf., 102. Inf. and the 8. Jäg.Div.* [see T78 R850 H36/157 for orders]
75. *Nachrichtenblatt der Panzertruppen*, Issue Nr.15 - Sep. 1944, p.27-28
76. These distinctions were also not always followed, depending on the commander of the unit and what sort of predecessor unit the element evolved from.
77. *OKH*/GenStdH/Org.Abt. Nr.I/15710/44 g.K., 14.2.44 [T78 R269 F6216933]; *OKH*/GenStdH/Org.Abt. Nr.I/15710/44 g.K. II. Ang., 25.2.44, p.1-3 [T78 R398 H1/39]
78. *AOK 7, Kriegsgliederung 7. Armee, Stand 14.2.44, 77. I.D. (In Neuaufstellung), Stand 18.2.1944* [T312 R1566 F124]; *265. Infanterie-Div., Stand: 1.2.44* [F105]; *266. Infanterie-Div., Stand: 1.2.44* [F116]; *343. Infanterie-Div., Stand: 31.1.44* [F104]
79. *OKH*, Anl.2 zu *OKH*/GenStdH Org.Abt.(I) Nr.4730/42 g.K., 7.10.42 [T78 R405 F6375223 & 6375229]; see chapter *"709. Infanterie-Division"*; *AOK 7, Kriegsgliederung 7. Armee*, Stand 18.5.44, *Kriegsgliederung) 709. I.D. Stand: 1.5.44* [T312 R1566 F217]; *AOK 7, Kriegsgliederung 7. Armee*, Stand 18.5.44, *716. Infanterie-Division, Stand: 1.5.44* [T312 R1566 F215]
80. *AOK 7, Kriegsgliederung 7. Armee*, Stand 18.5.44, *265. I.D., Stand: 1.5.1944* [T312 R1566 F228]; *AOK 7, Kriegsgliederung 7. Armee*, Stand 18.5.44, *343. I.D., Stand: 1.5.44* [T312 R1566 F227];

AOK 7, Kriegsgliederung *7. Armee*, Stand 18.5.44, *266. Infanterie-Division, Stand: 1.5.44* [T312 R1566 F225]
81. *OKH/Ch H Rüst u BdE/AHA Ia(I)* Nr.493/44 g.K., 11.1.44, p.1-2 [T78 R848 H36/153]
82. Anl.1 zu *OKH/GenStdH/Org.Abt.* Nr.I/16900/44 g.K., 20.5.44, p.2 [T78 R410 F6378466]
83. *OKH/Ch H Rüst u BdE AHA/Ia(I)* Nr.377/44 g.K., 15.1.44 [T78 R848 H36/153]
84. See chapters *"77. Infanterie-Division"* and *"91. Luftlande-Infanterie-Division"*
85. *H.Kdo.LX*, *Tätigkeitsbericht des H.Kommandos LX für Monat September 1941*, p.1 [T314 R1603 F26]; *AOK 7*, Ia Nr.830/44 g.K., 14.2.44, p.2 [T312 R1565 F112]
86. Examples of the transfer of full divisions: *OKH/GenStdH/II.Abt.* Nr.1011/43 g.K.Chefs., 16.2.43 [T78 R431 fr6403008-10]; *AOK 7*, *Tätigkeitsbericht der Abt.IIa/IIb für die Zeit vom 1.7. - 30.9.43*, p.1 [T312 R1562 F4] In 1943 many divisions of the former *6. Armee,* which had been destroyed at Stalingrad, were reconstututed under *Ob.West*. In the third quarter, all seven infantry divisions and the one armoured division that had been rebuilt under *AOK 7* again left that sector.
87. Examples for *OKH*: *OKH/GenStdH/Org.Abt.* Nr.I/4364/43 g.K., 20.9.43 [T78 R419 F6388545]; Examples for *7. Armee* : *AOK 7*, *Tätigkeitsbericht der Abt.IIa/IIb für die Zeit vom 1.7. - 30.9.43*, p.1 [T312 R1562 F4]; *AOK 7*, Ia Nr.6282/43 g., p.1-3, 7.12.43 [T312 R1559 F328-30]; Examples for *XXV. A.K.*: *AOK 7*, Ia Nr.131/42 g.K., 12.1.42 [314 R742 F84-7]; Examples for *LXXXIV. A.K.*: Gen.Kdo.*LXXXIV. A.K.*, *Tätigkeitsbericht IIa/IIb für den Monat Oktober 1942*, 31.10.42 [T314 R1603 F600]; Chef d Gen.St.d.*LXXXIV. A.K.*, Ia Nr.2832/42, 4.12.42 [T314 R1603 F726] A basic overview of who were not considered *ostverwendungsfähig* in October 1943 can be found in Gen.Kdo.*LXXXIV. A.K.*, Ia Nr.1882/43 g.K., 18.10.43, p.1 [T314 R1604 F1184]
88. When it concerns personnel, the *Ist* also includes personnel on leave, detached and those injured or sick but expected to return within eight weeks. [*OKH/GenStdH/Org.Abt.* Nr.I/16500/44 g.K., 25.4.44 with Anlagen in T78 R398 H1/36]
89. *AOK 7*, *Tätigkeitsbericht der Abt. IIa/IIb für die Zeit vom 1.7. bis 30.9.43*, p.1 [T312 R1562 F4]; *AOK 7 Tätigkeitsbericht der Abt. IIa/IIb für die Zeit vom 1.10. bis 31.12.43*, p.5 [T312 R1562 F18]
90. Gen.Kdo.*LXXXIV. A.K.*, Ia Nr.1882/43 g.K., 18.10.43, p.1 [T314 R1604 F1184]
91. *OKH/GenStdH/Org.Abt.* Nr.I/8088/43, 8.10.43 [T78 R527 F186]
92. Gen.Kdo.*LXXXIV. A.K.* IIa/IIb, *Tätigkeitsbericht IIa/IIb für den Monat Oktober 1942*, 31.10.42 [T314 R1603 R1603 F600]
93. Anl. zu Gen.Kdo.*LXXXIV. A.K.*, Ia Nr.1402/43 g.K., *716. I.D. (bodenständige Div. 15. Welle)*, 24.7.43 [T314 R1604 F718]; Anl. zu Gen.Kdo.*LXXXIV. A.K.*, Ia Nr.1402/43 g.K., *709. I.D. (bodenständige Division 15. Welle)*, 24.7.43 [T314 R1604 F719]
94. Der *Oberbefehlshaber West*, Ia Nr.550/43 g.K. Chefs., 28.10.43, p.35 [T78 R311 F6263262]
95. *AOK 7 IIa/IIb*, *Tätigkeitsbericht der Abt. IIa/IIb für die Zeit vom 1.7. - 30.9.43*, p.4 [T312 R1562 F7]; also see *OKH*, Ch H Rüst und BdE AHA Ia(I) Nr.2529/43 g.K., 20.5.43, p.3 [T78 R849 H36/156]
96. Anlage zu GenStdH. Org.Abt. Nr.I/3891/44 g. II.Ang., 26.4.44, *Soldaten aus den in das Deutsche Reich eingegliederten Gebieten* [T78 R420 F6389629]
97. *AOK 7*, *Tätigkeitsbericht der Abt. IIa/IIb für die Zeit vom 1.1. - 31.3.44*, p.3-4 [T312 R1566 F696-7]
98. *Heeresgruppe Süd-Ukraine*: 0.6% (incomplete); *H.Gr. Nord-Ukraine*: 0.4%; *H.Gr. Mitte*: 0.6%; *H.Gr. Nord*: 0.6%. [GenStdH/Org.Abt., Nr.I/3891/44 g. II.Ang, 26.5.44 and Anlage in T78 R420 F6389629-9]
99. Anlage zu GenStdH/Org.Abt. Nr.I/3891/44 g. II.Ang., 26.4.44, *Soldaten aus den in das Deutsche Reich eingegliederten Gebieten* [T78 R420 F6389629]
100. This is evident from prisoner of war interrogations.
101. For example, the difficulties with Styrians led *H.Gr. Mitte* to request their removal. At the same time, they could not be used in Southern Europe due to the risk of desertion, and their numbers were too high to be used exclusively in the West and Norway. [GenStdH/Org.Abt. Nr.I/25512/43, 28.12.43 in T78 R528 F965]
102. *OKH/GenStdH/Org.Abt.* Nr.I/8388/43 g., 8.10.43, p.1-2 [T78 R527 F187-8]; Anlage zu GenStdH/Org.Abt. Nr.I/3891/44 g. II.Ang., 26.4.44, *Soldaten aus den in das Deutsche Reich eingegliederten Gebieten* [T78 R420 F6389629]
103. *AOK 7*, *Tätigkeitsbericht der Abt. IIa/IIb für die Zeit vom 1.1. - 31.3.44*, p.4 [T312 R1566 F697]
104. Overmans, R. (1999), *Deutsche militärische Verluste im Zweiten Weltkrieg*, München: Oldenbourg Verlag, p.170-172, 228-232
105. It should be noted that not all Poles in the *Wehrmacht* belonged to *DVL III*. This makes the definition of "Pole" much more complex than it may appear at first glance.
106. *AOK 7*, *Tätigkeitsbericht der Abt. IIa/IIb für die Zeit vom 1.1. - 31.3.44*, p.3 [T312 R1566 F696]
107. *Ibid.*, p.1-3 [T312 R1566 F694-6]
108. Examples: *AOK 7*, *Tätigkeitsbericht der Abt.IIa/IIb für die Zeit vom 1.7. - 30.9.43*, p.1 [T312 R1562 F4]; Gen.Kdo.*LXXXIV. A.K.*, Ia Nr.1654/43 g.K., 6.9.43 [T314 R1604 F902]
109. Examples: Chef d Gen.St.d.*LXXXIV. A.K.*, Ia Nr.2832/42, 4.12.42 [T314 R1603 F726]; Gen.Kdo.*LXXXIV. A.K.*, Ia Nr.1882/43 g.K., 18.10.43 [T314 R1604 F1184-5]
110. *AOK 7*, Ia Nr.5207/43, 16.10.1943 [T314 R745 F96]
111. There were two sets of numbers. For the *7. Armee,* they only covered the static divisions, where they distinguished between combat and support troops. The first set merely gave the average age of these groups per division. The second set provided actual numbers for five different age groups: 1899 and older, 1900-05, 1906-13, 1914-22 and 1923 and younger.
112. PWIS(H)/194, German Military Manpower, June 1944, 16 July 1944 [TNA, WO 208/3622]; O.S.S., Research and Analysis Branch, R & A No. 2581.1, Nationality and Age of German Armed Forces Prisoners Captured in Northern France, June to August 1944. 4 Jan. 1945.
113. Leleu, J.L. (2022), *Combattre en Dictature*, Paris: Perrin, Appendix 13 (based on M.I.R.S. (b), Various age groups studies, 12.8.1944). A copy of the original report could not be accessed and Leleu's brief representation of it is taken as being accurate here.

114. Technically, not all deaths were "in action," as other facts may have been involved (e.g., DOW training or vehicular accidents), but for simplicity's sake, the term KIA will be used.
115. The *Vermisstenbildliste* can be accessed at https://vbl.drk-suchdienst.online/Feldpostnummer/FPN.aspx. The lists have been checked for the period June-August 1944, but May and September have also been included when individuals can reasonably be expected to have been with a unit during the fighting as the dates often represent last contact; The dead cards form the collection "Germany, Military Killed in Action, 1939-1948" at https://www.ancestry.com/search/collections/61641 {Original data in BaMa, B 563-2, Kartei der Verlust- und Grabmeldungen gefallener deutscher Soldaten 1939-1945 (-1948)]. The death cards have been checked for the period of D-Day to 25 July 1944 (Operation Cobra).
116. Leleu, J.L. (2022), Appendix 21
117. *AOK 7*, Ia Nr.1542/44 g.K., 14.3.44, p.1 [T312 R1565 F283]
118. *AOK 7*, Ia Nr.3000/44 g.K., 4.4.44, p.3 [T312 R1565 F421]
119. *K.St.N. (Heer)* 131F, *Schützenkompanie (bodenstandig)*, 1.12.43 [T78 R391 F6366295-8]
120. *K.St.N. (Heer) Nr. 131*, *Schützenkompanie (n.A.)*, 1.5.44 [CAMO, Bestand 500, Findbuch 12451, Akte 142]
121. *265. I.D., Zustandsbericht 265. I.D., Meldung vom 1.6.1944* [T314 R747 F9]
122. This estimate is based on known or comparable *KStN's* as well as known alterations, and it includes all three non-German battalions. In some cases, it is not known which *KStN* a unit used, or how the situation in the field differed from that on paper. This particularly concerns the bicycle units and part of the support troops.
123. *K.St.N. (Heer) Nr.131 n*, *Schützenkompanie (n.A.)*, 1.5.44 [CAMO, Bestand 500, Findbuch 12451, Akte 142]
124. Numbers for a division with: A *"2. Gliederungsart"* antitank battalion (headquarters, headquarters company, company of towed heavy AT guns, company of assault guns and a *Flak* company with self-propelled 2cm *Flak*); three of the light howitzer batteries and three heavy batteries were armed with three rather than four howitzers. If all artillery batteries had four guns, the number of horses would increase by another 111 [Anl.1 zu *OKH/GenStdH/Org.Abt.* Nr.I/16900/44 g.K., 20.5.44, p.7 in T78 R410 F6378471]; *K.St.N. (Heer) Nr.433, Batterie leichte Feldhaubitzen (zu 4 Geschützen) einer Infanteriedivision 44 / Batterie schwere Feldhaubitzen (zu 4 Geschützen) einer Infanteriedivision 44*, 1.3.44 [CAMO, Bestand 500, Findbuch 12498, Akte 25]
125. Anl.1 zu *OKH/Gen.St.d.H/Org.Abt.* Nr.I/16900/44 g.K., 20.5.44, p.6 [T78 R410 F6378470] The number of lorries includes the prime movers of the AT battaliuon, which could also be *Maultiere*, *RSO's* or halftracks.
126. *OKH/Chef H Rüst und BdE, AHA/Stab I(1)/I(3)* Nr.298/44 g.K., 4.5.44 [T78 R763 H19/56]
127. Anl. zu Gen.Kdo.*LXXXIV. A.K.*, Ia Nr.1402/43 g.K., *709. I.D. (bodenständige Division 15. Welle)*, 24.7.43 [T314 R1604 F719]
128. Gen.Kdo.*LXXXIV. A.K.* Ia, *Tätigkeitsbericht des Gen.Kdo.LXXXIV. A.K. für den Monat Juni 1942*, p.3 [T314 R1603 F212]
129. Gen.Kdo.*LXXXIV. A.K.*, Ia Nr.116/43 g.K., 15.1.43, p.1 [T314

[T314 R1604 F33]
130. Gen.Kdo.*LXXXIV. A.K.*, Ia Nr.303/43 g.K., 12.2.43, p.2 [T314 R1604 F153]
131. *Der Führer*, OKW/WFSt/Op. Nr.662656/43 g.K. Chefs., *Führerweisung Nr.51*, 3.11.43 [https://bunkermuseumhansltholm.dk/viden-om/dokumenter-1940-45/vaernemagtens-overkommando-OKW-vedr-danmark/fuehrerweisung-nr-51-3111943/]
132. *Oberbefehlshaber West*, Ia Nr.592/43 g.K.Ch., 8.11.1943 [T312 R1563 F766]
133. *AOK 7*, Ia Nr.124/43 g.K.Chefs., 11.11.943 [T312 R1563 F760-1]
134. *Ibid.*, p.1 [T312 R1563 F760]
135. *Beweglichmachung:* Making mobile, used as a noun. In the area of the *LXXXIV. A.K.*, the term had been used to cover efforts to provide mobility to the corps reserves.
136. *AOK 7*, Ia Nr.3000/44 g.K., 4.4.44, p.3-4 [T312 R1565 F421-2]
137. *Ibid.*
138. *Ibid.*, p.4 [T312 R1565 F422]
139. Obkdo.d.*H.Gr. B*, Ia Nr.4943/44 g.K., 18.7.44, p.3 [T311 R3 F7003815]
140. *AOK 7*, Ia Nr.1542/44 g.K., 14.3.44, p.2 [T312 R1565 F281]
141. *AOK 7*/O.Qu./A.O.Kraft/Ia Nr.2500/44 g.K., 7.5.44 [T312 R1565 F638-000656]
142. Obkdo.d.*H.Gr. B*, Ia Nr.4943/44 g.K., 18.7.44, p.3 [T311 R3 F7003815]
143. *AOK 7*, Ia Nr.6200/43 g.K., 1.12.43, p.4 [T312 R1559 F287]; Anl.2 zu *AOK 7*, Ia Nr.6200/43 g.K., 24.12.43 [T312 R1559 F444]
144. *AOK 7*, Ia Nr.1542/44 g.K., 14.3.44, p.1 [T312 R1565 F280]
145. *AOK 7* O.Qu., *Besprechungspunkte O.Qu. bei O.Qu.West.*, 12.5.44, p.2 [T312 R1571 F390]
146. See *Führerweisung Nr.51*
147. *AOK 7*, Ia Nr.1542/44 g.K., 14.3.44, p.1 [T312 R1565 F283]
148. BvTO b. *AOK 7*, *Tätigkeitsbericht für die Zeit vom 1. Januar bis 31. März 1944*, p.5 & 6 [T312 R1571 F881-2]; BvTO b. *AOK 7*, Anl. 15 zum Tätigkeitsbericht des BvTO beim *AOK 7* 1.1.1944 - 30.6.1944 [T312 R1571 F985]
149. *AOK 7* BvTO., *Tätigkeitsbericht für die Zeit vom 1. Januar bis 31. März 1944*. p.11 [T312 R1571 F887]
150. *AOK 7*, Ia Nr.2568/44 g.K., 19.5.44, p.1 [T312 R1565 F734]
151. See chapter *"265.Infanterie-Division"*; for the 275.Inf.Div. see **Zetterling, N. (2000)**, *Normandy 1944, German Military Organisation, Combat Power and Organisational Effectiveness*, Winnipeg: J.J.Fedorowicz Publishing, p.257
152. *AOK 7*, *Besprechung bei über Beweglichmachung 265. und 266. I.D.*, 11.2.44, p.1 [T312 R1565 F94]
153. *AOK 7*, Ia Nr.1542/44 g.K., 14.3.44, p.1 [T312 R1565 F283]
154. *AOK 7*/O.Qu./A.O.Kraft/Ia Nr.2500/44 g.K., 7.5.44, p.3 [T312 R1565 F640]
155. *Armee-Oberkommando* Ia Nr.900/44 g.K., *Befehl für Beweglichmachung und Verlastung von Reserven.*, 6.2.44, p.1-2 [T312 R1565 F45-6]
156. *AOK 7*/O.Qu./A.O.Kraft/Ia Nr.2500/44 g.K., 7.5.44, p.3 [T312 R1565 F640]; *AOK 7* O.Qu., *Besprechungspunkte O.Qu. bei O.Qu.West.*, 12.5.44, p.2 [T312 R1571 F390]
157. *AOK 7*, Ia Nr.2568/44 g.K., 19.5.44, p.1 [T312 R1565 F734]

77. Infanterie-Division

158. Tessin, G. (1972), *6.Band*, p.36; **Tessin, G. (1976)**, *13.Band*, p.227; *AOK 7*, Ia Nr.755/44 g.K., 9.2.44, p.4 [T312 R1565 F72]
159. *AOK 7* BvTO., *Tätigkeitsbericht für die Zeit vom 1. Januar bis 31. März 1944*. p.1 [T312 R1571 F877]; *AOK 7*, Ia Nr.755/44 g.K., 9.2.44 [T312 R1565 F69]
160. *AOK 7* BvTO, Anl.15 zum Tätigkeitsbericht BvTO *AOK 7*, *Zusammenstellung der in der Zeit vom 1.4. - 30.6.44 im Armeebereich durchgeführten Bewegungen.*, p.1 [T312 R1571 F982]
161. *AOK 7*, Ia Nr.2870/44 g.K., 7.6.44, p.1 [T312 R1565 F883]
162. *Gen.* Poppe commanded the *225. I.D.* from January 1942 to November 1943, receiving average performance reviews. On 28 April, *Gen.* Poppe was put in charge of the hradquarters responsible for standing up *Gren.Div. Ostpreußen* (1 or 2) on 5 July. [German general staff officers files, index cards of *Gen.Lt.* Poppe in T78 R891 H6/26]
163. *AOK 7* Ia, *Kriegstagebuch der Führungsabteilung AOK 7 für die Zeit vom 1.Jan. - 30.Juni 1944*, 11.2.44 [T312 R1564 F188] — Hereafter referred to as: *AOK 7* Ia, *KTB 1.1.-30.6.1944*; Kartei von Inf.-Kommandeuren, index cards of *Gen.Lt.* Poppe and *Gen.Lt.* Ortner [T78 R908 H6/354]
164. German general staff officers files, index cards of *Gen.Lt.* Stegmann [T78 R893 H6/26] *Gen.* Stegmann was in command of the *291.*, *263.*, *206.* and *36. I.D.* between May 1943 and January 1944, receiving above average performance reviews. In January he informed his corps commander that he was no longer fit, both physically and mentally, to properly lead his division. He was posthumously promoted to *Generalleutnant* as of 1 June 1944.
165. *AOK 7*, Ia Nr.3205/44 g.K., 18.6.44 [T312 R1565 F1109]; Volksbund
166. *AOK 7* Ia, *AOK 7 Kriegstagebuch Ia - 6 Jun 1944 - 25 Jul 1944*, p.57 [T312 R1569 F276] — Hereafter referred to as: *AOK 7* Ia, *KTB 6.6.-25.7.44*
167. C.S.D.I.C. (UK), S. R. Report, S.R.M. 806; **Wilbrand (1944)**, *Gefechtsbericht des Grenadier Regimentes 1050 (77. Infanterie-Division)*, p.17 [T78 R672 H41/61b]
168. *OKH*/Chef H Rüst u BdE AHA/Ia(I) Nr.377/44 g.K. 15.1.44 [T78 R848 H36/153]
169. Tessin, G. (1972), *6.Band*, p.75, 81, 106, 117 & 122
170. *AOK 7*, Ia Nr.433/44 g., 21.1.44, p.1 [T312 R1564 F482]; *AOK 7*, Kriegsgliederung 7. Armee, Stand 9.2.44, 77. I.D. (in Neuaufstellung), Stand 3.2.44 [T312 R1566 F88]
171. *AOK 7*, Ia Nr.38/44 g.K., 3.1.44 [T312 R1564 F401]
172. Gen.Kdo.*LXXXIV. A.K.* Abt.Ia Nr.098/43 g.K.Chefs., 1.1.44, Anlage [T312 R1564 F400]
173. *AOK 7*, Ia Nr.303/43 g.K., 15.1.44 [T312 R1564 F454]
174. *AOK 7*, Ia Nr.350/44 g.K., 18.1.44 [T312 R1564 F470]
175. *AOK 7*, Ia Nr.755/44 g.K., 9.2.44, Anl.3, p.1 [T312 R1565 F73-85]
176. Tessin, G. (1974), *9.Band*, p.304; Wehrkreiskommando Generalgouvernement Abt.Ia Nr.827/44 g. 23.1.44 [T501 R218 F517]; Oberfeldkommandantur 603 Abt.Ia, *Monatsbericht für die Zeit vom 16.1. - 15.2.1944*, 19.2.44. [T501 R218 F306]
177. *AOK 7*, Ia Nr.755/44 g.K., 9.2.44, Anl.3, p.1 [T312 R1565 F73-85]
178. Tessin, G. (1972), *6.Band*, p.36
179. *AOK 7*, Ia Nr.755/44 g.K., 9.2.44 [T312 R1565 F73-85]
180. Der Chef des Generalstabes des Heeres, Org.Abt.(I), Nr.I/3197/43 g.K.II.Ang., 2.10.43. [T78 R420 F6389106-9]
181. *AOK 7*, Ia Nr.755/44 g.K., 9.2.44, Anl.3, p.1 [T312 R1565 F82]; *AOK 7* Ia, *KTB 1.1.-30.6.1944* [T312 R1564 F189]
182. Tessin, G. (1973), *7.Band*, p.124; **Tessin, G. (1974)**, *9.Band*, p.271
183. Tessin, G. (1976), *13.Band*, p.247
184. *AOK 7*, Ia Nr.985/44, p.2 [T312 R1565 F115]; **Tessin, G. (1976)**, *13.Band*, p.236
185. *AOK 7*, Ia Nr.755/44 g.K., 9.2.44, Anl.1 [T312 R1565 F79]
186. Anl.2 zu *OKH*/GenStdH/Org.Abt. Nr.I/1299/44 g.K. Chefs., 6.6.44 [T78 R420 F6389914]
187. *OKH* Chef H Rüst und BdE, AHA Ia(I) Nr.510/44 g.K., 21.1.44, p.5 [T78 R848 H36/153]; *AOK 7*, Ia Nr.755/44 g.K., 9.2.44, Anl.1 [T312 R1565 F79]
188. Anl.1 zu *OKH*/GenStdH/Org.Abt. Nr.I/16900/44 g.K., 20.5.44, p.2 [T78 R410 F6378466]
189. Anlage 2 zu *OKH*/GenStdH/Org.Abt. Nr.I/1600/44.g.K., 20.5.44 [T78 R410 F6378462]
190. *OKH*/Chef H Rüst u BdE AHA/Ia(I) Nr.377/44 g.K., 15.1.44, p.1 [T78 R848 H36/153]; Anl.2 zu *OKH*/GenStdH/Org.Abt. Nr.I/1299/44 g.K. Chefs., 6.6.44 [T78 R420 F6389914]
191. *OKH*/GenStdH/Org.Abt. Nr.I/17239/44 g.K., 25.5.44 [T78 R526 F160]
192. *OKH*/GenStdH/Org.Abt. Nr.I/7281/44 g., 30.7.44 [T78 R526 F447]
193. *OKH* Chef H Rüst und BdE, AHA Ia(I) Nr.510/44 g.K., 21.1.44, p.5 [T78 R848 H36/153]; *AOK 7*, Ia Nr.755/44 g.K., 9.2.44, p.4 & Anlage 2 [T312 R1565 F72 & 80]
194. *AOK 7*, Ia Nr.1649/44 g., 11.3.44 [T312 R1565 F253]
195. *AOK 7*, Ia Nr.755/44 g.K., 9.2.44, Anl.3 [T312 R1565 F82-3]
196. *AOK 7*, Ia Nr.755/44 g.K., 9.2.44, Anl.1 [T312 R1565 F79]
197. Anl. Zu *OKH*/GenStdH/Org.Abt. Nr.I/3197/43 g.K., 24.7.1943 [T78 R399 F6368965]; Anl.1 zu *OKH*/GenStdH/Org.Abt. Nr.I/16900/44 g.K., 20.5.44, p.2 [T78 R410 F6378466]
198. Anl.2 zu *OKH*/GenStdH/Org.Abt. Nr.I/1299/44 g.K. Chefs., 6.6.44 [T78 R420 F6389914]
199. Gen.d.Art.i.*OKH*, *Kriegstagebuch Nr.4 des Stabes General der Artillerie im OKH*, 1.1.44-31.12.44 [T78 R269 F6216692]; *OKH*/GenStdH/Org.Abt. Nr.I/5895.44 g., 5.6.4 [T78 R526 F207]; *OKH*/GenStdH/Org.Abt. Nr.I/6430/44 g., 22.6.44 [T78 R526 F312]
200. *AOK 7*, Ia Nr.755/44 g.K., 9.2.44, p.5 & Anl.1 [T312 R1565 F73-85] 8.8 cm *Flak* were specifically ordered for the *84.* and *92. I.D.* [*OKH*/Ch H Rüst u BdE AHA Ia(I) Nr.510/44 g.K., 21.1.44 in T78 R848 H36/153]
201. *OKH*/GenStdH/Org.Abt. Nr.I/5895.44 g., 5.6.4 [T78 R526 F207]; The number of heavy howitzers was incorrectly given as six per battery in Anl.2 zu *OKH*/GenStdH/Org.Abt. Nr.I/1299/44 g.K.,Chefs., 6.6.44 [T78 R420 F6389914]. This was manually corrected in *OKH*/GenStdH/ Org.Abt.(I), Nr.I/18310/44 g.K., 24.7.44, Gliederung d. Inf.Div.(25th wave) [T78 R410 F6378477]

202. OKH/GenStdH/Org.Abt. Nr.I/6430/44 g., 22.6.44 [T78 R526 F312]
203. AOK 7, Ia Nr.755/44 g.K., 9.2.44, Anl.1 [T312 R1565 F73-85]
204. Anl.2 zu OKH/GenStdH/Org.Abt. Nr.I/1299/44 g.K. Chefs., 6.6.44 [T78 R420 F6389914]
205. OKH/GenStdH/Org.Abt. Nr.I/17239/44 g.K., 25.5.44 [T78 R526 F160]
206. OKH/GenStdH/Org.Abt. Nr.I/7281/44 g., 30.7.44 [T78 R526 F447]; C.S.D.I.C. (UK) S.IR 445, 2 Jul 44,p.10 [NARA, RG 165, Box 659, Folder 2]
207. 77. I.D., Ia Nr.273/44 g.K., p.1-2 & Anlage [T314 R1568 F946-9]
208. Report of unknown origin, possibly Ob.West, concerning status of newly formed divisions of the 25th wave [UKNA, HW 5/479, CX/MSS/T178/11, KV 3185]
209. 77. I.D., Ia Nr.273/44 g.K., 2.6.44, p.1 [T314 R1568 F946]
210. WFST/Op. (H) West, Nr.004662/44 g.K., 3.5.44, p.1 [T77 R1421 F237] Referred to in **Zetterling, N. (2000)**, p.242-3
211. C.S.D.I.C. (UK) S.IR 445, 2 Jul 44,p.2 [NARA, RG 165, Box 659, Folder 2]
212. AOK 7 Ia, KTB 6.6.-16.8.44, p.128 [T312 R1569 F131]
213. Data obtained from the German Red Cross Vermisstenbildliste and death cards in the Ancestry.com 'Germany, Military Killed in Action, 1939-1948' collection.
214. Leleu, J.L. (2022), Combattre en Dictature, Paris: Perrin, Appendix 13 (based on MIRS (b), Various age groups studies, 12.8.1944)
215. 77. I.D., Ia Nr.273/44 g.K., 2.6.44, p.1 [T314 R1568 F946]
216. Report of unknown origin, possibly Ob.West, concerning status of newly formed divisions of the 25th wave [UKNA, HW 5/479, CX/MSS/T178/11, KV 3185]
217. Anl.1 zu OKH/GenStdH/Org.Abt. Nr.I/16900/44 g.K., 20.5.44, p.2 [T78 R410 F6378466]; 77. I.D., Ia Nr.273/44 g.K., Anl. Gliederung 77. I.D. (25. Welle), Stand: 1.6.44, p.1 [T314 R1568 F948]
218. 77. I.D., Ia Nr.273/44 g.K., Anl. Gliederung 77. I.D. (25th wave), Stand: 1.6.44, p.2 [T314 R1568 F949]
219. 77. I.D., Ia Nr.273/44 g.K., Anl. Gliederung 77. I.D. (25th wave), Stand: 1.6.44, p.1 [T314 R1568 F948]
220. C.S.D.I.C. (UK) S.IR 445, 2 Jul 44,p.3 [NARA, RG 165, Box 659, Folder 2]
221. PWIS(H)/LF/191, 28.6.44, p.2 [UKNA, WO 208/3630]
222. 77. I.D., Ia Nr.273/44 g.K., Anl. Gliederung 77. I.D. (25th wave), Stand: 1.6.44, p.1 [T314 R1568 F948]; AOK 7, Kriegsgliederung 7. Armee, Stand 18.5.44, 77. I.D., Stand 1.5.1944 [T312 R1566 F223]
223. 77. I.D., Ia Nr.273/44 g.K., Anl. Gliederung 77. I.D. (25th wave), Stand: 1.6.44, p.1 [T314 R1568 F948]
224. PWIS(H)/LDC/132, 18.7.44, p.2 [UKNA, WO 208/3646]
225. C.S.D.I.C. (UK) S.IR 445, 2 Jul 44,p.4 [NARA, RG 165, Box 659, Folder 2]
226. 77. I.D., Ia Nr.273/44 g.K., Anl. Gliederung 77. I.D. (25th wave), Stand: 1.6.44, p.1 [T314 R1568 F948]
227. AOK 7, Kriegsgliederung 7. Armee, Stand 18.5.44, 77. I.D., Stand 1.5.1944 [T312 R1566 F223]; 77. I.D., Ia Nr.273/44 g.K., Anl. Gliederung 77. I.D. (25th wave), Stand: 1.6.44, p.1 [T314 R1568 F948]

228. C.S.D.I.C. (UK) S.IR 445, 2 Jul 44,p.4 [NARA, RG 165, Box 659, Folder 2]; PWIS(H)/LDC/132, 18.7.44, p.2 [UKNA, WO 208/3646]
229. AOK 7, Kriegsgliederung 7. Armee, Stand 18.5.44, 77. I.D., Stand 1.5.1944 [T312 R1566 F223]
230. C.S.D.I.C. (UK) S.IR 445, 2 Jul 44,p.4 [NARA, RG 165, Box 659, Folder 2]; PWIS(H)/LDC/132, 18.7.44, p.2 [UKNA, WO 208/3646]
231. C.S.D.I.C. (UK) S.IR 445, 2 Jul 44,p.4 [NARA, RG 165, Box 659, Folder 2]
232. 77. I.D., Ia Nr.273/44 g.K., Anl. Gliederung 77. I.D. (25th wave), Stand: 1.6.44, p.1 [T314 R1568 F948]
233. C.S.D.I.C. (UK) S.IR 445, 2 Jul 44,p.5 [NARA, RG 165, Box 659, Folder 2]
234. PWIS(H)/LDC/132, 18.7.44, p.1 [UKNA, WO 208/3646]
235. 77. I.D., Ia Nr.273/44 g.K., Anl. Gliederung 77. I.D. (25th wave), Stand: 1.6.44, p.1 [T314 R1568 F948]
236. PWIS(H)/LDC/132, 18.7.44, p.1 [UKNA, WO 208/3646]; PWIS(H)/LDC/145, 18 Jul 44, p.2 [UKNA, WO 208/3646]
237. PWIS(H)/LF/173, 23 Jun 44 [UKNA, WO 208/3630]; C.S.D.I.C. (UK) S.IR 445, 2 Jul 44,p.4 [NARA, RG 165, Box 659, Folder 2]
238. PWIS(H)/LDC/132, 18.7.44, p.1 [UKNA, WO 208/3646]; PWIS(H)/LF/173, 23 Jun 44 [UKNA, WO 208/3630]; PWIS(H)/LDC/145, 18 Jul 44, p.2 [UKNA, WO 208/3646]
239. PWIS(H)/LDC/132, 18.7.44, p.2 [UKNA, WO 208/3646]
240. C.S.D.I.C. (UK) S.IR 445, 2 Jul 44,p.5 [NARA, RG 165, Box 659, Folder 2]
241. PWIS(H)/LDC/132, 18.7.44, p.1 [UKNA, WO 208/3646]; PWIS(H)/LDC/145, 18 Jul 44, p.2 [UKNA, WO 208/3646]; C.S.D.I.C. (UK) S.IR 445, 2 Jul 44,p.4 [NARA, RG 165, Box 659, Folder 2]
242. PWIS(H)/LDC/145, 18 Jul 44, p.2 [UKNA, WO 208/3646]; PWIS(H)/LDC/132, 18.7.44, p.1 [UKNA, WO 208/3646]
243. C.S.D.I.C. (UK) S.IR 445, 2 Jul 44, p.5 [NARA, RG 165, Box 659, Folder 2]
244. PWIS(H)/LF/173, 23 Jun 44 [UKNA, WO 208/3630]
245. PWIS(H)/LDC/30, 27 Jun 44 [UKNA, WO 208/3645]
246. C.S.D.I.C. (U.K.) S.I.R. 445, 2 Jul 44,p.6 [NARA, RG 165, Box 659, Folder 2]
247. FID-DZ No.182, 8 July 44 [NARA, RG 498, Box 1326]
248. C.S.D.I.C. (UK) S.IR 445, 2 Jul 44,p.6 [NARA, RG 165, Box 659, Folder 2]
249. PWIS(H)/LF/190, 28 Jun 44 [UKNA, WO 208/3630]; **Wilbrand (1944)**, appendix: Kriegsgliederung der 77. I.D.
250. PWIS(H)/LF/190, 28 Jun 44 [UKNA, WO 208/3630]
251. 77. I.D., Ia Nr.273/44 g.K., Anl. Gliederung 77. I.D. (25th wave), Stand: 1.6.44, p.1 [T314 R1568 F948] Men from the division confirm that there were eight of these guns in total. C.S.D.I.C. (UK) S.IR 445, 2 Jul 44,p.10 in NARA, RG 165, Box 659, Folder 2]
252. OKH Chef H Rüst und BdE, AHA Ia(I) Nr.510/44 g.K., 21.1.44, p.5 [T78 R848 H36/153]; AOK 7, Ia Nr.755/44 g.K., 9.2.44, p.1 [T312 R1565 F73]
253. AOK 7, Ia Nr.2454/44 g.K., 13.5.44, p.2 [T312 R1565 F696]; 77. I.D., Ia Nr.273/44 g.K., Anl. Gliederung 77. I.D. (25th wave), Stand: 1.6.44 [T314 R1568 F948-9]
254. PWIS(H)/LDC/40, 28 Jun 44 [UKNA, WO 208/3645] If correct, the Russian heavy piece was most likely a 12,2 cm le.F.H. 388(r).
255. PWIS(H)/LDC/145, 18 Jul 44, p.2 [UKNA, WO 208/3646]

This officer claims they were German 7.5 and 15 cm guns. Since the Kriegsgliederung of 1 June lists all guns as Russian, his identification of the guns is not considered credible.
256. PWIS(H)/LDC/132, 18 Jul 44, p.1 [UKNA, WO 208/3646]
257. C.S.D.I.C. (UK) S.IR 445, 2 Jul 44, p.5 [NARA, RG 165, Box 659, Folder 2]
258. 77. I.D., Ia Nr.273/44 g.K., Anl. Gliederung 77. I.D. (25th wave), Stand: 1.6.44, p.1 [T314 R1568 F948]
259. AOK 7, Kriegsgliederung 7. Armee, Stand 14.2.44, 77. I.D. (In Neuaufstellung), Stand 18.2.1944 [T312 R1566 F124]; AOK 7, Kriegsgliederung 7. Armee, Stand 12.3.44, Kampfgr. 77. I.D., Stand 18.2.1944 [T312 R1566 F161] On 18 February, the division already had six 7.5 cm heavy AT guns, which can only realistically refer to the Pak 40, as no Pak 41's have been found in Normandy.
260. C.S.D.I.C. (UK) S.IR 445, 2 Jul 44, p.5 [NARA, RG 165, Box 659, Folder 2]; K.St.N. (Heer) Nr.188f n, Infanteriepanzerjägerzug (zu 3 Geschützen 7.5cm Pak (mot) (n.A.), 1.12.43 [CAMO, Bestand 500, Findbuch 12451, Akte 142]
261. Kuhle in C.S.D.I.C. (UK) S. R. Report, S.R.M. 596, p.5 [UKNA, WO 208/4138] — Hereafter referred to as: **Kuhle**, S.R.M.596. Kettenkräder are mentioned together with three AT guns that supported the III./1050 during the fighting. The origin of the AT guns is not clear. They may have belonged to a different division.
262. PWIS(H)/LF/190, 28 Jun 44, p.1 [UKNA, WO 208/3630]
263. PWIS(H)/LDC/40, 28 Jun 44, p.1 [UKNA, WO 208/3645]
264. AOK 7, Kriegsgliederung 7. Armee, Stand 14.2.44, 77. I.D. (In Neuaufstellung), Stand 18.2.1944 [T312 R1566 F124]
265. AOK 7, Kriegsgliederung 7. Armee, Stand 12.3.44, 77. I.D. (In Neuaufstellung), Stand 18.2.1944 [T312 R1566 F160]
266. AOK 7, Kriegsgliederung 7. Armee, Stand 18.5.44, 77. I.D., Stand 1.5.1944 [T312 R1566 F223]
267. C.S.D.I.C. (UK) S.IR 445, 2 Jul 44, p.5 [NARA, RG 165, Box 659, Folder 2]
268. PWIS(H)/LDC/40, 28 Jun 44, p.1 [UKNA, WO 208/3645]
269. 77. I.D., Ia Nr.273/44 g.K., Anl. Gliederung 77. I.D. (25th wave), Stand: 1.6.44, p.1 [T314 R1568 F948]
270. PWIS(H)/LDC/40, 28 Jun 44, p.1 [UKNA, WO 208/3645]
271. PWIS(H)/LDC/132, 18 Jul 44, p.1 [UKNA, WO 208/3646]
272. C.S.D.I.C. (UK) S.IR 445, 2 Jul 44,p.3-4 [NARA, RG 165, Box 659, Folder 2] These claims raise the question of what was meant by "light" and "heavy" platoons. Is any platoon with AT guns a heavy platoon? Is a "light" platoon one armed with Ofenrohre?
273. OKH/GenStdH/Org.Abt. Nr.I/15461/44 g.K., 25.3.44 [T78 R398 H1/39]; OKH/GenStdH/Org/Abt/ Nr.I/15461/44 g.K. II.Ang., 30.3.44 [T78 R398 H1/39]
274. It was actually listed under the heading "Panz.Jäg.Abt. 177", but no battalion staff was listed.
275. AOK 7, Kriegsgliederung 7. Armee, Stand 14.2.44, 77. I.D. (In Neuaufstellung), Stand 18.2.1944 [T312 R1566 F124]; AOK 7 Ia, KTB 1.1.-30.6.1944 [T312 R1564 F207]; AOK 7, Kriegsgliederung 7. Armee, Stand 12.3.44, 77. I.D. (In Neuaufstellung), Stand 18.2.1944 [T312 R1566 F160]
276. AOK 7 Ia, KTB 1.1.-30.6.1944 [T312 R1564 F187]
277. OKH/GenStdH/Op/Org.Abt./Nr.I/1595/44 g., 21.2.44 [BaMa, RH 10/20]
278. C.S.D.I.C. (UK) S.IR 445, 2 Jul 44,p.7 [NARA, RG 165, Box 659,

279. *AOK 7/O.Qu., Kriegstagebuch der Oberquartiermeisterabteilung AOK 7 für die Zeit vom 1.6.44 - 30.6.44* [T312 R1571 F502]
280. *Ibid.* [T312 R1571 F576]
281. *Ibid.* [T312 R1571 F527]
282. The document speaks of *"Neuaufstellung"*, which can refer to both an initial formation or a complete reconstitution of an existing formation. In this case, the former seems more likely.
283. See chapter *"91. Luftlande-Infanterie-Division"*
284. *77. I.D., Ia Nr.273/44 g.K., Anl. Gliederung 77. I.D. (25th wave), Stand: 1.6.44*, p.1 [T314 R1568 F948]
285. *AOK 7/O.Qu., Kriegstagebuch der Oberquartiermeisterabteilung AOK 7 für die Zeit vom 1.4.44 - 30.4.44* [T312 R1571 F19-20]
286. *77. I.D., Ia Nr.273/44 g.K., Anl. Gliederung 77. I.D. (25th wave), Stand: 1.6.44*, p.1 [T314 R1568 F948]
287. C.S.D.I.C. (UK) S.*IR* 445, 2 Jul 44,p.3 [NARA, RG 165, Box 659, Folder 2]
288. *OKH/AHA/Abwicklungsstab, Anl. z. Sachgeb. 91 Nr.6.44 g., Kampfgruppe 91. I.D. Stand vom 17.7.* [T78 R672 H41/61b] — Hereafter refered to as *91. I.D., Kriegsgliederung KG 91. I.D., 17.7.44* [T78 R672 H41/61b]
289. *OKH/AHA/Abwicklungsstab, Anl. z. Sachgeb. 91 Nr.6.44 g., Kampfgruppe 91. I.D., Stand vom 20.7.* [T78 R672 H41/61b] — Hereafter refered to as *91. I.D., Kriegsgliederung KG 91. I.D., 20.7.44* [T78 R672 H41/61b]; *OKH/AHA/Abwicklungsstab, Anl. z. Sachgeb. 91 Nr.6.44 g., Kampfgruppe 91. I.D., Stand vom 26.7.* [T78 R672 H41/61b] — Hereafter referred to as: *91. I.D., Kriegsgliederung KG 91. I.D., 26.7.44* [T78 R672 H41/61b]
290. PWIS(H)/LF/188, 28 June 1944 [UKNA, WO 208/3630]
291. *AOK 7, Ia Nr.1649/44 g., 11.3.44* [T312 R1565 F253]
292. Feldpostübersicht
293. *AOK 7/O.Qu., Kriegstagebuch der Oberquartiermeisterabteilung AOK 7 für die Zeit vom 1.3.44 - 31.3.44* [T312 R1570 F1013]; *AOK 7/O.Qu., Kriegstagebuch der Oberquartiermeisterabteilung AOK 7 für die Zeit vom 1.4.44 - 30.4.44* [T312 R1571 F9]
294. *77. I.D., Ia Nr.273/44 g.K., Anl. Gliederung 77. I.D. (25th wave), Stand: 1.6.44*, p.1 [T314 R1568 F948]
295. PWIS(H)/LF/188, 28 June 1944, p.1 [UKNA, WO 208/3630]
296. *Ibid.*; C.S.D.I.C. (UK) S.*IR* 545, 11 July 1944, p.1-2 [NARA, RG 165, Box 659, Folder 2]; C.S.D.I.C. (UK) S.*IR* 445, 2 July 1944,p.7 [NARA, RG 165, Box 659, Folder 2]
297. PWIS(H)/LF/188, 28 June 1944, p.1 [UKNA, WO 208/3630]
298. *AOK 7, Kriegsgliederung 7. Armee, Stand 18.5.44, 77. I.D., Stand 1.5.1944* [T312 R1566 F223]
299. *77. I.D., Ia Nr.273/44 g.K., Anl. Gliederung 77. I.D. (25th wave), Stand: 1.6.44*, p.1 [T314 R1568 F948]
300. Zetterling, N. (2000), *Normandy 1944, German Military Organisation, Combat Power and Organisational Effectiveness*, Winnipeg: J.J.Fedorowicz Publishing, p.230
301. *AOK 7, Kriegsgliederung 7. Armee, Stand 18.5.44, 77. I.D., Stand 1.5.1944* [T312 R1566 F223]
302. *OKH, Chef H Rüst und BdE, AHA/Stab I(1)/I(3) Nr.2987/44 g.K., 4.5.44, incl. Anl.* [T78 R763 H19/56]

303. PWIS(H)/LDC/101, 11 Jul 44 [UKNA, WO 208/3646]
304. *77. I.D., Ia Nr.273/44 g.K., Anl. Gliederung 77. I.D. (25th wave), Stand: 1.6.44*, p.1 [T314 R1568 F948]
305. PWIS(H)/LDC/102, 11 Jul 44 [UKNA, WO 208/3646]
306. *77. I.D., Ia Nr.273/44 g.K., Anl. Gliederung 77. I.D. (25th wave), Stand: 1.6.44*, p.1 [T314 R1568 F948]
307. PWIS(H)/LF/176, 24 Jun 44, p.1 [UKNA, WO 208/3630]
308. *AOK 7, Kriegsgliederung 7. Armee, Stand 9.2.44, 77. I.D. (In Neuaufstellung), Stand 3.2.1944* [T312 R1566 F88]
309. *AOK 7, Ia Nr.755/44 g.K., 9.2.44, Anl.3*, p.2 [T312 R1565 F83]; Tessin, G. (1973), 17.Band, p.192; Feldpostübersicht
310. *AOK 7, Kriegsgliederung 7. Armee, Stand 14.2.44, 77. I.D., Stand 18.2.1944* [T312 R1566 F124]
311. *AOK 7/O.Qu., Kriegstagebuch der Oberquartiermeisterabteilung AOK 7 für die Zeit vom 1.3.44 - 31.3.44* [T312 R1570 F1013]
312. *AOK 7, Kriegsgliederung 7. Armee, Stand 10.4.44, 77. I.D. (In Neuaufstellung), Stand: 1.3.44* [T312 R1566 F198]
313. *77. I.D., Ia Nr.273/44 g.K., Anl. Gliederung 77. I.D. (25th wave), Stand: 1.6.44*, p.1 [T314 R1568 F948]
314. PWIS(H)/LDC/101, 11 Jul 44 [UKNA, WO 208/3646]; C.S.D.I.C. (UK) S.*IR* 445, 2 Jul 44,p.7 [NARA, RG 165, Box 659, Folder 2]
315. *AOK 7, Kriegsgliederung 7. Armee, Stand 10.4.44, 77. I.D. (In Neuaufstellung), Stand: 1.3.44* [T312 R1566 F198]
316. PWIS(H)/KP/46, 22 Jun 44 [UKNA, WO 208/3623]; PWIS(H)/LF/176, 24 Jun 44, p.1 [UKNA, WO 208/3630]; *OKH/Chef H Rüst u. BdE, AHA Stab I(1) Nr.140747, 29.3.44* [UKNA, HW 5/468, CX/MSS/T156/110, KV 1214] The timespan that the battalion used the name Baumann is not clear. An *Oberleutnant* Baumann was linked to the battalion on 20 April, but he was serving with a different division at the time. [CX/MSS/T168/57, KV 2373 in UKNA, HW 5/474]
317. *OKH/Chef H Rüst u. BdE, AHA Stab I(1) Nr.140747, 29.3.44* [UKNA, HW 5/468, CX/MSS/T156/110, KV 1214]
318. *AOK 7, Kriegsgliederung 7. Armee, Stand 18.5.44, 77. I.D., Stand 1.5.1944* [T312 R1566 F223]
319. *77. I.D., Ia Nr.273/44 g.K., Anl. Gliederung 77. I.D. (25th wave), Stand: 1.6.44*, p.1 [T314 R1568 F948]
320. *AOK 7, Kriegsgliederung 7. Armee, Stand 18.5.44, 77. I.D., Stand 1.5.1944* [T312 R1566 F223]; *Sonderstab Oehmichen z.Zt. AOK 7, Ia/Stopak Nr.67/44 g.K., 13.5.44*, p.12 [T312 R1568 F694]; PWIS(H)/LF/176, 24 Jun 44, p.1 [UKNA, WO 208/3630]
321. PWIS(H)/LF/176, 24 Jun 44, p.1 [UKNA, WO 208/3630]; *Sonderstab Oehmichen z.Zt. AOK 7, Ia/Stopak Nr.67/44 g.K., 13.5.44*, p.12 [T312 R1568 F694]
322. PWIS(H)LDC/33, 28 Jun 44, p.1-2 [UKNA, WO 208/3645]
323. PWIS(H)/KP/46, 22 Jun 44 [UKNA, WO 208/3623]
324. PWIS(H)/LF/176, 24 Jun 44, p.1 [UKNA, WO 208/3630]; PWIS(H)/KP/46, 22 Jun 44 [UKNA, WO 208/3623]
325. PWIS(H)LDC/33, 28 Jun 44, p.2 [UKNA, WO 208/3645]
326. Poppe, W. (1954), MS # P-168, *Einsatz der 77. Infanterie-Division in Nordfrankreich vom 1.2. - 15.8.1944*, p.4
327. *Inv.-Gespräch Ia / Chef d.G. LXXIV. A.K., 25.4.44* [T312 R1565 F540]
328. *Sonderstab Oehmichen z.Zt. AOK 7, Ia/Stopak Nr.67/44*

g.K., 13.5.44, p.12 [T312 R1568 F694]
329. *AOK 7, Kriegsgliederung 7. Armee, Stand 18.5.44, 77. I.D., Stand 1.5.1944* [T312 R1566 F223]; **Block, M.**, message posted on 4.8.2005 at www.network54.com/Forum/47207/thread/1123152772/ (accessed 13.1.2017 [possibly based on records from BaMa RH 19 IV/39]
330. C.S.D.I.C. (UK) S.*IR* 445, 2 Jul 44,p.7 [NARA, RG 165, Box 659, Folder 2]; PWIS(H)/LF/176, 24 Jun 44, p.1 [UKNA, WO 208/3630]
331. *OKH/GenStdH/Org.Abt. Nr.I/5895.44 g., 5.6.4* [T78 R526 F207]
332. *AOK 7, Kriegsgliederung 7. Armee, Stand 18.5.44, 77. I.D., Stand 1.5.1944* [T312 R1566 F223]
333. *77. I.D., Ia Nr.273/44 g.K., Anl. Gliederung 77. I.D. (25th wave), Stand: 1.6.44*, p.1 [T314 R1568 F948]
334. PWIS(H)/LDC/38, 28 Jun 44, p.2 [UKNA, WO 208/3645]
335. PWIS(H)/LF/193, 28 Jun 44, p.1 [UKNA, WO 208/3630]
336. *Ibid.*
337. PWIS(H)/LDC/38, 28 Jun 44, p.2 [UKNA, WO 208/3645]; PWIS(H)/LF/193, 28 Jun 44, p.1 [UKNA, WO 208/3630] The interrogation reports mention "s.T. bombs". This presumably stands for "sticky bombs", which matches the magnetic *Hafthohlladungen*.
338. *77. I.D., Ia Nr.273/44 g.K., Anl. Gliederung 77. I.D. (25th wave), Stand: 1.6.44*, p.1 [T314 R1568 F948]
339. PWIS(H)/LDC/38, 28 Jun 44, p.1 [UKNA, WO 208/3645]; PWIS(H)/LF/193, 28 Jun 44, p.2 [UKNA, WO 208/3630]
340. PWIS(H)/LDC/38, 28 Jun 44, p.1 [UKNA, WO 208/3645]
341. C.S.D.I.C. (UK) S.*IR* 524, 7 Jul 44, p.1-2 [NARA, RG 165, Box 659, Folder2]
342. *LXXIV. A.K. Ia, Ia-Tagesmeldung, 16.5.44* [T314 R1568 F603-4]
343. *Gen.Kdo.LXXIV. A.K. Ia, no number, 18.6.44* [T314 R1568 F919]
344. *AOK 7, Ia Nr.2203/44, 15.4.44*, p.4 [T312 R1565 F489]
345. *Anlage zu Okdo.d.H.Gr. B, Ia Nr.10076/44 g.K., 20.11.44* [T78 R410 F6378764]
346. *OKH/GenStdH/Org.Abt. Nr.I/17239/44 g.K., 25.5.44* [T78 R526 F160]
347. *77. I.D., Ia Nr.273/44 g.K., Anl. Gliederung 77. I.D. (25th wave), Stand: 1.6.44*, p.1 [T314 R1568 F948]; C.S.D.I.C. (UK) S.*IR* 445, 2 Jul 44,p.8 [NARA, RG 165, Box 659, Folder 2]
348. *77. I.D., Ia Nr.273/44 g.K., Anl. Gliederung 77. I.D. (25th wave), Stand: 1.6.44*, p.1 [T314 R1568 F948]
349. C.S.D.I.C. (UK) S.*IR* 445, 2 Jul 44, p.8 [NARA, RG 165, Box 659, Folder 2]; Feldpostübersicht
350. C.S.D.I.C. (UK) S.*IR* 445, 2 Jul 44, p.8-9 [NARA, RG 165, Box 659, Folder 2]; *Feldpostübersicht*
351. C.S.D.I.C. (UK) S.*IR* 445, 2 Jul 44, p.8-9 [NARA, RG 165, Box 659, Folder 2]
352. *OKH/GenStdH/Org.Abt. Nr.I/7281/44 g., 30.7.44* [T78 R526 F447]
353. FID-DZ No.333, 28 July 44 [NARA, RG 498, Box 1326]
354. PWIS(H)/LF/172, 23 Jun 44, p.1 [UKNA, WO 208/3630]; C.S.D.I.C. (UK) S.*IR* 429, 26 Jun 44, p.1 [NARA, RG 162, Box 659, Folder 2]
355. *77. I.D., Ia Nr.273/44 g.K., Anl. Gliederung 77. I.D. (25th wave), Stand: 1.6.44*, p.1 [T314 R1568 F948]

356. PWIS(H)/LF/172, 23 Jun 44, p.1 [UKNA, WO 208/3630]; C.S.D.I.C. (UK) S.*IR* 429, 26 Jun 44, p.1 [NARA, RG 162, Box 659, Folder 2]
357. PWIS(H)/LF/176, 24 Jun 44, p.2 [UKNA, WO 208/3630]
358. *77. I.D.*, Ia Nr.273/44 g.K., 2.6.44, p.1 [T314 R1568 F946]
359. *AOK 7/O.Qu.*, *Besprechunspunkte O.Qu. bei O.Qu.West*, 12.5.44, p.2 [T312 R1571 F390]
360. *AOK 7/O.Qu.*, *Kriegstagebuch der Oberquartiermeisterabteilung AOK 7 für die Zeit vom 1.4.44 - 30.4.44* [T312 R1571 F27]
361. *77. I.D.*, Ia Nr.273/44 g.K., p.1 [T314 R1568 F946]
362. Ibid., 2.6.44, p.1-2 [T314 R1568 F946-7]
363. Anl. zu *AOK 7*, Ia Nr.3000/44 g.K. v. 4.4.44, *Übersicht über Bewegl. Truppenteile bei eingesetzten oder in Reserve befindlichen Div.* [T312 R1565 F428]
364. *AOK 7*, Kriegsgliederung *7. Armee*, Stand 18.5.44, *77. I.D.*, Stand 1.5.1944 [T312 R1566 F223]; **Kuhle**, S.R.M.596
365. *AOK 7*, Kriegsgliederung *7. Armee*, Stand 18.5.44, *Kampfgr. 77. I.D.*, Stand: 1.4.44 [T312 R1566 F224] The date of the Kriegsgliederung is 1 April 1944, but it was part of the overview of 18 May. This suggests no new information had been received or that there had been no changes. Still, it might have been outdated on D-Day.
366. **Tessin, G. (1972)**, *6.Band*, p.36; **Tessin, G. (1976)**, *13.Band*, p.227
367. C.S.D.I.C. (UK) S.*IR* 445, 2 Jul 44,p.2 [NARA, RG 165, Box 659, Folder 2]
368. *AOK 7*, Ia Nr.540/44 g.K., 3.2.44 [T312 R1565 F28]; **Tessin, G. (1974)**, *9.Band*, p.304; W.Kr.Kdo.Gen.Gouv. Abt.Ia Nr.827/44 g., 23.1.44 [T501 R218 F517]; Oberfeldkommandantur 603 Abt.Ia, *Monatsbericht für die Zeit vom 16.1. - 15.2.1944*, 19.2.44. [T501 R218 F306]; C.S.D.I.C. (UK) S.*IR* 445, 2 Jul 44, p.2 [NARA, RG 165, Box 659, Folder 2]; PWIS(H)/LF/191, 28 Jun 44, p.1 [UKNA, WO 208/3630]
369. Oberfeldkommandantur 603 Abt.Ia, *Monatsbericht für die Zeit vom 16.1. - 15.2.1944*, 19.2.44. [T501 R218 F306]; PWIS(H)/LF/191, 28 Jun 44, p.1 [UKNA, WO 208/3632]; C.S.D.I.C. (UK) S.*IR* 445, 2 Jul 44,p.2 [NARA, RG 165, Box 659, Folder 2]; **Poppe, W. (1954)**, p.1
370. Tessin, G. (1973), *7.Band*, p.124; **Tessin, G. (1974)**, *9.Band*, p.271; W.Kr.Kdo.Gen.Gouv. Abt.Ia Nr.827/44 g. 23.1.44 [T501 R218 F517]; Oberfeldkdtr. 603 Abt.Ia, *Monatsbericht für die Zeit vom 16.1. 15.2.1944*, 19.2.44. [T501 R218 F306]; PWIS(H)/LF/191, 28 Jun 44, p.1 [UKNA, WO 208/3630]
371. Kartei von Inf.-Kommandeuren, index card of Gen.Lt. Poppe [T78 R908 H6/354]; *AOK 7*, Ia Nr.881/44 g., 11.2.44, p.1 [T312 R1565 F89]
372. Leichtfuss, C.S.D.I.C. (UK) S. R. Report, S.R.M.602, p.2 [UKNA, WO 208/4138] — Hereafter referred to as **Leichtfuss**, S.R.M.602. The general's shortcomings are also reflected in the performance reviews by his superiors. He was deemed suitable for raising and training a division in rear areas but not to lead a division under difficult conditions.
373. Kartei von Inf.-Kommandeuren, index cards of *Gen.Lt.* Ortner [T78 R908 H6/354]; German general staff officers files, index cards of *Gen.Lt.* Ortner [T78 R891 H6/26]; German general staff officers files, index cards of *Gen.Lt.* Stegmann [T78 R893 H6/26]
374. AOK 7 BvTO, *Tatigkeitsbericht für die Zeit vom 1.Januar bis 31. März 1944*, p.1 [T312 R1571 F877]
375. *AOK 7* Ia, *KTB* 1.1.-30.6.1944, period 5-12 Febr 44 [T312 R1564 F188 F183, 187-189]
376. *AOK 7*, Ia Nr.382/44 g., 19.1.44 [T312 R1564 F474]
377. *AOK 7*, Ia Nr.433/44 g., 21.1.44, p.1 [T312 R1564 F482]
378. *AOK 7*, Ia Nr.759/44 g., 5.2.44 [T312 R1565 F38]
379. *AOK 7*, Ia Nr.832/44 g., 8.2.44 [T312 R1565 F63]
380. *AOK 7*, Ia Nr.861/44 g., 10.2.44 [T312 R1565 F87]
381. *AOK 7* Ia Nr.904/44 g., 12.2.44 [T312 R1565 F102]
382. *AOK 7*, Ia Nr.1288/44 g., 27.2.44, p.1 [T312 R1565 F180]
383. *AOK 7*, Ia Nr.1406/44 g.K., 2.3.44 [T312 R1565 F204]
384. *AOK 7*, Ia Nr.1517/44 g., 7.3.44 [T312 R1565 F221]
385. *AOK 7*, Ia Nr.222/44 g., 10.4.44 [T312 R1565 F458]
386. *AOK 7* Ia, Anlage zum K.T.B. Führungsabt. *AOK 7* Ia, Lage-Karten *AOK 7* vom 6.1.-5.6.44, *Stand: 8.4.44* [T312 R1570 F5]; **Poppe, W. (1954)**, Skizze 1
387. Ibid.
388. Ibid.
389. Ibid.; *AOK 7* Ia Nr.881/44 g., 11.2.44, p.1 [T312 R1565 F89]
390. *AOK 7*, Ia Nr.2063/44 g.K., 3.4.44 [T312 R1565 F414-5]; *AOK 7*, Ia Nr.2252/44 g.K., 23.4.44, p.1-2 [T312 R1565 F529-30]; *AOK 7*, Ia Nr.2243/44 g.K., 23.4.44, p.1-2 [T312 R1565 F531-2]
391. *AOK 7* BvTO, Anl.15 zum Tätigkeitsbericht BvTO *AOK 7*, *Zusammenstellung der in der Zeit vom 1.4. - 30.6.44 im Armeebereich durchgeführten Bewegungen.*, p.1 [T312 R1571 F982]
392. *AOK 7*, Ia Nr.2252/44 g.K., 23.4.44, p.1-2 [T312 R1565 F529-30]
393. *AOK 7*, Ia Nr.610/44 g., 6.5.44 [T312 R1565 F628]
394. See C.S.D.I.C. (UK) S.*IR* 545 [NARA, RG 165, Box 659, Folder 2]; *AOK 7* Ia, Anlage zum K.T.B. Führungsabt. *AOK 7* Ia, Lage-Karten *AOK 7* vom 6.1.-5.6.44, *Stand: 22.5.44 & Stand: 5.6.44* [T312 R1570 F7-10]
395. *AOK 7* Ia, *KTB* 1.1.-30.6.1944 [T312 R1564 F240-1]; *AOK 7* Ia, Anlage zum K.T.B. Führungsabt. *AOK 7* Ia, Lage-Karten A.O.K.7 vom 6.1.-5.6.44, *Stand: 5.6.44* [T312 R1570 F9-10, original in BaMa RH 20-7/138K] — Hereafter referred to as *AOK 7*, Situation map, 5.6.44; Gen.Kdo.*LXXIV. A.K.* Ia Nr.1049/44 g., 9.6.44 [T314 R1568 F892]
396. *AOK 7*, Ia Nr.798/44 g., 17.5.44 [T312 R1565 F714]
397. *AOK 7*, Ia Nr.988/44 g., 27.5.44 [T312 R1565 F777]; *AOK 7*, Ia Nr.586/44 g., 4.5.44, p.1 [T312 R1565 F619]
398. C.S.D.I.C. (UK) S.*IR* 545, 11 Jul 44, p.6 [NARA, RG 165, Box 659, Folder 2]; *AOK 7*, Ia Nr.714/44 g., 12.5.44 p.2 [T312 R1565 F690]
399. C.S.D.I.C. (UK) S.*IR* 545, 11 Jul 44, p.6 [NARA, RG 165, Box 659, Folder 2]
400. *AOK 7*, Ia Nr.714/44 g., 12.5.44 p.2 [T312 R1565 F690; C.S.D.I.C. (UK) S.*IR* 545, 11 Jul 44, p.6 [NARA, RG 165, Box 659, Folder 2]; PWIS(H)/LF/188, 28 Jun 44, p.1 [UKNA, WO 208/3630]
401. C.S.D.I.C. (UK) S.*IR* 545, 11 Jul 44, p.6 [NARA, RG 165, Box 659, Folder 2]
402. Ibid., p.1; *AOK 7* Ia, *KTB* 1.1.-30.6.1944 [T312 R1564 F241]

403. The "Po" is a geographical reference to Coastal Defence Group Pontrieux.
404. C.S.D.I.C. (UK) S.*IR* 433, 27 Jun 44 [NARA, RG 162, Box 659, Folder 2]
405. C.S.D.I.C. (UK) S.*IR* 545, 11 Jul 44, p.1 [NARA, RG 165, Box 659, Folder 2]
406. C.S.D.I.C. (UK) S.*IR* 561, 4 Jul 44 [NARA, RG 165, Box 659, Folder 2]
407. C.S.D.I.C. (UK) S.*IR* 545, 11 Jul 44, p.1 [NARA, RG 165, Box 659, Folder 2]
408. Referred to officially as the *15 cm sFH 13/1 (Sf.) auf Geschützwagen Lorraine Schlepper(f)*
409. LXXIV. A.K., Ia-Tagesmeldung, 31.5.44 [T314 R1568 F613]
410. C.S.D.I.C. (UK) S.*IR* 545, 11 Jul 44, p.1 [NARA, RG 165, Box 659, Folder 2]; Gen.Kdo.*LXXIV. A.K.*, Ia Nr.967/44 g.K., 12.6.44, p.1 [T314 R1568 F897]
411. C.S.D.I.C. (UK) S.*IR* 445, 2 Jul 44,p.7 [NARA, RG 165, Box 659, Folder 2]
412. Rolf, R. (2014), *Atlantikwall - Batteries and Bunkers*, Middelburg: PRAK publishing, p.422-3; Anl.3 zu *AOK 7/A.Pi.Fü.*, map titled *K.V.Abschnitt A.1., K.V.Gr.Lamballe* [T312 R1569 F726-7] The location of the 1st Battery might have been a temporary field position, before it moved to a casemated site. Rolf places the *3./AR 177* at the casemated *La.Wn.376*, about 2 km west of *La.Wn.374*. This is odd, since this battery did not exist. Was this the actual fortified position of the 1st Battery that had been referred to?
413. Essentially, a type of combat engineer battalion, it was entrusted with preparing coastal defences and plans for flooding areas to deny access.
414. C.S.D.I.C. (UK) S.*IR* 545, 11 Jul 44, p.1 [NARA, RG 165, Box 659, Folder 2]
415. Ibid., p.2; *AOK 7*, Ia Nr.6156/43 g., 1.12.43 [T312 R1559 F279]; *AOK 7*, Kriegsgliederung *7. Armee*, Stand 18.5.44, *266.Infanterie-Division*, Stand 1.5.44 [T312 R1566 F225]
416. C.S.D.I.C. (UK) S.*IR* 545, 11 Jul 44, p.2 [NARA, RG 165, Box 659, Folder 2]; *AOK 7*, Ia Nr.872/44 g., 21.5.44 [T312 R1565 F740]
417. Gen.d.Art.b.*Ob.West* Ib Nr.1077/44 g.K., *Divisions-Artillerie: Stand v.1.4.44*, 18.4.44 [CAMO, Bestand 500, Findbuch 12451, Akte 418]
418. C.S.D.I.C. (UK) S.*IR* 545, 11 Jul 44, p.2 [NARA, RG 165, Box 659, Folder 2]; *AOK 7*, Ia Nr.834/44 g., 19.5.44 [T312 R1565 F731]
419. PWIS(H)/LDC/132, 18 Jul 44, p.2-3 [UKNA, WO 208/3646]
420. The "Ra" is a geographical reference to Coastal Defence Group Rance.
421. C.S.D.I.C. (UK) S.*IR* 545, 11 Jul 44, p.3 [NARA, RG 165, Box 659, Folder 2]; *AOK 7*, Ia Nr.988/44 g., 27.5.44 [T312 R1565 F777]; *AOK 7*, Ia Nr.1035/44 g., 30.5.44 [T312 R1565 F800]
422. C.S.D.I.C. (UK) S.*IR* 545, 11 Jul 44, p.2-4 [NARA, RG 165, Box 659, Folder 2]
423. Ibid. p.4
424. *AOK 7*, Ia Nr.6076/43 g., 27.11.43 [T312 R1559 F249]; *AOK 7*, Kriegsgliederung *7. Armee*, Stand 18.5.44, *77. I.D.*, Stand 1.5.1944 [T312 R1566 F223]; BvTO b. *AOK 7*, Anl.15 zum Tätigkeitsbericht BvTO *AOK 7*, *Zusammenstellung der in der Zeit vom 1.4. - 30.6.44 im bearbeiten und durchgeführten grösseren Einzeltransporte.*, p.1

[T312 R1571 F986]

425. *AOK 7, Ia Nr.2538/44 g., 13.5.1941944*, p.2 [T312 R1565 F694]; *AOK 7, Ia Nr.457/44 g., 25.4.44* [T312 R1565 F543]; *AOK 7, Ia Nr.834/44 g., 19.5.44* [T312 R1565 F731]

426. *AOK 7 BvTO, Anl.15 zum Tätigkeitsbericht BvTO AOK 7, Zusammenstellung der in der Zeit vom 1.4. - 30.6.44 im bearbeiten und durchgeführten größeren Einzeltransporte.*, p.2 [T312 R1571 F987]; *AOK 7, Ia Nr.971/44 g., 26.5.44* [T312 R1565 F773]

427. *AOK 7, Ia Nr.988/44 g., 27.5.44* [T312 R1565 F777]

428. C.S.D.I.C. (UK) S.*IR* 545, 11 Jul 44, p.4 [NARA, RG 165, Box 659, Folder 2]

429. Rolf, R. (2014), p.422

430. C.S.D.I.C. (UK) S.*IR* 545, 11 Jul 44, p.4 [NARA, RG 165, Box 659, Folder 2]; *LXXIV. A.K., Ia-Tagesmeldung, 30.5.44* [T314 R1568 F613]; *LXXIV. A.K., Ia-Tagesmeldung, 31.5.44* [T314 R1568 F613]

431. C.S.D.I.C. (UK) S.*IR* 545, 11 Jul 44, p.4-5 [NARA, RG 165, Box 659, Folder 2]; *AOK 7 Ia, KTB 1.1.-30.6.1944* [T312 R1564 F240]

432. C.S.D.I.C. (UK) S.*IR* 545, 11 Jul 44, p.5 [NARA, RG 165, Box 659, Folder 2]; PWIS(H)/LF/190, 28 Jun 44, p.1 [UKNA, WO 208/3630]

433. Gen.Kdo.*LXXIV. A.K.* Ia, *Ia-Tagesmeldung, 16.5.44* [T314 R1568 F603]; **Rolf, R. (2014)**, p.422-3

434. Gen.Kdo.*LXXIV. A.K.* Ia, *Ia-Tagesmeldung, 16.5.44* [T314 R1568 F603-4] "*II./1049*" was possibly at typo for the *III./1049*, which held the *Landfront West*, while the 2nd Battalion was not in the fortress.

435. Okdo.d.*H.Gr. B* Ic Nr.426/44 g.K., 5.5.44 [T314 R1568 F820-3]; Gen.Kdo.*XXV. A.K.* Ia, *Kriegstagebuch Nr.13 Gen.Kdo.XXV. A.K. Führungsabteilung (Ia) 1.4.44 - 5.6.44* [T314 R746 F56]; C.S.D.I.C. (UK) S.*IR* 520, p.1 [NARA, RG 165, Box 659, Folder 2]

436. Anl.1 zu Gen.Kdo.*LXXIV. A.K.* Abt Ia Nr.1488/44, 2.6.44, *Abschlussbericht zur Aktion "Landgraf"* [T314 R1568 F861-5]

437. C.S.D.I.C. (UK) S.*IR* 520, p.1 [NARA, RG 165, Box 659, Folder 2]; Gen.Kdo.*LXXIV. A.K.*, Abt. Ia Nr.709/44 g.K., 8.5.44 [T314 R1568 F817-8]; list of troops selected for *Akton Landgraf*, attached to Obko.d.*H.Gr. B* Ic Nr.426/44 g.K., 5.5.44 [T314 R1568 F823]; Anl.1 zu Gen.Kdo.*LXXIV. A.K.* Abt Ia Nr.1488/44, 2.6.44, *Abschlussbericht zur Aktion "Landgraf"* [T314 R1568 F861-5]

438. *AOK 7, Ia Nr.2750/44 g.K., 31.5.44* [T312 R1565 F806]

439. Anlage zu *AOK 7, Ia Nr.2710/44 g.K.*, p.1, 28.5.44 [T312 R1565 F794]

440. *AOK 7, Ia, KTB 6.6.-25.7.44*, p.15 [T312 R1569 F233]

441. *Ibid.*, p.17 [T312 R1569 F235]

442. *Ibid.*

443. *Ibid.*
AOK 7, Ia Nr.2870/44 g.K., 7.6.44 [T312 R1565 F883]

444. Communication between Ia *LXXIV. A.K.* and Ia *77. I.D.*, 7.6.44 [T314 R1568 F872-3]; Gen.Kdo.*LXXIV. A.K.* Ia, no number, 7.6.44 [T314 R1568 F876];

445. Warning order from Ia *LXXIV. A.K.* to Ia *77. I.D.* at 09:30 on 7.6.44 [T314 R1568 F868]; **Kuhle**, S.R.M.596

446. Kuhle gives the time as 14:00 on 8 June, while official *AOK 7* records state that the first divisional units started moving at 14:00 on 7 June. *AOK 7 Ia, KTB 6.6.-25.7.44*, p.18 [T312 R1569 F236]; **Kuhle**, S.R.M.596.

447. Kuhle, S.R.M.596

448. *AOK 7 Ia, KTB 6.6.-25.7.44*, p.20 [T312 R1569 F238]

449. Gen.Kdo.*LXXIV. A.K.*, Ia Nr.941/44 g.K.,7.6.44; Gen.Kdo.*LXXIV. A.K., Kriegsgliederung des Gen.Kdo.74.A.K.*, Stand: 1.6.44 [T314 R1568 F664]

450. *AOK 7 Ia, KTB 6.6.-25.7.44*, p.22 [T312 R1569 F240]; *AOK 7* order at 11:35 on 8.6.44 [T314 R1568 F879-80]

451. Gen.Kdo.*LXXIV. A.K.* Ia, *Ia-Tagesmeldung, 9.6.44* [T314 R1568 F618]

452. *AOK 7 Ia, KTB 6.6.-25.7.44*, p.23 & 25 [T312 R1569 F241 & 243]; *AOK 7 Ia Nr.2924/44 g.K., 9.6.44* [T312 R1565 F911]

453. *AOK 7 Ia, Ia-Morgenmeldung, Teil 3, 11.6.44*, p.2 [T312 R1565 F956]

454. Kuhle, S.R.M. 596

455. *Ibid.*

456. Brandt, C.S.D.I.C. (UK) S.R. Report, S.R.M.612 [UKNA, WO 208/4138] — Hereafter referred to as **Brandt**, S.R.M.621

457. Gen.Kdo.*LXXIV. A.K*, Ia Nr.1348/44, 9.6.44 [T314 R1568 F618]

458. *AOK 7 Ia, AOK 7 Kriegstagebuch Ia, 6 June 1944-16 August 1944*, p.21 [T312 R1569 F24] — Hereafter referred to as: *AOK 7 Ia, KTB 6.6.-16.8.44*

459. Anl. zu OKH/AHA/Abwicklungsstab, Anl. z. Sachgeb. 91 Nr.6.44 g., *Kriegsgliederung (91. LL.D.), Unterstellungen Stand: 10.6.44* [T78 R672 H41/61b]; **Brandt**, S.R.M.612

460. *AOK 7 Ia, KTB 6.6.-25.7.44*, p.30 [T312 R1569 F248]

461. Wilbrand (1944), p.4; Anl. zu OKH/AHA/Abwicklungsstab, Anl. z. Sachgeb. 91 Nr.6.44 g., *Kriegsgliederung (91. LL.D.), Unterstellungen Stand: 10.6.44* [T78 R672 H41/61b] — Hereafter referred to as *91. I.D., Kriegsgliederung 91. I.D., Unterstellungen, 10.6.44*

462. HQ 90th Infantry Division, *IPW Report # 3*, 14 Jun. 44 [NARA, RG 407, Box 3282, File 207-2.1]

463. HQ 82nd Infantry Division, *Total number of POW captured*, 17 Jun. 44 [NARA, via Egbert van de Schootbrugge]

464. *AOK 7 Ia, KTB 6.6.-16.8.44*, p.21 [T312 R1569 F24] Wilbrand says these arrived on 10 June. This seems quite early, but the first units from the division reportedly reached the area south of Valognes that evening. As an example of mis-dropped airborne troops, much of the 377th PFAB (101st AB) had been misdropped in the Montebourg - Valognes area. See **Bando, M. (2007)**, *101st Airborne - The Screaming Eagles in World War II*, St.Paul, MN: Zenith Press, p.72]

465. Wilbrand (1944), p.5

466. *AOK 7, Ia-Morgenmeldung, Teil 3, 11.6.44*, p.2 [T312 R1565 F956]

467. *AOK 7, Ia Nr.2988/44 g.K., 11.6.44* [T312 R1565 F959

468. *AOK 7 Ia, KTB 6.6.-16.8.44*, p.21 [T312 R1569 F24]

469. Hoffmann (1944), *Bericht über Kampfgruppe v. Schlieben*, p.9-10 [T312 R1566 F368-369]

470. HQ 4th I.D., AG 319.1, *Action Against Enemy, Reports After/ After Action Reports*, 22 Jul. 44, Sec III - Intelligence, p.4-5 [MCoE HQ Donovan Research Library, D328/I2179]; **Wilbrand (1944)**, p.6; **Hoffmann (1944)**, p.9 [T312 R1566 F368]; **Schwellenbach (1944)**, *Erlebnisbericht über Kampfhandlungen des II./GR 729 im Kampfraum Cherbourg (Cotentin-Halbinsel)*, p.4-5 [T78 R672 H41/61a]; **Historical Division, Department of the Armee (1948)**, *Utah Beach to Cherbourg (6 June-27 June 1944)*, United States Army, Washington, D.C., p.94. Wilbrand, the later regimental adjutant, states that the front ran from Montebourg along the highway to Ste. Mère-Église, facing east. At Éroudeville it then turned west, facing south. This description does not appear to be entirely accurate as there is no evidence to support a front on the highway, and Éroudeville actually lies some distance to the west of it.

471. Wilbrand (1944), p.4; **Baret, J. (2014)**, *Une Tombe en Normandie - Vie et Mort du Sergent Adolph Greter*, Valognes: Imprimerie ICL, p.96. The poor Allied intelligence gathering in this sector is indicated by the fact that on 15 June the 8th IR (4th ID) still believed it was facing the *II./729* and the *II./921* in this sector.

472. Hoffmann (1944), p.9 [T312 R1566 F368]; **Wilbrand (1944)**, p.4 & 6-7; **Poppe, W. (1954)**, p.11-12

473. Hoffmann (1944), p.9 [T312 R1566 F368]; **Schwellenbach (1944)**, p.2 & 4; **Stadlhofer (1944)**, *Bericht über den Einsatz der III./AR 243 vom 6.6.1944 bis 25.6.1944*, p.2 [T78 R672 H41/61b]; also see the chapter *"709.Infanterie-Division"*

474. HQ 82nd Airborne Div., Interrogation Report No.6, 11 Jun. 44, p.1-2 ; HQ 505th Infantry Regt., *S-2 Report*, 12 Jun. 44 [both NARA, via Egbert van de Schootbrugge]; also see the chapter *243. Infanterie-Division* for information about KG Simon.

475. 90th Inf.Div., *IPW Summary No.5*, 16 Jun. 44 [NARA, RG 407, Box 3282, File 207-2.1]; 90th Inf.Div., *IPW Summary No.5*, 17 Jun. 44 [NARA, RG 407, Box 3282, File 207-2.1]

476. *77. I.D.*, orders issued by Gen. Stegmann regarding the division's move south, 17.6.44, copied and translated in Annex 1 to G-2 Periodic Report Nr.9, HQ First US Army, 19 June 1944 [Available at https://firstdivisionmuseum.nmtvault.com/jsp/viewer.jsp?doc_id=iwfd0000%2F20141124%2F165&page_name=799 & 800, accessed on 4 Aug. 2018]

477. *AOK 7 Ia, KTB 6.6.-25.7.44*, p.24 [T312 R1569 F242]; Unnamed AOK 7 document, 12.6.44 [T312 R1565 F983]

478. Nordyke, P. (2005), *All American All the Way*, St.Paul, MN: Zenith Press, p.369-372; *AOK 7, Ia Nr.3052/33 g.K., 13.6.44* [T312 R1565 F1002]

479. *AOK 7 Ia, KTB 6.6.-25.7.44*, p.37-38 [T312 R1569 F256-7]; *AOK 7, Ia Nr.3083/44 g.K., 14.6.44* [T312 R1565 F1020-1]

480. *AOK 7 Ia, KTB 6.6.-25.7.44*, p.36 [T312 R1569 F255]

481. *Ibid.*, p.38 [T312 R1569 F257]

482. *Ibid.*, p.40 [T312 R1569 F259]; Kampfgruppe Eitner, *Kampfgruppenbefehl für die Verteidigung im Abschnitt la Rivière - les Moitiers*, 15.6.44. [T78 R672H41/61b]; *AOK 7, Kriegsgliederungen zum KTB der Führungsabteilung AOK 7 ab 6.6.44 bis 30.6.44, Stand: 23.6. 14 Uhr*, 23.6.44 [T312 R1566 F16] – Collection hereafter referred to as: *Kriegsgliederungen z. KTB 6.-29.6.44*

483. OKH/AHA/Abwicklungsstab, Anl. z. Sachgeb. 91 Nr.6.44 g., *Kriegsgliederung Kampfgruppe 91. I.D., Stand: 18.6.44* [T78 R672 H41/61b]

484. *AOK 7, Kriegsgliederungen z. KTB 6.-29.6.44, Stand: 23.6. 14 Uhr*, 23.6.44 [T312 R1566 F16]

485. *AOK 7 (Polo) Ia Nr.2989/44 g.K., 11.6.44.* [T312 R1565 F963]; Gen.Kdo.*LXXIV.A.K*, Ia Nr.1379/44 g., 12.6.44 [T314 R1568 F695];

259

Gen.Kdo.LXXIV.A.K, Ia Nr.967/44 g.K., 12.6.44 [T314 R1568 F697-8]; *AOK 7*, Ia Nr.3167/44 g.K., 17.6.44 [T312 R1565 F1097]
486. Wilbrand (1944), p.6-7
487. Historical Division, Dept. of the Armee (1948), p.94, 102-104, 115; HQ 4th I.D., AG 319.1, *Action Against Enemy, Reports After/After Action Reports*, 22 Jul. 44, Sec IV - Operations [MCoE HQ Donovan Research Library, D328/I2179]; 4th ID, *Montebourg*, p.1-2 [MCoE HQ Donovan Research Library, D328/I2180, The Invasion of France, file titled "Miscellaneous Notes"]
488. 90th Inf.Div., *G-2 Report No.6*, 15 Jun. 44; 90th Inf.Div., *IPW Summary No.5*, 16 Jun. 44; 90th Inf.Div., *G-2 Report No.7*, 16 Jun. 44; 90th Inf.Div., *IPW Summary No.5*, 17 Jun. 44. All of these are in NARA, RG 407, Box 3282, File 207-2.1
489. Leichtfuss, C.S.D.I.C. (UK) S. R. Report, S.R.M. 576 [UKNA, WO 208/4138] — Hereafter referred to as **Leichtfuss**, S.R.M.576
490. *Ibid*.
491. *AOK 7* Ia, *KTB 6.6.-25.7.44*, p.38 [T312 R1569 F257]
492. *AOK 7* Ia Nr.80/44 g.Kdos Chefs., *Weisung an LXXXIV. Korps*, 14.6.44 [T312 R1565 F1026]
493. Maj. i.G. Prinz zu Holstein, *Besprechung zwischen dem Oberbefehlshaber der 7. Armee und dem Komm. General des LXXXIV. A.K. am 14.6.1944 in St. Lô*, 15.6.44, p.2 [T312 R1565 F1028]
494. The date is not clear. Von Criegern puts it on 14 June, but the *AOK 7* war journal first mentions the creation of *Gruppe von Schlieben* on 15 June. This is supported by the corps order of the same date. However, it is also mentioned in a report from a meeting between *Gen.* Dollmann and Fahrmbacher at the corps headquarters on 14 June. This suggests that it may have been discussed before becoming official on the 15th. [Maj.i.G. Prinz zu Holstein, *Besprechung zwischen dem Oberbefehlshaber der 7. Armee und dem Komm. General des LXXXIV. A.K. am 14.6.1944 in St. Lô*, p.2 in T312 R1565 F1027]
495. Criegern, F. von (1948), MS # B-784 (Germ.), *Teil I, Die Kämpfe des LXXXIV. A.K. in der Normandie von der alliierten Landung bis 17.6.44*, p.30; Captured *Korpsbefehl* of Gen.Kdo. LXXXIV. A.K., 15.6.44, copied and translated in Annex 1 to G-2 Periodic Report Nr.9, HQ First US Army, 19 June 44 [Available at https://firstdivisionmuseum.nmtvault.com/jsp/viewer.jsp?doc_id=iwfd0000%2F20141124%2F165&page_name=798, accessed on 4 Aug. 2018]
496. *AOK 7* Ia, *KTB 6.6.-25.7.44*, p.41 [T312 R1569 F260]
497. *AOK 7*, Ia Nr.3119/44 g.K., 16.6.44 [T312 R1565 F1059]
498. *AOK 7* Ia, Ia-Vormittagsmeldung, 16.6.44 [T312 R1565 F1064]
499. *AOK 7*, Ia Nr.1436/44 g., 16.6.44, p.1 [T312 R1565 F1061]
500. In 1954, Poppe contributed a monograph to the Foreign Military Studies. In it, he reconstructed the order of events with the help of individuals, who had been involved at the time. While it is difficult to match this to other versions, it does include important details, which is why it is included here separately:
The withdrawal plans were introduced by the *LXXXIV. A.K.* on the morning of the 15th but were cancelled that afternoon as having been a merely theoretical exchange of ideas. This is supported by an officer on the division staff who confirms that *Gen.* Fahrmbacher himself had called it a "tactical exchange of thoughts", but gave no date. The plans were re-activated on the afternoon of the 16th but yet again revoked within hours. They were finally approved in the early hours of the 17th.
All these dates have been corrected from Poppe's claims, which appear to be one day too late. The last three times the orders came in via *Gen.* von Schlieben. This indicates that *Gruppe von Schlieben* was both operational — which was reported on the morning of 16 June — and included the 77. I.D. [**Poppe, W. (1954)**, p.13-14; C.S.D.I.C.(UK) S.R.M.576, 21 Jun 44 in UKNA, WO 208/4138; *AOK 7* Ia, *KTB 6.6.-25.7.44*, p.44 in T312 R1569 F263]
501. Wilbrand (1944), p.7; **Hayn, F. (1954)**, *Die Invasion - Von Cotentin bis Falaise*, Scharnhorst Buchkameradschaft der Soldaten, Heidelberg, p.54
502. *AOK 7* Ia, *KTB 6.6.-25.7.44*, p.44 [T312 R1569 F263]; *AOK 7*, Ia, *KTB 6.6.-16.8.44*, p.42 [T312 R1569 F46]
503. *AOK 7* Ia, *KTB 6.6.-25.7.44*, p.44-45 [T312 R1569 F263-4]; **Hayn, F. (1954)**, p.53
504. *AOK 7* Ia, *KTB 6.6.-25.7.44*, p.45 [T312 R1569 F264]
505. *Ibid*.
506. *Ibid*., p.46 [T312 R1569 F265]
507. *Ibid*.
508. *Ibid*., p.46-47 [T312 R1569 F265-6]
509. Viebig, C.S.D.I.C. (UK) S.R. Report, S.R.M. 846, p.2 — Hereafter referred to as: **Viebig**, S.R.M.846
510. Hayn, F. (1954), p.53
511. *AOK 7* Ia, *KTB 6.6.-25.7.44*, p.46-47 [T312 R1569 F265-6]
512. *Ibid*., p.48 [T312 R1569 F267]
513. *Ibid*., p.46 [T312 R1569 F265]
514. Wilbrand (1944), p.7
515. *AOK 7* Ia, *KTB 6.6.-25.7.44*, p.49 [T312 R1569 F268]
516. *AOK 7* Ia, Nr.3169/44 g.K., 17.6.44, p.1 [T312 R1565 F1095]
517. *AOK 7* Ia, *KTB 6.6.-25.7.44*, p.49 [T312 R1569 F268]
518. Criegern, F. von (1948), *Teil I*, p.34
519. *AOK 7* Ia, 22.6.44 [T312 R1565 F1233-4] For support regarding the order to build defensive positions also see **Wilbrand (1944)**, p.7 [T78 R672 H41/61b]
520. *AOK 7* Ia, *KTB 6.6.-25.7.44*, p.49 [T312 R1569 F268]
521. Criegern, F. von (1948), *Teil I*, p.35-36
522. 77. I.D., orders issued by *Gen.* Stegmann regarding the division's move to the south, 17.6.44, copied and translated in Annex 1 to G-2 Periodic Report Nr.9, HQ First US Army, 19 June 44 [Available at https://firstdivisionmuseum.nmtvault.com/jsp/viewer.jsp?doc_id=iwfd0000%2F20141124%2F165&page_name=799 & 800, accessed on 4 Aug. 2018] The order was captured, but the translated version only gives the day, not the time.
523. *Ibid*.
524. Poppe, W. (1954), p.15
525. Wilbrand (1944), p.7
526. Hayn, F. (1954), p.56. Pages 56 and 57 quote a report from the intelligence officer of the division, *Hptm.* Schreihage
527. Fahrmbacher, W.K. (1946), MS # B-371 (Germ.), *Bretagne 6.6.44-10.6.44 und Normandie 12.6.44-25.6.44*, p.38
528. Wilbrand (1944), p.8
529. Hayn, F. (1954), p.56
530. 9th I.D., *Report of operation, 14 June - 1 July 1944*, p.9
531. Wilbrand (1944), p.8
532. Hayn, F. (1954), p.56
533. Wilbrand (1944), p.8-9; Headquarters Ninth Infantry Division, APO No.9, *Report of operation conducted by Ninth Infantry Division US Army - Cotentin peninsula France - 14 June - 1 July*, 14.7.44, p.9 — Hereafter referred to as: 9th I.D., *Report of operation, 14 June - 1 July 1944*; Deutsches Rotes Kreuz
534. Wilbrand (1944), p.9
535. Brandt, S.R.M.612
536. Wilbrand (1944), p.9 [T78 R672 H41/61b]
537. 9th I.D., *Report of operation, 14 June - 1 July 1944*, p.8-9
538. Hayn, F. (1954) p.56; **Wilbrand (1944)**, p.8; *AOK 7*, Ia Nr.3205/44 g.K., 18.6.44 [T312 R1565 F1109]
539. *AOK 7* Ia, Nr.3238/44 g.K., p.2 [T312 R1565 F1133]
540. Choltitz, D. von (1947), MS # B-418 (Germ.), p.17; Report at 08:00 on 18 Jun 1944 [UKNA, HW 5/506, CX/MSS/T 220/54]
541. The exact timing of the Serenade is surprisingly difficult to find. Based on the logs of the 60th IR, it probably took place in the late morning.
542. 9th I.D., *Report of operation, 14 June - 1 July 1944*, p.7-8 ; *AOK 7*, Ia Nr.3238/44 g.K. p.2 [T312 R1565 F1133]
543. Wilbrand (1944), p.9
544. *Ibid*., p.9-10. According to *Hptm.* Schreihage, the *Kampfgruppe* started moving at 01:00. [**Hayn, F. (1954)**, p.56]
545. Hayn, F. (1954), p.56-57
546. *Ibid*., p.57
547. Wilbrand (1944), p.10
548. *AOK 7*, Ia Nr.3238/44 g.K., p.2 [T312 R1565 F1133]; *AOK 7* Ia, 22.6.44 [T312 R1565 F1234]
549. *AOK 7* Ia, *KTB 6.6.-25.7.44*, p.63 [T312 R1569 F282]
550. Wilbrand (1944), p.11
551. *AOK 7*, Ia Nr.1481/44 g., 17.6.44 [T312 R1565 F1089]
552. With the possible exception of *Gen.* von Schlieben, whose own force was weakened by the departure of the 77. I.D. The general did not mention any kind of plan in his post-war monograph.
553. *AOK 7* Ia, *KTB 6.6.-25.7.44*, p.52 [T312 R1569 F271]
554. Hayn, F. (1954), p.56
555. Schlieben, K.W. v. (1948), MS # B-845 (Germ.), *Die deutsche 709.Infanterie - Division vor und während der anglo-amerikanischen Invasion vom 6. Juni 1944*, p.60-61
556. *Ibid*., p.68
557. Call from *OKW*/WFSt/Major Friedl to *Ob.West*, 22.6.44 - 15.55 Uhr [T311 R25 F7029759]
558. *Ob.West* Ia Nr.4836/44 g.K., 22.6.44 [T311 R25 F7029760]
559. *AOK 7* Ia, *KTB 6.6.-25.7.44*, p.63 [T312 R1569 F282]
560. *Ibid*.
561. *AOK 7* Ia, 22.6.44 [T312 R1565 F1233-4]
562. Okdo.d.H.Gr. B, Ia Nr.illegible/44 g.K., 22.6.44, p.2 [T311 R3 F7003681]
563. Judicial rank within the military equivalent to *Generalmajor*.
564. Ose, D. (1982), *Entscheidung im Westen 1944*, Stuttgart *Der Oberbefehlshaber West und die Abwehr der alliierten Invasion*, Stuttgart: Deutsche Verlags-Anstalt, p.154; Viebig, S.R.M.846, p.2; Mittagsmeldung *H.Gr. B.* to *Ob.West* on 3 Jul 44, p.146 [T311 R16

565. *H.Gr. D (Ob.West), Kriegstagebuch (Text) 1.-31.7.44*, p.146 [T311 R16 F7016742] On 3 July, *Ob.West* records mention *Gen. Theissen*'s conclusion. Von Rundstedt formally cancelled the investigation, referring to Rommel's meeting with Keitel.
566. *AOK 7, Ia Nr.1607/44 g.*, 20.6.44, p.2 [T312 R1565 F1179]
567. *AOK 7, Ia Nr.3241/44 g.K.*, 20.6.44, p.1 [T312 R1565 F1174]; *AOK 7 Ia, KTB 6.6.-25.7.44*, p.54 [T312 R1569 F273]
568. *AOK 7*, Anlage zum *KTB* Führungsabteilung, Lagenkarten A.O.K.7 vom 6.6.44-30.6.44, *Lage Normandie, Stand: 28.6.44, 22.00 Uhr* [T312 R1570 F37]; **Nauroth, H.S. & B. Steinberg (2017)**, *Die Geschichte der 91. Luftlande-Division - Rekonstruktion eines Großverbandes der Deutschen Wehrmacht*, Hamburg: tredition GmbH, p.118-119
569. *AOK 7, Ia Nr.1772/44 g.*, 24.6.44, p.2 [T312 R1565 F1287]
570. *WFSt. Op.(H), Lage West, Stand: 4.7.44*, Chef WFSt (1:200.000) [NARA, via www.wwii-photos-maps.com]
571. For one, see CX/MSS/R.228 (C), 20 June 44, p.24 [UKNA, HW 5/514]
572. *OKH/AHA/Abwicklungsstab, Anl. z. Sachgeb. 91 Nr.6.44 g., Kriegsgliederung Kampfgruppe 91. I.D., Stand: 18.6.44* [T78 R672 H41/61b]
573. *AOK 7 Ia, KTB 6.6.-25.7.44*, p.63 [T312 R1569 F282]
574. **Brandt**, S.R.M.612. The quote comes from a conversation between regimental commanders *Obst. Rohrbach* (*GR 729*), *Brandt* (*GR 1050*) and *Hermann* (*Flak-Rgt. 30*), and is given to *Rohrbach*. The information does not match his regiment, but does match *GR 1050*.
575. *AOK 7, Ia Nr.3282/44 g.K.*, 21.6.44 [T312 R1565 F1219]
576. Schlieben, K.W. v. (1948), Germ., p.68
577. Harrison, G.A. (1951, reprint 1984), p.415
578. *AOK 7, Ia Nr.3238/44 g.K.*, p.2 [T312 1565 F1133]; *AOK 7/O. Qu., Kriegstagebuch der Oberquartiermeisterabteilung AOK 7 für die Zeit vom 1.6.44-30.6.44* [T312 R1571 F523] One of these documents, albeit somewhat ambiguous in its phrasing, suggests that it was the artillery with the troops north of the penetration line that was lost, not that of the entire division.
579. 9ᵗʰ I.D., *Report of operation, 14 June - 1 July 1944*, p.7-8. The equipment encountered included two "105 mm" guns and two "57 mm" guns. In addition one howitzer and five guns were not described in detail.
580. *AOK 7, Ia Nr.3454/44 g.K., 3.Teil*, 27.6.44, p.1 [T312 R1565 F1381]
581. Hayn, F. (1954), p.56
582. *AOK 7, Ia Nr.3454/44 g.K., 4.Teil*, 27.6.44, p.2 [T312 R1565 F1381] Other numbers from the same document put these losses respectively at 57%, 30%, 30% and 40%. This may refer to units north of the Douve, with or without units supposed to be with *Gruppe von Schlieben*. [*AOK 7, Ia Nr.3454/44 g.K.*, 27.6.44, p.2 in T312 R1565 F1376]
583. *AOK 7, Ia Nr.3454/44 g.K., 3.Teil*, 27.6.44, p.1-2 [T312 R1565 F1378-1379]
584. *77. I.D., Ia Nr.325/44 g.K.*, 3.7.44, Anlage - quoted in **Wilbrand (1944)**, p.11
585. Poppe, W. (1954), p.18
586. CX/MSS/R.239 (C), p.14, 8 July 44, p.14 [UKNA, HW 5/524]
587. *OKH/AHA/Abwicklungsstab, Anl. z. Sachgeb. 91 Nr.6.44 g., Kriegsgliederung Kampfgruppe König, Stand: 18.6.44 - 28.6.44* [T78 R672 H41/61b]
588. *AOK 7, Kriegsgliederungen z. KTB 6.-29.6.44, Stand: 27.6.44 14 Uhr* [T312 R1566 F19]; *AOK 7, Anlage zum KTB* Führungsabteilung, Lagenkarten A.O.K.7 vom 6.6.44-30.6.44, *Lage Normandie, Stand: 28.6.44, 22.00 Uhr* [T312 R1570 F37]
589. *AOK 7, Kriegsgliederungen z. KTB 6.-29.6.44* [T312 R1566 F21]; also see chapter "*243.Infanterie-Division*"
590. *OKH/AHA/Abwicklungsstab, Anl. z. Sachgeb. 91 Nr.6.44 g., Kriegsgliederung Kampfgruppe König, Stand: 18.6.44 - 28.6.44* [T78 R672 H41/61b]; **Kreibig (1945)**, *Ergänzung zu taktischem Bericht für 265.Inf.Div. des Hauptmann Kastner vom 29.10.1944*, p.2 [T78 R672 H41/61b]; **Nauroth, H.S. & B. Steinberg (2017)**, p.118-119
591. *AOK 7, Ia Nr.3454/44 g.K.*, 27.6.44, p.2 [T312 R1565 F1376]
592. *AOK 7, Ia Nr.3454/44 g.K., 3.Teil*, 27.6.44, p.1 [T312 R1565 F1378]
593. *Gen.d.Art.b.Ob.West Ib Nr.1077/44 g.K., Landeabwehrgeschütze: Stand v. 1.4.44*, 18.4.44 [CAMO, Bestand 500, Findbuch 12451, Akte 418]
594. Telephone Journal 60th Infantry, 17 June 44 [NARA]
595. *91. I.D., Kriegsgliederung KG 91. I.D.*, 17.7.44 [T78 R672 H41/61b]; *91. I.D., Kriegsgliederung KG 91. I.D.*, 20.7.44 [T78 R672 H41/61b]; *91. I.D., Kriegsgliederung KG 91. I.D.*, 26.7.44 [T78 R672 H41/61b]
596. 21 AGp/Int/1070, App. Y to 21 Army Group Intelligence Summary No. 143, Part II, 8 Jul 44 [UKNA, WO 171/131]
597. *AOK 7, Ia Nr.3363/44 g.K.*, 24.6.44 [T312 R1565 F1295]; **Choltitz, D. von (1947)**, MS # B-418 (Germ.), *Kämpfe des LXXXIV. A.K. in der Normandie vom 18.6.144 ab*, p.10; **Hausser, P. (1945)**, MS # A-907 (Germ.), *Seventh Army 29 June - 20 Aug 44*, p.7; **Hausser, P. (1946)**, MS # A-974 (Germ.), *Normandie - 7. Armee vom 29.6. - 24.7.1945*, p.4
598. Wilbrand (1944), p.12; *AOK 7 Ia, Anlage zum KTB* Führungsabteilung, Lagenkarten A.O.K.7 vom 6.6.44-30.6.44, *Lage Normandie, Stand: 29.6.44, 22.00 Uhr* [T312 R1570 F38]; *Ibid., Lage Normandie, Stand: 30.6.44, 22.00 Uhr* [T312 R1570 F39]
599. *AOK 7, Ia Nr.3538/44 g.K.*, 30.6.44 [T312 R1565 F1467]
600. *Marschbataillon*: Originally a replacements transfer formation, not a combat battalion. By late 1943, the Germans had realised that circumstances could force these units straight into action and, for 1944, it was intended to prepare them for combat. In Normandy these battalions were usually about 1,000-1,200 men, but there were no fixed numbers.
601. *AOK 7 Ia, KTB 6.6.-16.8.44*, p.118 [T312 R1569 F121]
602. PWIS(H)/LF/404, 31 Jul 44 [UKNA, WO 208/3633]
603. *AOK 7, Ia Nr.3537/44 g.K.*, p.2 [T312 R1565 F1473]
604. PWIS(H)/LF/404, 31 Jul 44 [UKNA, WO 208/3633]
605. Wilbrand (1944), p.11-12. *Oblt.* Wilbrand was appointed regimental adjutant and put in charge of the reorganisation. Apparently this officer had previously been in the *II./1050*. The officer is also the author of the combat report of his regiment.
606. Nauroth, H.S. & B. Steinberg (2017), p.118-119
607. *AOK 7, Ia Nr.3505/44 g.K.*, 29.6.44 [T312 R1565 F1432]
608. Mahlmann, P. (1946a), MS # A-983 (Germ.), *353. Inf. Division*, p.14-15 & Anl.7
609. Wilbrand (1944), p.12-13; Mahlmann indeed states that the *I./942* remained on the *Mahlmann-Linie* east of Mont-Castre, but also identifies it as the *II./942*. The *I./942* is mentioned by *AOK 7* and *77. I.D.* sources. Mahlmann links the *I./AR 353* to the *243. I.D.* and the 4ᵗʰ Battalion of the *91. LL.D.* but, unless it was later changed, this contradicts period records.
610. *Ibid.*, p.14
611. PWIS(H)/LF/404, 31 Jul 44 [UKNA, WO 208/3633]
612. Wilbrand (1944), p.12-13
613. Blumenson, M. (1961, 1993 reprint), *Breakout and pursuit*, Center of Military History, United States Army, Washington D.C., p.53-55 & Map 3
614. Blumenson, M. (1961, 1993 reprint), p.64
615. *AOK 7 Ia, KTB 6.6.-25.7.44*, p.91 [T312 R1569 F311]; *LXXXIV. A.K.* on 3.7.44 at 22:00 [UKNA, HW 5/520, CX/MSS/T235/23, XL 697]; **Hausser, P. (1946)**, p.10; **Mahlmann, P. (1946a)**, Anl.8; WFSt Op.(H), *Lage West (LXXXIV. A.K.), Stand: 4.7.44* (1:50000) [NARA, via www.wwii-photos-maps.com]
616. Wilbrand (1944), p.14-15
617. *AOK 7 Ia, KTB 6.6.-16.8.44*, p.108 [T312 R1569 F111]
618. *LXXXIV. A.K.* on 3.7.44 at 22:00 [UKNA, HW 5/520, CX/MSS/T235/23, XL 697]; **Hausser, P. (1946)**, p.11-12; **Choltitz, D. von (1947)**, p.32 & 34-35
619. WFSt Op.(H) zu Lage West, Stand: 4.7.44 (1:50.000) [NARA, via www.wwii-photos-maps.com]
620. *AOK 7 Ia, KTB 6.6.-16.8.44*, p.112 [T312 R1569 F115]
621. Wilbrand (1944), p.15-16
622. Flivo LXXXIV. A.K., 4.7.44 at 09:40 [UKNA, HW 5/520, CX/MSS/T235/39, XL 711]; Flivo LXXXIV. A.K., 4.7.44 at 15:30 [UKNA, HW 5/520, CX/MSS/T235/84, XL 750]; *AOK 7 Ia, KTB 6.6.-16.8.44*, p.112 [T312 R1569 F115]; *AOK 7 Ia, KTB 6.6.-25.7.44*, p.95 [T312 R1569 F315]
623. Wilbrand (1944), p.16
624. *AOK 7 Ia, KTB 6.6.-16.8.44*, p.113 [T312 R1569 F116]
625. *Ibid.*, p.115-116 [T312 R1569 F118-9]; **Blumenson, M. (1961, 1993 reprint)** p.67
626. *AOK 7 Ia, KTB 6.6.-25.7.44*, p.97 [T312 R1569 F317]
627. *AOK 7 Ia, KTB 6.6.-16.8.44*, p.116-118 [T312 R1569 F119-21]
628. Message of Flivo LXXXIV. A.K. on 5.7.44 at 16:30 [UKNA, HW 5/521, CX/MSS/T236/95]
629. *AOK 7 Ia, KTB 6.6.-16.8.44*, p.116-117 [T312 R1569 F119-20]; *AOK 7 Ia, KTB 6.6.-25.7.44*, p.97-98 [T312 R1569 F317-8]; **Weidinger, O. (1954)**, *Bericht über den Einsatz bei La Haye de Puits*, p.30-33 [in Anlagenband A to **Stückler, A. (1954)**, MS # P-159, *2.SS-Panzer-Division "Das Reich", Juni bis September 1944*]
630. *AOK 7 Ia, KTB 6.6.-16.8.44*, p.119-120 [T312 R1569 F122-3]
631. *AOK 7 Ia, KTB 6.6.-16.8.44*, p.125 [T312 R1569 F128]; *AOK 7 Ia, KTB 6.6.-25.7.44*, p.101-102 [T312 R1569 F321-2]; **Blumenson, M. (1961, 1993 reprint)**, p.70-71
632. *AOK 7 Ia, KTB 6.6.-16.8.44*, p.125 [T312 R1569 F128]; **Weidinger, O. (1954)**, p.31 [part of Anlagenband A to **Stückler, A. (1954)**, MS # P-159]
633. *AOK 7 Ia, KTB 6.6.-16.8.44*, p.126 [T312 R1569 F129]; **Blumenson, M. (1961, 1993 reprint)**, p.69-72; After action Report 90th Inf.Div. for July 1944, p.10-12 [Available at

www.90thdivisionassoc.org/History/AAR/index.html, accessed on 9 October 2014]; Okdo.d.*H.Gr. B*, Tagesmeldung, 9.7.44, p.6-7 [T311 R3 F7002516]

634. *AOK 7* Ia, *KTB 6.6.-16.8.44*, p.128 [T312 R1569 F131]; Okdo.d.*H.Gr. B*, Tagesmeldung, 9.7.44, p.6-7 [T311 R3 F7002516]

635. 82d Airborne Division, Interrogation Report No.21, 6 Jul 44, p.1 [NARA, via Egbert van de Schootbrugge]

636. *AOK 7* Ia, *KTB 6.6.-25.7.44*, p.103 [T312 R1569 F323]

637. PWIS(H)/LF/404, 31 Jul 44 [UKNA, WO 208/3633]

638. *AOK 7* Ia, *KTB 6.6.-16.8.44*, p.127 [T312 R1569 F130]

639. *AOK 7* Ia, *KTB 6.6.-25.7.44*, p.104-105 [T312 R1569 F324-5]; *AOK 7* Ia, *KTB 6.6.-16.8.44*, p.129 [T312 R1569 F132]

640. *AOK 7* Ia, *KTB 6.6.-16.8.44*, p.109, 117, 142 & 146 [T312 R1569 F112, 120, 146, 150]; *AOK 7* Ia, *KTB 6.6.-25.7.44*, p.106 [T312 R1569 F326]

641. Okdo.d.H.Gr,B, Ia Nr.4109/44 g.K., 27.6.44 [T311 R3 F7002302]; Okdo.d.*H.Gr. B*, Ia Nr.4434/44 g.K., 5.7.44 [T311 R4 F7003778]

642. *AOK 7* Ia, *KTB 6.6.-16.8.44*, p.130-131 [T312 R1569 F133-4]; *AOK 7* Ia, *KTB 6.6.-25.7.44*, p.106-107 [T312 R1569 F326-7]; Okdo.d.*H.Gr. B*, Ia Nr.4541/44 g.K., 8.7.44 [T311 R3 F7002514-5]

643. *AOK 7* Ia, *KTB 6.6.-16.8.44*, p.135 [T312 R1569 F138]

644. Wilbrand (1944), p.16; Biography of *Obst.* Dropmann in the Pe*rso*nenregister of Lexikon der Wehrmacht [Available at www.lexikon-der-wehrmacht.de/Pe*RSO*nenregister/D/DropmannJ.htm, accessed on 3 March 2019]

645. Poppe, W. (1954), p.18; PWIS(H)/LDC/271, 24 Aug 44, p.1 [UKNA, WO 208/3647] On 15 June, *Maj.* Karsten was appointed the new commander of *GR 1058* (*91. LL.D.*), but he never took the post. [Alph. Kartei von allen Inf. Offizieren einschliesslich Oberst, index card of *Maj.d.R.* Karsten in T78 R912 H6/355]

646. Flivo *LXXXIV. A.K.* 10.7.44 at 01:00 [UKNA, HW 5/526, CX/MSS/T251/63, XL 1526]; *AOK 7* Ia, *KTB 6.6.-16.8.44*, p.137 [T312 R1569 F140]

647. Flivo (*LXXXIV. A.K.*) on 10.7.44 at 01:00 [UKNA, HW 5/526, CX/MSS/T241/39, XL 1498]

648. *AOK 7* Ia, *KTB 6.6.-16.8.44*, p.136 [T312 R1569 F139]

649. *Ibid.*, p.137 [T312 R1569 F140]; **Hausser, P. (1946)**, p.20

650. *AOK 7* Ia, *KTB 6.6.-25.7.44*, p.108-109 [T312 R1569 F328-9]

651. *AOK 7* Ia, *KTB 6.6.-16.8.44*, p.139 [T312 R1569 F143]

652. *AOK 7* Ia, *KTB 6.6.-25.7.44*, p.110-112 [T312 R1569 F330-2]; *AOK 7* Ia, *KTB 6.6.-16.8.44*, p.139-140 & 142 [T312 R1569 F143-4 & 146]

653. WFSt Op.(H), *Lage West, Stand: 11.7.44*, Chef WFSt (1:200.000) [NARA, via www.wwii-photos-maps.com]; *AOK 7* Ia, *KTB 6.6.-16.8.44*, p.144 [T312 R1569 F148]

654. *AOK 7* Ia, *KTB 6.6.-16.8.44*, p.144-146 [T312 R1569 F148-50]

655. *Ibid.*, p.146 [T312 R1569 F150] The exact date of the *Führerbefehl* is unclear.

656. *Ibid.*, p.148 [T312 R1569 F152]

657. *AOK 7* Ia, *KTB 6.6.-16.8.44*, p.148-149 & 155 [T312 R1569 F152-3 & 159]; *AOK 7* Ia, *KTB 6.6.-25.7.44*, p.117-118 & 120 [T312 R1569 F337-8 & 340]

658. Gen.Kdo.LXXXIV.A.K, Ia Nr.1758/44 g.K., 13.7.44 [Published in **Wind, M. & H. Günther (2004)**, *Kriegstagebuch 17.SS-Panzer-Grenadier-Division „Götz von Berlichingen" - Auswahl von Dokumenten - 30. Oktober 1943 bis 6. Mai 1945*, St.Ingbert: Dengmerter Heimatverlag]; Okdo.d.*H.Gr. B*, Ia Nr.4753/44 g.K., 14.7.44, p.4 [T311 R3 F7002544]

659. *AOK 7* Ia, *KTB 6.6.-25.7.44*, p.118 [T312 R1569 F338]; *AOK 7* Ia, *KTB 6.6.-16.8.44*, p.149 & 154 [T312 R1569 F153 & 158

660. Wilbrand (1944), p.16

661. *AOK 7* Ia, *KTB 6.6.-25.7.44*, p.152 [T312 R1569 F156]; *AOK 7* Ia, *KTB 6.6.-25.7.44*, p.120 & 124 [T312 R1569 F340 & 344]

662. *AOK 7* Ia, *KTB 6.6.-25.7.44*, p.152 [T312 R1569 F156]

663. *Ibid.*, p.154 [T312 R1569 F158]

664. *AOK 7* Ia, *KTB 6.6.-25.7.44*, p.120 [T312 R1569 F340]

665. Message Flivo *LXXXIV. A.K.* on 15.7.44 at 10:30 [UKNA, HW 5/531, CX/MSS/T246/49, XL 2173]; Okdo.d.*H.Gr. B*, Ia Nr.4924/44 g.K., 18.7.44, p.7 [T311 R3 F7002569]

666. See *AOK 7* Ia, *KTB 6.6.-16.8.44*, p.162-173 T312 R1569 F166-77]

667. Gen.Kdo.LXXXIV.A.K, *Ia-Tagesmeldungen der Divisionen*, 16.7.44, p.1 [T314 R1604 F1364]; Okdo.d.*H.Gr. B*, Ia Nr.4924/44 g.K., 17.7.44, p.6 [T311 R3 F7002568]

668. *AOK 7* Ia, *KTB 6.6.-16.8.44*, p.168 [T312 R1569 F172]

669. Okdo.d.*H.Gr. B*, Ia Nr.4961/44 g.K., 19.7.44, p.6 [T311 R3 F7002578]; *AOK 7* Ia, *KTB 6.6.-16.8.44*, p.168 [T312 R1569 F172]

670. Poppe, W. (1954), p.20

671. Okdo.d.*H.Gr. B*, Ia Nr.4961/44 g.K., 19.7.44, p.7 [T311 R3 F7002579]

672. 21 AGp/Int/1070, App. A to 21 Army Group Intelligence Summary No. 147, Part II, 20 Jul. 44 [UKNA, WO 171/131]

673. *91. I.D.*, *Kriegsgliederung KG 91. I.D.*, 17.7.44 [T78 R672 H41/61b]

674. *Ibid*.

675. German battalion classifications: "*stark*" ("strong") - combat strength of more than 400 men; "*mittelstark*" ("medium strong") more than 300; "*durchschnittlich*" ("average") more than 200; "*schwach*" ("weak") more than 100; "*abgekämpft*" ("worn out") under 100 [T78 R421 F6390283].

676. *91. I.D.*, *Kriegsgliederung KG 91. I.D.*, 17.7.44 [T78 R672 H41/61b]; *91. I.D.*, *Kriegsgliederung KG 91. I.D.*, 20.7.44 [T78 R672 H41/61b]; *91. I.D.*, *Kriegsgliederung KG 91. I.D.*, 26.7.44 [T78 R672 H41/61b]

677. *91. I.D.*, *Kriegsgliederung KG 91. I.D.*, 17.7.44 [T78 R672 H41/61b]

678. *91. I.D.*, *Kriegsgliederung KG 91. I.D.*, 20.7.44 [T78 R672 H41/61b]

679. Gen.Kdo.*LXXXIV. A.K.*, Ia Nr.035/44 g.K., 22.7.44 [T314 R1604 F1388]

680. *Ibid*.; referred to in **Zetterling, N. (2000)**, p.240

681. *91. I.D.*, *Kriegsgliederung KG 91. I.D.*, 17.7.44 [T78 R672 H41/61b]; *91. I.D.*, *Kriegsgliederung KG 91. I.D.*, 20.7.44 [T78 R672 H41/61b]; *91. I.D.*, *Kriegsgliederung KG 91. I.D.*, 26.7.44 [T78 R672 H41/61b]

682. *91. I.D.*, *Kriegsgliederung KG 91. I.D.*, 26.7.44 [T78 R672 H41/61b]

683. PWIS(H)/LF/525, 16 Aug 44, p.1 [UKNA, WO 208/3635]; Kartei von Inf.-Kommandeuren, index card of *Obst.* Einstmann [T78 R908 H6/354]

684. *91. I.D.*, *Kriegsgliederung KG 91. I.D.*, 26.7.44 [T78 R672 H41/61b]

685. *H.Gr. D (Ob.West)*, *Kriegstagebuch (Text) 1.-31.7.44*, p.286 [T311 R16 F7016882]

686. König, E. (1946), MS # B-010 (Germ.), *Kämpfe in der Normandie*, p.10

687. Gen.Kdo.*XXV. A.K.* Ia, Anl.2 z. *KTB* Nr.15(II), Algemeines vom 16.7. - 31.7.1944 [T314 R747 F546] — Hereafter referred to as: Gen.Kdo.*XXV. A.K.* Ia, Anl.2 z. *KTB* Nr.15(II)

688. König, E. (1946), p.10; Gen.Kdo.*XXV. A.K.*, Abt. Ia, *Kriegstagebuch Nr.15 (II.Teil) Gen.Kdo.XXV. A.K. Führungsabteilung (Ia) vom 11.7.-31.7.44* [T314 R747 F275] — Hereafter referred to as: Gen.Kdo.*XXV. A.K.* Ia, *KTB* Nr.15(II)

689. Poppe, W. (1954), p.20

690. WFSt Op.(H), *Lage West, Stand: 23.7.44*, Chef WFSt (1:200.000) [NARA, via www.wwii-photos-maps.com]; Gen.Kdo. *XXV. A.K.* Ia, *KTB* Nr.15(II) [T314 R747 F275]

691. PWIS(H)/LF/525, 16 Aug 44, p.1 [UKNA, WO 208/3635]

692. PWIS(H)/KP/238, 10 Aug 44 [UKNA, WO 208/3625]; PWIS(H)/LDC/257, 21 Aug 44 [UKNA, 208/3647]; PWIS(H)/LF/505, 14 Aug 44, p.2 [UKNA, WO 208/3635]; PWIS(H)/LF/525, 16 Aug 44, p.1 [UKNA, WO 208/3635]; PWIS(H)/LF/534, 17 Aug 44 [UKNA, WO 208/3635]

693. PWIS(H)/LF/525, 16 Aug 44, p.1 [UKNA, WO 208/3635]

694. Anl.1 zu OKH/GenStdH/Org.Abt. Nr.I/1348/44 g.Kdos Chefs., *Übersicht über die in Aufstellung und Umgliederung befindlichen grossen Verbänden*, 5.8.44, p.4 [T78 R421 F6390493]

695. Gen.Kdo.*XXV. A.K.* Ia, *KTB* Nr.15(II) [T314 R747 F273]

696. *Ibid.* [T314 R747 F275]; **Poppe, W. (1954)**, p.20

697. Gen.Kdo.*XXV. A.K.* Ia, *KTB* Nr.15(II) [T314 R747 F277]

698. *Ibid.* [T314 R747 F283]

699. Poppe, W. (1954), p.21 & 30

700. Gen.Kdo.*XXV. A.K.* Ia, *KTB* Nr.15(II) [T314 R747 F283]

701. Gen.Kdo. *XXV. A.K.*, Abt. Ia Nr.2660/44 g., 31.7.44 [T314 R747 F542]; Gen.Kdo.*XXV. A.K.* Abt. Ia, Ia-Morgenmeldung, 31.7.44 [T314 R747 F560]

702. Gen.Kdo.*XXV. A.K.* Ia, Anl.2 z. *KTB* Nr.15(II), Anruf Oberst Bacherer, *77. I.D.*, 30.7.44 [T314 R747 F532]

703. Poppe, W. (1954), p.21

704. C.S.D.I.C. (UK), S.R. Report, S.R.M. 804

705. Gen.Kdo.*XXV. A.K.* Ia, *KTB* Nr.15(II) [T314 R747 F283]; Gen.Kdo. *XXV. A.K.*, Abt. Ia Nr.2661/44 g., 31.7.44 [T314 R747 F551]; *AOK 7*, *Zusammenstellung der Telephongespräche, Lage Orientierung u. Entschlüsse, 16 Juli 44 - 16 Aug 44, Ferngespräche Gen.Feldm. v. Kluge*, phone call with *Gen.* Fahrmbacher (01:45), 31.7.44 [T312 R1568 F630]; *H.Gr. D (Ob.West)*, *Kriegstagebuch (Text) 1.-31.7.44*, p.329 [T311 R16 F7016925]

706. Gen.Kdo. *XXV. A.K.*, Abt. Ia Nr.2660/44 g., 31.7.44 [T314 R747 F542]

707. Ferngespräch Gen. Fahrmbacher – GenLt. Ramke at 02:35 on 31 Jul 44 [T314 R747 F545]

708. *Ob.West* Ic Nr.5285/44, 31.7.44 [T311 R20 F7022736]; *AOK 7*, Zusammenstellung der Telephongespräche, Lage Orientierung u. Entschlüsse, 16 Juli 44 - 16 Aug 44, *Ferngespräche Gen.Feldm. v. Kluge*, phone call with GenLt. Speidel (9:20), 31.7.44 [T312 R1568 F633]

709. Gen.Kdo.*XXV. A.K.* Ia, Anl.2 z. *KTB* Nr.15(II), Ferngespräche Gen.Feldmarschall Kluge - General Fahrmbacher, 31.7.44 [T314 R747 F543]
710. Blumenson, M. (1961, 1993 reprint), *Breakout and pursuit*, Center of Military History, United States Army, Washington D.C., p.317
711. *AOK 7*, Zusammenstellung der Telephongespräche, Lage Orientierung u. Entschlüsse, 16 Jul 44 - 16 Aug 44, *Ferngespräche Gen.Feldm. v. Kluge*, 31.7.44 [T312 R1568 F629]; Gen.Kdo.*XXV. A.K.* Ia, Anl.2 z. *KTB* Nr.15(II) [T314 R747 F533]; *77. I.D.*, Ia Nr.1063/44 g., 31.7.44 [T314 R747 F552]
712. Gen.Kdo.*XXV. A.K.* Ia, KTB Nr.15(II) [T314 R747 F285]
713. Communication XXV.AK. [T314 R747 F549-550]
714. Blumenson, M. (1961, 1993 reprint), p.320-321
715. Fahrmbacher, W.K. (1946), p.23
716. Poppe, W. (1954), p.22
717. *AOK 7*, Ia Nr.460/44 g., 1.8.44 [T315 R1841]
718. *H.Gr. D (Ob.West)*, *Kriegstagebuch (Text)* 1.8. - 31.8.44, p.349 [T311 R16 F7017045]; **Fahrmbacher, W.K. (1946)**, p.24
719. Gen.Kdo.*XXV. A.K.*, Ia Nr.932/44 g.K., 2.8.44 (14:32) [T315 R1841 F77]; Kampfgruppe Spang Ia Nr.2475/44 g., 3.8.44, 03:00 [T315 R1481 F93]
720. Poppe, W. (1954), p.22
721. Radio contact between Ia *XXV. A.K.* and Ia *266. I.D.* on 4.8.44 at 10:00 [T315 R1841 F88]; Report from Ia *XXV. A.K.* to *AOK 7* on 5.8.44 at 01:00 [UKNA, HW 5/552, CX/MSS/T267/22, XL 4798 and XL 4811]
722. Order from *XXV. A.K.* Ia to Obst. Bacherer on 4.8.44 at 16:30 [UKNA, HW 5/551, CX/MSS/T266/103, XL 4726]
723. Report from *XXV. A.K.* Ia to *AOK 7* on 4.8.44 at 21:30 [UKNA, HW 5/551, CX/MSS/T226/160, XL 4787]
724. *AOK 7*, Ia Nr.562/44 g., 6.8.44 [T312 R1569 F398]; Situation report of *XXV. A.K.* on 6.8.44 at 09:00 [UKNA, CX/MSS/T268/45, XL 4969]; [T311 R4 F7003898]
725. Poppe, W. (1954), p.23 & 31
726. Message from about 03:30 on 7.8.44 [UKNA, HW 5/554, CX/MSS/T269/101, XL 5148]
727. Poppe, W. (1954), p.23
728. Kdt. d. Festung St. Malo, Abt. Ia, 6.8.44 [T501 R157 F7]
729. Blumenson, M. (1961, 1993 reprint), p.400-410; see *Ob.West*, Okdo. *H.Gr. D*, Anlagen zum Kriegstagebuch, Befehl, Meldungen, 11-20 Aug 44 [T311 R29 F7035408-85]; see daily reports from *H.Gr. B* for 5-16 Aug 44 [T311 R3 F7002699-778]; see periodic reports for 10-16 Aug 44 [T311 R4 F7004296-331 & 589-590]
730. C.S.D.I.C. (UK) GRG.G. 176, p.1 [UKNA, WO 208/4363]
731. *Ob.West*, Okdo. *H.Gr. D*, Anlagen zum Kriegstagebuch, Befehl, Meldungen, 11.8-20.8.1944, *Abendmeldung vom 14.8.44*, p.2 [T311 R29 F7035530]
732. Poppe, W. (1954), p.23-24
733. Blumenson, M. (1961, 1993 reprint), p.402; C.S.D.I.C. (UK), S.R. Report, S.R.M. 804
734. Poppe, W. (1954), p.24-26
735. Blumenson, M. (1961, 1993 reprint), p.409 & 413
736. C.S.D.I.C. (UK), S.R. Report, S.R.M. 804
737. *OKH*/GenStdH/Org.Abt.I Nr.19995/44 g.K., 16.10.44 [T78 R432 F6403685]
738. *OKH*/GenStdH/Org.Abt. Nr.I/10381/44 g., 13.9.44 [T78 R398 H1/38]; Übersicht über aufgelöste Divisionen, H.Gr. Ob.West [T78 R410 F6378876]
739. Anlage zu Okdo.d.*H.Gr. B*, Ia Nr.10076/55 g.K., 20.11.44 [T78 R410 F6378764]
740. CX/MSS/R, 273 (C), 12 Aug. 44, p.27 [UKNA, HW 5/558]
741. Poppe, W. (1954), p.20
742. Anlage zu Okdo.d.*H.Gr. B*, Ia Nr.10076/55 g.K., 20.11.44 [T78 R410 F6378764]

91. Luftlande-Division

1. Only one similar division existed in the Wehrmacht: the *22. LL.Div*. Its *Luftlande* designation dated back to 1939, and the division participated in the air assault on the Netherlands in 1940. The *Luftlande* designation was permanently cancelled in October 1942. [**Tessin, G. (1965)**, *4.Band*, p.176]
2. Tessin, G. (1972), *6.Band*, p.171; *OKH*/Chef H Rüst u BdE AHA/Ia(I) Nr.377/44 g.K., 15.1.44, p.1 [T78 R848 H36/153]; *Div. Verbände, II. Teil, 91.Inf.Div.* [T78 R412 F6380194]
3. *OKH*/GenStdH/Org.Abt. Nr.I/15946/44 g.K., 4.3.44 [BaMa, RH10/20]
4. Ibid.; Anlage 2 zu *OKH*/GenStdH/Org.Abt. Nr.I/1600/44 g.K., 20.5.44, p.2 [T78 R410 F6378462]
5. Heydte, F.A. von der (1952), MS # B-839 (Germ.), *Das Fallschirmjägerregiment 6 in der Normandie., I. Die Kämpfe im Raum von Carentan*, p.13-14
6. *Gen.* Ortner commanded the *69. I.D.* from September 1941 to February 1944. On paper he briefly commanded the *77. I.D.*, before he was put in command of the *(44.) Reichsgrenadier-Div. "Hoch- und Deutschmeister"* on 1 May. [German general staff officers files, index cards of *Gen.Lt.* Ortner in T78 R891 H6/26]
7. Nauroth, H.S. & B. Steinberg (2017), *Die Geschichte der 91. Luftlande-Division - Rekonstruktion eines Großverbandes der Deutschen Wehrmacht*, Hamburg: tradition GmbH, p.6, 9 & 18; German general staff officers files, index cards of *Gen.Lt.* Falley [T78 R885 H6/26]; Kartei von Inf.-Kommandeuren, index card of *Gen.Lt.* Poppe [T78 R908 H6/354] From September 1943 to April 1944 *Gen.* Falley commanded the *36., 330.* and *246. I.D.*, receiving excellent performance reviews. From August 1942 to June 1943, he led a school for officer candidates.
8. German general staff officers files, index cards of *Gen.Lt.* Falley [T78 R885 H6/26]; *AOK 7*, Ia Nr.1415/44 g.K., 15.6.44, p.2 [T312 R1565 F1052]
9. König, E. (1946), MS # B-010 (Germ.), *Kämpfe in der Normandie*; German general staff officers files, index cards of *Obst.* König [T78 R888 H6/26]
10. König, E. (1946)
11. See T78 R672 H41/61b
12. Nauroth, H.S. & B. Steinberg (2017), *Die Geschichte der 91. Luftlande-Division - Rekonstruktion eines Großverbandes der Deutschen Wehrmacht*. The book is an extensive collection of records and other documents, sorted by date. Any narrative takes second place to this.
13. Tessin, G. (1977), *1.Band*, p.77; **Tessin, G.** (1972), *6.Band*, p.171; **Tessin, G. (1976)**, *13.Band*, p.230; PWIS(H)/LDC/39, 28 Jun 44, p.1 [UKNA, WO 208/3645]; *OKH*/Ch H Rüst u BdE AHA Ia(I) Nr.6065/43 g.K., 6.11.43 [T78 R851 H36/159]
14. Tessin, G. (1976), *13.Band*, p.230-231; **Tessin, G. (1973)**, *7.Band*, p.259; Anl. 1 zu *OKH*/Ch H Rüst u BdE AHA Ia(I) Nr.6065/43 g.K., 6.11.43 [T78 R851 H36/159]
15. *OKH*/Chef H Rüst u BdE AHA/Ia(I) Nr.377/44 g.K., 15.1.44, p.1-2 [T78 R848 H36/153]
16. Nauroth, H.S. & B. Steinberg (2017), p.5
17. *OKH*, Chef H Rüst und BdE, AHA Ia(I) Nr.540/44 g.K., *Durchführungsbestimmungen Nr.2*, 21.1.44, p.1 & Anl. p.5 [T78 R848 H36/153]
18. *OKH*, Chef H Rüst und BdE, AHA Ia(I) Nr.528/44 g.K., *Durchführungsbestimmungen Nr.3*, 21.1.44, p.1 [T78 R848 H36/153]; *OKH*, Chef H Rüst und BdE, AHA Ia(I) Nr.510/44 g.K., *Durchführungsbestimmungen Nr.1*, 21.1.44, p.1 [T78 R848 H36/153]
19. *OKH*/Ch H Rüst u BdE AHA/Ia(I) Nr.377/44 g.K., 15.1.44, p.1 [T78 R848 H36/153]; Anl. Zu *OKH*/Ch H Rüst u BdE AHA/Stab I(1) Nr.1231/44 g.K., 16.2.44
20. Tessin, G. (1976), *13.Band*, p.230-231; **Tessin, G. (1973)**, *7.Band*, p.259
21. Anl.1 zu *OKH*/GenStdH/Org.Abt. Nr.I/16900/44 g.K., *Grundgliederung der Inf.Div.44 mit Stärkeberechnung*, 20.5.44, p.2 [T78 R410 F6378466]; *OKH*/Ch H Rüst u BdE AHA/Ia(I) Nr.377/44 g.K., 15.1.44, p.1 [T78 R848 H36/153]; the *Sollgliederung* of the *77. I.D.* provides an excellent example of a 25th wave division in early 1944, see *AOK 7*, Ia Nr.755/44 g.K., 9.2.44, Anl.1 [T312 R1565 F79]
22. *OKH*/GenStdH/Org.Abt.I/15946/44 g.K., 4.3.44, p.1 [BaMa, RH10/20]
23. Ibid.; *OKH*/GenStdH/Org.Abt.I/15946/44 g.K., 21.3.44 [BaMa, RH 10/20] The 4 March document mentions the "*Geb.Haub. 36*", but this weapon did not exist. On 21 March it was corrected to the *7,5 cm Gebirgsgeschütz 36*.
24. *OKH*/GenStdH/Org.Abt.I/15946/44 g.K., 4.3.44, p.1-2 [BaMa, RH10/20]
25. *OKH*/GenStdH/Org.Abt. Nr.I/17239/44 g.K., 25.5.44 [T78 R526 F160]
26. *OKH*/GenStdH/Org.Abt. Nr.I/5895.44 g.K., 5.6.4 [T78 R526 F207]
27. *OKH*/AHA/Abwicklungsstab, Anl. z. Sachgeb. 91 Nr.6.44 g., *91.Inf.Division (Div. 25. Welle), Stand v. 6.6.44* [T78 R672 H41/61b] — Hereafter referred to as *91. I.D., Gliederung*, 6.6.44
28. Captured *Kriegsgliederung* of the *91. I.D.*, issued with SHAEF, G2 Division, SHAEF Intelligence Notes #18, 13 Jul. 44, A-17 [UKNA, WO 219/5229] — Hereafter referred to as *91. I.D., Kriegsgliederung*, 15.4.44 [UKNA, WO 219/5229]
29. *OKH*, Chef H Rüst und BdE, AHA/Stab I(1)/I(3) Nr.2987/44 g.K., 4.5.44, incl. Anl. [T78 R763 H19/56]
30. Zetterling bases his estimate on the 32 trains needed to transport the division. When the same logic is applied to the *77. I.D.*, this division should be weaker since it only required 29 trains. However, he already gives a higher number of men for that division. [**Zetterling, N. (2000)**, p.229 & 239; *AOK 7*/O.Qu., *Kriegstagebuch der Oberquartiermeisterabteilung AOK 7 für die Zeit vom 1.5.44 - 31.5.44* [T312 R1571 F296]]

31. SHAEF, G-2 Summary, Nr.10, 15 June 1944, p.2 [UKNA, WO 208/5562]

32. Data obtained from the German Red Cross *Vermisstenbildliste* and death cards in the Ancestry.com 'Germany, Military Killed in Action, 1939-1948' collection. A few additional KIA were added from IPW-43, IPW Report, 6 June 44 [82AB, G-2 Message File "Neptune", 6-12 June 1944]

33. The number of weapons is a close match to those of the *Kriegsgliederung* of 15 April. This suggests that it did not precede the *Gliederung* by much.

34. SHAEF, G2 Division, *SHAEF Intelligence Notes #18*, 13 Jul. 44, p.A-5 [UKNA, WO 219/5229]; *91. I.D., Gliederung*, 6.6.44; OKH, Chef H Rüst und BdE, AHA/Stab I(1)/I(3) Nr.2987/44 g.K., 4.5.44, incl. Anl. [T78 R763 H19/56]

35. AOK 7, Armee-Nachrichten-Führer 7, *Tatigkeitsbericht für die Zeit vom 1.5. - 5.6.44*, 5.6.44, p.1 [T312 R1566 F642]; See monthly reports (*Tätigkeitsbericht*) from the Armee-Nachrichten-Führer 7 for the period Jan-May 1944: [T312 R1566 F407-8, 466, 565, 483 & 642]

36. Triepel, G. (1946), MS # B-260 (Germ.), *I.Abschnitt, Cotentin (6.Juni - 18.Juni 1944)*, p.3-4

37. PWIS(H)/LDC/239, 16 Aug 44, p.1-2 [UKNA, WO 208/3647]

38. *91. I.D., Kriegsgliederung*, 15.4.44 [UKNA, WO 219/5229]; *91. I.D., Gliederung*, 6.6.44; Alph. Kartei von allen Inf. Offizieren einschliesslich Oberst, index card of *Obst.* Beigang [T78 R917 H6/355]; Alph. Kartei von allen Inf. Offizieren einschliesslich Oberst, index card of *Obstlt.* v. Saldern [T78 R913 H6/355]; Feldpostübersicht: **Nauroth, H.S. & B. Steinberg (2017)**, p.5 & 8

39. *91. I.D., Kriegsgliederung*, 15.4.44 [UKNA, WO 219/5229]; *91. I.D., Gliederung*, 6.6.44

40. *Ibid.*; PWIS(H)/112, PWs taken 9 Jun 44 [UKNA, WO 208/3622]; C.S.D.I.C. (UK) S.*IR* 465, 29 Jun 44 [NARA, RG 165, Box 659, Folder 4]

41. PWIS(H)/112, PWs taken 9 Jun 44, p.1 & App. A [UKNA, WO 208/3622]

42. *91. I.D., Kriegsgliederung*, 15.4.44 [UKNA, WO 219/5229]

43. C.S.D.I.C. (UK) S.*IR* 362, 16 Jun 44, p.1-2 [NARA, RG 165, Box 660, Folder 4]; *K.St.N. (Heer) Nr.111 n, Stab eines Infanteriebataillons (n.A.)*, 1.12.43 [CAMO, Bestand 500, Findbuch 12451, Akte 142]

44. PWIS(H)/112, POWs taken 9 Jun 44, App.A [UKNA, WO 208/3622]; PWIS(H)/125, 13 Jun 44, p.1 [UKNA, WO 208/3622]; C.S.D.I.C. (UK) S.*IR* 368, 16 Jun 44 [NARA, RG 165, Box 660, Folder 4]

45. PWIS(H)/LDC/39, 28 Jun 44, p.2 [UKNA, WO 208/3645]

46. PWIS(H)/112, POWs taken 9 Jun 44, p.1 & App.A [UKNA, WO 208/3622]

47. *91. I.D., Kriegsgliederung*, 15.4.44 [UKNA, WO 219/5229]

48. PWIS(H)/125, 13 Jun 44, p.1 [UKNA, WO 208/3622]

49. PWIS(H)/112, POWs taken 9 Jun 44 [UKNA, WO 208/3622]

50. *Ibid.*, p.1; PWIS(H)/125, 13 Jun 44, p.1 [UKNA, WO 208/3622]

51. AOK 7 Ia, *Kriegstagebuch der Führungsabteilung AOK 7 für die Zeit vom 1.Jan. - 30.Juni 1944* [T312 R1564 F270-1] — Hereafter referred to as: AOK 7 Ia, KTB 1.1.-30.6.1944

52. PWIS(H)/112, POWs taken 9 Jun 44, App.A [UKNA, WO 208/3622]; C.S.D.I.C. (UK) S.*IR* 345 [UKNA, WO 208/3590]; PWIS(H)/LDC/39, 28 Jun 44, p.1 [UKNA, WO 208/3645]

53. C.S.D.I.C. (UK) S.*IR* 345 [UKNA, WO 208/3590]

54. C.S.D.I.C. (UK) S.*IR* 362, 16 Jun 44, p.1 [NARA, RG 165, Box 660, Folder 4]

55. PWIS(H)/112, POWs taken 9 Jun 44, p.1 [UKNA, WO 208/3622]

56. PWIS(H)/125, 13 Jun 44, p.1 [UKNA, WO 208/3622]

57. PWIS(H)/188, POWs taken 8-9 Jun 44 [UKNA, WO 208/3622]

58. PWIS(H)/LDC/39, 28 Jun 44, p.1 [UKNA, WO 208/3645]

59. C.S.D.I.C. (UK) S.R.REPORT, S.R.M.545, 14 Jun 44, p.1-2 [UKNA, W0 208/4138]

60. PWIS(H)/LDC/39, 28 Jun 44, p.1 [UKNA, WO 208/3645]

61. C.S.D.I.C. (UK) S.*IR* 368, 16 Jun 44 [NARA, RG 165, Box 660, Folder 4]

62. PWIS(H)/112, POWs taken 9 Jun 44, p.1 [UKNA, WO 208/3622]

63. PWIS(H)/188, POWs taken 8-9 Jun 44 [UKNA, WO 208/3622]

64. PWIS(H)/125, 13 Jun 44, p.1 [UKNA, WO 208/3622]

65. PWIS(H)/LDC/39, 28 Jun 44, p.1 [UKNA, WO 208/3645]

66. C.S.D.I.C. (UK) S.*IR* 362, 16 Jun 44, p.1 [NARA, RG 165, Box 660, Folder 4]

67. C.S.D.I.C. (UK) S.*IR* 368, 16 Jun 44 [NARA, RG 165, Box 660, Folder 4]; PWIS(H)/112, POWs taken 9 Jun 44, p.1 [UKNA, WO 208/3622]; PWIS(H)/125, 13 Jun 44, p.1 [UKNA, WO 208/3622]

68. PWIS(H)/112, POWs taken 9 Jun 44, p.1 [UKNA, WO 208/3622]

69. PWIS(H)/125, 13 Jun 44, p.1 [UKNA, WO 208/3622]

70. C.S.D.I.C. (UK) S.*IR* 362, 16 Jun 44, p.1 [NARA, RG 165, Box 660, Folder 4]; *K.St.N. (Heer) Nr.131 n, Schützenkompanie (n.A.)*, 1.5.44 [T78 R391 F6359520-22]

71. OKH, Chef H Rüst und BdE, AHA/Stab I(1)/I(3) Nr.2987/44, g.K., 4.5.44, Blatt 1 [T78 R763 H19/56]; *K.St.N. (Heer) Nr.131 n, Schützenkompanie (n.A.)*, 1.5.44 [T78 R391 F6359520-22]; SHAEF, G2 Division, *SHAEF Intelligence Notes #18*, 13 Jul. 44, A-3 [UKNA, WO 219/5229]

72. *91. I.D., Kriegsgliederung*, 15.4.44 [UKNA, WO 219/5229]

73. *91. I.D., Gliederung*, 6.6.44

74. SHAEF, G2 Division, *SHAEF Intelligence Notes #18*, 13 Jul 44, A-5 [UKNA, WO 219/5229]

75. *91. I.D., Kriegsgliederung*, 15.4.44 [UKNA, WO 219/5229]

76. PWIS(H)/LF/168, 22 Jun 44 [UKNA, WO 208/3630]

77. *K.St.N. (Heer) Nr. 171 n, Infanteriegeschützkompanie (n.A.) (2 s.I.G. 6 le I.G.)*, 1.12.43 [CAMO, Bestand 500, Findbuch 12451, Akte 142]

78. PWIS(H)/112, POWs taken 9 Jun 44, App.A [UKNA, WO 208/3622]

79. OKH/AHA/Abwicklungsstab, Anl. z. Sachgeb. 91 Nr.6.44 g., *Kriegsgliederung KampfGruppe König, Stand: 18.6.44 - 28.6.44* [T78 R672 H41/61b] — Hereafter referred to as *91. I.D., Kriegsgliederung KG König*, 18.-28.6.44

80. OKH Chef H Rüst und BdE, AHA Ia(I) Nr.510/44 g.K., 21.1.44, p.5 [T78 R848 H36/153]

81. Compare KStN 177 and KStN 428a. [*K.St.N. (Heer) Nr.177, Schwere Gebirgsjägerkompanie*, 1.3.44 in T78 R391 F6359688-94]; *K.St.N. (Heer) Nr.428a, Batterie 7,5cm Gebirgsgeschütze 36 (zu 54 Geschützen) einer Jägerdivision*, 1.11.43 in T78 R392 F6360104-7]

82. This conflicts with a captured regimental order from 8 June, which refers to three platoons with *I.K.H.'s*, but a translation or transcription error cannot be ruled out.

83. PWIS(H)/LDC/96, 10 Jul 44, p.1 [UKNA, WO 208/3645]; *91. I.D., Kriegsgliederung KG König*, 18.-28.6.44. It should be noted that this information was provided in July 1944, after the remnants of the *13./1057* had joined the *13./1058*. It still seems likely that his description of the organisation of the *13./1057* refers to the situation on D-Day.

84. OKH/AHA/Abwicklungsstab, Anl. z. Sachgeb. 91 Nr.6.44 g., *Kriegsgliederung Kampfgruppe 91. I.D., Stand*: 18.6.44 [T78 R672 H41/61b] — Hereafter referred to as *91. I.D., Kriegsgliederung KG 91. I.D.*, 18.6.44; *91. I.D., Kriegsgliederung KG König*, 18.-28.6.44

85. PWIS(H)/LDC/96, 10 Jul 44, p.1 [UKNA, WO 208/3645]; *91. I.D., Kriegsgliederung KG König*, 18.-28.6.44

86. PWIS(H)/LF/168, 22 Jun 44 [UKNA, WO 208/3630]

87. *91. I.D., Kriegsgliederung*, 15.4.44 [UKNA, WO 219/5229]; SHAEF, G2 Division, *SHAEF Intelligence Notes #18*, 13 Jul. 44, A-6 [UKNA, WO 219/5229]; PWIS(H)/188, PWs taken 8-9 Jun 44 [UKNA, WO 208/3622]; PWIS/LDC/96, 10 Jul 44, p.1 [UKNA, WO 208/3645]; C.S.D.I.C. (UK) S.*IR* 459, 26 Jun 44 [NARA, RG 165, Box 659]

88. C.S.D.I.C. (UK) S.*IR* 459, 26 Jun 44, p.1 [NARA, RG 165, Box 659]

89. PWIS(H)/188, POWs taken 8-9 Jun 44 [UKNA, WO 208/3622]; C.S.D.I.C. (UK) S.*IR* 459, 26 Jun 44, p.1 [NARA, RG 165, Box 659, Folder 2]

90. *K.St.N. (Heer) 1140 n, Panzerjägerkompanie (n.A,) (zu 12 Geschützen 7.5cm Pak)*, 1.10.43 [T78 R393 F6361777-9]

91. PWIS(H)/188, POWs taken 8-9 Jun 44 [UKNA, WO 208/3622]; C.S.D.I.C. (UK) S.*IR* 459, 26 Jun 44, p.1 [NARA, RG 165, Box 659, Folder 2] He claims that the first platoon in his company also had two or three lighter guns than *Pak 40's*. It is possible that the ad hoc 4th Platoon was attached to the 1st Platoon, without him realising this. Currently there is no evidence that, despite the plans from March, the company had anything more than two *Ofenrohr* platoons with 18 launchers each; PWIS/LDC/96, 10 Jul 44, p.1 [UKNA, WO 208/3645]

92. KStN 154b also called for a man in each section to lead a horse. Such a man was also in the platoon headquarters as well as a messenger and two machine-gunners.

93. C.S.D.I.C. (UK) S.*IR* 459, 26 Jun 44, p.1 [NARA, RG 165, Box 659, Folder 2]

94. SHAEF, G2 Division, *SHAEF Intelligence Notes #18*, 13 Jul. 44, A-6 [UKNA, WO 219/5229]

95. C.S.D.I.C. (UK) S.*IR* 459, 26 Jun 44, p.1 [NARA, RG 165, Box 659]

96. PWIS(H)/LDC/96, 10 Jul 44, p.1 [UKNA, WO 208/3645]

97. C.S.D.I.C. (UK) S.*IR* 459, 26 Jun 44, p.1-2 [NARA, RG 165, Box 659]

98. *Ibid.*, p.1. The document mentions platoons instead of sections, but then the numbers would not add up.

99. *K.St.N. (Heer) Nr.154 b, Panzerzerstörerzug einer Infanterie-Panzerjägerkompanie*, 1.2.44 [CAMO, Bestand 500, Findbuch 12451, Akte 142]

100. PWIS(H)/188, POWs taken 8-9 Jun 44 [UKNA, WO 208/3622]
101. Nauroth, H.S. & B. Steinberg (2017), p.18
102. *Ibid*., p.32; *OKH*, Chef H Rüst und BdE, AHA/Stab I(1)/I(3) Nr.2987/44, g.K., 4.5.44, Blatt 1 [T78 R763 H19/56] The invasion time numbers, per the *Inf.Div. 44 KStN's*, would be: 13, 2, 116, 597 (including 98 *Hiwi's*). This includes another medium mortar platoon, while replacing one of its NCO's with an officer.
103. Nauroth, H.S. & B. Steinberg (2017), p.14
104. SHAEF, G2 Division, *SHAEF Intelligence Notes #18*, 13 Jul 44, A3 & A-5 [UKNA, WO 219/5229]
105. Nauroth, H.S. & B. Steinberg (2017), p.32; *OKH*, Chef H Rüst und BdE AHA/Stab I(1)/I(3) Nr.2987/44, g.K., 4.5.44, Blatt 1 [T78 R763 H19/56]
106. *91. I.D., Kriegsgliederung*, 15.4.44 [UKNA, WO 219/5229]; *91. I.D., Gliederung*, 6.6.44
107. Nauroth, H.S. & B. Steinberg (2017), p.16; PWSI(H)/LF/212, 2 Jul 44 [UKNA, WO 208/3631]; *91. I.D., Kriegsgliederung*, 15.4.44 [UKNA, WO 219/5229]; SHAEF, G2 Division, *SHAEF Intelligence Notes #18*, 13 Jul 44, A-6 [UKNA, WO 219/5229]; *K.St.N. (Heer) 1140 n, Panzerjägerkompanie (n.A.) (zu 12 Geschützen 7.5cm Pak)*, 1.10.43 [T78 R393 F6361777-9]
108. SHAEF, G2 Division, *SHAEF Intelligence Notes #18*, 13 Jul 44, A-3 & A-5 [UKNA, WO 219/5229]
109. *91. I.D., Gliederung*, 6.6.44; PWIS(H)/LF/199, 29 Jun 44, p.1-2 [UKNA, WO 208/3630]
110. *OKH/Org.Abt.(I), Nr.I/18310/44 g.K., 24.7.1944, Gliederung d. Inf.Div.(25th wave)* [T78 R410 F6378477]; *91. I.D., Gliederung*, 6.6.44
111. Nauroth, H.S. & B. Steinberg (2017), p.12 & p.16
112. Feldpostübersicht
113. Nauroth, H.S. & B. Steinberg (2017), p.18; *91. I.D., Kriegsgliederung*, 15.4.44 [UKNA, WO 219/5229]
114. Feldposübersicht
115. See chapter *"77. Infanterie-Division"*
116. PWIS(H)/LF/199, 29 Jun 44, p.1 [UKNA, WO 208/3630]
117. *Ibid*.
118. SHAEF, G2 Division, *SHAEF Intelligence Notes #18*, 13 Jul. 44, A-3 [UKNA, WO 219/5229]
119. Zetterling (2000), p.239
120. *Div.Füs.Kp. 191, Tätigkeitsbericht der Div.Füs.Komp.191*, 17.5.44 [BAMA, RH 26-91/11].
121. PWIS(H)/LDC/32, 27 Jun 44, p1 [UKNA, WO 208/3645]
122. *OKH/GenStdH/Org.Abt. Nr.I/17239/44 g.K., 25.5.44* [T78 R526 F160]
123. PWIS(H)/LDC/32, 27 Jun 44, p.1 [UKNA, WO 208/3645]
124. PWIS(H)/179, POW taken 9 Jun 44) [UKNA, WO 208/3622]
125. PWIS(H)/LDC/32, 27 Jun 44, p.1 [UKNA, WO 208/3645]; PWIS(H)/179, PW taken 9 Jun 44) [UKNA, WO 208/3622]. The medic claimed that there were actually four sections per platoon and that each had a machine gun. The information from the company commander is considered more reliable.
126. PWIS(H)/LDC/32, 27 Jun 44, p.1 [UKNA, WO 208/3645]
127. *91.I.D., Kriegsgliederung*, 15.4.44 [UKNA, WO 219/5229]
128. *Div.Füs.Kp. 191, Tätigkeitsbericht der Div.Füs.Komp.191*, 17.5.44 [BAMA, RH 26-91/11]
129. PWIS(H)/LDC/29, 27 Jun 44 [UKNA, WO 208/3645];
PWIS(H)/179, POW taken 9 Jun 44) [UKNA, WO 208/3622]
130. *91.I.D., Kriegsgliederung*, 15.4.44 [UKNA, WO 219/5229]
131. *OKH/Ch H Rüst u BdE AHA/Ia(I) Nr.377/44 g.K., 15.1.44, p.1 [T78 R848 H36/153]; OKH/Ch H Rüst u BdE AHA/Ia(I) Nr.510/44 g.K., 21.1.44, p.1* [T78 R848 H36/153]; an early *Gliederung* of a regular 25th wave division can be found in *AOK 7, Ia Nr.755/44 g.K., 9.2.44, Anl.1* [T312 R1565 F79]
132. Anl.2 zu *OKH/GenStdH/Org.Abt. Nr.I/1299/44 g.K. Chefs., 6.6.44* [T78 R420 F6389914]; *OKH/GenStdH/Org.Abt., Nr.I/18310/44 g.K., 24.7.44, Gliederung d. Inf.Div.(25th wave)* [T78 R410 F6378477]
133. *OKH/GenStdH/Org.Abt.I/15946/44 g.K., 4.3.44, p.1* [BaMa, RH 10/20]; *OKH/GenStdH/Org.Abt.I/15946/44 g.K., 21.3.44* [BaMa, RH 10/20]
134. *Feldpostübersicht*
135. C.S.D.I.C. (UK) S.IR 370, 16 Jun 44, App. [NARA, RG 165, Box 660]; SHAEF, G2 Division, *SHAEF Intelligence Notes #18*, 13 Jul 44, A3 & A-5 [UKNA, WO 219/5229]; *91. I.D., Kriegsgliederung*, 15.4.44 [UKNA, WO 219/5229]
136. Nauroth, H.S. & B. Steinberg (2017), p.18
137. *91. I.D., Kriegsgliederung*, 15.4.44 [UKNA, WO 219/5229]
138. *Feldpostübersicht*; PWIS(H)/LDC/39, 28 Jun 44, p.1 [UKNA, WO 208/3645]; **Nauroth, H.S. & B. Steinberg (2017)**, p.13
139. Nauroth, H.S. & B. Steinberg (2017), p.12
140. PWIS(H)/LDC/39, 28 Jun 44, p.1 [UKNA, WO 208/3645]
141. Nauroth, H.S. & B. Steinberg (2017), p.17
142. *OKH/GenStdH/Org.Abt.(I), Nr.I/18310/44 g.K., 24.7.44, Gliederung d. Inf.Div.(25th wave)* [T78 R410 F6378477]; See chapter *"77. Infanterie-Division"*
143. *OKH/Ch H Rüst u BdE AHA/Ia(I) Nr.377/44 g.K., 15.1.44, p.1* [T78 R848 H36/153]
144. *AOK 7, Ia Nr.3454/44 g.K., 2.Teil, 27.6.44* [T312 R1565 F1377]; Situation report from *Fj.Rgt. 6* to *17. SS-Pz.Gren. Div.*, 10.7.44 [Published in **Wind, M. & H. Günther (2004)**, *Kriegstagebuch 17.SS-Panzer-Grenadier-Division „Götz von Berlichingen" - Auswahl von Dokumenten - 30. Oktober 1943 bis 6. Mai 1945*, St.Ingbert: Dengmerter Heimatverlag]
145. Post referring to "General der Artillerie beim Chef Gen. St.d.H.(Ib) Nr.2570/44 g., 5.4.44" [https://forum.axishistory.com/viewtopic.php?f=50&t=227060&p=2064047#p2064047, accessed on 2 May 2022]
146. PWIS(H)/LDC/109, 12 Jul 44 [UKNA, WO 208/3646]
147. SHAEF, G2 Division, *SHAEF Intelligence Notes #18*, 13 Jul. 44, A-3 [UKNA, WO 219/5229]
148. *91. I.D., Kriegsgliederung*, 15.4.44 [UKNA, WO 219/5229]
149. PWIS(H)/LDC/109, 12 Jul 44 [UKNA, WO 208/3646]
150. *Ibid*.
151. C.S.D.I.C. (UK) S.IR 370, 16 Jun 44 [NARA, RG 165, Box 660]
152. Triepel, G. (1947), MS # B-469 (Germ.), *II.Teil, (18.6.-31.7.44), Artillerie-Führer 91.Infanterie-Division*, p.1; **Choltitz, D. von (1947)**, MS # B-418 (Germ.), *Kämpfe des LXXXIV. A.K. in der Normandie vom 18.6.144 ab*, p.13; **König, E. (1946)**, p.2-3; *AOK 7/O.Qu., Kriegstagebuch der Oberquartiermeisterabteilung AOK 7 für die Zeit vom 1.6.44 - 30.6.44* [T312 R1571 F481]
153. *AOK 7/O.Qu., Kriegstagebuch der Oberquartiermeisterabteilung AOK 7 für die Zeit vom 1.6.44 - 30.6.44* [T312 R1571 F481]; *AOK 7/O.Qu., Kriegstagebuch der Oberquartiermeisterabteilung AOK 7 für die Zeit vom 1.6.44 - 30.6.44* [T312 R1571 F503]; Anl.1 zu *AOK 7, O.Qu./Qu.1, Nr.2081/44 g.K., 5.6.44*, p.2 [T312 R1571 F598]
154. *AOK 7/O.Qu., Kriegstagebuch der Oberquartiermeisterabteilung AOK 7 für die Zeit vom 1.6.44 - 30.6.44* [T312 R1571 F491]
155. Triepel, G. (1947), p.1
156. König, E. (1946), p.3; **Triepel, G. (**1947), p.2-3
157. *91. I.D., Kriegsgliederung KG 91*, 18.6.44; *OKH/AHA/Abwicklungstab, Anl. z. Sachgeb. Nr.91.6.44 g., (Kriegsgliederung) 91. I.D. (Div.25th wave) mit Unterstellungen, Stand vom 20.6.44* [T78 R672 H41/61b] — Hereafter referred to as *91. I.D., Kriegsgliederung 91. I.D. mit Unterstellungen*, 20.6.44; *AOK 7, Ia Nr.3454/44 g.K., 2.Teil, 27.6.44* [T312 R1565 F1377]; *Gen.Kdo.LXXXIV. A.K., Ia Nr.035/44, Takt. Gliederung der Artillerie, Stand: 21.7.44*, 22.7.44 [T314 R1604 F1388]; **Nauroth, H.S. & B. Steinberg (2017)**, p.157
158. *Gen.d.Art.b.Ob.West Ib Nr.1077/44 g.K., Landeabwehrgeschütze: Stand v. 1.4.44*, 18.4.44 [CAMO, Bestand 500, Findbuch 12451, Akte 418]
159. *Gen.Kdo.LXXXIV. A.K., Ia Nr.1370/43 g.K., 19.7.43*, p.2 [T314 R1604 F705]; Report of the *91. I.D.* on a conference with the commander of the *LXXXIV. A.K.* on 11.5.44, 11.5.44, copied and translated in Annex 1 to G-2 Periodic Report Nr.9, HQ First US Army, 19 June 44 [Available at https://firstdivisionmuseum.nmtvault.com/jsp/viewer.jsp?doc_id=iwfd0000%2F20141124%2F165&page_name=800, accessed on 4 Aug. 2018]
160. *91. I.D., Kriegsgliederung*, 15.4.44 [UKNA, WO 219/5229]; *91. I.D., Gliederung*, 6.6.44
161. SHAEF, G2 Division, *SHAEF Intelligence Notes #18*, 13 Jul. 44, A-3 [UKNA, WO 219/5229]
162. *OKH/GenStdH/Org.Abt. Nr.I/17239/44 g.K., 25.5.44* [T78 R526 F160]
163. *OKH/GenStdH/Org.Abt. Nr.I/7281/44 g., 30.7.44* [T78 R526 F447]
164. SHAEF, G2 Division, *SHAEF Intelligence Notes #18*, 13 Jul. 44, A-3 [UKNA, WO 219/5229]
165. *Ibid*.
166. PWIS(H)/143, POW taken 7 Jun 44 [UKNA, WO 208/3622]
167. SHAEF, G2 Division, *SHAEF Intelligence Notes #18*, 13 Jul. 44, A-3 [UKNA, WO 219/5229]
168. For example, see **DeTrez, M. (2004)**, *Sainte-Mere-Eglise - Photographs of D-Day*, Wezembeck-Oppem, D-Day Publishing, p.175-179, 186-189; The 325th GIR (82AB) alone captured 13 of these vehicles in one area on 8 June. [HQ 325th Glider Infantry, *S-2 Journal - Operation Neptune, Cotentin Peninsula, France*, p.2]
169. SHAEF, G2 Division, *SHAEF Intelligence Notes #18*, 13 Jul. 44, A-4 & A-5 [UKNA, WO 219/5229]
170. PWIS(H)/188, POWs taken 8-9 Jun 44 [UKNA, WO 208/3622]; *K.St.N. (Heer) 188a n, Teileinheit, Führer einer Infanteriepanzerjägerkompanie (tmot) (n.A.)*, 1.12.43 [CAMO, Bestand 500, Findbuch 12451, Akte 142]; *K.St.N. (Heer) Nr.188f n, Infanteriepanzerjägerzug (zu 3 Geschützen 7.5cm Pak (mot) (n.A.)*, 1.12.43 [CAMO, Bestand 500, Findbuch 12451, Akte

142]; *K.St.N. (Heer) Nr.154 b, Panzerzerstörerzug einer Infanterie-Panzerjägerkompanie*, 1.2.44 [CAMO, Bestand 500, Findbuch 12451, Akte 142]
171. PWIS(H)/112, POWs taken 9 Jun 44, App.A [UKNA, WO 208/3622]; *K.St.N. (Heer) Nr.130 n, Stabskompanie eines Infanterieregiments (n.A.)*, 1.4.44 [CAMO, Bestand 500, Findbuch 12451, Akte 142]
172. SHAEF, G2 Division, *SHAEF Intelligence Notes #18*, 13 Jul. 44, A-3 & A-4 & A-5 [UKNA, WO 219/5229] The authorised number of vehicles for regular 25th wave divisions, based on the *KStN's*, can be found in *OKH/Chef H Rüst und BdE, AHA/Stab I(1)/I(3) Nr.298/44 g.K.*, 4.5.44 in T78 R763 H19/56]
173. *Ibid.*
174. *Ibid.*
175. *Ibid.*
176. *Ibid.*
177. Der Generalinspekteur der Panzertruppen, Nr.810/44 g.K., *Führervortrag am 27.3.44 (Anl. 1 z. Teil A)*, 28.3.44 [T78 R622 F805]
178. Nauroth, H.S. & B. Steinberg (2017), p.4-8, 10-12, 14 & 16
179. OKW/WFSt/Op. Nr.771370/44 g.K. Chefs., 27.4.44, p.1-2 [CAMO, Bestand 500, Findbuch 12450, Akte 115]; *OKH, Organisationabteilung I P, Beitrag zu KTB*, 7.6.44 [T78 R420 F63890532]
180. OKW/WFSt/Op. Nr.771370/44 g.K. Chefs., 27.4.44, p.1-2 [CAMO, Bestand 500, Findbuch 12450, Akte 115]
181. *AOK 7* Ia, *KTB* 1.1.-30.6.1944 [T312 R1564 F246]
182. *AOK 7* BvTO, Anl.15 zum Tätigkeitsbericht BvTO *AOK 7, Zusammenstellung der in der Zeit vom 1.4. – 30.6.44 im Armeebereich durchgeführten Bewegungen.*, p.1 [T312 R1571 F982]
183. *AOK 7* BvTO, Anl.15 zum Tätigkeitsbericht BvTO *AOK 7, Zusammenstellung der in der Zeit vom 1.4. – 30.6.44 im Armeebereich durchgeführten Bewegungen.*, p.1 [T312 R1571 F982]; *AOK 7/O.Qu., Qu.1 Nr.8419/44 g., Besondere Anordnungen für die VeRSOrgung anlässlich des Eintreffens der 91. LL.D.*, 6.5.44 [T312 R1571 F349]; *AOK 7*, Ia Nr.2347/44 g.K., 1.5.44 [T312 R1565 F580-1]
184. *Ibid.*
185. *AOK 7*, Ia Nr.2430/44 g.K.II.Ang., 8.5.44 [T312 R1565 F636]
186. *AOK 7* BvTO, Anl.15 zum Tätigkeitsbericht BvTO *AOK 7, Zusammenstellung der in der Zeit vom 1.4. – 30.6.44 im Armeebereich durchgeführten Bewegungen.*, p.1 [T312 R1571 F982]
187. *AOK 7* BvTO, Anl.15 zum Tätigkeitsbericht BvTO *AOK 7, Zusammenstellung der in der Zeit vom 1.4. – 30.6.44 im Armeebereich durchgeführten Bewegungen.*, p.1 [T312 R1571 F982]; *AOK 7*, Ia Nr.680/44 g., p.1, 10.5.44 [T312 R1565 F672]; *AOK 7*, Ia Nr.696/44 g., p.1, 11.5.44 [T312 R1565 F687]; *AOK 7*, Ia Nr.714/44 g., 12.5.44 [T312 R1565 F689]; *AOK 7*, Ia Nr.25386/44 g.K., 13.5.44, p.1 [T312 R1565 F693]; *AOK 7*, Ia Nr.2546/44 g.K., 14.5.44 [T312 R1565 F700]; *AOK 7*, Ia Nr.773/44 g., 15.5.44 [T312 R1565 F705]
188. *AOK 7*, Ia Nr.2546/44 g.K. [T312 R1565 F700]; *AOK 7* Ia, Anlage zum K.T.B. Führungsabt. *AOK 7* Ia, Lage-Karten A.O.K.7 vom 6.1.-5.6.44, *Stand: 5.6.44* [T312 R1570 F9-10, original in BaMa RH 20-7/138K] — Hereafter referred to as *AOK 7*, Situation map, 5.6.44
189. *AOK 7*, Ia Nr.2567/44 g.K., 16.5.44, p.1 [T312 R1565 F710]
190. Report of the *91. I.D.* in a conference with the commander of the *LXXXIV. A.K.* on 11.5.44, copied and translated in Annex 1 to G-2 Periodic Report Nr.9, HQ First US Army, 19 June 44 [Available at https://firstdivisionmuseum.nmtvault.com/jsp/viewer.jsp?doc_id=iwfd0000%2F20141124%2F165&page_name=800, accessed on 4 Aug. 2018]
191. Gen.Kdo.*LXXXIV. A.K.*, Ia Nr.1370/43 g.K., 19.7.43, p.2 [T314 R1604 F705]
192. Report of the *91. I.D.* in a conference with the commander of the *LXXXIV. A.K.* on 11.5.44, copied and translated in Annex 1 to G-2 Periodic Report Nr.9, HQ First US Army, 19 June 44; *AOK 7* (Maj.i.G. Johannes) Ia Nr.6001/43 g., *Anl.1 zum Bericht über Reise O.B. v. 17. – 20.11.43*, 22.11.43, p.1 [T312 R1559 F162]
193. Gen.Kdo.*LXXXIV. A.K.*, Ia Nr.1168/44, 12.5.44 [T312 R1565 F682] (document incorrectly dated 12.4.44)
194. PWIS(H)/125, 13 Jun 44, p.1 [UKNA, WO 208/3622]; **Heydte, F.A. von der (1952)**, p.8
195. *91. I.D.*, Ia Nr.145/44 g.K., 5.6.44 [copied and translated as enclosure No.3 to 82nd Airborne Division, *G-2 Report No.65*, 14 Jun 44, NARA] The accompanying map with the exact area is missing. Also, the composition of the motorised combat team was specified in a previous order, which has not been found.
196. *Ibid.*
197. *AOK 7*, Situation map, 5.6.44
198. order from *Ob.West* (*H.Gr. D*) Ia on 13.5.44 [UKNA, HW 5/489, CX/MSS/T197/31, KV 5416]
199. *AOK 7*, Ia Nr.2546/44 g.K., 14.5.44 [T312 R1565 F700] ; *AOK 7*, Situation map, 5.6.44
200. *AOK 7*, Ia Nr.2546/44 g.K., 14.5.44 [T312 R1565 F700]; *AOK 7*, Situation map, 5.6.44; **Keil, G. (1948b)**, MS # B-844 (Germ.), *Bericht zu der Anfrage der Historischen Division über den Einsatz des Inf. Regiments 1058 und der Kampfgruppe Keil*, p.2
201. Keil, G. (1948b), p.2 & 4
202. PWIS(H)/125, 13 Jun 44, p.2 [UKNA, WO 208/3622]; PWIS(H)/188, PWs taken 8-9 Jun 44 [UKNA, WO 208/3622]; C.S.D.I.C. (UK) *S.IR* 345 [NARA, RG 165, Box 660]; PWIS(H)/125, 13 Jun 44, p.2 [UKNA, WO 208/3622]; Message from 7 PW Cage (Sgt. Berland) to CG 82nd Airborne Div., 8 Jun 44 at 21:10 [NARA, via Egbert van de Schootbrugge]
203. Keil, G. (1948b), p.2 & 5
204. Nauroth, H.S. & B. Steinberg (2017), p.40; **Keil, G. (1948b)**, p.5
205. Keil, G. (1948b), p.2
206. Message CG 82nd Airborne Div. To CG VII Corps, 7 Jun 44 at 21:10 [NARA, via Egbert van de Schootbrugge]
207. *AOK 7*, Situation map, 5.6.44
208. PWIS(H)/130, 14 Jun 44 UKNA, WO 208/3622]
209. Gren.Rgt.1057, Ia, 20.5.44 [copied and translated in 82nd Airborne Division, *Interrogation Report No.7*, 14 Jun 44, NARA]
210. PWIS(H)/LDC/32, 27 Jun 44, p.1 [UKNA, WO 208/3645]; *91. I.D.*, Ia Nr.145/44 g.K., 5.6.44 [copied and translated as enclosure No.3 to 82nd Airborne Division, *G-2 Report No.65*, 14 Jun 44 & Message from IPW-43 to S-2 508th PIR, 6 Jun 44 [both NARA, via Egbert van de Schootbrugge]
211. Gen.Kdo.*LXXXIV. A.K.*, Ia Nr.1168/44, 12.5.44 [T312 R1565 F682] (document incorrectly dated 12.4.44); **Nauroth, H.S. & B. Steinberg (2017)**, p.39 & 50; HQ 82nd Airborne Div., Interrogation Report No.1 6 Jun 44 [NARA, via Egbert van de Schootbrugge]
212. *AOK 7*, Ia Nr.1093/44 g., 2.6.44 [T312 R1565 F827]
213. *AOK 7*, Ia Nr.575/44 g., 3.5.44 [T312 R1565 F596]
214. Anl. zu OKH/AHA/Abwicklungsstab, Anl. z. Sachgeb. 91 Nr.6.44 g., *Kriegsgliederung (91. LL.D.), Unterstellungen Stand: 10.6.44* [T78 R672 H41/61b] — Hereafter referred to as *91. I.D., Kriegsgliederung 91. I.D., Unterstellungen*, 10.6.44
215. PWIS(H)/LDC/32, 27 Jun 44, p.1 [UKNA, WO 208/3645]
216. Gen.Kdo.*LXXXIV. A.K.*, Ia Nr.1168/44, 12.5.44 [T312 R1565 F682] (document incorrectly dated 12.4.44); PWIS(H)/LDC/32, 27 Jun 44, p.1 [UKNA, WO 208/3645]
217. Nauroth, H.S. & B. Steinberg (2017), p.36; *AOK 7*, Situation map, 5.6.44
218. *91. I.D., Kriegsgliederung 91. I.D., Unterstellungen*, 10.6.44; Annex No.1 to G-2 Report No.66: HQ 82nd Airborne Div., *Interrogation Report No.9 (correct)*, 15 Jun 44, p.1 [NARA, via Egbert van de Schootbrugge]
219. Nauroth, H.S. & B. Steinberg (2017), p.36 & 39; *91. I.D., Kriegsgliederung 91. I.D., Unterstellungen*, 10.6.44
220. *AOK 7*, Situation map, 5.6.44; PWIS(H)/LDC/32, 27 Jun 44, p.1 [UKNA, WO 208/3645]
221. C.S.D.I.C. (UK) *S.IR* 370, 16 Jun 44, p.1 [NARA, RG 165, Box 660, Folder 4]
222. Gen.Kdo.*LXXXIV. A.K.*, Ia Nr.1168/44, 12.5.44 [T312 R1565 F682] (document incorrectly dated 12.4.44)
223. Griesser, V. (2007), *Die Löwen von Carentan, Das Fallschirmjäger Regiment 6 1943-45*, Herne: VS-Books, p.103 & 126
224. PWIS(H)/LDC/109, 12 Jul 44 [UKNA, WO 208/3646]
225. Gren.Rgt.1057, Ia, *Regimental order for the defence of the Merderet Sector*, 8.6.44 [copied and translated as Enclosure No.2 to 82nd Airborne Division, *G-2 Report No.61*, 11 Jun 44, NARA]
226. *91. I.D.*, Ia Nr.145/44 g.K., 5.6.44 [copied and translated as enclosure No.3 to 82nd Airborne Division, *G-2 Report No.65*, 14 Jun 44, NARA]
227. *Fj.Rgt. 6*, After action report for 6-11 June 1944, 17.6.44 [collection Greg Way] The 9th Battery was linked to the *KG Bohnenkamp* sector in the plans from mid-May and several members of the battery were killed in the Pont-l'Abbé area on D-Day.
228. Nauroth, H.S. & B. Steinberg (2017), p.34 & 39. Unfortunately, the authors provide no actual evidence for the attachment of the *Sturmbataillon* battery or for its supposed location south of Cauvin. This location has also been linked to the *13./919*. Without evidence, a mix-up cannot be ruled out.
229. Gen.Kdo.*LXXXIV. A.K.*, Ia Nr.1168/44, 12.5.44 [T312 R1565 F682] (document incorrectly dated 12.4.44)
230. *AOK 7*, Situation map, 5.6.44
231. Gen.Kdo.*LXXXIV. A.K.*, Ia Nr.1168/44, 12.5.44 [T312 R1565 F682] (document incorrectly dated 12.4.44); PWIS(H)/LDC/96, 10 Jul 44, p.1 [UKNA, WO 208/3645]
232. *AOK 7*, Ia Nr.1288/44 g., 27.2.44, p.1 [T312 R1565 F180]
233. König, E. (1946), p.5
234. *Luftlandegeschwader*: airlanding wing.

235. *OKH*/GenStdH/Org.Abt.I/15946/44 g.K., 4.3.44, p.1-2 [BaMa, RH10/20]
236. *Ob.West* **(Okdo.d.**H.Gr. D**), Ia Nr.2537/44 g.K., 26.3.44** [T78 R311 F6262808]
237. *OKW*/WFSt/Op., Nr.003217/44, 29.3.44 [UKNA, HW 5/466, CX/MSS/T152/54, KV 828]
238. *OKW*/WFSt/Op. Nr.771370/44 g.K. Chefs., 27.4.44, p.1-2 [CAMO, Bestand 500, Findbuch 12450, Akte 115]; *OKH*, Organisationabteilung I P, *Beitrag zu KTB*, 7.6.44 [T78 R420 F63890532]
239. **Nauroth, H.S. & B. Steinberg (2017)**, p.24-25. This includes the map WFSt Op.(H), *Vorgesehene Kräfteverschibungen bei feindlichen Großlandungen, Stand: 4.5.44* (not identified in the book); **Office of Naval Intelligence (1950)**, *War Diary – German Naval Staff, Operations Division, Part A, Volume 53, January 44*, Washington, D.C., p.225
240. *AOK 7*, Ia Nr.2430/44 g.K.II.Ang., 8.5.44 [T312 R1565 F636]; *AOK 7*, Situation map, 5.6.44
241. Anlage zu *AOK 7*, Ia Nr.2710/44 g.K., p.1, 28.5.44 [T312 R1565 F794]
242. **Harrison, G.A. (1951, reprint 1984)**, *Cross-Channel Attack*, Office of the Chief of Military History United States Army: Washington D.C., p.280, 286-7, 289 & Map VIII, IX & X
243. *Ibid.*, map IX & X
244. **König, E. (1946)**, p.1-2
245. *AOK 7*, Ia Nr.1415/44 g., 15.6.44, p.2 [T312 R1565 F1052]; **Nauroth, H.S. & B. Steinberg (2017)**, p.45-46 & 48; C.S.D.I.C. (UK) S.*IR* 389, 17 Jun 44, p.1 [NARA, RG 165, Box 660, Folder 4]; **Nordyke, P. (2005)**, *All American All the Way*, St.Paul, MN: Zenith Press, p.275-6; HQ 325 Infantry, Supplement to Interrogation Report #3, 11 Jun 44 [NARA, via Egbert van de Schootbrugge] It is sometimes claimed that the driver was *Gefr. Vogt*, but this is questionable. Allied records identify him as *Uffz*. Baumann. As a prisoner he was also able to provide the make and registration number of the car, which lends credibility to his information.
246. **Pickert**, *Reisebericht*, 10.6.44, p.5 in *Ob.West*, *Anlage zum K.T.B., Befehle Meldungen, 6.6.-18.6.44* [T311 R25 85434.1 F7029433]
247. Armeefeldpostmeister beim *AOK 7*, III 2975 – O Bfb 1185/44 g.K., p.3, 18.6.44 [T312 R1571 F732]; Anl.3 z. Bericht Nr.86 des APM 7 2975-), BfB 1070/44 g.K., 5.6.44 [T312 R1571 F631]
248. 506th Parachute Infantry, *Operation Neptune S-1, S-2, S-3 Journals*, 1944, p.2-4 [NARA]; *AOK 7*, Ia Nr.1162/44 g., p.1 [T312 R1565 F861]; **Nauroth, H.S. & B. Steinberg (2017)**, p.34; **History Section, United States Army, European Theater of Operations (ETO)**, *Regimental Unit Study Number 3, 506 Parachute Infantry Regiment in Normandy Drop*, p.25-26, 30-33 [available at: https://history.army.mil/documents/wwii/506-nor/506-nor.htm, accessed 2 Aug. 2018] — Hereafter referred to as **History Section, United States Army,** *506th PIR in Normandy Drop*
249. **Nauroth, H.S. & B. Steinberg (2017)**, p.34
250. *AOK 7 Ia, AOK 7 Kriegstagebuch Ia – 6 Jun 1944 – 25 Jul 1944*, p.1-2 [T312 R1569 F219-20] — Hereafter referred to as: *AOK 7 Ia, KTB 6.6.-25.7.44*
251. *AOK 7* Ia, *KTB 6.6.-25.7.44*, p.3 [T312 R1569 F221]; **Criegern, F. von (1948)**, MS # B-784 (Germ.), *Teil I, Die Kämpfe des LXXXIV. A.K. in der Normandie von der alliierten Landung bis 17.6.44*, p.10-11; **Nauroth, H.S. & B. Steinberg (2017)**, p.58; PWIS(H)/LDC/239, 16 Aug 44, p.1 [UKNA, WO 208/3647]; PWIS(H)/LDC/39, 28 Jun 44, p.1 [UKNA, WO 208/3645]
252. *AOK 7* Ia, *KTB 6.6.-25.7.44*, p.3 [T312 R1569 F221]
253. *Ibid.*, p.6 [T312 R1569 F224]
254. *AOK 7* Ia, Morgenmeldung, 6.6.44 [T312 R1565 F860]
255. *AOK 7*, Ia Nr.1162/44 g., p.2 [T312 R1565 F862]
256. *AOK 7* Ia, *KTB 6.6.-25.7.44*, p.14 [T312 R1569 F232]
257. **Harrison, G.A. (1951, reprint 1984)**, p.289-93; 82d Airborne Division, *Action in Normandy, France, June-July 1944, Section II – Narrative*, p.2-6 [McoE HQ Donovan Research Library, D78/I2011] — Hereafter referred to as 82nd AB, *Action in Normandy, Narrative*
258. *AOK 7*, Ia Nr.1162/44 g., p.2 [T312 R1565 F862]
259. **Nordyke, P. (2005)**, p.256-265
260. *Ibid.*, p.250, 324 & 326; **Harrison, G.A. (1951, reprint 1984)**, p.291-3
261. **Keil, G. (1948b)**, p.2-3
262. *AOK 7* Ia, Morgenmeldung, 6.6.44 [T312 R1565 F860]
263. **Keil, G. (1948b)**, p.3-4
264. *AOK 7*, Ia Nr.1162/44 g., *Ia-Mittagsmeldung vom 6.6.44*, p.2 [T312 R1565 F862] The report says "east of Émondeville" but this may be an error (should be west of Émondeville where the highway to Ste. Mère-Église was) or they may have been attempting to come to the aid of *Batterie Azeville* (2./H.K.A.R. 1261) as has been mentioned by *Obstlt.* Keil (commander of *GR 919*). Instead, *Sturm-Btl. AOK 7* would be brought up to deal with the airborne forces around Azeville. [**Keil, G. (1948b)**, p.4; *AOK 7* Ia, *KTB 6.6.-25.7.44*, p.10 in T312 R1569 F228]
265. **Keil, G. (1948b)**, p.4
266. *Ibid.*; **Nordyke, P. (2005)**, p.234, 241-245; **Schlieben, K.W. v. (1948)**, MS # B-845 (Germ.), *Die deutsche 709.Infanterie – Division vor und während der anglo-amerikanischen Invasion vom 6. Juni 1944*, p.28
267. **Schlieben, K.W. v. (1948)**, p.28
268. **Keil, G. (1948b)**, p.4
269. **Nordyke, P. (2005)**, p.282-3; **Historical Division, War Dept. (1948)**, p.53-4
270. *91. I.D., Kriegsgliederung KG 91. I.D.*, 18.6.44; **Heydte, F.A. von der (1952)**, p.15-16
271. US Army, History Section, European Theater of Operations (1945), *Regimental Study Number 2, Fight at the Lock*; US Army, History Section, European Theater of Operations (1945), *Regimental Unit Study Number 3, 506 Parachute Infantry Regiment in Normandy Drop* (in particular page 4-6)
272. **Heydte, F.A. von der (1952)**, p.15
273. *AOK 7*, Ia Nr.1162/44 g., p.2 [T312 R1565 F862]
274. **Heydte, F.A. von der (1952)**, p.16-17; *Fj.Rgt. 6*, After action report for the period 6-11 June 1944, 17.6.44
275. Conversations of the Ia *AOK 7* on the evening of 6.6.44 with *LXXXIV. A.K.* [T312 R1565 F866]; *AOK 7*, Situation map, 5.6.44
276. **Heydte, F.A. von der (1952)**, p.17
277. *Fj.Rgt. 6*, After action report for the period 6-11 June 1944, 17.6.44
278. *AOK 7*, Ia Nr.1162/44, g., 6.6.44 [T312 R1565 F863]
279. *AOK 7*, Ia, Ia-Tagesmeldung, 6.6.44, p.2 [T312 R1565 F868]
280. **Criegern, F. von (1948)**, p.16
281. See the chapter *"243.Infanterie-Division"*
282. *Ibid.*; **Schlieben, K.W. v. (1948)**, p.29 & 31; **Stadlhofer (1944)**, *Bericht über den Einsatz der III./AR 243 vom 6.6.1944 bis 25.6.1944*, p.1-2; **Criegern, F. von (1948)**, p.16
283. **Nordyke, P. (2006)**, *Four Stars of Valor – The Combat History of the 505th Parachute Infantry Regiment in World War II*, St.Paul, MN: Zenith Press, p.181-195
284. *91. I.D., Kriegsgliederung KG 91. I.D.*, 18.6.44
285. **Schlieben, K.W. v. (1948)**, p.32-33; **Stadlhofer (1944)**, p.3
286. **Nordyke (2005)**, p.298-300
287. *Ibid.*, p.288-291 & 326
288. **Heydte, F.A. von der (1952)**, p.17-18; *Fj.Rgt. 6*, After action report for the period 6-11 June 1944, 17.6.44
289. **Heydte, F.A. von der (1952)**, p.18-20; **Griesser, V. (2006)**, p.105-107, 109, 113-114; **History Section, United States Army,** *506th PIR in Normandy Drop*, p.36-39, 50 & 52
290. The document actually states Hiesville, not Houesville, but this would have left its rear and left flank unprotected and the N13 highway into St.Côme-du-Mont open.
291. *Fj.Rgt. 6*, After action report for the period 6-11 June 1944, 17.6.44
292. **Heydte, F.A. von der (1952)**, p.19-20
293. 82nd AB, *Action in Normandy, Narrative*, p.7; **Harrison, G.A. (1951, reprint 1984)**, p.328 & 342
294. *AOK 7*, Ia Nr.2879/44 g.K., 7.6.44, p.3 [T312 R1565 F880]
295. *AOK 7*, Ia Nr.2941/44 g.K., 10.6.44, p.3-4 [T312 R1565 F930-1]; **Criegern, F. von (1948)**, MS # B-784, p.17
296. *AOK 7*, Ia Nr.2941/44 .g.K., 10.6.44, p.3-4 [T312 R1565 F930-1]; **Schlieben, K.W. v. (1948)**, p.33-34
297. **Hoffmann (1944)**, *Bericht über Kampfgruppe v. Schlieben*, p.9 [T312 R1566 F368]
298. See the chapter *"709.Infanterie-Division"*
299. **Hoffmann (1944)**, p.1 & 9 [T312 R1566 F360 & 368]
300. **Neugebauer (1944)**, recording of information provided by *Lt.* Rösgen regarding certain individuals in the fighting between Ste. Mère-Église and Montebourg [T78 R672 H41/61a]; **Keil, G. (1948a)**, MS # C-018 (Germ.), *Bericht über die Kämpfe des hessisch-thüringischen Grenadier-Regiments 919 under der Kampfgruppe Keil*, p.53; HQ 82d Airborne Division, G-2, *Interrogation Report No.9*, 16 Jun 44, p.3 [NARA, RG 407, Box 1396, File 101-2.2]
301. **Nordyke, P. (2005)**, p.327; 82nd AB, Action in Normandy, Narrative, p.9
302. C.S.D.I.C. (UK) S.*IR* 413, 23 Jun 44, p.1 [UKNA, WO 208/3591]
303. **Heydte, F.A. von der (1952)**, p.20-22; *AOK 7*, Ia Nr.2911/44 g.K., 8.6.44, p.1 [T312 R1565 F898]; **History Section, United States Army,** *506th PIR in Normandy Drop*, p.52-70; *Fj.Rgt. 6*, After action report for the period 6-11 June 1944, 17.6.44
304. *Fj.Rgt. 6*, After action report for the period 6-11 June 1944, 17.6.44
305. *Ibid.*
306. *Ibid.*
307. 91.Inf.Div., Ia, 8.6.44, copied and translated in the G-2

records of the 82nd Airborne Div. [NARA, via Egbert van de Schootbrugge]
308. *91. I.D., Kriegsgliederung KG König*, 18.-28.6.44; *Fj.Rgt. 6*, After action report for the period 6-11 June 1944, 17.6.44
309. *91. I.D., Kriegsgliederung 91. I.D. mit Unterstellungen*, 20.6.44
310. *91. I.D., Kriegsgliederung KG König*, 18.-28.6.44
311. Situation report from *Fj.Rgt. 6* to *17. SS-Pz.Gren.Div.* on 10 July 1944 [Published in **Wind, M. & Günther, G. (2004)**]; Gen. Kdo.*LXXXIV. A.K.*, Ia Nr.048/44 g.K., 23.744, p.2 [T314 R1604 F1374]
312. Gren.Rgt.1057, Ia, *Regimental order for the defence of the Merderet Sector*, 8.6.44 [copied and translated as Enclosure No.2 to 82nd Airborne Division, *G-2 Report No.61*, 11 Jun 44, NARA]
313. *Ibid.*
314. *Ibid.* The translated document mentions three *le.I.G.*-platoons armed with *I.K.H.'s*
315. C.S.D.I.C. (UK) S.*IR* 362, 16 Jun 44, p.2 [NARA, RG 165, Box 660]; C.S.D.I.C. (UK) S.*IR* 465, 29 Jun 44 [NARA, RG 165, Box 659, Folder 2]
316. Gren.Rgt.1057, Ia, *Regimental order for the defence of the Merderet Sector*, 8.6.44 [copied and translated as Enclosure No.2 to 82nd Airborne Division, *G-2 Report No.61*, 11 Jun 44, NARA]
317. Nordyke, P. (2005), p.326, 328-9
318. *AOK 7*, Ia Nr.2911/44 g.K., 8.6.44, p.2 [T312 R1565 F899]
319. Gen.Kdo.*LXXXIV. A.K.*, Ia Nr.1273/44 g.K., p.3 [T312 R1565 F939]; **Criegern, F. von (1948)**, MS # B-784, p.21
320. *AOK 7* Ia, Anlage zum *KTB* Führungsabteilung, Lagenkarten A.O.K.7 vom 6.6.44-30.6.44, *Stand: 8.6.44, 22 Uhr* [T312 R1570 F17]
321. Nordyke, P. (2005), p.330-342
322. (Unknown Ia) 09:30 on 9.6.44 [UKNA, HW 5/498, CX/MSS/T212/122, KV 7557]; **Nordyke, P. (2006)**, p.335
323. Historical Division, Department of the Armee (1948), *Utah Beach to Cherbourg (6 June-27 June 1944)*, United States Army, Washington, D.C., p.120-126; **Harrison, G.A. (1951, reprint 1984)**, p.398-401; **Nordyke, P. (2005)**, p.343-359
324. *AOK 7* Ia, *KTB* 6.6.-25.7.44, p.24-25 [T312 R1569 F242-3]; *AOK 7*, Ia, Ia-Vormittagsmeldung, 10.6.44 [T312 R1565 F921]
325. *AOK 7* Ia, Ia-Tagesmeldung, 9.6.44 [T312 R1565 F907]; report from unknown authority at 00:15 on 10.6.44 [UKA, HW 5/497, CX/MSS/T211/644, KV 7335]
326. *Fj.Rgt. 6*, After action report for the period 6-11 June 1944, 17.6.44
327. *AOK 7*, Ia, *KTB* 1.1.-30.6.1944 [T312 R1564 F297]; *AOK 7* Ia, *KTB* 6.6.-25.7.44, p.27 [T312 R1569 F245]
328. *91. I.D., Kriegsgliederung 91. I.D., Unterstellungen*, 10.6.44.
329. Captured document, presumed to be from around 10 June 44, copied and translated in SHAEF, G2 Division, *SHAEF Intelligence Notes #17*, 6 Jul. 44, p.A-4 [UKNA, WO 219/5228] The numbers are incomplete and sometimes unclear. It is assumed that the "Division HQ" does not include the mapping detachment or military police. Also, the document does not list *Fla-Kp. 191*. Without a definition, it is impossible to know exactly which units are included in the support troops (referred to as "services") numbers. Combined, these were probably stronger, which may suggest the loss of several hundred men. Units may have been excluded.; *OKH*, Chef H Rüst und BdE, AHA/Stab I(1)/I(3) Nr.2987/44, g.K., 4.5.44 [T78 R763 H19/56]
330. *91. I.D., Kriegsgliederung 91. I.D., Unterstellungen*, 10.6.44; C.S.D.I.C. (UK) S.*IR* 362, 16 Jun 44, p.2 [NARA, RG 165, Box 660]; C.S.D.I.C. (UK) S.*IR* 465, 29 Jun 44 [NARA, RG 165, Box 659, Folder 2]
331. *91. I.D., Kriegsgliederung 91. I.D., Unterstellungen*, 10.6.44; see the chapter *"243.Infanterie-Division"*
332. Stadlhofer (1944), p.5 [T78 R672 H41/61b] ; see the chapter *"77. Infanterie-Division"*; see the chapter *"243.Infanterie-Division"*
333. *AOK 7* Ia, *AOK 7 Kriegstagebuch Ia – 6 Jun 1944 – 25 Jul 1944*, p.30 [T312 R1569 F248]
334. *91. I.D., Kriegsgliederung 91. I.D., Unterstellungen*, 10.6.44
335. *Ibid.*; *Fj.Rgt. 6*, After action report for the period 6-11 June 1944, 17.6.44
336. *Fj.Rgt. 6*, After action report for the period 6-11 June 1944, 17.6.44
337. *91. I.D., Kriegsgliederung 91. I.D., Unterstellungen*, 10.6.44; *AOK 7*, Ia Nr.1093/44 g., 2.6.44 [T312 R1565 F827]
338. *91. I.D., Kriegsgliederung 91. I.D., Unterstellungen*, 10.6.44
339. Historical Division, War Dept. (1948), p.125-128 & Map No.24; 90th Infantry Division, Report of operations June 1944, p.3 [available at: www.90thdivisionassoc.org/afteractionreports/Scans/junjul44/90th%20Div%20AAR%20June%2044%20pt%201.htm, accessed 6 May 2020]
340. Unknown authority, Ia/c at 11:00 on 10.6.44 [UKNA, HW 5/497, CX/MSS/T211/96]
341. *AOK 7* Ia, Ia-Vormittagsmeldung, 10.6.44 [T312 R1565 F921]; *AOK 7*, Ia Nr.1276/44 g., 10.6.44 [T312 R1565 F924]; *AOK 7*, Ia Nr.1282/44 g., 10.6.44 [T312 R1565 F950]
342. See the chapter *"243.Infanterie-Division"*
343. Historical Division, War Dept. (1948), p.79-81, 87-88, Map No.17
344. *Fj.Rgt. 6*, After action report for the period 6-11 June 1944, 17.6.44; *91. I.D., Kriegsgliederung 91. I.D., Unterstellungen*, 10.6.44
345. König, E. (1946), p.1; *AOK 7*, Ia Nr.2949/44 g.K., 10.6.44 [T312 R1565 F925]
346. Pickardt, *Reisebericht* (for 8-9 Jun 44), 10.6.44, p.5 [T311 R25 F7029433]
347. *AOK 7*, Ia Nr.2941/44 g.K., 10.6.44 [T312 R1565 F925]; **König, E. (1946)**, p.1. *Obst.* König was in command of several regiments on the Eastern Front from June 1942 to April 1944. By 1944 his performance reviews noted his potential to become a very good divisional commander. [German general staff officers files, index cards of *Gen.Maj.* König in T78 R888 H6/26]
348. *AOK 7*, Ia Nr.2941/44 g.K., 10.6.44, p.5 [T312 R1565 F932]; **Pickardt**, *Reisebericht* (for 8 9 Jun 44), 10.6.44, p.5 [T311 R25 F7029433]
349. *AOK 7*, Ia Nr.2976/44 g.K., 11.6.44, p.2 [T312 R1565 F958]; *AOK 7*, Ia-Morgenmeldung ,*Teil 1*, 11.6.44 T312 R1565 F954]; *AOK 7*, Ia Nr.1319/44 g.K., 12.6.44 [T312 R1565 F977]; *AOK 7* Ia, *AOK 7 Kriegstagebuch Ia – 6 Jun 1944 – 25 Jul 1944*, p.30 [T312 R1569 F248]
350. Historical Division, War Dept. (1948), p.128; 90th Infantry Division, Report of operations June 1944, p.3
351. Historical Division, War Dept. (1948), p.128
352. See the chapter *"243.Infanterie-Division"*; **Nordyke, P. (2005)**, p.362-364; **Harrison, G.A. (1951, reprint 1984)**, p.338 & Map XXI
353. Historical Division, War Dept. (1948), p.82-85, 88-89 & Map 17; *Fj.Rgt. 6*, After action report for the period 6-11 June 1944, 17.6.44
354. *AOK 7* Ia, Nr.2988/44 g.K., 11.6.44, p.1-2 [T312 R1565 000959-60]
355. Historical Division, War Dept. (1948), p.85
356. *AOK 7* Ia, *KTB* 1.1.-30.6.1944
357. Heydte, F.A. von der (1952), p.24; *AOK 7* Ia, *KTB* 1.1.-30.6.1944 [T312 R1564 F305]
358. *Fj.Rgt. 6*, After action report for the period 6-11 June 1944, 17.6.44; **Heydte, F.A. von der (1952)**, p.25 & 27-28
359. *AOK 7* Ia, Nr.2988/44 g.K., 11.6.44 [T312 R1565 000959-60]
360. *AOK 7* Ia, Ia-Morgenmeldung, *Teil 3*, 11.6.44 T312 R1565 F956]
361. *AOK 7* Ia, *KTB* 1.1.-30.6.1944 [T312 R1564 F304]
362. *AOK 7* Ia, Ia no number/44 g., 12.6.44, p.1 [T312 R1565 F978]; *AOK 7*, Ia 3032/44 g., 12.6.44, p.1 [T312 R1565 F978]; *AOK 7* Ia, *KTB* 1.1.-30.6.1944 [T312 R1564 F305-9]
363. *AOK 7* Ia, Nr.1356/44 g., 13.6.44 [T312 R1565 F1001]; *AOK 7* Ia, *AOK 7 Kriegstagebuch Ia, 6 June 1944 – 16 Aug 1944*, p.32 [T312 R1569 F35] — Hereafter referred to as: *AOK 7* Ia, *KTB 6.6.-16.8.44*; *AOK 7* (Polo), Ia Nr.3037/44 g.K., 13.6.44, p.1 [T312 R1565 F999]; **Historical Division, War Dept. (1948)**, p.128-129
364. *AOK 7* (Polo), Ia Nr.3001/44 g.K., 12.6.44 [T312 R1565 F976] The records state that the town was in American hands from 18:00 on the 11th, but this was a misinterpretation.
365. Harrison, G.A. (1951, reprint 1984), p.361 & 364; **Heydte, F.A. von der (1952)**, p.27-28; **Historical Division, War Dept. (1948)**, Map No.18; **Bando, M. (2007)**, *101st Airborne – The Screaming Eagles in World War II*, St.Paul, MN: Zenith Press, 89-90
366. According to the regimental After-Action-Report, it was subordinated to the division as of 19:30 on the 11th. This appears not to have been formally acknowledged by the *LXXXIV. A.K.* until the next day.
367. *AOK 7* (Polo), Ia Nr.3023/44 g.K., 12.6.44 [T312 R1565 F992]; Message Flivo *LXXXIV. A.K.* at 08:30 on 12.6.44 [UKNA, HW 5/5499, CX/MSS/T213/43, KV 7678] This message gives the time as 10:00 and a slightly different dividing line.
368. *AOK 7*, Kriegsgliederungen zum *KTB* der Führungsabteilung *AOK 7 ab 6.6.44 bis 30.6.44, Stand: 22.6.44, 14 Uhr* [T312 R1566 F13] – Collection hereafter referred to as: Kriegsgliederungen z. *KTB* 6.-29.6.44
369. *91. I.D., Kriegsgliederung KG 91. I.D.*, 18.6.44
370. *91. I.D., Kriegsgliederung KG König*, 18.-28.6.44; *AOK 7* Ia, Anlage zum *KTB* Führungsabteilung, Lagenkarten A.O.K.7 vom 6.6.44-30.6.44, *Lage Normandie, Stand: 22.6.44, 2200 Uhr* [T312 R1570 F30]
371. Nordyke, P. (2005), p.369-372; 508th PIR, *Unit Journal, 508th Parachute Infantry Regiment, Operation "Neptune", Normandy, France, 28 May to 8 July 1944*, p.5-6 [NARA]
372. *AOK 7* Ia, *KTB* 6.6.-25.7.44, p.35 [T312 R1569 F254]
373. *AOK 7*, Ia Nr.3052/33 g.K., 13.6.44 [T312 R1565 F1002]; *AOK 7*

Ia, *KTB* 1.1.-30.6.1944 [T312 R1564 F311]
374. *AOK 7* Ia, *KTB* 6.6.-25.7.44, p.36-37 [T312 R1569 F255-6]
375. **Nordyke, P. (2005)**, p.371-372; 508th PIR, *Unit Journal, 508th Parachute Infantry Regiment, Operation "Neptune", Normandy, France, 28 May to 8 July 1944*, p.6 [NARA]
376. **König, E. (1946)**, p.5-6
377. *AOK 7* (Polo), Ia Nr.3037/44 g.K., 13.6.44, p.1 [T312 R1565 F999]
378. **Historical Division, War Dept. (1948)**, p.128-129; **Harrison, G.A. (1951, reprint 1984)**, p.403
379. *AOK 7* Ia, *KTB* 6.6.-25.7.44, p.38 [T312 R1569 F257]
380. Der Oberbefehlshader der *7. Armee*, *AOK 7* Ia Nr.80/44 g.K. Chefs., *Weisung an LXXXIV. A.K.*, 14.6.44 [T312 R1565 F1026]
381. *AOK 7* Ia, *KTB* 6.6.-25.7.44, p.40 [T312 R1569 F259]
382. Also see the chapters *"77. Infanterie-Division"* and *"265. Infanterie-Division"*
383. **Harrison, G.A. (1951, reprint 1984)**, p.403-404; 82nd AB, *Action in Normandy, Narrative*, p.15
384. 9th I.D., *Report of Operation conducted by Ninth Infantry Division US Army – Cotentin Peninsula, France 14 June-1 July 1944*, 14 July 1944, p.3-4 – Hereafter referred to as 9th I.D., *Operations Report, 14 Jun – 1 Jul 44*
385. **Harrison, G.A. (1951, reprint 1984)**, p.403-404
386. *AOK 7* Ia Nr.3083/44 g.K., 14.6.44, p.2 [T312 R1565 F1021]
387. *AOK 7* Ia, *KTB* 1.1.-30.6.1944 [T312 R1564 F315]
388. *Maj.i.G.* Prinz zu Holstein, *Besprechung zwischen dem Oberbefehlshaber der 7. Armee und dem Komm. General des LXXXIV. A.K. am 14.6.1944 in St. Lô*, p.2 [T312 R1565 F1027]
389. *Ibid.*; *AOK 7*, Ia Nr.3116/44 g.K., 15.6.44 [T312 R1565 F1048] The number of 2,212 could also refer to *Gefechtsstärke* (fighting strength), which is the case for the other units in the document. König stated that the losses were about 3,000 when he took command of the division on 10 June. Considering this was from memory, it is reasonably close to the reported number.
390. See the chapters *"77. Infanterie-Division"*, *"243.Infanterie-Division"* and *"709.Infanterie-Division"*
391. Actually shown on the document as the *III./922*, which was further east under the *709. I.D*
392. Members of the battalion were killed in the area, including the battalion commander. Volksbund; **Baret, J. (2014)**, p.97
393. Message from the *243. I.D.* to the *77. I.D.*, 16.6.44 at 16:11, copied and translated in Annex 1 to G-2 Periodic Report Nr.9, HQ First US Army, 19 June 44 [Available at https://firstdivisionmuseum.nmtvault.com/jsp/viewer.jsp?doc_id=iwfd0000%2F20141124%2F165&page_name=800, accessed on 4 Aug. 2018]
394. See the chapters *"77. Infanterie-Division"*, *"243.Infanterie-Division"* and *"709.Infanterie-Division"*
395. *Kampfgruppe Eitner, Kampfgruppenbefehl für die Verteidigung im Abschnitt la Rivière – les Moitiers*, 15.6.44 [T78 R672H41/61b]
396. *AOK 7* Ia, *KTB* 6.6.-16.8.44, p.40 [T312 R1569 F43]; *AOK 7* Ia, *KTB* 1.1.-30.6.1944 [T312 R1564 F318]
397. *AOK 7* Ia Nr.3105/44 g.K., 15.6.44 [T312 R1565 F1036]; *AOK 7* Ia, *KTB* 6.6.-25.7.44, p.41 [T312 R1569 F260]
398. *AOK 7* Ia, *KTB* 6.6.-25.7.44, p.41 [T312 R1569 F260]

399. *AOK 7* Ia, Nr.3114/44 g.K., 15.6.44 [T312 R1565 F1046]; *AOK 7*, Ia Nr.3113/44 g.K., p.2-3 [T312 R1565 F1041-2]
400. *AOK 7* Ia, *KTB* 6.6.-25.7.44, p.42 [T312 R1569 F261]
401. *AOK 7* Ia, *KTB* 1.1.-30.6.1944 [T312 R1564 F320]
402. *AOK 7* Ia, Nr.1436/44 g.K., 16.6.44, p.1 [T312 R1565 F1062]; Flivo *LXXXIV. A.K.* at 23:00 on 15.6.44 [UKNA, HW 5/503, CX/MSS/T217/18, KV 8303 & KV 8324] The reports state that the line north of the Douve included the main road north of Neuville, which would put it further east. [*LXXXIV. A.K.* late on 15.6.44 in UKNA, HW 5/503, CX/MSS/T217/18, KV 8473]
403. HQ Ninth Infantry Division, *Report of Operations*, 14 July 1944, p.4
404. *AOK 7* Ia, 16.6.44 [T312 R1565 F1064]; Flivo *LXXXIV. A.K.* at 23:00 on 15.6.44 [UKNA, HW 5/503, CX/MSS/T217/18, KV 8303 & KV 8324]; *LXXXIV. A.K.* late on 15.6.44 CX/MSS/T217/18, KV 8473]
405. The boundary was now west of the Merderet while the *77. I.D.* had been deployed either side of the river. Comments from the corps commander indicate that the *77. I.D.* was part of *Gruppe von Schlieben*. [*AOK 7* Ia, *AOK 7 Kriegstagebuch Ia – 6 Jun 1944 – 25 Jul 1944*, p.44 in T312 R1569 F263]
406. See chapter *"709.Infanterie-Division"*; *AOK 7* Ia, *Kriegstagebuch Ia – 6 Jun 1944 – 25 Jul 1944*, p.44 [T312 R1569 F263]
407. 82nd AB, *Action in Normandy, Narrative*, p.16-18
408. 9th I.D., *Operations Report, 14 June-1 July 1944*, p.4-5
409. **König, E. (1946)**, p.4
410. *AOK 7* Ia, *KTB* 6.6.-25.7.44, p.43 [T312 R1569 F262]
411. *Ibid.*, p.44 [T312 R1569 F263]
412. *Ibid.*, p.45 [T312 R1569 F264]; *AOK 7*, Ia Nr.3131/44 g.K., 16.6.44 [T312 R1565 F1063]
413. *AOK 7* Ia, *KTB* 6.6.-25.7.44, p.45 [T312 R1569 F264]
414. *AOK 7* Ia, *Ia-Vormittagsmeldung*, 16.6.44 [T312 R1565 F1064]
415. Message from the *243. I.D.* to the *77. I.D.*, 16.6.44 at 16:11, copied and translated in Annex 1 to G-2 Periodic Report Nr.9, HQ First US Army, 19 June 44 [Available at https://firstdivisionmuseum.nmtvault.com/jsp/viewer.jsp?doc_id=iwfd0000%2F20141124%2F165&page_name=800, accessed on 4 Aug. 2018]
416. *AOK 7* Ia, *KTB* 6.6.-25.7.44, p.46 [T312 R1569 F265]
417. Flivo *LXXXIV. A.K.* at 21:00 on 16.6.44 [UKNA, HW 5/504, CX/MSS/T218/103, KV 8568]; *AOK 7*, IA NR.3147/44 g.K., 16.6.44, p.3 [T312 R1565 F1068]; *AOK 7* Ia Nr.3136/44 g.K., 16.6.44, p.2 [T312 R1565 F1075]
418. *AOK 7* Ia, *KTB* 6.6.-25.7.44, p.46-47 [T312 R1569 F265-6]
419. *Ibid.*, p.48 [T312 R1569 F267]
420. 82nd AB, *Action in Normandy, Narrative*, p.18-19
421. 9th I.D., *Operations Report, 14 Jun – 1 Jul 44*, p.5-6
422. *AOK 7* Ia Nr.3147/44 g.K., 16.6.44, p.2-3 [T312 R1565 F1067-8]
423. Okdo.d.H.Gr. B., Ia Nr.3612/44 g.K., 17.6.44, p.4 [T311 R3 F7002397]
424. 82nd Airborne Division, *Interrogation Report No. 9 (correct)*, 15 Jun 44, p.1 & 82nd Airborne Division, *Interrogation Report No. 9*, 16 Jun 44, p.1-2 [both NARA, via Egbert van de Schootbrugge]
425. *AOK 7* Ia, Nr.3169/44 g.K., 17.6.44, p.1 [T312 R1565 F1095]; *AOK 7* Ia, *KTB* 6.6.-25.7.44, p.49 [T312 R1569 F268]

426. *AOK 7* Ia, *KTB* 6.6.-25.7.44, p.49 [T312 R1569 F268]; *AOK 7*, Ia Nr.1481/44 g., 17.6.44 [T312 R1565 F1089]; *AOK 7* Ia, *KTB* 1.1.-30.6.1944 [T312 R1564 F328-9]
427. 9th I.D., *Operations Report, 14 Jun – 1 Jul 44*, p.6-9; **Harrison, G.A. (1951, reprint 1984)**, p.415 & Map XXII
428. *AOK 7*, Ia Nr.3282/44 g.K., 21.6.44 [T312 R1565 F1219]
429. 82nd Airborne Division, *Interrogation Report No.11*, p.4 [NARA, via Egbert van de Schootbrugge]
430. **Harrison, G.A. (1951, reprint 1984)**, p.415-416; **Plumenson, M. (1961, 1993 reprint)**, *Breakout and pursuit*, Washington D.C.: Center of Military History, United States Army, p.37; **Choltitz, D. von (1947)**, p.4-10; **Pemsel, M. (1948)**, MS #B-763, *Die 7. Armee in der Schlacht in der Normandie und in den Kämpfen bis Avranches (6.6.-29.7.44)*, p.40
431. Tannhauser (*243. I.D.*) Ia, 18.6.44 at 07:00 [UKNA, HW 5/506, CX/MSS/T220/12, KV 8776]; *AOK 7*, Ia Nr.1526/44 g., 19.6.44 [T312 R1565 F1128]; for examples of the term *"Nordfront"* see T312 R1565 F1110 & T312 R1569 F115, 118, 127, 130
432. *AOK 7*, Ia Nr.3205/44 g.K., p.2, 18.6.44 [T312 R1565 F1110]
433. **König, E. (1946)**, p.4
434. Still called *"Kampfgruppe 91. I.D."* in the document, rather than *"KG König"*.
435. *91. I.D., Kriegsgliederung KG 91. I.D.*, 18.6.44
436. *Ibid.*
437. *Ibid.*; *91. I.D., Kriegsgliederung KG König*, 18.-28.6.44
438. *91. I.D., Kriegsgliederung KG 91. I.D.*, 18.6.44
439. AR 191, *Regimentsbefehl Nr.29*, 24.6.44 [**Nauroth, H.S. & B. Steinberg (2017)**, p.111-112]
440. See chapter *"77. Infanterie-Division"*
441. *91. I.D., Kriegsgliederung KG 91. I.D.*, 18.6.44
442. *Ibid.*
443. *Ibid.*
444. See chapter *"77. Infanterie-Division"*
445. *91. I.D., Kriegsgliederung KG 91. I.D.*, 18.6.44
446. *91. I.D., Kriegsgliederung KG König*, 18.-28.6.44; *AOK 7*, Ia Nr.3454/44 g.K., 2.Teil, 27.6.44 [T312 R1565 F1377]; AR 191, *Regimentsbefehl Nr.29*, 24.6.44 [**Nauroth, H.S. & B. Steinberg (2017)**, p.111-112]
447. *91. I.D., Kriegsgliederung 91. I.D. mit Unterstellungen*, 20.6.44; *91. I.D., Kriegsgliederung KG König*, 18.-28.6.44
448. **Nauroth, H.S. & B. Steinberg (2017)**, p.157
449. *91. I.D., Kriegsgliederung KG 91. I.D.*, 18.6.44. II./AR 177 (Maj. Hartung) was mistakenly identified as I./AR 177.
450. **Triepel, G. (1947)**, p.1
451. See chapter *"243.Infanterie-Division"*
452. *AOK 7*, *Kriegsgliederungen z. KTB 6.-29.6.44, Stand: 23.6.44, 14 Uhr* [T312 R1566 F16]
453. *91. I.D., Kriegsgliederung KG 91. I.D.*, 18.6.44
454. See chapter *"243.Infanterie-Division"*
455. *91. I.D., Kriegsgliederung KG 91. I.D.*, 18.6.44
456. *AOK 7* Ia, *KTB* 6.6.-25.7.44, p.51 [T312 R1569 F270]; **König, E. (1946)**, p.4; *LXXXIV. A.K.*, 18.6.44 at 08:00 [UKNA, HW 5/505, CX/MSS/T219/104, XV 8721]
457. *AOK 7*, Ia Nr.3241/44 g.K., 20.6.44, p.2 [T312 R1565 F1175]
458. *AOK 7*, Ia Nr.3205/44 g.K., p.2, 18.6.44 [T312 R1565 F1110]; *AOK 7*, Ia Nr.1513/44 g., 18.6.44 [T312 R1565 F1108]

459. Flivo *LXXXIV. A.K.* at 10:30 on 20.6.44 [UKNA, HW 5/508, CX/MSS/T222/80] The report aitbout the battlegroup is from 10:30 on 20 June, but seems to refer to events on 19 June; [UKNA, WO 208/4138, C.S.D.I.C. S.R. Report, S.R.M.587]; PWIS(H)/LDC/39, 28 Jun 44 [UKNA, WO 208/3645]
460. *AOK 7 Ia, AOK 7 Kriegstagebuch Ia – 6 Jun 1944 – 25 Jul 1944*, p.53 [T312 R1569 F272] It is not clear if this refers to just the centre of the *Nordfront* or everything west of *U.Gr. Eitner*.
461. *AOK 7 Ia, KTB 6.6.-16.8.44*, p.25 [T312 R1569 F28]; Polo (*AOK 7*), Ia Nr.1308/44 g., 11.6.44 [T312 R1565 F968]
462. Polo (*AOK 7*) Ia Nr.1515/44 g.K., 18.6.44 [T312 R1565 F1121]
463. *AOK 7*, Ia Nr.3041/44 g.K., 20.6.44, p.3 [T312 R1565 F1177]
464. *Ibid.*; **Choltitz, D. von (1947)**, p.7
465. *AOK 7*, Ia Nr.3041/44 g.K., 20.6.44, p.3 [T312 R1565 F1177]
466. **Choltitz, D. von (1947)**, p.10; **Hausser, P. (1945)**, MS # A-907 (Germ.), *Seventh Army 29 June – 20 Aug 44*, p.7; **Pemsel, M. (1948)**, p.60
467. *LXXXIV. A.K.*, 19.6.44 at 14:00 [UKNA, HW 5/506, CX/MSS/T220/72, KV 8835]
468. *AOK 7, Kriegsgliederungen z. KTB 6.-29.6.44, Stand: 23.6.44, 14 Uhr* [T312 R1566 F16]
469. *AOK 7, Kriegsgliederungen z. KTB 6.-29.6.44, Stand: 27.6.44 14 Uhr* [T312 R1566 F19]
470. *AOK 7, Kriegsgliederungen z. KTB 6.-29.6.44, Stand 29.6. 17 Uhr* [T312 R1566 F24]; *AOK 7, Anlage zum KTB Führungsabteilung, Lagenkarten A.O.K.7 vom 6.6.44-30.6.44, Lage Normandie, Stand: 28.6.44, 22.00 Uhr* [T312 R1570 F37]
471. *AOK 7, Kriegsgliederungen z. KTB 6.-29.6.44, Stand: 23.6.44, 14 Uhr* [T312 R1566 F16]
472. *Ibid.*, *Stand: 28.6.44* [T312 R1566 F21]
473. *AOK 7, Anlage zum KTB Führungsabteilung, Lagenkarten A.O.K.7 vom 6.6.44-30.6.44, Lage Normandie, Stand: 25.6.44, 22.00 Uhr* [T312 R1570 F34]
474. *Ibid.*, *Lage Normandie, Stand: 28.6.44, 22.00 Uhr* [T312 R1570 F37]; *Ibid.*, *Lage Normandie, Stand: 29.6.44, 22.00 Uhr* [T312 R1570 F38]
475. **Triepel, G. (1947)**, p.1-3
476. 82nd AB, *Action in Normandy, Narrative*, p.21-22
477. *AOK 7*, Ia Nr.1526/44 g., 19.6.44 [T312 R1565 F1128]
478. *LXXXIV. A.K.*, 19.6.44 at 14:00 [UKNA, HW 5/506, CX/MSS/T220/72, KV 8835]
479. Flivo *LXXXIV. A.K.* at about 14:00 on 19.6.44, [UKNA, HW 5/506, CX/MSS/T220/71]
480. **Nordyke, P. (2005)**, p.385-6
481. *AOK 7 Ia, KTB 6.6.-25.7.44*, p.54 [T312 R1569 F273]; *AOK 7*, Ia Nr.3238/44 g.K., p.2 [T312 R1565 F1133]
482. *AOK 7*, Ia Nr.3241/44 g.K., 20.6.44, p.1 [T312 R1565 F1174]
483. Flivo *LXXXIV. A.K.* at 10:30 on 20.6.44 [UKNA, HW 5/508, CX/MSS/T222/80]
484. *AOK 7 Ia, KTB 6.6.-25.7.44*, p.55 [T312 R1569 F274]; 82nd AB, *Action in Normandy, Narrative*, p.23
485. Flivo *LXXXIV. A.K.*, 20.6.44 at 16:30 [UKNA, HW 5/508, CX/MSS/T222/64, KV 9075]
486. *Ibid.*
487. *AOK 7*, Ia Nr.1595/44, 20.6.44 [T312 R1565 F1172]
488. *AOK 7*, Ia Nr.1607/44 g., p.1-2 [T312 R1565 F1178-9]; 82nd AB, *Action in Normandy, Narrative*, p.22-23; *AOK 7*, Ia Nr.1645/44 g., 21.6.44, p.2 [T312 R1565 F1207]
489. *AOK 7*, Ia Nr.1645/44 g., *21.6.1944*, 21.6.44, p.1 [T312 R1565 F1206]
490. *OKH/AHA/Abwicklungsstab, Anl. z. Sachgeb. 91 Nr.6.44 g., Kampfgruppe 91. I.D., Stand vom 20.7.* [T78 R672 H41/61b] — Hereafter referred to as *91. I.D., Kriegsgliederung KG 91. I.D., 20.7.44*
491. The order to send the *II./894* to Normandy was not given by *AOK 7* until 21 June, but the option appears to have been discussed as early as 18 June. [Gen.Kdo.*XXV. A.K.*, Ia Nr.746/44 g.K., 18.6.44 in T314 R746 F884; *AOK 7*, Ia Nr.3268/44 g.K., 21.6.44, p.1 in T312 R1565 F1215]
492. *91. I.D., Kriegsgliederung KG 91. I.D., 20.7.44*
493. *Ibid*.
494. **Harrison, G.A. (1951, reprint 1984)**, p.415-6; 82nd AB, *Action in Normandy, Narrative*, p.23-25; 90th Infantry Division, Report of Operations June 1944, p.6-7
495. For a summary of this period see the daily reports (*Tagesmeldungen*) for 21 Jun – 2 Jul 44 [T312 R1565 F1205-466]; 1.-2 Jul 44 is covered in the daily reports of *H.Gr. B* [T311 R3 F7002471-9]
496. CX/MSS/R.223 I, p.27 [UKNA, HW 5/509]
497. Unknown authority, 21.6.44 [CX/MSS/T225/9, KV 9378, KV 9395]; *AOK 7* Ia, *KTB 6.6.-25.7.44*, p.55 [T312 R1569 F274]
498. *AOK 7*, Ia Nr.1687/44 g. II.Ang., 23.6.44, p.1 [T312 R1565 F1230]; *AOK 7*, Ia Nr.1698/44 g., 23.6.44, p.2 [T312 R1565 F1256]; 90th Infantry Division, Report of operations June 1944, p.6-7
499. *AOK 7*, Ia Nr.1735/44, p.2 [T312 R1565 F1262]; Okdo.d.*H.Gr. B*, Ia Nr.3878/44 g.K., 23.6.44, p.1 [T311 R4 F7004909]
500. It is not clear when *U.Gr. Lewandowski* joined the front, but it was not mentioned on 21 June and first appeared on the map late on 22 June. This is assumed to be correct.
501. *AOK 7* Ia, Anlage zum *KTB* Führungsabteilung, Lagenkarten A.O.K.7 vom 6.6.44-30.6.44, *Lage Normandie, Stand: 22.6.44, 2200 Uhr* [T312 R1570 F30]; *AOK 7*, Ia Nr.3492/44 g.K., 29.6.44, p.2 [T312 R1565 F1429]; *AOK 7, Kriegsgliederungen z. KTB 6.-29.6.44, Stand: 23.6.44, 14 Uhr* [T312 R1566 F16]
502. CX/MSS/R. 226 (C), 27.6.44, p.21 [UKNA, HW 5/512]
503. *AOK 7*, Ia Nr.1772/44, p.2, 24.6.44 [T312 R1565 F1287]
504. Report from *LXXXIV. A.K.*, Ia, 25.6.44 [UKNA, HW 5/514, CX/MSS/T228/81, KV 9864]
505. *AOK 7*, Ia Nr.3454/44 g.K., 2.Teil, 27.6.44 [T312 R1565 F1377]; *AOK 7*, Ia Nr.3454/44 g.K., p.2, 27.6.44 [T312 R1565 F1381] The personnel strength reported for these units on 1 July is typically higher. Without reinforcements, it seems likely that the numbers of 27 June refer to actual fighting men, not the men in the support echelons of the infantry, artillery, antitank or engineer units.
506. *OKH/AHA/Abwicklungsstab, Anl. z. Sachgeb. 91 Nr.6.44 g., 91.Inf.Division (Div. 25. Welle), Stand v. 1.7.44* [T78 R672 H41/61–] — Hereafter referred to as: *91. I.D., Gliederung, 1.7.44*
507. *91. I.D., Kriegsgliederung KG König, 18.-28.6.44*; *91. I.D., Gliederung, 1.7.44*
508. The position of the *II./895* conflicts with *AOK 7* records for 29 June, which shows all three battalions from *KG 265* under *U.Gr. Eitner*. It is possible that the field army's information was outdated. [*AOK 7*, Ia Nr.3492/44 g.K., 29.6.44, p.2 in T312 R1565 F1429]
509. The *II./1049*'s relief was ordered on 29 June by the *LXXXIV. A.K.*, which indicates that the *Gliederung*, at least partially, presents a situation after 28 June. [See the chapters *"77. Infanterie-Division"* and *"265.Infanterie-Division"*]
510. *91. I.D., Kriegsgliederung KG König, 18.-28.6.44*
511. *Ibid.*; 90th Inf.Div., PWI Report No 5, 6 Jul 44 [NARA, RG 407, Box 3282, File 207-2.1]
512. PWIS(H)/LDC/96, 10 Jul 44, p.1 [UKNA, WO 208/3645]
513. The number of 7.62cm guns is difficult to read.
514. *91. I.D., Kriegsgliederung KG König, 18.-28.6.44*; *91. I.D., Gliederung, 1.7.44*
515. *91. I.D., Kriegsgliederung KG König, 18.-28.6.44*
516. *Ibid.*
517. Ib *2. SS-Pz.Div.* to *AOK 7*/ O.Qu., Q1/Munition on 14.7.44 [UKNA, HW 5/536, CX/MSS/T251/72]
518. *91. I.D., Kriegsgliederung KG König, 18.-28.6.44*
519. *Ibid.*
520. *AOK 7 Ia, KTB 6.6.-16.8.44*, p.95 [T312 R1569 F98]; *AOK 7*, Ia Nr.3492/44 g.K., p.2 [T312 R1565 F1429]
521. *AOK 7*, Anlage zum *KTB* Führungsabteilung, Lagenkarten A.O.K.7 vom 6.6.44-30.6.44, *Lage Normandie, Stand: 29.6.44, 22.00 Uhr* [T312 R1570 F38]; also see the chapter *"243.Inf.Div."* for more information
522. **Nauroth, H.S.& B. Steinberg (2017)**, p.118-119
523. See the chapters *"77. Infanterie-Division"* and *"353.Infanterie-Division"*
524. *AOK 7*, Ia Nr.3492/44 g.K., 29.6.44, p.3 [T312 R1565 F1430]; *AOK 7*, Ia Nr.3538/44 g.K., 30.6.44 [T312 R1565 F1467]
525. *AOK 7*, Ia Nr.3538/44 g.K., 30.6.44 [T312 R1565 F1467]
526. *91. I.D., Gliederung, 1.7.44*
527. *Ibid.*
528. *Ibid.*
529. *Ibid.*
530. *Ibid. Same document in BaMa, RH 15/441*
531. The document refers to the antitank units as a battalion but, since *Fla-Kp. 191* is mentioned separately in a later report, this must be *Pz.Jg.Kp. 191*.
532. Flivo *LXXXIV. A.K.* at 11:10 on 2.7.44 [UKNA, HW 5/519, CX/MSS/T233/53, XL 509]
533. Flivo *LXXXIV. A.K.*, evening 2.7.44 [UKNA, HW 5/519, CX/MSS/T234/3, XL 557 & XL 559]
534. See chapter *"265.Infanterie-Division"*
535. HQ 508th Parachute Inf., *IPW Repo-t - Consolidated*, 4 July 1944 [NARA, via Egbert van de Schootbrugge]
536. 82nd AB, *Action in Normandy, Narrative*, p.26-27
537. 90th Infantry Division, Report of operations July 1944, p.2-3 [available at: www.90thdivisionassoc.org/afteractionreports/HTML/Jul44/index.html, accessed 6 May 2020]
538. See the chapters *"77. Infanterie-Division"* and *"353.Infanterie-Division"*
539. *LXXXIV. A.K.* on 3.7.44 at 22:00 [UKNA, HW 5/520, CX/MSS/T235/23, XL 697]; *AOK 7* Ia, *KTB 6.6.-16.8.44*, p.113 [T312 R1569

F116]; **Choltitz, D. von (1947)**, p.32

540. This period is discussed in more detail in the *"77. Infanterie-Division"* chapter.

541. Triepel, G. (1947), p.1-3

542. 82d Airborne Division, *Interrogation Report No.21*, 6 Jul 44, p.1 [NARA, via Egbert van de Schootbrugge]

543. 21 AGp/Int/1070, App. A to 21 Army Group Intelligence Summary No. 147, Part II, 20 Jul. 44 [UKNA, WO 171/131]

544. König, E. (1946), p.7. König identifies the location as "La Fresnie, 20 km west of Périers" and La Fresnerie is the best match.

545. AOK 7 Ia, *KTB 6.6.-16.8.44*, p.113 [T312 R1569 F116]

546. Choltitz, D. von (1947), p.34-35

547. AOK 7 Ia, *KTB 6.6.-16.8.44*, p.113 & 115 [T312 R1569 F116 & 118]

548. *Ibid.*, p.137 [T312 R1569 F140]

549. AOK 7 Ia, *KTB 6.6.-25.7.44*, p.109 [T312 R1569 F329]

550. See the chapters *"77. Infanterie-Division"*, *"243.Infanterie-Division"* & *"353.Infanterie-Division"* for an overview of this period

551. AOK 7 Ia, *KTB 6.6.-16.8.44*, p.168 [T312 R1569 F172]; see the chapter *"77. Infanterie-Division"*; Okdo.d.*H.Gr. B*, Ia Nr.4924/44 g.K., 18.7.44, p.7 [T311 R3 F7002569]; **König, E. (1946)**, p.7

552. OKH/AHA/Abwicklungsstab, Anl. z. Sachgeb. 91 Nr.6.44 g., *Kampfgruppe 91. I.D., Stand vom 17.7.* [T78 R672 H41/61–] — Hereafter referred to as: *91. I.D., Kriegsgliederung KG 91. I.D.*, 17.7.44

553. *91. I.D., Kriegsgliederung KG 91. I.D.*, 20.7.44

554. *91. I.D., Kriegsgliederung KG 91. I.D.*, 17.7.44

555. *Ibid.*

556. LXXXIV. A.K. Ia, *Ia-Tagesmeldungen der Divisionen*, 16.7.44, p.1 [T314 R1604 F1364]

557. *91. I.D., Kriegsgliederung KG 91. I.D.*, 17.7.44

558. *Ibid.*

559. AOK 7 Ia, *KTB 6.6.-25.7.44*, p.113 [T312 R1569 F333]

560. *Ibid.*, p.126 [T312 R1569 F346]

561. Document (page 1 missing) [UKNA, HW 5/540, CX/MSS/T255/136]

562. *91. I.D., Kriegsgliederung KG 91. I.D.*, 20.7.44

563. *Ibid.*

564. *Ibid.*

565. Gen.Kdo.*LXXXIV. A.K.*, Ia Nr.035/44, *Takt. Gliederung der Artillerie, Stand: 21.7.44*, 22.7.44 [T314 R1604 F1388]; **Nauroth, H.S. & B. Steinberg (2017)**, p.157

566. Gen.Kdo.*LXXXIV. A.K.*, Ia Nr.035/44, *Takt. Gliederung der Artillerie, Stand: 21.7.44*, 22.7.44 [T314 R1604 F1388]

567. AOK 7 Ia, *KTB 6.6.-16.8.44*, p.180 & 185 [T312 R1569 F184 & 189]

568. Gen.Kdo.*LXXXIV. A.K.*, Ia, 23.7.44 [T314 R1604 F1371]; Gen.Kdo.*LXXXIV. A.K.*, *Ia-Tagesmeldungen*, 27.7.44 [T314 R1604 F1377]

569. AOK 7 Ia, *KTB 6.6.-16.8.44*, p.183 [T312 R1569 F187]; also see the chapter *"353.Infanterie-Division"*. The transfer of *Fs.Art.Abt. 5* may explain why it was crossed off on the overview of the 21st.

570. *Kampfwert III:* one of five possible ratings to give the combat effectiveness of a formation. III means a formation is only capable of defensive operations.

571. Gen.Kdo.*LXXXIV. A.K.*, Ia Nr.048/44 g.K., 23.7.44, p.2-3 [T314 R1604 F1374-5]

572. Gen.Kdo.*LXXXIV. A.K.*, Ia Nr.048/44 g.K., 23.744, p.2 [T314 R1604 F1374]; *91. I.D., Kriegsgliederung KG 91. I.D.*, 17.7.44; *91. I.D., Kriegsgliederung KG 91. I.D.*, 20.7.44; OKH/AHA/Abwicklungsstab, Anl. z. Sachgeb. 91 Nr.6.44 g., *Kampfgruppe 91. I.D., Stand vom 26.7.* [T78 R672 H41/61–] — Hereafter referred to as: *91. I.D., Kriegsgliederung KG 91. I.D.*, 26.7.44

573. Gen.Kdo.*LXXXIV. A.K.*, Ia Nr.048/44 g.K., 23.744, p.2 [T314 R1604 F1374]; *5. Fj.Div.*, Ia, 06:30 at 23.7.44 [UKNA, HW 5/540, CX/MSS/T255/19, XL 3307]

574. Gen.Kdo.*LXXXIV. A.K.*, Ia Nr.048/44 g.K., 23.744, p.2 [T314 R1604 F1374]

575. *Ibid.*

576. *91. I.D., Kriegsgliederung KG 91. I.D.*, 26.7.44

577. *Ibid.*

578. *Ibid.*

579. *Ibid.*

580. *Ibid.*

581. *Ibid.*; **Triepel, G. (1947)**, p.5

582. Document (page 1 missing) [UKNA, HW 5/540, CX/MSS/T255/136]

583. Okdo.d.*H.Gr. B*, Ia Nr.5177/44 g.K., 26.7.44 [T311 R4 F7004699]; Okdo.d.*H.Gr. B*, Ia Nr.5185/44 g.K., 26.7.44 [T311 R4 F7004698]; Okdo.d.*H.Gr. B*, Ia Nr.5194/44 g.K., 26.7.44, p.2 [T311 R4 F7004696]

584. Obkdo.d.*H.Gr. B*, Ia Nr.5201/44 g.K., 27.7.44, p.5 [T311 R3 F7002629]

585. see chapter *"243.Infanterie-Division"*; Okdo.d.*H.Gr. B*, Ia Nr.5272/44 g.K., 28.7.44 p.2 [T311 R4 F7004686]

586. *H.Gr. D (Ob.West), Kriegstagebuch (Text) 1.-31.7.44*, p.286-7 [T311 R16 F7016882-3]

587. *Ibid.*, p.293 [T311 R16 F7016889]

588. *Ibid.*, p.295 [T311 R16 F7016891]

589. message Flivo *LXXXIV. A.K.* at 09:00 on 28.7. [UKNA, HW 5/544, CX/SS/T259/40, XL 3818]

590. Okdo.d.*H.Gr. B*, Ia Nr.5272/44 g.K., 28.7.44 p.2 [T311 R4 F7004686]

591. Okdo.d.*H.Gr. B*, Ia Nr.5288/44 g.K., 29.7.44, p.2 [T311 R4 F7004684]

592. Okdo.d.*H.Gr. B*, Ia Nr.5306/44 g.K., 29.7.44, p.2 [T311 R4 F7004681]

593. König, E. (1946), p.7-8; II.Jagdkorps, Ic, at 06:00 on 3.7.44 [TNA, HW 5/546, CX/MSS/T261/90, XL 4112] König mentions the *Wolga-Tat.Inf.Btl.* (627) from memory, but it seems more likely he confused it *Georg.Inf.Btl. 797*, which was reported at Granville in OB West records. *H.Gr. D (Ob.West), Kriegstagebuch (Text) 1.-31.7.44*, 30.7.44, p.321 in T311 R16 F7016917; AOK 7 Ia, *KTB 6.6.-25.7.44*, p.95-6 in T312 R1569 F315-6]

594. König, E. (1946), p.8-9

595. *Ibid.*, p.9

596. *Ibid.*

597. *H.Gr. D (Ob.West), Kriegstagebuch (Text) 1.-31.7.44*, 30.7.44, p.321 [T311 R16 F7016917]

598. König, E. (1946), p.9-10

599. *H.Gr. D (Ob.West), Kriegstagebuch (Text) 1.-31.7.44*, 30.7.44, p.322 [T311 R16 F7016918]

600. Blumenson, M. (1961, 1993 reprint), *Breakout and Pursuit*, Center of Military History, United States Army, Washington D.C., Map VII

601. König, E. (1946), p.10

602. Gen.Kdo.*XXV. A.K.* Ia, Anl.2 z. KTB Nr.15(II), *Algemeines vom 16–7 - 31.7.44* [T314 R747 F54–] — Hereafter referred to as: Gen.Kdo.*XXV. A.K.* Ia, Anl.2 z. *KTB* Nr.15(II)

603. König, E. (1946), p.10; Gen.Kdo.*XXV. A.K.* Ia, Anl.2 z. *KTB* Nr.15(II), 31.7.44 [T314 R747 F548]

604. Message LXXXIV. A.K. at 11:30 on 31.7.44 [UKNA, HW 5/548, CX/MSS/T263/11, XL 4299]

605. Achilles (AOK 7), Ia Nr.432/44 at 16:00 on 31.7.44 [UKNA, HW 5/548, CX/MSS/T263/43, XL 4338]

606. Fahrmbacher, W.K. (1946), p.23, 73-77; *XXV. A.K.*, late on 7.8.44 UKNA, HW 5/555, CX/MSS/T270/60, XL 5263]; unknown authority [UKNA, HQ 5/558, CX/MSS/T273/37, XL 5917]

607. OKH GenStdH/Org.Abt. Nr.I/18 681/44 g.K., 10.8.44 [T78 R398 H1/38]

608. Tessin, G. (1972), 6.Band, p.118; **Tessin, G. (1974)**, 9.Band, p.233

609. The period to November 1944 is quite well covered by **Nauroth, H.S. & B. Steinberg (2017)**.

610. German general staff officers files, index cards of *Gen.Maj.* König [T78 R888 H6/26]

611. Anl. Z. Okdo.d.*H.Gr. B*, Ia Nr.10076/44 g.K., 20.11.44 [T78 R410 F6378772]; **Tessin, G. (1974)**, 9.Band, p.233; **Tessin, G. (1976)**, 13.Band, p.253 & 255

A fine example of a German propaganda photo: From their positions on the Atlantic Wall the German forces await the arrival of the Anglo-Americans. (Archives du Calvados 10Fi/1, photo 32 Fama, France et Atlantic, Berlin)